NOT BY BREAD ALONE

NOT BY BREAD ALONE

Russian Foreign Policy under Putin

ROBERT NALBANDOV

Potomac Books
An imprint of the University of Nebraska Press

Manufactured in the United States of America.

Library of Congress Cataloging-in-Publication Data
Names: Nalbandov, Robert.
Title: Not by bread alone:
Russian foreign policy under Putin /
Robert Nalbandov.
Description: Lincoln, Nebraska: Potomac Books,
an imprint of the University of Nebraska Press, 2016.
Includes bibliographical references and index.
Identifiers: LCCN 2015035263
ISBN 9781612347103 (cloth: alkaline paper)
ISBN 9781612347981 (epub)
ISBN 9781612347998 (mobi)
ISBN 9781612348001 (pdf)
Subjects: LCSH: Putin, Vladimir Vladimirovich, 1952—
Political and social views. | Putin, Vladimir Vladimirovich, 1952—
Influence. | Russia (Federation)—Foreign relations—21st century. |
National interest—Russia (Federation) | Strategic culture—Russia
(Federation) | Great powers. | Russia (Federation)—Politics and
government—21st century. | Political culture—Russia (Federation)—
History—21st century. | Identity politics—Russia (Federation)—
History—21st century.
Classification: LCC DK510.766.P87 N36 2016 |
DDC 327.47—dc23 LC record available at
http://lccn.loc.gov/2015035263

Set in Garamond Premier Pro by L. Auten.

To Seta Iskandarian, the love of my life

CONTENTS

ACKNOWLEDGMENTS

I appreciate invaluable contributions provided by Dr. Artyom Tonoyan in the matter of Russian Church history and the place of Christianity in Russian political culture. I also would like to thank Dr. Irakli Machaidze for his inputs regarding the philosophical parts of the political cultural content.

NOT BY BREAD ALONE

1

Continuity without Change

In 1990, in the wake of the fall of the Berlin Wall, a German rock band, the Scorpions, came up with perhaps its most famous song, "The Wind of Change." The iconic words "The world is closing in / Did you ever think / That we could be so close / Like brothers" were the closest depiction of the spirit of expectation of drastic and—at that time—positive transformations in the world. Globalization was still too far on the political horizon to talk about, but the conflict between civilizations, as described by Huntington at the dawn of the bipolar era, was long gone.[1]

With its first breath as a newly reborn state, Russia resembled Ilya Murometc, its fairy tale hero, staring at the stone on the three-prong road and choosing between three equally destructive options: imminent death (physical extermination), losing the horse (economic deprivation), or staying alive but forgetting himself (identity oblivion). Dimitri Simes added political context to the Russian trilemma regarding the three possible outcomes of the situation in the new post-Soviet geopolitical environment, predicting "the restoration of the Russian empire under an authoritarian, xenophobic, anti-Western regime; the splintering of the region into different groupings with widely divergent foreign policies and cultures; instability and possibly even civil war; or the emergence of truly independent democratic nations united by some form of a common market and collective security framework."[2] The independent Russian state survived, notwithstanding two bloody wars in Chechnya and sporadic outbursts of separatist feelings in Tatarstan, one of its major Muslim enclaves. This was achieved, however, not at the expense of societal consolidation and strengthening of the social contract between the citizens and the government, but as a result of titanic efforts on the part of President Putin's government to build the "vertical of power," a famous euphemistic cliché of neoauthoritarianism.

Life after the Union Empire

The Soviet Union did not die in 1991: it lapsed into a quarter-century-long lethargy and was awakened by Putin's calls for the *Russkii Mir* (Russian world), a thinly veiled reference to the *Pax Romana* by the Roman emperor Octavian Augustus in 27 BC. At the end of 2006, speaking prior to the start of the Year of the Russian Language, Putin said, "And the Russian world can and should unite all those who cherish Russian words and Russian culture, no matter where they live, in Russia or abroad, and no matter what ethnic group may belong. Use more often this phrase—'Russian world'!"[3] The problem lay in the Russian semantics, in which the words "peace" as *pax*, and "world" as *mundus* are complete homonyms: *mir*. The Roman version of *pax* meant a time of stability that spanned two centuries, in which multiple tribes under the rule of Rome lived in relative peace, fighting neither one another nor their metropolis. *Pax Romana* was, in a way, an archaic version of the Soviet Union: probably that is why it is so appealing to the contemporary Russian political establishment. In the case of Putin's Russian world, we see the attempt to violate the regional and possibly worldwide *pax* with the purpose of bringing narrow *mundus* to a single dominant ethnic group: the Russians.

Poetically speaking, the Soviet Union has been a Sleeping Beauty waiting for her Prince to kiss her awake and return her to her previously unblemished glory. Hans Morgenthau was right: unlike individuals who possess some degree of morality, countries, especially empires, do not commit suicide out of moral considerations.[4] They die for many reasons: because of internal systemic collapses, like the Mayan civilization in the ninth century. Or they may experience the crisis of overexpansion, such as the Mongol empire in the fourteenth century. Or they may be conquered by outside forces, as Urartu in the sixth century BC. Or they may collapse due to all of the above factors, the convergence of which led to the collapse of the Roman empire in the fifth century.

The Soviet Union's retreat from the global arena was different. A quarter century of foreign policy implosion initially led to the truncated views of Russia regarding the world around it. After the collapse of the Soviet Union, the country was still struggling to keep the Soviet bits and pieces together, while limiting its role to a mere spectator in the international world order. First Russian president Boris Yeltsin was tasked with the enormous agenda of preserving foreign policy status quo in whatever forms possible, even if it led to a tighter rapprochement with the West by possibly jeopardizing the future of the "Great Russia." Initially, as Andrew Kutchins and Igor Zevelev noted, "The idea was that Russia should subordinate its foreign policy goals to those of the West since the hope, and even the expectation for many, was that Russia would soon become a fully Western country. Becoming part of the West greatly overshadowed traditional Russian images of the country as a great power, and the sovereignty and role of the state were diminished by the goal of transforming into a market democracy."[5] At the birth of a new nation, Russia was thus ready and eager to end the civilizational confrontation with the West and to rejoin the European family of nations after almost a century of self-inflicted isolation.

In the early 1990s, there was a common desire among Russian liberals, including their first foreign minister, Andrey Kozyrev, to take the upper hand in their country's foreign policy. Kozyrev, who on numerous occasions lamented the negative consequences of the Soviet empire on the future Russian foreign policy, was known for his ultra-liberal (in the Russian sense, of course) positions regarding Russia's role in world politics.[6] At first, Russia willingly undertook the role of the second, if not the third, violin in the world concert of states. Such a foreign policy stance was, to a certain degree, stipulated by the domestic processes under way in Russia in the early 1990s. The phantom pains from economic collapse logically ensued after the dissolution of the command-and-control economy of the Soviet Union accompanied by the overwhelmingly popular defeatist sentiments. Such a stance prevented Russia from exercising its foreign policy in various directions, be it active opposition to NATO's intervention in the former Yugoslavia and full participation in the settlement of the conflict there, or mediation in the ethnic conflicts next door in Georgia, Nagorno-Karabakh, and Moldova, in which Russia may have exerted her power with a "big brother" influence.

With Putin's ascent to power, starting from his lead of the FSB, followed by his first prime ministership in 1999, and ending with his continuous presidential reign, the realists of all sorts may finally breathe freely. "The game of 'high politics' is the same game it always was," as Colin Gray once famously put it.[7] The end of the Soviet Union rendered a supposedly lethal blow to this school of thought, which was unable to rationally predict self-destruction of a nation-state. After all, a state so supreme and so intractable in the international system should keep going forever. The problem was that the Soviet Union was not a nation-state in its standard sense. For more than seventy years, it was unable to mold a new but consolidated *Homo sovieticus* nation where "national in form, socialist in content" would homogenize fifteen ethnicities, several of which had had negative historical narratives of bloody confrontations.[8]

After a rather unexpected knockdown resulting in the rapid transformation of the international world order at the end of the twentieth century, the realists were almost finished with their incredibly myopic outlook on international processes. Theirs was a vision of the world where, according to John Mearsheimer, "for every neck there are two hands to choke it."[9] Such a mind-set could not withstand the attacks coming from the followers of social constructivism. Constructivism was a rather new offspring in the family of theories of international relations, which praised identity over rationalism.[10] It replaced both realism and liberalism with its rather rosy view of world affairs based on mutual respect for human rights controlled by international organizations via economic interdependence between the growing numbers of democracies who preferred to cooperate rather than to fight one another.[11] Due to the conflicts in the former Yugoslavia, the former Soviet Union, and Africa, the scope and focus on the international arena had slowly shifted to the second image, a subsystemic level of intrastate interactions.[12] Domestic actors represented by ethnic groups brought in the notion of "societal security," thereby replacing the hegemony of states.[13]

Putin's Contributions to Russian Foreign Policy

This was the time when Vladimir Putin, an almost unknown former midlevel KGB functioneer, rose to power. In less than a decade he had become the alpha and omega of Russian politics or, for a better word, an institution of his own. His power style, or *Putinism*, soon became associated with the state-controlled oligopoly, where the majority of decision-making tools are concentrated in the hands of the closest entourage of the leader's friends, but which still allows for certain degrees of freedom to the majority of its population—only to prevent them from changing the existing state of the distribution of wealth by satisfying their primary needs with limited benefits. Without a doubt, no major decision in Russian foreign policy is taken without Putin's personal touch, be that the war against Georgia in August 2008 (while he accompanied his national team to the Beijing Olympic Games) or the "hybrid war" in Crimea in March 2014 where the "polite green men" (the term given to unidentified soldiers in Russian military uniform who occupied the peninsula) in 2014 "facilitated" the referendum on Russian annexation of the peninsula.[14] Putin is usually known for his reticence in giving immediate feedback for his country's behavior. For instance, his first speech on Crimean annexation was as late as three weeks after the actual, unofficial Russian intervention, and during the 2008 war against Georgia, he largely remained in the shadows as prime minister, giving the first violin role to President Dmitry Medvedev. Nevertheless, Putin remains the major power actor at home, projecting his influence onto the actions of his government in the international arena.

Domestically Putin gave his fellow Russians just what they have long been craving: the feelings of moral superiority over others and belief that "they hate us because they ain't us," that everyone else is envious of the "Russianness," their moral values, and military might. Deep inside, however, this viewpoint is somewhat similar to Nietzsche's *ressentiment* discussed in his *Genealogy of Morals*, only in its reverse meaning.[15] This feeling is based on two conditions: "fundamental comparability between the subject and the object of envy, or rather the belief on the part of the subject in fundamental equality between them," and "the actual inequality . . . of such dimensions that it rules out practical achievement of the theoretically existing equality."[16] *Ressentiment* was somewhat absent during the Soviet era, when Russia acted as "big brother" and the *primus inter pares* in the happy Soviet family of incarcerated nations. After Russia revived from the collapse of the Soviet Union in the early 1990s, this feeling started slowly but surely to appear in popular Russian nationalism. It became an amalgamation of the primordial form of "a spiritual principle," in which the newly formed views of the Russian nation go back to early Christianity, Peter the Great's conquests, and the victories of the Russian military in various wars it fought for survival.[17] It is also somewhat modernist, bringing together growing numbers of Russian citizens by "imagining" their communities as a unity of all Slavs, a vision embodied by the "Russian world" that their government strives to create in the international arena.[18]

Starting from the end of Putin's second term in 2008 and beginning with his third one in 2012, growing Russian *ressentiment* finally arrived at the logical point of its progression. It found its archenemies embodied by the Western world, in general, and Americans, in particular, whom Putin called nouveau riche for getting the wealth and the power in the international affairs that they did not deserve. Previously praised and accepted democratic practices became almost obsolete within months; even "liberalism" became a swear word in the Russian popular pro-Kremlin culture. The contemporary Russian political discourse had long engaged in nationalistic clichés, turning liberals into "liberasts" (a semi-homophone combination of a "liberal" with a "pederast"); Europe into "Gay-rope" (an allusion to the freedom of sexual orientation, as a universal human right, but one faced with particular popular resentment and hatred in the mass culture in Russia); Americans into *Pindos* (a pejorative term for the Greek settlers along the Black Sea coast given to them by Ukrainians in the nineteenth century); the

United States into *Pindostan*, and the culmination of all derogatory labeling—"fascists" and "national traitors" for all those who opposed Russia's international and domestic policies.

Transformations in Foreign Policy

The change in Russia's view of itself and the rest of the world coincided with the transformation of Russian foreign policy priorities and the ways in which to achieve them. The first Foreign Policy Concept Paper adopted during Putin's presidency in 2000 noted the underlying and irreconcilable difference between two outlooks on international relations: that of the West and Russia's own, hidden by the guise of liberalist thinking. Its further reading, according to Lawrence Caldwell, introduced realism: "As the Foreign Policy Concept of 2000 looks westward toward the developed states of Europe and North America, it carefully adopts the language of realism."[19] Yet in 2000 Russia was more open to international cooperation and viewed its place in the world through the prisms of this cooperation. The 2000 Concept declared relations with the European Union as its foreign policy priority: "The main goal of Russian foreign policy in Europe is creation of a stable and democratic system of European security and cooperation. Russia is interested in the further balanced development of the multifunctional character of the Organization for Security and Cooperation in Europe (OSCE)." By allowing liberalism into its foreign policy thinking, Russia emphasized the need to reinforce various intergovernmental structures, allowing its voice to be heard on the intraregional arena and also to further develop bilateral contacts with single states.

Russia was also more malleable in its relations with the United States. The 2000 Concept focused on Russia-U.S. relations concerning the need to deepen bilateral cooperation for the greater common good: a very liberalist notion. The Concept reads, "The Russian Federation is prepared to overcome considerable recent difficulties in relations with the United States, to retain the infrastructure of the Russian-American cooperation created for the past ten years. Despite the existence of serious, in some cases fundamental, differences, Russian-American cooperation is a prerequisite for improving the international situation and ensuring global strategic stability." Russia was striving to cement its place in the international society of states and was open to cooperation as never before or after.

When the domestic chaos of the 1990s settled down and the legacy of the Chechen wars began to fade away followed by the success of the "vertical of power," Russia adopted a more forthright stance with regard to regional and international affairs. This opened up the Pandora box of *ressentiment*. In his speech at the 2007 Munich Security Conference, Putin attacked the postulates of global security because of dissatisfaction with Russia's role within that realm: that of a follower rather than a leader. Putin blamed all involved, and specifically the United States, for turning the OSCE, the organization through which Russia dreamed of playing a key role, "into a vulgar instrument of ensuring the foreign policy interests of one country." He also attacked NATO for expanding beyond its borders and threatening the projection of the Russian political ego on the European continent by building "One single center of power. One single center of force. One single center of decision making. . . . [T]he world of one master, one sovereign."[20] It was back in 2007 that Russia had shown the first signs of unwillingness to play in the international security game, the rules of which, as he presumed, were written by the winners of the Cold War: the United States.

Domestic political processes, leading to the consolidation of Russian power within Putin's inner circle, led to a considerably rough international policy rhetoric. In 2012, as Dmitri Trenin claimed, "Putin's formal return to the Kremlin has ushered in yet another iteration of his foreign policy, which might be called 'sovereignization.'"[21] In simple terms, this meant reassertion of power in the international arena by Russia and a renewal of its attempts to reshape the international environment in accordance with its own vision of the world. Back in 1992, when commenting on the nature of Russian foreign policy, former minister of foreign affairs Andrey Kozyrev mentioned its path-dependent and repetitive character. In his article in *Foreign Affairs*, Kozyrev said, "Historical analysis brings out a certain cyclical pattern in the evolution of Russia: major periods of modernization were always brought about by a brutal collision with the outside world, which only tended to underscore the inadequacy of a backward and xenophobic Russia."[22] Those who ignored the signs of discontent in Putin's 2007 tone were served with Putin's speech at the meeting of the Valdai Discussion Club in 2014.

The year 2014 (coincidentally, a centennial jubilee from the start of World War I) marked a turning point in Russian foreign policy. In his speech at the Valdai Discussion Club, Putin took the issues pertinent to Cold War confrontation out of the closet of history and put them on public display. He compared the United States with the nouveaux riches, bestowed with riches of global leadership but destined to "squander them." It was there that Putin made reference to the Russian Bear, who views the Taiga (a very vague term) as his natural habitat and refuses to share it with anyone.[23] This was the primary stumbling block in Russia-U.S. relations, which Putin best explained by describing U.S. foreign policy: "What is allowed to Jupiter is not allowed a bull." Such a worldview foreshadows a continuation of Russia's actions, directed at reshaping the map of the world, at least in its regional Eurasian dimension.

What Happened to Russia, and Why?

The question is not so much what happened in the last fifteen years to cause a resurgence of Russian popular visions on its place and role in the world. The question is why. Why is a country once striving to become a full-fledged member of the democratic family of states in Europe now actively and deliberately juxtaposing itself to the notion of democracy? And why has democracy become in Putin's understanding the process of European colonization of aboriginal nations instead of individual and collective liberation?[24] What happened in Russia, which in the early 1990s was eager to establish itself as "a reliable partner in the community of civilized states" and now is consciously trying to place itself on the outskirts of the very community it was seeking to join?[25] Why did Yeltsin's Russia, advocating for "several degrees warmer relations" and perhaps a future membership with NATO, take a 180-degree turn by showcasing NATO and the United States as its nemeses?[26] And why do the Russian people continue to support their government's anti-European/anti-American stance while witnessing daily deterioration of their lifestyle?

The variable of Putin is, without question, a very potent factor in Russian foreign and domestic policy. It would be, however, quite myopic to concentrate foreign policy motivators exclusively on the personalities of the country's leaders. Individual qualities, likes, and dislikes matter, of course, in fine-tuning foreign policies, but they act as intervening spectators and not full-fledged independent variables in shaping priorities. Even in a hard-core realist vision, one which espouses the power-relative rhetoric and rational choice reasoning, "the balance of power is not so much imposed by statesmen on events as it is imposed by events on statesmen."[27] Liberalism, on the other hand, praises common norms and values as governing the international world order, rather than individual preferences of the statesmen. In social constructivism, too, leaders act as secondary figures, subordinate to their nation's much greater forces of collective identity constructs. From the point of view of rules, norms, ideology, and beliefs comprising the notion of "strategic culture," the present volume sides with a so-called third generation, which postulates that "the sources of . . . cultural values are . . . less deeply rooted in history, and more clearly the product of recent practice and experience."[28] These values play an enormous role in understanding the behavior of Russia on the international arena; they are key to finding answers to the numerous "whys" of Russian foreign policy. Finally, cultural visions of oneself, one's place in the world, and the views of other members of the international system help shape the very subjective prisms through which objective reality is translated.

The questions about Russian foreign policy decisions and the causes for its specific behavioral patterns demand answers. This book is yet another attempt to crack open the Russian puzzle, as described by Churchill: "It is a riddle, wrapped in a mystery, inside an enigma; but perhaps there is a key. That key is Russian national interest."[29] Unlike Churchill and his realist followers, such as Hans Morgenthau, who claimed that a nation's interests are "defined in terms of power," the present volume postulates that the main motivator behind the actions of the current Russian government is not power (or rather, not power alone) but the Russian political culture that defines its modus operandi in the international arena.[30] In this political culture construct, power is merely a subordinate intervening variable, one that may take different forms depending on specific situations within the Russian state but that is primarily defined, framed, and implemented as a result of the intricate convergence of Russian cultural traits that lie at the core of its political behavior.

In an attempt to solve Churchill's triple puzzle, this book will take an unorthodox approach in discussing the motivators of Russia's foreign actions by bringing it the domestic political, economic, and cultural. Russian political culture is an inherent part of its national culture; therefore, domestic affairs have a profound effect on how the country behaves internationally. Russia views international relations through the prism of its domestic policy and vice versa. Its foreign policy actions are primarily directed toward its own constituencies. As Viacheslav Morozov claims, "If security concerns previously focused on Russia's status in the international system and alleged Western attempts to undermine this status, now Russian authorities came to view Western intervention anywhere in the world as a step toward regime change at home and hence as a direct security threat."[31] This is evident in its many foreign policy decisions, including the desire to contain the threat of numerous "color" revolutions that struck first in Georgia and then in Ukraine and Kyrgyzstan—far away from Russian borders, in order to protect Russian citizens from the "corrupting influence" of the West.

Russian political culture is viewed here as the meta-variable affecting the structural core of its foreign policy decisions and making Russian international behavior unique, enigmatic, and so unpredictably vague. Russian political culture is a historically developed product molded by generations of people and influenced by multiple forces. The first force is the crisis within the Russian identity construct, based on Russia's quest for self-determinism and crisis with the definition of its place in the world. The second force is application of the foreign policy vision almost exclusively by the "hard" power. The third force with a colossal impact on traditional foreign policy behavior within the Russian state is the absolute, unabridged, unchecked, and unrestrained domestic power derived from multiple sources of legitimacy (inheritance, power transfer, succession, takeover, etc.), but lacking the main one: people. In democratic societies, people are the focus of the social contracts, since they empower their governments to serve them. In Russia, the people serve not as sources of power but as its targets. Finally, the fourth force is its pursuit of unabridged global influence determined exclusively in terms of territorial dimensions.

The existing scholarship on Russian foreign policy largely ignores the political culture as an important variable. Contemporary research on Russian politics keeps traditional interest-based rationales at the center of the foreign policy "vectors," focuses on the revival of the Cold War confrontational model's influence on contemporary foreign policy decision making, provides historic perspectives for Russia's international behavior, or traces its functional area-specific aspects, such as arms control, natural resource polities, human rights, and the influence of economic factors on its foreign policy.[32] Views on Russian foreign policy tend to cover "strategic interests and the factors that influence Russian foreign policy broadly . . . [and] examine Russia's domestic policies, economic development, and views of the world," or they stress power politics, those which force Russia to "continue to insist on having a seat at the table in addressing threats and challenges across the world."[33] Political culture remains overshadowed by grand foreign policy schemes concentrating on the tangible aspects of international relations, while leaving out the identity construct factor.

Yet the four factors discussed above, which appeared as a result of the realist/constructivist merger and now form the Russian political culture, give answers to several puzzling features of the contemporary Russian political life. For instance, why do Putin's domestic ratings continue to rise, notwithstanding the ongoing antagonism his policies have created in the international arena and the declining quality of life at home? Russian actions in Ukraine, including the annexation of the Crimean Peninsula in March 2014 and the hybrid war waged by Russian paramilitaries in its southeastern regions, caused an uproar in the international community—no doubt one of the loudest and most uniform reactions since the collapse of the Soviet Union. In response to this overwhelmingly negative reaction, according to the Levada Center's opinion poll, a majority of the Russian population, unified beneath the constructed image of enemies surrounding Russia, continue to support Putin as president (84 percent) and believe that the country is "moving in the right direction" (66 percent).[34]

Another notable feature of the present volume is its structure, which deconstructs Russian foreign policy into its primary and peripheral regional dimensions and explains how political culture influences the choices Russia makes and the foreign policy instruments it uses in diverse geographic locales. Primary dimensions of Russian foreign policy include the geographical areas that belong to Russia's sphere of geopolitical interest (Europe, Asia, and Near Neighborhood—the former Soviet states) or it feels particularly threatened by the external hostile forces (the United States, in particular). Periphery dimensions of Russian foreign policy are those geographic regions in which Russia is less involved or does not feel essential to its revived national identity constructs or sees no threat to its sovereignty. These are Latin America, Africa, and the Middle East, which Soviet Union used quite well for its proxy wars against the United States. Now, however, Russia is quickly making up for its absence from these regions in the first decade after its independence by accelerating political and economic involvement in former Cold War partners—all in spite of the United States.

Viewing foreign policy in the primary and peripheral regional dimensions offers a comprehensive, all-inclusive regional guide to Russian foreign policy. Regional dimensions showcase the variety of policy "means" Russia uses to achieve its foreign policy objectives. The book presents the specifics of foreign policy goals, engagement practices, and tools used by Putin's administration to promote Russia's national and strategic interests in each of these geographic locations, as influenced by its own utilitarian and identity views on each region. The purpose of having such a structure is to present foreign policy decision making as a result of a carefully deliberated and calculated agenda, focused on reinstituting Russian strategic dominance in all parts of the globe rather than a series of detached and hectic moves. The volume begins by introducing the scope and parameters of its specific vision of Russian political culture. Chapter 2 analyzes this phenomenon as a product of Russia's three historical heritage roots: its evolution in terms of territorial expansion, its messianic view of its rulers, and its internal identity crisis. It explains the mechanisms behind foreign policy decision making through Russian identity constructs: the role of power in the historical foreign policy discourse, the place of fear in shaping double identity lenses, the issue of transience of authority, and the importance of territorial possessions as the immediate foreign policy objective.

The discussion of the highest priority geographical dimensions of Russian foreign policy must begin with the country that has become the newly constructed nemesis of Russians in its current domestic political discourse: the United States. Chapter 3 talks about the place of the United States, its policies, military, policy makers, and diplomats, in the contemporary Russian foreign policy discourse as its primary target, number one rival, and the biggest threat to Russian statehood and sovereignty, internationally, and the integrity of the Russian nation, domestically. The short-lived *détente* with the United States after the dissolution of the Soviet Union in the 1990s was gone by 2007. Putin's ascent to power in 2000 marked a steady but deliberate decline in such bilateral relations. Along with building the vertical of power internally, Putin needed to develop a vision of a significant external threat to ensure that domestic institutional actors would rally around his rule. This was accomplished by exploiting Russia's own identity crisis. In order to attain superpower status, a goal to which Russia currently aspires, it needs to construct a superpower nemesis on the other side of the international relations field. In a way, it follows the methodological tool of "falsification" described by Lacatos: a phenomenon can only be proven if it is disapproved by the presence of the counter-phenomenon.[35] Growing anti-Americanism is evident in large-scale moves, such as systematic blockage of the U.S.-sponsored resolutions at the UN Security Council, as well as less significant "backstabs," as New York senator Charles Schumer called the Edward Snowden affair.[36]

The relationship with former cellmates of the Soviet prison is another high-priority geographical area in Russian foreign policy making, which is discussed in chapter 4. After the dissolution of the Soviet Union, all its former republics began developing separate identities as independent nations. Russia, as the legal heir to the USSR, was unsuccessful in trying to reconsolidate the derelict union by keeping the same nations in a different form. This includes Russia's failed attempts to forge the Commonwealth of Independent States, the Warsaw-type Collective Defense Treaty Organization, and more recently the Eurasian Customs Union. The failure to build up a new institutional bondage with the former members of the Soviet Union is explained herein by diverse and sometimes conflicting relations, ranging from friendly (Azerbaijan and Kyrgyzstan) to cooperative and partnering (Kazakhstan and Turkmenistan), paternalistic (Armenia), brotherly but suspicious (Belarus), formerly amiable but recently mistrusting and now openly hostile (Ukraine), antagonistic (Georgia), unfriendly (Moldova), lukewarm (Uzbekistan), and protective (Tajikistan).

Next in line is chapter 5 with another direction of foreign policy: Europe. The European vector has long been influenced by three main aspects of Russian political culture: relations with NATO, energy exports, and the quest for establishing its *Europeanness*. The North Atlantic Alliance has traditionally been Nemesis Number One for Russia, and the fear of losing the battle to NATO during the Soviet times was quite successfully translated to the contemporary Russian mentality. The matter of deployment of NATO's antimissile defense systems in Europe was also skillfully securitized by the Russian establishment to present it to the general public as inherently hostile. Regarding oil and gas exports, Russia strives to prove to Europe that it is a reliable trade partner; however, the reality of ongoing gas battles with Ukraine shows that "who controls the export routes, controls the oil and gas; who controls the oil and gas, controls the Heartland," with the Heartland being Europe.[37] Finally Russia's desire to enter and remain within the family of European nations collides with the numerous cases of human rights violations that run contrary to the letter and spirit of the European Union, as well as acts in opposition to the wishes of other post-Soviet states (namely, Georgia, Ukraine, and Armenia) in closer integration and association with the EU.

Chapter 6 focuses on Russia's relations with the countries of Asia-Pacific. The most important actor in the region for Russia is China, with its growing economic might and geopolitical power. Rapprochement with China is not a new sign in the Russian foreign policy, but recently accelerated efforts to harmonize its economic trade with China and attract the investments of the former in the oil and gas projects show a slow drift toward the Asian part of the "Eurasian" Russian identity. Japan is another power player in the region with which Russia has an uneasy history in one of the longest ongoing territorial disputes in the region—the possessions of the Kuril Islands. Finally, North Korea is close to the Russian identity in its fierce opposition to all-American notwithstanding considerable economic hardships this country is going through because of its authoritarian leadership.

Periphery directions of Russian foreign policy are covered in chapter 7 with a focus on the countries of Latin America, the Middle East, and Africa. Russia's relations with Latin America resemble its relations with African countries. The primary difference is that the Soviet Union was a bit more "involved" in the domestic affairs of some Latin American countries, due to their proximity to its Cold War rival, the United States. In the Middle East, the three-prong character of the Russian political culture is best revealed: territory, power, and identity. Russian involvement in Africa is a rediscovered terra incognita since Putin's times.

Finally, chapter 8 reviews the evolution of Russian foreign policy as historically galvanized by its political culture. It resumes the discussion of transformations in Russian political culture from its independence through the early stages of Putin's governance and its current moves in the international arena.[38] The chapter also touches upon the question of whether Russian political culture has been influenced in any form by the growing forces of globalization, or whether it is, in fact, too rigid to be changed.

A few words about methodology used in preparation of the present book. This is a single-case study, in which various aspects pertinent to the studied case are brought together to create an analytical framework focusing on key explanatory variables unique to the specific case.[39] The meta-variable on which the book bases its analysis of Russian foreign policy is Russian political culture. Therefore, the task is not to meticulously document all the more or less important events in Russian foreign policy since the ascendance of Putin to power, but to explain the driving forces behind Russia's patterned and repeated behavior in the international arena.

In applying the notion of political culture to the contemporary Russian foreign policy priorities, the contextual and discourse analysis help a lot to understand the forces behind some of the decisions the country makes on the international political arena. In additional to existing academic scholarship on the Russian political, cultural, and economic studies, the book reviews statements by Russian leaders, their interviews to mass media, independent analyses of think tanks, Internet blogs of political analysts, and the public opinion polls, which provide useful tools for creating a holistic picture of Russian foreign policy. In doing so, it also relies heavily on the academic publications of the Russian scholars—experts in the fields of Russian foreign policy, domestic public administration, and the comparative politics of the regions in which Russia is currently involved. Without the acknowledgment of the Russian side of international relations scholarship, building an all-inclusive outlook on the Russian foreign policy is next to impossible. I did most of the translation of the materials from these works as well as numerous Russian state websites, online mass media sources, think tanks, and blog posts of individual contributors to the Russian domestic and foreign policy.

2

Fear and Loathing in Russian Political Culture

You will not grasp her with your mind
Or cover with a common label,
For Russia is one of a kind—
Believe in her, if you are able . . .

—A quatrain by FEDOR TUTCHEV, translated by ANATOLY LIBERMAN

In his annual address to the Federal Assembly of the Russian Federation in 2005, Vladimir Putin uttered the words that became the leitmotif of his subsequent years in power: "The collapse of the Soviet Union was the biggest geopolitical catastrophe of the century." To many, this was a highly utopian message with the agenda to harness domestic support and beef up Putin's own ratings after the terrorist attack at the Beslan school in 2004 and to counter general discontent among the Russian population with the political insecurity and economic collapse of the country. In reality, however, this was perhaps Putin's most important program statement after the decrepit Boris Yeltsin handpicked him with the mega-goal of reviving the lost grandeur of the Russian land.

Putin, however, can claim neither the authenticity of this statement nor being the sole source of the overwhelming sentiment in the majority of the Russian population that "we were cheated by the West." When the Soviet Union collapsed in 1990, the dawn of a new era of democracy, respect for fundamental freedoms, and human rights protection came into view for the Russian polity. New realities of transformed relationships within Russia, between its citizenry and the government, and outside with foreign partners were epitomized by former president Boris Yeltsin at the conference formally ending the Cold War in 1992, when he said, "[We have] crossed out all of the things that have been associated with the Cold War. . . . From now on, we do not consider ourselves to be potential enemies. . . . [I]n the future there will be full frankness, full openness, [and] full honesty in our relationship."[1] The Cold War ended, and the new Russian political establishment was painstakingly trying to show the rest of the world its clear intentions to start its new history with a clean slate.

In almost two decades from that historical moment, Russia is back to square one: the West, which is a collective depiction of the United States, Europe, and NATO, is showcased for the Russian state as the greatest villain in mass media and open political discourse. Visions of the West conquering the hearts and minds of ordinary Russians haunt the delusional imagination of powerful actors in Moscow. Recently acquired "friends" have become "enemies" in the quasi-official Russian political discourse, and the desire to join the family of democratic nations and to build the common European House was replaced by threats to "burn America down to nuclear ashes" uttered by Dmitri Kiselev, Putin's chief propaganda man in 2014.[2] A return to anti-Western rhetoric was the cover of the unfriendly steps of Russia undertaken toward its former Soviet friends and even those who claimed to be its brethren, including the war in Georgia in 2008 and the annexation of Crimea in the aftermath of the Ukrainian crisis of 2014. These were not, however, unrelated cases of "supporting international law," as relayed to the international community by Russian leadership. On the contrary, ever since Putin's third presidential term, the consolidated "vertical of power," a set of measures directed at improving the administration's efforts and the accountability of public administration units, which, in simple terms, means institutionalizing the bureaucracy in Russia, started showing its true colors as the "Third Rome."[3] This was not, however, a slight tilt or fine-tuning of the political agenda since "castling" in the Putin-Medvedev-Putin tandem of 2008 or even Putin's first two terms. These are all links of the intricately entangled, historically molded, and path-dependent variable that institutionalize Russian behavior in the global arena: its *political culture.*

Multiple Dimensions of Political Culture

Countries are like people: their behavior in various situations is defined by many factors, the most potent of which is culture. Culture interprets human essence and, in turn, is defined by such components as language, ethnicity, religion, customs and traits, and visible and invisible behavioral standards. In the words of Jerome Hanley, culture is an "integrated pattern of human behavior that includes thoughts, communication, action, customs, beliefs, values, and instructions of a racial, ethnic, religious, or social group."[4] Not so long ago the Iceberg model of culture became a popular tool for understanding the cultures of different nations.[5] As the tip of an iceberg is its only visible part while most of it is hidden under the water, so is the surface culture, which can be easily seen and distinguished. Surface culture includes such visual signs as arts, languages, cuisine, religion, dances, and community customs. They can be very easily seen but do not give much information about how the groups developed these specific cultural traits. Layers of deep cognitive waters cover most of the iceberg—the real variable behind what is visible. The "DOS behind Windows" factor-variables that cannot be seen by an untrained eye include such abstract notions of sin and justice, work ethics, specific problem-solving, definitions of sanity, friendship, and love, concepts of time and space, and many more that are always content-specific.

When politics is merged with culture, the result—political culture—is a product of complex interactions of national institutional actors (governments, civil society, businesses, nonprofits, media, etc.) domestically, among themselves, and internationally, with the rest of the world. On a domestic level, they define the modes of communications of these actors within various levels through their reactions to the internal political processes. On a broader scale, political cultures presuppose responses of the local polity to external challenges and disturbances. Political cultures are the necessary ingredients for defining the longevity of governance regimes in general and individual rulers in particular, as well as in the matter of predicting possible behavioral patterns in the international arena.

The notion of political culture goes beyond North's definition of culture, which is a "language-based conceptual framework for encoding and interpreting the information that the lenses are presenting to the brain."[6] Lowell Dittmer defines political culture as "a system of political symbols . . . nest[ing] in a more inclusive system that we might term 'political communication,'" which is deeply embedded in the identities of the actors reflected in their political behavior.[7] Political behavior, according to Claude Ake, is "ubiquitous. Members of society behave politically insofar as, in obeying or disobeying the laws of the society, they support or undermine the power stratification system."[8] David Laitin and Aaron Wildavski view political culture as a three-pronged phenomenon: it instills "points of concern to be debated"; it guides people "by the symbols of their culture and is instrumental in using culture to gain wealth and power"; and it contains symbols that "must be interpreted in full ethno-graphic context."[9]

In the present volume, political culture is defined as *modes of responses by institutional actors to the challenges emanating from internal and external environments*. These modes are *historically developed and remain persistent through generations*. This is similar to the definition of political culture developed and applied by James Wilson et al. to American society: "a patterned and sustainable way of thinking about how political and economic life ought to be carried out."[10] Perhaps the closest definition to political culture used in the present volume belongs to Gabriel Almond and Sidney Verba: "particular distribution of patterns of orientation toward political objects among the members of the nation."[11] Based on those wordings, political culture becomes essentially the symbolic medium of political behavior—what Stephen Chilton calls "all publicly common ways of relating within the collectivity" or the ways in which institutional actors interact with their governance regimes and react to presented political agendas, both domestic and international.[12]

Symbolic communications between institutional actors within specific governance regimes make political culture the product of their identities.

Political culture of a country is similar to individual culture in a sense that it brings national-identity components into the behavioral equation, largely corresponding to the same cultural characteristics on the individual level of its citizens. On the domestic level, political culture includes actors' sets of behavioral responses to changes in their governance regimes. The same applies at the level of international systems, except that in this case changes in the governance are substituted by fluctuations of the regional and/or global environment, depending on the roles the countries in question play in it. Political culture thus becomes the meta-variable that glues together the individual cultural variables and affects the behavior of institutional actors through their subjective opinions and views on the objectively existing reality.

Application of the Iceberg model to political culture produces the patterns that can easily be identified by looking at the specific behavior of countries on the international level: how they respond to changes in the political environment around them and how they treat other countries and the community groups within them. On the deeper underwater level lie perhaps the most important factor-variables that define the behaviors of countries: the rationales behind each and every international action. The submerged factors of political culture are the variables that permeate the very core of the societal fabric and profoundly impact the ways countries respond to external disturbances, challenges, and threats.

In largely primordialist societies, where a nation is a "a soul, a spiritual principle," the underwater variables are the complex products of convoluted interactions of the actors at the political, economic, and cultural layers intertwining the society fabric that have been created as a result of centuries of existence and interactions with other cultures.[13] According to modernists, who view nations as "a contingency, and not a universal necessity," political culture comes about as a result of the conscious choices of countries and not historical occurrence on their evolutionary path of industrial training, improvement of the manufacturing process, and introduction of shared industrial responsibilities.[14] Finally, postmodernists (as well as constructivists) consider a nation as something that cannot be embraced holistically but can only be viewed in the form of "imagined communities," fluid constructs the matter and essence of which depend on the individual preferences and cognitive frameworks of reference.[15]

Russian Political Culture

Russian political culture did not appear overnight or during the last two decades of the new Federation. It was molded by years of the nation-building process that transcended significant historic milestones. The making of the Russian political culture started from the ancient East Slavic tribes that conglomerated around the Kievan Rus', the first Slavic country. It saw the inception of one of the world's longest-lasting royal dynasties and the first Russian one, the Rurikovichi of the ninth century, by invitation from Scandinavia. It witnessed the creation of the Russian empire through centuries of territorial conquests in all directions. It suffered through the renaissance of the Soviet Union as the superpower ruling half of the world in the twentieth century. Very recently, it started the quest to form a new but not novel Russian identity, which would possibly embrace its rich history, its diverse cultural landscape and ethnic composition, rediscovered spirituality, and unique view on the world and their place there.

In the case of Russia, its political culture is the variable that stipulates its modus operandi in the global arena and has led it to some recent actions on the international level that many would find quite strange or unusual. Russian political culture rests on four pillars: its identity, which is still in the process of being molded; the notion of power, both domestic and international; views on the origins and types of authority; and the historically developed place and role of "territory" in the nation-building process. National identity in political culture is not developed overnight. It requires centuries of repetitive cycles of responses to the internal and external challenges that have been historically proven to create generalizable patterns that can and will be duplicated under similar circumstances in the future.

Two Logics in Russian Foreign Policy

Russia has undergone several changes in its view of itself, others, and its place in the world. Andrei Tsygankov identifies three schools of thought on Russian foreign policy: Westernizers, placing emphasis on the similarity of Russian domestic politics, culture, and economy with the West; Statists, who stressed "the state's ability to govern and preserve the social and political order"; and Civilizationists, who advocated a view of Russia as completely different from the West and projected Russian values abroad.[16] Presence of the identity component in foreign policy is a significant departure from the previously accepted rational-choice reasoning toward the constructivist view of the decision-making mechanisms related to actions in the international arena. Discourse on the differences in the motivators for countries was pioneered by James March and Johan Olsen in their seminal works on neo-institutionalism.[17] According to them, two logics govern the behavior of actors and organizations: the *logic of expected consequences* and the *logic of appropriateness*, which are juxtaposed and used separately to explain the behavior of institutional actors.

When transferred to the realm of international affairs, the two logics have a similar, if not increased, role in states' behavioral patterns. Under the logic of expected consequences, as argued by Alexander Hicks, states reveal an "instrumental behavior—perceived as semiautonomous—of rational individuals under institutional constraint."[18] Decisions are made based on the actors' rational choices, and this assumes "some model of individual action, often one based on subjective-expected utility theory."[19] A number of preconditions must be present in such a strategy: the actors should be aware of their own capacities, should see several options for action, should calculate beforehand the costs and benefits of moving in any direction, and should act in the way that maximizes their own benefits.

States, similar to organizations, guided by this logic, also calculate the expected utility and possible losses they could suffer from their actions. In the words of Kjell Goldmann, weighing expected consequences "essentially leads us to derive actions from given preferences."[20] If states think they stand to benefit more than they stand to lose, they decide to intervene. The questions states ask themselves are "What is the situation we are faced with? What are the available options for our actions? What benefits would our interventions bring us and what costs would we incur? How can we design our actions to bring the highest expected benefits and least possible costs? What consequences would we face if we intervened and if we did not intervene?"

In foreign policy, according to Patrick Regan, states evaluate carefully "the cost and benefits of alternative action along with their estimations of the probability that any action will achieve the desired outcome."[21] In short, if states see that the utility from their actions is high enough to outweigh the costs they would incur, they decide to intervene. Similarly, states would refrain from intervening if the costs of intervention are unacceptably high in comparison with the benefits they would receive.

The second logic—of appropriateness—is based on normative beliefs that make behaviors or actions appropriate under certain conditions and inappropriate under others. The notion, levels, categories, and types of (in)appropriateness are set by actors themselves either alone or together under institutional settings that would set norms and standards for all their members. From a neo-institutional perspective, the emphasis is made, according to Hicks, "on the orienting or energizing role of the social—or, at least, of other individuals—rather than stressing the casual exogeneity of ego."[22] States possess their own social identities that guide their actions in the international arena. The logic of appropriateness thus "essentially leads us to derive actions from given identities," which are also—similar to interests in the previous case—given, fixed, and rigid.[23]

Individually, states may act on the basis of their own sense of appropriateness, which might differ from that of others. States act jointly, in the words of March and Olsen, "according to the institutionalized practices of a collectivity, based on mutual, and often tacit, understandings of what is true, reasonable, natural, right, and good."[24] States evaluate the situation in accordance with the norms, rules, morality, and ideational settings they are themselves governed by. In a similar fashion, Mark Weber et al. define three factors behind the logic of appropriateness: "recognition and classification of the kind of situation encountered, the identity of the individual making the decision, and the application of rules or heuristics in guiding behavioral choice."[25]

Equipped with the logic of appropriateness, states, according to March and Olsen, "seek to fulfill the obligations and duties encapsulated in a role, an identity, and a membership in a political community. Rules are followed because they are perceived to be adequate for the task at hand and to have normative validity."[26] The questions that states ask themselves when deciding to intervene are "What is the situation we are faced with? Who are we? Who are the other actors? Does this situation violate the moral principles our society is based on? What are our obligations to our own people, those involved in conflicts, and wider community of states? How will our behavior affect us? Is the intervention appropriate?"

In essence, states decide to act if they view a particular situation as a threat to their identities and a violation of the principles or "rules and practices [that] specify what is normal, must be expected, can be relied upon, and what makes sense in a community."[27] Having assessed the issue-areas from the point of view of their own and the collective moral basis, states take certain actions if they think that the situations have exceeded the threshold of ethical and normative permissibility. They may still act in the international arena in a certain way even if their cost-benefit calculus is negative: they would intervene, in the words of Franklin Weinstein, "regardless of what the particular situation involved would dictate in light of national interest."[28] States would do so because it is morally unacceptable for them to do otherwise, and they can do otherwise. Similarly, states might abstain from intervention in the domestic affairs of other countries if they believe that the situation is within the limits of moral and normative acceptability.

The problem with this separation of logics is twofold: first, there is considerable difficulty in their unilateral application to the philosophy of decision-making deliberations of states, and, second, they suffer from insufficiency of their independent usage for explaining diverse behavior of states. Neither of these logics alone fully explains the whole complex array of situations that states face and the options available for them. Much in the same line, Martha Finnemore and Kathryn Sikkink argued, "Rationality cannot be separated from any politically significant episode of normative includence or normative change, just as the normative context conditions any episode of rational choice. Norms and rationality are thus intimately connected."[29]

Russian foreign policy is driven by both logics with varying degrees of their convergence. It is next to impossible, however, to draw a clear line separating one from the other. In some actions, for example, in the policy of trading energy carriers and using them as a foreign policy tool, Russia reveals the logic of carefully calculated consequences. In other words, as a rational actor, Russia possesses credible information about the options available to it and to the buyers of oil and gas as strategic commodities. It further ranks these options based on the expected utility and makes decisions as a result of all actors' choices assuming that the one chosen will have the most expected utility. On the other hand, Russia may act on the basis of its multiple identity constructs, which would mean a lower degree of instrumentally rational outcome but a much higher degree of emotional and moral satisfaction from its actions.

Russia and Its Identity Abyss

Victor Pelevin, one of the most prominent Russian modernists and *l'enfant terrible* of Russian literature, gave the following description of the new Russian identity in a dialogue of the characters in his iconic novel *Generation P*:

> "Our national business goes international. And there are all sorts of dough—Chechen, American, Colombian.... And if you look at them just as dough, they are all the same. But each of them has some sort of a national idea. We used to have Orthodoxy, Autocracy and Nationalism. Then there was com-

> munism. And now, when it is finished, there is no idea at all, except for dough. . . . We lack national i-den-ti-ty. . . . We need a clear and simple Russian idea to tell any bitches from any Harvard very simply: blah-blah-blah and nothing else. . . . We also need to know where we are coming from."[30]

The problem of not knowing where to come from is the fundamental in understanding the current excruciating question of the Russian nation to locate the birthplace of its identity. But looking into the past is not its goal. The paramount objective is to use or, rather, to construct the historical factsheets to "anchor" the future of the Russian identity. Multiple identity constructs of the Russian nation play an enormous role in the projection of "Russianness" to the level of the international system. Discourse on Russian identity occupies the centerpiece of the Russian foreign-policy decision-making mechanism at the highest level. Identity, on its own, is an intricate construct that is convoluted in multiple historical events that shaped the contemporary reality in Russia. Identity is a very important factor-variable stipulating certain behavioral patterns in many societies, including Russian. According to Sonia Roccas and Marilynn Brewer, "Through such collective identities, individuals become connected to others by virtue of their common attachment to the group rather than their personal relationships."[31] Identity connects an individual to a larger group of like-minded, like-looking, and like-behaving individuals and creates strong in-group solidarity.

Quite similar to individual identity, in the case of countries, the "collective 'self'" is juxtaposed with the "collective 'other'" but with a much larger notion of group solidarity based on collective memories, myths, and fables.[32] Kay Deaux identified five human identity types that unite several more subcategorized identities: ethnicity and religion, political affiliation, vocation and avocation, relationships, and stigmatization.[33] Nearly all of them apply to the Russian political identity, which can be grouped into two related constructs: *internal* and *external* identities. In turn, these identities are projected through two lenses: the *concave* lens of self-image and views on its place in the world, and the *convex* lens projecting the constructed identity outward via foreign policy.

The first category of identity refers to the inner vision of a nation on itself and its place in the world. This is what Stella Ting-Toomey and Leeva Chung call "self-concept": personal identity constructs that encapsulate unique characteristics of individuals that form the given society.[34] Depending on how each community chooses to identify itself versus others, the "self-concept" can include ethnicity, race, specific personality traits, language, and religion. The "self-concept" is similar to what Naomi Ellemers et al. call "collective self": individual subjectivization with the group.[35] Internal identity is a highly subjective construct of how a nation views itself and how it projects its vision to the outside environment, be this the immediate regional neighbors or the world.

The second form of identity is external—the "convex" lenses of constructed vision on itself as projected to the outer environment. Erving Goffman calls this "a dramatic effect": a daily performance of internal identity for the purposes of showcasing it to the external audience.[36] Simon Clarke gives more insights to external identity, which is directly relevant in the case of Russian political culture: "Identity is . . . projected at the target audience in a theatrical performance that conveys self to others. . . . [T]he performer can be completely immersed in his own act and sincerely believe that the version of reality he is projecting is actually correct."[37] This is especially important for in-group identities when they are projected outward. In essence, this sort of identity does not mean who you are in reality; it shows, however, to others who you want to be taken for.

Russian internal identity constructs have been traditionally viewed by the Russian political establishment as the interplay of Western and Eastern civilizational traditions. They were presented to the domestic audience as bridges connecting two geographic areas in a positive vision or as a split or a gap separating these two directions in a negative way. A special role in the quest for Russian identity is allotted to the school of thought called "Eurasianism," which claimed the unique place for the Russian nation as located between Europe and Asia.[38]

Another outlook on the Russian identity connects it with the collective nature of the Russian nation. At a meeting of the two presidential councils, on foreign affairs and on interaction with religious groups, the matter of Russian national identity was placed within the realm of national security. Even though identity constructs remain fluid, such a view means that any deviations from a given form and content of the notion of Russian identity will be considered national treason. The other form of promotion of the Russian identity is primordialist and rather nationalistic. The promoters of this view in the Sobor (Christian Orthodox Congregation) view the Russian nation as "global, peacebuilding; bearing salvation to the world; open to assimilation by others with whom it shared its being; striving to bring harmony to conflict- torn humanity. The Russian nation has raised the torch of spiritualized humanity in the name of all peoples."[39] This ecumenical vision of Russian identity places the "Russian" over any other cultures by presenting it as "high" and ready to accept the willing (or force the unwilling) "lower" ones.

Yet, from its historical perspective, modern Russian political thought lacks consensus as to what the starting point should be in the quest for Russian identity. The quest for a unique Russian identity is based on a marvelous mélange of primordialism, modernism, and postmodernism—diverse and mostly conflicting views on nationalism that agree on a single starting point: the greatness of the Russian national identity spreading beyond the centuries of dynasties of rulers who contributed to the visionary construct of "Great Russia."

The matter is not so much in the disagreement of various societal factions on where the Russian concave identity starts. It is about where it ends. Several contending "anchors" can appear: the ninth century when various warring East Slavic tribes decided to invite Rurik, a Varyagian tribal leader, to rule them; the times of Peter the Great's "hack[ing] through" the window to Europe in the seventeenth century; the progressive reforms of Tsar Alexander II, who abolished serfdom in Russia; the martyrdom of Tsar Nicholas II, whose execution by his communist jailers in 1918 led to seventy years of the Empire of Evil; the era of Stalinism, which by the most prudent estimates took the lives of 20 million of its own citizens.[40] Or the Russian identity is modern, after all, and it started with the sole victory of the Soviet Union over Nazi Germany (as presented by Soviet and, later, modern Russian propaganda) and ended with the annexation of the Crimean Peninsula from Ukraine in 2014.

There is a common "anchor" in this odyssey into the history of the Russian soul: *velikoderzhavnost'*—the greatness of the Russian National Power, as such, as revealed through the centuries of its existence on the Eurasian map. The identity quest sometimes brings quite unexpected and unforeseen results. In going way back in history and looking for the cultural and spiritual roots, none other but the mystical Aryan race was found as the predecessor of the Russian race. Vyachelsav Nikonov, a member of the Russian Duma (parliament) and head of the Duma Committee on Education (and incidentally the grandson of Vyacheslav Molotov, minister of foreign affairs of the USSR who signed the infamous Ribbentrop-Molotov Pact in 1939) found the *Übermensch* background in the Russians. On his official website belonging to the Duma, this MP writes, "We must always remember what country we live and work in; we must know our traditions. Our Fatherland has a great past. The Aryan branch of the tribe descended from the Carpathian Mountains; peacefully populated the Great Russian plain; Siberia, the coldest part of the planet; came to the Pacific, established Fort Ross; absorbed the traditions of the richest cultures of Byzantium, Europe, Asia."[41] Even though these multiple references are made to completely different historical times, what unites them all is the general line of Russia's *velikoderzhavnost'* playing the role of the regional and possibly global superpower.

Ghost of the USSR

Popular Russian narratives connect Soviet times as an extremely significant "anchor" and the point of reference to the domestic source and forms of power even for a comparatively younger generation of Russians, who should not have an actively conscious memory of the Soviet period. This is perfectly understandable since, according to Veljko Vukacic, "the Soviet experience, however contradictory and ambivalent, is the main historical storehouse from which a usable Russian past can be constructed, for the simple reason that it is the only one within living collective memory."[42] It is only within the Soviet Union that Russians, as a nation, felt venerated on a daily basis by the host of fourteen other Soviet nationalities. It was, in a way, the "daily plebiscite" in the Soviet context when the Russian nation was elevated in the average Soviet *komunalka* (common house) for being "Big Brother."[43] And the Russians gladly accepted the role of the *primus inter pares*, which was greatly missed once the Soviet jail broke.

The Soviet Union's place as a superpower in the contemporary Russian identity-in-the-making is clearly visible in the social construct of the modern Russian military and society. Putin changed the music of the Russian national anthem back to the old Soviet Union anthem's soon after he became president of Russia for the first time in 2000. In the 2000s other important institutional structures of the Soviet mental upbringing were reanimated: the DOSSAF (Voluntary Society for Assistance to the Army, Air Force, and Navy), a quasi-military youth sports organization, abandoned during the early years of Russian independence, received a new life in 2009. So did the GTO (Ready for Work and Defense), a patriotic athletic training program in educational, professional, and sports organizations giving health-based certification required for enrollment in the universities for the Russian students in 2014. Above all, as a crowning event, the VDNKh (Exhibition of Achievement of National Economy) made a sparkling comeback as the point of pride for the Soviet Union's economic performance, in an overly ambitious project of turning the Russian international exposition center back to its original activities.

The most recent development in the list of Soviet comebacks for finding the concave lenses of Russian identity was the reinstatement in 2014 of the statue of Felix Dzerzhinsky, the founding father of the *CheKa*, the Extraordinary Committee, the notorious predecessor of the NKVD and later the KGB. The monument was originally erected in 1958 in front of the ominous KGB building in Lubyanka Square, associated by many in the Soviet Union and abroad with grim memories of massive human repressions. In 1991 the monument was taken down by the democratizing forces of new Russia, and a quarter of a century afterward it was returned by the Communist party leaders. All these steps are directed toward the resuscitation of Soviet nostalgia, together with the Russian imperial coat of arms and the tricolor flag, which would solidify Russian identity.

The same "Great Russia" construct in today's identity quest is embodied in the draft law submitted to the Russian Duma to create a new holiday in Russia, the Day of Military Glory, which is the day when the Russian troops occupied Paris (March 31) as the result of the European campaigns of the Russian army in 1813 and 1814. The reason for going that far in glorifying their past, according to the law's creators, is "the need to revive the historical traditions of the celebration of Russia's victory in the Patriotic War of 1812 and to reduce the numbers of attempts to falsify historical facts and events associated with this period."[44] Similar to the spirit of obsession over glorifying and guarding their past is the recent mass move to build monuments to the heroes of World War I, such as Drozdovsky, Kolchak, Denisov, and Denikin. These are the generals of the tsarist era who were associated with the Russian military victories in the war that they had exited from as a loser after the Bolshevik coup of 1917. By this Russia wants to commemorate its 1.5 million deaths and stand on par with the United States and Europe, which have numerous monuments dating back to this war. This is yet another attempt to create Russian identity and to foster national consolidation by historically referencing it with past glory or defeats.

Russian Orthodoxy as a National Anchor

Another significant domestic player is used by the Russian political establishment and mainstream social circles to reinforce the sense of uniqueness of the Russian nation and the "Russian World": the Russian Orthodox Church. It has undergone some turbulent times since the end of tsarist rule in 1917. During the Soviet period, any religion was banned as being "opium for the masses," and priests were severely mistreated by the communist regime, which advocated for increasing oppressions against the clergy and viewed them as class enemies.[45] While there is no exact aggregate figure of the persecuted Russian Orthodox priests during Soviet times, some sources list as many as

42,000 deaths in detention facilities between 1918 and 1930.[46] This figure includes 3,000 sanctioned executions in 1918 alone, which amounts to more than 95 percent of actively employed clergy.[47] These data do not incorporate sporadic and unsanctioned cases of tortures and killings of the clergy, such as 958 priests buried in a single location in the outskirts of Moscow in 1918 or the massive numbers of closed churches during the first decades of Soviet rule, which are all appalling in their gruesome nature as state-sponsored tyranny against religious representatives and against the general public who considered themselves true religious believers.[48]

Starting in the early 1990s, the revival of the Russian state marked a slow resumption by the Church of its previously held positions in the everyday lives of common Russian citizens by reviving the traditions of Sunday liturgy, baptism, church-held weddings, and other religious rites. In addition to the popular return to spiritual roots, the Church also entered into domestic political discourse as an actor in its own right. Soon Orthodoxy attracted the government, which started to use it to galvanize Russian society around the patriotic ideas of uniqueness and grandeur. Dmitri Trenin et al. view this process as a mutually beneficial relationship between the church and the state: "The Russian Orthodox Church has emerged for the first time in post-Communist times as an open political ally of the Kremlin. This relationship is now officially termed a partnership. The authorities hope that the church's blessing will shore up their legitimacy, which was questioned during the recent protests."[49] The first several years of consolidation of Putin's vertical of power in Russia marked an unprecedented convergence of the religious and secular interests directed toward the revival of "Great Russia," both domestically and internationally.

New Russian leaders soon espoused their lost Christian roots and used this as the engine of consolidation of the masses around the "vertical of power." Christian values, in the words of Sergey Lavrov, are based on the "thousand-year-old traditions common to the world's main religions," whose receptacle is Russia and its people.[50] This rapid convergence of the church and the state, according to Trenin, led to "the conservative version of Russian nationalism, which is becoming the Kremlin's new mainstream, [and] is closely related to Orthodox Christianity. Religion is being upgraded to be a centerpiece of Russia's national identity, and its traditional ethics are being adopted as a foundation of Moscow's foreign policy."[51] Both sides, it seems, benefited equally from such closeness.

The most recent quest to amalgamate the Orthodox Church and Russian identity happened at the All-Russian People's Sobor in 2014, which designed and adopted the so-called Declaration of Russian Identity. According to this Declaration, a Russian is someone "who considers himself/herself a Russian; has no other ethnic preferences; speaks and thinks in Russian; recognizes the Orthodox Christianity as the basis of national spiritual culture, and has conscious solidarity with the fate of the Russian people."[52] This definition creates strict entry frameworks, since a person who is ethnically Russia but is, for instance, a Buddhist or who satisfies all the requirements but otherwise does not fully share in the excitement of the Battle of Kulikovo of 1380, which started liberation of the Russian lands from the Mongol Horde, would not fully enjoy the ethnic membership.

Close interactions with the clergy led to the point where religious celebrations were praised and observed by top-level Russian officials, including Putin himself, for "bringing people back to their primordial spiritual values that play a special role in the history of Russia and nourish our national culture."[53] The Orthodox Church positively responded to such an elevated role in modern-day Russian life by giving, on multiple occasions, its unyielding support to the Russian government's general foreign and domestic political line. As a token of the its servitude in the Russian political establishment's quest for greatness, the Church published a 2014 calendar with twelve pictures of Stalin, from youth to adulthood, with short descriptions of his deeds and famous statements. The calendar was produced by the official print shop of the Russian patriarchy, Patriarchal Publishing and Printing Center, Holy Trinity St. Serge Monastery, and soon became a national best seller.

Stalin: Godfather of the Modern Identity Construct

Stalinism and the personality cult of Stalin occupy a special place in the power-laden constructs of the Russian political collective identity. The roots of Stalinism go much deeper into the mental history and are connected with the fact that criticism of Stalin in Russia left intact the main principle of the Soviet system of government—disregard for an individual at the expense of collective benefits. It is not difficult to understand the growing popularity of Stalin as a brand-name among Russian citizens. During the 2000s, public response to Stalin's personality fluctuated insignificantly. According to the Levada Center, the leading Russian public opinion study, more than twofold (from 16 to 7 percent) decreased the numbers of those who feared and hated him (from 9 to 5 percent); 1.5 times (from 18 to 12 percent) lowered the numbers who had the feelings of irritation and hostility toward Stalin. Positive attitudes for the most part remained at the same level (23 percent viewed Stalin with respect, 7 percent with sympathy, and 2 percent with admiration). Negative feelings against Stalin gave way to indifference (from 12 to 38 percent).[54] Sarah Mendelson and Theodore Gerber's independent study conducted in Russia corroborated the same major trend: Russians do miss the times of Stalin. Their data gathered in 2006 show "one-quarter or more of Russian adults say they would definitely or probably vote for Stalin were he alive and running for president."[55]

Starting with Putin's third presidential term, however, public opinion changed drastically. In 2008 the state TV channel Rossiya held an online competition on the "Name of Russia" where the participants cast their votes by text messages, telephone, and over the Internet on which historic figure, in their view, is most closely associated with Russian identity.[56] Stalin led the charts for quite some time, gave way to the third-century tsar Alexandr Nevsky and a reformer from the last tsarist era, Stolypin, but still ended up as the third personality most closely associated with Russia, ahead of Pushkin, Peter the Great, Suvorov, Lenin, Mendeleev, Dostoyevsky, and Ivan the Terrible. In Levada's repeated poll in 2010, 48 percent of respondents viewed Stalin's role in the history of the country as positive, and only 22 percent considered his personal legacy negative—this is versus over 60 percent of those who viewed Stalin's legacy negatively in 1989.[57]

Not only the period of Stalinism but also the whole Soviet era is treated by many in Russia as the "back to the future" point of reference. Dmitry Rogozin, deputy prime minister of Russia and a stout opponent of everything Western, very eloquently expressed this nostalgia in one of his Twitter posts in 2014: "24 years ago the Soviet rock had its first crack. Then came the rock fall. Who knew that it would continue for ¼ of a century? But the time has come to pick up the rocks."[58] Illusionary or sincere, Stalin's skyrocketing popularity in the second decade of the twenty-first century can be explained, to a certain degree, by the feeling of *ressentiment*—blaming the West for its own inferiority complex after the collapse of the Soviet Union. The Cold War ended with the disappearance of the Soviet state, but memories of the Soviet Union as feared by opponents and venerated by followers are still vivid in the imagination of not only senior Russians but also the representatives of much younger generations. Notwithstanding his non-Russian background and his heavy Georgian accent, the mainstream Russian political culture takes Joseph Stalin-Jughashvili as the Great Russian. This is puzzling since, according to David Brandenberger, "Stalin was not a Russian nationalist and had historically opposed all efforts to promote Russian self-rule."[59] Ethnicity does not matter here, and neither do the lives of millions of Soviet citizens who one way or another disagreed with the general political line of their country and who were sentenced to rot in the GULAG labor camps. What matters is the grandeur that Stalin brought to the Soviet Union and the feelings of the masters of the Universe that he gave to the Soviet nation.

Selective Historical Oblivion

Together with the quest to locate the identity anchors, Russian historical memory is quite selective. The country is consciously and selectively sunk in the waters of Lethe about its past, which makes it well remember certain points in time while purposefully forgetting others. David

Satter contends, "Failure to memorialize the victims of Communist terror has contributed to the moral corrosion of the Russian society. Disregard for human life exists in many countries, but in Russia it is unsurprising to see it carried to grim extremes."[60] Millions of lives sacrificed on the altar of Soviet civilization are forgotten, while collective glory is revered. At the same time, there are several monuments to the victims of political repressions in Russia, including the famous sphinxes in St. Petersburg with human heads facing the apartment houses and with rotten skeleton faces looking at the local penitentiary (one of them was vandalized in February 2015). There are only a handful of museums commemorating the victims of Stalin's repressions, including the State Museum of Gulag History in Moscow and the Perm-39 (included as a foreign agent in the lists of unwelcome organizations by the controversial Foreign Agents Law) on the site of one of the labor camps in Siberia. These commemorative signs are, without a doubt, a positive development in the general tendency: the mysterious Russian soul seems to settle the two opposing approaches in one historical receptacle.

There is not a single museum to the wrongful deeds of the Soviet Union or Russia in the international arena. Unlike Germany, which has Holocaust museums where its younger generations are told about the horrendous crimes against humanity committed by the Nazis, similar monuments in Russia, commemorating past negativity, such the Katyn massacre of over 21,000 Polish POWs in 1940 by Stalin's functionaries, are quite rare. The issue is not only in forgetting past negative deeds but in the impunity of the perpetrators as such. Perhaps it has to do with the fact that Russia, as a country, transcends the value of individual human lives, which makes Russian political culture immune to what Karl Jaspers calls "metaphysical guilt": "a solidarity between men as human beings that makes each co-responsible for every wrong and every injustice in the world, especially for crimes committed in his presence or with his knowledge. If I fail to do whatever I can to prevent them, I am too guilty."[61] This is the ultimate self-victimization where the people share on the level of their DNA the burden for the *mala in se*—inherently evil crimes—even if they were hundreds of miles away.

Russian political culture, however, is devoid of such feelings of metaphysical collective remorse mostly toward the external environment but also in relation to its own domestic context. That is why there are calls to rehabilitate Stalin's and the general Soviet past. Lenin's corpse is still displayed on the central square of the country. That is why the criminal inquiry into the dissolution of the Soviet Union, sponsored by the three major parties in the Duma (the ruling "United Russia," communists, and liberal democrats) was launched, ultimately opening a criminal case against Gorbachev as guilty for illegal dismantlement of the country. That is why Putin's call to put the issue of reverting the name of the Russian city of Volgograd back to Stalingrad up for public referendum in 2014 appeared quite legitimate. All these seem well along the lines of the group identity frameworks of Russian political culture. It does not matter how many millions perished at the hands of the Soviet punitive machine for the whole period of its existence: the country was strongly feared abroad, and this is all that mattered on the collective level.

Many countries tend to protect their past. This is normally done on the legislative level by enacting certain laws that prohibit acknowledgment or denial of certain facts or behavior that are considered illegal by state institutions. For instance, there is a common view in many countries that denial of the Holocaust and other crimes against humanity represents a grave crime. There are certain laws against Holocaust denial in different forms in Austria, Belgium, the Czech Republic, France, Germany, Israel, Liechtenstein, Lithuania, the Netherlands, Poland, Romania, Slovakia, Spain, and Switzerland, to name a few. Most if not all of them condemn this horrible deed: denial of the facts of mass murders of innocent populations.

Russia has enacted a similar law: on April 23, 2014, the Duma included the article "Rehabilitation of Nazism" in the Russian Criminal Code. In addition to penalizing the denial of the crimes against humanity committed during World War II, the new law institutes criminal punishment for "distribution of information expressing clear disrespect for society about the days of glory and anniversaries of Russia related to the protection of the Fatherland, as well as the desecration of the symbols of military glory of Russia" done either publicly or via Internet media.[62] The law contains a wide interpretation of the facts of "rehabilitation" and what constitutes "Nazism" and allows for prosecution of a wide variety of speech, including Internet blogging. Six months later, Putin signed the law banning propaganda or public display of attributes or symbols of organizations that have collaborated with the Nazis, as well as those who do not accept the verdict of the Nuremberg Tribunal. These laws have a dual purpose: to cultivate the sense of triumph and the identity of a victor among the new generations of Russians and to direct public outrage and the legislative machine against Ukraine, the embodiment of which has recently become the UPA (Ukraine Rebellion Army), the ultra-nationalist militia collaborating with Nazi Germany during their occupation of the republic from 1941 to 1943.

Quite notable regarding selective oblivion was Foreign Minister Lavrov's call at the UN Security Council in 2014 not to acknowledge governments that came to power as a result of a coup d'états against any government—even the most despotic ones—as legitimate in direct reference to the Euromaidan in Ukraine in 2014. To make things even more interesting, Lavrov advocated for institutionalizing individual sovereignty at the international level, asking, "Why not adopt a declaration of the General Assembly on noninterference in the internal affairs of sovereign states, nonrecognition of a coup d'état as a method of regime change?"[63] The motion was, without a doubt, directed toward the current government in Ukraine that came into power, as Russia claims, as a result of the illegal overthrow by the "fascist junta" in early 2014 and is based on the Roman legal principle *nullum crimen sine lege* (no crime without law) on the nonretroactive effect of international law. As Article 28 of the Vienna Convention on the Law of Treaties states, "Unless a different intention appears from the treaty or is otherwise established, its provisions do not bind a party in relation to any act or fact which took place or any situation which ceased to exist before the date of the entry into force of the treaty with respect to that party."[64] In essence, this principle protects the legal actors from their past deeds that in the time of their committing were not banned.

The blissful historical oblivion that the Russian authorities are so skillfully trying to cover up has two aims. On the one hand, Russia wants to institutionalize at the international level the changes in the map of Europe and in regional politics that they had done themselves, including the de jure annexation of Crimea, which Putin called "a righteous act" and "restoration of historical justice" at Seliger in 2014. The same stands true on the de facto Russian ownership of Abkhazia and South Ossetia. In simple terms, Russia is always right: it is historically just to take away the Peninsula, which was transferred to Ukraine in 1956, as well as repossession of Kalinigrad, which became Russian only eight years prior to the Crimean transfer. On other hand, they want to preclude any changes in the same geopolitical locale that are under way and might be initiated by actors other than themselves, with direct reference to the biggest boogeymen of the current regime—the "colored revolutions" pioneered in Georgia, Ukraine, and Kyrgyzstan.

The Role of the Superpower in Russian Political Culture

The quest for identity construct is inextricably linked with the vision of Russian greatness in contemporary Russian political discourse. The two behavioral logics discussed above are closely related to the role and place of the notion of superpower in the constructs of global and regional politics of Russia. There is a commonly accepted vision that superpowers are not born by universal contingencies. They become such by building up forces of power as the viable bases for survival and the elimination of other hegemons, which are the two true tasks every hegemon faces. In the Gramscian view, a superpower should possess two types of hegemonic power on the level of the international system: the power of the dominant group to effectively coerce the opponent (a kind of "direct domination") and the power to gain the consent of other actors to follow the presented course of action (somewhat "indirect"), which a true hegemon showcases.[65]

The form, substance, and purpose of such influence, however, remain within the competence of this political culture. Superpower can either use pure "hard power" in Bismarck's famous term *Blut und Eisen* (blood and iron), employing traditional and conventional military means of warfare, or "soft power," which in simple terms means "the ability to get what you want through attraction rather than coercion or payment."[66] The notion of "soft power" was born at the end of the twentieth century out of the emergence of new "trends," as Joseph Nye calls them, on the international scene: economic interdependence, transnational actors, nationalism in weak states, the spread of technology, and changing political issues.[67]

Being a superpower carries a dual burden that is oriented both inward and outward. The inward orientation means that a superpower needs to be recognized as such at home, by own citizens, who would feel proud of their country's actions in the international arena. It boosts the morale of its own people and instills feelings of confidence at being a citizen of and being protected by their country. The outward orientation, as it follows from its name, means that a superpower needs to be acknowledged as such on the regional and global levels. It projects the superpower identity toward other actors in the international system and also means that from the liberalist/constructivist perspective, a superpower becomes a role model and a trendsetter for others to follow.

There are different and even conflicting views on what constitutes a superpower, highlighting diverse categories and approaching the matter from diverse theoretical angles. They all, however, tend to agree on two commonalities, by which the hegemonic qualities can be evaluated: the concepts of "coercion" and "appeal," which are synonyms for "hard" and "soft" powers, respectively. In order to be a true superpower, a nation must possess both of these qualities: "hard" coercion will foster the establishment of a superpower nation as a winner of the years of confrontation against other countries with similar aspirations. However, it is the "soft" appeal that would cement the power achievements and provide for the longevity of the superpower. In simple terms, a superpower should be feared by some and admired by others.

The notion of "coercion" directly follows the realist school of thought and its rational logic of consequentiality, which evaluates the pros and cons by the actors of following or rejecting the hegemonic options imposed on them. Even if we assume, as Harold Lasswell did in 1930, that "the role of politics is to solve conflicts when they have happened," the hegemon can still employ the "political methods of coercion, exhortation, and discussion" to engage in compellence to peace.[68] The quality of compellence as enjoyed by a hegemon can be viewed in its relative power to effectively impose its own will on the other actors and, conversely, to withstand the imposition of the will of the others onto itself. In the wake of human civilization, Greek historian Thucydides provided the all-embracing definition of a hegemon as a power actor: "The standard of justice depends on the equality of power to compel and that in fact the strong do what they have the power to do and the weak accept what they have to accept."[69] Much in the same line of reasoning, Andreas Antoniades believes that "the concept of hegemon may imply a great capacity for coercion and/or a great degree of influence or control of the structures of the international system and the international behaviour of its units."[70] John Ikenberry and Charles Kupchan also focus on the "hard power" qualities of a hegemon by arguing, "The constitutive elements of hegemonic power include military capabilities; control over raw materials, markets, and capital; and competitive advantages in highly valued goods."[71] These capabilities are indispensable for the establishment of a true superpower in the international arena.

In promoting its own vital national interests, a superpower can use its coercive force legitimately (or not) in any of its embodiments, ranging from economic sanctions, diplomatic or other forms of blockade, or even an open war, which, as we know from Carl von Clausewitz, is "an act of force to compel our enemy to do our will."[72] What matters here is the will of a hegemon to compel, based on its power capabilities, those who consider themselves hegemons: a true hegemon must prove to itself and to others that it is in a position to project its power outwards.

The second characteristic of a superpower—"appeal"—can be seen in the mix of liberalism and social constructivism in international relations. It reflects some work of the logic of consequentiality in that it contains seeds of voluntary acceptance of the hegemonic options and lifestyle by others (usually weaker actors in the international arena) who willingly decide to follow the political course defined by "their" superpower. It also invokes the logic of appropriateness in following the political "appeal" of the hegemon out of the desire to openly swim in the superpower's waters. This latter category is more interesting, since it represents a clear departure from the power-infused rhetoric and actions of the rational choice-based logic of consequentiality and involves more or less the free will of the actors to follow the presented course of action or to resist. According to Antonio Gramsci, "There exists democracy between the 'leading' group and the groups which are 'led,' in so far as the development of the economy and thus the legislation which expresses such development favour the (molecular) passage from the 'led' groups to the 'leading' group."[73] Here, the notion of democracy negates coercion as the main tool for spreading hegemonic dominance and provides for the voluntary "appeal" needed to persuade the actors to follow the courses of action offered (and not imposed) by the hegemon. It also brings the notion of identity into compellence discourse: actors choose to side with a hegemon because they are associating themselves with it. This reflects Robert Gilpin's view on the hegemon, who distinguishes between "dominance" and "leadership," where the former involves a certain degree of coercion and forces acceptance of the hegemon's options and the latter reflects mostly a voluntary decision by the actors to follow the hegemon, who acts here as a role model.[74]

There is nothing wrong per se on the normative level with the notion of the superpower in the international arena. The word itself does not mean that the country that views itself as a superpower and is considered as such by other actors of the international system should be necessarily menacing the stability and integrity of those actors by posing constant threats to their sovereignty. Different countries at various junctures were superpowers in the contemporary sense of the word: ancient Rome, Persia, the Mongol Horde, Great Britain, France, and Spain all had enough economic might supported by their numerous colonial possessions and enough military land and sea powers to protect their own sovereignty and to successfully project their own vision on the work. They fought, of course, with each other and with others, but their wars that were primary to their true superpower nature, within the contemporary international environment, have gone into a deep coma in the rapidly globalizing world.

The Territory Construct

The notion and meaning of territory plays, perhaps, the biggest role in building the superpower construct in contemporary Russian political culture. Throughout its history Russia had to defend its own land from foreign invaders and itself waged numerous wars with the purpose of territorial expansion. To put it simply, size matters for Russia, and the essence of Russian identity has always been linked with the territory it covers. John Thompson places the territorial variable at the center of Russian foreign policy in his seminal book on Russia: a country that has "[s]ix thousand miles and eleven time zones from east to west, three thousand miles from north to south, with the world's largest coastline"[75] is destined to be a superpower simply by its gigantic size. Territorial expansionism is thus a *sine qua non* of the Russian superpower nature. It is puzzling, however, why the country with one of the lowest population densities in the world (#15 with only 9 people per square km of land area in 2009–2013) would ever want to increase its territorial possessions at the expense of someone else's land and end up having no human capital to essentially use it.[76] But true connoisseurs of Russian political culture know that its essence is domination and its form is the land expansionism.

In the nineteenth century a French aristocrat, Astolphe-Louis-Léonor, marquis de Custine, wrote a book, La Rusiie en 1839," in which he described the territorial dimensions of the Russian political culture:

> At the heart of the Russian people there boils strong, unbridled passion for conquest—one of those passions that grow only in the mind of the oppressed and nourish only on the nationwide disaster. This nation, predatory by its very nature; greedy from all the deprivations that it had suffered; by humiliating submission at home redeems in advance its dream of a tyrannical power over other nations; expectations of fame and wealth distract it from

disgrace it is going through; the kneeling slave dreams of the world domination, hoping to wash away the stigma of failure from renunciation of all public and personal liberties.[77]

Starting with Tsar Ivan III, who effectively ended the 250-year Mongol rule, Russia engaged in what became known as "Gathering the Land"—consolidation of the Russian principalities around Moscowia. The first wave of territorial expansion hit Russia's own Slavic kin: Moscowia forcefully annexed the city of Yaroslavl in 1471, then Novgorod in 1478, which had the first prototype of a consultative government in Russia, the *Novgorod Veche*. After that came the victorious war with Tver' in 1485, the principality ruled by Ivan III's brother; followed by the cities of Uglich (1491), Volotsk, Ryazan', and Pskov.[78] It was during the reign of Ivan III that the philosophical view of Moscow as the "Third Rome" was born out of the writings of the monk Filafei.

Ivan's grandson, the notorious Ivan IV the Terrible, continued the territorial expansionist policy with the outside beyond the already "gathered" Russian world. The sixteenth century marked Russia's territorial wars with its immediate neighbors in all directions: with Sweden in the northwest; Poland and Lithuania in the west; the Tatars and Siberian nomads in the east; and Turkey and Iran in the south. In less than thirty years, Ivan IV incorporated the lands of the Kazan, Astrakhan, Siberian khanates, and the lands formerly owned by the Great Nogai Horde.[79] After the deaths of the real and fake heirs to the Russian throne after Ivan, the Times of Troubles thwarted the territorial expansion of Russia but only for seventy years when the tsar from a new (and the last) dynasty, Peter the Great, started his victorious evolutionary change in Russia.

Peter I became the first emperor of Russia, the title "usually given by the Roman Senate to people for their famous deeds and embodied in statues for generations to come."[80] The change of title from a "tsar" to an "emperor," apart from the usual verbal grandeur attached to it, made a very important and far-reaching political statement: a country led by an emperor becomes an empire in the real and perceptional sense, a superpower that is not shy to make its grand entrance into the regional and possibly international arena. The only hurdle on the way of that entry was the fact that Russia was essentially a land-locked country, geographically and politically speaking. To become a true empire it needed to state its economic and political dominance, and the only way to do so was through water: Russia needed seaports to trade with and conquer others.

The target of Peter's expansionist policies became the seaports of the Black, Azov, Caspian, and Baltic Seas. As Gordon Smith argues, "Over the years, much has been made of the quest for warmwater ports as a primary motivating force in Russian and Soviet territorial expansion in the Balkans and the Far East."[81] Peter's most notable military actions leading to territorial acquisitions include the Azov Raid (1695–96), the North War with Sweden (1700–1721), the Russian-Turkish War (1710–17), the Caspian Raid (1722–23), and the eastward enlargement toward Siberia and India. True to his new emperor status, Peter was "settling" Russia down in its newly acquired superpower imperial status. His controversial and, as now widely accepted, fake last will and testament, including fourteen points on Russia's territory-driven hostile stance, falls very much in line with the past and present performance of Russia in the international arena.[82]

Territory is the only form that the Russian *velikoderzhavnost'* construct has taken through generations of Russian rulers. The greater the territory, the greater the power. That is why Russia ultimately and de facto annexed two regions of Georgia in 2008 and annexed Crimea and took the southeastern territories of Ukraine under its actual control in 2014. When commenting on the sense of multilateralism within territorial borders of Russia, a prominent modern political journalist, Semen Novoprudsky, said, "Russia has never been either a national, in the sense of a single civic nation, or a mono-ethnic state. Always empires in different forms. She has never had a long-established territory. She developed exclusively by the addition . . . of land. Therefore, Russia does not acknowledge any boundaries—geographical, moral, political, or legal. It is used to being boundless."[83] The current mottos of Russian nationalists, "Russia's borders are where Russians are," and "Whom does Russia border? Anyone it pleases!" follow the specific view of the country on the territory surrounding it and sets a very dangerous motive for subsequent aggressive actions in the international arena.

The Hard Power Construct

In our modern world the superpower characteristics have shifted from pure "hard force" to its "softer" and sometimes "smarter" versions.[84] No longer do the countries that see themselves as powerful enough to exert pressure on other actors directly take over their land. They use Nye's "soft power" concepts to attract their followers and to impose their will on others. Most contemporary powers like China and the United States prefer to cooperate with each other (China is the #2 trading partner for the United States, and the United States is the #1 trading partner for China). Another good example of the modern superpower is the United States, whose global involvement is based on promotion of the moral and normative standings on which the country is based. The fact of growing international interdependence drove Fukuyama to proclaim the "end of history" after the Cold War, which is the result of the rapid and somewhat unexpected onslaught of the Western liberal democracies on the rest of the world. Influenced by Fukuyama, James Mittelman calls the United States the only "hyperpower" and argues that the globalized environment will contain one omnipresent conflict: the hyperconflict in multiple directions that would be unveiled between the hyperpower and the rest of the world.[85] The notion of a superpower using its military and economic force to threaten the rest of the world and by doing so reinstate its superpower status by annexing the territories of other equally sovereign states has long been gone for most of the handful of countries that meet the superpower criteria. Most, but not for Russia.

The form of power in the current Russian political culture domestically and in international affairs is usually "hard," and its application is traditionally framed in terms of territorial possessions. Hard power is also the only method of territorial augmentation. In a different article Novoprudsky contends, "We [Russians] have a completely distorted view on the power of a state. A strong state for us is the one that 'solves problems' in a purely criminal sense: it annihilates (instead of educating and healing) its own people and the rest; it annexes the territory of others (instead of normally developing its own); it strikes fear (instead of building bridges of friendship)."[86] This was the standard modus operandi of solving political issues during the medieval times when the strong countries took over their neighbors' land. The Soviet Union, too, was not free of this fallacy. Even with the Soviet allies it used hard power coercion to keep them from possible ideological deviance. It intervened in 1956 in Hungary to keep it under its heel.[87] It almost intervened in the same year in Poland with the same reason, "to prevent changes in the Politburo which they feared might lead to Poland's secession from the Soviet bloc."[88] It intruded in 1968 in Czechoslovakia, to keep it within the Soviet sphere of influence, let alone its open military interventions outside its nominally European camp—in 1975 Angola and the occupation of Afghanistan in 1979.[89] The same view continues in the Russian state in the twenty-first century, specifically as a response to its occupation of Ukraine, but it has far deeper roots in the turbulent history of application of brute force for the purpose of territorial and political dominance.

When the Russian empire collapsed in 1917, the nations occupying it were given a chance for national sovereignty. Russia was uniquely placed to use this momentum and to use its appeal in order to keep the remnants of tsarist Russia together. Instead, as Revaz Gachechiladze writes, "The democratic ethic that was just about to develop in the first decades of the twentieth century was abruptly cut short by Sovietization."[90] This was a coercive process of forcefully dragging most of the post-tsarist nations back to a new entity, the Union of the Soviet Socialist Republics. First, the Russian Eleventh Army entered Azerbaijan on April 28, 1920, and proclaimed it a Soviet republic.[91] Armenia met the same fate in December, and on February 16, 1921, the same Eleventh Army annexed Georgia after a short but bloody war.[92] Two decades later the northwestern enlargement of the Soviet Union happened at the expense of the military occupation of the Baltic states of Estonia, Latvia, and Lithuania, which under the Ribbentrop-Molotov Pact were included under the influence of the Soviet Union.[93] In 1939–40, as a result of the Soviet-Finnish war, from which the Soviet Union left victorious, some of the territory formerly included in the Grand Duchy of Finland, as a part of the Russian tsarist empire, was transferred to the Soviet Union.[94]

Collapse of the Soviet Union gave Russia a unique chance to exercise its political influence on the former Soviet republics in any way other than open military force. It could act as the role model setting the democratization precedent for the other former Soviet republics, or it could undertake a role of another Brussels and lead the nations that have the experience of living together for decades if not centuries. Yet it chose the least peaceful and productive way of creating the superpower "appeal" and focused exclusively on its "coercive" aspect. Examples of application of the "hard power" politics by the new Russia seemingly independent from the Soviet Union legacy include its invasions in the early 1990s in Moldova's disputed Transdniestria region and its participation in the conflicts in the Abkhazian and South Ossetian regions of Georgia.

After a decade of frozen conflict, the situation in the Georgian breakaway regions aggravated to a point where Russia openly intervened in 2008 on the side of the separatist governments of Abkhazia and South Ossetia, de facto cutting them off from Georgia and de jure recognizing their independence and state sovereignty. The Russian "appeal" in this particular action spread over a handful of countries, including Nicaragua, Venezuela, and the island nations of Nauru, Vanuatu, and Tuvalu, who joined the Russian Federation in celebration of this new "parade of sovereignties," to borrow the expression from Hale, about the post-Soviet space.[95] The rest of the world, including the majority of multilateral and intergovernmental organizations and, most importantly, all other former Soviet Union brotherly republics—even Belarus, Russia's closest strategic ally and a member of the intergovernmental union with the latter—were impermeable to both Russian "appeal" and "coercion." The most recent case of the aggressive politics launched by Russia against its other closest ethnic "relative," Ukraine, included annexation of the Crimean Peninsula and the "hybrid" war against this country in 2014.

The *Velikoderzhavnost'* Construct

The constructed concept of "Great Russia" could well be a myth instilled and cultivated in the minds of the Russian citizens by their governments. What people think, however, about themselves as members of the political community of their nation-state is even more important. Their path-dependency comes from self-conscious posturing in relation to non-Russians, which in turn leads to subjective reactions to the changes happening in the objective reality around them. The word "great" (*velikaya*) in the Russian language has the territory-related root of "great in size." It cannot afford engaging in the thrifts of small-scale regional skirmishes and power muscling in with its immediate neighbors. Just like a large atom attracting the smaller particles around it which had no choice but to eventually end up tied to it by its centrifugal force, or a gigantic planet whose force of gravity draws in smaller satellites and influences their own gravity fields, so does Russia strive to project its overwhelming influence on the global scale. Its size predisposed Russia to its high level of involvement in global politics: being the largest country in the world bears the heavy burden of responsibilities that cannot be discarded.

Despite variations of Eurocentrism, Eurasianism, or Russophilia, Eastern or traditional Orthodox Christianity or an Islam-centric orientation, the uniting element in contemporary Russian political culture is self-image as a superpower. But due to the unfortunate but presumably reversible concatenation of circumstances (mostly the collapse of the Soviet Union), the nation was heavily truncated to a country with regional interests. This is why when in March 2014 President Obama called Russia "a regional power that is threatening some of its immediate neighbors—not out of strength but out of weakness," it was so negatively received in Putin's entourage.[96] This was a serious affront to Putin's own views on "Great Russia" and the "Russian World."

The task for Putin is to reanimate the great superpower image in the hearts and minds of its own citizens and to project it abroad. In this sense, his logic is very close to that of the Athenians visiting the leadership on the Isle of Mellos in Greece in the fifth century BC as depicted by Thucydides in his *History of the Peloponnesian War*. There, the Athenian envoys tried to justify their attack on the Mellians in case the Mellians refused to support them in their war with Sparta by referring to their domestic constituencies, "because it is not so much your hostility that injures us; it is rather the case that, if we were on friendly terms with you, our subjects would regard that as a sign of weakness in us, whereas your hatred is evidence of our power."[97] Similarly, Putin is trying to re-create a concept of a superpower, a vision of Great Russia by appealing to its own citizens. A clear message of this was the grandiose Olympic Games in Sochi in 2014, which cost Russian society the fantastic sum of 1.5 trillion rubles, equivalent to more than $37 billion.[98] These efforts are directed both to formerly existing signals of lost grandeur as well as creation of new internal identity constructs in all layers of Russian society.

The Concept of Fear and Social Contract

In the matter of constructed Russian national identity, a separate role is played by the notion of fear between the government and its citizens on the domestic level and between the Russian state and the rest of the world. A superpower cannot have the prefix "super" without two important attributes that are related to the comparative military and economic standings of the actors: its own citizens and other countries recognizing its greatness. These are the essential parts of the concave and convex lenses of Russian identity, respectively: you are how you see yourself and how others see you. The tools available for such a dual superpower construct are "coercion" and "appeal," which can be reflected on both levels. On the domestic level, a government exerts what Max Weber called the necessary condition for a normally functioning state: "a human community that (successfully) claims the monopoly of the legitimate use of physical force within a given territory."[99] The citizens both voluntarily and forcefully accept the supremacy of the state over their own sovereignties, which is the core of a social contract between the state and the citizens. Internationally, a country that posits itself as a superpower showcases its military and economic might to attract followers and to scare away potential adversaries. Historical reality shows that on both levels, Russia consciously chose the coercive option.

The concave and convex identities in the Russian context are inextricably linked to two notions embedded in traditional views that Russians have of themselves, their governments, and how they want the rest of world to view them: the concept of "fear" and its role and place in the "social contract." The form and essence of the social contract and the prevalence of fear as the strongest motivator in keeping the terms of the contract in the Russian realities are important for understanding the intricacies existing between the citizens themselves and the state.

First appearing in the "Trial of Socrates,"[100] the "social contract" was presented as a mode of citizen/government interaction, which is essentially made between the citizens themselves and the government acting as an external arbiter and guardian of domestic stability. John Locke further viewed the political power of citizens as vested in government as "a right of making laws with penalties of death, and consequently all less penalties, for the regulating and preserving of property, and of employing the force of the community, in the execution of such laws, and in the defence of the common-wealth from foreign injury; and all this only for the public good."[101] An interesting aspect of any social contract is that it can exist under both autocratic and democratic regimes. The difference is its durability and the fulfillment of the obligations of governments and their constituencies.

Traditionally, in the Hobbesian sense of the world, the social contract is a pledge among citizens themselves not to violate each other's rights, liberty, and property, and the state stays as the guarantor of this pledge. The essence of the "State of Nature," according to Thomas Hobbes, is fear born out of constant competition for resources and wealth, which are by definition limited. The Hobbesian fear results in a "warre of every man against every man [where] . . . nothing can be Unjust. The notions of Right and Wrong, Justice and Injustice, have there no place. Where there is no common Power, there is no Law; where no Law, no Injustice."[102] To Locke, too, the power and authority of government come from people, who, unlike for Hobbes, are living in a "State of Reason." Locke introduces moral and normative constraints on the state of nature, contrary to the "unconstrained" Hobbesian vision. Locke contends, "The state of nature has a law of nature to govern it, which obliges every one, and reason, which is that law . . . [that] no one ought to harm another in his life, health, liberty or possessions."[103] In most of these traditional forms of social contracts, the motivating forces behind governments to rule people and people to obey governments are the inherently rational desires for both parties to be better off in the future.

Effectiveness and Legitimacy of Governance

Longevity of the social contract ultimately defines the durability of the governance regime. This view on stability fulfills Seymour Lipset's requirement for the legitimacy of a state, where "groups will regard a political system as legitimate or illegitimate according to the way in which its values fit in with their primary values," and Aaron Wildavski's political socialization, where "shared values [are] legitimating social practices."[104] These views on political stability include both prerequisites: internal (societal "fit" and legitimacy) and external (recognition of the international community). Problems in providing these prerequisites by governments are referred to by Charles Call as the "internal" and "external" legitimacy gaps "where a significant portion of its political elites and society reject the rules regulating the exercise of power and the accumulation and distribution of wealth" and "when other states fail to recognize or accept its borders or its internal regime," respectively.[105]

Modern scholarship on the social contract focuses on the mechanisms creating the incentives for both parties to continue existence under the set institutional frameworks. These mechanisms are present in any government-citizen interactions regardless of the nature of the governance regimes; their character and nature are, however, different in each case. For governance regimes to be successful and sustainable with regard to political stability and economic and social development, two qualities are necessary, according to Lipset: effectiveness and legitimacy. By effectiveness Lipset means "the actual performance of a political system, the extent to which it satisfies the basic function of government as defined by the expectations of most members of a society, and the expectations of powerful groups within it which might threaten the system." Legitimacy in this context is the "capacity of a political system to engender and maintain the belief that existing political institutions are the most appropriate or proper ones for the society."[106] Jack Goldstone capitalizes on Lipset's model and argues, "Effectiveness reflects how well the state carries out state functions such as providing security, promoting economic growth, making law and policy, and delivering social services. Legitimacy reflects whether state actions are perceived by elites and the population as 'just' or 'reasonable' in terms of prevailing social norms."[107] The combined legitimacy and effectiveness of governance is a prerequisite for political stability in most societies, regardless of their governance regimes. The difference is in the sources of internal and external stability.

In democracies, internal political stability is based on "the rule of law, strong institutions rather than powerful individuals, a responsive and efficient bureaucracy, low corruption, and a business climate that is conducive to investment."[108] These institutions serve a dual purpose: they cut transaction costs for its actors (citizens) and, at the same time, limit the options available to them. The first task is achieved by offering greater opportunities for self-expression and active participation in the decisions vital to their communities and countries. Citizens would have fewer incentives to revolt against their governments if they felt that they received due protection concerning law and order. The legitimacy is created via the free and fair expression of their choice. Fulfillment of the second task is more complicated. Yi Feng assumes that the more developed the democracy, the lower the level of internal political disturbances, thus "democracy will increase the probability of major regular government change, lessen the chances of irregular government change, and, in the long run, decrease the propensity for minor regular government change."[109] This means that the institutional arrangements in place limit the changes for sporadic political activity while increasing the steady flows of political processes based on effective dialogues between governments and their citizens.

Democracy is an evolutionarily more effective form for achieving domestic and international political stability on the basis of Kantian arrangements developed by citizens and vested in their governments.[110] Politics in democracies depends on the "democratic resilience" of the regime, which is based on the willingness and ability of its citizens to participate in political processes and, similar to autocracies, the benefits offered to them by their democratically elected government. Coercion is, by definition, absent from the toolbox of democratic resilience, and the effectiveness of the regime is nondiscriminatory. In modern forms of democratic governance, where the decision- and law-making are done through the collaborative participation of states and their citizens, "both are expected to justify the laws they would impose on each other. In a democracy, leaders should therefore give reasons for their decisions and respond to the reasons that citizens give in return."[111] The social contract in democracies becomes what Habermas calls the most advanced forms of "popular sovereignty": always a two-way street with mutual checks and balances as well as limitations to the options for political participation imposed on each other by both parties of the contract.[112]

Mostly similar to its form and inherently different with regard to substance, the social contract is also present in modern autocracies around the globe. The key variable that differentiates the democratic social contract from the autocratic one is the source of power. In autocratic regimes, according to Vital Silitski, the social contract "is asymmetrical in its nature. . . . [T]he state proposes the social contract in order to nip public discontent in the bud, without resorting to excessive punitive actions. . . . The asymmetrical nature of the social contract is caused by the inability of social groups to self-organize and elaborate horizontal contractual agreements."[113] Whereas in democracies the power vested in governments comes from their subjects, in autocracies "it is the state, and not civil society, that sets the framework of the consensus by offering material and nonmaterial benefits in exchange for citizens' loyalty."[114] Much of the loyalty to the ruler thus depends on the degree of popular intimidation.

Autocracies have their own paths to political stability achieved by their resilience, but this time it is "authoritarian."[115] "Authoritarian resilience" refers to the tenaciousness of leaders to stay in power by providing for the basic needs of most of their subjects and by employing effective mechanisms of coercion. In most cases, authoritarian resilience is based on two pillars: coercing the population and providing them limited benefits. People are prevented from revolting against the regime, which will continue as long as the coercion is effective. The fruits of the effectiveness of governance are offered to limited groups of elite individuals closely affiliated with the ruling autocrats, creating the unique rational choice-based societal "fit": the more benefits these groups receive from governance, and the higher the acceptance level of the regime's domination, the "fitter" and more legitimate the regime will be. The elite in the Russian case includes the *siloviki* (actors from powerful ministries of the interior, defense, FSB, etc.) and the "pocket oligarchs" whose finances can be used for political purposes by the ruling elite in exchange for political favors. Hence the government's legitimacy is acknowledged by these "close circles," who receive most of the benefits, and the rest of the citizens who could endure the coercion levels long enough to fear even worse consequences.

In autocracy these larger population groups also receive some benefits. However, while in democracy "citizens both decide the size of government and have a right to the fiscal residuum, [in] autocracy . . . the state apparatus both decides the size of government and can appropriate the fiscal residuum."[116] Due to the limits established by autocracy on civil participation in the political and economic lives of their countries, the benefits are provided to a much narrower extent. Autocracies aim to satisfy the basic needs of larger populations while keeping the better and ultimately lavish lifestyles of the close circles, allowing them to enjoy disproportionally larger benefits. That is why the middle-class layers in these societies are extremely thin. The individuals from the privileged groups, on the other hand, enjoy free and flexible interpretation of both the letter and the spirit of the law, including economic legislation, and receive preferential treatment by the institutions of governance—all of which falls under the umbrella of "corruption."

The stronger the punitive mechanism of governance, in other words, the more "resilient" the regime is, the "fitter" it feels within the society. Autocracies use the government apparatus, commonly referred to in post-Soviet societies as "administrative resources," to limit the freedoms of their citizens and to disregard general human rights. In most instances, they seem to succeed: according to a public opinion poll conducted by the FOM (Public Opinion Fund), only 9 percent of Russians viewed individual freedoms as an important value in 2000 with an increase to only 14 percent in 2013.[117] Use of law and order as punitive mechanisms coerces subjects to the point where any expression of free will is punishable by definition. In comparison, the durability of societal "fit" for democracies depends on the constant political exchange between the government and the electorate, which is accomplished through wide civil participation in the institutional frameworks offered by democracies.

The process of democratic governance is a reciprocal dialogue between the ruling regime and institutional actors. In order to be effective, democracies must provide for the protection of the rights of their citizens and also ensure their free and uninterrupted participation in the political life of their country. The second part of effective governance is contained in the efforts the citizenry makes to contribute to this process. Bo Rothstein and Jan Teorell call these two components of democracy "inputs" and "outputs." According to them, "A state regulates relations to its citizens on two dimensions. One is the 'input' side, which relates to access to public authority. The other is the 'output' side and refers to the way in which that authority is exercised."[118] On the more contextual level, outputs and inputs are closely connected with the notion of the social contract discussed above, where outputs are about the benefits the citizens will get from the government in case of their compliance as well as the punishments they would receive in case of defection from their government's rule, and inputs are enshrined in the process of participation of the citizenry in governance processes.

Effective interplay between outputs and inputs has direct consequences for the overall sustainability of the governance regimes discussed by Lipset. In his equation, outputs are tantamount to the regime's effectiveness and inputs are related to the notion of a government's legitimacy. Democracies exercise political equality on the combined inputs and outputs of their social contracts. Equal democratic participation of citizens in the form of inputs provides for the basis of norms, rules, and practices of democratic institutionalization. Impartial outputs cement the equality among citizens as exercised by democratically elected authorities. "Inputs," in a sense, are the basis of the fulfillment of the social contract, since they represent the media of participation by institutional actors in the lives of their countries. Citizenship in such settings is "active" and it is the source of power, and not its recipient or a witness.

In autocracies, the links between inputs and outputs are distorted by authoritarian resilience. On the one hand, autocracies do not allow for outputs to be available to all layers of society. Unlike democratic equality, autocracies provide higher outputs for close circles of governance and discriminate against all the rest and much lower outputs for the rest of the population. Correspondingly, the effectiveness and legitimacy of authoritarian regimes are based on inputs from those circles alone, which mostly have to do with individual loyalty to the regimes and their leaders. Under autocratic governance, institutional actors do not produce or are restricted from full provision of inputs, whereas outputs are skewed in favor of the ruling elites. Citizenship in such settings becomes "passive": it is the recipient of the power and not its source.

Autocracies may remain stable for some time by providing lone outputs, which will satisfy the main human requirements for institutional actors given by Abraham Maslow.[119] They would, at the same time, have to compensate for the inputs by mimicking the democratic institutional forms without creating viable conditions for full and equal participation of actors in the political processes. In situations with high output but low input, there is a risk that the government will turn into some form of authoritarian regime. Not fearing popular discontent, governments may provide for the basic or even higher needs of their societies while keeping their political participation to a minimum. On the contrary, low output combined with high input, which is a perfect precondition for state failure, would increase the proclivity of popular uprisings. Not satisfied with current economic conditions, the public may unite against their governments.

For most of its history, starting from the times of Rurik, the first known form of a central government in Russia, Russia has been an autocratic state. The absolutism of power was first introduced by the Great Prince of Moscow Vasily III and was institutionalized by his son Ivan IV, who crowned himself the tsar (a Russian word derived from the Latin word *Caesar*) in 1547 to equalize his title with that of the European monarchs, followed by the first emperor of Russia, Peter I. The monarchy was toppled institutionally in 1917 with the dethroning of the last tsar, Nikolay II, and physically a year later with the assassination of the whole royal family by the Bolsheviks. The vision of autocratic rule as an inherent and irreversible part of Russian political culture, however, survived in the form of the Soviets. During the Soviet Union, the "small body of leading policy officials and ministers, chaired by the General Secretary, and staffed by the party Secretariat, took the key policy decisions" of vital national importance (such as the military interventions in Hungary in 1956, deployment of missiles in Cuba in 1962, Czechoslovakia in 1968, and the last Soviet military intervention in Afghanistan in 1979) with complete exclusion of the people as the true source of power in the decision-making process.[120]

Civil society has been historically the mere witness and ex post facto recipient of the results of grand political decisions of government, which it has little if any control over. The notion of checks and balances, inherent to democratic governance, was absent from the Russian public administration equation. People used to express their view on government decisions not through the mechanisms of deliberation and participation but by spontaneous outbursts of massive unrest. The most famous of these were the uprisings of Don Cossacks under Stepan Rasin in 1667, Kondratii Bulavin (1707–9), and the civil war (1773–75) led by Yemelyan Pugachev against the harsh social and economic conditions of the peasant population.[121] Both of these major rebellions, together with lesser and more localized cases of civil riots, were brutally stifled. During the times of the Soviet Union, too, any deviation from the "general line of the party and the Government" was considered a serious crime, especially if it was committed on a group scale, such as stifling the protest action in Tbilisi, Republic of Georgia, in 1956, against the destruction of Stalin's personality cult by Khrushchev, or some three decades later, in 1989, when demonstrations of politically active Georgian citizens demanding independence from the USSR were violently disbanded by Soviet tanks.

The historically developed authoritarian nature of the social contract in Russia has blocked most avenues for civic participation in the decisions vital to their individual and collective well-being. Individual sovereignty and human rights have never been popular, and neither has the social contract been fully executed when it comes to respecting its terms and conditions. The Russian social contract has always been based on reciprocal fears of the parties involved. Individual or group autocrats feared popular uprising, at worst, and even the growth of the feelings of discontent among their citizens has been put down with extreme prejudice. Civil society has lived in a constant state of fear, which has, paradoxically, two mutually exclusive forms. The Hobbesian fear of losing their lives and possessions eliminated even the slightest chance for self-expression and the statement of their rights, looking at the brutal past performance of autocrats against their citizens.

The other side of their fear is an existential horror at losing the cause of their fears—the autocrats. Ken Kesey's character in his masterpiece *One Flew over the Cuckoo's Nest* gave quite a vivid account of this type of the social contract that is applicable to the historical and contemporary Russian realities and very close to the world in which Thucydides lived several millennia before. Kesey's character Harding, a mental patient, says, "This world belongs . . . to the strong, my friend! The ritual of our existence is based on the strong getting stronger by devouring the weak. . . . We must accept it as a law of the natural world. The rabbits accept their role in the ritual and recognize the wolf as the strong. . . .

[W]e're all here because we can't adjust to our rabbithood. We need a good strong wolf . . . to teach us our place."[122] The citizens, in a way, fear that they will be left without a single potent ruler who is capable of protecting them from multiple external threats by taking most of their sovereignty, thus creating the phenomenon of "individual sovereignty" as opposed to its Habermasian "popular" form.

Fear as directed inward, domestically, has been used by many Russian governments throughout its history to keep the citizens in check at all times and to prevent any signs of popular freethinking and discontent with the outputs that the governments were providing to their own citizens. Such was the docile reaction of the populace when Ivan the Terrible decided to relinquish the powers and to retreat to his village home in 1565. The Russian people begged him to return and gave him carte blanche for governance (to which he hesitantly agreed and introduced the Oprichnina to punish them).[123] This resulted in the brutal years of state-led terror and the Times of Troubles following his death and subsequent tsarlessness.[124] During this period the Russian people felt they were left without a father, who would be harsh in punishment but loving in reward. Nikolay Sanyakov brings up a very interesting point related to the role of fear in medieval Russia during Ivan's reign and his Oprichnina, the tsar's personal execution squads and precursors of the KGB: "The purpose of Oprichnina was to gain recognition of and love toward Ivan the Terrible as a Tsar, no matter how far from ideal he could have been."[125] Fear is here more as a necessary tool for ensuring effectiveness and legitimacy of governance than as an actor on its own.

In the modern history of Russia, fear was first institutionalized in the form of the Red Terror by Lenin.[126] Between 1918 and 1923, in the effort to protect the new state from the revanchist monarchic remnants of tsarist Russia, the communist government looted, tortured, and killed tens of thousands of its own citizens—ideological rivals, those who were less sympathetic with the new regime or those who were simply richer than the average Russian populace. According to Orlando Figes, "Licensing popular acts of plunder and retribution was an integral element of this system, a means of 'terrorizing the bourgeoisie' into submission to the

Proletarian State."[127] It was Lenin who "treated the working class much as a metalworker treated iron ore" to serve some higher purpose.[128] He cemented the totalitarian nature of collective governance in the contemporary Russian mentality through massive state-led repressions. In Ukraine alone, which may have suffered most of all nations from the policies of *dekulakization* (resettlement of the wealthy peasants to the northern territories) and *collectivization* (expropriation of the land and its transfer into the collective ownership, basically abolition of private property), nearly 5 million people vanished in what became known as the Ukrainian holocaust, or the Holodomor.[129] Lenin's suppressive tactics were further perfected by Stalin, who locked up in the GULAGs thousands of Soviet intelligentsia, artists, military, workers, peasants—all those who were suspected of disloyalty to the regime.[130]

The domestic terror and intimidation started by Lenin was perfected by Stalin a decade later in a form of the Great Terror. In his book *Stalin's Police: Public Order and Mass Repression in the USSR, 1926–1941,* Paul Hagenloh traces the origins of Stalin's policing practices back to Lenin's Red Terror, when initially most dissidents were severely repressed.[131] The popular submissive consent of the majority of Soviet citizens to the mass repressions of the Stalinist regime allowed Stalin to build the empire of labor concentration camps where millions of Soviet citizens worked their lives away for the prosperity of the Soviet Union. Terror, which, according to Timothy Snyder, "was the *sine qua non* of Stalinism," had different forms: *dekulakization* practices inherited from Lenin; mass famine on the largest scale ever known; ethnic deportations of "disloyal" groups (Greeks, Chechens, Turks, etc.) from the west to the east of the Soviet empire; extermination of ideological rivals and all those who were vocally unhappy with the regime; and the purges of power figures within the inner communist circles, the so-called *nomenklatura*, accused of disloyalty to Stalin.[132]

The Great Terror was, indeed, an institutionalized form of terrorizing Russia's own people, with its established norms, rules, standards, and best practices. Barry McLoughlin writes, "*Massoperacii* [mass operations] was the internal cypher used by . . . the NKVD to denote major and ubiquitous offenses against certain groups in society. . . . The victims were convicted *in absentia* and *in camera* by extra-judicial organs—the *troiki* [consisting of three people] sentenced indigenous 'enemies.' . . . This strict division of labor in implementing state terror was also adhered to at the highest echelons of power."[133] The so-called processes were devoid of any due process of law: the gruesome statistics of the Great Terror, given by Gregory, include 1.5 percent of the adult population having been exterminated or imprisoned between 1930–32 and 1937–38, the worst years of Stalinism, with approximately 2.5 million arrests within this period and over 2 million deaths while some reports from the State Archives of the Russian Federation reference as many as 7 million perished by the ruthless regime of the state-sponsored and-led domestic terror.[134]

In those relationships born out of state-level fear, the horrors are amplified when, by mutual acceptance of state and citizens, fear of the state is institutionalized as the basis for the social contract in Russia. Essentially, the population resembles a wife who is being abused by her husband but still refuses to divorce. She consciously accepts the hardships and ill treatment just for the sake of having a husband instead of having none. On the other side of this relationship is the abusing husband, who inflicts pain upon his wife . . . out of love. As a hugely politically incorrect Russian saying goes, *B'et znachit lubit*—he is beating his wife because he loves her. The effectiveness in such love-hate relationships depends on the durability and duration of fear and on the sense of legitimacy—on the willful acceptance of coercion.

Internal Fear

By the time of Putin's grand entrance in politics in 1999, the Russian political scene was craving a strong leader unbendable to the external pressure and domestic opposition—an avatar for an autocratic (i.e., good) ruler. That is not to say that Putin's current governance style can in any way be compared with or even related to the scale and character of tsarist suppressions or communist atrocities. It is an extremely "light" and civilized version of governance when juxtaposed with the methods of the Russian autocrats. However, the main idea here is the same:

people should feel happy when collectively seeing the ability of the government to punish regime defectors. If Putin's first term was marked by milder treatment of the opposition, his third coming in 2012 had a goal of "tightening the screws" by making public signs of protest illegal. "The nation needs decades of stable and calm development without any sharp movements and ill-conceived experiments" based on liberal policy, declared Putin as a part of his 2012 election campaign, and he embarked on the task of building the vertical of power.[135]

The first and perhaps most controversial domestic public show of intimidation in Putin's Russia was the imprisonment of Mikhail Khodorkovsky in 2003, one of the richest men in Russia, who showed aspirations for power and, according to Richard Sakwa, "was advancing an alternative vision of a pluralist democracy with an active civil society within the framework of national liberalism, thus challenging the administrative regime's basis of power."[136] The keyword here is "active" versus the "passive" civil society that has traditionally been as such under the Russian autocratic settings. The Khodorkovsky affair was a clear message sent to all those who decided to mess with Putin's regime: don't. The same messages were reiterated over and over again in a number of laws adopted in 2013 to limit expression and speech (the anti-gay law of banning the "propaganda of nontraditional sexual relations" and the "pro-religious" law punishing "public actions expressing explicit disrespect toward society and committed with the purpose of insulting the feelings of believers."[137] The laws on freedom of movement (control over dual citizenship), assembly (changes in the law on demonstrations and rallies severely limiting public expression), and public activity (the notorious "foreign agent" law regulating the activities of Russian civil society—a copy/paste from the U.S. Foreign Agents Registration Act (FARA).[138]

The Putin regime's reaction to the antigovernmental actions of protests, including the Bolotnaya Square demonstrations in 2011 and 2012, the March of Millions in 2012, and detention of over 5,000 Russian citizens for disagreeing with the political situation in the country in 2012 show a different form of fear, but it is essentially still projected inward.[139]

The mass actions gathering thousands of protesters on Bolotnaya Square and Sakharov Avenue in 2011 preceded Putin's second coming as president. By their numbers the protesters did not represent a force in any way able to affect the decisions of the government, let alone pose a threat to its raison d'être. They send, however, strong messages to the top echelons of power that public discontent is growing and may even pose significant challenges to the vitality of the current regime.

On top of that, the successful "color revolutions" in Georgia (2003), Ukraine (2004–5) and Kyrgyzstan (2005) proved to Putin that no regime, with however strong and tenacious autocratic governance, can be toppled by the will of the people, provided there are certain preconditions for that. This is probably what he meant when he explained his view on geopolitical and individual rivalry in an interview for the documentary *Philosophy of Soft Power*: "I won't say about myself; I will say about Russia. Russia has no rivals. Russia has only one rival: itself, our internal problems, our turmoil."[140]

One of the most successful Russian revolutionaries, Lenin gave the following outline of the circumstances under which regimes can be forcefully taken down: "For revolution, it is not enough that the lower classes ['the bottoms'] do not want to live like before. It requires also the upper classes' ['the tops'] unwillingness to rule and govern as before" together with "subjective change: the ability of the revolutionary class to take revolutionary mass action."[141] These conditions were applicable directly to the Russian context since, once successful in 1917 against the tsarist regime and in 1990 against the Soviet Union's decrepit rule, it can be duplicated a century later in a perfectly controlled experimental environment, research-methodologically speaking. This was one of the main reasons for "tightening the bolts," as the Russian saying goes, when Putin came to power again in 2012 against the politically active members of the Russian polity. He feared the consequences of civil activity, as he called "national traitors" and the "fifth column" during his famous Crimean speech in March 2014: as domestically initiated and grown as well as supported from the outside, in the form of Western assistance to the strengthening of Russian civil society.

External Fear

The fear projected by Russian rulers domestically upon their own people had another area of application: international level. There is a saying in the Russian language, which is difficult to grasp for a foreigner: "*Bei svoix chto b chujie boyalis.*" Its closest equivalent would be the Chinese "Beat the dog before the lion." Even this expression, however, does not fully reflect the controversy in applying fear domestically with the aim of delivering the message of intimidation and coercion to the rest of the world.

A story that would shed some light on this saying and its relevance to the current discussion on the role of fear as projected outwardly to the external environment happened thousands of years ago and a thousand miles away from Russia, in ancient Rome. In 508 the Roman Empire was waging a war against the Cluvian leader Lars Porsena. A young Roman patrician, Gaius Mucius Scaevola, sneaked into the enemy camp with the aim of assassinating Porsena but mistakenly killed his scribe. When caught, and facing the grim prospects of violent death, he defiantly declared, "I am Gaius Mucius, a citizen of Rome. I came here as an enemy to kill my enemy, and I am as ready to die as I am to kill. We Romans act bravely and, when adversity strikes, we suffer bravely. . . . Look upon me and realize what a paltry thing a body is for those who seek great glory." Scaevola then put his right hand into the fire burning in front of him and kept it there without any visible signs of pain in his face or body. Utterly shocked by this relentless show of self-mutilation, Porsena let his manqué killer go with the following words: "Leave this place. You have proved a stouter foe against yourself than against me."[142] Scaevola won his life back due to such an exorbitant amount of self-inflicted pain that made any other forms of violence against him simply useless.

This is the point in Russian political culture where internal fear and intimidation are transferred to the external environment. Similar to Scaevola's self-mutilation, which aimed at the external environment, the institutionalized domestic tyranny was meant to send a clear message to foreign enemies and friends alike: if Russian rulers can terrorize their own people, imagine what they could do to the rest of the world! Within the historically path-dependent Russian social contract, the concept of external fear had a double meaning: almost existential fear of being surrounded by enemies and living under the constant threat of annihilation and the wish to turn the situation around and to be feared by others. A poll run by the Levada Center brings additional insights into the internal/external dichotomy of fear in the Russian political culture. In September 2014, 84 percent of the respondents thought Russia was surrounded by enemies—that is, exactly the same ratio of people supporting Putin's foreign policy, and 79 percent believed the source of threat is the West.[143] Together with that, 59 percent did not care about Russia being isolated from the Western world.

History plays an immense role in the concept of external fear in Russia. Since its very inception Russia has been under constant threat of being conquered by enemies along its borders while trying to conquer them in return. The world has proven time and again to be a fundamentally unsafe place for Russians where anarchy and lawlessness prevail. The normal state of nature is thus an omnipresent sense of existential anarchical threat that cannot be controlled. The convex lenses of Russian identity are inextricably connected with the notion of anarchy on the international level, which creates multiple "security dilemmas" for the systemic actors. As described by Robert Jervis, the phenomenon of the security dilemma had its roots in antiquity and came into its own in the modern era.[144] Typical security dilemmas arise in an environment of systemic anarchy where there is no ultimate arbiter capable of punishing those who defect from the world order and rewarding those who comply. Under such conditions, the relative power of actors (nation-states) matters in defining their roles and place in the international arena and the tenor of their interactions with others.

A classic example of the nature of the anarchic system was given by Thucydides: "The standard of justice depends on the equality of power to compel and . . . in fact the strong do what they have the power to do and the weak accept what they have to accept."[145] Under the anarchic nature of the international system, communication channels between actors are limited, which decreases the propensity for them to frankly discuss their differences. Lack of honest interactions further decreases trust between them and presents the actions of "the other" as inherently hostile. Failure to properly communicate each other's true intentions creates reciprocal fear about the ultimate goals behind states' actions. The more separated the countries are from each other identity-wise, the fewer contacts they have on international grounds. Even the little they know of each other becomes distorted. Customs and rituals acquire fictitious images of hostility due to lack of information. Increasing uncertainty of each other's future actions contributes to a fear of mutual intention, the true nature of which—evil or good—cannot easily be distinguished.

Mutual misinterpretation of the real situation leads to an increase in reciprocal fear between ethnic groups, posing any actions by counterparts as a priori hostile and requiring unnecessary extra protection. Buildup of fear and mistrust fuels uncertainty in each other's actions, leaving the states in self-help situations. Under such conditions, states first try to increase their own defensive capabilities, which is viewed across the broad range of other states as innately malicious. A security dilemma unfolds a foggy screen on those defensive capabilities, further blurring the distinction between offensive and defensive use of force: states by definition view others as building up their offensive power and thus resort to building their offensive powers in return. This phenomenon finds its roots in Hobbesian "equality" between all men in their desires to possess greater utility in conditions of inherent economic scarcity. Eventually, there is no security anymore.

Fear has a dual nature in Russian political culture: fear of being obliterated by external actors and, in return, fear caused to external actors by the threat of obliterating them. To Russians, the world is an unfriendly environment, the main goal of which is to destroy the Russian nation. John Thompson identified three variables salient to the consolidation of Russian lands around the Moscovite state in the fourteenth to sixteenth centuries, which are very much aligned with the triple Russian identity construct: "security and unity," a highly valued sense of "community preservation and cohesion," and the fear of annihilation in the extremely hostile outside environment.[146] The last factor is instrumental in understanding the reverse identity: how Russians think that the rest of the world views them—as an ideological threat and as a territorial target. In response to the hostile and anarchic environment, Russians have to deal with the world with a similar degree of hostility and lawlessness. This was their rationale in numerous wars against their neighbors.[147]

Indeed, the world has always been a dangerous place for Russians. Russia has constantly fought for its existence while being "[s]urrounded on all sides by powerful enemies" or being attacked by all sorts of hostile forces: Polovci, Vikings, the Livonian Order, the Polish-Lithuanian state, Sweden, Turkey, the Tatars, France, Germany, and, most recently, the United States and NATO on a political level.[148] The situation continued until the Soviet Union could "clear its backyard" by installing anti-NATO buffer zones around its European perimeter by creating puppet Soviet regimes in Eastern Europe. During Soviet times, skillful communist propaganda represented the world as having a single agenda of destruction of the USSR. The practice of name-calling and verbal demonization was overwhelming at all times, be it against Yugoslav leader Tito, presenting him as a puppet of American imperialism, or the "fascist" Hungarian revolutionary movement, or Lech Walesa, Polish opposition leader, as being trained by Americans in the early 1980s, or the Baltic States as "the citadel of fascism and historical den of European enemies" and finally former Georgian president Mikheil Saakashvili as the embodiment of evil.[149] Ukraine, too, had its share of Russian propaganda: fascists; *maidanutie*, a derogatory name combining "those who go on Maidan" (opposing the government) and a curse word; *Banderovci* (the followers of Stepan Bandera, the leader of the Ukrainian nationalist movement from the 1930s through the 1950s), and *ukropi* ("dill" in Russian is "ukrop"–a curse word homonymous to a "Ukrainian"), to mention a few.

One of the results of projecting fear toward external actors is a violated social contract on the international level. The legal principle *pacta sunt servant* does not seem to have the same standing in Russian political culture as in many Western countries. Several examples of keeping international promises give a good idea of the path-dependent application of fear. As a part of his Decree of Peace of 1917, Lenin urged the warring sides in World War I to cease hostilities and start negotiations on a free and fair peace treaty. The Brest-Litovsk treaty concluded in March 1918 and laid the grounds for subsequent peaceful processes in Europe but left the Soviet Union without significant prior holdings in the former Russian empire, including Ukraine, Finland, Kars (in modern-day Turkey), and Batumi (currently in western Georgia). However, within seven months Lenin denounced the treaty: according to Richard Pipes, he "has been widely credited by the Bolsheviks with prophetic vision in accepting a humiliating [Brest-Litovsk] treaty that gave him the time he needed and then collapsed on its own weight. . . . Nothing he had done contributed more to his reputation for infallibility."[150] As a result of violating the treaty, the Soviets gained badly needed respite and conducted large-scale advances in Ukraine, leading to the capture of Kiev.

Eighty years and a collapse of the Soviet Union later, in December 5, 1994, Russia, the United States, Great Britain, and Ukraine, concluded the Budapest Memorandum on Security Assurances. The High Contracting Parties jointly promised to guarantee to Ukraine, among others, its independence and sovereignty within its existing borders in exchange for renouncing its nuclear-power status as a remnant of the Soviet Union and transferring its entire nuclear arsenal to the Russian Federation. Also, the parties pledged to refrain from the threat or use of force against Ukraine, including conventional military, nuclear, or economic pressure. In early 2014 Russia violated the treaty by (allegedly) conducting a hybrid (i.e., unofficial) military intervention and annexing the Crimean Peninsula and later supporting the irredentist aspiration of pro-Russian rebels in southeast Ukraine by providing them with economic and military support. The word "allegedly" has to be used here since so far there are no Russian flags hovering above the Russian tanks seen in Ukraine. This is all true to a famous Russian saying, *Ne Poiman—Ne Vor*: You are not a thief until you are caught red-handed.

Another outcome of the outward projection of fear is aggressive and threatening rhetoric in the international arena, which continues with remarkable path-dependency in Russian political culture from the times of the Soviet Union. In 1960 Khrushchev was reportedly weaving and banging his shoe at the UN General Assembly to disrupt discussion on the Hungarian uprising.[151] Fifty-two years later, the current Russian UN envoy, Vitaly Churkin reportedly responded to the criticism of his colleague from Qatar on Russia's blocking the UN Security Council resolution on Syria: "I dare you to talk to me once again in such a tone—and your Qatar will not make it until tomorrow."[152] More recently, Russia's most notorious politician, Vladimir Zhirinovsky, threatened to destroy Poland and the Baltic countries if they deployed NATO bases: "The Baltics, Poland—they are all doomed. They will be swept away. There will be nothing left of them if they don't come to their senses, these leaders of the dwarf states! . . . We'll have to destroy them . . . [by] carpet bombings. . . . That's it: no Baltics, no Poland anymore."[153] He also called for annihilation of Germany and France. "Who is spoiling out blood today? Angela Merkel. It's because of her we have sanctions and everything else. . . . We must burn down the whole Paris. . . . We must bomb the whole Germany: bomb Germany completely, to destroy everything there: not a single stone, not a single German. . . . Only then we will feel as a country-victor."[154]

Apart from causing a serious diplomatic scandal between Russia and these countries, these hostile speech acts remained largely unnoticed in the international media. This cannot be said about Putin's direct threat to take over Ukraine that he allegedly made in his phone conversation with José Manuel Barroso, head of the European Commission, in September 2014: "If I want, I would take Kiev in two weeks."[155] Putin made similar threats, but on a considerably larger scale against the European security architecture, in his conversations with Petr Poroshenko, president of Ukraine. According to Poroshenko, Putin said, "If I wanted to, Russian troops could take in two days not only Kiev but also Riga, Vilnius, Tallinn, Warsaw, and Bucharest."[156] The Russian side refuted the facts of such language used by saying that these words "were taken out of context."

Threat is also used as the preferred tactic in dealing with even the most loyal friends and partners. Armenia is Russia's quasi-satellite and a country overly dependent on its trade and investments.[157] In early September 2014 Armenian president Serzh Sargsyan tried to decide the economic and trade fate of his country—which aggravated domestic opposition forces—by agreeing to accede to the Customs Union with Russia only weeks after Putin had visited Azerbaijan, Armenia's long-term rival. While the trip was considered a protocol event between the two countries, and no major military or defense agreements or contracts were signed between the two countries, it was a clear tactic of psychological pressure, said Russian political analyst Sergei Markedonov.[158] The preventive message sent and duly received by Armenia was to side with Russia in its economic orientation or face vague but quite possible negative consequences of military rapprochement with Azerbaijan. Another show of "hard-power" saber-rattling in Armenia happened in December 2013: when Putin visited the country, he went directly to the Russian military base in the city of Gyumri instead of meeting with Sargsyan, thus violating the standard protocol of presidential foreign visits, but showing his value of hard power.[159]

The outward projection of fear became clearly visible in Russian actions resulting from recent events in Ukraine. After President Viktor Yanukovich was ousted by the coalition of opposition forces followed by a bloody standoff in the country's capital, Kiev, Russia intervened in Crimea, an autonomous region of Ukraine on the Black Sea mostly populated by Russian speakers. As a result of a completely theatrical display of force by deploying Russian uniformed soldiers (but without identifying marks) in support of their Russian brethren, according to Masha Gessen, Putin showed that he "intends to save the world from the West. He has started with Crimea. When he says he is protecting ethnic Russians in Ukraine, he means he is protecting them from the many terrible things that come from the West."[160]

The response of the international community to these actions in Ukraine was limited to the cautious escalation of economic sanctions and willingness to accept the Russian annexation of the Crimean Peninsula provided there are credible promises by the Russian government not to proceed even further into western Ukraine. This is a vivid proof of success of the policy of intimidation of opponents routinely applied by Russia. The world is afraid of any unforeseen steps Russia, a nuclear power, might undertake. The fear, however, is more perceptional than real: it is not connected with actual growing Russian influence in the world or even regionally. It is hidden in the fact that Russia is a country that possesses large military nuclear potential in the hands of a government whose actions are difficult if not impossible to predict. In this sense, the world is afraid of Russia just as it is afraid of North Korea, which also may threaten to toss a nuclear bomb at someone: the fear of rogue unpredictability.

In the construct of convex lenses of Russian identity as projecting outward fear, the North Atlantic Treaty Organization is given a special role as the nemesis. This subjectification, at first glance, seems quite paradoxical. On no occasion did NATO reveal any hostile behavior toward Russia or take unfriendly steps to decrease its security. On the contrary, the existing frameworks of the NATO—Russia Council provided viable mechanisms for mutual cooperation and assistance. Nevertheless, NATO is viewed in Russia as villain #1. In his Crimean speech (the one that officially announced the annexation of the region), Putin said, "We are against . . . NATO's ruling the roost near our fence, next to our houses or on our historical territories. You know, I just cannot imagine that we would drive to Sevastopol to visit NATO sailors there."[161] It was against NATO that Putin on the pro-Kremlin youth forum Seliger 2014 claimed Russia was continually building up its nuclear and conventional military.[162] This sentence, and the whole speech, is the epitome of fear-based rationales in Russian foreign policy behavior.

Collectivism

An inherently anarchic geopolitical environment infused with fear and uncertainty deeply imprinted the security dilemma in Russian political culture. The resulting modus operandi is framed by prevalence of offensive over defensive strategies. Similarly, the Machiavellian concept that "one ought to be both feared and loved, but as it is difficult for the two to go together, it is much safer to be feared than loved" seems to have taken a firm foothold in the collective Russian political culture as projected outward.[163] In a public opinion survey conducted by the Levada Center in 2014, on the question, "What would you like to see Russia become—a great power, which is respected and feared by other countries, or a country with high domestic standards of living?" 48 percent chose the first option.[164] At that time, such a high number of those who are ready to surrender individual well-being to collective feelings of greatness was largely due to the annexation of Crimea, but most certainly this should not be considered a one-time case of accidental growth of patriotism.

In this convex construct of superpower as exerting massive collective menace to the surrounding environment, the Soviet Union phantom plays a significant role. It offers Russian citizens the unique reminiscence of the great power status that their country once played in the international arena. As a leading piece of propaganda, young journalist Ulyana Skoybeda's showcase of the revival of Russian imperial identity after having been inspired by Putin's speech on the Crimean annexation deserves to be presented here. In an article in the *Komsomol'skaya Pravda*, the mainstream newspaper intended for younger Russians, she said, "Stepping into a confrontation with the whole world for the sake of truth and the protection of its interests—this is what the USSR was about. Being prepared to live in poverty (for the sanctions of the international community mean poverty)—this is what the USSR was about. It is when all people are ready to walk in rubber boots to save Crimea; when it is more important not to betray your brethren than to have thirty types of sausages in your refrigerator; when the humiliation of Perestroika is finally over. . . . No big deal that Russia had lost its place in the G8: this is exactly how, always isolated, the USSR had existed. . . . Yes, this is the country I know. Hello, Motherland. I missed you so much. . . . The Soviet Union, like a phoenix, has risen from the ashes. . . . It is not the Crimea that came back to us. We did. We came back home. In the USSR."[165]

The mix of power rhetoric with the psychology of superiority in the matter of confronting the rest of the world at the expense of individual freedoms brings the notion of "collectivism" into the equation of Russian political culture. In 1924 the poetic herald of communism, Vladimir Mayakovski, attacked Western and capitalist individualism by opposing to it the Communist Party power of unity and uniformity:

> One!
> Who cares about it?!
> One's voice
> Is thinner than squeal
> Who would hear it?-
> Only one's wife!
> If not in a market,
> But close
> The Party—
> this
> is a single hurricane,
> Of condensed voices.[166]

During the communist era, collectivism was an answer to the hardships that the Russian people went through as a result of the October Revolution and World War II. Even today, the fact that considerable numbers of Russian citizens are willing to forsake individual tangible comforts, economic stability, and social well-being in exchange for some shared intangible goods, such as satisfaction from the feeling of menace their country holds to the rest of the world, reflects on the notion of "collectivism" in Russian political culture.

This masochistic nature of Russian political culture was noted by Russian author and thinker Fyodor Dostoyevsky in his *Diaries* of 1873:

> "I think that the principal and most basic spiritual need of the Russian People is the need for suffering, incessant and unslakeable suffering, everywhere and in everything. I think the Russian People have been infused with this need to suffer from time immemorial. A current of martyrdom runs through

> their entire history, and it flows not only from the external misfortunes and disasters but springs from the very heart of the People themselves. There is always an element of suffering even in the happiness of the Russian People, and without it their happiness is incomplete. Never, not even in the most triumphant moments of their history, do they assume a proud and triumphant air; they have an air of tenderness that almost reaches the point of suffering; the People sigh and attribute their glory to the mercy of the Lord. The Russian people seem to take delight in their suffering."[167]

Russia has historically been willing to put high quality of life on the altar of the concept of *velikoderzhavnost'*, and the people, as Dostoyevsky noted, were willing to sacrifice their individual economic wealth for the sake of moral suffering that stems from the feeling of living in a stronger and more menacing country: a true paradox.

When personal egoistic well-being ceases to be an important criterion for considering a great power status, the country in question chooses an essentially different developmental path. This means shifting budgetary priorities from public welfare, health, and education to defense from external threats and domestic law enforcement against those individuals who do not comply with the collective opinion of the many. The end of the Soviet Union led to a drastic fall of individual economic indicators: according to a report by the Higher School of Economics of the Russian Federation, "The rapid rise in prices for consumer goods and services . . . exceeding the increase in nominal income (11.3 times more), led to a fall in real incomes in 1992 by more than two times—up to 43.7 percent from the previous year."[168] In 2009, according to the same report, the Russian GDP only slightly exceeded that of 1990.

Russia is located at the far end of Geert Hofstede's "Collectivism" cultural value scale with the transcendence of the collectivist into collectivist political thinking.[169] Two factors influenced the development of collectivist thinking in Russian political culture: the natural habitat of the Russian nation and Orthodox Christian values and practices. Starting from the times of the primitive Slavic tribes, the surrounding world has been cold and unwelcoming where the struggle for survival has been their daily activity. According to Thompson, "For most of its history, Russia was a very poor country, its people struggling to survive and improve their way of life while supporting, with limited resources, a government-organized defense against recurrent enemies."[170] Renowned Russian historian Vasilii Kluchevsky also notes the environmental difficulties in molding the Russian nation: "Great Russia, with all of its forests, marshes, and bogs at every step, presented to settlers thousands of minor dangers, unforeseen difficulties, and unpleasant things with which it was constantly necessary to cope and struggle."[171] Harsh climatic conditions due to the northern location of the country; long and cold winters and the impossibility of carrying out most agricultural activities coupled with the struggle for survival against a plethora of external invaders presupposed a collectivist economic and political lifestyle.

Also bringing collectivism into Russian political culture are the Christian traditions of the Russian nations. The order of Orthodoxy heightened the sense of community and also influenced the level of isolation from the other Christian traditions of the West. More specifically, the etymology of the word "cathedral" in Russian—*sobor* (*sbor*: congregation)—is closely related to the term *obshchina*, the communal nucleus of the early Russians. Yale Richmond claims, "The Orthodox vision of sobornost is the main driving force behind all the social and political endeavors of the Russians . . . the expression of the desire to treat their rapidly expanding state as one big family."[172] Communal religious rites galvanized Russian society in the Middle Ages, where the Church stood on par with the secular government in controlling the everyday lives of the *obshchina* members.

More recent Russian/Soviet history associated economic collectivism with communal management of agriculture, the *kolkhoz*, and political collectivism "with violence [which] is appropriated and monopolized by the authorities who appoint themselves as the guardians and protectors of the interests of the whole national essence."[173] During the Soviet Union, the country harassed its own citizens on the individual level, promising them increased collective benefits, the pinnacle of which was the ultimate equalizer, the nuclear mace. Stalinism gave birth to a political neologism: "public enemies," who were all those who opposed the general politics of the party—these were severely persecuted. The level of state terror against defectors was evident in the inclusion of the corresponding notion as an infamous article in the main law of the state, the Soviet constitution.[174] This tradition of prevalence of the collective over the individual essence was revived in 2014 when Putin reworded the term "public enemy" in his Crimean annexation speech: "traitors of the nation." In describing Putin's view on collectivism, Svetlana Alexievich contends, "He who does not rejoice is an enemy of the people. They belong to the fifth column, to the obscurantists from the State Department. The Stalinist vocabulary is fully restored: traitors, renegades, accomplices of the Fascists. With the only difference that the Stalinists are now orthodox."[175] Of course, the current situation in Russia is still far from the total state terror of Stalinism, but the grim resemblance in the rhetoric puts the domestic "non-systemic" (i.e., not part of the Duma) opposition in a dangerous position.

Skoybeda's statements above reflect not only the superpower nostalgia: they also show an attitude toward political events that has been framed in terms of a historically developed and cemented Russian collectivist view. This excerpt relays the main message that Russian political culture sends to the outside world: being a Soviet Union means having enough power to oppose the whole world and to present a sufficiently viable force to intimidate others by employing a realist view on superpower. The collectivist view also means that Russia is enjoying its menacing status as a compelling superpower and is simply incapable of having its quality of "appeal" for others.

Origins and Transience of Authority

Russia is a country of political jokes. People used to tell jokes about their governments and its officials all the time, even during Stalinist times and Brezhnev's less despotic era. It would be wrong to assume that Putin's regime took the phenomenon of political jokes to a substantially different level, but it also made its contribution to the ability of the Russian people to take the political processes with a healthy grain of humor. One such event where facetious comments were slung was the presidential–prime ministerial "castling" between Putin and Medvedev in 2008 and back from Medvedev to Putin in 2012. As one of the most illustrious jokes goes, Putin is making his annual New Year's presidential address on December 31, 2007, to the Russian people, talking about all the achievements and progress the country has made over the past year. He then steps down from the pulpit and a camera follows him. Putin comes up to Medvedev standing aside, bites him in his neck, and Medvedev becomes . . . the new president of Russia.

This political quip describes one of the most important components of Russian political culture: the transition of power between the existing/past ruler to the forthcoming one. It is the very meta-variable that glues all the above factors in the intricate cobweb of Russian political culture where the government's accountability for its citizens is nonexistent. In societies with either direct or representative democracy, the people directly or through their representatives participate in the decision-making processes vital to their everyday life, and there is nothing more important than selection of the country's top executive. The process of democratic governance is a two-way street that allows the people to keep their elected representatives constantly accountable—through the tools of governance, the most potent of which is impeachment—for their good or bad deeds as well as the specific policy products they offer. This way, the people also become active producers and creators of policy and not its mere recipients. Here is where the Latin saying "*Vox populi suprema lex*" comes into play: "The voice of the people is the highest law." On the opposite side of the governance spectrum are autocracies, where the people have limited or no control over the ultimate effects of the decision-making process. They are not policy producers or creators but policy recipients, without proper participation in governance at most of its levels.

The balance struck between inputs and outputs, historically created in the case of Russia, turned it into what North et al. call "a natural state," where the main if not the only decision-makers are located in the upper echelons of power. "A natural state," according to Douglas

North et al., "reduces the problem of endemic violence through the formation of a dominant coalition whose members possess specific privileges. . . . Elites—members of the dominant coalition—agree to respect each other's privileges, including property rights and access to resources and activities. By limiting access to these privileges to members of the dominant coalition, elites create credible incentives to cooperate rather than fight among themselves."[176] The problem with the natural state is that both the producers and main recipients of policy outputs are available to the ruling elites, which are the main producers of the legitimacy of the state apparatus. This means a stagnant political life, since the authority transition happens within the internally competing but largely externally peaceful elites who are repeatedly excluding the population from this process.

There is, indeed, little that is evolutionary in the process of authority transition in Russia. The first mechanism of power transfer traditionally happened through official invitation in 862 when the Scandinavian chieftain Rurik was invited with his brothers to lead local Slavic tribes who were living in a classical state-of-nature situation, suffering from omnipresent security dilemmas. As the first Russian historical chronicle, *The Tale of Bygone Years,* describes the situation between the tribes, "There was no law among them but tribe rose against tribe. . . . They said to themselves, 'Let us seek a prince who may rule over us and judge us according to the Law.' . . . They thus selected three brothers, with their kinfolk, who took with them all the Russes and migrated. The oldest, Rurik, located himself in Novgorod; the second, Sineus, at Beloozero; and the third, Truvor, in Izborsk."[177] The foreign Rus' tribe thus settled down upon external invitation of the locals, ultimately giving their name to the country of Russia.

Rurik and his descendants (Rurikovichi) ruled the country for centuries through the second medium of power transfer in Russia: hereditary lines, from a tsar to his son, and so on. This process was not without the usual bumps and hiccups that were common in heraldic reign in practically all parts of the world with dynastic rule. With short interruptions and swings from one regional offshoot of the Rurikovichi to another, including assassinations of members of the royal family and the whole line of impostors, this was the longest royal realm in the history of Russia, lasting for seven and a half centuries. In 1612 the last Rurikovich, Vasiliy Shuisky, a highly loathed tsar among Russians, accused of poisoning his more popular contender, General Skopin-Shuisky, was deposed and transferred to Poland, a medieval nemesis of Russia.[178]

The short tzarless intermission between 1598 and 1613 (not counting two impostors from Poland: False Dmitry I and II), known as the Times of Troubles, created another means of power transfer, which, however, was not practiced until the twentieth century by the communists: narrow elite circles-led elections. In 1613 Mikhail Federovich Romanov was elected tsar by Zemsky Sobor, a group of boyars, clergy, and provincial representatives who feared the absence of monarchical rule more than the rule itself. The House of Romanov spawned five tsars and ruled until 1917 when the last one, Nicholas II, was deposed as a result of the bourgeois revolution—a new medium of power transfer in Russian history. Another revolution occurred in October 1917, in this case led by the lumpenproletariat inspired by inflammatory populist speeches and slogans of Vladimir Lenin and other Bolsheviks. The revolution revived the one-off method of power transfer in Russia: the elite election within a single-party system of the CPSU (Communist Party of the Soviet Union).[179] Sakwa traces the mystery of election/appointment of the Soviet leaders back to the turbulent and path-dependent Russian history, which, according to him, "is littered with examples of savage court intrigues and murders as one monarch gave way to another. The Soviet period was no different."[180] Communist leaders were selected and appointed in the intricate game of "Kremlinology," where the reading-between-the-lines techniques of trying to define who is next in line in the Politburo focused on who stood closest to the first figure and who was rumored to succeed him in the aftermath; placement/removal of the portraits of communist leaders; other discourse and visual signs in the Soviet media.[181]

Gorbachev was loosening the communist grip on the lives of people and was conniving for the revelation of their free will. The coup staged by dying-out hardcore communists organized around the GKChP (State Committee on the State of Emergency) was supposed to reinstate the authoritarian resilience of the Communist Party, but it failed. For the last time in Russian/Soviet history, the Russian people, led by another democratizer, Yeltsin, took matters into their own hands and went out on the streets of Moscow protesting against being dragged back to the Stone Age by the CPSU in its last agonizing convulsions.[182] This was the first step toward reinstatement of the *vox populi*. According to Herbert Ellison, "It was an overwhelming victory for Russian democrats in their long struggle against the power of the Communist party and the Soviet government—a victory that opened the way to Russian democracy."[183] The "way" or the "door" to governance through which the public voice should be heard was closed by the same person who opened it, Boris Yeltsin, who was the second-most-hated modern Russian ruler after Gorbachev.

The popular narrative of the early 1990s pictures Gorbachev and Yeltsin both as villains and national traitors. The general public accused them of collapsing the Soviet Union and putting the country into a decade of domestic political turmoil and economic devastation, coupled with the significantly minimized foreign prestige of a former superpower whom no one considered seriously any more in the international arena. By the end of the second term in 1999, Yeltsin, according to Masha Gessen, "had no legal right to seek a third term, nor was he well enough to try. . . . [He] had every reason to fear an unfriendly successor. Yeltsin was not just an unpopular president: he was the first politician whom Russians had ever trusted—and the disappointment his people felt now was every bit as bitter as the support he had once enjoyed had been inspiring."[184] Senescent Yeltsin had no other choice but to handpick his *preemnik* (successor), the most contemporary form of power transfer in Russia: a person whom he would wholly entrust with not only governance of the country but also his family. This person turned out to be Vladimir Putin, a former KGB lieutenant colonel and a Russian *apparatchik* relatively unknown even on the local political scene. It is largely rumored that it was Boris Berezovsky, a Russian oligarch (who committed suicide in

London's ritzy suburbs in 2013 under mysterious circumstances) who advised Yeltsin to consider the candidacy of a young Petersburgian, who (taking into account his tarnished reputation for shady overseas oil sales) could be easily controlled.[185] As history shows, they were both wrong.

When the time came for Putin to end his second consecutive term as president, "operation successor" was enacted for the second time. Thereafter came the meteoric rise of Medvedev, a fellow Petersburgian, to power largely copying Putin's own. Having been appointed by the latter as the head of the Securities and Exchange Commission in 1999, Medvedev soon led Putin's election campaign, after which he became the deputy head of the presidential administration and the head of the Russian state gas giant Gazprom. In 2005 Medvedev was appointed the first deputy prime minister of Russia, responsible for such important national projects as housing, healthcare, agriculture, and education. Yet he was an unlikely presidential candidate: "too soft, too pro-Western, too liberal."[186] However, as it sometimes happens even with the least likely personalities to fit within a specific position, the odds were in Medvedev's favor. Since then the expression "tandem" acquired a substantially new meaning in the Russian political lingo.[187] Medvedev became president in 2008 and appointed Putin as his prime minister "to play the key role . . . in strengthening our tandem".[188] He "warmed the seat" for Putin for another four years and loyally gave it back to him in 2012.

In all of the abovementioned transfers of power from the predecessor to the successor, wider civil society was mostly excluded from participation in the power (re)distribution with its roles limited to nominal "yay-sayer" in the political transitions, including numerous façade elections. Putin continues this tradition of being the alpha and omega of Russian politics. His solo decisions on national and foreign issues meet little if any opposition from the domestic political establishment. Even the appointment of Medvedev as his successor happened via purely personal views: Daniel Treisman quotes Putin commenting on Medvedev's candidacy, saying, "I am confident that he [Medvedev] will be a good president and an effective manager. But besides other things, there is this personal chemistry: I trust him. I just trust him."[189] Internationally, too, all key political decisions are made without involvement of the larger stakeholders. The Russian parliament's lighting-speed approval of Putin's request to send troops to Ukraine's Crimea in 2014 heralds only one thing: that the decision to intervene in the domestic affairs of this sovereign state had already been made by Putin, and its "deliberations" were merely conniving lip-service.

Group Elites vs. an Individual

Centuries of excluding the Russian population from authority transitions brought a unique apathy to its mentality toward the general political processes under way in the country, as well as affecting it from outside. In 1969 Andrei Amal'rik wrote a prophetic book, *Will the Soviet Union Last beyond 1984?* in which he predicted the collapse of the Soviet order with only a six-year error. Amal'rik used the exclusion of the citizenry from the political process as the main variable that would eventually lead to collapse of the Soviet giant. Here is what he said: "The Russian people, by virtue of their historical traditions . . . are almost completely unable to understand the idea of self-governance, equality of the law and personal freedom—and the related responsibility. . . . The very word 'freedom' is understood by most people as a synonym for 'disorder.'"[190]

By excluding the people from policy inputs, the elites in the natural Russian state also eliminate their feelings of proprietorship over outputs. Even more so, when the people do not view themselves as owners of the full benefits that are available to a limited number of individuals, they have limited responsibility for what is going on in their lives. In comparison to the high collectivism when it comes to overall pride for the country, on the individual level the population paradoxically suffers from the lack of responsibility for their lives.

In Russian political discourse, just as in any country with absolutist public administration structures, elites at the highest levels have always been visually separated from those whom they govern. Even though they could not have bragged to have the most impeccable performance, both as managers and simply as human beings, people would generally prefer to have the highest decision-making authorities rather than live without them. The same reason guiding people to beg Ivan IV to return to power has survived until contemporary times when the dualist relations between an autocratic ruler and the citizenry are cherished as something idolatrous. In the best traditions of authoritarianism, the "bottoms" should love and venerate their "tops," who would mercifully bestow their grace upon the latter and punish them, but lovingly. This was the situation with serfdom in Russia, which lasted for almost four centuries before it was abolished in 1861 by Russian reformer Tsar Alexander II. The relationships between serfs and their owners are depicted in current Russian political discourse as increasingly positive and as the icon for the traditional public administration setting in patriarchal Russia. In September 2014, Valery Zor'kin, chairman of the Supreme Court and one of the nominally most powerful civil servants in Russia, made the following comment in an article on Alexander II's reforms: "With all the cons of serfdom, it was the very 'clip' holding the inner unity of the nation. It is no accident that the peasants, according to some historians, told their former masters after the reform: 'We were yours, and you—ours.'"[191] Historian Boris Mironov echoes Zor'kin in delivering panegyrics to serfdom as an integral part of Russian identity: "Serfdom . . . was an organic and a necessary component of the Russian reality. . . . It was the flip side of the breadth of Russian nature."[192] This creates an idealistic picture of a caring autocrat who was, in the words of Richard Wortman, "not only the anointed of God, he would be the guardian of his nation's well-being."[193] In return, not only should the "rabbits" be content with the rule of the "wolf," but it is required of them to be genuinely happy with what is given to them and with what is withheld.

The conditions for the reenactment of serfdom are rapidly coming into view: of course, it is in a different form and shape but with similar content, the sharp division of the domestic social and economic landscape into the "haves" and "have-nots." In authoritarian societies, typical examples of this were tsarist Russia and the communist Soviet Union, where, to retain an aura of supremacy and imperviousness to the people's choices, the ruling elites stood far and above the ordinary plebs. The whole idea of governance, as Kordonsky claims, is built on the philosophy of serfdom, where the administrative divisions, starting from the smallest ones, households, and extending as far as whole regions of Russia are governed as "estates" during serfdom. "An estate becomes a part of the "real" space, separated by any borders. . . . Thus the regions of the Russian Federation, especially the republics, being 'de facto' its subjects, 'in reality' are the estates of their presidents and heads of administrations. A substantial part of municipal districts . . . are 'in reality' the estates of the heads of municipalities where practically all income-generating property is in ownership of the members of their families and trustees."[194] The estate division of governance in Russia re-created what Yevgenii Minchenko calls "Politburo 2.0," with direct reference to the elitist management style of the communists. For him, governance in Russia is represented by "a conglomerate of clans and groups that compete with one another over resources. Vladimir Putin's role in this system remains unchanged—he is an arbiter and a moderator, but a powerful arbiter who has the last word (at least for the time being) in conflict situations."[195] In the governance scheme, Putin is a real tsar reincarnate: he hovers above the mutually competing groups, which are too weak and too disunited to challenge his rule.

In such "estate" relationships, the phenomenon of social distance plays an important role in establishing and maintaining autocratic governance. Russia fits perfectly well within Geert Hofstede's "Large Power Distance" category with the following definition of the social balance between the Russian autocracy and its people, given by Harriet Murav: "The ruler's superiority to and distance from the people enhanced his or her right to autocracy."[196] According to Mauk Mulder's "Power Distance Theory," a typical autocrat, by definition being "the more powerful individual[,] will strive to keep or increase the distance to the less powerful person. He will avoid association with less powerful persons and his feelings toward them are negative. He cannot recognize himself (i.e., the picture he has made for himself) in less powerful persons and experiences any increase of power of the less powerful person as a threat to his own, relatively more powerful, position."[197]

Under large social power-distance settings, autocrats would normally delegate their tasks and duties to their henchmen, who were held responsible by popular judgment for all deeds, bad or good. What is interesting to note is that society plays an enormous role in bestowing future autocrats with power. As Jan Bruins and Henk Wilke noted, "In hierarchically structured groups where subjects are acting in terms of selves, power processes are not so much the result of group members' desire for power, but of the feeling of entitlement they have on the basis of the bureaucratic rule."[198] The more the entitlement that the group's members allow the autocrat to have, the larger the social power distance between him/her and the group.

The paragon of social power-distance theory was the Soviet Union, where major decisions were made behind the closed doors of the Communist Party Central Committee. The secrecy was overwhelming. When Soviet premier Nikita Khrushchev read his famous report "On the Cult of Personality and Its Consequences" in 1956, dethroning Stalin from the Soviet Union pedestal and ending the era of mass fear, suppressions, and terror, it was a shock to even his closest communist entourage. Needless to say, the report has the stamp "Top Secret" and "Not for Publication" on it, and not until it happened to reach the Israeli Security Service Shin Bet and through them the United States did the Soviet people learn about it and the huge transformations that would result.[199] Essentially, in autocratic societies it was not the citizens who "owned" policies (as it should be in more open and democratic countries). Rather, the policies, made backstage in complete detachment from the existing community realities on the ground, "owned" the citizens.

In eighteenth-century Russian bureaucratic tradition, there was a strictly stratified system of ranks established by Peter I, which was "based . . . on the notion of scales and the recognition of an ego-centered level of 'people who are just like us' versus those more select and those more vulgar."[200] To a much lesser degree, this bureaucratic stratification system during the Soviet Union was somewhat similar to the notion of the caste system of *songbun* in North Korean culture, where, according to Robert Collins, "Each and every North Korean citizen is assigned a heredity-based class and socio-political rank over which the individidual exercises no control but which determines all aspects of his or her life. Under this classification system, all citizens become part of one of three designated classes—the 'core' or loyal class, the 'wavering' class, or the 'hostile' class."[201] The difference with the Soviet Union was, of course, absence of the birthright variable and a higher mobility across the social strata, but the philosophy and the spirit of social distancing between the rulers and their citizens remained essentially the same.

Even on an individual level, the members of the Supreme Soviet of the Communist Party were fully separated from the realities of the ordinary people and led their lives as the pharaohs in ancient Egypt. Not much was known of their personal lives, their families, their likes or dislikes. In fact, anything personalized was carefully removed from the communist governance setting, leaving the leaders as nothing more than impersonal and emotionless images hovering in the communist sky. An article from the newspaper *Hour*, published in 1984 in the immediate aftermath of the death of one of the least known leaders of the Soviet Union, Constantine Chernenko, sheds some light on the social power distance in the USSR between the ruling elite and the lower classes: "There is no 'first family' concept in the Soviet Union, and the private lives of the elite are carefully screened from the general public. . . . There is no campaigning for office in the Soviet Union, wives do not stand alongside their husbands at ceremonial occasions, and official biographies seldom contain the kind of personal details that are taken for granted in the United States or other Western countries."[202] Keeping the family out of the spotlight was yet another tool of social elevation of the autocratic rulers in the Soviet Union.

Daily Portions of Lies

Putin continues the noble tradition of his predecessors of detachment from the people. He stands far above the general crowd, who has three times already delegated the responsibility for their lives into his hands. To start with, the very aura of Putin is drenched in mystery. In fact, more is known about his Labrador Koni than about his family, including his former and current wives and his two daughters. The causes of his sudden divorce in 2013 and his courting of (or lack thereof) and marriage to Alina Kabayeva, an Olympic bronze and gold medalist and an MP, are being kept by Putin's entourage under the strict regal veil of secrecy. These facts—divorces and marriages—in all reality, are ordinary milestones in regular human interactions, even though these humans might be country leaders. In the case of Putin, however, such events should, in principle, belong to a wider public domain. The reasoning is pretty simple here: the people elected him and the people must know what is going on with their choice on the emotional level. However, loyal to the Russian tradition of attaching divine qualities to the leaders, Putin's life events were enveloped in obscurity and elevated to the status of state secrets. As the presidential press secretary Peskov once commented on the numerous rumors on Putin's nuptials, "It's his decision and he's not obliged to talk about his personal life. . . . He works so much I don't know where he finds time for it."[203] This was an obvious lie, since Putin is not an ordinary citizen and cannot elope with his sweetheart without his secretary or the guard knowing it. The common people, too, knew very well it was a lie, but they prefer to be content with that lie rather than question it, which is another integral part of the individual leadership component of Russian political culture. Another example is Putin's absence from the political scene for ten days in March 2015. No public explanations were made on what the ruler of the largest country in the world was doing for those days.

Blatant lies have been elevated to the highest level of governance in modern Russia to cope with domestic and international challenges. There is a dual connection here between the state lying to its people and the people knowingly believing the lies. On the one hand, allowing lies to permeate the very core of society happens because of the historically developed tradition of disregard to individual interests for the sake of the ephemeral common good, which follows collectivism in Russian political culture. The logic here goes in the direction of "the rulers know best" what an average citizen needs; thus they enjoy unquestioned leeway in their actions. On top of taking much of the individual freedom and sovereignty away from citizens for the sake of common happiness, the

Russian social contract also gives rulers carte blanche for their actions. The citizens' indulgence of government reflects the old *Tsar-Batushka* (Tsar-Father) approach where human and material costs of governance are given the absolute charter from the people.

The other reason for condoning the state's lies to its citizens is hidden deep within the fabric of Russian society and also has to do with collective versus individual existential approaches. By accepting rulers' lies, citizens relegate the gravity of the reality around them and vest responsibility for their individual lives into the hands of their rulers. This way, reality with its problems and hardships seems less problematic and easy to live in when there is knowledge that some distant Leviathan is carrying the daily decision-making burden on its broad governance shoulders. To a certain degree, allowing the lies to happen has to do with fear of potentially negative consequences that may arise from questioning the validity of the arguments and the facts promulgated by the government. On the other hand, however, it is a genuine ostrich-like behavior of shunning reality by assuming that once the lies are accepted, with the passage of time, they will become truth, partly or wholly.

Letting the governments lie became the modus operandi of citizen-government relations in Russia. It is, in a way, more comfortable to have your government lie to you: living a lie takes personal responsibility away from the citizenry, allowing them to lie to their government in return, which becomes a universally acceptable habit in relations with the state. Lying makes the state collectively responsible for the situation within the country, which means that at some point in the future, people will start blaming the state (and not themselves) for their hardships. This happened with the Soviet Union, when the whole population, first forcefully and later quite voluntarily, delegated responsibility for their lives to a small group of geriatric apparatchiks who appeared twice a year on the Kremlin wall and greeted the consenting herds of Soviet people from above. In the late 1980s the slowing growth in numbers of dissident cohorts and their sympathizers began revising the "sanctions to lie" of the Soviet government, and this eventually led to its demise.

Being on the outskirts of Russian foreign policy, individuals can be lied to by the authorities without much forethought. Soviet propaganda used this attitude every now and then when it poured tons of lies upon citizens about the "rotting" state of the Western economy, society, politics, and culture as well as its own operations abroad. Most of the facts about military operations in Afghanistan, especially the real number of casualties, were kept secret from the Soviet people and the outside world. In the wake of the Chernobyl disaster in 1986, the Soviet government convoluted the reality of its deadly natural/manmade catastrophe from the Soviet people, especially those who lived close to the nuclear power plant, to avoid panic on a mass scale. Russian MP Alla Yaroshinskaya, who at the time of the Chenobyl explosion was a journalist working in Ukraine, brings up the number of 148,000 who died within the decade following the disaster and 100,000 of those who helped with the immediate aftermath.[204] Most of them could have been saved had the Soviets timely evacuated the population. Alexander Shlyakhter and Richard Wilson also noted the factor of secrecy in misinforming the population about the deadly consequences of the radiation, the "failure [to manage technology] is due in large part to the secrecy that was endemic in Soviet society and to a lesser extent in the tsarist Russian society before it. Society existed in compartments, with little communication between them. Secrecy was often justified by the desire to avoid panic."[205] The real scale of the disaster leading to unnecessary deaths was one that could have been avoided had the government duly informed its people.

In modern-day Russia, with the same MO, the government continues to spread deliberate lies. For example, in September 2000, Putin answered, "It sunk" to Larry King's question "What happened to [the submarine] the *Kursk*?"[206] And the Russian public was perfectly content with 118 lives wasted onboard the submarine without proper investigation.[207] The recent hybrid war in Ukraine in 2014, starting with the Russian annexation of Crimea and paramilitary guerilla operations in its southwest, revealed the whole kaleidoscope of lies the Russian government has been feeding its citizens. In March 2014, during the press conference in the aftermath of the Crimean annexation, Putin flatly denied any presence of Russian troops on the peninsula, and the heavily armed and uniformed soldiers and the heavy military machinery—but without the regular Russian army—he called "self-defense forces who went to the nearest supermarket and bought their uniforms there."[208] Two decades after Pavel Grachev, Yeltsin's minister of defense, blatantly disavowed any presence of Russian troops in the military operation in Chechnya in 1994, his successor, Sergei Shoigu, remains loyal to the culture of disinformation.[209] When asked at a press conference in March 2014 whether there were Russian troops in Crimea, Shoigu replied, "It is a bunch of baloney. . . . There are absolutely no Russian troops in the Crimea," and he called pictures of the Russian military vehicles with license plates from the 21st region (Chuvash Republic) "a provocation."[210] "They are lost" or "they are on vacation."[211] These were the strawman cover-ups of the presence of multiple Russian regular troops in Ukraine.

State- originated and-sponsored lies are saturated with appallingly and deliberate fake stories for the domestic public, which it readily swallows. One of them was aired on the Russian First State Channel of a phony "refugee from Slavyansk." There, she spoke of a three-year-old Russian boy whom the "Ukrainian fascists" crucified, like Jesus, in his underwear, and then cut his flesh open with knives to make him suffer. They let his mother watch, and eventually tied her to a tank and dragged her around the central square for three kilometers.[212] Another "credible" story aired on the NTV on November 2, 2014: a teenage boy claimed that the Ukrainian military had kidnapped him from his house, injected him with an unknown medicine to make him obedient, put electronic GPS chips into his jacket, and sent him to the pro-Russian militia, which would make him a live target for Ukrainian guided missiles.[213] In reality, he was a mentally disabled runaway from an eastern Ukrainian village.[214]

The problem here is not that the government is blatantly lying to its people. It is that the people are allowing these lies to exist without properly questioning the nature and the sources of information. Another issue, which is much worse, is that such policy is deliberately targeting the people, knowing that they will accept it no matter what. The Russian government seems to know its people quite well. With regard to the situation in Ukraine, there is an overwhelming free pass given to the Russian leadership by their citizens, epitomized by Vladimir Nikitin, head of the Pskov Regional Branch of the Union of Paratroopers: "There are things that you don't talk about. Since there is some political will, something done up there, let them bear the full responsibility. If the president deems it necessary, he will address the people; if he does not—so be it: politics is politics. War is war. If they decided not to divulge some information, it means there is nothing there."[215] Such a view on the President-*Batushka* can well be generalized to a wider public spectrum: according to a recent public opinion poll conducted by the Fund of Public Opinion (FOM), 72 percent of Russian citizens are fine with state censorship of mass media. Moreover, respondents are convinced that there are important social issues during coverage of which the state may lie to its people. In comparison with 2013, the numbers of those who consider it normal to distort information in mass media in the interest of the state doubled and reached 54 percent.[216] With the enemies of Russian statehood consolidating around and against it, nothing seems to shake the unerring support of the Russian populace to its leader, even the most outrageous and blatantly deliberate lies.

Role of an Individual

Rulers and individuals with power have always been venerated in Russia, especially if the power comes not only with their positions and ranking but is also backed up by their characters, genuine or purposely showcased. Personal health and longevity of a ruler is another factor affecting the durability of the social contract in Russia. The resilience of the Soviet Union as an institution replaced the individual longevity by the efficacy of the one-party state apparatus. It successfully preserves and monopolizes inputs by providing the limited outputs to the close circles of loyal party officials. In return, such actions were considered legitimate as long as the population enjoyed some degree of the protection of lives and property in the face of potential troubles that would follow the absence of such a menacing Leviathan. In the input-output policy dichotomy, inputs are the strategies and the tactics that governments use to perpetually bully their citizens into complete submission and political anabiosis whereas outputs (effectiveness) are represented by rabbitlike consent to governmental actions on the part of the population and their unconditional and blindfolded support to what the rulers do.

Not only did the state hold the monopoly over the real national security-related materials, classified as "state secrets," but it also conducted overwhelming and all-encompassing censorship in nearly all spheres of life, including such seemingly public information as the five-year plans.[217] Indeed, as Georgi Bovt notes in drawing parallels between the informational policies of Putin's and the Soviet regimes, the majority of the documents related to the economic performance of the Soviet Union were withheld from the general public with the stamp "classified."[218] This way the Soviet autocracy could keep its hand on the pulse of the nation by severely limiting its outputs even in the form of public goods, such as the information that is normally available in democratic societies. This way the government was withholding one more sovereign right of the people's social contract with it: the right to know what the government is doing.

When in 1999 Putin came to the Russian political scene, it had long been accustomed to state violence against own people. There was already well-established authoritarian political culture. Lionel Posard concurs: "Autocracy was one of the main characteristics of Russian political culture. Indeed, successive reigns and rulers all were of autocratic nature. This became so common through history that, in the eyes of the average Russian citizen, autocracy is inseparable from the notion of legitimate government."[219] A synonym for autocracy in Russian political culture is power and the ability to use it indiscriminately. Those who have those qualities are revered, feared, and, as a result, loved. Those who don't are collectively loathed. That is why neither Gorbachev nor Yeltsin are fully respected in Russian society: they were both embodiments of powerlessness and wussiness—the former for not being able to preserve the Soviet empire and the latter for giving in too much to the West.

Putin is not an exception from the President-*Batushka* style of reverence given to him by the very virtue of the position he has been holding since 2000. The new millennium gave new Russia a leader whose task, as he defined it, was to help get "Russia off its knees and whack everybody hard."[220] The process started in 1999 when Putin became prime minister for the first time. This task has two objectives: collection and retention of Russian lands, started by Ivan III in the fifteenth century, and rebuilding the image of Russia as the true superpower. Putin has become the institution of collective responsibility for the fate of Russian citizens—just as it always was with the tsars since the Ruriks.

Ever since the dissolution of the Soviet Union, Russia has embarked on a titanic domestic journey to reinvest itself as a new nation but with roots going back to the messianic vision of its role as defender of the Slavic race and Eastern Orthodoxy. The same identity quest was directed outward, since for a decade after its independence, Russian foreign policy has been undergoing the growing pains of defining its role in the international system. Putin has a Sisyphean task facing him: to create a whole new Russian identity on the shambles of the Soviet Union, thus avoiding the inherent mistake that led to its collapse—the absence of nationalism. Since his ascent to power, Russia has started two grandiose projects—building its domestic vertical of power and reinstating its superpower status internationally. One can argue, however, that one is inseparable from the other. Putin thus acts out of the reinvented identity of his nation and his own as its leader. In 2010 when commenting on the contribution of the Soviet nations, specifically Ukraine, in the victory of the Soviet Union in World War II, Putin said, "I disagree with [the statement] that if we had been separated, we would not have won the war. We still would have, because we are the country of victors."[221] Putin's statement resonated far beyond Russian borders and made people related to the war—the participants and their posterity—in the ex-Soviet republics harshly negative about this statement of ethnic superiority.

One of the most frequently used references for "Great Russia" is the Soviet Union, which has high personal emotional value for Vladimir Putin. For him, as a KGB officer working on the forefront of his country's national defense, the primary task was preservation of integrity and national sovereignty of the country that had collapsed. Hence comes

Putin's regret in the dissolution of the USSR and, in a way, personal stigma in allowing the "greatest geopolitical catastrophe of the twentieth century" to happen. This is his personal reference point in Russian greatness, his individual fault and self-victimization. Disintegration of the Soviet Union is increasingly presented in Russian domestic narrative as a result of the loss in the Cold War against the United States. This makes the United States the culprit in Putin's personal loss and target for his personal revenge. The form of this revenge is simple: to gain the Soviet lands back.

Putin's actions show perfectly well that he has undertaken the task of gathering up the land that he considers to be Russian. The recent Russian wars in the post-Soviet space that ended up with augmenting its territory at the expense of former Soviet war brethren mean that Putin, as a ruler, is on the messianic path to undo the events of the early 1990s and to put Russia on the road to resurrecting tarnished glory. The shot-run tactical targets are, without a doubt, the post-Soviet republics, but the grand strategic and long-run target is the USSR's archenemy, the United States. Hillary Clinton gave a very fitting description of the driving forces behind the general stance of revival of Russian grandeur: "Putin's worldview is shaped by his admiration for the powerful czars of Russian history, Russia's long-standing interest in controlling the nations on its borders, and his personal determination that his country never again appear weak or at the mercy of the West. . . . He wants to reassert Russia's power by dominating its neighbors and controlling their access to energy. . . . Putin sees geopolitics as a zero-sum game in which if someone is winning then someone else has to be losing."[222] For Putin, the Russian presidency is a "mission" and not a regular job. As political journalist Natalia Gevorkian noted, "There are presidents who want to leave behind a museum or library. Putin wants to keep the empire restored, at least partially"—a legacy that any autocrat ruler can jealous of.[223]

Seen by one of his aficionados as "the White Knight, sent by God to save Russia from hostile takeovers," Putin has the state-building mission of reviving Russia, both internally and externally.[224] It all started in 2000 with strengthening the vertical of power that brought along so-called managed democracy, described by Putin as "the vast majority of our [Russian] citizens . . . . rely[ing] on their historical traditions, their history, and, if I may say so, on their traditional values."[225] It is this "back to the future" quest that Russia is undertaking. For her, standing on the trident fork of fate and trying to define Russia's future, it really does not matter which road it chooses as long as the road ends in *velikoderzhavnost'*.

The contemporary social contract in Putin's Russia is based on essentially diverse sets of government-citizen relations. As Dmitry Nikolayev, head of the Institute of Strategic Analysis, elaborated, it is "a high tide of patriotism in exchange for limiting democracy and the start of a decline in living standards of the people."[226] Putin's governance has brought the social contract in Russia to a qualitatively different level, where, as Russian philosopher Vladimir Solov'ev noted when referring to the English patriotism of Samuel Johnson, "better to abandon patriotism than your conscience."[227] Alexander Auzan sees several social contracts that Putin's regime has offered to its citizens. First, during the early 2000s, there was the "domestic order in exchange for taxes" contract where the main task of the government was to end the war in Chechnya and the chaos in Russia proper. From 2000 through 2008 the terms of the social contract changed into "stability in exchange for loyalty." The end of this form of contract coincided with the global financial crisis and the war against Georgia, as a result of which a new social contract appeared: "social guarantees in exchange for loyalty." The annexation of Crimea and the hybrid war in Ukraine led to another change in citizenry-government relations, in which the former are willing to sacrifice well-being for the sake of the feelings of moral superiority over others or what Auzan called "self-austerity in exchange for a superpower status."[228] In this sense Russian patriotism replaced the craving of the middle class for economic stability, if not economic development.

The political future for Russia as defined by its leadership remains unclear. This quest may end up in a new type of serfdom already eulogized by the "spiritual staples" and mutual "ownership" praised by Zor'kin.

Or it could be lead to complete abolition of constitutionalism in Russia, which some of the leading Russian politicians think is detrimental to the Russian state. In the summer of 2014, speaking at the All-Russian Youth Forum "Seliger," Zhirinovsky addressed patriotic Russian youth with the following message: "Democracy will destroy us. As long as we have democracy, we will crawl. To start walking, not crawling, we need to move away from democracy to the imperial form of governance.... We should ban all the parties! Let it be an elected monarchy where 5,000 to 6,000 of the best people would elect their emperor!"[229] This is basically a call back to 1613 when the first Romanov was elected as a tsar by a group of boyars.

The view that, ever since the collapse of the Soviet Union, democracy has brought Russia all possible hardships, however questionable and out-of-this-world may sound, is widespread in the Russian society. According to the research conducted by the Russian economist Evgeni Yasin, "Russians consider democracy, accompanying the market economy in our country, as defective, and the retirees generally oppose it, believing that here it leads to anarchy and banditry. At the same time, many of them would like to see a tsar as the head of the country."[230] Zhirinovsky, however blatant he may be, was simply verbalizing the general stance in the Russian social contract where the population allows for the existence of autocratic and oligarchic leadership in exchange for personal security and order.

With all the modern-day perks of a globalized society, it seems that the Russian people are still looking for someone considerably superior to tell them what to do and how to live their lives. Having Putin's strong personality allowed the majority of Russian citizens to find self-worth and a new destiny. The duality of "loser before" and "winner after" Putin was quickly cemented in the concave and convex lenses of Russian society. Putin is, without a doubt, the national leader of the overwhelming majority of Russian citizens. According to the Levada Center's polling in August 2014, 84 percent support Putin.[231] Support here is linked with the moral values the Russian people hold: according to FOM's poll in 2014, the supreme leadership in Russia enjoys the highest trust among the Russian people: 36 percent polled hold Putin as their personal highest "moral authority," with the Patriarch Cyril, head of the Russian Orthodox Church, having the lowest "weight" in Russia—only 1 percent, next to Stalin.[232] Whether he goes to the bottom of Finnish Bay in a bathyscaphe, or fishes out a 21-kg pipe in Tuva River, or gets two Greek amphora from the bottom of the Taman Gulf (previously planted there by his functionaries), or hangglides as a leader of a flock of Siberian cranes in Yamal, Putin is the newly created avatar of Russian strength and the receptacle of everything positive in the Russian nation. Soviet-style eulogizing of its leaders, including elevating to the level of a personality cult, just started for Putin. In the fall of 2014, the Network of Supporters of Putin organized a Facebook exhibition of portraits, "12 Feats of Putin," where Putin is performing a dodecathlon of miracles following the storyline of the twelve labors of Hercules.

There are several explanations for the revival of the personality cult in Russia. Most of them are connected to the annexation of Crimea and standing tall in front of its main nemesis, the West, which was the culmination of Russia's decade-long "getting off its knees." Minister of Culture Vladimir Medinsky summarized the cause of the skyrocketing public support for Putin: "What is the biggest change we saw in Russia in Putin's era? The fact that Russia has started to win. We have not won for a few decades—nowhere. We got used to the defeats and very often—to humiliations."[233] The sense of collective gains (at the expense of someone's loss), moral superiority, and the ecstasy of living in a superpower has blinded citizens to the point where even the most obvious economic hardships in their lives can be endured for the sake of their ruler's longevity.

Much could be said about governmental "fit," "legitimacy," and "effectiveness" as the main parameters according to which a government's durability and general political stability can be predicted. Political analyst and journalist Stanislav Kucher put it quite well: "People suddenly 'got' the government that they 'deserve.' Strong, independent from the 'sleek West,' good and fair. Now everyone who supports Putin feels a part of this large, independent, and fair power."[234] Support for Putin—

the president who alleviated humiliation from the defeat in the Cold War and gifted the sense of superiority to his people—has spilled over the borders of reality into the virtual world. A state-run Internet community called "Russia-Reborn" was created "at these difficult times for Russia, when almost all the evil forces of modern humanity are united against her, pouring dirt on [her], lies and misinformation."[235] It split Russia-related pages in VKontate (a Russian version of Facebook) into the "patriots" and "enemies" and found more than one hundred patriotic online communities, the top three of which have up to 300,000 subscribers. People answered the call for Russian renaissance launched by Putin. Kucher is absolutely right. How could they not support the leader who makes them think better of themselves?

Superpower construct in the Russian political culture has immense importance on the longevity of the social contract. Russians' opinions about their country and themselves fluctuated with Putin's progress up the executive power ladder. A public opinion poll conducted by VCIOM in 2007 showed that 12 percent of the country's population considered it a great country.[236] Seven years later their numbers more than doubled: 25 percent thought that they were living in a great country and 50 percent believed that in fifteen years Russia would be a great power.[237] A report from the Levada Center in March 2014 brought up similar numbers: 63 percent of respondents viewed Russia as a superpower. According to another poll by VCIOM in September 2014, most people believed that life in general was better in Russia than anywhere else. Most respondents (68 percent) thought that they could meet much nicer people in Russia than in other parts of the world. More than half of them also considered Russia to be the best place to raise children, to have the most secure personal environment, to enjoy the best food and consumer products, and to live as freely as one desired.[238] Another important indicator of the overall situation in the country is the Happiness Index, which, according to VCIOM, has reached an unbelievable 78 percent.[239] Coincidentally, another poll by the Levada Center showed that 72 percent of the respondents had never been outside of Russia, and 78 percent had never visited any country outside of the USSR.[240] The figures above are difficult for a rational mind to comprehend: the lack of comparisons with other existing realities seems to not to bother the mainstream population who are firmly convinced of the righteousness of their beliefs.

Regime Mimicry and the Problem of Governance

In Russia, the longevity of the ruling regime and hence the durability of the contract itself still depend on the personal wellness of the ruler. Neither Yeltsin nor Putin—essentially, the two most prominent leaders of modern Russia—have created the system of governance that would go beyond the "natural state" and have the citizens as the very basis for its legitimacy and the recipients of its effectiveness.

After the collapse of the Soviet Union, the new Russian state chose a path toward developing its own democratic institutions. Russia "opened up" to democratic ideas and frameworks and tried to implement them and adjust to the rapidly changing Russian reality. Since democracy was neither a Russian trademark nor authenticated by it in the process of the evolution of its political thought, the democratic institutional frameworks had to be taken from somewhere else. Democratic institutions were transplanted into the Russian domestic reality by means of *regime mimicry*—a comprehensive process of political, economic, and cultural identity change.[241] The process is similar to isomorphic mimicry in biology, where "one organism mimics another to gain an evolutionary advantage."[242] Specifically, the "individuals of a more palatable species (the mimic) gain advantage by resembling members of another, less palatable species (the model)" in order to evolve into a seemingly dangerous form (usually a predator) to attain increased protection from other predators, while retaining the non-malevolent traits.[243]

Countries engage in regime mimicry for a variety of reasons. They may adopt the practices of institutions foreign to their popular "fit" because they would expect to receive purely tangible benefits from "joining the club" of democratic countries. These benefits may include developmental milestones through increased socialization with the countries whose institutions are adopted, such as memberships in international organizations (for instance, in IMF, WTO, or NATO) by implementing institutional reforms. In this case, the mimicking countries will follow the logic of expected consequences. They may also mimic existing structures and undertake reforms because they started associating themselves with the advanced democratic countries they want to look like. Here the benefits may also be available, but they are not the primary rationale for the regime mimicry; it is the identity construct that matters in building associations with other regimes. Such a behavior fits well within the logic of appropriateness.

In matters of public governance, even the most authoritarian regimes opt for democracy to survive in new and vastly unfamiliar settings of the institutional jungle they are plunged into. Regime mimicry develops, where the whole governance structure mimics advanced democratic institutions and notionally reflects externally implanted and not organically developed rules, norms, and practices. In the field of democratic institutionalization, regime mimicry would mean adoption of comprehensive forms of democratic governance (courts and the legal system, in general; offices of ombudsmen; systems of human rights protection; elections; local self-governance agencies, etc.). This usually happens when newly independent or created nations, after the sometimes painful process of gaining sovereignty, suddenly side with the institutions of other countries that have been developed in the process of cognitive evolution. These nations are faced with the normative conundrums of defining their developmental paths and, while making the choice toward democracy, adopt the institutions of more democratically developed countries without properly grasping their purpose and content.

The process of regime mimicry is a dangerous path: a developing country could be dragged into the vortex of mimicked settings and, furthermore, into state failure. According to Philipp Krause, "Part of the reason fragile states are hopelessly stuck is precisely because they try to mimic the formal institutions of success, rather than figuring out the functions of statehood on their own."[244] In order for mimicry to be successful, it should fully and completely transcend the fibers of society and become an inherent part of the political cultures of the mimicking nations. Regime mimicry can, indeed, turn into full-scale cognitive socialization, and this is where its greatest paradox lies: the fuller the mimicry, the higher the chances for it to turn into full normative socialization that would eventually end the mimicry.

An ideal condition for full mimicry is the simultaneous existence of all three variables. For a country to start copying institutional designs, there should be high enough external pressure on the parts of external and internal agents of change. In other words, "International organizations, local policy makers, and private consultants [should] combine to enforce the presumption that the most advanced countries have already discovered the one best institutional blueprint for development and that its applicability transcends national cultures and circumstances."[245] The political cultures of the recipient societies should be highly conducive to change. Finally, countries must be economically more or less stable to sustain the institutional change, which as a transformation process is always costly. These variables should be under the influence of both logics—appropriateness and consequentiality. This means that such societies should be willing to identify themselves with the democratic institutions and be individually interested in receiving tangible benefits from the regime mimicry.

Russia, like all of the ex-Soviet Union republics, had chosen the path toward democratic development. At the beginning, Russia welcomed the ideas of democracy and got supported by external "donors" agencies. In this matter, starting with the very first years of its independence, Russia had received considerable institutional and financial assistance from outside, especially from the United States and Europe, related to strengthening democratic governance and civil society. The United States Agency for International Development, for example, spent over $4.5 billion between 2008 and 2012 alone for "promotion of an open and innovative society" in Russia.[246] The European Commission, too, spent about €2.8 billion through the TACIS program "to smooth Russia's transition to democracy and market economy."[247] The money was channeled in so-called common spaces: economy and environment; freedom, security and justice, external security; research and education, for the purpose of supporting the institution-building efforts, providing technical assistance, and promoting higher education and regional cooperation with Russia.[248] The biggest donor to the Russian economy was the International Monetary Fund, which spent over $22 billion in support of its economic reforms.[249]

At that time the Russian political elite viewed the steps directed toward democratic institutional developments in Russia and helping revive its economy with suspicion and discontent. As Sergey Glaz'ev and A. Velichenkov separately noted in 1996, the reforms were drafted by the Americans, and the economic and policy indicators were developed from above and then merely translated into Russian.[250] As a result, many blamed the government of Russia for a "lack of pride and honor" and for being *kholops* (a category of serfs) of the West by following the steps of their foreign patrons.[251] Just as democracy and liberalism are collectively viewed as synonymous to an existential evil aimed at destroying the Russian nation, so are all efforts to help her economically. The United States is blamed for the creation of

> material and spiritual poverty; destruction of its statehood, economy, science, education, the armed forces; prevention of the revival of the country and turning it into a raw oil and gas appendage of the West, and put the security of the country in direct dependence on the price of oil and gas in the world market . . . ; paralysis of production . . . ; flow of enormous financial resources and national wealth of Russia abroad . . . ; mass exodus [of people] from poverty to the West . . . ; collapse of the armed forces, undermining the scientific, technical and educational potential; decline of agriculture.[252]

That includes basically every possible trouble and hardship the country had encountered after its independence.

The governance reality in Russia, however, tells us that Russia's economic failure was due to "the government's chronic refusal to reform. . . . Because of mismanagement, inertia, and outright corruption, such vital changes as trimming the budget, overhauling the tax code and tax collection, land reform, and otherwise providing conditions to stem capital flight and attract foreign investment have not been implemented."[253] In other words, regime mimicry in Russia had the effect of water poured in the sand: its intentions were noble, but the receiving media could not sustain change. The sarcasm is unavoidable. Apparently, as presented by the contemporary elite, Russia was seriously suffering from all the help and assistance it got after the collapse of the inherently detrimental and parochial command-and-control economy of the Soviet Union. Among other actions forced upon it by the evil West, Russia was forced to sell its natural resources, which currently bring most of the money to its state budget. Indeed, the country was waiting for a savior to come and salvage it from the deadly democratic and market economy clutches of the West.

The problems with the regime mimicry started with Putin's second term. One of the first harbingers of removal of the foreign political and cultural presence in Russia was closure of most of the regional offices of the British Council after accusing them of conducting "illegal" activities, evading Russian taxes, and violating the Vienna Convention on Diplomatic Relations. Some experts, however, suspect this action to be a continuation of the diplomatic scandal between the United Kingdom and Russia and an act of retaliation for the harsh British reaction to the murder of the ex-FBS agent Alexander Litvinenko in 2007. The *Guardian* quotes former UK ambassador to Russia Tony Brenton: "This is a continuation of the exchange of measures which resulted from the Litvinenko murder. Why do the Russian authorities want to do something that their own people will suffer from?"[254] Ambassador Brenton was apparently not fully aware of the Russian political cultural trait of punishing its own people to threaten others.

The third coming of Putin led to the thwarting of all U.S. technical and democratic assistance in Russia in 2014 by disbanding the USAID office. The culminating blow to the Western efforts to help the population of Russia by educating it was the closure of the FLEX program, which had educated more than 8,000 young Russian schoolchildren in the United States in its twenty-one years of existence. The reason: failure of 15 children to return from their yearlong studies in American schools, including one "outrageous" case of a Russian boy being illegally retained in by a gay male couple.[255]

To the detriment of its subjects, the Russian state started closing its society to everything "Western." This did not come out of nowhere. One possible reason for reversal of the democratic reforms might well be hidden in the complex nature of the domestic environment. Yasin, who was in charge of economic reforms in Yeltsin's government in 1990s, claims, "It was impossible to implement market reforms and to create real democratic government at the same time. Painfully uneasy were the reforms, and it was impossible to surpass these difficulties."[256] On the other hand, perhaps the country was deliberately closing Peter I's window, with an emphasis on all that was traditionally Russian and therefore right by definition. This is evident in Putin's claim that Russia does not embrace "so-called tolerance, neutered and barren," as practiced by many countries that are sloughing off ethnic, spiritual, and other traditional values and that are recognizing "the equality of good and evil."[257] As a result, the country is stuck, as described by Michael McFaul et al., between "a full-blown dictatorship" and "a consolidated democracy."[258] Putin's reign, especially his second and third terms, marked further stagnation of regime mimicry for Russia in most of directions: public administration, social, and economic.

Individual versus Collective Sovereignty

If a single sentence were to describe Russian from the point of view of its political culture constructed through the concave and convex lenses of the contemporary Russian identity, it would look something like this: *The biggest nuclear state in the world, surrounded by existential enemies, created by historically developed traditions of centralized, individually monopolized state power, with aspirations of regional and possibly global domination embodied in territorial enlargement through application of coercive power.* The current situation in Russia and its responses to the changing international climate around it are, however, much too complicated to be squeezed into a sentence or two.

The conflict with the West, represented by the United States and Europe, which Russia started visualizing in 2005, is existential, indeed, but it is not civilizational, as presented by Samuel Huntington at the dusk of the twentieth century.[259] The history has not ended with the Cold War, and the times of the last men have yet to come.[260] Even the Russian leadership would not relinquish enjoying the full spectrum of Western civilizational perks: Medvedev would not refuse to get all the newest iProducts so far, and neither would Putin reject the idea of wearing the most expensive A. Lange & Söhne watches on his wrist instead of a Russian Komandirskie. The conflict is in the differences in values between Russian political culture and the Western world.

In the new millennium with Putin in power, Russia jump-started the zero-sum game of Realpolitik by putting the notion of "nation-state" on the pedestal of the international system. The focus once again is shifting from the sub-systemic to the level of the global arena, where the main participants are no longer the non-state actors but states with their own, and sometimes conflicting, ideologies and views on themselves, their place in the world, and others. Russia is thus on a steady path to reanimating neo-realism but in a peculiar fashion: it is post-realism where the main forces behind rivalry and competition in the international arena are not the states' vital national interests per se but the Constructivist values that are the true driving forces behind them.

There is a clash of values that Russia has been promoting with the West that is no less serious or more malleable than the civilizational conflict. In the scale of Shalom Schwartz's Theory of Basic Values, conflicts are inevitable, since "some actions in pursuit of any value have consequences that conflict with some values but are congruent with others."[261] Just as goals in Johan Galtung's classical conflict model can be incompatible and thus zero-sum, so are the value constructs in contemporary Russian political culture.[262] For the local Russian nationalist audience, convergence of the convex and concave identity lenses presents the westerners (Americans, Europeans, etc.) as selfish and mercantile, spiritless and lewd, parochial and warmongering, deceitful and treacherous, while the Russians are presented as selfless and altruistic, spiritual and chaste, boundless and peaceful, trustworthy and honest.

There is, however, nothing unusual and extraordinary in this: most of the primordial nations use cultural categories to draw the line between "us" and "them" where they tend to present the former in a better light than the latter. Tobias Theiler extends this argument to a broader social identity theory and confirms that "people distinguish their ingroups from outgroups in ways that they perceive favorably to reflect upon the ingroup and . . . negatively upon their outgroup. . . . [T]hey continuously compare their ingroup to outgroups along dimensions that make their groups look good to them."[263] Further, according to Jimy Sanders, "The ways in which insiders and outsiders go about characterizing a group, and thereby positioning it and its members in the larger society, are responsive to the social and historical context within which intergroup interactions take place."[264] Marc Ross brings in the psychological dimension of culture and argues, "Psychocultural interpretations are the shared, deeply rooted worldviews that help groups make sense of daily life and provide psychologically meaningful accounts of a group's relationship with other groups, their actions and motives. They are at the core of shared systems of meaning and identity that define cultural communities."[265] A group thus becomes a bank of emotions, a repository of common heritage, which is positive toward its own kin and negative to all the rest with whom it had bad history.

The conflict with the West presented by the identity construct of Russian political culture lies through the faults of specific views on the matter of national sovereignty and self-determination. Russia is promoting an idea of individual sovereignty where it is "the right of governing its own body, [which] . . . ought to be considered as an independent state."[266] This principle espouses the infallible rights of the states to deal with their own problems and situations of domestic concern according to their views on governance and their societal "fit" without any interference from outside by other sovereign states. Such states, in Alexander Dugin's words,

> "are not happy to lose their independence to a supranational exterior authority—not in the form of an open American hegemony, nor in the Western-centric forms of world government or governance, nor in the chaotic dissolution of a failed international system. . . . They do not like transition

> at all, suspecting, with good reason, the inevitable loss of their sovereignty.... What they all want and share in common is a desire to preserve the international status quo as enshrined in their present form, adjusting and modernizing them as an internal and sovereign process as necessary."[267]

From a Western perspective, however, the states that Dugin lists—China, Russia, Iran, India, and South American and Islamic states—are stuck in the past where "what's mine is mine and what's yours is negotiable." In other words, Russia and Co. is promoting the idea of unabridged autocratic power that resists any external advice and exhortations. Indeed, why would he/she, since the entire country is in his/her personal eminent domain and not subject to sharing with anyone? Secretary of State John Kerry gave the perfect quintessence of the Russian foreign policy referring to Russia's actions in Ukraine: "You just don't in the twenty-first century behave in nineteenth-century fashion by invading another country on a completely trumped up pretext."[268] To this, the apologists of the Russian World point to the American actions in Iraq, asking, "If they could do it, why can't we?" completely missing the point of incomparability between these two cases of interventions.

Individual sovereignty also extends to the international arena, which states approach on the basis of their best national interests as well as their values and views on objective reality. Alliances under such sovereignty are minimal due to the inherently anarchic nature of interstate relations: they are created for the purposes of the individual sovereign interests of the states and exist as long they satisfy those interests. They are not glued by the supranational identity constructs, such as in the case of the European Union. This view on sovereignty as the main component of the social contract essentially means "What happens in Vegas stays in Vegas," where "Vegas" can be Moscow, Beijing, Teheran, Pyongyang, Caracas, or any other place where the rulers can do whatever they want with their own people and successfully preclude foreign intrusions into their domestic affairs and foreign policy.

The other side of sovereignty—shared—denotes "arrangements under which individuals chosen by international organizations, powerful states, or ad hoc entities would share authority with nationals over some aspects of domestic sovereignty" and "legitimated by a contract between national authorities and an external agent."[269] One of the pioneers in the study of collective international action, Hedley Bull, gave the following definition of the "society of states": "a group of states, conscious of certain common interests and common values [and which] conceive themselves to be bound by a common set of rules in their relations with one another, and share in the working of common institutions."[270] The highly normative context of such a commonwealth of states follows directly from this definition: the community of states is based on common values, which also means that the community is bound to protect those values in dealings with other states, even those that may not share the same values.

The concept of "shared sovereignty" is applied by Stephen Krasner to matters of external governance in collapsed and failed states, which are incapable of solving domestic issues on their own and have to "share" their social contract with outside agents. Such agents can be international, multinational, or supranational organizations (such as the European Union), subject-specific alliances (OPEC is one of examples), or even individual states acting as external powers. When transferred into the realm of peaceful interactions of more or less stable states, shared sovereignty denotes the specific mode of problem-solving where states no longer deal with problems and situations of domestic concern individually but collectively, according to the views of their joint governance, agreed upon by other sovereign states.

Globally, the states with collective security no longer individually approach vital matters on the basis of their best national interests but do so out of their combined values and views on objective reality. International alliances last longer because they are based not on self-interests (which often conflict) but on shared interests and are meant to solve the matters of a wider international community of states. Such actions, according to David Carment and Frank Harvey, "require the stamp of institutional legitimacy upon which long-term measures depend."[271] This factor was stressed by Charles Fenwick at the very birth of the United Nations, who considered that "[w]hat would be arbitrary for the individidual state would in the case of the whole body of states be no more than the exercise of the higher right of the community to maintain law and order and to see to the observance by separate states of their obligations as members of the community."[272] The resulting global social contract on the international level in the countries with shared sovereignty are also "split" between the members of this order in a sense that "what happens in Vegas" does not stay there but is a matter of common concern.

In Russian political culture, the notion of individual sovereignty equally extends to the domestic and international realms. Inside the country, the national government acts as the only point of reference and the source of legitimacy and legal remedy for the population. Individual sovereignty for rulers means that their people should accept whatever the government is giving them from above and whatever outputs are thrown down for public consumption. Moreover, they should be content with existing conditions and not hope to change the order of things. The institutional rigidity of individual sovereignty on the domestic level depends on the "effectiveness" of the coercion of the population and their protection from the detrimental influences from outside. Any institutional transformation going against the ruling regime is viewed as the work of the "fifth column" and "national traitors" who have been skillfully brainwashed by someone from outside—in the Russian case, by the United States. At the 2014 Valdai Club meeting in Sochi, much in the same communist tradition, Vyacheslav Volodin, first deputy chief of staff of the president, said, "With Putin, there is Russia. Without Putin, there is no Russia."[273] The individual sovereignty is indeed vested upon the individual, the Sovereign, who is the true embodiment of his/her people.

Individual sovereignty at the international level allows a country to undertake unilateral actions vis-à-vis other states without paying attention to the actual geopolitical situation, local context, and the opinions of peers. Legitimacy in the case of applying individual sovereignty outside the state borders is created by a single state and solely defied by its ruler. A restraining factor in this case can be multilateral alliances where decisions are jointly made and legitimacy is diffused or "shared" by the member states. This option is rejected by countries with individual sovereignty, like Russia, which thinks that cooperation with other countries is detrimental to Russian national interests and hence it undermines its individual approach to the important issues of international relations. In July 2014, at the meeting of the National Security Council, Putin proudly declared, "Russia, thank God, is not a member of any alliance. This is, to a large degree, the guarantee for our sovereignty. Any country that enters into alliances immediately gives away part of its sovereignty."[274] While other countries traditionally consider alliances as joint and thus rationally justifiable solutions to the existing issues of world concern, Russia views them as the very causes of those issues.

Ultimately, it is for the respective political cultures of nations to choose what type of sovereignty they would like to have, individual or collective. The problem is that these two versions of essentially the same thing are inherently conflictual. They cannot peacefully coexist: the collective sovereignty would be unhappy to see violations of the moral standings it is based on in the countries with individual sovereignty whereas the latter would view the countries with collective sovereignty as endangering their raison d'être by definition. This inevitably brings the countries to the brink of conflict. This is what Alexei Fedorov, one of the proponents of the individual sovereignty, had to say about the inherent confrontation between the two outlooks on sovereignty:

> The Cold War is still not over on planet Earth; there are still two poles of power, using different models of international law. Russia and the whole world (except for the West) are using the classical Westphalia model, postulating the factual sovereignty, which means that the opponent is legitimate, moral, and sovereign on the territory that he actually rules. Far-reaching philosophical messages stem from this about the rules of the common existence within the national scale (elections) and global (wars). Euro-Atlantic, i.e., the Western world, uses the other type, the Versailles system, created after World War I, whose main goal was the destruction of the Soviet and now Russian liberal statehood. This system of international relations is based on the sovereignty of recognition. This means that the enemy and the friend are each assigned randomly depending on the current circumstances and benefits.[275]

The grim outlook that Fedorov brings into Galtung's notion of a structural conflict as "an incompatibility." None of the versions of sovereignty are ready to back off, turning the international relations into a zero-sum game.

Conclusion

Political cultures of nations are strong determinants of their responses to internal and external disturbance. Cultures can be "flexible" (open and allowing change), "bifurcate" (undetermined and ambiguous), or "rigid" (rejecting change).[276] The longevity of political cultures largely determines the acceptance or rejection of transformations in the domestic or outside environments. The plurality of national identities across the globe and many nation-specific variables affecting diverse political cultures permit the existence of cross-cuts between these categories. Russian political culture represents one such example, where it can be both allowing for changes to happen and accepting them initially but then reversing to its previous state. It is both flexible and rigid, which has allowed for multiple social experiments to happen: fluctuations between the Western and Eastern political, cultural, and economic orientations; double political suicide in the twentieth century when the Russian and Soviet empires suddenly decided to collapse; and moving from feudalism to socialism, bypassing capitalism as a more advanced political-economic formation, to name a few. Each of these social experiments was accepted at the initial stage and then rejected after institutional actors refused to change.

By the inception of the new millennium, all the necessary conditions were present for the evolution of Russian identity formation into the *komunalka* mentality where individual benefits were forsaken for collectively existing but belonging to no "public goods." Feelings of moral superiority groomed on the fertile grounds of a resource-oriented, traditional estate-based nuclear country have created a deviant political culture. This is not to say at all that the word "deviant" bears a negative—or positive, for that matter—connotation. Deviation is a step away from the existing international order where multilateralism and collective reasoning matter more than individual actions, where the self-interests of states are provided by sharing them with others, and where the notion of "sovereignty" loses its "sovereign" root in the jointly managed system. Perhaps if the world were built of states using the traditional realists' blueprints, cooperation and multilateralism would themselves become deviations.

Until then Russia is desperately trying "to make a point" in the international arena, even though the expected consequences of such "points" might be detrimental to its overall vital national interests. Russia acts out of what it considers appropriate and rightly fitting the concave and convex lenses of its identity. Sometimes, such steps are carefully calculated; in most cases, however, their expected utility would not be revealed even in the long run. But what is "the long run" for a primordial state that wants to trace its origins from ancient Rome but is just a mere blink in the momentary gaze of history? In equating their historical, cultural, and societal heritage to that of Rome, the adepts of Russian political culture must remember that it was "the Romans' certainty of their superiority over the barbarians [which] justified merciless cruelty in defence of the civilized world," and this eventually brought perhaps the only truly global empire down.[277] The picture is cut and dried. Russia wants to remap the world in accordance with its vision of itself and others, while not allowing others to do so and even disregarding its own territorial quest.

3

Russia and the United States

> The United States has its own interests; Russia has its own. Notwithstanding personal relations, these are some obstacles that cannot be overcome.
>
> —SERGEI IVANOV, head of the presidential administration, 2013

> America does not want to humiliate us: it wants to subjugate us. It wants to solve its problems at our expense. In the entire history of Russia no one has succeeded in this, and no one will.
>
> —VLADIMIR PUTIN, at the All-Russian United People's Forum, 2014

In 2007 I was teaching at the Smolny College of Arts and Sciences in St. Petersburg, Russia. In addition, I was also working part-time for a local business consulting agency. I was interested in learning Russian political culture, and engagement in "Russian business" seemed like a good start. The first project I worked on was already under way. It was in a small suburban town about a half-hour drive to the south of St. Petersburg. My company had already conducted a SWOT analysis of the factory, and for me, working on large-N statistics as a part of my own research, it was always interesting to get a feel for the real-life application of this quantitative methodology. One of the questions asked in the survey was "What is, in your opinion, the biggest threat to your factory?" This question was designed to find out whether or not the workers had long-term trust in the financial viability and institutional stability of their factory, which would say much about possible costs associated with worker retention. Some of the answers, however, were quite startling: a surprisingly high number of the respondents said, "NATO and its enlargement."

At that time I could not find an answer to this seemingly strange choice for an external threat. What does NATO, thousands of kilometers away from the factory in the middle of Russian backwoods, have to do with its stability? This question has boggled my mind ever since I left St. Petersburg. Only after I had spent several years researching Russian foreign policy did I understand. There is no bigger enemy for Russia than the United States of America and NATO as a military tool of American influence.[1] Both threats are completely perceptional, however, and fully detached from reality on the part of the United States. The threat is constructed by skillful leadership in the Russian government to rally society around its leader in the times of troubles that it had caused in the first place. Russian anti-Americanism is a growing and incredibly potent phenomenon. It permeates the very societal fabric of the contemporary identity construct of Russia. It is seen, sometimes clearly and in other cases subtly, in the very careful built-up and developed role of the nemesis. Since the second coming of Putin in 2004, anti-Americanism has been nurtured on the highest echelons of the Russian political establishment and then translated farther down the societal ladder to Russian citizens in the form of *mala in se*: the inherent and existential evil. It is, in a way, a mirror image of everything Russian: a malicious, devilish superpower that aims to destroy the Russian essence.

Battle of Two Exceptionalisms

In many ways, Russia is similar to America. Both are home to diverse societal groups with significant ethnic, cultural, linguistic, and religious peculiarities. At different times these groups, sometimes voluntarily, sometimes forcefully, have been molded together to form a single nation. But the significant interracial and interethnic issues underlining their domestic politics still remain. Sometimes the differences can be overwhelming, leading to sporadic clashes of individual or group violence, such as in Sanford, Florida, in 2012 and Ferguson, Missouri, in 2014, or the mass disturbances on ethnic grounds between the Russians and the "Caucasians" (from the Caucasus) in Kondogopa in 2006 and ethnic pogroms in Burulevo in 2013. Russia and America also have their entourage of foreign followers who joined them by different means and with diverse aims. During the Cold War the two superpowers had more or less parity with regard to the support they could harness in the international arena.

Yet there are some fundamental differences that put these nations on opposing ends of the political spectrum and that to a certain extent predestined their conflict. America was forged through the process of colonization of its indigenous tribes; continental explorations in all possible directions; land acquisition by purchase, wars, or voluntarism; immigration of hordes from continental Europe and other parts of the world; the suffering of dark centuries of slavery and the glorious decades of its civil rights movement. As the vanguard of the technological progress and spearheading globalization with all its perks and challenges, America managed to create a uniform nation based on the civic values of democracy, respect for fundamental human freedoms and values, transparency and accountability of public servants, free expressions of political will, due process of law, and many more indispensable attributes of a free society. The American version of a melting pot or a salad bowl, depending on the individual cultures and the degrees of assimilation, was created by various civic molds, which led to the true American exceptionalism.

American exceptionalism is both different and special but not unique per se.[2] There are different types of exceptionalism that many nations have or want to possess to differentiate themselves from others. After all, who does not want to feel special? The notion of exceptionalism can consist of civic values as opposed to ethnic (Greece), clan-based (Somalia), family ideology-driven (North Korea), or religious (Iran). It can have different forms and representations, such as in Charles Murray's view: geography, ideology, traits (industriousness, egalitarianism, religiosity, philanthropy, and volunteerism), and political context.[3] Even the term "American Exceptionalism" in its modern understanding is not an endemic American term, for it was born in probably the most unlikely place: in the Soviet Union. It was, in fact, Stalin who coined this term, which he used to criticize not Americans themselves but members of the American Communist Party for their deviation from the general party line.[4]

Civic values and not ethnic superiority over the rest make American exceptionalism unique. It is the latter that Putin mistakenly took for the meaning of American exceptionalism in his op-ed in the *New York Times* published (coincidentally?) on September 11, 2013.[5] Unable or unwilling to fully embrace the democratic values and principles presented to it by the Western world soon after its independence, Russia is struggling to define its newfound identity that it seems to use as the cornerstone of its own exceptionalism. This term, of course, is not copied by the diverse Russian political spectrum, but its essence—in tsarist or Soviet times—is based on the same ethnic values. The Soviets tried to eradicate the ethnic components of their various nations by creating a new nation "ethnic in form and Soviet in context," the *Homo sovieticus*, but failed. The Soviet discourse throughout the seventy years of its existence was not less exceptional, although it was completely based on ideology and opposition to the rest of the world. Soviet exceptionalism failed because of the inability of its multiple societal groups to step beyond their ethnic bonds into something far more universally acceptable.

Exceptionalism in the Russian political context is inextricably linked to the three main driving forces of progress in Russia: its religious views, ethnic compositions of the nations filling its vast territory, and its ideological visions. Van Herpen identifies three similar components as legitimizing the case of Russian exceptionalism: the Russian Orthodoxy (depicted as the symbiosis of the church and the state), pan-Slavism (manifested in racism and anti-Semitism), and the communist ideology.[6] The merger of these factors had an extraordinary effect of the concave and convex lenses of the Russian identity and predisposed specific patterns of reaction on external and internal challenges. The three-prong vision on the Russian identity molded its political culture in a way that was to embrace its uniqueness, that is, its own version of exceptionalism, which by definition is different than others.

As the popular Russian saying goes, Russian political culture seems to be intentionally stepping twice on the same Soviet rake. It is promoting the motto "Russia's borders are where the Russians are" by capitalizing on the concept of the "Russian world" as "ourness." The "otherness" is embodied by such terms as the "Caucasian origins" to differentiate people with darker skin and hair from the clichéd blue-eyed and blond Russians and by socially marginalizing anyone who does not fit the general political line dictated by Kremlin by dubbing them "fascists," "traitors of the nation," and "liberasts." According to Marie Mendras, national exceptionalism of the Russian nation "is becoming [its] new doctrine and pattern of conduct, in a fragile combination of political protectionism and necessary adjustment to economic globalization and the Internet."[7] Russian exceptionalism, which is being coined by Putin's entourage at various levels, is ethno-religious and not civic for one simple reason. In a sovereign democracy, the regime that is currently being promoted by the Russian political elites, the societal "fit," and legitimacy of the regime are based not on the durability of civic ties between the citizenry and the government but on the duration of the regime's ability to cover the primary needs of its vast populations and the personal health of the ruler.

It is these fundamental differences between Russian and American exceptionalism that put the two countries on opposing sides. Under the inherent systemic anarchy, such differences would inevitably lead to the conflict. Alexis de Tocqueville found interesting parallels between the nineteenth-century United States and Russia. In *Democracy in America,* based on his trip to the United States, Tocqueville described the conflicting Russian and American identities:

> The American fights against natural obstacles which oppose him; the Russian is at grips with men. The former combats the wilderness and barbarism; the latter, civilization with all its arms. America's conquests are made with the plowshare, Russia's with the sword. To attain their arms, the former relies

> on personal interest and gives free scope to the unguided strength and common sense of individuals. The latter in a sense concentrates the whole power of society in one man. One has freedom as the principal means of action; the other has servitude. Their point of departure is different and their paths diverse; nevertheless, each seems called by some secret design of Providence one day to hold in its hands the destinies of half of the world.[8]

The destinies of the two nations—manifest (civic) in America and divine (ethnic, religious, and ideological) in Russia—are taking them back to the verge of the averted global nuclear extinction in the mid-twentieth century.

The international arena is where the two exceptionalisms directly clash in the attempts by the two nations to cement their global influence on world politics. In many respects, the aims of the two exceptionalisms are similar: to achieve world dominance. The differences, however, between the American and Russian foreign policy toolboxes are striking. In many of its foreign policy choices, the United States is following the Democratic Peace Principle, which means that the more democracies there are in the world, the less violent and volatile it will become.[9] This does not mean that democracies are particularly malleable and more peaceful by definition: they care, just like autocracies and other types of regimes, about protecting themselves. They do so by using the liberalist tenets of global peace and human rights protection and by applying a combination of powers: hard, soft, and smart, depending on specific circumstances and domestic political terrains of the target countries they are dealing with. The democratic domination, that is, a desire to have more democracies than any other regimes, is channeled via multiple communication passages: bilateral (the multidimensional missions in Iraq and Afghanistan), international (the UN), intergovernmental (within NATO), and supranational (cooperation with the European Union). Autocracies, too, strive for domination, but in Russia's case the power is always "hard," no matter where it is applied: its own citizens in Chechnya, the formerly brotherly Georgians, or practically ethnic kin, Ukrainians. From a domestic perspective, it is much easier to start the war for the autocracies than democracies, since the former are not under the time constraints of the cumbersome democratic decision-making mechanisms of the latter.

The application of American and Russian exceptionalism to the same geopolitical environment means that the actions of the two countries always contradict one another. In many aspects of international relations, Russia has been acting as a follower of U.S. foreign policy choices. Ivan Kurilla in his op-ed brings up numerous cases from Russian history when the American experience was positively implanted in the Russian context. He contends that "comparison with the United States and direct reference to their experience was a way of improving the governance system or the Russian economy. The American example was closely associated with the modernization agenda."[10] It all started changing in 2000 with Putin's ascent to power but even more so with his second presidential term. By launching the massive anti-Western propaganda campaign demonizing American and European values as detrimental to Russian "spiritual staples," by banning the foreign movements of certain officials and freezing their foreign accounts, by enacting the "anti-anti-Magnitsky law" prohibiting adoption of Russian orphans by Americans, and by adopting the law on foreign agents copying the American Foreign Agents Registration Act (following the logic, "if Americans can, why can't we?"), Putin's Russia cemented the ideological grounds for future political and economic confrontations with the United States.

A vivid example of such a quid pro quo foreign policy practice is the case of Kosovo, which affected the political settings in Europe for generations to come. At the turn of a new millennium, in the aftermath of the Kosovo conflict, Putin warned the West and the United Nations, in particular, that he would do exactly the same with the breakaway territories of Georgia. The recognition of the part of Serbia being in Europe and under completely different causal variables of the potential European supranationalism was "continuously portrayed [by Moscow] as an unacceptable Western political demarche, which would encourage separatism in the CIS."[11] During the process of Kosovo sovereignty,

"Moscow worked hard to de-legitimize the Kosovo model."[12] In 2008 Russia did precisely what it was scolding the United States and NATO for when it attacked Georgian forces in South Ossetia.

In an interview posted on the official presidential website on March 4, 2014, Putin gave the usual denialist spiel by negating the possibility for Crimea to join Russia and compared it with Kosovo independence. He said, "And I do believe that only the citizens living in a given territory, under the conditions of freedom of expression, and in safety can and must determine their future. And if the Kosovars were allowed to do (which also happened in many parts of the world as far as I know), no one had canceled the right of nations for self-determination, also given in the relevant UN documents."[13] Two weeks later, Putin issued the law annexing Crimea to Russia. With Crimean annexation, the Russian government seems to have mastered the double standards it has been accusing the West of every time it does not agree it. It even used exactly the same verbiage as NATO during its bombings of the capital of Serbia, a brotherly Slavic nation, calling it a "morally justifiable humanitarian operation." In his speech to the Valdai Discussion Club in 2014, Putin also placed the Crimean annexation on the same scale with Kosovo independence. Crimea, he said, "on the basis of the referendum, just like Kosovo, appealed to the Russian Federation for incorporation into Russia." What Putin meant was that if Kosovars can proclaim their independence, so can the Russian-speaking minority of Crimea and the eastern Ukraine.

The situation revealed a serious cognitive dissonance in Russian foreign policy. First, if Russia was advocating upholding sovereign rights of each nation for its self-determination, which includes the Abkhazians, South Ossetians, and now the Russians in Crimea, the same logic should apply in the case of Chechnya prior to the Russian victory there in 2000, which was making the same demands as the Kosovars in former Yugoslavia and now the Russian kin in Ukraine. Double standards are also deeply implanted in the Russian political culture.

In this particular situation, Russia was comparing Kosovo with Crimea, not the outcomes or the dependent variable but the process of separatism or the tools. As a matter of fact, after the war, Kosovo did not become the fifty-first American state while Crimea was de facto annexed by Russia. Comparing Kosovo with Crimea would be valid under several conditions. First, the United States should have beforehand concluded a peace agreement with the government of Yugoslavia, pledging to protect its territorial integrity—exactly what Russia did with Ukraine in 1994 under the terms of the Budapest Memorandum. Second, the United States should have introduced its unidentified troops in Kosovo in support of the Albanian ethnic minority—similar to the Russian "polite green men" in Crimea. Third, the United States should have run a referendum where the overwhelming number of Kosovar Albanians expressed their wish to join America—following Russia's own referendum in Crimea. Finally, the United States should have accepted Kosovo as the fifty-first state—just as Russia did with Crimea. Only under those conditions the comparisons between Kosovo and Crimea would have run in parallel universes. In this case, however, what we have is the comparison between an apple and a ballpoint pen; while the handling process is similar (both can be held in a hand), the results are drastically different.

The second part of the cognitive dissonance tells the observer that Russia does not really care about upholding the supreme principles of the international law it was advocating. What it is seriously concerned with is throwing a monkey wrench into the works. There was a clear message sent here: if you do not accept Kosovo's independence, we will not accept independence of Abkhazia and South Ossetia, and vice versa. Commenting *ex post facto* acknowledgment of these nations as sovereign, Putin said, "We recognized the independence of South Ossetia and Abkhazia in the same way as many European countries have recognized Kosovo's independence. In our opinion, it is absolutely unreasonable and in violation of existing international law."[14] That means that Russia knowingly and deliberately violated the international law, closely following U.S. foreign policy. This was done, of course, in Russia's own self-interests but also to backstab America: to mix business with pleasure. While opposing the dual standards of the West, Putin created his own dual standards based on the right of the power: whoever has more power in a given situation wins.

Commenting on the differences between the American and Russian "ways" of foreign influence, political columnist Yulia Latynina gave a very good description of the polarity of American and Russian involvement in foreign affairs: "When the United States gets involved in something abroad, they do so intending to solve the problem. . . . The United States did not go into Iraq and Afghanistan to create bloody chaos there. . . . The United States gets involved to resolve the problem. Kremlin—to create it."[15] It seems that by creating problems in Ukraine and Georgia, Russia was testing the international grounds the only way it can—by realist hard power. The newly acquired sense of the Russian exceptionalism tries to answer one of the most important Russian civilizational questions raised by the genius Dostoyevsky in his *Crime and Punishment*: "Whether I am a trembling creature or whether I have a right?"[16] In essence, this question translates into the quest for Russian exceptionalism: Russia wants to be as exceptional as the United States by mirror-copying its actions in the international arena.

The reason for the diverse application forms of exceptionalism in the United States and Russia lies in the different treatment of the individual. David Satter gives an excellent explanation of the prevalent collectivism that fits well within the discussion on Russian exceptionalism and its clash with the American one. According to him, the main problem is the historically developed disregard for an individual life: "Russia differs from the West in its attitude towards the individual. In the West, an individual is treated as an end in himself. His life cannot be disposed of recklessly in the pursuance of the political schemes, and recognition of its value imposes limits on the behavior of the authorities. In Russia, the individual is seen by the state as the means to an end and a genuine moral framework, for political life does not exist."[17] The individual is the pinnacle of the American lifestyle. The individual is the driving force behind progress, and in a sense American exceptionalism is the embodiment of truly exceptional individualism. The driving force behind Russian exceptionalism is the collective power of the masses where the individual is just another faceless screw in the system.

Perceptional Security Dilemma

During the annual presidential conference aired in April 2014, a month after the annexation of the Crimean Peninsula by the Russian Federation, the following dialogue took place between Putin and his chief media man, Dmitry Kiselev. With a few cuts to save space, the dialogue deserves to be shown.

KISELEV: Since we have problems with connection here, I will show what I mean.

He curves the index fingers and thumbs on his hands to form a circle.

KISELEV: Here's a circle, and I think our country is in this circle. I personally sense this choking feeling that someone is trying to suffocate me. I think this is NATO ...

Kiselev then points to his finger circle.

KISELEV: ... because NATO is growing like a cancer, and for the past twenty-five years has swallowed our Warsaw Pact allies, and then some parts of the Soviet Union, the Baltic states, and now opened its mouth trap to gobble Georgia and Ukraine. . . . Of course, you can say I am paranoid. But, as they say, if you are paranoid this does not mean that nobody is after you ...

PUTIN *(laughing)*: What are you afraid of so much? We will choke anyone we want.

Audience bursts into applause and laughter.[18]

Kiselev's passage on NATO stifling Russia is a perfect example of the revived ghost of security dilemma after a short-lived, post–Cold War bliss. First introduced by John Herz in 1950, security dilemma is a "structural notion in which the self-help attempts of states to look after their security needs tend, regardless of intention, to lead to rising insecurity for others as each interprets its own measures as defensive and measures of others as potentially threatening."[19] Robert Jervis took this point further in presenting security dilemma as having a realism-inspired, equally pessimistic outlook on the international system.[20] A perfect nutrient medium for security dilemma is the systemic anarchy where "no central government exists to insure order, no police or judicial system remains to enforce contracts, and groups have divided into independent armed camps."[21] Anarchy limits communications between the countries, increases fear and uncertainty in each other's intentions, and reciprocates fears of mutual annihilation. States en masse misinterpret the objective reality and the outgoing signals from others; this results in a distorted vision of the actions of their counterparts presented as a priori hostile. Parties to security dilemma try to outrun each other in building up their defensive capabilities, which are viewed by their rivals as offensive. They fear that if they do not strike first, others will, and the offense-is-the-best-defense approach takes over. Eventually, no one is completely secure.

With all the picturesque metaphors and allegories used, Kiselev is right in one thing: there is, indeed, a paranoid fear of being surrounded by enemies in the modern Russian political culture as inherited from its past. The avatar of the Russian existential fears is NATO, being driven, as in James Cameron's film *Avatar,* by the United States of America. For the Russians, NATO is the embodiment of all evil and earthly negativity that can be in the international relations. This approach has not changed since the Cold War era. For instance, according to Gvozdev and Marsh, a NATO-led regular military exercise, Able Archer, conducted in 1983 to simulate possible U.S. defensive actions in case of an actual conflict with the Soviet Union, was "perceived by the leadership of the USSR as a prelude to an actual attack."[22] In Putin's reign, the same story continues with attempts to include Russia as the main threat to America's own identity.

In his address to the Federal Assembly on December 4, 2014, Putin gave the following explanation of the Western sanctions on Russia's involvement in Ukraine:

> This is not just a nervous reaction from the United States or its allies for our position in relation to the events and the coup d'état in the Ukraine and even in the so-called Crimean spring. I am sure if none of that had happened . . . they [the United States] would have come up with some other excuse in order to restrain the growing capacities of Russia to influence it or, even better, to take advantage of it. The policy of containment was not invented yesterday. It has been carried out against our country for many, many years—always, we can say, for decades, if not centuries. In short, whenever someone thinks that Russia has become too strong, independent, these tools are immediately enacted.[23]

This statement shows desperate attempts to include Russia within the policy discourse of the United States and to present it as a threat to U.S. statehood—exactly as the United States itself has been considered the existential boogeyman for Russia.

Although over thirty years have passed since the Able Archer, any eastward move by NATO and the United States is seen as a priori hostile and anti-Russian. In her autobiography, Hillary Clinton noted, "Putin's claim that NATO's open door is a threat to Russia reflects his refusal to accept the idea that Russia's relations with the West could be based on partnership and mutual interest."[24] By proudly stating in 2014 that Russia does not belong to any alliances, the membership in which might question its sovereignty, Putin refuses to include the notions of "multilateralism" and "partnership" in the political lingo of his country.

In the present anarchic world, with the absence of universal authority to credibly punish the defectors and credibly reward the compliers of peace, the condition of security dilemma prevails. The United Nations, as a multilateral political organization, should not be considered an aspirant here, since this organization has long discredited itself with the sluggishness of its decision-making process with regard to its actions in the international arena, the lack of will of the key players and the rest of the international community to support and to commit to its decisions, and the utter impotence to properly fulfill them. It is, therefore, extremely important to understand the essence and the purpose of the mutually directed assurances of (non)aggressive intents. Under the conditions of the security dilemma, even the most positive messages of nonviolent behavior are considered hostile.

During the NATO summit in Wales in September 2014, the alliance members sent an overly positive message to Russia, keeping in mind its pirate behavior in Ukraine. Their concluding declaration reads, "We continue to believe that a partnership between NATO and Russia based on respect for international law would be of strategic value. We continue to aspire to a cooperative, constructive relationship with Russia, including reciprocal confidence building and transparency measures and increased mutual understanding of NATO's and Russia's nonstrategic nuclear force postures in Europe, based on our common security concerns and interests, in a Europe where each country freely chooses its future."[25] In such a clearly optimistic and cooperative declaration, Russia suspected a malicious intent. In response, the Russian Foreign Ministry blamed NATO for being puppeteered by the "hawks from Washington" in its "inability to alter its genetic code as having been created during the 'Cold War.'"[26] This exchange of "niceties" shows the depth of the security dilemma in which the Russian political elites are submersed.

The real—not perceptional—picture with regard to the military standing of Russia is quite different from how it is perceived. Together with regaining the Soviet Union's status came all the "perks" of the Cold War with its super rival, including the arms race and security dilemma, which Russia seems to succeed in. According to the Global Firepower Index 2014, second only to the United States and surpassing China, with the PwrIndx of 0.2355, the Russian state exceeds the United States by its number of nuclear warheads and tanks, but substantially lags behind in the number of aircraft, aircraft carriers, and submarines.[27] Russia is also a leader in the contemporary military buildup: SIPRI notes a 16 percent rise in the Russian military expenditures in 2012 with the largest share (4.4 percent) of the GDP spent on the military, equal to the United States.[28] According to the IHS Aerospace, Defense, and Security Consulting, "Russia has more than doubled its defense budget in nominal terms since 2007 and will have tripled since that time by 2016," which "coincided" with Putin's second presidential term and the economic boost following the increase in prices on the global oil markets.[29]

This is a growing trend in the current Russian military buildup: the main objective of the Russian State Armament Program 2020 is to modernize the old weapons and military equipment by 70 percent. These modernization efforts are planned at the rate of 20.73 trillion rubles (a bit more than a half trillion USD), which is a considerable leap from the obsolete Soviet military legacy.[30] And this is only according to the available data. According to the analysis of the financial information agency FINMARKET, which got hold of the secret annex to the state military budget document, in real terms by the end of 2014 the country will have spent 18.3 percent more than was initially planned in 2013.[31]

The steady buildup of its military potential unilaterally engulfed Russia, fresh from the classic security dilemma of the Cold War, in the so-called perceptional security dilemma. This happens when the threat calculations are wrong for a number of reasons, mostly the lack of communication and the record of past interactions. In the anarchic world, states do not communicate with each other and, keeping in mind the history of negativity, they expect the worst. Under such settings, as Stephen Van Evera notes, "Misperceptions are common: states often exaggerate the size of first move advantages, the size of window of opportunity and vulnerability, the degree of resource cumulatively and the ease of conquest. They then adopt war-causing policies in response to these illusions."[32] Charles Glaser also applies perceptional security dilemma to the military context of weighing possible odds of winning the potential confrontation: "States are inclined to do a poor job of updating [their military buildup or restraint], with a bias toward exaggerating the hostility of others. When they suffer from these biases, states will act as though the security dilemma is more severe than it actually is."[33] The bottom line here is that the spiraling of misperceptions leads to the inevitability of the conflict, for which all participants are equally blamed.

In the matter of creating and sustaining the perceptional security dilemma, a huge role is given to the domestic political establishment, which should support the militaristic policies of the decision makers in order for the latter to maintain the perceptive part of it. These "norm entrepreneurs" have the task of convincing their electorate of the righteousness of their choice by creating norms, rules, and practices for others to follow. Martha Finnemore and Kathryn Sikkink call them "critical for norm emergence because they call attention to issues or even 'create' issues by using language that names, interprets, and dramatizes them."[34] "Norm entrepreneurs" are thus crucial in consolidating the wide political spectrum, including inevitable veto players, for supporting their foreign policy misperceptions. All the categories of perceptional security dilemma mentioned by Robert White—diabolical enemy image, virile and moral self-images, selective inattention, absence of empathy, and military overconfidence—require undeniable backing of the domestic institutional actors.[35]

The paradox of application of the perceptional security dilemma in the case of Russian-American relations is in its causes. The interactions between the two countries follow the perceptional security dilemma scenario on the part of Russia, while it is absent in the United States. There are two reasons for this: first, since the end of the Cold War there has been no lack of communication between the two countries and problems of delivery of credible information about the true intentions. And second, in order for the security dilemma to "flourish," there must be at least two conflicting sides with Galtung's "incompatibilities" in a single action system; in other words, the security dilemma thinking should prevail on both sides of interstate relations. There are several issue-areas contributing to the buildup of the perceptional security dilemma on the side of Russia: growing anti-Americanism in Russian society; American "meddling in" the Russian domestic politics, traditional security aspects (such as nuclear security), and American policies toward former NIS nations, as presented by the conflicting views on the theories of international relations. None of that is present in the contemporary American discourse related to Russia, which makes the perceptional security dilemma seem lopsided.

Anti-Americanism

If a world championship on anti-Americanism had been held in 2014, Russia would have taken one of the three honorary places. There are several mutually complementary and equally negative narratives in modern Russia political discourse directed toward the United States. These narratives are created, nurtured, supported, and promoted by the political establishment at various levels and spread around the general public by practically all means of mass communication: television, newspapers, and the Internet. The Russian segment of Facebook and social networks (VKontake, and Odnoklassniki-based online communities) rapidly mushroomed with the worsening of relations between the United States and Russia and especially after the aggravation of the political situation in Ukraine. Some of them are directly linked to the Russian government propaganda machine, such as *Russia Today* (formerly known as *Surkovskaya Propaganda* after Russian gray cardinal Vladislav Surkov, former head of the presidential administration and the author of the "sovereign democracy" concept), or "We are against the USA. Anti-Maidan," and numerous USSR/Russia–related pages. While the forms and contents of these public opinion tools are in most cases different, the concept is the same: to tarnish the view of the common Russians on America and to eulogize their country as opposing the universal evil that America represents.

Dominating Narratives

Anti-Americanism is deeply grounded in the defeatist feelings dominant in Russian political culture immediately after the collapse of the Soviet Union causing Nietzsche's *ressentiment* in the Russian society. In purely technical terms, removal of a party of the conflict from the confrontation equation (and even more so—its self-pulverization) means by definition the defeat of that party and the victory of the remaining one. In absolute terms, the collapse of the Soviet Union and its Warsaw Pact meant its defeat in the Cold War against the United States and NATO, and many in Russia have been blaming the United States for the downfall of the USSR and the subsequent economic, political, and identity problems the new republic has suffered ever since.

The narratives and myths about America are centered on several key issues serving the grand purpose of the Russian renaissance. Some of them focus on the history of Cold War interactions; some direct the manageable audience to its aftermath while others cover the more contemporary points of concern. It is presented to the Russian audience that America was methodically plotting anti-Russian schemes while hiding behind the guise of friendship and cooperation, which lasted two decades after the end of the Cold War. It did have some success due to the impotence of Boris Yeltsin's governance, giving in to the United States and the West and the "fifth column," the *liberasts* who had sold their souls for the American dollar. This grand stratagem of aspirations for world domination was uncovered only after the arrival of Putin in Russian politics. It is, therefore, the messianic mission of Russia and Putin to stop the spread of parochial "democracy" and "human rights," which are nothing but items in the toolbox of American fascism.

A cursory overview of the narratives prevailing in the mass political discourse of Russia depicts the gloomy picture of Russia being trapped by the treacherous America, whose sole reason for existence is to destroy All-Russian. To start with, America destroyed the Soviet Union. It always wanted to destroy the Russian land, no matter what that country was called. In general, the United States specializes in bringing great misfortune to the world: bloody chaos and wars all over the planet are their business. As such, it was America who twisted the minds of naïve Ukrainians and Georgians, supporting and feeding the fascists and separatists there. Ukraine is just one example of American imperialism. America has used brute force and blackmail to subdue the peaceful Europeans by holding them hostage to NATO's will. Nazism and fascism are a new American ideology, and the only nation that can withstand its onslaught is Russia. Finally, although America is spearheading globalization and technological progress, this is done with malicious intent to control the Internet and its servers (most of which are located in the United States).

A special role in hate-tagging America in modern Russian political propaganda is given to ridiculing its military personnel. American soldiers, regardless of their ranks and service, are presented to the general Russian public as weak, effeminate, and cowardly, whereas Russian military personnel are brutish, virile, and laughing in the face of death. An interesting part of it is that there has been no occasion for direct military confrontation in the history of interactions between these two nations to prove or disprove these myths of Russian invincibility and American vulnerability. During World War II, America and the Soviet Union were allies in fighting Nazi Germany. The Cold War was "cold" by definition, which meant the superpower rivalry in the declaratory form and proxy ideological wars raged away from each other's borders. The Cuban Missile Crisis of 1962 was an exception, but even then the emotions never filled the nuclear cups of the two countries.

Negative depictions of the American military in popular Russian discourse started as early as 2008 in the aftermath of the conflict with Georgia. The Russian military left victorious after the five-day war against a nation of 3 million. Georgian military was trained by the American side, which had spent some $518 million in military assistance, including the Train and Equip Program, from 2002 to 2009.[36] Victory over the Georgian military thus indirectly meant victory over the Americans, which, too, was presented to boost Russian morale. Ever since then, the views on American soldiers have been mostly denigrating. In April 2014, an unnoticed incident for a general public in the West took place in the Black Sea involving an American warship and a Russian bomber airplane. The USS *Donald Cook* was cruising the Black Sea international waters when a Russian SU-24 fighter jet made several low-altitude passes in the close vicinity of the American ship. Pentagon official representative Steve Warren called these moves "provocative and unprofessional."[37] Several dozen Russian media outlets gave almost the same coverage of this seemingly insignificant incident but added details; apparently Colonel Warren described the Russian flight as "menacing and demoralizing." Most of the Russian media outlets also reported that thirty members of the American crew had filed resignations while aboard. These sailors explained the reasons for their actions in fearing for their lives and were allegedly being assisted by a group of psychologists immediately sent to calm their fears.[38]

Another notable example of the anti-American rhetoric—now in general political terms—was given by Sergey Glaz'ev, presidential advisor in charge of the Customs Union, in a TV program, *Politika,* in the aftermath of the annexation of Crimea. In this interview Glaz'ev, when referring to the situation in Ukraine in 2014, directly accused the United States of supporting Nazi Germany against the Soviet Union during World War II:

> We need to understand that this [the situation in Ukraine] is not a war of the Banderovtsi against Slavyansk [a Ukrainian city], but the war of the special agencies and the government of the United States against Russia . . . against the whole Russian world organized and financed from Washington. . . . It is their normal way of using radical people against their enemies. . . . Why are they attacking us? There is no rational explanation for this. . . . Why did they set Hitler against us in 1942? . . . It is the element of the American geopolitics: to steer up chaos and to damage all those countries who independently decide their fate.[39]

Such statements coming from such a high-level official, who has direct contacts with Putin, shows that the growing anti-Americanism in Russia is sanctioned at the highest echelons of power.

Such demonizing oratory is quite different from the general Soviet era anti-American propaganda. During the Cold War, when the two superpowers were more or less on equal footing with the numbers of nuclear warheads and conventional military power, the Soviet Union's popular messages were somewhat impersonal and devoid of direct name-calling and demonizing of the opponents. The Cold War confrontation went along the ideological lines with no particular hatred against the Americans as a nation and their president as their leader. There was no blind fury of negativity sent overseas from the Soviet Union, since there were no feelings of *ressentiment* and no inferiority complex against the American power, which was matched by the Soviet one. The Soviet Union was truly a superpower sure in its own might and with the feelings of the leader of at least some hemispheric parts.

Putin made it all personal, and he does not miss a chance to "stick a finger in the eye of the United States—whether it is Syria, Iran and now of course with Snowden."[40] This elaborate parlance came from New York senator Charles Schumer during the height of the scandal around the defector IT employee of the U.S. National Security Agency, Edward Snowden, in 2013. It was during Putin's rule that the Russian Internet space and the social networking websites were flooded with denigrating and demonizing images of the United States as a country, Barack Obama as its president, and average Joes or Janes as its citizens. To Putin's credit, as a master of public opinion, Russian citizens eagerly responded to the dehumanization and demonization of their country's former partner. Interesting results are given in Levada's public opinion poll in 2014, "Foreign Policy Foes and Partners of Russia," which showcases the remarkable fluctuation of the views of Russian citizens since Putin's second coming. If in 2004 22 percent of the respondents considered the relations with the United States "friendly" and "good neighborly" and 41 percent viewed them as "normal and calm," their joined indicator dropped down to 5 percent in 2014. Thirty-nine percent of the respondents think of the United States as their "enemy"; 43 percent believe that relations are "tense," and 11 percent consider them "lukewarm."[41] Consolidation of Russian society to jointly respond to the political challenges created by their leadership helped the people to finally decide whom to blame for its internal and external problems.

The apogee of demonization of All-American so far is equalizing America with the global terrorism it has been fighting against for several decades now. America is increasingly presented to the Russian public as a terrorist state itself. In *Vesti Nedeli*, the main news program of the Russia 1 state TV channel, aired on October 19, 2014, host Dmitry Kiselev compared President Obama to the ISIS leader Abu Bakr Al-Baghdadi. By presenting both men on the split screen with the "key bullet points" of their respective programs, Kiselev stressed Obama's middle name, apparently with the desire to emphasize the similarities between the Muslim names of Hussein and Abu. Here is an excerpt from this program, which shows the rock bottom of Russian-American relations presented with a highly personal character assassination of the leader of America:

> The Islamic State . . . is building a new caliphate and does not acknowledge the modern system of law, including international and state borders. There are striking similarities with the United States. . . . Barack Hussein Obama thinks he can spread his jurisdiction on the whole world, and so does Caliph Abu Bakr Al-Baghdadi. Barack Hussein Obama is convinced he can kill people without due process of law—Caliph Abu Bakr Al-Baghdadi agrees with him. Barack Hussein Obama is ready to forcefully impose his vision of perfection onto others, and Caliph Abu Bakr Al-Baghdadi follows him. [American] violence is hidden in the bird's-eye views [of drone attacks], and we do not see mutilated bodies and cut off heads, and the Caliph prefers public shows of violence. Finally, Barack Hussein Obama is obsessed by the messianic spirit and exceptionalism, and so is Caliph Abu Bakr Al-Baghdadi.[42]

Even a year prior to this program, such blatantly belligerent anti-Americanism on the Russian state-owned TV channel was simply impossible to imagine, which means that it was allowed and nurtured at the highest echelons of power. If deconstructed into the internal (domestically cultivated) and external (coming from outside of Russia), anti-Americanism in Russia shows its true colors of having been elevated to the state-level policy practices.

Internal Anti-Americanism

On the domestic level, America is blamed for most if not all the problems of Russian society. These include its economic downfall of 2008 and 2014; the support to the "fifth column" and "national traitors"; promotion of the liberal sexual lifestyle to degrade, thus endangering, the traditional pillars of Russian society; and loosening the grip of the "spiritual staples" of the mysterious Russian soul. The aggravating factor for this was, of course, Russia's open intervention into Ukrainian domestic political affairs and annexation of the Crimean Peninsula in

March 2014. Six years prior to that and also around the time when the countries were supposed to keep "Olympic peace" during the Olympic games, Russia attacked Georgia and took its two breakaway regions—Abkhazia and South Ossetia—under its de facto and de jure control. Not even the war against Georgia opened the eyes of the West: it took Russia's military actions closer to the EU's borders to be seriously considered in Brussels. After Georgia, Russia got the famous "reset" red button presented to Foreign Minister Lavrov by his American counterpart, Hillary Clinton, in March 2009, as a token of peaceful American intentions. The reset button carried an unintentional typo: the English word was translated into Russian as an "overload" (*peregruzka*) instead of the correct *perezagruzka*, which caused peals of amused laughter at the ceremony.

Little did both foreign affairs tsars know how prophetic the 2009 "overload" event would turn in five years. The relationship between Russia and America had fallen below freezing by the end of 2014 and seems to have no prospects for a possible rapprochement in the immediate future. As the sides agree that a new "re-reset" is unlikely, the tensions are slowly escalating. In his address to the UN General Assembly in 2014, President Obama corrected his negation of Russia as a major security threat for the United States, made at the televised presidential debate by the Republic contender Mitt Romney in the 2012 campaign. The events in Ukraine made Obama recalculate the geopolitical vision and place Russia, the Ebola virus, and ISIS in Iraq and Syria as the most dangerous threats to global peace. The head of the Duma's foreign relations committee, Alexei Pushkov, shared Obama's pessimism by blaming America and tweeting, "Reset-3, which would have improved the relations of Russia and the United States, is highly unlikely, as Obama's administration has firmly 'saddled the horse' of the Cold War. Not our choice."[43] Russia seems genuinely unaware of the changing attitudes of the West and the United States, in particular, and tends to blame the latter for all the evils that have befallen it since its independent existence.

The list of those evils comprises diverse economic, ethnic, and cultural areas of lives of everyday Russians. In his book published at the dusk of Yeltsin's era, Sergey Glaz'ev blamed the United States and the West, in general, for the genocide of the Russian nation. He wrote, "When American politicians, for example, say that the USA is interested in a strong and prosperous Russia, they are proceeding from the standpoint of the national interests of the American people; when they conduct an actual policy toward Russia, of wrecking, dismemberment, and destruction, they are acting in the interests of the world oligarchy, which guides their decisions. That is why they often say one thing, and do something directly opposite."[44] This was, to a certain degree, a reference to the U.S. desire to transfer the Western democratic institutional frameworks, including in the economic sphere, for the Russians to mimic.

Back in the day, Victoria Nuland, aide to Undersecretary of State Strobe Talbott, called this "the spinach treatment," referring to that highly unpopular vegetable among children who are force-fed by their parents who "know better": "The more you tell them it's good for them, the more they gag."[45] Echoing Glaz'ev's comments in 2014, Russian MP Yevgeny Fedorov, the founder of the anti-American "National Liberation Movement," presented his organization's viewpoints: the U.S. government is conducting genocide of the Slavs in Ukraine and plans to do so in Russia; Russia has been an economic colony of the United States since 1991 and has been paying the toll of $1 million a day ever since; the Russian constitution as written by the American advisors infringes on the national interests of the citizens of Russia; the Russian mass media are under American control and are translating their parochial propaganda; and the United States has developed the plan of military aggression against Russia.[46] If coming from an average citizen, such ideas would sound like nothing more than a paranoid stream of consciousness, but in the case of the elected member of the country's supreme legislator, these words acquire a completely different meaning.

Putin and his entourage grew skeptical of Western influence with the rise in oil prices after the financial market collapsed in 2008. It was the time when the desire not to depend on foreign money or listen to Western advice started to grow in Russian society. In 2012, at the demand of the Russian government, the U.S. Agency for International Development, which had been active in the country since 1992 and had spent about $3 billion in assistance, ended its existence.[47] In 2014, to protect Russian teenagers from being brainwashed in America, the Russian government ended the Future Leaders Exchange (FLEX) program. According to U.S. ambassador John Teft, "For over two decades... [the FLEX] has brought more than 8,000 Russian high school students to the United States to live with American host families, attend high school, and experience community life for an academic year."[48] The formal explanation for the closure of the program was the failure of fifteen children to go back to Russia and the adoption of one of them by a gay couple. The informal explanation, however, is connected to the wish to protect Russian children from the "corrupting influence" of Western culture and its values.

Expulsion of the USAID was followed by the rapid growth of anti-Putin sentiments in Russian society. Various laws were passed that limited opportunities for Russian citizens to be influenced from outside, including the "Foreign Agent Law" with the purpose of controlling the nonprofit organizations that received foreign funding in 2012; the amendments to the "State Treason Law," which defined treason as "providing financial, logistical, consulting, or other assistance to a foreign state, international or foreign organization, or their representatives in activities directed against the security of the Russian Federation"; and the "Dual Citizenship Law," forcing all those with multiple citizenship to register with the Federal Migration Agency in 2014. These legislative actions undertaken by the Russian government between 2005 and 2014 were aimed at limiting outside American and Western influences over the hearts and minds of adult Russians. In the digital age, access to information sharing is practically unrestricted, with the rare exception of North Korea, China, and Iran. Russia is thinking of joining them with the invention of the death-switch that would cut the country off the Internet (being, as Putin thinks, "developed as the special project of the CIA") in case of a major attack on its digital grid.[49] This led to adoption of the amendments to the "Law on Information, Information Technology, and Protection of Information" in April 2014, ordering IT companies and especially IP telephone companies to store and provide the personal information of users to law enforcement agencies.

Mostly, however, the Russian political establishment worried that the Americans would fund the opposition parties capable of attracting enough supporters to represent viable power against the ruling regime. The United States is suspected of financially and ideologically supporting the "fifth column" and "national traitors"—those who do not agree with the general line of the presidential party, Edinnaya Rossiya. Among these actors the most prominent are Drugaya Rossiya (The Other Russia), Yabloko (Apple), the United Democratic Movement Solidarnost, and Parnas (headed by the outspoken opposition leader Boris Yavlinsky and formerly by the thirteenth world chess champion Garry Kasparov). All of them are referred to in Russia as "non-systemic opposition," i.e., the parties that remain outside of the Duma quorum, as well as radical organizations. According to N. P. Medvedev and A. B. Borisenko, "Support to the non-systemic opposition by the Western community is an important factor of the current political situation in the Russian Federation, which is expressed both in sympathizing to the disgruntled Russian oligarchs and the leaders of 'Other Russia' by the Western political and economic elite as well as in certain informational and geopolitical pressure."[50] The situation is further aggravated by the vision of the United States as supporting the opposition parties leading to regime changes in former Soviet republics in the form of the color revolutions, which the ruling party views as the harbingers of the domestic problems.[51]

Even the word "Maidan," as the central square in Kiev, Ukraine, entered the Russian language as a neologism that means "a forceful overthrow of the government conducted by rogue opposition groups with Western funding." In fact, the whole idea behind extending the reset's olive branch of peace to Russia was considered the wittingly treacherous act of luring Russia into submission. According to Veronika Krashennikova, head of the Institute of Foreign Policy Research and Initiatives, "The reset was nothing but a tactical move from the United States to engage Russia in the role of a junior partner, serving the interests of Washington."[52] The culmination of the U.S. intervention in the domestic affairs of Russia was considered its "involvement" in the second Ukrainian revolution in 2013–14. The overthrow of the corrupt President Viktor Yanukovich and the subsequent positioning of the Ukraine (a country that Russian nationalists have long denied the raison d'être) by its new leaders close to Europe and the West, hence away from Russia, is perceived as being directly funded, organized, and puppeteered from Washington. The fact that once successful and replicated somewhere else, the Maidan can also happen in Russia, which brings out the worst fears of the Russian political establishment.[53]

Finally, America is blamed for supporting terrorist organizations in Chechnya. Such a belligerent rhetoric comes from Putin's famous "Valdai" speech, where he places responsibility for supporting the Chechen terrorists squarely on American shoulders: "They once sponsored Islamic extremist movements to fight the Soviet Union. Those groups got their battle experience in Afghanistan and later gave birth to the Taliban and Al-Qaeda. The West, if not supported, at least closed its eyes and, I would say, gave information, political and financial support to an international terrorists' invasion of Russia: we have not forgotten this."[54] Criticism of the United States as the country sponsoring terrorism is not new. Back in 2000 Foreign Minister Igor Ivanov accused the U.S. Department of State of "supporting terrorists and separatists, and not only in Russia."[55] This statement was made nine months prior to 9/11, upon meeting the American diplomats with Ilyas Akhmedov, foreign minister of self-proclaimed "Republic of Ichkeria"—Chechnya, which is currently the fiefdom of Putin's loyal supporter Ramzan Kadyrov, head of Chechnya.

After 9/11 Putin was among the first foreign leaders to support the American Global War on Terror, including facilitation of "the deployment of American forces to Central Asia as a staging ground for Operation Enduring Freedom in Afghanistan."[56] This, however, as S. V. Bespalov noted, was done partly out of a pragmatic viewpoint, "to present its own struggle with the Chechen separatists and their supporters among the representatives of international Islamist groups as one of the 'fronts' in this 'war' and, accordingly, to reduce the pressure of criticism of its policies in Chechnya by the Western political and intellectual elites."[57] The same accusations coming from Russian leaders fourteen years later revealed long-standing rancor against the United States and its inability to stand with Russia in its own domestic problems. Such belligerent outbursts, clearly aimed at consolidating the wide spectrum at home around the American threat, also signify the start of another upsurge of domestic anti-Americanism.

"Meddling" in Russia

The area of human rights has traditionally been a stumbling block in relations between the advanced democratic states and their autocratic counterparts. As Michael Doyle notes, democracies or "liberal republics are prepared to protect and promote—sometime forcibly—democracy, private property, and the rights of individuals overseas in non-republics."[58] This is the convex lens of the democratic regimes: they want others to be equally democratic to avoid possible confrontations. Among other attributes of well-functioning democracies, human rights play a crucial role in the matter of democratizing external governances. Much in the same line of reasoning, the analysis of David Sobek et al. shows that the "governments which respect human rights at home are less likely to become involved in violent international disputes with one another."[59] They may, of course, promote the respect of human rights in other non-democratic regimes. For example, Andrew Moravcsik talks about "established" democracies as having "an incentive to promote [democracy] for others . . . in order to bolster the 'democratic peace' by fostering democracy in neighboring countries. . . . In such cases, established democracies can be expected to support rhetorical declarations in favor of human rights and regimes with optional enforcement."[60] Promotion of human rights and fundamental freedoms, the very essence of the American projection of its democratic values, is depicted in Russia as hostile and directed against Russia's own traditional values.

The cause of this part of the perceptional security dilemma is in the clash between the collective sovereignty promoted by the United States and individual sovereignty safeguarded by Russia. In their countermeasures to the intrusion into their internal affairs, Russia applies its preferred tactics of punishing its own people for the sake of attaining a menacing impact in the international arena. Human rights were not put in the center of the U.S.-Russian interactions after Putin came to power; they were, in fact, always one of the key approaches, which the United States used in its political, social, and economic interactions with the USSR. One of the tools for applying pressure on the Soviet Union was the Jackson-Vanik Amendment, which "was included in the Trade Act of 1974 to protect religious freedom in the former Soviet Union."[61] The legislative act limited trade with the Soviet Union because the latter stifled the rights of its Jewish population and denied them freedom of religion, speech, and movement.

According to Anders Aslund et al., once Russia became a member of the World Trade Organization in 2012, the United States had two options: revoke the amendment completely or use the "non-application principle," which would mean separate fulfillment of the WTO statutes.[62] The impending decision to repel the amendment coincided with the human rights scandal that exploded in 2009 in Russia when the Russian lawyer for the investment advisory firm Heritage Capital Management was put in prison for investigating multimillion dollar fraud involving the Russian tax officials and died there without due process of law.[63] The Magnitsky Act, which Angus Roxburgh called "a death-knell of the reset policy," was a legislative move to urge Russia to provide the rule of law to their citizens by offering them the carrots (repelling the Jackson-Vanik Amendment) and the sticks (individualized punitive mechanisms).[64] As with other subsequent actions of the United States, including the sanctions imposed on Russia for its intervention in Ukraine, the Magnitsky Act "specified that individuals connected to Sergei Magnitsky's death should be placed on a visa ban list and their assets in the United States should be frozen."[65] It was indeed a sign of doors of interstate cooperation slowly closing, but the Russian retaliatory reaction to the Magnitsky Act startled even the most pessimistic observers of Russian political culture.

In December 2012 Russia banned the import of American meat for the sum of $500 million per year after finding a chemical element, ractopamine; it shut down the operations of USAID; it tried to limit the influence of foreign money in domestic Russian nongovernmental organizations and increased the pressure on its domestic opposition.[66] But the most incredible retaliatory reaction, also targeting American individuals but with much larger connotations and area of coverage, was the law "On Sanctions for Individuals Violating Fundamental Human Rights and Freedoms of the Citizens of the Russian Federation." The law, named after Dmitry Yakovlev, a two-year-old Russian adoptee who died in a locked car as a result of excessive heat in 2008, banned the adoption of Russian children by American citizens, together with "suspending the activities of nonprofit organizations that receive cash and other assets from American citizens (organizations), and are involved in political activities in Russia . . . that act as a threat to Russian interests."[67] With this, Russia put together its own list of eighteen persona non grata Americans, as suspected by Russia of ill treatment of Guantanamo detainees and "lawyers and judges involved in prosecuting Russian organized crime figures"—all for the sake of the tit-for-tat foreign policy.[68]

The span of four years between the tragic death of a child and its use for political purposes by the Russian establishment puts the "Dima Yakovlev Law" in the same arsenal of counterpunitive measures taken by Russia against the United States by punishing its own people. It was, in a sense, a "Santa Claus present" to the Russian children—the law came into force on January 1, 2013—who were about to be adopted by Americans and taken away from horrible asylums. The law clearly reflects the self-mutilation nature of the Russian political culture in its responses to the international actions that it deems hostile to its domestic idyll.

External Anti-Americanism

Russia was traditionally weary of U.S. international military involvements, viewing them as violating the balance of power on the global level and tarnishing the prestige of Russia as a country that is incapable of the same scale military actions as the United States. Notwithstanding the fact that officially the United States/NATO and Russia "do not view each other as adversaries," according to Andrey Makarychev, "Russia openly treats the Alliance as its major military threat.... The [NATO-Russia Founding] Act mentions 'aggressive nationalism' as a common threat, yet this is the exact characterization of Russia's policies today. It goes without saying that today any debate regarding Russia's moves toward democracy and political pluralism remain hollow and meaningless."[69] Having purposely located itself on the opposing international political spectrum, Russia is prepared to re-create the Cold War confrontation with the Western world.

Putin's evolution from the Munich 2007 to Valdai 2014 is also significant in showcasing the growing anti-Americanism in the Russian political culture directed against the American actions outside the state borders of the Russian Federation. In 2007 it was the attacks on the unipolar world dominated by the United States when Russia felt uncomfortable being on the edge of the global processes: Putin was accusing the United States of "uncontained hyper use of force—military force—in international relations" and "greater disdain for the basic principles of international law." At Valdai, Putin reiterated the danger emanating from America's encroachments on the national sovereignties of the countries by imposing "unilateral dictate" of power and loyalty to the democratic principles, so much disdained by the institutional actors in Russia. Using very plain language, Putin compared the United States to the French nouveau riche who "unexpectedly end up with a great fortune... in the shape of world leadership and domination." For him, the "so-called victors in the Cold War had decided to pressure events and reshape the world to suit their own needs and interests."[70] Putin's message to the world and the United States in particular was a harbinger of upcoming significant changes in Russia's outlook in the outward projection of its national security.

Changes in the attitude of Russian authorities toward the actions of the United States on the international arena are reflected in Russia's new military doctrine in 2014. The "old" version was adopted in 2010 and drew heavily on the National Security Strategy 2020 (adopted in May 2009). There, Russia pledged to respect international law for the benefit of global peace. With regard to its national security interests directed toward America, "Russia will seek to build an equal and full strategic partnership with the United States on the basis of shared interests and taking into account the influence that Russian-American relations have at the international situation, as a whole."[71] The military doctrine 2010 defined NATO enlargement, possible deployment of foreign troops, and Anti-Ballistic Defense (AMD) systems in Eastern Europe as some of the grave threats to the national security of Russia.[72]

The Doctrine promoting international cooperation in the field of collective security with the major intergovernmental institutions, including the European Council and NATO, was adopted the same year as its American counterpart. It reflects a more liberalist vision than its upcoming successor in 2014. Jacob Kipp notes that the 2010 doctrine followed the U.S. Quadrennial Defense Review (QDR) 2010, which did not discuss Russia in terms of the military confrontation; the overall document "does not focus on Russia as a threat to the United States and seems more focused upon the current conflicts and the global struggle against terrorism than upon preparing to fight major regional wars by conventional means. Russian commentators judged this to be a potential development of significance for Russia's security interests."[73] This was very much in line with the general "thawing" of the Russian-American relations after their 2008 freeze.

The new Military Doctrine 2014 makes the Russian military outlook for the next several years substantially more concentrated around the West as the new rival for Russian statehood. The document, according to Mikhail Popov, deputy secretary of the NSC, responds to the augmented threats coming from NATO, and the United States and the AMD are the focal points of the new document.[74] In many respects the new document resembles its much older versions. The military doctrine of 2003 also contained the "deployment of foreign troops in the territory of new NATO members and countries that aspire to join the bloc; armed force used by ad hoc coalitions; persistence of Cold War stereotypes that aggravate the international situation; . . . demonstration of military power close to the borders of Russia; expansion of military blocs" as security threats.[75]

The 2014 doctrine thus reemphasized the negative perceptions of the Russian political establishment of the United States as playing the key role in the military part of NATO. The first national security threat is "augmenting of the power capacity of the North Atlantic Treaty Organization (NATO) and giving it global functions carried out in violation of the international law; proximity of the military infrastructure of members of NATO to the borders of the Russian Federation, including its further expansion."[76] In protecting its sovereignty and independence, Russia defines the same sovereignty to others, mainly its neighbors: "deployment (buildup) of military contingents of foreign states (groups of states) in the territories of states adjacent to the Russian Federation and its allies" is a direct reference to the NATO expansion and the cementing of the missile defense systems in Europe.[77]

Russian-American relations, after the failed "reset," dropped below the freezing point in the aftermath of violation of the sovereignty of the Ukrainian nation by Russia. Now Russia is trying to build up an anti-American coalition on the international level by rapidly expanding its cooperation with the BRICS countries: Brazil, Russia, India, China, and South Africa. During the BRICS summit in Brazil in July 2014, Putin tried to harness support against the "frequent cases of massive application of unilateral sanctions" of the United States and its allies and to create "a system of measures that would prevent the persecution of countries not agreeing with various U.S. foreign policy decisions."[78] This multilateral organization, in the view of Russian authorities, can present a viable counterbalance to the onslaught of the West, including its economic and financial influence.

To offset the dominance of the American dollar, Putin also suggested that BRICS could create their own Development Bank by 2020 with the starting capital of $50 billion, soon to be doubled. The bank would give annual credits to the companies of the member countries and regulate the interbank exchanges. With the most ambitious start, at the present stage the BRICS bank's assets and its credit portfolio ($35.6 billion and $16.3 billion) would be ten times less than those of the World Bank and three times less than those of the Asian Development Bank.

Similar to the World Bank, the BRICS Development Bank would contain the pool of foreign exchange reserves to "bail out" its members in times of need, but as Lucy O'Carroll of Aberdeen Asset Management notes, "The biggest challenge to the BRICS Bank comes from the BRICS themselves. The new institutions may give more representation and identity to the issues of concern to the founder members, but not necessarily much more than that. . . . Another hindrance to the BRICS Bank is that it is ultimately a bloc, rather than having a role of global scope."[79] While the desire may sound noble, at least, on the part of Russia, the future of the BRICS Bank is far too clear.

Reverse Blame Game

One of the most effective instruments of anti-Americanism in contemporary Russian political culture is blaming the United States for its own deeds. Russia has deliberately placed itself in the Kingdom of Crooked Mirrors depicted by a 1964 Soviet fairy tale about the place where everything gets its negative distorted image. One of the most commonly used narratives is accusing the current U.S. government for inhumane treatment of the indigenous population of North America during its medieval explorations during the fifteenth through eighteenth centuries.

The conquests of the Native Americans that started with Columbus's voyage and the first settlements of the Europeans on the new continent play a crucial role in the contemporary Russian domestic political discourses focusing on the American devilish role while forgetting its own. Most frequently, the ill treatment of the Native American tribes and the age of slavery are the narratives especially dear to the hearts and minds of the Russian political elites. Applying the preferred tactics of selective memory to objective historical narratives, Russia places the blame on the United States for mistreatment of the Native American tribes but completely forgets how it got all that land to the east of the Ural Mountains. The legislative branch is not an exclusion from the general rule. In October 2014, at a meeting of the "Patriotic Platform" of the ruling party, Edinnaya Rossiya, dedicated to one of the main Russian holidays, the National Unity Day celebrating the victory of the Russian guerrillas against the Polish invaders, its head and chair of the Duma Anti-Corruption Committee, Irina Yarovaya, gave the following description of the Russian multiculturalism as opposed to the American society: "We, as multinational people, never absorbed each other's cultures; we have no experience of colonization; Russia has always been progressing on the path of unification, faith, and honor!"[80] At the same meeting the leadership of the ruling party decided to toss away the notion of democracy as detrimental to the Russian rule of people: "love and loyalty to the Fatherland, friendship, morality, and ethics," according to Yarovaya.

Most Russian claims against America are centered on the issue of land possession, the core of the Russian raison d'être. What the apologists of the Russian imperial construct tend to forget is that the American conquest by the European nations roughly coincided with Russia's own expansions eastward, toward Siberia and beyond. The Russian onslaughts, pioneered by the Cossacks led by Ermak, were not less brutal. Just like the European countries that viewed America as a source of new income and resources, "The Russians were driven east by fur, the 'soft gold' that accounted for one-third of the Imperial coffers at the height of the fur trade. . . . Russia's colonial expansion was a massive hunt for bears and minks, sables, ermines, foxes, and otters"—the medieval raw resources that Russia used for subsequent trade with Europe.[81] Similar to the conquest of America, the Russian occupation of Siberia was "the victory of modern guns against primitive bows and arrows and the triumph of Christianity over paganism" of the local indigenous tribes.[82] Bruce Lincoln gives a vivid description of the less publicized Russian occupation of Siberia: "The coming of the Russians replaced that [preexisting] harmony with a system of exploitation based upon greed and arrogance. Draining one Siberian resource after another, the Russians over the next four hundred years would turn Siberia into one of history's greatest ecological catastrophes. Arrogantly, and with all the self-righteous certainty of men and women who had proclaimed it their mission to bestow the blessings of their way of life upon the other peoples of the world, the Russians dated the beginnings of Siberia's history from October 26, 1582, the day of Ermak's 'conquest.'"[83]

The Russians subjugated hundreds of local tribes west of the Ural Mountains to the Russian tsarist rule, including Buryats, Nentsi, Chukchi, Kolmyki, Ukagiri, Koryaki, and Samoedi—who were wiped out or completely assimilated. In essence, it was the same slavery as in America, but much less institutionalized and discussed. The euphemism that the Soviet and then Russian historiography uses for colonization of Siberia is *osvoenie*, which can be translated as "mastering": "dissemination of socioeconomic relations new for Siberia and the introduction of new types of economic activities," as the popular vision on the idolatrous symbiosis of the indigenous Siberian and the newcomer Russian populations goes.[84] What *osvoenie* meant in reality, in the words of D. N. Verkhoturov, was "cleaning all western, central and partly southern part of the Siberian Khanate from its 'excess population.' . . . [All] the villages and towns along the rivers Tura, Tavda, Tobol and Irtysh were plundered and their populations were annihilated."[85] This was the modus operandi of most of the medieval conquerors, and Russian explorers did not stand out from their European counterparts.

The notion of territory, as a part of the Russian political culture, is given an important role in the reverse blame. The calls to return Alaska as illegally purchased from Russia in 1867 and unlawfully possessed ever since are regularly made in the Russian mass media. There is even an interregional political movement of ultraorthodox Russians, Pchelki (Bees), who have submitted a lawsuit claim in the Moscow Arbitrage Court on acknowledging the purchase contract of Alaska as false because instead of the promised $7.2 million in gold coins, the Russian side received a bank check for the same amount.[86] The Russian Internet space and social networking sides are full of memes and demotivators with the map of Alaska painted in pink with the logo "Ice-Cream," comparing the Russian demands for this cold area with their annexation of the warmer Crimea (*Krim* in Russian) from Ukraine.

Some Russian politicians are determined to take the matter of territorial claims against America to a qualitatively higher level. In September 2014, Mikhail Degtyarev, a nationalist hardliner MP from the Liberal-Democratic Party, submitted a parliamentary query to the Ministry of Foreign Affairs of Russia requiring it to take an international action. The purpose of the query was to force the United States to return Fort Ross and its adjacent land, currently a historic landmark located in Sonoma County, California, which was established by the Russians in the early 1800s and sold to the American side in 1841. According to Degtyarev, "The whole history of American relations in the sphere of state-building and ownership of land and property is murder, robbery, and terrorism. But we are not Indians, which the Americans had evicted. We are Russians, and we just want to get money for our land in accordance to the law. Fort Ross is a Russian property, the sales operation is negligible, and its details are covered in darkness." He stated that Russia should "reclaim its land and put our Iskanders [tactical ballistic missiles known in the West as SS-26 Stone] there."[87] This statement is apparently viewed as peaceful and friendly in Russia, while American calls for "partnership" and "cooperative, constructive relations" apparently have some convoluted evil context.

The reality, however, is not as it seems for Russia. America did not punish Russia as a loser in the Cold War, as presented by its views on the past, economically or territorially. Together with this, America is often presented as breaking international agreements, but it was Russia that violated the Budapest Treaty of 1994 by holding a public referendum under the guns in the Crimea and sending its well-armed and trained "volunteers" to Ukraine, thus endangering the peace in Europe that had lasted for seventy years. It is, in fact, Russia that brims with defeatist sentiments after the end of the Cold War, not the United States, as Sergei Ryabkov, deputy foreign minister of Russia, accused the United States of missing the "winner's" label.[88]

Today Russia continues to blame America for its actions in the world, seeing its roots in abuse of the indigenous North American population. Speaking at the Seliger 2014, Putin turned attention to the historically negative impact of America on the global peace: "Anything that Americans touch they turn into Libya or Iraq." He forgets Russia's military interventions in Georgia in 2008 and Ukraine in 2014, as well as earlier actions of the Russian Fourteenth Army in Transdniestria in early

1990s.[89] On the personal level, too, Russia has been systematically demonizing the United States and NATO on all possible fronts, attributing to American and its people the "hobby of killing children, the elderly, and women anywhere as it pleases."[90] The United States is blamed for instigating World War II, but it was the Soviet Union (the political descendant of which Russia proudly considers itself) that designed plans of co-domination in Europe with Hitler's Nazi regime. Stalin's Russian Soviet Federative Republic supported the Nazi military machine, held regular military training for the German officers in Russia, sent Russian officers to Germany, and awarded medals of honor for participation in joint military exercises.[91] With these reverse blame actions, Russia is trying hard to present its actions as a priori righteous, rightful, and justified, and whoever dares to oppose the main course chosen by Russia is seen as wrong and unjust.

Traditional (Nuclear) Security Concerns

The first and most important military area of cooperation was the nuclear weapons issue, which is the holy of the holies of every nuclear power's national security. After the collapse of the Soviet Union, several of its former republics—Russia, Ukraine, Kazakhstan, and Belarus—ended up having significant nuclear potential. Not only was this negative from the point of view of the institutional stability of the European continent, but it was also detrimental to the newly created nations in question. Nuclear warheads would present significant challenges to their owners; neighboring countries would be concerned about safe and secure storage, transportation, destruction, and prevention of illegal access and possible sales by organized crime groups.[92] Russia, as a successor to the USSR and militarily the strongest of all the ex-republics, undertook the responsibility of "cleaning" its immediate nuclear neighborhood by the Budapest Treaty.

Under the Nunn-Lugar Cooperative Threat Reduction program initiated after the collapse of the largest nuclear country in the world in 1991, the nuclear potential of the former Soviet republics had to be dismantled and destroyed on the spot or transferred to Russia for elimination. This included such programs as strategic arms elimination, chemical weapons destruction, nuclear weapons, missile materials storage, and transportation security. To ensure the implementation of these programs, according to the program report, "The United States has the right to examine the use of any material, training, or service provided. For nuclear weapons storage sites in Russia, DOD is authorized to make three visits to each site where security upgrades are being installed. . . . In addition to the site visits, DOD is allowed to audit equipment through alternative means, including data on locations (by site designator) of equipment, in situ photographs, documentation, letters from the Ministry of Defense (MOD) attesting to intended use, and examination of sample equipment."[93]

Current Russian political discourse sees the deployment of the Anti-Missile Defense (AMD) radars in the territories of the former Soviet camp in the Eastern Europe as a direct threat coming from the United States and NATO. The initial rift between the United States and Russia appeared in 2001 with the withdrawal of the Bush administration from the Anti-Ballistic Missile Treaty (ABM) signed in 1972 in the midst of the Cold War crisis between the United States and the Soviet Union. The Bush administration withdrew from the treaty because it desired to create its own missile defense system, which would protect the continental United States against potential attacks from the "rogue" nations of Iran and North Korea. Russia responded negatively to the United States abandoning the Treaty, especially in light of ongoing NATO expansion. According to Jeffrey Mankoff, this decision "had already forced Moscow to confront its loss of influence on the European continent; now the United States appeared to be seeking to undermine strategic parity and weaken one of the few remaining bases on which Russia could claim major power status. Moreover, Russia did not share the United States' perception that Tehran and Pyongyang posed imminent missile threats."[94] Russian fears went back to the Cold War confrontation and imagined the United States wanting to capitalize on the "weak" Russia by fencing it off from the European heartland.

These fears found a real target when in 2007 the United States announced it was building the new Ballistic Missile Defense (BMD) systems in Poland and the Czech Republic, in a continuous effort to protect both the United States and its allies in Europe from possible aggression from Iran and North Korea. Russia reacted harshly: for her it was clearly a hostile move "threatening the national security." This move would be followed by counterdeployment of the Iskanders in Kaliningrad, close to the European capitals and retargeting them at the countries with the American AMD radars.[95] In 2009 the Obama administration announced a new "European Phased Adaptive Approach" (EPAA) in its AMD in Europe, as a part of the NATO missile defense system. The task of protecting U.S. personnel and assets in Europe was given to several BMD installations: Standard Missile (SM) 3 Interceptor Block IA and the so-called Aegis BMD SPY-1 Radar systems for countering short-, medium-, and long-range ballistic missiles, full deployment of which is planned to be completed by 2018.[96] The system is unique in that it will be able to intercept multiple targets (up to fifty) of the missiles launched at European soil.

The plans to deploy the BMDs in Europe hit the very center of the concave lenses of Russia's superpower construct taking it to the bipolar confrontation in Europe. The issue of the deployment of the missiles and antimissile defense systems goes directly back to the times when the balance in the numbers of warheads defined the future of the continent. Although it is difficult to think of a future nuclear war in Europe or elsewhere, or even about the possibility of a terrorist organization hijacking a nuclear bomb, the possession of the ultimate equalizer strongly reverberates in the hearts and minds of the Russian political establishment seeking to return to the great power politics. Unilateral withdrawal of the United States from the ABM treaty threatened to endanger Russian superpower status. According to Robert Donaldson and Joseph Nogee, Russia "views missile defense as a threat to its own nuclear deterrent and by implication to its status as a great power. Russia's nuclear arsenal is one of the elements that distinguishes it as a great power. To diminish that arsenal is to diminish its possessor. The problem is not a genuine loss of power . . . so much as it is a loss of prestige."[97] In line with its superpower construct, Russia cannot be bordered even by the defensive weapons of the adversaries.

The superpower convex vision of itself made Russia respond so feverishly to the news on the AMD in Europe. Russia felt cornered by the U.S. plans because "in its eyes this disrupts the power balance and evokes a feeling of endangerment."[98] According to Major General Lyaporov, commander of the Moscow AMD, "The only guarantee for . . . [Russia] is the complete halt by the United States of deploying its missile defense systems in Europe."[99] The problem is that no guarantees, written or verbalized, by the United States and NATO would be enough for Russia, who is very closely following the perceptional security dilemma scenario.

Russia's views on nuclear weapons are defined by its perception of the huge role these weapons have in the overall defense of their country, which are not different from the American view on its own security. The National Security Strategy 2010 states, "There is no greater threat to the American people than weapons of mass destruction, particularly the danger posed by the pursuit of nuclear weapons by violent extremists and their proliferation to additional states."[100] Similar to these views on the paramount importance of nuclear weapons in the country's defense, Russian National Security Strategy 2009 gives the following list of military threats: "the policy of a number of leading foreign countries aimed at achieving overwhelming superiority in the military sphere, primarily in strategic nuclear forces . . . unilateral development of the global missile defense system."[101] In a sense, not having been outnumbered or overpowered in nuclear potential strengthens the feelings of security and the ability to breathe freely.

Quite a significant aspect fueling the perceptional security dilemma was that the United States undertook the task to protect the European continent unilaterally, without due consultations and involvement of Russia in the process. In the documentary *Cold Politics*, Putin made this point crystal clear: "The BDM system is clearly directed toward neutralizing the nuclear missile potential of the Russian Federation. Because the radars put along the borders of our country and missile defense systems they would cover our territory up to Urals . . . , the deployment locations of our land nuclear systems. . . . And they [NATO] do not want to give us any written guarantees that these systems would not be used against us."[102] In layman's terms, the translation of this message from Russian into diplomatic language is centered on the following argument: "We cannot commit not to attack you but want you to commit not to defend yourself against our possible future attack."

Russia has taken several steps to force itself into the European defense framework by creating a common defense system in which it would be an active participant. In 2007 it offered the United States joint operation of the radar station in Gabala, Azerbaijan. This was one of the dozens of radar stations operated on the former territory of the Soviet Union, out of which only four are currently in Russia. The United States and NATO, however, refused to put their stakes in the outdated radar systems in Azerbaijan.[103] The United States had already made preliminary arrangements with Poland and the Czech Republic for deployment of the radar systems there. In response to this "hostile" act, Putin took the Cold War ghost of the Cuban Missile Crisis out of the closet: "Similar actions by the Soviet Union, when it deployed missiles in Cuba, provoked the Caribbean crisis. For us, technologically, the situation is very similar."[104] To make things even worse, he threatened European security on a completely different level: as a response to potential ABMDS deployment, Putin suggested that Russia would stop complying with the 1990 Conventional Forces in Europe (CFE) treaty, which restricts deployment of conventional military forces across the European continent until the NATO countries ratify it.[105] NATO insists that the Russian troops stationed in the contested regions of Georgia [Abkhazia and South Ossetia] and Moldova [Transdniestria] violate the treaty.

Despite repeated assurances from the American side that the BMD is incapable of reaching the Russian ICMBs, and despite the cancellation of Phase IV of the EPAA in 2013, Russia ignited the mechanism of the security dilemma. This would mean the ability to launch land-based cruise missiles, which are, indeed, banned by the ABM. It is the hypothetical technical possibility that frightens Moscow and fuels its perceptional security dilemma with the United States and NATO. States engulfed in perceptional security dilemmas would consider purely defensive moves of their opponents as hostile and threatening their own national security, if not now, then definitely in the near future. Ivan Konovalov, director of the Center for Strategic Conjuncture, in an interview with the Voice of Russia, called the quarrel around the ABM "political gambling": "Russia demands legally binding guarantees that this system is not directed against its strategic potential. The West refuses to provide such guarantees. . . . In a situation where the West needs tools to exert pressure on Russia, missile defense is again being pushed to the foreground."[106] Thus the only viable security guarantee for Russia as verbalized by its government is a complete thwarting of the antimissile defense system in Europe or full-fledged participation in the European defense architecture.

NATO also saw providing legally binding guarantees to Russia as "unnecessary. The adoption and the ratification of such documents would also be complicated, as the parliaments of each member state would have to ratify it and there is no precedent of ratification of this kind."[107] What this means is that NATO does not want to give a veto power in the inter-Alliance decision-making process to a nonmember state, not necessarily being Russia. Instead, NATO proposed assurances to the highest political levels in the member countries, which Russia, in return, consider insufficient.

In the matter of nuclear defense in Europe, Russian officials may come up with self-assurances of their own invincibility, such as the famous folklore response to the EPAA plans given by then Russian ambassador to NATO and current vice prime minister Dmitry Rogozin in his twitter, "How many times do you need to be reminded how dangerous this is? The Russian bear will get out of his den and will kick asses of those ill-fated hunters."[108] It was Rogozin who sent a visually menacing message of planting a poplar tree in his residence while representing his country to NATO—a clear reference to an ICMB RT-2PM2 Topol'-M ("poplar" is Topol' in Russian), known in the West as the SS-27 Sickle B. The bottom line is that the driving force, however, remains the same as during the Soviet Union, before that the tsarist empire, and the Slavic tribes in the medieval Rus': fear. Any hypothetically unfriendly move that seems to jeopardize the Russian national interests reanimates the primeval fears of being surrounded by hostile forces willing to destroy the Russian nation.

The United States in the Former Soviet Space

Involvement of the United States in the political processes of the ex-Soviet republics is another irritant for the Russian authorities. American activities in the region known by Russians as the "Near Abroad" and Eastern Europe contribute to the formation of the perceptional fears in Russia of possible intrusion into their own affairs as well as those of its immediate spheres of influence. With this, there is a widely accepted opinion that the United States and NATO betrayed Russia after the end of the Cold War and did not fulfill their alleged promise not to incorporate post-Soviet and formerly communist countries of the Eastern bloc. There are ongoing claims in Russian power circles that NATO continued its *Eröffnung* ("opening" in German) eastward despite pledges not to do so. Putin himself confirmed this myth of NATO's betrayal:

> They once promised us that after the unification of Germany, NATO would not expand eastward. But then its expansion began, first by taking over former Warsaw Pact countries, and then at the expense of the former Soviet Union. We were told that it had nothing to do with us, because the states can choose for themselves how to ensure its safety. However, when the infrastructure of the military bloc is approaching our borders, we have the right to take any steps in response—and nobody can deny this right.[109]

The picture of the United States and NATO as betraying Russian trust is meant to drill the Russian population in the defensive nature of the Russian hostile expansionism in Eastern Europe, namely, Ukraine and Georgia, and present its actions as just. In reality, however, "the promise not to station any additional foreign troops or nuclear weapons only applied to the former East Germany. Of the 275,000 U.S. soldiers that used to be stationed in Germany, only around 43,000 remain today," which cannot realistically represent any viable threat to the integrity of the Russian borders.[110]

It is constantly presented by the Russian political establishment to its public that, after the collapse of the Berlin Wall in 1990, NATO and the United States "made just such a promise [not to expand eastwards] in exchange for the Soviet troop withdrawal from East Germany—and then betrayed that promise as NATO added 12 eastern European countries in three subsequent rounds of enlargement."[111] Mark Kramer, however, makes this point very clear: the non-enlargement issue "never came up during the negotiations on German reunification, and Soviet leaders at the time never claimed that it did. Not until several years later . . . did former Soviet officials begin insisting that the United States had made a formal commitment in 1990 not to bring any of the former Warsaw Pact countries into NATO. These claims have sparked a wide debate, but they are not accurate."[112] Anne Applebaum continues this point on the pages of the *Washington Post*: "No treaties prohibiting NATO expansion were ever signed with Russia. No promises were broken. Nor did the impetus for NATO expansion come from a 'triumphalist' Washington. On the contrary, Poland's first efforts to apply in 1992 were rebuffed. . . . No NATO bases were placed in the new member states, and until 2013 no exercises were conducted there."[113] Even the man in charge of the dissolution of the Soviet Union, Mikhail Gorbachev, refuted the fable of NATO's nonexpansion. In a TV interview he said, "This is a myth; it was created by mass media."[114] He also noted that the Soviet leadership did not even raise the question of such guarantees during its negotiations with the Western leaders.

Besides, no East European state that joined NATO did so under coercion or as a result of military intervention. On the contrary, Russia is closing in on NATO by its hybrid quasi-intervention in Ukraine. It also blames NATO for its deployment of AMD in Europe in defense of a potential confrontation with Russia and accuses President Obama of "mental aberration" when he referred to Russia's expansions in European as a growing threat of global scale at the UN General Assembly in 2014.[115] It seems that Russia, which had begun the process of forceful reincorporation of the chunks of formerly Soviet nations into its neocolonial realm, is genuinely expecting Western countries to approve of its actions.

The reason for such groundless accusations is that Russia continues to consider the former Soviet republics as its own backyard and even beyond, the Eastern Europe, as the sphere of its vital national interests. Consequently, it treats their pro-Western choices as being influenced by the United States' financial and political backing. The convex lens of the democratic identity of the United States dictated its active involvement in the lives of the newly independent states on the basis of the neo-institutional reasoning. According to this view, the behavior of a system is "the consequence of interlocking choices by individuals and sub-units, each acting in terms of expectations and preferences manifested at those levels."[116] Through their actions to share the political systems of the newly reborn nations, the United Stated applied the logic of appropriateness through which the transplanted democratic political institutions in a new institutional soil of postcommunist countries "realize both order, stability, and predictability, on the one hand, and flexibility and adaptiveness, on the other."[117] Because the end of the Soviet Union somewhat unexpectedly "enriched" the international system with fifteen new nation-states, there was an urgent need to integrate them into the newly acquired family of nations by making them democratic.

As Edward Kolodziej and Roger Kanet pointed out, the problem was that most of the former Soviet states still "largely remain[ed] within Russia's sphere of power and influence."[118] This statement does not apply to the Baltic nations, who have been very quickly reintegrated into the European family they had been forcefully taken from in 1940. But for the rest there was simply no avoidance of the Russian factor: stepping into the post-Soviet space meant that the West was also getting on Russia's highly skeptical and suspicious radar. This was the land that Russia owned literally for centuries, some as a result of the blood conquests and others by the conscious willful or forceful choices of their populations. Mostly, however, the cause of the primordial views of Russians on the post-Soviet space is the nature of the former interethnic relations within the Soviet Union. The Russian nation was the Big Brother in all possible senses. Not only was it a *primus inter pares* among the other republican-level nations and smaller ethnic groups of the Russian empire and later the Soviet Union but also it was put on the ethnic pedestal by them and collectively revered. Coming directly from primordialist reasoning, Russia thinks that it continues to "own" all the Near Abroad just as it used to own it in the Russian empire and then in the Soviet Union. It is an extremely path-dependent construct of its concave identity that views itself as the leader of the nations around its borders, regardless of the actual desires of these nations to stay or to leave the sphere of Russia's political influence.

In this geopolitical area, too, Russia blames the United States for meddling in the foreign, political orientations of these nations without paying due attention to its own actions. The "color revolutions," as they were generally called, were the actions of the people who were tired of the corrupt or otherwise static government that precluded further human development. In Georgia, Ukraine, and Kyrgyzstan, the people rose against their governments because they were seeking positive change. Real or putative participation by the United States in the more or less peaceful changes of the government in these countries was received with harsh negativity on the part of the ruling Russian elites who viewed these countries as tools of American imperial expansionism and believed they were next.

The Rose Revolution in Georgia in 2003 was the wake-up call for the Russian government in seeing a regime change orchestrated from outside.[119] Another example is the Orange Revolution in Ukraine in 2004–5, which is viewed in Russia as a direct product of the American financial and political intervention in Russia's "own."[120] Finally, the Tulip Revolution that followed in Kyrgyzstan was, according to Stephanie Ortmann, "further proof that a U.S. plan to topple irksome regimes in the region existed and ultimately was centered on Russia itself."[121] All these color revolutions bore for the Russian government the similarities of having the Western/American interference in the domestic affairs of independent states. Some even see the long-term results of the color revolutions in the collapse of the Commonwealth of the Independent States completely or its desegregation into smaller units: just as Russia always suspected, another sign of America's closing in on it.[122]

The Russian establishment is afraid of the possibility of exporting the "color" spirit at their home via manipulation of the population from outside. The process of color revolutions is well described by I. V. Shamin, as "used by the U.S. ruling circles to successfully overthrow undesirable regimes in the former Yugoslavia, Georgia, Ukraine, and Kyrgyzstan, and to establish its full or partial control over these countries. The main feature of this model geopolitical struggle is in its designation for 'illegitimate' overthrow of the political power in the 'attacked' country. It is implemented by the use of . . . grievances the citizens have towards the policies of the ruling authorities and sociopolitical activity of certain population groups."[123] Perceptional security dilemma would dictate that potentially pro-American governments that would come into power as a result of color revolutions are kinetically anti-Russian.

There is ample evidence—mostly on the part of the United States itself—in its work to build democratic governance structures in post-Soviet space and to contribute to its own security by strengthening the security of the new and potentially unstable states. The United States has been the primary lobby state of several former communist nations, and not only those that left the tight Soviet family in 1991 but also in Eastern Europe, in their aspirations for democratizing their society by helping them financially and politically. According to the USAID "Greenbook," Ukraine received approximately $1.7 billion in economic assistance with an additional $103.593 million in 2012, $104.407 million for 2013, and $95.271 million in 2014.[124] Georgia, according to a Congressional Research Service note, regularly led the list of world states in terms of per capita U.S. economic aid. Between 1992 and 2010, Georgia received $3.3 billion. In 2001, the economic support was $87.1 million; another $87 million was earmarked for 2012, with a subsequent budgetary appropriation request for $68.7 million in 2013.[125] These contributions were directed in support of Georgian democratic institutions, cultural heritage retention, economic development, and military aid.

A bit different was the American strategy in Kirgizstan, a country where it had its military transit center in Manas from 2001 to 2014 and which is in dangerous proximity to known terrorist hotspots. According to Robert Tian, "The American strategy of 'Greater Central Asia' is directed toward . . . cooperation in energy resource supplies, transport, and infrastructure with the purpose of removing the region from its current Russia-China influence orbit."[126] For that, as Jim Nichol's Congressional Research Service report notes, "with Kyrgyzstan ranking third in such aid per capita among the Soviet successor states," the cumulative U.S. assistance to Kyrgyzstan between 1992 and 2002 was more than $3.5 billion in support of their governance, economic development, and civil society.[127] Besides, the proximity of the Central Asian republics to the failed states of the Middle East and Asia that have been known for harboring terrorist groups place this region firmly within the U.S. vital national interests of protecting the country from Muslim extremism.[128] Such a stance should be beneficial to Russia, since the stronger buffer zones also mean stronger borders for Russia.

Another concomitant fear stems from possible loss in the target countries for the Russian businesses that were "covered" by the corrupt government. For instance, according to Forbes's estimates, Russian banks have lost $25 billion as direct and indirect risks in Ukraine between January and October 2014.[129] Seeing such developments as threatening the Russian vital national interests in the areas of *blizhnee zarubezh'e* (the "near neighborhood"—the name given to the former Soviet republics) by definition, Russia took matters into its own hands. In the words of Nikolay Patrushev, National Security Council secretary, copying the spirit and the letter of the Soviet-era paranoiac propaganda on "rotting capitalism," "Ukrainian crisis was a widely anticipated outcome of the systemic actions of the United States and its closest allies. The last quarter of the century, these actions were aimed at a complete separation of Ukraine and other former Soviet republics away from Russia, total reformatting of the post-Soviet space to fit the American interests."[130] Russia's foreign policy was directed toward bringing the ex-Soviet nations back to its sphere of influence and was activated in all directions to undo the results for American interests.

With this, Russia has been somewhat successful in reversing some of the effects of the "color revolutions." According to David Goldman, after the failure of Yushenko's government to stand up to its democratic promises, the "Ukrainian voters elected a pro-Russian government [in 2010], effectively burying the Orange Revolution. Russia reversed the 2005 'Tulip Revolution' in Kyrgyzstan by supporting a coup against the American-sponsored government. And America's attempt to build up Georgia as a toehold in the Caucasus came to grief after Russia's military intervention in 2008."[131] To a point, Russia was triumphant. Turmoil in Ukraine, pro-Russian government in Kyrgyzstan, almost complete reversal of democratization in Georgia—these results can be written off as a success in the Russian foreign policy registry.

The fact that Russia views the spread of democracy in its adjacent territories by mass actions—mostly bloodless—of popular protest as jeopardizing its vital national interests shows the pitch black abyss separating the country from democracy. The external efforts and help of the international community to build the democratic society in Russia met the fate of water being poured on hot sand; although the intentions were good, the recipient environment was hostile.

American Sanctions and Russian Embargo Selfies

The annexation of Crimea and the hybrid war in Russia led the West to reconsider its mostly conniving attitude toward recent Russian actions in the international arena. New "appeasement" followed the "reset" policy after the victorious Russian war against Georgia in 2008. This included resumption of bilateral and multilateral military cooperation under the aegis of NATO, multibillion dollar trade contracts, and the sale of military equipment, such as the four *Mistral*-class helicopter carriers by France. The events in Ukraine served as a warning for those in the United States who refused to view Russia as a security threat let alone as a potent regional actor in Eurasia.

After weeks of negotiations regarding the annexation of Crimea and the hostilities in Ukraine, first the United States and then the European Union introduced economic sanctions against Russia. At first these were restrictions imposed against individual members of Putin's entourage, Russian banks sponsoring state actions in Ukraine, and select companies that were directly or indirectly involved in the conflict in Ukraine. The choice of the economic sanctions as the tool of pressure was not accidental: the United States, as a liberal democracy, keeps the application of the military force as a last resort. Besides, neither the United States nor the European Union countries are tied with Ukraine in a binding treaty to evoke the "all-for-one" principles of mutual defense. The sanctions, according to Peter Wallensteen, may include "general trade bans between nations, where most of the trade between the parties is affected. It presupposes no use of military means. . . . [T]he focus is on international, negative (value-depriving) actions of one nation . . . against another nation."[132] Sanctions are the obvious choice here, since they represent the least costly international response when compared with boots-on-the-ground interventions. Sanctions thus carried both preemptive and preventive weight: to quarantine the existing territorial gains Russia made in Crimea and to prevent its further expansion.

The first round of U.S. sanctions was announced prior to Putin's Crimean annexation speech in March 2014. These sanctions surgically targeted the people who directly or indirectly participated in Russia's hostile takeover actions in Ukraine. Presidential Executive Order 13600 "Blocking Property of Certain Persons Contributing to the Situation in Ukraine" established "sanctions on individuals and entities responsible for violating the sovereignty and territorial integrity of Ukraine, or for stealing the assets of the Ukrainian people."[133] Another executive order followed in eleven days and expanded both the scope and the depth of the economic means of pressure on Russia. These sanctions included the no-travel list for the Russian political leadership (except for those on the top level, including Putin himself), the most prominent of whom are Sergey Narishkin (chair of the State Duma), Dmitry Rogozin (deputy head of the government), Sergey Ivanov (chief of presidential administration), Ramzan Kadyrov (head of the Chechen Republic), Vladislav Surkov (presidential aide), Sergey Glaz'ev (presidential advisor), Valentina Matvienko (chair of the Council of Federations),

Viktor Ozerov (head of the Duma defense and security committee), and Vladimir Yakunin (president of the State Railroad).[134] Targeted sanctions included imposing trade restrictions (production, export, and re-export of goods and services) on large Russian companies and suspending their credit financing. These were applied against Russia's largest banks (Sberbank, Bank of Moscow, Gazprombank OAO, Russian Agricultural Bank, VEB, and VTB Bank), companies engaged in the production, transportation, and sales of energy carriers (Gazprom, Gazprom Neft', Lukoil, Surgutneftegas, and Reset), and state-owned defense industry firms (OAO Dolgoprudny Research Production Enterprise, Mytishchinski Mashinostroitelny Zavod OAO, Kalinin Machine Plant JSC, Almaz-Antey GSKB, and JSC NIIP).[135]

The U.S. sanctions were followed individually by key world players (Canada, Japan, Australia, United Kingdom, Germany, France) and collectively within the frameworks of the intergovernmental organizations (the G7, NATO, the European Union, Council of Europe, the European Bank for Reconstruction and Development) canceling various forms of sector-specific international cooperation with Russia. The purpose of the sanctions was to punish Putin's inner circle in hopes that it would, in turn, put pressure on Putin to abandon the selected course of actions disrupting regional peace in Europe.

After some deliberations, Russia reciprocated with its own sanctions, but its retaliation stood true to a part of its political culture of self-punishment. Russia's initial sanctions placed nine Americans on its no-travel list, including Harry Reid (Senate majority leader), John Boehner (Speaker of the House of Representatives), Robert Menendez (chairman of the Senate Committee on Foreign Relations), and several senators, including perhaps the most outspoken critic of Putin's foreign policy, John McCain.[136] Blaming the United States and NATO for the unveiling confrontation, Russian Foreign Minister Sergei Lavrov stated at the UN General Assembly, "Western alliance led by the United States, acting as the champion of democracy, rule of law and human rights within separate countries, acts in directly opposite ways in the international arena, rejecting the democratic principle of the sovereign equality of states as enshrined in the UN Charter and tries to judge for everyone what is good and what is evil."[137] Interestingly enough, Lavrov's own daughter Ekaterina has been living in the United States for many years, apparently preferring the climate of parochial democracy to the Russian spirituality.

What happened next stunned the international community but apparently not Russian citizens who were ready, as their reaction showed, to support its government's seeking the greater public good, which is international prestige and superpower status for the country, at the expense of individual rational well-being. On August 6, 2014, Putin signed decree #560, "On the Use of Specific Economic Measures," which mandated an effective embargo for a one-year period on imports of most of the agricultural products whose country of origin had either "adopted the decision on introduction of economic sanctions in respect of Russian legal and (or) physical entities, or joined same."[138] Countries against which the import embargo was established included the United States, the European Union, Norway, Canada, and Australia.

Prior to the embargo, food exports from the EU to Russia were worth around €11.8 billion, or 10 percent of the total. Food exports from the United States to Russia were worth around €972 million, almost twelve times less. Food exports from Canada are even smaller: around €385 million, which is thirty times less than European exports.[139] Essentially, this was a self-inflicted embargo that the Russian government placed on its citizens by banning the import of major foodstuff (fruit, vegetables, meat, fish, milk, and dairy imports) as well as industrial goods from the sender-states, and it placed sanctions against specific individuals in Putin's entourage.[140] In simple terms, in return for the punishment of select individuals, the Russian side decided to punish the whole nation.

It is difficult to evaluate the full-scale effect of the embargo, but one thing is obvious: the consequences of this act will hit hardest the average Russian citizens who are tacitly or actively backing up the foreign policy choices that their country's government had been making. The sanctions may not be as hard as they seem for the Russian oligarchs. In accordance with the recent changes in the federal law on the compensations for the violation of the due process of law, the billionaires affected by the sanctions against Russia will be compensated from the state budget; that is, they will be paid by the Russian citizens. This law is popularly known in Russia as the "Rotenberg Law," named after Putin's judo sparring partner and a Russian oligarch, whose bank accounts and villas in Italy, including a four-star hotel in Sardinia, were seized by Italian authorities in compliance with European Union sanctions.

The American sanctions are individualized and mostly indirectly targeting Putin via his immediate entourage. The Russian sanctions are collectively targeting their own people by linking the fate of their country to the well-being and fate of Putin, as a "strong leader able to consolidate . . . a predominant portion of society, [who is] not comfortable for those who would prefer to deal with a gutta-percha country with gutta-percha Russia."[141] By attempting to fortify Russian society facing hard economic conditions, the authorities are reinforcing the autocratic resilience of the regime by making the individual sanctions a collective burden. Russian society in its mass, with the exception of those who are in opposition to the ruling regime, responded by rallying around its leadership and treating the sanctions as mosquito bites. In doing so, even popular Russian culture revealed the preference for the "hard power" discourse in responding to the sanctions. In September 2014 an art show was staged on the streets of Moscow distributing free T-shirts aimed at boosting the morale of ordinary citizens in withstanding the American and Western sanctions. The T-shirts had a stylized depiction of the Topol intercontinental ballistic missiles and Islander mobile theater ballistic missiles with "My Topol Is Not Afraid of Sanctions" and "Sanctions? Please, Don't Make My Iskanders Laugh" placed directly on the chest.

If prolonged, the sanctions against property, assets, and businesses owned by the current Russian leaders or affiliated individuals will eventually affect the economic well-being and stability of the average Russian citizen. The logic goes back to the notion of the American exceptionalism: it is deeply rooted within the American mentality that people are producers of policy, not its recipients. The policy "inputs" of the constituencies, therefore, are believed to be directly affecting the domestic and foreign policy "outputs." People are the main engines of change, whether positive or negative. Since, according to Daniel Drezner, the "sanctions are a rational choice when the sender perceives future conflict with the target," they are evaluated in economic terms and are aimed at achieving certain calculated outcome.[142] As a democracy, the United States has certain institutional choices and "constraints [that] allow leaders of democracies to use sanctions as signals of resolve," as noted by Robert Hart, who found that the economic sanctions imposed between 1914 and 1989 by democracies were more successful than those by other regimes.[143] The reason for this is that the long-term envisaged policy effect of the sanctions is perceived in the West as forcing people in Russia to realize that their government is wrong (specifically in relation to Ukraine) and then press upon it to initiate a policy change, just as it has done in their domestic policy landscape.

In autocratic governance regimes, the situation with the response to the sanctions is quite different. The onslaught of globalization cannot be disregarded here. Regardless of the governance regime, according to Susan Allen, "As states become more politically open, the domestic public can and does, to some degree, create political costs for leaders who resist sanctions. Conversely, in autocratic states, leaders may actually benefit from sanctions, as domestic publics are unable to impose political costs, and the economic constraints of sanctions often allow leaders to extract greater rents while overseeing the trade of scarce goods."[144] Similarly, the elites in autocracies may actually benefit from the imposed sanctions, at least in the short run. Further along in her article, Allen writes, "In autocratic states, key supporters of the government (such as the military) may be shielded from the pain of sanctions, making them unlikely to rebel. . . . Economic sanctions can have the perverse consequence of strengthening the regime in power, increasing its ability to limit the activities of opposition forces. In these societies, there is often a strong relationship between those with political power and those with economic power."[145] In the case of Russia, which has turned into a "natural state" with its elite, supporting the government, and "pocket oligarchs," such as Rotenberg, the closest entourage to the ruling circles will even benefit, at least temporarily, from the consolidated support of their citizens united against common enemies. When autocratic regimes are threatened from the outside, as is the case with economic sanctions imposed on Russia, they often do whatever is possible to limit concurrent internal threats. To do so, autocracies play to their strengths, and states that choose repression typically have strong tools of force at their disposal.[146] These arguments are directly applicable to the Russian auto-sanctions during which Putin's popularity ratings skyrocketed despite the slowly worsening economic life of ordinary Russian citizens.

From the point of view of economy of numbers, however, this is not so problematic to achieve. After all, given the volume of the mutual trade balance, the United States, as a sanctions sender, is in better condition than Russia as their recipient. Effectiveness and utility of economic sanctions are widely debated in academia and policy circles. In the matter of evaluation of the outcomes, according to Robert Pape, the criterion or the "standard for judging the success of economic sanctions requires that the target state concede 'to a significant part of the coercer's demands.'"[147] Further, as David Baldwin and Pape are convinced, "Estimating the effectiveness of a policy instrument in achieving various goals is necessary but not sufficient for judging the utility, usefulness, or efficiency of employing a given technique of statecraft in a given situation. Only the combined analysis of costs and effectiveness allows one to make judgments about the utility, usefulness, or efficiency of economic sanctions."[148] In the matter of evaluating success of the sanctions, others believe in the lower long-term utility of the "soft power" concerning domestic politics of the sending state. According to A. Cooper Drury, "First, there is some general public attention paid to sanction use that limits his ability to act. Second, certain groups that find some sanctions to be particularly salient will also constrain the president's actions."[149] When the logic of Robert Putnam's two-level game eventually kicks in, the local businesses affected by the sanctions will put pressure on their government to provide for the economic cushions for the loss of the profits from mutual trade.[150]

This view would be true if the volumes of the mutual trade affected by the sanctions would be prohibitively high for both sides of the sanctions equation. According to the Russian Federal Customs Agency of the Russian Federation, only 3.8 percent of the total foreign trade turnover between January and August 2014 was with the United States.[151] The same is confirmed from the American side: the information provided in the U.S. embassy communiqué on the Russian-American business cooperation mentioned the bilateral trade turnover between the United States and Russia in 2012 as worth $39.9 billion (down by $3 billion from 2011), which further decreased by a half in 2013 to $19 billion.[152] Notwithstanding such a low level of mutual interdependence, the Russian side is quite optimistic with regard to the U.S.-imposed sanctions. According to A. V. Zimovec, "The only viable sanction that the United States can apply to Russia is freezing its foreign currency reserves and its companies. However, even this measure cannot be fully effective, since it is simply unreal to cut off all links of such a large country as Russia."[153] He also claimed that some sanctions, including freezing the accounts, can even be positive for Russia, because it will be easier for the government to control large offshore companies and develop its own payment system.

With the relatively small amount of bilateral trade turnover between the United States and Russia in comparison with that of the European Union, the long-term consequences of the sanctions should be fully taken into account. First of all, sanctions mean disruption of the future oil supplies in the world market, since they are applied against one of the largest producers and transporters of energy carriers in the world, as well as against their own companies servicing oil productions.[154] In such a case, as Robert Mitkowski noted, "The fear is that widening sanctions against Russia will escalate to the point where oil supplies from the former Soviet Union are disrupted. . . . It is not only oil supplies that are at risk. Natural gas shipments from Russia to Europe are being threatened. Russia pipes in about one-third of Europe's natural gas, with much of the continent's southern tier fed by pipelines that traverse Ukraine."[155] Also, as Capital Economics senior commodities economist Caroline

Bain notes, "Most severe possible consequence of deteriorating relations [with] Russia would be a disruption to Russian energy supplies to the EU—whether as a result of . . . sanctions or Russian manipulation."[156] However, the real negative effects of the disruption of oil and gas supplies from Russia to the global markets, beyond the fearful estimates of the experts, are yet to be clarified. Moreover, the reality with the energy carriers' prices is quite the opposite.

Two indirect but concomitant factors will contribute to the effectiveness of the Western sanctions imposed on Russia: the ongoing fall in the prices for oil and gas and the avalanche fall of the exchange rate of the Russian ruble to the U.S. dollar and euro. Prices started plummeting in June 2014, when the price per barrel of "Brent" oil, to which Russian oil is tied, fell from $107.52 per barrel to $78.77, or down by 27 percent.[157] In February 2015, the oil price stopped at $60 per gallon.[158] If the drop continues, this will have grave consequences on the Russian state budget, which is overly dependent on foreign sales of its resources. At the end of the 1980s, as Jacob Mirkin, one of the leading Russian economists, notes, the consecutive four-year fall in oil prices in the global markets was a death sentence for the Soviet Union.[159] Revenues from the sales of energy carriers (oil and gas) comprised, on average, 40 percent of the state budgetary revenues and 40–45 percent of the Russian GDP between 2011 and 2013.[160] As Nadejda Saygadachnaya's allegory goes, "The 'Russian Roulette' performed by the Ministry of Finance is, in fact, the fiscal roulette where the role of the fateful cartridge is carried by the price of oil, and all the slug slots in the holder are filled by other types of revenues, which, in reality, play no significant role, and that is why there are no shots made."[161] Although for a number of years the draft budgetary outlooks were designed to decrease the state budget's dependence on the revenues from oil and gas sales, the energy hurdle seems difficult to overcome.

The same fate is prognosticated for future budgetary revenues. According to Antanina Azarova, "In 2012, the federal budget [was] balanced only at the high price of oil not less than $120 per barrel. . . . [D]ecline in oil prices could lead to an increase in the budget deficit and capital outflows, deterioration of the current operations, despite the drop in the exchange rate, and slowing growth. . . . If oil prices fall by 10 percent, this will increase the government deficit by 1.4 percent of GDP."[162] An influential independent economic think tank, the Institute of Economic Policy, popularly known in Russia as the Gaidar Institute, named after one of the main economic reformers of the Yeltsin era, issued a similarly gloomy forecast on the budgetary revenues. According to its report, between 2013 and 2015, the "oil and gas revenues will account for 44 to 46 percent of the budgetary revenues. . . . [A] $1 change in the average price for crude oil 'Urals' leads . . . to a change in the value of oil and gas revenues by more than 1 percent (70–75 billion rubles). If in the next three years the average oil price will equal the average in 2005–12 (about $80 billion), the budgetary revenues will decrease by 9 to 11 percent, or about 2 percent of GDP annually."[163] Coupled with the ongoing sanctions against the major Russian oil companies and the banks financing them, this could be a significant problem for the Russian government to deal with in the short-term future.

The other factor is the collapse of the Russian ruble exchange rate against the U.S. dollar and euro that started in January 2014. This fall can be compared to the economic crisis of 1998 when the Russian ruble severely devaluated as a result of the drop in the world raw material prices, caused by the Asian fiscal crisis.[164] The current dynamics of the drop in the exchange rate is alarming: from 32.86 rubles per $1 in January 2014 to 62 rubles and from 45 rubles to 1 euro to almost 70 in January 2015, causing the Russian Central Bank to spend "billions of its reserve dollars every day to prop up the Russian currency."[165] Yelena Tregubova brought up the following factors affecting the situation with the Russian currency leading it to its ongoing devaluation: unstable geopolitical factors (the situation in Ukraine), drops in the oil prices, and weak domestic economy. According to her, "If [the negative] prognoses are fulfilled, the annual inflation will reach its maximum [for the first time] since the 2008 crisis."[166] Overall, according to Dmitry Bulin, by the end of October 2014 the Russian Central Bank will have spent $22 billion to keep the ruble from further collapse.[167]

One of the reasons for such a poor performance of the ruble is the number of cheap credits that were available for Russian banks from Western financial institutions. The statistics from the Central Bank of Russia mentioned the 350 percent increase in the foreign debt from $213 billion in 2005 to $731 billion in 2014, as oil prices were rising.[168] The sanctions imposed the ban on long-term financing for the Russian companies, which caused the drop in the long-term credit rating by the Moody from Baa1 in June 2014 to Ba1/Not Prime with a negative prognosis in February 2015.[169] The resulting situation would require serving the credits at the expense of other loans, which the banks and companies cannot apply for under the climate of ongoing sanctions. The credits can, in principle, be covered by the foreign currency reserves, which suffered from a more than 13 percent drop in a year of the Ukrainian affair: from $524 billion in November 2013 to $454 billion in October 2014.[170] This means that there is less money to pay back to the foreign creditors. According to the Sberbank CIB, "By the end of 2015, the Russian companies will have to pay $106.7 billion of foreign debt. . . . Currently the Russian banks have $48 billion of liquidity that can be used to cover this debt. Thus the deficit of foreign currency liquidity is $58 billion."[171] Unlike the pre-sanction years, foreign debts were covered by additional loans, and currently they have to be served at the expense of the foreign currency reserves and the monies that would have otherwise been spent on developing their own businesses.

Theoretical Bases for Dissention

The root cause of tension between Russia and the United States is hidden in the clashes between the two theoretical approaches of the countries to their places, roles, and destinies in the international arena and in the personal views on the cooperation and conflict of their leaders. The stance Russia has taken reflects a mélange of purely realist "instrumental rationality" reasoning based on relative power considerations it holds between itself and the United States, with the significant presence of social constructivism based on identity formation. This mix of rationalism and identity-based politics has been the *sine qua non* of Russia's dealings with the United States during all three of Putin's presidential tenures, but especially after his Munich and Valdai speeches, which he delivered nine years apart and which reflect his personal evolution from a moderate *sterkh* to an accomplished hawk.[172]

Realism, in simple terms, "emphasizes the constraints on politics imposed by human nature and the absence of international government . . . [making] international relations largely a realm of power and interests."[173] Power, according to Hans Morgenthau, is the main variable that defines the interests: "the objectives of foreign policy [are] defined in terms of national interest and must be supported by adequate power."[174] The individual plays an important but negative role here. Kenneth Waltz sees the causes of war "in the nature and behavior of man. Wars result from selfishness, from misdirected aggressive impulses, from stupidity."[175] Realism further assumes that the actors are utility maximizers who aim at achieving higher utility at all costs. In the words of Kjell Goldmann, weighing pros and cons in purely rational calculus schemes "essentially leads us to derive actions from given preferences."[176] These preferences are set for all current and future actors who engage in assessment of anticipated costs and benefits of specific actions and usually choose the most cost-effective ones. The international system in realists' understanding represents a rational choice institution where the preferences are "fixed and exogenously determined" for the actors.[177] The sources of these preferences are secondary: rationality discards such variables as norms, values, and identities of the actors and brings in a nothing-personal-just-business approach to the international system.[178]

Another key assumption in realism is that the world is essentially anarchic and represents the "war of every man against every man," to quote Hobbes's *Leviathan*.[179] In this state of nature, dictated by the systemic anarchy, everyone (in this particular case, the countries) is out for themselves. The mix of anarchy with self-help situations, set preferences, and imminent conflict as a normal state of affairs creates a gloomy and pessimistic outlook of realists on international relations.[180] In the fifth century BC, Thucydides gave a great example of the unavoidable nature of the international environment: "Of the gods we believe, and of men we know, that by a necessary law of their nature they rule wherever they can. And it is not as if we were the first to make this law, or to act upon it when made: we found it existing before us, and shall leave it to exist for ever after us."[181] This is a classical view of a Greek tragedy on the world where none the actors are in full control of their fate (in the ancient beliefs, a work of the gods or Providence) which inescapably brings them to reciprocal destruction.

The views on international affairs are fundamentally different in liberalism. This theory stems from Rousseau's views on the Social Contract, which can be reduced to the following utterance: "Each of us puts in common his person and his power under the supreme direction of the general will; and in turn we receive every member as an indivisible part of the whole."[182] Kantian vision on liberalism extends beyond the level of domestic politics and proposes application of the notion of a social contract on the international system's level. In the preliminary and definite articles of his *Perpetual Peace*, Kant draws the causal linkages between the republican (democratic) form of government, as "founded in accordance with the principles of freedom of a society of men . . . [and] constructed according to the fundamental idea of the dependence of all subjects upon a common legislature," on the one hand, and absence of wars in the international arena, on the other.[183]

Liberalism in the international arena starts by placing individuals and their interests at the center of international politics. Unlike realism, where individuals are forced to commit crimes of war because they are doomed to the life, which is "solitary, poor, nasty, brutish, and short," under liberalism they are considered to be capable of positive and peaceful interactions, even under the conditions of systemic anarchy.[184] Mostly, however, the difference is in the ability to control their lives: individuals are the witnesses of what is going on around them—they have no choice for action. In liberalism, on the contrary, individuals define the reality around them and not vice versa. For liberalism, human rights and freedoms as well as harmony and interdependence represent the very forces that prevent conflicts from occurring. Individuals under liberalism are also rational actors, but there "it is the faith in human reason that leads . . . international liberals to believe that efforts to overcome the problems of anarchy are not inevitably doomed."[185] As a result, liberals view the state as the product of the interactions of individuals, which shape foreign policy preferences in accordance to their views on the better world.

Liberals believe that "even though states exist in a condition of anarchy, progress away from a state of perpetual war can be fashioned by creating informal 'institutions' of modernization—of economies, of technology, of human morality, and of communication within and between states."[186] It is the emphasis on the international institutions that brought up the notion of "Democratic Peace," which states that the democracies, constrained by international and intergovernmental organizations and regimes, tend not to fight with each other.[187] Another key variable of liberalism in the matter of constraining the potentially hostile actions of the states under the systemic anarchy is the economic and political interdependence.[188] Interdependent states prefer to foster mutual cooperation with the purpose of individual economic benefits and collective political stability of the system. The institutional approach is present here, too, but in this case the preferences are not given: they are created and shared by the states having the common task of universal peace. As it is clear from the main premises of liberalism discussed above, it strives to constrain the role of an individual under the collective settings of the universally accepted peace and prosperity.

A relative newcomer to realm of theories is constructivism. In 1992 Alexander Wendt published an international relations groundbreaker, "Anarchy Is What States Make of It," where he launched a structural criticism of the realist world of rigid preferences and effervescent conflict. There, he claimed, "self-help and power politics do not follow either logically or causally from anarchy and that if today we find ourselves in a self-help world, this is due to process, not structure."[189] In the same line of reasoning, Audie Klotz and Cecelia Lynch put the agents in the center of the institutional structures of the international system: "Constructivists stress that both structural continuities and processes are based on agency. Agency, in turn, is influenced by social, spatial, and historical context."[190] It is the context and identities which drive constructivism —and not the interests, which are given and defined in terms of power in realism or framed by mutually beneficial projects of trade and cooperation in liberalism. Similar to liberalism, the interests of actors are endogenous and determined by their corresponding identities, but here they are individualized for each actor. In this meaning, according to J. Samuel Barkin, "the interests are shared within an identity group and form the basis for political interaction."[191] In another article Wendt argues that international politics itself is constructed—not preset—by the identities and interests of the actors.[192] Rationality is also present in the constructivists' lens, but here "an action or belief may be called 'rational' when it makes sense to act that way."[193] The constructivist views, therefore, form the basis for relative rationality, which means that what is rational for one action could be completely irrational for others.

Identity constructs are key to understanding how the constructivist world operates. Decision-making mechanisms in social constructivism embrace normative patterns and identity constructs that make actors' behavior acceptable under certain conditions and intolerable under others.[194] The notion, the levels, the categories, and the types of acceptable behavior are constructed by the actors themselves and not provided, which "leads us to derive actions from given identities."[195] The preferences are not set; they are fluid and constantly changing. Interests and identities in constructivism, as laid down by Wendt, are "endogenous to interactions."[196] The actions depend not on the objective reality as such but on the result of its subjective interpretations through the individual identity constructs. The constructivist view, therefore, turns the objective reality into as many subjective interpretations as there are actors.

The main theoretical reason for the Russian-American confrontation is not in the inherent difference in the grounds for national interests, whether power or norms, but in the identity clashes between the nations, which makes constructivism the meta-theory of the dyadic interstate relations. Henrikki Heikka rejects this idea, claiming that both neorealism and constructivism fail to account for Russian foreign policy, and she proposes a deeper quest into the Russian identity based on the discourse analysis. She claims, "The causal origins of anti-Western construction of Russian national interests can be traced to the cultural identification process and discursive strategies rather than to current Russia-Western interaction or to the structure of international relations."[197] However, when analyzed even on the deep level of verbal discourse and implied meaning, Russia and America remain constructivist nations. Both promote their own visions of exceptionalism, but the form of application of their constructed identities in world politics is drastically different and in many aspects conflicting. The conflict can be visualized on the level of the states and on the interpersonal level of the country rulers.

The discussion on the theoretical premises of the interstate rivalry between Russia and the United States reveals an interesting paradox underlying the very foundations of their foreign policies. As a collectivist state domestically, in the international arena Russia is promoting the position of individual sovereignty on the basis of the realist narrow vision of its own national security. As an individualist state domestically, in the international arena the United States is promoting the position of collective sovereignty on the basis of the liberalist broad vision on the global security. In October 2009 Secretary of State Clinton clearly stated the administration's worldview succinctly and directly in an interview with the Ekho Moskvy radio station during her visit to Moscow: "I believe in a world in which our interdependence and our interconnectedness are recognized. And we're not living in a bipolar world; we're not even living in a multipolar world. We're living in a world of interdependence, and we need multiple partners. I like to think of it as a multipartner networked world."[198] The incompatibility between these theoretical foundations places these states on different levels that do not cross, since they exist in parallel ontological dimensions. This is probably what Sergey Ivanov meant by his comment used in the epigraph for this chapter on the differences in interests and insurmountable obstacles.

Powerful individuals in Russian society have always played significant roles in managing the perceptional security dilemmas. Based on the leaders' own visions, perceptional security dilemmas appear where there is "a discrepancy between the psychological environment of the decision-makers and the operational environment of the real world.'"[199] John Stoessinger identifies several types of perceptional security dilemmas based on the leadership variable, which are synonymous with the concepts of the concave and convex lenses used here: the self-view of the leader, his or her views on the counterparts, including their intentions, their existing military capabilities, and the empathy of the leader with the counterparts.[200] All these types of perceptional security dilemmas are applicable to the personality of Putin, who quite willingly and deliberately has plunged his country into the previously nonexisting rivalry with the United States and its leadership.

As for individual leadership—the views on oneself and one's destiny—Putin and Obama also exist in parallel dimensions. Years of interactions between these leaders revealed no personal chemistry, such as existed between "Friend Boris" Yeltsin and "Friend Bill" Clinton or between Putin and George W. Bush, who looked into Putin's eyes and was able to "get a sense of his soul" at their first meeting in Slovenia in 2001. This was the very turning point in the relationship between the two countries. Like Bush, Putin is a classical old school hardliner. George Bovt noted this similarity: "Bush, despite all odds, was closer to Putin as a human being. He was easier to deal with, more open. In a fairy tale . . . [Putin] in the context of American politics could even become a very successful Republican."[201] In an earlier article entitled "Bush Is Like Putin," Bovt claimed that in the foreign policy actions of Bush's administration, "Putin supported Bush not out of calculated or political self-interest. He supported him unconditionally. Because he had PERSONAL sympathy toward Bush. Because for him Bush is one of his own. Bush is essentially Putin, only an American one."[202] Personal attractions and "clicks" for Putin were essential in supporting U.S./NATO military operations abroad, including allowing NATO to establish its transit base not only in Kyrgyzstan, close to its borders, but inside Russia proper in Ulyanovsk in 2012.

Completely different is Putin's interaction with Obama. Obama is a neoliberal whose National Security Strategy 2010 states that "nations that respect human rights and democratic values are more successful and stronger partners, and individuals who enjoy such respect are more able to achieve their full potential."[203] This stance and the whole strategy do not resonate much with Putin, who laments the dissolution of the Soviet Union. Saying during the presidential debate of 2012 that Russia is not a threat or dismissing Russia as "a regional power that is threatening some of its immediate neighbors—not out of strength but out of weakness," right after the Crimean annexation would not be mended by naming Russia one of three global threats along with Ebola and ISIS.[204]

Conclusion

Not everything is absolutely bad in Russia-U.S. relations. The talks on military cooperation continue—perhaps not with the present pre-2008 and even pre-2014 intensity, but they are not off the table completely. There were bilateral visits of the disarmament team and reciprocal flyovers of the Russian and American territories under the "Open Skies Treaty" in February 2015. The two countries also cooperate in such highly sensitive fields as space exploration, which was a "state secret" during the Cold War. By 2014 most of the cooperation programs were under way, including the signing of the agreement on threat reduction under the Nunn-Lugar program for 2013. The purpose of them all is to alleviate uncertainty in each other's actions and to ease mutual fears—essentially, to decrease potential interstate security dilemmas between the two nuclear powers.

The perceptional security dilemma, however, is in full swing. Most of the tensions between Russia and the United States have to do with the irreconcilable clash of the value systems of the two countries. For Russia, the country, which lived for more than ten centuries under absolutism and monarchy, it is very difficult to understand the United States, a country that never had it. The primordial identity of Russia as a powerful actor has created the alternative reality where every step of the United States in the international arena has a hidden subcontext fueled by hatred toward Russia. The power construct of the Russian political identity dictates that Russia can become a superpower again only if it is recognized as such by the United States. For a country that spent most of its history under the constant fear of annihilation, external recognition of a superpower state by the United States (and the European Union, for that matter) has to bear the component of fear.

A famous Latin expression comes to mind, *Aquila non captat muscas*, which translates into English as "The eagle does not capture flies." Russia came out of the Cold War as a severely truncated eagle whose wings (former Soviet republics) had been clipped by the West. It aspires to be reborn as a new and potent eagle, perhaps the one that is now in its coat of arms, to be duly and on a par recognized by the United States. Absence of fear in Russian political culture's view signifies no superpower respect. By enticing the United States into a confrontation, Russia is aiming to leave the camp of flies and join that of the eagles. It is therefore fundamental for Russia to re-create the Cold War style of fear within the United States, which would elevate it to superpower status in its own eyes. Recognition as a superpower is desperately needed for keeping the domestic rating of the current government high and for satisfying the power cravings of its own populations. For this grand purpose it will continue its disruptive actions in Europe and beyond with a dual purpose: to fill the gap between the real and perceived power constructs and to satisfy the demands of its domestic constituencies, if not economically, then imperially, for sure.

4

Russia and Its Near Abroad

> They [Ukrainians] say that they could sit well on two chairs . . . enjoy them both and get dividends. This will never happen!
>
> –DMITRI MEDVEDEV, September 2013

> The bear won't ask anyone's permission. . . . It is not going to . . . move to other climatic zones, where it is uncomfortable. But it will not give up its taiga to anyone.
>
> –VLADIMIR PUTIN, meeting of the Valdai Club, October 2014

In explaining the key variables driving Russian foreign policy in the new millennium toward its Near Abroad, that is, the former Soviet Union republics, the rich past of interactions between Russia and these nations occupies a central theme. There are a plethora of variables affecting the Russian stance toward these countries, which cannot be considered separately in a specific context. In simple terms, the "theory of everything" explaining Russian attitudes toward its former Soviet brethren consists of multiple factors, which sometimes duplicate and overlap but are never simple to explain.

Relations with the former Soviet Union have been the priority direction of Russian foreign policy ever since its independence. This is quite understandable: modern Russia keeps the memory of seventy years of living together with current Newly Independent States (NIS) in one common Soviet house and several centuries more with some of them within or under the wings of the Russian empire. In the attempt to build relations with these nations, the very crux of Russian identity is revealed. Russia is guided by the purest type of primordialism, which keeps that "the nations are an ancient, necessary, and perhaps natural part of the social organization, an organic presence whose origins go back to the mists (or myths?) of time."[1] On the other hand, it is trying to build bridges into a modernist future but, in doing so, is guided by the grip of its "past imperfect" that it is not willing or ready to give up.[2]

The end of the Soviet Union came unexpectedly to those realists who, like John Mearsheimer, preached about the persistence of the struggle in Europe in one form or another.[3] The heads of three Soviet republics—Ukraine, Belarus, and Russia—signed the Belovezhskaya Declaration at the end of December 1991. The resulting turmoil has lasted in different shapes for every former Soviet nation, ranging from economic collapse to interstate and intrastate wars and domestic terrorism. Except, perhaps, for the three Baltic States—Lithuania, Latvia, and Estonia—which had firmly decided to align their domestic and foreign policies with the European family from which they were extracted by the Soviet Union in the 1940s, most newly created nations were in limbo with regard to their future paths. To borrow Indiana senator Richard Lugar's famous 1993 assessment of NATO's future, the former Soviet Union "either goes out of area or out of business."[4]

Several scenarios were possible from the very onset. I. N. Burganova mentioned five: complete integration of the former Soviet nations under its substitute, the Commonwealth of Independent States (CIS); restitution of the Soviet Union; "diverse speed integration"; the CIS functioning as an interest-based club; and dissolution of the CIS.[5] At the beginning of the 1990s, some versions of the future seemed quite unlikely, such as returning to the Soviet Union. For nations too weary of communist rule, including Russia itself, even the thought of going back to one-party rule and supremacy of its ideology was ruled out. However, developments of the first decades of the new millennium in Russia and their impact on the Near Abroad nations proved that politics is not void of "never say never" reasoning.

Neocolonial Primordialism

Primordial memory is very difficult to erase because Russia strives to act as the nucleus for those nations with whom Moscow has played a role starting from the early-medieval stages of its territorial expansionism. In doing so, Russia had developed what Sandra Joireman calls "soft primordialism," where the attachments are those "evolving from history and a myth of common homeland rather than blood types or cultural heritage. Essentially, this means that the defining elements of ethnic identification are psychological and emotional rather than biological."[6] Within Russia proper, civil identification takes place slowly: after all, the nations forming the Russian federalist state are referred to by their political center and establishment as *rossiyane* (Russians by citizenship) versus *russkie* (Russians by ethnic origin).

Russia's "soft primordialism," as the main force behind the formation of the NIS direction of Russian political culture, identifies the mix of political and emotional characteristics that it draws its power from. On the domestic level, the precursor for *rossiyane* was the *sovetskii narod* (the "Soviet people"), which, to many, was not artificial at all. Manuel Castells considers this collective national connotation to have "some reality in the minds and lives of the generations born in the Soviet Union, in the reality of people making families with people from other nationalities, and living and working throughout the former Soviet territory."[7] To a greater extent, collective identity was sustained and nourished not only by the Russians per se but also by all other Soviet nations.

Identity that Goes a Long Way

The strongest explanation for success in constructing the collective Soviet identity is given by its communist ideology. The collective phenomenon of an ordinary Soviet citizen, the *Homo sovieticus*, was cemented by the communist ideology of the center. According to Russian economist Yegor Gaidar, "Messianic communist ideology shifted the center of political conflict from a confrontation between ethnic groups to a struggle among social classes. That struggle garnered support from people in the non-Russian regions, who fought for a new social order that would open the way to a brilliant future, and played a large role in forming the Soviet Union within borders resembling those of the Russian empire. Russia succeeded owing to a unique combination of circumstances. No one else in the twentieth century managed to do it."[8] By artificially constructing a class-led struggle, the Soviets shifted the allegiances of multiple diverse nations from ethnic, linguistic, or religious centers to the common and single ideological one. Nations included in the Soviet Union, voluntarily or not, could keep their ethnic backgrounds—"national in form"—but filled it up with ideological ingredients—"soviet in content." They were, in fact, encouraged to do so through the process called *korenizatsiya* (many translate it as *nativization*, but the closest meaning to it is *back to one's roots*): a policy that "actively encouraged the use of native languages in schools, newspapers, courts, and soviets."[9] On the international level, too, the fears—real or perceived—of being surrounded by enemies were actively cultivated by the Soviet leadership, which drew people together under the umbrella of collective threat. During the Soviet Union, NATO was as feared in the Soviet Caucasus (which actually bordered Turkey, a NATO state) as it was in the Central Asian republics.

Too much, in the primordialist view, unites the former parts of the Russian/Soviet empire: inseparable identity constructs (between three Slavic nations: Russians, Ukrainians, and Belarusians); Orthodox Christian identity and struggle for survival (with Georgians and Armenians); common collectivization efforts during the Soviet Union; early achievements in the Soviet Union; the *likbez* (enlightenment and education programs, mostly in the Central Asian republics); electrification of the country; economic revival of some areas (for instance, building the irrigation channels in Central Asia, allowing for increased cotton production); joint victory over Nazi Germany and postwar reconstruction efforts; and later achievements of the Soviet Union (military progress including development of nuclear weapons; the first nuclear power plants; space exploration programs; athletic victories).

Contemporary accomplishments and myths of the Soviet Union

united the Soviet nation: Anderson's "imaginary communities" had sprung up all over the USSR regardless of their ethnic origins, cultural backgrounds, and language peculiarities, which drew their feelings of belonging together from the Stakhanov feat, Gagarin's conquering of the cosmos, or triumphs of Soviet athletes at the Olympic Games.[10] Even though for a quarter of a century post-Soviet countries have existed on the world map as independent sovereign states, they are, in the view of Egor Kudryavcev, due to their common past, also similar when it comes to their political, economic, and social lives. He asserts, "Belonging to a single country . . . means that there is a general economic space. This means established manufacturing process chains between enterprises; common transport infrastructure. The common-for-all sharp transition from a planned economy into a market led one to the existence of similar types of management."[11] Although, in terms of political determination and human rights, the USSR represented what many called a "prison of nations," life inside common Soviet cells was not completely detrimental, economically and socially speaking.[12] Babak Rezvani was right to mention that "its prisoners, at least the largest ones, did not suffer death, but rather were fed and were, in fact, stronger when they were released."[13] This kept the Soviet state afloat, since it provided minimum outputs for their populations to keep them from asking for their inputs into the governance matters.

Many of the nations, indeed, after joining the USSR, had significantly elevated their standards of living, including satisfying contemporary requirements for housing, health care, education, and social services. Nevertheless, Soviet times meant different things for different nations: while some looked up to Moscow for guidance, support, and money, others, such as the Baltic nations, Georgians, and Ukrainians (in the later years of the USSR with their respective National Fronts), were pushing for their sovereignty and self-determination. They genuinely abhorred communist rule and were successful in jailbreak only when the Soviet Union allowed doing so by all the transformations it went through in the late 1980s. For Russians, it meant a leadership role in the largest country in the world, which they carried on for seventy years.

An abundance of psychosocial and economic signs of living together, especially for the past century, is very sensitively guarded by Russia, which is afraid of losing the memory of being the *paterfamilias* for the diverse Soviet bunch. To a certain degree, this is quite understandable. In all of them, Russia was not merely an equal partner, participant, or a spectator; it was their core and the reason for all those achievements. Russia was the true engine of progress for the Soviet nations, but for Russia it would be extremely difficult for some (such as Armenia) to withstand devastating external forces. These points in joint history represent the "anchors" for modern Russian identity. Russia uses them to build its future statehood. Therefore, not only their rejection as something that never happened but even attempts to revise their substance and present them in any other light that portrays Russia in a less than favorable way are considered sheer blasphemy in Moscow. A good example is the law on countering the attempts to undermine the historical memory of World War II. Basically, the law is "criminalizing the denial of the facts established by the verdict of the International Military Tribunal for the trial and punishment of the major war criminals of the European Axis countries, the approval of the offenses established by the said judgment, as well as for the dissemination of false information on the activities of the Soviet Union in World War II."[14] The last part is what makes this law very liberal in punishing those who somehow try to diminish the role the Soviet Union played in the victory of World War II. Here, Russia tries to protect its past with the purpose of building its future: a very primordialist move.

To a certain degree, the importance of the past in the present-day Russian political culture can be explained by its ethnic composition. For most of its existence, Russia has not been a solitary ethnic nation-state but was the imperial metropolis for its multiple nations. Like France or Britain, who date their colonial empires back to Columbus's explorations, Russia's existence as a colonial power also reaches back to the fifteenth century, when the country started rapid territorial expansion after the end of Mongol rule. In the early twentieth century, the Russian empire was replaced by the Soviet. In all these imperial forms, Russia has united multiple larger nations and smaller ethnic groups under the umbrella of its statehood. The end of the Soviet Union brought a different form to Russia: it lost its imperial possessions and could freely engage in building its nation-state with different ethnicities on the basis of their civil identities. The process was stalled in 2008 after the Georgian war when Russia started taking back its Soviet debris, which essentially started its neocolonialism.

Never-Ending Empire

In its desire to keep the ex-Soviet republics under its influence, Russia is held hostage in its post-imperial liturgy. The memories are sweet indeed. An example: in 1983, at the two hundredth anniversary of the unification of Georgia with Russia, Georgian president Eduard Shevardnadze (also former minister of foreign affairs of the USSR) said, "Georgia is called the country of the sun. But for us the true sun rose not in the east but in the north, in Russia—the sun of Lenin's ideas."[15] In 1999 the same Shevardnadze included the promise of potential membership of Georgia in NATO by 2005 as a part of his election campaign (if elected).[16] This was just one of the cases where Russians were taken down from the Soviet pedestal put there by other nations—a memory that is very difficult to forget, let alone to reverse.

A quarter century after the collapse of the Soviet Union, Russia has not yet fully awakened from the feeling of living in a common house of nations. It is slowly realizing that previous forms of center-periphery relations can no longer be imposed on them. Many past empires were in Russia's shoes after the decolonization process. Starting from the empires of Alexander the Great, the Romans, Persians, Byzantines, and Mongols, the colonial metropolia conquered surrounding nations and established their rule mostly with the power of their swords and fire. When their empires collapsed, the colonial centers, with different speed, also went into decline. It is too early to compare them with the medieval and even modern empires, such as those of Great Britain, France, Spain, Portugal, and Italy. However, one similarity is that none of them has ended up following the fate of postcolonial decomposition.

Another striking resemblance between the European colonial powers is that most of them never bordered their colonial possessions. With several exceptions (such as turning the colonial border into a national one when Spain changed the status of Sahara and declared it as its province in 1958, yet even this step was more political than territorial), the colonial metropolia used to rule lands thousands of miles away from their national borders.[17] This factor had enormous consequences for the future postcolonial existence of both the metropolia and the former colonial periphery. Due to the absence of "porous boundaries" discussed at length by Donald Horowitz, between them and their colonial possessions, the metropolia were shielded from the insecurities and domestic chaos, and that ensured the imperial collapse.[18] Most of these cases of state failures in ex-colonies were inevitable consequences of the centers' letting go of their peripheries, and any political, economic, and cultural vulnerabilities were largely contained if not to a single country's borders (as was the case with the Somali civil war of 1991) then spilled over only to fellow former colonies nearby (the Rwandan genocide of 1994 is a good example of intraregional proliferation of insecurity).[19] The distance between the colonial center and the periphery thus played a positive role in preventing the former from being the target of the angered populations of the latter. Undeniably, many of the former metropolia went through the waves of postcolonial migration, both invited and unexpected, but this is in no way comparable to uncontrolled flows of desperate refugees across borders.

Territorial separation from the colonial core and the periphery had an additional positive effect on both sides of the imperial dyad. After the end of their imperial existence, most of the metropolia maintained qualitatively limited political contacts with their former colonial possessions, letting them fly solo in their new lives as independent countries. Here, again, there are exceptions, such as concurrent French military interventions in its "private African domain," as Elizabeth Schmidt calls its former possessions on the African continent.[20] Yet, even there, the direction of military, political, and economic support was strictly regulated on the basis of bilateral agreements between France and the African countries in question, which were responsible for calling in French support.[21] This prevented the metropolia from getting bogged down in the (usually) turbulent domestic politics of the newly created states, which were on the path to political maturity. Absence of immediate borders with their ex-colonial patrons also turned out to be beneficial for these nations. With all the difficulties concomitant upon postcolonial transformations, no land connection with their former metropolia meant that they would fully assume responsibility over their own lives and could stand up for the decisions they made themselves.

Russia is unlike most of the most recent colonies in that it would just not let it go: neither mentally, of its own bittersweet colonial memories, nor politically, culturally, and economically. Russia itself was one big empire that used to incorporate diverse nations, most of which it directly borders. Even where there are no common borders, like with Tajikistan, it still views the outer borders of the region of Central Asia as its own. These are sweet memories because they never ended: Russia has never shrugged off its colonies and continues independent existence away from them. They were always there, at arm's reach, and the feelings of territorial proximity to the land that once belonged to Russia were not easy to leave behind. Besides, in most of its imperial existence Russia was looked up to by its colonial subjects, eulogized as a savior, and praised as the guiding light in their political, economic, and cultural evolution. The memories are also bitter because some of them, as Anatoly Korolov and Mansur Mukhamedjanov lamented, "being in captivity to ethnocratic intoxication . . . took a sharp turn to break current economic, political, and cultural ties and start making territorial or some other claims" upon the Russian nation, which was previously admired and venerated.[22]

Post-imperial phantom pains in Russia, to a certain degree, are similar to what other empires were going through during their times of decolonization. In its foreign policy regarding the New Independent States, Russia resembles France, which, as Gérard Prunier puts it, has always considered Africa *le pré carré* (our own backyard) and viewed itself as "a large hen followed by a docile brood of little black chicks" that needed always to be taken care of.[23] When Putin made his program speech at the Valdai Discussion Club in October 2014, he allegorized the taiga bear as the embodiment of Russia: "The bear won't ask anyone's permission [for anything]. In general, it is considered the master of the taiga, and it is not going to—and I know this for sure—move somewhere, to other climatic zones, where it is uncomfortable. But it will not give up its taiga to anyone."[24] Russia continues to view the former Soviet republics as its own taiga in terms of the natural extension of its *velikoderzhavnost'*. Such an attitude is defined by extending its territorial coverage and including parts of other post-Soviet republics or reinforcing its ability to influence the decisions of governments, including their future political orientations.

A significant difference between Russia and most of the recent-day colonial empires is that in order to be truly great, neither France nor Great Britain (pardon the tautology here) needed to have colonial possessions. In fact, Charles de Gaulle's *grandeur*, described by Andrew Moravcsik as a combination of "his war-time suspicion of the 'Anglo-Saxons,' his commitment to a unilateral foreign policy backed by nuclear weapons, his nationalist obsession with the preservation of sovereignty, and, above all, his search for a European foreign policy free from superpower influence" appeared in the late 1950s and early 1960s, the time when France, the last of the European colonialists, started letting go of its African possessions.[25] Close to the French political identity of *grandeur* in mid-twentieth century, Russian *velikoderzhavnost'* remains at the core of its concave identity. The difference: its identity construct is impossible without its colonies.

For Russia to feel truly great, it has to go beyond its nation-state's borders and surround itself with obedient peripheries, as buffers, against the rest of the world. With loyal and dependent neighboring countries willing to promote Russia's cultural values, its foreign policy, and economic interests, Russia would view itself truly as a great country—a superpower that has both the ability of coercion and the charm of appeal. This image would overshadow the ongoing economic and social hardships facing its population. Without its imperial entourage, Russia would be just another ordinary country: still the largest one on the planet but with mediocre social development and economic performance comparable with that of an average Latin American nation—neither of which completely satisfies the contemporary Russian political establishment.[26]

The nations surrounding Russia's borders are among the most important factor-variables comprising vital national (Russian) interests and are in the center of its foreign policy priorities. Apart from the quest for the neocolonial political identity, Dmitry Dolenko, Zhana Konichenko, and Alexey Petukhov gave the following account for the additional variables stipulating Russia's active involvement in the lives of neighboring countries: first, the NIS is home to "25 million Russian compatriots; they have vital communications with Russia; they have natural resources, in the development of which the whole USSR, first of all Russia, had invested; they have vital Russian economic and military facilities necessary to ensure its national security; they are the sources of human labor for Russia; and, lastly, their territories may act as a buffer zone against drug trafficking, arms smuggling, terrorism, etc."[27] These are all diverse issue-areas and definitely are not equally applicable to each of the post-Soviet countries. Nevertheless, the profusion of those factors targeted by Russian vital interests, indeed, postulates active and long-term involvement of Russia in the domestic politics of the countries located along its borders.

An important aspect to keep in mind when analyzing the confluence of events and happenings in the NIS with Russia's participation is that in the territory of the former Soviet Union, Russia does not only want to play the mere *primus inter pares* role. Russia strives at uniting and leading the "band of misfits," as Bliakher refers to the NIS countries, in the conflict over the values that it is involved in with the Global West.[28] Keeping Soviet traditions firmly in place, Russia aspires to regional leadership in the Eurasian continent by spearheading the "anti-" movement, which can be against many of the successful projects in the West: anti-American, anti-Western, anti-European, anti-anything that does not contribute to the greatness of the Russian nation.

The Role of Borders

The phenomenon of state borders plays another, indirect role in defining specific modus operandi of Russia toward certain countries of the Near Abroad. Their proximity to European borders is an important factor stipulating the distinct foreign behavior of the Russian government. The closer a post-Soviet nation is to Europe (and the United States, for that matter), the more sensitive Russia becomes to the possibility of the reversal of its political orientation and the more involved it strives to be in the domestic affairs of the country in question. The Russian political mainstream views the Western parts of the former Soviet Union as buffer zones and extensions of its territory, just like the continental shelf stretches landmasses out into hostile, dark seawaters. Likewise, the farther a former Soviet nation is from Europe (where the main ground zero of the threat to Russian statehood is being constructed), the less likely Russia is to engage in a substantive foreign policy quarrel with its government.

A good example of the dual vision existing in Russian foreign policy thought toward the former brotherly republics is its diverse reactions to the involvement of the European Union and the United States in the countries adjacent to the EU. For instance, to a certain degree, the Ukrainian crisis was ignited by Russia out of its fears that the Ukrainian government would turn the country's wheel in the direction of Brussels (including closer association with Europe and ultimately its membership in NATO), which was viewed in Moscow as an attempt to drift away from Russia's sphere of influence. On the other hand, Russia was not merely indifferent but actually accommodating of NATO's presence in Uzbekistan and Kyrgyzstan during their operations in Iraq and Afghanistan in the early 2000s. It even proposed that NATO troops use one of its airports in Ulyanovsk as a transit facility for extraction of nonlethal cargo and personnel from Afghanistan, but this was never implemented.[29] Perhaps it thought that due to the long distance separating European political institutions from Central Asian nations, the EU and NATO would be "like two elephants running through the same city . . . while never meeting each other," meaning rationally unjustifiable prospects for close integration of the region in either of them.[30] Or maybe the existence of such a giant as Kazakhstan between Russia and the aforementioned countries ensured Russia of no long-term political consequences for bases in the region. In either case, Russia applied custom-made foreign policy designs in each specific post-Soviet country, which reveals its commitment to multidimensional engagement in the Near Abroad. This stance does not fit with the Baltic States, which are in the European Union and NATO; yet these countries were never truly viewed as Russia's own.

The variables of past economies, former joint political belonging, and cultural affiliations linking Russia with Near Abroad nations were influenced by the superpower identity and feelings of *velikoderzhavnost'* being contracted and cultivated under Putin. Finally, these influences were reinforced by the need to defend Russian statehood against external challenges, magnified into a vision of overwhelming threats. Thus was created the Grand National policy objective: the revival of the Soviet Union in any suitable form with borders as close as possible to the former ones. Back in the 1990s, the head of the Communist Party of Russia, Genadiy Zyuganov, noted the zero-sum character of the political future facing Russia: "The main task of Russia in the immediate future is 'gathering the lands' and reviving a new Soyuz state. There is no other way. Either we, one step at a time, peacefully and voluntarily are able to integrate the 'post-Soviet space' and reinstate control over the geopolitical heart of the world, or we are facing degradation and a colonial future."[31] At that time, such statements seemed outdated if not bizarre in Russian society, which was rapidly transforming from tight communist rule and economic austerity to adopting democratic principles and living in a market economy. By his second presidential term, Putin, a former KGB operative and a member of the Communist Party (the second was inseparable from the first), seemed to have mastered the teachings of the Russian communist guru and decided to put them to work.

As a part of Russian political culture, pariah thinking is reflected in the institutional approaches in its foreign policy directions toward the Near Abroad. As was the case with both prior empires, having aligned itself in opposition to all things western, Russia also expects to turn the NIS countries into a loyal "entourage" of nations, translating its decisions to European and American counterparts. This also means that the political courses taken by Russia's neighbors, especially those closer to the EU and NATO, are treated with extremely close scrutiny. Their actions, if not supervised by or at least aligned with Moscow, are considered indigent attempts to defy the strategic direction of Russia and ultimately shake the identity pillars of Russian *velikoderzhavnost'*. Their defiance can differ in form and content, and range from the wish of some of them to join NATO (mostly Georgia and Ukraine) or to become more closely associated with the European Union (here the Ukrainian crisis fits well, as well as Armenia), or even not to elect Moscow's protégé during their elections (as Abkhazia dared to choose Sergey Bagapsh over Putin's former KGB colleague Alexander Ankvab in the 2004 presidential elections).

Triangulation of Russian "soft primordialism" with modernism and postmodernism creates specific foreign policy patterns embracing the past, present, and future of Russian foreign policy in the region. The nations unwilling to follow Russia in their modern-day domestic and international policy choices are seen as attempting to erase Russian inputs in their historic milestones, as encroaching on the current raison d'être of the Russian nation and, ultimately, as denying its potential political future. Following its "soft primordialist" attitudes toward the twelve NIS states (minus the three Baltic members of the EU), Russia wants to establish qualitatively new relationships with the former Soviet nations by giving them at least some institutionalized form of multilateralism, which would mirror the letter and the spirit of political-economic-cultural cohesion in the European Union and military cooperation in NATO.

Institutionalized Neo-Imperialism

When the Soviet Union was created in December 1922, it inherited a vast empire of nationalities with their own cultures, religions, languages, and customs. With that, the imperial institutional arrangements also came along, with the center in Saint Petersburg/Moscow deciding the fates of its populations in the multimillions. Not willing to reinvent the wheel, Soviet leaders kept the main institutional arrangements of the former Russian empire, turning it into a "prison of nations," or what President Ronald Reagan once famously called the Evil Empire. Neither the Russian empire nor its successor, the Soviet Union, in the words of Rogers Brubaker, was

> conceived in theory nor organized in practice as a nation-state. Yet while it did not define the state or citizenry as a *whole* in national terms, it did define the component *parts* of the state and the citizenry in national terms. . . . No other state has gone so far in sponsoring, codifying, institutionalizing, even (in some cases) inventing nationhood and nationality on the sub-state level, while at the same time doing nothing to institutionalize them on the level of state as a whole. (emphasis in original)[32]

The institutional legacies of the Russian empire and the Soviet Union separately meant two things for the new Russian nation-state at the brink of the century. First, if the common institutional arrangements had worked twice (and they have all failed because of external factors—Lenin was a German spy and Gorbachev an American spy—both conspiracy theories have widest application in Russia), there is no reason why they should not work for the third time, at the end of the twentieth century, now led by a reborn Russia. Second, the lessons from the demise of both empires should be learned and their institutional design drawbacks can always be improved upon to allow for the existence of some forms of multilateralism or even supranationalism.

Commonwealth of Indifferent States

There were several institutional attempts to resurrect the reformed Soviet Union from the world of fallen empires, where Russia would again play the leading role and act as the main engine of multiethnic cohesion. The first one was the Commonwealth of Independent States, or CIS. Created on December 8, 1991, even before the dissolution of the Soviet

Union, the CIS included only three Slavic republics: Russia, Belarus, and Ukraine. The same month the founding legal document, the Alma Ata Declaration, was concluded among eleven former Soviet republics: Azerbaijan, Armenia, Belarus, Kazakhstan, Moldova, Kyrgyzstan, the Russian Federation, Tajikistan, Turkmenistan, Uzbekistan, and Ukraine. The composition of the newly created entity almost entirely copied that of the Soviet Union without the EU-oriented Baltic States and Georgia, which in the early 1990s was torn between two civil wars with its ethnic minorities, Abkhazians and South Ossetians, who it suspected were supported by Russia.

From the perspective of regional security, by signing the Declaration, the newly created nations pledged, among other things, "to build democratic law-governed states, the relations between which will develop on the basis of mutual recognition and respect for state sovereignty and sovereign equality, the inalienable right to self-determination, principles of equality and noninterference in internal affairs, the rejection of the use of force, the threat of force, and economic and any other methods of pressure,"[33] Two years after its inception, the CIS was enriched by bringing in Georgia. This country was clearly losing in its internal conflicts against its South Ossetian and Abkhazian minorities, which were politically, economically, and militarily supported by Russia.[34] Eduard Shevardnadze had no choice but to come under the multilateral wings of the CIS to retain its sovereignty and territorial integrity, which Russia, the main driving force behind the institution, undertook upon itself to protect.

Unlike its territorial predecessor, the CIS is not a static organization. Vladimir Vorob'ev identified three stages of its institutional development, which appeared as a result of the evolution of bilateral relations between its member states, the integration process within the CIS, and external influences. The first stage (1991–93) can be described as "preliminary institutionalization" when "former Soviet republics were gaining independence, recognition, and legal and international formulation of their statehood." During the second stage of "active institutionalization" (1993–96), "new independent states strengthened their political sovereignty, entered into the international community and international financial institutions, and started developing trade and economic links with their closest neighbors." Finally, in what can be named "established institutionalization" (1997–2000), "CIS member states entered a stage of relative political and socioeconomic stability."[35] Ol'ga Biryukova also presents the integration of the CIS as a two-stage process, the first part of which (for her it is 1991–96) suffered from "inertia, having exhausted its potential from the economic and political ties that did not collapse." The second stage (1996–2001) was marked by "the transition to a 'search' integration model characterized by its instability, imbalance between the interests of national elites and the needs of the population."[36] This was also the period when subregional institutions of economic and political cooperation started to appear: the Collective Security Treaty Organization in 1992 (CSTO); the Organization for Democracy and Economic Development in 2001 (GUUAM: Georgia, Ukraine, Uzbekistan, Azerbaijan, and Moldova); the Russia-Belarus Union State in 1997; and the Organization of Central Asian Cooperation between 2002 and 2005 (OCAC), which later became a part of the Eurasian Economic Community (EEC, 2011–14) and was replaced by the Eurasian Economic Union (2015 forward).

Both Vorob'ev and Biryukova are right: the period up until the middle of the first decade of the 2000s can be characterized as "institutional bliss" for the CIS and its members. There were no major ongoing conflicts between or within the member states, and the unresolved ones (in Georgia, Nagorno-Karabakh, and Moldova) were frozen. Also, the processes of European integration and NATO's enlargement were less frightening for Russia, which was dealing with its own domestic economic hardships and war in Chechnya. As the world started to slowly globalize in the new millennium, the CIS began feeling negative vibes that threatened to shake the institutional foundations of the newly born multilateral organization.

CIS, as a multilateral organization, suffered from problems that appeared at the more advanced stages of its institutional development. The preconditions for the future of the CIS were, however, seemingly bright. The historical memories of cohabitation were still vivid among the majority of the former Soviet population living now in independent countries. On top of that, in their early independent years many of the new nations were, and some continue to be, ruled by former Communist Party buddies—Kuchma in Ukraine, Yeltsin in Russia, Shevardnadze in Georgia, Makhamov and Rakhmonv in Tajikistan, Niyazov in Turkmenistan, Aliyev in Azerbaijan, Karimov in Uzbekistan, and Nazarbayev in Kazakhstan. These former party bosses shared past communist beliefs, including many similar traits in management style and thus were, at least theoretically, more predisposed to peaceful and mutually beneficial economic cooperation among themselves. From the point of view of domestic governance, all decided to implement some elements of democratic frameworks, which should have predisposed political closeness. Finally, the economies of CIS countries were also similar in the sense of their transformation processes from command-and-control centralized mechanisms to liberalized markets. In addition, the well-functioning supply-and-demand system in the Soviet Union provided them with already existing networks for the sale of raw materials and manufactured commodities.

With all the clearly visible advantages for the effective existence and flourishing of the CIS, the organization suffered from a single but significant drawback that crossed all the pros out: it was the design flaw that made all the subsequent efforts of its actors to keep it alive doomed to an eventual washout. The historical memory of the common Soviet past has been keeping the CIS countries together by sheer inertia without offering them tangible benefits from rational choice institutionalism perspectives.[37] The economic drawbacks of the CIS, according to Katrin Elborgh-Woytek, included "slow progress in transition; severe restrictions to trade, including trade blockades in the Caucasus and Central Asia; geographic and topographic features; weaknesses in physical infrastructure; and corruption and governance problems in customs and transport services. Political tensions among the CIS countries and restrictions to market access in some of the CIS countries' main trading partners add to the difficulties."[38] The Soviet Union compensated its members for the lack of economic incentives of a free market and capitalist relations by offering a strong coercive grip and punishment in case of defection; this was a contrasting mirror image of another multilateral organization, the European Union, which provided tangible benefits for willing cooperation.

Needless to say, when the USSR collapsed, its former members started developing economic ties outside of the CIS. Stanislav Chernyavsky explains this process of growing anti-Russian nationalism within the Near Abroad: "The CIS countries have adapted to independent existence in the context of a weakening or complete absence of economic ties between them, different reforms of their governance styles. The process of gaining sovereignty became irreversible, where the independence of the states is understood primarily in terms of freedom from Russia."[39] Even the Free Trade Area of the CIS member states (CISFTA) proposed in 1993 only materialized in 2011 with its signing and ratification in 2014.[40] It is too early to assess its performance, whether positive or negative, especially within the light of the Ukrainian debacle and the concomitant Western sanctions and self-sanctions against Russia.

Internally, CIS suffered from mismanagement when it came to implementing the decisions of its summits. Being its most active member, according to Stina Torjesen, "Russia was among the worst offenders when it came to putting policy into practice. Agreements signed by the CIS heads of state would often face difficulties when sent to the Russian State Duma, where deputies refused or postponed ratifying many agreements."[41] This shows how little Russia was interested in keeping the CIS alive. Even Putin himself talked about the design flaw in the CIS in 2005. According to him, "CIS never had a super task of economic integration. . . . If in Europe the EU countries worked together for unification, the CIS was created for civilized divorce."[42] After that, Russia accelerated working in bilateral dimensions and promoting other integration projects, such as the Customs Union. This move reinforced the failure of regionalization of the CIS, where its members simply could not agree on many of the points of proposed supranational structures or the legal paperwork. As a result, according to Paul Kubicek, "the CIS was handicapped on many fronts, including emergent multi-polarity in the post-Soviet space and domestic level political consideration in many post-Soviet states."[43] Retreat from the CIS for them thus became only a matter of time.

The first harbinger of the CIS's demise was Turkmenistan, which left the official ranks of the organization at the 2005 Kazan Summit but kept the status of an associated observer member. Its long-term president, Turkmenbashi (Father of All Turkmen) Saparmurat Niyazov, explained this decision on the grounds of his country's preference for bilateral versus multilateral relations. There is, however, an opinion that "the Commonwealth members themselves pushed Turkmenbashi out of the CIS by regularly criticizing him at previous summits."[44] Regardless of the reasons, Turkmenistan's misbehavior turned out to be contagious, and other members used it as a precedent to leave or threaten to leave the CIS. Turkmenistan's exit was followed by Georgia's, whose membership in the CIS ended on a much more painful note. As a result of the 2008 war with Russia, it left the CIS seeing no benefit of being with the latter for its inability to enforce sovereignty and territorial integrity clauses upon Russia, which violated them against Georgia.[45] The fact that one state of the commonwealth violated its founding principles of respect for the territorial integrity and sovereignty of another Commonwealth member, in the words of M. Wesley Shoemaker, "probably dealt a death-knell to the CIS."[46] In 2014 in the aftermath of the Euromaidan, Ukraine decided to abandon its presidency of the CIS and its parliament in planning to consider the country's complete withdrawal from the organization.[47] Withdrawal of such a heavyweight actor from the CIS would mean another nail in its coffin.

Eurasian Union

By the late 2000s, instead of the moribund CIS, Putin engaged in promoting the idea of the Eurasian Union, which was borrowed from Kazakhstan president Nursultan Nazarbayev. Back in 1994 in his speech at Moscow State University, Nazarbayev spoke of some kind of post-Soviet European Union, replacing the modifier with "Eurasian."[48] At that time this was just a very hypothetical idea of how an ideal picture of interstate cooperation in the territory of the former Soviet Union could look. This thought had been gathering dust on the shelves of the post-Soviet archives until 2011 when Putin reanimated Nazerbayev's idea "in the process of being upgraded into a single economic space, with the goal of an economic union among the three by 2015."[49] In his interview to the newspaper *Izvestiya*, Putin mentioned the founding role of the CIS in unifying the ex-Soviet republics in different directions: economic (through the EEC and the Customs Union), political, and military (still through the CIS and the CSTO). In pointing to the European experience of creation of a supranational entity, Putin alluded to the ultimate goal of the Eurasian Union as a possible counterpart of the EU: "It took forty years for the Europeans to evolve from the European Coal and Steel Community to the full-fledged European Union. The formation of the Customs Union and the Common Economic Space is much more dynamic, as it considers the experience of the EU and other regional entities. We see their strengths and weaknesses. And this is our clear advantage to avoid errors, to prevent the reproduction of all sorts of bureaucratic hurdles."[50] In 2011 Putin seemed quite committed to jump-starting cooperation among the Near Abroad on a qualitatively different level.

The economic component of the newly created entity is, indeed, seen by many as its real foundation. After all, if the EU started from sector-specific economic cooperation between limited numbers of its future members and later expanded across the European continent, why can't Russia do the same and take the spirit of supranationalism further east? The Eurasian Economic Community (EEC), created in 2001 as a precursor to the Customs Union (2010) and the Common Economic Space (2012), was given exactly this task: effective promotion of ideals of economic integration and ultimate harmonization of the institutions of its member states: Russia, Belarus, Kazakhstan, Kyrgyzstan, and Tajikistan. Ukraine, Armenia, and Moldova were given observer status. With this spirit of multilateralism in place, the EEC was, indeed, "designed and modeled on the EU's structure, including the institutional mechanisms in place. Thus the Eurasian Economic Integration Commission should be analogous to the European Commission in terms of structure and functions," as Andrey Makarychev and Andre Mommen explained.[51] Similar to the initial goals of the European Coal and Steel Community, the major aim of the EEC, as noted by Piotr Dutkiewicz and Richard Sakwa, was "expediting the building of a common economic space, coordinating the process of integration of its member states into the world economy and harmonized economic legislation."[52] These all were noble tasks, which, with careful planning and implementation, were supposed to bring the desired results to the new social contract that Russia was striving to execute among post-Soviet states. The example of the European Union was, at minimum, reassuring.

To a certain degree, the EEC was, indeed, successful in creating a common policy stance with regards to foreign trade. According to Rowe and Torjesen, its members managed to come up with a list of products—over 11,000 commodities—that they agreed to establish common tariffs on. However, as they noted, "Decision-making power [in the EEC] is weighted according to financial contribution rather than based on the one-state-one-vote principle of the CIS. The differential voting mechanism clearly favored Russia, in effect enshrining its great power [*velikoderzhavie*] dominance in the organization."[53] The main decision-making body, the Interstate Council, would thus be unevenly skewed in its preferences toward Russia, which goes against the very spirit of multilateralism and even supranationalism.

This should not be surprising to hear, especially if taking into account Shoemaker's definition: "The essential purpose of the Eurasian Economic Union will be to unite the various countries in the area of the former Soviet Union into a new economic bloc under Russian leadership."[54] The new entity would thus diverge from the EU's supranational governance because of its design incompatibility. Russian post-Soviet imperialism has a fundamental difference from its Soviet predecessor *korenizatsiya* and the European supranational model: it is designed to be ethnic in form (as led by none else but the Russians) and imperial in content (forcefully imposed on its members). Liliya Shevtsova comments, "The Kremlin is building support for its great power aspirations in exchange for financial, economic, and military bonuses to the Eurasian Union members."[55] The problem is that these bonuses are not yet clear and readily available for the members, and they do not feel completely free from the memories of Russia's dominating role in the Soviet Union.

As the form of a new social contract, in the CIS Russia had to deal with sovereign nations and not gutless victims of the Soviet punitive machine. Russia had to show to the members of the Commonwealth that it is striving to act as a truly unifying force that they could rely on in case of economic hardships (within the Eurasian Economic Community) and political and military problems (within the Collective Security Treaty). In reality, however, as Dmitry Trenin correctly noted, "For each of the CIS members their independence is, first and foremost, viewed in terms of independence from Moscow."[56] With these views, any forceful "dragging" of the countries into the CIS, EEC, and potentially the Eurasian Union is fraught with negative consequences for proposed Russian multilateralism. Due to its sheer size, Russia dominates the other EEC members, and as Zhanis Kembayev concluded, it actively worked to bring Ukraine into the Community as some sort of a counterbalance to its power to disperse the fears of the EEC's lesser member states.[57] The myth and reality of living under one common Soviet roof are still vivid in the governance of the Near Abroad. Most of them have already undergone generational changes and are free from the communist legacy but are nevertheless aware of the internal "prison" regime.

The main problem in Russia's attempts to bring the former Soviet countries together is the very post-Soviet neo-institutionalism that it aspires to bring. This notion is characterized by incompatibility of two qualities of a superpower, which was discussed in chapter 2 on Russian political culture: the ability to effectively impose its will on followers and to attract their willing adherence to its will. The CIS countries are treating Russia's actions with increased suspicion, especially with the wave of growing support for the Russian world and Eurasianism. A loyal adherent of them both, Russian novelist Alexander Prokhanov, views Russia's attempt to create the Eurasian Union as a step in the direction of institutionalizing Russia's neo-imperialism. In the article in the newspaper *Zavtra* (Tomorrow), where he is a chief editor, Prohanov sang the following praises to Putin's Eurasianist direction:

> On the territory of the shattered Soviet empire, among the imperial debris, on the orphaned scraps of the disappeared Red kingdom, Putin promises to build a new imperial community. . . . But even if it proves to be a bluff, this bluff is associated with a yearning for Empire. The desecrated spaces, oppressed peoples, plundered developmental potentials, [and] wailing sacred stones of the Empire speak up through Putin's voice. . . . The ideology of justice as the main resource of the upcoming Empire will become attractive to all peoples inhabiting Eurasia. . . . Put your ear to the cobblestones of the Red Square. And you hear the roar of the Fifth Empire.[58]

Another popular Russian writer, Sergey Lukianenko, echoed Prokhanov's notion of gathering up the imperial stones in a peculiar way, revoking the senses of divine revelation: "We should firmly and clearly understand: we, Russia, are now the bearers of truth, freedom, and kindness. All those who oppose us are bringing lies, slavery, and evil. There is no middle ground; those undecided are, at minimum, unwitting accomplices of the enemy."[59] Here, too, allusions are made to the notions of justice and righteousness, which are innate parts of Russian political culture.

The statements above were made in relation to the Ukrainian crisis and are not the official position of the Russian Federation, nor are they coming from official state representatives. They are made by prominent private citizens who have their own loyal audiences. However, in the context of the ongoing project of post-Soviet institutionalism initiated and championed by Russia, they bear a less than convoluted message to their readers. Connected with Russia's actions in Georgia in 2008, its repeated denial of autonomous identity to Ukraine culminating in 2014–15, its infringements upon the state sovereignty of Moldova—all this shows that Russia is trying to reshape the institutions of the newly proposed post-Soviet order in accordance with its individual interpretations of the memories uniting the Near Abroad, its own understanding of right and wrong, and its own visions of historical justice. This is the new social contract that Russia, as an up-and-coming superpower, wants to offer to its followers.

Political-Military Institutionalism

The military component of institutionalized neo-imperialism is enshrined in the Collective Security Treaty Organization (CSTO), which was supposed to be yet another step in reanimating the Soviet Union or, to be more precise, its military hypostasis. The founding document, the Collective Security Treaty (CST), was modeled after the Warsaw Pact and the NATO Treaty in a sense that it established common security and defense principles, although in a much smaller geographical space. Article 4 of the CSTO treaty introduced the same "all for one, one for all" clause as Article 6 of the NATO treaty: "If a State-member is under aggression (an armed attack that threatens its security, stability, territorial integrity, and sovereignty), this will be considered by the States-members as aggression (and armed attack that threatens their security, stability, territorial integrity, and sovereignty) against all States that are Parties to this Treaty."[60] Initially, six states of the former Soviet Union signed the treaty (Russia, Armenia, Kazakhstan, Kyrgyzstan, Uzbekistan, and Tajikistan), later joined by three more (Azerbaijan, Georgia, and Belarus).

In May 2002 the treaty turned into a full-scale organization, the CSTO, which, according to some views, had a number of positive traits. First, it "contributed to 'peaceful divorce' of the former Soviet republics," legally binding them from attacking each other. Second, due to Russia's agreement to "share" its military, the strongest one on ex-Soviet land, with the rest of the team, the organization "became a viable guarantee of the external security of the member states." Lastly, its collective forces could be used "in the interests of international security and outside the territories of the member states, provided these actions comply with the UN Charter."[61] Despite these seemingly beneficial results that participation in the CSTO promised its members, from its very inception there were serious disagreements on the form and substance of membership.

Since its membership in the CIS, Georgia felt threatened by Moscow due to their conflicts of the early 1990s. For its part, Azerbaijan criticized the CST for its inefficiency in light of the unresolved issue of Nagorno-Karabakh, which it viewed as an interstate conflict with Armenia. Uzbekistan, too, started dwindling in its orientation toward its ex-Soviet brothers, on the one hand, and the United States and Pakistan, on the other.[62] But the biggest *enfant terrible* of the CSTO was Belarus, which was expected to follow Russia in most if not all its decisions. In June 2009 at the session of the Collective Security Council, the highest decision-making body in the CSTO, it was decided to create the Collective Rapid Reaction Forces to be available to CSTO members as a 9/11 tool. However, Belarus declined participation at the session in light of the "Dairy Wars" going on with Russia as a protest to the embargo of Belarusian dairy products to Russia. The explanation given by Mink was that "without ceasing the actions that undermine the foundations of economic security of the partners, decision-making on other aspects of security is impossible."[63] Later on, Belarus agreed to sign the document, which did not stop the "minority view" of its president: in 2010 Lukashenka claimed that the future of the CSTO had "no prospects" due to its "inability to properly react to the coup in one of its members," meaning the disturbances in Kyrgyzstan in 2010.[64]

Neither the high promises of collective security nor the prospects of sharing the burden of collective security managed to keep its initial members in place. There were countries that were more decisive than Belarus: Georgia left the CSTO in 2008 in the aftermath of the war with Russia, and the CSTO was quick to call its actions there a "genocide."[65] Technically, the conflicts represented "threats to the territorial stability, territorial integrity, and sovereignty" of Georgia, which the CST member states pledged to protect. In 2012 another country left the CSTO—Uzbekistan, the reason for which, as some experts consider, was "Tashkent's desire to resume their 'passionate romance' with the United States, which they replaced for several years by 'flirting with Russia'—and U.S. military support."[66] The reality of CSTO was that the multinational organization had turned into the tool for keeping a

Russian military presence in the Near Abroad and projecting it beyond CIS borders.

No other CSTO member but Russia deployed its troops in the partners' territories. Russia had placed different levels of defense units in the territories of CSTO members: the Regional Group in Belarus where the local armed military are reinforced by the Twentieth Army; the 102nd Military Base in Gyumri (Armenia); the 201st Military Base in Dushanbe (Tajikistan); the 999th Air Force Base in Kant (Kyrgyzstan); the Seventh Military Base in Abkhazia; and the Fourth Military Base in South Ossetia. Russia is especially interested in extending the Early Warning Systems (EWS) of its missile defense system. In particular, Russia deployed three radar stations in Belarus, Azerbaijan, and Kazakhstan capable of "launch detection of land and sea ballistic and cruise missiles, and to ensure the integrity of their trajectory and the time of their flight."[67] Russian domination in the CSTO, both in political and military terms, has turned this organization into its foreign policy tool.

Neighbors to the West

The Western part of the Near Abroad occupies a special place in contemporary Russian foreign policy. The three countries bordering the European Union—Ukraine, Belarus, and Moldova—"deserve" close attention from Moscow due to their proximity to the threats to Russian statehood emanating from the EU and NATO. Russia strives to achieve multiple goals in the western vector of its future foreign policy. The best possible future scenario for Russia is to have a loyal entourage of the Slavic nations plus Moldova that would be completely dependent on Russia economically and politically and would translate its "cultural staples" beyond their borders to the rest of Europe. This scenario would entail incredible effort on the part of Russia to bring under its umbrella the former Soviet nations who are more exposed than others to Western values and are more closely integrated with European economic networks. This option thus belongs to the distant and vague future due to the fact that Russia is not in a position to force it upon them militarily or economically to follow its foreign policy course.

The second, more likely and shorter-term scenario for Moscow is to achieve political and economic destabilization in Ukraine, Moldova, and Belarus to delay their closer affiliations with the West as much as possible and thus to extend its own influence over their foreign and domestic policies. The situation is different in each case, which calls for customized choices and application of foreign policy tools on the part of Russia. Ukraine suffers from the ongoing involvement of Russia in its various southeastern parts adjacent to its own territory and is the first case of de jure large-scale territorial remapping in the former Soviet Union. Unlike the disputed areas in Nagorno-Karabakh and Abkhazia/South Ossetia, Russia officially included the Crimean Peninsula as administratively its own in March 2014. In the case of Belarus, Russia already has a like-minded actor that plays its own games with Europe. Lukashenka is a strong and witty leader who would not easily bend under economic or political pressure from Moscow and would not hesitate to play both sides of the European game—the EU/United States and Russia—to keep his personal rule as long as possible. Moldova has an open wound in the form of a frozen conflict in Tiraspol, Transdniestria, its breakaway region that enjoys strong economic and political support from Moscow. Destabilization in Moldova for Russia would be easier to achieve, especially taking into account the Russian annexation of Crimea, which brought Tiraspol even closer to Moscow, militarily speaking.

The third and least likely scenario is Russia's withdrawal from domestic politics in the three countries and its own return to the family of European nations as a responsible member. This option is unlikely to happen for two reasons. First, withdrawal from parts of Ukraine and the return of Crimea to its legal owner would decrease the status of Russia as a rising superpower: an image that has been constructed domestically during Putin's last two presidential terms and translated overseas. Steps in this direction would mean that Russia succumbed to outside (European and American) pressure and that the sanctions had reached their intended target. These actions of the international community have been widely ridiculed in the Russian mainstream and political establishment as something that Russia is doing "right." A 180-degree reversal of foreign policy, however, would mean that Russia was very much "wrong," which is unacceptable for its political culture built on self-righteousness delivered domestically and abroad. The second reason this course of action is unlikely is that it would also render a significant blow to the national self-awareness and self-esteem of the Russian nation. This move will seriously jeopardize Putin's own domestic standing, as he is currently enjoying all-time high approval from his people, and it would derail the train of his pocket oligarchs. If Putin were removed for failing to fulfill his promises to the "Russian world," they would fear the loss of their assets.

Ukrainian Debacle

Russian foreign policy in Ukraine encompasses multiple issue-areas and is directed toward achieving control over political decisions in this neighboring country. Ukraine is the second-largest post-Soviet nation, which puts it by definition in the line of potential rivals to territorially conscious Russia. Russia needs Ukrainian territory to use for transit routes of its energy carriers to European markets. Thus having a loyal government in Kiev would give viable guarantees for nondisruption of Russian oil and gas sales, both by not impeding their physical flows and not blackmailing by raising transit tariffs. Another consideration here is that Ukraine is the buffer zone between Russia and the European Union, as the geopolitical entity, and NATO, as the military organization. Having the government in Kiev translate Russia's own views on regional foreign affairs toward the West would cover its back and afford a certain degree of peace and stability, militarily speaking. Lastly, there is a sizable Russian (17 percent) and Russian-speaking population in Ukraine, as mentioned in the last all-Ukrainian census in 2001.[68] This makes Russia both an "external homeland" for ethnic Russians and a "surrogate lobby state" for those who want to align themselves with Russia, especially those living close to the national border between Russia and Ukraine.[69]

Relations between Russia and Ukraine have never been easy. Russian foreign policy in Ukraine is composed of several key issue-areas, which are simultaneously accessed to achieve the ultimate policy results for Moscow: to keep Kiev within its spheres of influence, at minimum, and to incorporate Ukraine, or at least parts of it, at best. These issue-areas include the combination of identity denial for Ukrainians as a separate nation; sovereignty denial for Ukraine as a separate country; demonization of Ukrainians as fascists and puppets of the West; and the economic collapse of Ukraine and slow encroachment on its territory, started from Crimea and ongoing in its southeastern parts.

The causes of the 2014 crisis in Ukraine and Russia's (alleged) participation in its civil war in 2014 go way back in the history of the interactions between these nations. The Ukrainian debacle is not a one-off event in Russian foreign policy. On the one hand, it is a logical part in the chain of actions in continuation of Russia's "getting off its knees" and reinstating its superpower status. On the other, it is a direct consequence and continuation of the centuries-long nationalistic policies of the Russian empire and later the Soviet Union against the indigenous populations of their western parts. Understanding the dual nature of Russian involvement in Ukraine, especially the intricacies of the identity peculiarities of this "brotherly kinship," as well as the historical peripeteia in the region, including external interests, is fundamental to interpreting the roots of contemporary Russian foreign policy toward its neighbor.

The first part of Russia's multifaceted policy in Ukraine is framed by the historically developed patterns of denying the raison d'être of the Ukrainian nation and presenting Ukrainians as a non-nation and a lesser offspring of Russians. Historically molded Ukrainian identity is composed, according to Sergei Shtukarin, of three parts: "national," where its bearer reacts positively to the maxim "Ukraine for Ukrainians"; "civil," which implies loyalty to Ukraine's statehood regardless of ethnic background; and "alien," which regards both Ukrainian ethnicity and statehood as foreign.[70] Similarly, as Serhy Yekelchyk noted, Ukrainian national identity encompassed three components, being "a direct descendant of medieval Kyivan Rus', the seventeenth-century Cossack polity, and the 1918–20 Ukrainian People's Republic."[71] The current geographic divide in Ukrainiano society into the pro-European west and pro-Russian east was born of centuries of interactions with both sides of its bipolar identity equation.

With its historical core of the Kievan Rus', which gave birth to the medieval Slavic fiefdoms, Ukraine represents the basis for and the cradle of the common eastern Slavic identity and was the center, which the future Russian empire would build around.[72] Having sprung out of the Kievan Rus' at the end of the thirteenth century, the Grand Duchy of Moscowia later expanded to a full-scale empire and eventually engulfed Ukraine. Together with its core essence, Ukraine has always been perceived as the outskirts of the great Russian empire: the name itself in the eastern Slavic dialects means "at the edge" or "the borderland."[73] Ukraine had a short period of independence during medieval times in the form of the Galicia-Volhynia political entity in the thirteenth and fourteenth centuries, which the Ukrainian historian Stefan Tomashivsky named "the first undeniably Ukrainian state."[74] In the fifteenth and sixteenth centuries, the western part of present-day Ukraine was included in the powerful Polish-Lithuanian Commonwealth, after which some of its territories became semi-independent under the rule of the Cossacks.[75] These were groups of paramilitaries who were "Orthodox men roaming the steppes, and . . . famously independent minded."[76] Cossacks were the military regiments gathered at a distant and well-protected place called Zaporojskaya Sich'. These daredevils pledged no allegiance to any their neighbors, be it the Polish-Lithuanian union, the Ottoman empire, the Crimean Khanate, or Moscovia. In 1710 the Sich' produced one of the first prototypes of a modern-day democratic constitution under Hetman Orlyk, with real attributes of democracy, including the separation of powers and an elective governance style.[77]

After their bloody defeat by the Polish army in 1651, the Cossacks appealed to Alexei I, tsar of Moscovia, to accept them under his protectorate.[78] They were seeking a temporary military alliance, fearing the ultimate subjugation under the Polish reign. The initial arrangements provided for mutual loyalty of the Cossacks and Alexei I, wide autonomy, and keeping the internal composition of Ukraine. Later on, however, these accords were broken by Moscovia, which completely subordinated the land it initially promised to (temporarily) defend from external threats. This marked the period of Ukrainian history under Russian rule, which transitioned to Soviet governance after the October Revolution of 1917. Ukraine did have its early independence, though, in the form of the Ukrainian People's Republic in 1918 and the West Ukrainian People's Republic, which joined the former in 1919 with the loss of its territory to Poland, Romania, and Czechoslovakia in the Polish-Ukrainian War of June 1919. Ukrainian independence, however, turned out to be short-lived, and the nation was ultimately vanquished by the Soviet army in midsummer 1920, creating the Ukrainian Soviet Socialist Republic.

The initial process of Russification (making it Russian) in Ukraine was much stricter than in any other part of the Russian empire. It started with the so-called *Valuevskiy Cirkulyar* ("Circular Letter of Valuev," Minister of the Interior, 1863) and *Ems Ukaz* ("Order of Ems," 1876), which banned the use of the Ukrainian language and dialects in the western provinces. During Soviet times, sovietization (making it Soviet) replaced large-scale Russification in most parts of the Soviet Union, keeping the process of turning all into Russians relatively mild. It remained, however, in Ukraine, where Anna Reid identified two reasons for its more rigorous assimilation by Russia: comparatively early existence under the Soviet geopolitical umbrella and denial of a unique Ukrainian identity by Russian nationalists. According to her, "Russians deny their [Ukrainians'] existence. Ukrainians are a 'non-historical nation,' the Ukrainian language is a joke dialect. . . . The very closeness of Ukrainian and Russian culture, the very subtlety of the differences between them, is an irritation."[79] The denial of the ethnic uniqueness of Ukrainians, which Chaim Kaufmann considers the "strongest" identity of all, became an integral part of the systematic nationalism policy toward Ukraine in the Soviet Union.[80]

The process of sovietization also included eradication of the Ukrainian language and culture and embraced the identity factor, which extended far beyond mere linguistic subordination of the Ukrainian languages to the Russian one as its western dialect. Since Ukraine was historically considered a core and the birthplace of Russian identity, having this holy of holies belong to another nation or its worship being narrated in the language other than its own would mean deprecation of Russia's own identity. As Zbigniew Brzezinski rightly observed, "Without Ukraine, Russia ceases to be an empire, but with Ukraine suborned and then subordinated, Russia automatically becomes an empire."[81] There was thus a political reasoning behind Soviet identity denial: the stronger the Russian/Soviet cultural linkages were with the Ukrainians, the stronger the cultural cleavage between Ukrainians and the Western world, especially with its immediate neighbors, Poland and Lithuania. Systematic identity denial by the Russian imperial and then Soviet authorities created long-lasting stigmatization in Ukraine and had its part in the regional divide in Ukraine.

With the collapse of the Soviet Union, Ukraine was blessed in comparison with some ex-Soviet republics, which experienced the "charms" of the imperial collapse to the very bitter end. Although Ukraine received large economic and industrial resources from the Soviet Union as a part of its independence inheritance, this potential appeared to be obsolete and an ill fit under the burden of independent existence. Inflation skyrocketed; the tentacles of a command-and-control economy that had provided both the demand and supply lines for the Soviet economy were completely severed. These conditions were coupled with thoughtless economic reforms, which led to a rapid economic downfall, including hyperinflation, severe GNP crush, corruption in privatization policies, and chronic budgetary deficit.[82] Except for the unavoidable economic problems during transformation from one economic managed style (here: the command-and-control top-down planned economy) to another (free-market economic relations), Ukraine did not suffer from a civil war (unlike Georgia), internal conflicts (again, unlike Georgia with its minorities), or intra-/interstate wars (as Moldova in Transdnistria and Armenia/Azerbaijan in Nagorno-Karabakh). With all the differences, its society remained more or less consolidated against the economic hardships, which it carried on with different degrees of success and failure.

The overthrow of former president Kuchma's corrupt regime, which was notorious for preferential political and economic regionalism, nepotism, corruption, and even crime as a result of the Orange Revolution in 2004–5, marked the slow decline of the country into domestic chaos.[83] The ensuing turmoil slowly culminated in Russia's cutting off a part of its Black Sea land and the ongoing disastrous conflict in its southeastern parts. The public protests in November 2004 staged as a response to mass election fraud allegedly committed by the forces acting against the presidential pro-Western runner-up Viktor Yushchenko enjoyed wide popular support. Already then the regional split was present here: while Yushchenko was mostly considered a pro-Western politician and enjoyed the support of western and central Ukraine, Viktor Yanukovych, then prime minister of Ukraine and the principal contender in the presidential race in November 2004, had his electorate largely based in eastern pro-Russian Ukraine. The democratic part of Ukrainian society predominantly viewed Yanukovych as a "Kuchma reincarnate" with the same Soviet-style bureaucracy and Kuchma's backing. Yushchenko, who according to independent exit polls won by a margin of 10 percent in the second round, was put behind Yanukovych by the Central Election Committee. This sparked mass protest rallies by Yushchenko's supporters in Kiev and elsewhere in Ukraine except for its eastern regions.[84] The third round of elections held in December confirmed Yushchenko's victory.

The promises of political change and economic revival made by incoming President Yushchenko appeared to be short-lived, and the democratic path was too difficult to continue. Because of internal struggle between powerful political and economic forces, Yushchenko appointed Yanukovych as prime minister in 2006. Four years later, as a result of the next presidential elections, Yanukovych became president of the country, marking an almost 180-degree reversal from volatile democracy to possibly stable but stagnant rule.[85] The result of the 2010 elections further widened the regional political divide in Ukraine between pro-democratic West and pro-Russian East.

A clear sign of the fluctuations of the bifurcate political course of

Ukraine was the conclusion in May 2013 of the memorandum on obtaining observer status in the Customs Union of the Eurasian Economic Community and the failure to sign the Associated Agreement with the European Union on the free trade zone in November 2013. This agreement, together with the initial Partnership and Cooperation Agreement of 1994, was seen by many as the "'road map' for gradual economic rapprochement" with the EU.[86] The agreement was initiated by Yanukovych, who was struggling to keep balance between the two gravity centers in his country, but in November 2013 he backed off the deal with the European Union.[87] For many in Ukraine, this automatically meant a move toward the Customs Union with Russia, which was a threshold to tighter affiliation within the upcoming Russia-dominated Eurasian Union.

At that point the Ukrainian government did not want to "upset" either the EU or Russia: according to Suzdalcev, Ukraine "wants to have all the benefits of the Customs Union but is not going to join it; instead, it wants to enter the European Union."[88] In a similar manner, Trenin, Lipman, and Malashenko explain, "Putin has offered membership in the customs union to Ukraine, which is torn between the appeal of short-term gains in the East, such as lower gas prices, and its long-term aspirations to join the West. Essentially, Kiev has continued its old game of trying to get the most from relations with both of its big neighbors—the EU and Russia—without making a clear and unambiguous choice."[89] These were, essentially, mutually exclusive directions: as Russia's leaders repeatedly noted, "After the signing of the Association Agreement—this is our open position, very simple and a sincere attitude—it will be very difficult for Ukraine to join the Customs Union, if it wants to."[90] East and West clashed in Ukraine, and this was not merely an allegorical description of the situation in Ukraine at the end of 2014. In Miszlivetz's view, these opposite geographical directions represented "[t]wo mutually exclusive worldviews and aspirations. . . . The first one is stretching the borders, the second is desperately trying to close and seal them."[91] As the events following this fateful decision show, the incompatibility between the two diametrically opposed foreign policy directions of Ukraine would define its political future for generations to come.

It was not only international indecisiveness and dwindling relations between Russia and the European Union, however, that brought the people in Ukraine to a second revolution in 2014. Yanukovich's regime, as Oxana Shevel et al. noted, was characterized by elitism, suppressions of human rights, nepotism, "family" reign, and a massive level of corruption.[92] To prove this point, the World Wide Governance Indicators 2010 and the Transparency International Corruption Perception Index 2012 jointly named Ukraine as one of the most corrupt countries in the post-Soviet space.[93] The inability of Yanukovich's government to provide effective governance domestically and to choose firmly either way for the country's international orientation (be that in the European or Russian direction) led to the second revolution in Ukraine, which turned out to be much bloodier from the onset and with grave consequences for Ukrainian statehood.

The main cause of the mass protests in 2014, known as Euromaidan, an evolved name of the 2004 protests that happened in Kiev's central square, Maidan, was frustration as a result of the inability of Yushenko's government to stand loyal to its promise of the democratic restructuring of the country. This protest made the initial Maidan look like a pale and much "lighter" version of its 2014 successor. Andrew Wilson notes, "If anything, things were worse than in 2004," with modern-day Internet technology including the Facebook, Twitter, and Russian social media websites, such as "VKontakte," with Ukrainian opposition politicians, journalists, and ordinary activists calling for demonstrations in support of the country's European course.[94]

On November 21, 2014, the first groups of Ukrainians unhappy with Yanukovich's choice to drop the Association Agreement started flooding the Maidan Square. Slowly the situation escalated as several attempts by opposition leaders—the newly released from prison Yulia Timoshenko, former prime minister of Ukraine in the Yushenko government; former world champion boxer Vitaly Klichko; and young Ukrainian politician Arseniy Yatsenyuk—to communicate the will of the people to

Yanukovich and negotiate a mutually acceptable deal were repeatedly turned down by a relentless Yanukovich. In the midst of the crisis, "Yanukovych pushed through draconian 'anti-protest' laws that limited free speech, assembly, and media rights," which additionally aggravated the Euromaidan.[95] The confrontation escalated with mutual attacks on both sides—from the police and special forces armed with firearms, "water cannons, stun grenades, and rubber bullets," on the one side, and the protesters, armed by Molotov cocktails and boulders, on the other.[96]

By 2015 protests were held all over Ukraine, but mostly in its central and western parts, against Yanukovich's regime, as a whole, and not only against its foreign policy. On February 21 the opposition leaders and the government managed to sign the Agreement of Settlement of Political Crisis in Ukraine, which would allow for early presidential elections in 2014 and constitutional changes revoking important powers of the president gained by Yanukovich and vesting them back to the parliamentary republic.[97] Such a state of affairs, however, did not satisfy most of the radical opposition of the self-defense units, including the nationalist organization Right Sector, which stormed the governmental buildings of the Parliament, cabinet of ministers, the presidential administration, and the Interior Ministry.[98] The same day Yanukovich fled Kiev in the eastern direction, briefly appeared in his stronghold of Kharkiv, and eventually, with Russia's help, ended up in the Russian city of Rostov-Na-Donu.[99]

There is a completely different official narrative from the Russian government, which it delivers domestically to the local electorate and translates internationally. According to numerous sources, the conflict in Ukraine has been provoked by the West (largely defined as the European Union and the United States), with the active involvement of American diplomats (such as Victoria Nuland, assistant secretary of state for European and Eurasian affairs at the United States State Department, who visited the Euromaidan and distributed cookies to its participants) and implemented by the Ukrainian Nazis, the Right Sector. Stanislav Byshok et al. explain, "When democratic Euromaidan all over the country entered its 'hot' stage, *maidanarbeiters* and common 'angry citizens' constituting the main body of protesters were not suitable for the clashes with the police, armory seizure, or attacking municipal administrations. That was when neo-Nazi militants under disguise of the Right Sector that upon closer examination turned out to be a union of previously known right-wing radical paramilitary units took the stage."[100]

There is no denying that right-wing Ukrainian nationalists participated in the Euromaidan and the ensuing overthrow of President Yanukovich. Nancy Naples and Jennifer Mendez present both sides of the story here: "While Russia justifies its actions by pointing to the hypocrisy of U.S. and NATO foreign policies, the western media has glossed over the complexities of the popular and nationalist Euromaidan movement, especially the central role played by its far-right contingents in the protests in the streets."[101] However, the Right Sector party and its leader, Dmytro Yarosh, were among the least popular political forces in Ukraine. As shown by the results of the presidential elections held in May 2014, shortly after the emotions and the grief of the Euromaidan had calmed down, Yarosh managed to gain the support of only 0.7 percent of the electorate and not 37 percent as presented for domestic viewers by the Russian state propaganda distributor, Channel 1.[102]

Russia's domestic and foreign action after the ousting of Yanukovich reflected conflicting values for Russia. These actions included support for and sheltering of Ukraine's exiled president and quite long abstinence from recognizing the newly elected president Poroshenko and the post-Euromaidan government, as well as its annexation of the Crimean Peninsula in March 2014 and (alleged) involvement in the civil war in the southeastern parts of Ukraine. For example, there are no signs of personal sympathy between Putin and Yanukovich. Putin's initial support to Yanukovich does not mean that he approves the lifestyle (among others, having a gold loaf of bread, alleged gold toilets, and other luxury accessories in his residence) or management modus operandi of his Ukrainian colleague. Putin supported Yanukovich back in 2004 and in early 2014 out of his views on Realpolitik: just because the latter was pro-Russian and he considered the forces that beat him in the Orange Revolution and in the Euromaidan to be on the West's paycheck.[103] Yanukovich was clearly Russia's man in Ukraine. On numerous occasions Russian official representatives rendered open support to their protégé, including pre–Orange Revolution elections in 2004, where "the involvement of Putin in Prime Minister Yanukovich's campaign [was] the most obvious foreign involvement."[104] Eric Miller brings up the figure of $600 million worth of Russian contributions to Yanukovich's election campaign in 2004.[105] After the elections, according to Liliya Shevtsova, "Ukraine president Viktor Yanukovich's willingness to opt for marriage with Russia cost Moscow $15bn and a promise to export gas to Ukraine at discounted prices."[106] Even after the events of February 2014, Russia continued to support Yanukovich in his position of an elected president. Slowly, however, the discourse around Yanukovich started diminishing in official Russian channels and gave way to other issues, such as Crimea.

From the point of view of Russian domestic politics, there are serious fears in the Russian political establishment that Ukraine's Euromaidan represents a dangerous precedent for Putin himself and the people in public service and businesses who support him. The fact that a brotherly nation—almost Russians—took matters into their own hands and, by means of a civil action of protest and revolution, solved their own fate could poison the hearts and minds of the local population in Russia proper. The 84 percent who support Putin's course will last as long as they do not see potential positive developments in Ukraine; therefore, those developments are discredited through the character assassination of Ukraine's new leaders and by ridiculing Western support for the Euromaidan. The events of 2014–15 in Ukraine clearly showed what a civil society can do to its government when it violates the very postulates of the democratic social contract with the citizens it pledged to safeguard. This is a stark contrast with the culture of governmental lies and deception omnipresent in contemporary Russian life.

Russia's actions to harbor Yanukovich and to support him, as well as its initial nonrecognition of the Ukrainian leadership, revealed the autocratic reciprocity with which the Russian political establishment treated the corrupt government of its neighbor. To a certain extent, this brings up historical anecdotes of the mutual respect medieval royals had for even the most unyielding rivals. One of them was given by brilliant Austrian writer Stefan Zweig in his historical novel *Mary Stuart* in his explanation of the hesitations English queen Elizabeth I had in relation to ordering capital punishment of her archenemy, Mary, Queen of Scots, in 1587. To allow Mary to live would mean prolongation of the conflict with Scotland; to allow her to die would jeopardize Elizabeth's own legitimacy, as a queen, in the eyes of her subjects. The following passage is particularly notable from the point of view of autocratic reciprocity:

> To send an anointed queen to the scaffold was a plain demonstration to the hitherto servile people . . . that even a monarch was subject to doom at the hands of the executioner, and could not be regarded as sacrosanct. Thus Elizabeth's decision implied, not merely the doom of a fellow creature, but the doom of an idea. For centuries the slaughtering of this idea would work havoc.[107]

The same logic applied to Putin's support for Yanukovich. To accept, at least tacitly, the new Ukrainian government to rule as a result of the bloody coup over Yanukovich and his "family" would be tantamount to allowing the same seditious thoughts to get hold of the heads in Russia proper, which would ultimately bring the same havoc as in Ukraine. This would also mean weakness of the central government in Moscow, which had "permitted" its own "Maidan" to succeed. Ultimately, there are fears that the Euromaidan would fine-tune the will of people at home in Russia, which would jeopardize the legitimacy of its current government. Various groups of concerned citizens have been mobilized from time to time to safeguard the ruling regime in Russia, including the notorious youth group Nashi, but they had mostly peaceful forms of governmental support and proved incapable of effectively preventing mass actions of protest in 2011. In January 2015 a new group was created, the name of which speaks for itself: Anti-Maidan.[108] The group is quite a motley bunch of some 10,000 former military, Cossacks, athletes, and bikers. Under the guidance of Russian senator Dmitry Sablin, the Anti-Maidan members would train in specially designated camps to learn and to teach others how to oppose the "orange" threat. In February 2015 the Russian Anti-Maidan held thousands of demonstrations all over Russia with the slogan "Anniversary of Maidan. We Will Not Forget. We Will Not Forgive."[109] Mostly with anti-American, anti-European, and anti-Ukrainian shades, they marched on the main streets of the Russian cities protesting against something that had happened thousands of miles away from them, in another sovereign country.

From the standpoint of international politics, relevant insights about Russian actions in Ukraine after the Euromaidan can be found in Andrei Tsygankov's comments back in 2004 concerning Russia's involvement in Ukrainian domestic politics prior to and after the Orange Revolution. According to him, "Putin's support to Yanukovich never amounted to an effort to build a new empire or to incorporate Ukraine into Russia. . . . Although the Russian president badly miscalculated Yanukovich's chances of winning, and although he provided strong support for Yanukovich's elections, Putin was never willing to sacrifice his relations with the West over the crisis in Ukraine, and he did not let his readiness to stand for Russia's strategic interests to be turned into confrontation."[110] Marlène Laruelle corroborates these important points: in addition to open and almost immediate congratulation of the winners of the 2004 elections, Russia sent messages to the Ukrainian and international audience that it "had no objections to Ukraine's joining the European Union. . . . At no point has Russia tried to support separatist trends in eastern Ukraine. Sanctions, too, were excluded from the Kremlin's arsenal."[111] In other words, the policy was hit-and-miss: good if it works with Yanukovich, but no big deal if it does not.

That was back in 2004: three years prior to Putin's Munich speech, in which he for the first time laid down the basis for Russia's foreign policy as crushing the "unipolar domination" of the United States. Far ahead was also his Valdai speech of 2014 in which he professed Russia's own path as being based on nationalism, patriotism, and opposition to all things American and Western. The main event that characterized the reflection of this policy shift in the case of Ukraine was intervention in Crimea in February and March 2014. Shortly after the success of

Euromaidan, groups of similarly uniformed and armed people, whom the popular Russian narratives call "Green People" and "Polite People," occupied the main administrative building in the capital of Crimea, Simferopol, hoisting Russian flags. On February 27 Sergey Aksenov, a local leader with the interesting nickname "Goblin" and head of the Russian Unity Party, was appointed head of the government of Crimea.

The referendum on joining Russia was held on March 14 under the vigilant eyes of the green and polite people. Ten days prior to that, Putin declared that Russia did not consider inclusion of Crimea as a separate part.[112] Before that, Russian defense minister Sergey Shoigu also denied the presence of Russian troops in Crimea, which Putin later refuted, admitting to the presence of the Russian military, which were "maintaining order."[113] During the meeting with the Department of Defense on December 19, 2014, Putin stated, "Russia, as always, will consistently defend its interests and sovereignty, will seek strengthening international stability, and will advocate for equal security for all states and peoples," which was achieved at the expense of the security and sovereignty of Ukraine and its people. Further, he thanked the Russian military leadership for "clear, discreet, targeted actions, for their courage and professionalism" during the Crimean referendum, which went contrary to the official Russian denialist policy at the beginning of the crisis.[114]

The denial of participation in the Ukrainian conflict extended to active military operations in the southeastern parts of the country populated predominantly by a Russian ethnic or linguistic majority. In the aftermath of Yanukovich's fleeing the country and the Crimean annexation, in April and May 2014, two cities—Lugansk (formerly Voroshilovgrad) and Donetsk—conducted their own referenda and declared their independence from Ukraine and announced the creation of the People's Republics, provoking the start of the Anti-Terrorist Operation from Kiev. After initial military actions, the conflict slowed down to a latent phase by September 2014, only to resume in January 2015. Russia continues to abstain from any participation on the side of the "volunteers," declaring that it only sends humanitarian cargo, and Ukrainian authorities continue to blame Russia for supporting the insurgency.[115]

Total casualties by November 2014, according to a UN report, had reached 4,300 military and civilian deaths, with an additional half-million refugees and internally displaced persons.[116]

With regard to the actual course of action prior to and after the referendum, as narrated by the Russian side, the most important description is offered by Igor Girkin (aka Strelkov), former minister of defense of the Donetsk People's Republic. In the TV talk show *Polit-Ring* aired on January 21, 2015, he admitted that he was in Crimea on February 21 to prepare the referendum—the very day that the fate of President Yanukovich was sealed. He also said, "No troops chose to side with the people [supporting the referendum]. . . . They continued subordination to Kiev and did not comply with the new government's orders. I did not see any support of the state representatives. . . . Members of parliament were all collected [for the referendum] by the militia who brought them all into the rooms so that they could vote. . . . Yes, I was one of the commanding officers of this militia." To the question "Why didn't you do the same in Donetsk and Lugansk?" he replied, "Because in the suburbs of Simferopol and in Sevastopol there were Russian soldiers and there was a hope that they would support us. So they did. Had the BTRs with Russian marines been stationed in Donetsk and Lugansk, trust me, everything would have been the same."[117] This confession of a high-ranking political and military officer of the irredentists directly implicates Russian in enticing the political change in Ukraine. Strelkov's statements mean that (a) he, together with the Russian troops, was in Crimea prior to the end of the Euromaidan and (b) that the Russian troops contributed to the forceful pro-Russian voting at the referendum. This also means that the decision to annex Crimea was made prior to Yankovich's escape: the soldiers and Strelkov were sent there "just in case" he was ousted. In fact, Yanukovich's fleeing the scene in Kiev turned out to be a blessing in disguise for Russian leadership, who used it as an excuse for getting involved in Crimea.

Two days after the referendum and based on its results, Russia officially incorporated the Republic of Crimea as a new administrative unit into Russia. The tangible result of this bloodless Anschluss was annexation of the irredentist Crimean Peninsula with its subsequent incorporation as a federal entity in the Russian Federation. The intangible results, however, have exceeded all possible expectations. Applying selective historical memory to the fact of handing Crimea over to the Ukrainian Soviet Socialist Republic in 1954, Putin motivated the annexation of Crimea by the illegality of Ukraine's possession of the peninsula. In his historical speech at the ceremony incorporating Crimea into Russia on March 18, 2014, Putin blamed the present situation on the now-extinct Soviet Union (the country whose collapse he once considered "the biggest geopolitical catastrophe of the twentieth century") and its nontransparent transfer of Crimea to Ukraine (which was a normalcy with the elite-led Politburo).

In his historical game-changing speech held on March 18, 2014, Putin declared, "In people's hearts and minds, Crimea has always been an inseparable part of Russia. This firm conviction is based on truth and justice and was passed from generation to generation, over time, under any circumstances, despite all the dramatic changes our country went through during the entire twentieth century."[118] Public opinion polls in the immediate aftermath of the Crimean annexation revealed sky-rocketing support of the ordinary Russian population for the actions of its government, both past and potential, and their president. When responding to a question on Russia's possible future annexation of the territories of the former Soviet Union, 58 percent of respondents said, "Russia has a right to this; it must protect our people." Even more so, the Crimean "operation" boosted the public morale of Russians who believed that the annexation of Crimea is evidence of Russia's "returning to its traditional role as a great power, and asserting its interests in the post-Soviet space."[119]

Annexation of Crimea brought several tangible and emotional benefits for Russia. According to Grigorii Vanin and Alexander Zhilin, "By the end of May [2014] Crimea should have become the central base of NATO in the region or . . . the stationary unsinkable aircraft carrier near the Russian fence. For that purpose, reinforcement works on the facilities had already been started on the peninsula to accommodate troops, headquarters, warehouses, and other infrastructures."[120] Russia thus feared that the new government of Ukraine, which was clearly pro-Western (pro-European and pro-American), would deny Russia the only military foothold on the Black Sea: Crimea and its peninsula. With them in hand, Russia possesses a strategic naval point that will allow it to control the flow of personnel and goods across the sea. As Paul Schwartz notes, "Operating from Sevastopol, the Black Sea Fleet provides Russia with the ability to project power in and around the Black Sea, while also serving as a potent symbol of Russian power. . . . The Black Sea Fleet provides Russia with substantial operational capability within the immediate area. . . . Sevastopol also provides the Russian navy with access to the Mediterranean and to the South Atlantic and Indian Oceans beyond."[121] The annexation of Crimea also bears serious mid- to long-term implications for European energy security because Russia can expand its energy carriers' cache and distribution networks. According to Frank Umbach, "It is . . . expected that Russia will claim large parts not just of Crimea's, but also of Ukraine's continental shelf and Exclusive Economic Zone (EEZ), which may seriously complicate the division of the Black Sea continental shelf and EEZs with Romania and Turkey."[122] Full possession of Sevastopol (prior to the annexation, Russia's Black Sea fleet was stationed there under a contract with the Ukrainian government) and Crimea, as a whole, would allow Russia to both boost its *velikoderzhavnost'* domestically and project its status abroad as a full-fledged naval power.

During his annual address to the Federal Assembly on December 4, 2014, Putin once again referred to the Ukrainian affair, but in a peculiar fashion. The matter was presented to the audience of Russian legislators as a part of returning to the historical Orthodox roots of the Russian nation: "It was thanks to this spiritual unity [in Crimea] that our forefathers for the first time and forevermore saw themselves as a united nation. All of this allows us to say that Crimea, the ancient Korsun or Chersonesus, and Sevastopol have invaluable civilizational and even sacral importance for Russia, like the Temple Mount in Jerusalem for the followers of Islam and Judaism. And this is how we will always consider it."[123] This part of the address bears several important implications for the future of Crimea within the Russian Federation, since it institutionalized the unilateral Russian vision of its own place in the world justified by divine revelation.

The stale conflict with no clear winner or loser in the southeast is characterized by many observers as a "hybrid war," which is "a mixture of classical warfare with irregular armed groups. A state . . . makes a deal with non-state actors—boyeviks, locals, other organizations—and officially denies any links with them. These actors can do what the state itself cannot."[124] Even though Russian troops appear from time to time in Ukraine, pictures from the battlegrounds posted to online social networks are detained by the Ukrainian military, the entry of the official military in the territory of the sovereign state is explained by the Russian officialdom as if they "have accidentally lost their way" and come to Ukraine by mistake.[125] For its part, Russia, on the highest level, mentions the international character of the conflict but, much in line with its political culture, with the reverse blame. Commenting on the escalation of violence in the region in January 2014, Putin directly accused NATO troops of fighting in Ukraine on the side of the government: "Mostly there are so-called voluntary nationalist battalions—not even an army—this Foreign Legion, in this case, the Foreign Legion of NATO, which is, of course, not pursuing the national interests of Ukraine."[126] In reality, however, the reverse is happening: Russian and foreign social media are flooded with pictures of ultra-right and ultra-left volunteers from Serbia, Spain, France, Chechnya, and other parts of Russia who are fighting against the regular Ukrainian troops.[127] The denial and reverse blame also extend to the tragic incident with the Malaysian Airways airplane MH 17, which was shot down in the skies over Donetsk with 298 people aboard on July 17, 2014.

Not only does Russia deny at every possible opportunity its involvement in the conflict but it blames the United States for instigating the conflict in Ukraine. The West, in the Russian political narratives, has intervened in Ukraine within the context of geopolitical confrontation against Russia led by America and aimed at destroying Russian statehood through Ukraine. A few examples fill the gaps in Russian policy toward the West, broadly defined. Deputy Foreign Minister Sergey Ryabkov's statement in relation to the Ukrainian conflict is notable from the point of view of Russia's aspiration to lead the anti-American movement around the world. According to the diplomat, "The U.S. desire to impose its will on the whole world and the sanctions will meet harsh resistance from Russia."[128] His boss Sergey Lavrov called Ukraine a "victim of Western politics": "The situation [in Ukraine] has exposed the continuing deep, systemic flaws in the existing architecture of the Euro-Atlantic area. The West took the course of 'vertical restructuring of mankind' under its (far from harmless) standards . . . aiming to expand their ownership of the geopolitical space without balancing the legitimate interests of all the peoples of Europe," meaning Russian interests in Ukraine.[129]

Specifically with reference to American support of the new Ukrainian government, Eurasianist Alexander Dugin gave the following explanation of the causes of the Ukrainian crisis: "The ultimate task [of the United States] was to tear all of Ukraine (along with Crimea) away from our country, to accelerate the processes of Eurasian integration; to roughly block Kremlin's claims on leadership in the multipolar world. All these are critical for Americans. . . . That is why Putin with his dreams of 'Great Russia' is an existential threat to them."[130] Russian politician Iskander Valitov was more blunt: "They [the West] are getting straight with us. Also, through Ukraine, dragging us into what they have done. . . . This is not a conflict between its western and eastern parts, and not a conflict between Russia and Ukraine. For twenty years the United States has been raising this vicious animal, the only purpose of which was to bite Russia. . . . This is an aggression carried out by an artificially operated puppet."[131] By pushing the blame for Ukraine onto the United States and the European Union, as well as anti-Russian sanctions, Russia desperately tries to justify its own actions as defensive (much in line with the "Just War" theoretical postulates) and claim it was forced by them to annex Crimea.[132]

The general public in Russia seems to share this viewpoint. In a poll conducted by the Levada Center in November 2014, 84 percent of respondents supported annexation of Crimea and 70 percent believed that the conflict was imposed on Russia by the United States and other Western countries.[133] Along the same lines, 78 percent think that Russia, by doing so, has not violated international law or any international treaties, and 66 percent do not care if the Western countries and Ukraine think so. In reality, however, it was Russia who broke international law with its annexation of Crimea. On December 5, 1994, the United States, Great Britain, the Russian Federation, and Ukraine concluded the Budapest Memorandum on Security Assurances. In exchange for Ukraine's giving up its nuclear arsenal, the parties pledged "to respect the independence and sovereignty and the existing borders of Ukraine . . . to refrain from the threat or use of force against the territorial integrity or political independence of Ukraine . . . [and] to refrain from economic coercion designed to subordinate to their own interest the exercise by Ukraine of the rights inherent in its sovereignty."[134] Naturally this agreement can be turned upside down to justify Russia's intervention in Ukraine as a response to its perception of U.S. and European actions as violating the memorandum by forcing Ukraine into their own geopolitical and economic wings. When asked at a press conference what the official position of Russia was with regard to its fulfillment (or lack thereof) of the terms of the Budapest Memorandum, Lavrov gave a very peculiar retort: "There are political obligations, including respect for the sovereignty, territorial integrity, and political independence of Ukraine. There are obligations to respect the result of the military coups [in Ukraine]."[135] That statement tells the international community (especially the OSCE) that Russia had a very "liberal" treatment of the international law and is committed to shaping it according to its likes or dislikes toward particular ruling regimes in a sovereign country, which it may or may not consider legitimate and may choose to intervene in the future.

Belarus: An Uneasy Partnership

Russia's relations with its other Slavic kin, Belarus, resembled that of a dysfunctional family, but were less volatile than with Ukraine. The name "Belarus," or "White Russia," as noted by Jan Zaprudnik, "originated in the twelfth century and initially designated various parts of northwestern Russia or Ukraine." Similar to Ukraine, Belarus had its first independent states of Polatsk, Turai, and Navahradak between the ninth and thirteenth centuries.[136] In later centuries, largely owing to the Mongol conquest of the Kievan Rus' in 1240, the lands populated by the Belarusian tribes were taken over first by the Grand Duchy of Lithuania and, later, in the sixteenth century, by the Polish-Lithuanian Commonwealth. The Commonwealth lasted until the late eighteenth century, when, as a result of the three partitions of Poland, according to Andrew Wilson, "Belarus was swallowed almost whole by the Romanov Empire," owing to the growing strength of tsarist Russia.[137]

With all the long history of Belarus, scholars stumble over multiple roadblocks in defining Belarusian identity: it is Russian, similar to Russian, or something else. Historically, its origins, as Serhii Plokhy notes, go back to the medieval times of "the Ruthenian identity that had previously developed in the Grand Duchy of Lithuania but failed to produce a distinct identity in modern times."[138] Among the possible reasons for the limbo of Belarusian identity was the systematic policy of Russification of tsarist rule. In the push to eradicate the national consciousness of the Belarusians, Nicolai I prohibited the use of the term "Belarusia" and renamed the land the "Northwestern Territory," simultaneously banning the use of Belarusian as a distinct language in the 1840s with the same purpose of identity denial to the Belarusians and cutting them off from the influence of Catholic Poland and Lithuania.[139] The Belarusian Soviet Socialist Republic was formed in 1918, marking an era of new communist governance. Russification was replaced by *korenizatsiya*, giving the Russian language the status of "second" language while Belarusian retained its official language status.[140] The manual on "Cultural Policy in the Byelorussian Soviet Socialist Republic," as quoted by David Marples, had the purpose of "introduc[ing] a 'Socialist attitude' among the population and [developing] the ideological base of the working class."[141] This was a significant milestone for Belarusian identity, which was "watered down" by the growing Soviet one.

The end of Soviet rule in Belarus brought along the phenomenon of Alexander Lukashenka, who is considered by many to be the last European dictator.[142] His heavy-handed autocratic governance replaced in 1994 the latent rule of Shushkevich and Hryb, the first post-Soviet heads of Belarus. Lukashenka, being against any opposition, according to Juri Čavusau, shut down 347 nongovernmental organizations between 2003 and 2005, while most of the remaining ones were forced to go underground or to retreat to the Baltic States.[143] Economically Belarus did not "get out" of the Soviet Union in complete shambles, unlike many other post-Soviet republics. The country kept most of its industrial potential intact and working, including oil refineries processing Russian oil and transporting it further to Europe; valuable natural resources processing, such as potash mines and metallurgical and chemical plants; and heavy industrial equipment factories, such as the Soviet giant MAZ truck factory and MZKT, manufacturing heavy military machinery. These industrial capabilities, together with most of the economic potential of the country, are controlled by Lukashenka and his loyal oligarchs who have good working relations with their counterparts in Russia.

Russia remains one of the main supporters of Belarus, economically and politically speaking. Strong historical and linguistic ties between the two countries stipulate their current good neighborly relationship. Lukashenka himself has often stated that "Belarus is Russia itself but with a stamp of quality."[144] Similarities between the leaders of the two countries in their domestic management styles (with Lukashenka being more of a hardliner) and their foreign policy (as in opposition to all things Western) bring the two countries together and create fertile preconditions for their peaceful cohabitation. Finally, exogenous factors, such as increased interest on the part of the international community in human rights and the state of civil society in the two countries, equally terrify Putin and Lukashenka at the prospects of the West exporting the "colored revolutions" into their respective countries.

Russian foreign policy in Belarus pursues several interconnected aims. First, it is in Russia's best interests to keep Belarus as its loyal and devout partner in its opposition against NATO. Political closeness between Russia and Belarus was institutionalized on a number of levels. On February 21, 1995, Russia and Belarus signed the "Treaty of Friendship, Good Neighborly Relations and Cooperation" and erased their common borders. Between 1996 and 1998 a number of agreements were reached that paved the way to their further integration. The crowning moment was on December 8, 1999, with the conclusion of the Union State Treaty that aimed at future harmonization of the political, economic, and cultural lives in Russia and Belarus. Both nations are traditionally stout anti-NATO actors with military cooperation treaties reinforcing defense partnerships.[145] On top of that, Belarus is constantly being portrayed domestically and internationally by its leadership as "the frontline against an expansionist NATO," which is very much in line with Russian's own views on Belarus as far as serving as the buffer zone between itself and NATO.[146]

From an economic perspective, there are, indeed, very close ties between the two countries, each of which is interested in mutual cooperation. Traditionally, Russia's share in the economy of Belarus has been very high. For example, in 2004 Russia's direct investments in Belarus had 23.5 percent of the total FDIs, which was explained by "the unity of territorial borders and the unity of the customs space."[147] In 2011, Russia had more than 75 percent of the FDIs in the economy of Belarus.[148] In 2012 the FDIs decreased by almost a quarter, but Russia's share was the highest at 46.7 percent.[149] For example, in 2009 Russia invested $4 billion in the Belarusian economy.[150] In 2011, Belarus became the sixth most attractive foreign investment location for the Russian capital.[151] That space was turned into the Customs Union during the summer of 2010, which makes trade between its members, including Belarus, "considerably easier and facilitates creation of joint enterprises and mutual investments."[152] In 2010, for example, according to the Belarus state information agency Belta, Russian investments in the Belarusian economy reached $6.555 billion, out of which direct investments amounted to $5.55 billion (an increase of 25.5 percent from the previous year).[153] With that, Russia owns large shares in many Belarusian strategic enterprises, such as "Beltrangas," the natural gas distribution company, 50 percent of which belongs to the Russian giant Gasprom.[154]

A separate part in Russia's economic policy in Belarus is the transit of oil and gas through the territory of the latter to European markets as a viable option for bypassing stubborn Ukraine. The transit routes have been in place since the Soviet Union coupled with the oil-refining business. According to Margarita Balmaceda, "Belarus . . . plays an important role in oil transit. Druzhba, the most important pipeline, transporting Russian oil to Europe, passes through Belarus. In 2004 about half of Russian oil exports . . . went through Belarus."[155] Besides, as she notes, "Belarus's oil refining capacity is comparable to Ukraine's. . . . Oil refined in Belarus is easier to export to the West than oil refined in Russia."[156] Although some minor quarrels arise from time to time between Russia and Belarus over ownership of the pipeline, Russia has significant leverage in the form of transit dollars that it threatens to withdraw.[157]

Keeping its good relations with Belarus would also allow Russia to strengthen and promote further integration processes within the post-Soviet space, which is another goal of its foreign policy toward Belarus. Interactions with Minsk would be a litmus indicator for the other members of the Customs and Eurasian Unions of what the future holds for them. A positive spirit would send attractive messages to existing and potential members of the post-Soviet integration processes of Moscow's true and benevolent intentions to act as a leader of the free union of sovereign states. Conversely, if these interactions seem uneasy for Belarus, as a lesser member of the tandem, especially leading to potential disruption of the Union State, this would deliver completely different and mostly negative messages to the members of Russia-dominated multilateral-cooperation frameworks.

The seemingly blissful road to further integration of Russia and Belarus is not without bumps. Although Belarusian identity as a middleman between Russia and Europe fits well within Russia's own plans for this country, Lukashenka's government has its own foreign policy, which causes uneasiness in Moscow. Belarus's approach to integration processes with Russia is based on a rational calculus of the pros and cons of balancing against the West. Although Minsk wants to keep its alliance with Russia, expecting clear benefits from economic cooperation, it still is not fully committed to severing links (mostly economic) with the European Union, which is a constant irritant for Russia. With all the difficulty of dealing with Europe and the recent worsening of relations with Russia over the possession of and control over Belaruskalii, one of the Belarusian industrial giants producing significant amounts of the world's potassium, Belarus is turning elsewhere for political and economic help.[158] The recent economic rapprochement with China (to the amount of $5.5 billion and another projected $30 billion) marked another round in the political games of Lukashenka with the rest of the world. By calling China "the global empire," "the leading power of the world," and "the world's center," Lukashenka is sending clear political messages both to the West and to Russia that he is keeping his options open and actively looking for a patron.[159]

The same abstinence is seen with the question of closer integration with Russia, where Belarus, even if it does want to play second fiddle, wants to choose its own notes while doing so. It would welcome increased involvement of Russia in the post-Soviet integration as well as in its own economy on its own terms, knowing that it is perhaps the closest modern strategic ally of Russia, in the post-Soviet space in general and in the Western direction in particular. Loyalty costs; in the case of Belarus's riding Russia's economic current, this cost is "between $7bn and $12bn annually. Periodic threats from the Belarusian president to withdraw from the Eurasian project are usually met with further Russian largesse. For example, Moscow has promised Minsk $2bn in low-interest loans, apparently to reward Mr. Lukashenka for softening his demands on sovereignty."[160] Blackmail seems to be working fine in the matter of the international orientation of Belarus as well as strengthening the feelings of sovereignty among its own citizens.

Russia is also irritated at the unwillingness of Belarus to follow its foreign policy in its broad strokes. Lukashenka proved to be a consistent supporter of Georgian sovereignty and territorial integrity and has repeatedly refused to recognize the de facto or de jure results of Russian intervention in Abkhazia and South Ossetia. The situation repeated with Crimea: commenting on the situation in Ukraine, Lukashenka recalled the Budapest Memorandum and declared, "No state should violate the territorial integrity or take a part of another state, which was guaranteed" by the Budapest Memorandum.[161] At the same time, he blamed Ukraine for "asking for" what has been coming to it from Russia after the Euromaidan and their desires to deploy NATO troops there. The Russian response was asymmetrical, as usual: the ups and downs of the anti-Belarusian campaign in Russia closely followed the Belarusian stubbornness. Recently, however, Lukashenka's stance toward NATO has taken an interesting turn. In February 2015 he declared willingness to cooperate with NATO: "As a sovereign state we are open to a constructive dialogue with NATO on the principles of parity and transparency. We have many common issues; we collaborate on what fully are within Belarusian interests."[162]

The targets for Russian anti-Belarusian propaganda is always easy to find, whether it be shadowy deals and political persecution in Belarus, or omnipresent corruption and political pressure, or even character assassination against Lukashenka due to his lavish lifestyle and the shadowy gains of his pocket oligarchs.[163] One of the most notable cases was a movie, *Godfather*, which was supposedly a political blockbuster in Russia. In it the pro-governmental Russian TV station NTV talked about mysterious disappearances and assassinations of political opponents to the regime and also quoted Lukashenka's statements on Hitler's regime being a model for his own governance.[164] Interestingly enough, the movie was made in 2010, and the events it covers go back to 1999; this shows the level of political manipulation and control between the two "brotherly" nations. In return, the Belarusian state channel ONT had a special program that criticized Putin's propaganda drive in a Russian car and openly called him "a fool on the road" in reference to his test-driving a new Lada.[165] The most recent invective circulated in Russian political mainstream mass media was news of alleged growing anti-Russian sentiments in Belarus for its attempts to rewrite the history of World War II, the biggest no-no in Russia's convex identity construction of the European liberators.[166]

Such a sensitive treatment of Belarusian domestic politics in Russia gives Lukashenka some leeway in dealing with the latter and a strong bargaining point. In January 2013, when referring to the Eurasian Union's integration processes, he declared, "Perhaps Russia would like to accelerate some steps, become even more radical. But neither Kazakhstan nor Belarus will do so out of the blue. . . . We see the landmarks of the world economy, and we are directed to them, of course. But we have our own interests."[167] Lukashenka also stresses that his country would insist on "equal standing, like in the EU" between all the members of the Union, particularly referring to the prospects of common currency within the Eurasian Union.[168] Driven by those self-interests, Belarus reinstated customs control with Russia in December 2014, which many consider to be the first sign of the Eurasian Union's failure from inside.[169]

An additional headache for Moscow is the politicization of Russian involvement in Belarus by its leadership in order to consolidate support for its domestic clientele for its "strong" stance against Russia, as well as send a message of independence in its foreign policy decisions to the international public. According to Alexandra Koval'chuk, high tides and ebbs in Russia-Belarus relations are synchronized by the election rounds in the two countries, but especially so in Belarus. "By studying the specifics of Russian-Belarusian relations, there are cycles of tension between Moscow and Minsk. These tensions are directly dependent on the election calendar, because usually before the elections both sides are more likely to compromise due to the popularity in both countries of the idea of integrating Russia and Belarus."[170] The politics and economy in Russian-Belarusian relations are entangled to a point when Lukashenka's domestic political support closely correlates with the fluctuation of Russian's financial backing. According to Balmaceda, the Russian oil giant "Lukoil supported Lukashenka's 2001 reelection campaign in exchange for promises that Naftan [the major Belarusian state-owned oil company] would be privatized."[171] So-called rent relations with Russia where it pays for Belarusian royalty are used to support the government at a level sufficient to ensure the loyalty of the populace. Both presidents seem to be very keen on keeping power and are using the issues of bilateral political agreement for personal benefit.

The sanctions imposed by Western governments against Russia coupled with the Russian embargo on European commodities created additional economic sources for Belarus to raise its voice firmly. Belarusian businesses either increased their production of substitutive goods for the Russian market or reexported European food products to Russia under local Belarusian labels. The products vary from "Mink oyster" to "Gomel salmon" and Polish cream, which suddenly became Belarusian by the label.[172] Overall, for ten months in 2014, most of which were marked by the sanctions climate, Belarusian entrepreneurs had increased exports to Russia by 15 percent, most of which are, in fact, reexported food products from Europe and elsewhere.[173] This is happening due to the nonexistent borders between the two countries due to the Union State and the Customs Union, notwithstanding Russian bans on foreign products with Belarusian origins.

Economic tensions between Russia and Belarus were quite common even before the European sanctions. Just as Belarus uses its geopolitical location to blackmail Russia and to extort additional finances by threatening to swing between it and Europe, Russia does not hesitate to apply "soft power" tools to tame its Western brother. There are numerous examples of the economic sticks used to bring Belarus to order, for instance, the concurrent "Dairy Wars" between the two countries in 2009, when Russia banned up to five hundred types of dairy products in June. Another type of punishment for Belarusian pigheadedness are the "Gas Wars" over the cost for transit of Russian gas, which entail double standards for payments coming from the Russian and Belarusian sides and mutual accusations of dirty business practices.

Politically, Belarus is very sensitive to the Ukrainian situation and does not feel fully safe with the growth of Russian nationalism. Discussing foreign threats to Belarusian statehood at the National Security Council meeting, Lukashenka named Russia alongside its traditional NATO sources of menace: "The behavior of our eastern brother cannot but alarm. . . . [W]hat is the reason for such a policy of the Russian Federation toward Belarus? . . . Everyone should understand that nobody can talk with our country from a position of strength. We are not a huge state, do not have the power of nuclear weapons, but our army is efficient enough to respond to any threat."[174] Commenting earlier on the growing rumors of discrimination against ethnic Russians and Russian speakers, Lukashenka said, "We will fight for our country against any invaders. And there is another thing: if Putin comes here, nobody knows whose side the [Belarus] Russians will take."[175] Coming from one of the most loyal Russian adherents of anti-Western politics, such statements should alarm Moscow. This is no mere game that Belarus is playing to quell signs of discontent in the domestic electorate. Lukashenka is seriously troubled by the growing entrenchments of the "Russian world" cultivated at the highest echelons of power in Moscow.

Paralyzing Limbo in Moldova

Like many of the former Soviet republics, Moldova became a part of the tsarist empire as a result of its expansionist war against the Ottoman empire in 1815, when annexation was approved by the Congress of Vienna.[176] The influence of its eastern neighbor on political and cultural life in the newly gained land, as the pro-Russian view explains, was framed by "conducting advanced European thought, especially educational concepts, under the banners of which the irreconcilable struggle with medieval obscurantism took place."[177] The Russian "enlightenment" mission in Moldova, including bringing the Russian language, went far beyond the nominal annexation of the land and also impacted the public administration and economic stance of a land that had been under prolonged Ottoman influence.

Prior to the transfer of the land under Russia's wings, the Moldova principality included part of modern-day Romania. A part of that possession, called at that time Bessarabia, was proclaimed a republic after the October Revolution and then showed an aspiration to join Romania. The Molotov-Ribbentrop Pact of 1939 placed Moldova under Soviet control. The Romanian government, in coalition with Nazi Germany, gained control over Moldova in 1941 and kept it until 1944 when it lost the province to the Soviet Union.[178] Similar to other Soviet republics, Moldova experienced the influence of *Russification*, only in this case it meant turning its script from Latin into Cyrillic and changing the name of the language from Romanian into "Moldovan." Steven Roper adds to the *korenizatsiya* policy "a new mythology [that] was created in which Soviet scholars spoke of a distinctive Moldovan language that was a foundation of distinctive non-Romanian Moldovan national identity."[179] These steps followed the general Soviet stance to create the new *Homo sovieticus* on the shambles of previously existing national identities destroyed by the Soviets in the first place.

At the end of the 1980s, seeing pro-Romanian forces gaining momentum in Moldova, predominantly Russian-speaking groups feared that it might eventually join Romania, which went against their desire to preserve the Soviet lifestyle and the political, cultural, and economic orientation toward Moscow. The situation escalated in August 1989 with adoption of the language law by Chisinau, the capital of Moldova, which brought back the initial name of the language and its Latin script.[180] Political self-awareness aggravated previously dormant interethnic tensions within Moldovan society under Soviet rule, where people of different ethnic backgrounds were divided, according to Nikolay Bibilunga, into the castes of "locals," "title nations," "immigrants," "newcomers," and "occupants."[181] When the new country was faced with the choice of defining its future geopolitical orientation, these tensions boiled down to open ethnic hatred. N. I. Kharitonova notes that during pro-independent rallies, anti-Russian and anti-communist slogans were frequently heard, such as "Russians, get out!" "Down with the Russian empire!" "Down with the communists!" and "Suitcase—Railroad Station—Russia!"[182] In June 1990 the Moldova Soviet Socialist Republic declared independence; in September their example was followed in Transdniestria, where the Moldovan Transdniestrian Soviet Socialist Republic was an entity equal to Moldova within the USSR. This decision was promptly annulled by the Supreme Soviet in Moldova. In response, in September 1990 the pro-Russian population on the left bank of the Dniester River proclaimed independence from Moldova and took the name of the Transdniestria

Moldovan Republic. The ethnic composition of the region is of interest: Nataliya Nechayeva-Yuriychuk brings up the figures of 33.5 percent ethnic Moldovans, 30 percent Ukrainians, and 30 percent Russians.[183] This makes the conflict in Moldova not a typical interethnic strive but more like an ideological-geopolitical confrontation.

After small-scale skirmishes in November 1990 with minimal casualties, the leadership of Transdniestria signed a petition to join the Soviet Union and decided to take over governmental buildings in nearby cities. This culminated in a large-scale military confrontation from March through July 1992 between the separatists, allegedly supported by the Russian Fourteenth Army, who provided weapons and ammunition, and the Moldovan state military.[184] To resolve the conflict, the CIS heads decided to engage in conflict resolution using the CIS peacekeeping force, consisting of the neighboring Russian, Ukrainian, Byelorussian, Romanian, and Bulgarian forces, which never materialized with its initial design.

Matters now turned to bilateral negotiation between Moldova and Russia, which agreed to stop the conflict with simultaneous respect for the territorial integrity of Moldova but to allow the Transdniestrians to decide their allegiance in case Moldova decided to join Romania in the future. The Joint Control Commission (JCC), composed of the Moldovan, Russian, and Transdniestrian representatives (with the balance of power skewed 2:1 against Moldova) was established in July 1992. The JCC also provided for the deployment of a joint peacekeeping force, again outnumbering the Moldovans: six battalions from Russia, three battalions from Transdniestria, and only three from Moldova.[185] In 2005 the JCC was joined by the U.S. and EU troops to provide for the impartial monitoring of the situation.[186] In 2011 the new peacekeeping/negotiation format was defined: 5 + 2, where the first five actors were Moldova, Transdniestria, Ukraine, Russia, and OSCE, and the last two members—the United States and the EU—had observer status.

Four years after its independence, in 1994, Moldova acceded to the Commonwealth of Independent States. This move, however, did not help the country to solve its internal conflict with the breakaway region of Transdniestria, populated mainly by non-Moldovan minorities. So far the participation of Russian troops on the Transdniestrian side has not been properly documented. The Fourteenth Soviet Army deployed in Moldova during the Soviet Union was split between the right and left banks of the Dniester River, with the part on the left bank integrating into the Russian forces. After several unsuccessful negotiations, Russia agreed on the principles of removal of its troops from Transdniestria but insisted on prior political settlement of the matter. According to the OSCE, the Russian presence in Moldova amounts to five thousand troops, "extremely well-armed . . . and the only armored force in Moldova capable of offensive action."[187] These forces are viewed from diametrically opposing standpoints in Chisinau and Tiraspol, the capital of Transdniestria. Whereas in the former they are considered occupants, for the latter they represent the only viable force keeping peace and preventing possible further aggression on the part of the Moldovan government.

The official role of Russia was that of an unprejudiced and neutral mediator, although with its support to the Transdniestrian regime, traditional sympathies toward Russian-speaking "compatriots," as well as its imbalanced presence in the peacekeeping forces, it was hard to hold up a veil of transparency and impartiality.[188] In 1997 the sides to the conflict signed the so-called Moscow Memorandum, which laid down the framework for normalization. The problem preventing the resolution of the conflict is a discrepancy of ideas regarding the future of the Moldovan state. According to Tsukanova, "Moldova understands the single territorial integrity of a unitary state under the 'common state' provision together with giving broad autonomy to Transdniestria. The authorities in Tiraspol are in favor of an 'equal subjectivity' clause in a single but composite state, with the establishment of their own customs space, creation of the delimitation commission, and demarcation of Transnistria."[189] These diametrically opposing views have been reiterated over and over again during the conflict-resolution process, which prevents its ultimate settlement.

In 2003 Moscow tried to seal the deal with Chisinau and proposed the document known as the Kozak Memorandum after Putin's inner-circle politician Dmitry Kozak. According to the proposed frameworks of agreement, Moldova would become a federal state retaining its breakaway part on equal footing with the center and with the continuous presence of Russian troops.[190] Essentially the memorandum, eventually rejected by the Moldovan government, meant defeat for the Moldovan aim of reuniting the country, because it neither solved the matter of the preservation of Moldovan statehood nor ended the presence of Russian peacekeepers in Transdniestria.

The aspirations of the two sides are in 180-degree opposition while applying the same postulates of international law. Moldova approaches the conflict from the point of view of the integrity of its borders and state sovereignty. For Transdniestria the same principles apply, where their thoughts on separation and independence coincide with irredentism and joining Russia. There were several referenda held in Transdniestria: in 1991 the majority of people voted for independence. In response to the referendum in Moldova proper to join Romania or not (most of the participants voted for sovereignty), in 1994 Transdniestria held its own where they overwhelmingly voted for joining the CIS as a sovereign state.[191] In 1995 Transdniestria also voted to keep the Russian troops in place, and at the last referendum in 2006, most of them also chose independence over being a part of Moldova—a possible response to Putin's earlier argument made "if Kosovo could gain its independence from Russia's ally Serbia as the western powers wanted, then Abkhazia and South Ossetia should also be granted independent statehood."[192]

The most recent move was made in April 2014 by the Transdniestrian foreign minister and vice prime minister, Nina Shtanki, who declared, "The fact that Transdniestria wants to be a part of Russia is not a decision after a Maidan, but solves the problems after the Maidan and is the will of the people expressed in the referendum of 2006. Besides, it is no secret that we are a part of the 'Russian world.' We insist on it: historically, mentally, and legally."[193] Her Russian colleague Lavrov added fuel to the Moldovan fire in his comment on the influence of NATO in the region: "The Chisinau authorities are clearly trying to move in an undemocratic direction. . . . Transdniestria has the right to decide about their future on their own, if Moldova does not retain nonaligned status. And we will defend this basis."[194] The message sent to the government in Chisinau and the European and American side was clear: in case of further closeness of Moldova with the EU or NATO, it would meet the same fate as Ukraine.

Back in 1999 at the OSCE summit in Istanbul, Moscow pledged to remove its military base from Transdniestria by 2002. This caused a harshly negative reaction in the region, which is extremely pro-Russian and anti-Western. The Russian Duma supported the multiple petitions of the Transdniestrian because "the unresolved conflict and NATO expansion demanded preservation of the Russian military presence [in Transdniestria]. Transdniestria, which, unlike the Republic of Moldova, sides with Russia and the CIS, needs firm guarantees of its future special status within the single Moldovan state."[195] A part of promoting cultural links with the former, in 2001 Russia lobbied the treaty, giving a "prominent status" to the Russian language in a country where the majority of the population (about 65 percent) speaks Romanian, 14 percent are Ukrainians, another 13 percent are Russians, and 8 percent are from other nations.[196] To many, especially the pro-Romanian forces, this was considered a "creeping" neo-Russification in Moldova, leading to numerous actions of protest.[197]

Preventing and or even strongly inhibiting Moldova's closeness with the Alliance is one of the strategic objectives of Russia's foreign policy toward the country in question. Russia needs non-allied Moldova, much as it needs non-allied Ukraine, to use as buffer zones between itself and NATO. Russia is also very sensitive to political processes in Moldova, since a loyal government there would mean fewer problems for Russian foreign policy in Europe. A soft power tool that Russia could use, especially under the conditions of the sanctions and self-embargo of 2014, is Moldova's energy dependence on gas and oil from Russia. Currently only 3 percent of Moldova's energy use is from local sources, and gas consumption is at 65 percent of total energy supplies.[198] Russian Gazprom is both the gas supplier and, as in Belarus, the owner of 50 percent of MoldovaGaz, the national gas company.

Under such conditions, using gas supplies as leverage in Moscow is a cheap alternative to military pressure in Transdniestria, especially seeing the closeness of Moldova as it signed and immediately ratified the Association Agreement with the European Union in July 2014. As V. V. Ogneva and L. A. Brysyakina write, "As a proper response to attempts to diversify supply routes of fuel in the EU bypassing Russia and the policy of double standards against Russian energy correction, it could act asymmetrically [in Moldova] in favor of the eastern and southern directions."[199] Moldova could well become another target of Russian energy politics in the case of Europe's continuous efforts to look for alternative sources of energy. Seeing Russian energy politics in another country that is being used as a transit zone in Europe, Moldova started to receive gas supplies from Romania in August 2014 through the Iasi-Ungheni pipeline. The new energy route would not completely eliminate its dependence on Russian gas, since it would provide only 5 percent of the total needs of Moldova, but it is a step in the direction of its energy independence, which could be potentially punishable by Moscow.[200]

The legal presence of its troops as a part of the peacekeeping forces allows it to keep its finger on the pulse of events and also to control local officials of the unrecognized breakaway region from any possible rapprochement with Moldova proper. As history has shown, recognition of a part of another country as independent, as in the cases of Abkhazia and South Ossetia, is the first step toward their eventual incorporation with Russia. At the present stage, however, Russia is content with the ambiguous status of Transdniestria because it allows her to have the upper hand over the government in Chisinau with minimal headache of having to engage the West, as is the case with its involvement in Ukraine. Interesting developments appeared in January 2015 when Moscow suddenly stopped economic support for Transdniestria: for the first time since its de facto independence, Moscow refused donations of $100 million that Tiraspol was expecting for pension remittances and other social payments. Some experts suggest this could be a move Moscow is making to show to the West its goodwill in Moldova in exchange for its acceptance of the presence of Crimea within Russia.[201] This was the first sign of some positive developments in the country, which, however, had to be tested by actual steps Moscow would (or would not) take to ease tensions.

Neighbors to the South

The Caucasian land is inextricably linked to the Russian convex identity construct, dominated by imperial views of stretching across the seas. The relationship with three southern post-Soviet republics—Georgia, Armenia, and Azerbaijan—is characterized by diverse levels of animosity among themselves, on the one hand, and between them and Russia, on the other. Similar to the western direction of its foreign policy, Russia feels threatened in the south by the growing might of Turkey. For its part, Turkey is showing signs of becoming one of the key political and economic actors in the Middle East and Southern Caucasus regions, and it is one of the most active NATO members. It hosts two U.S. military bases: the first one is the Incirlik Air Base, which is the home of "the most forward deployed land-based American aircraft[s] in the Eastern Mediterranean that are capable of launching a tactical nuclear strike in the event of conflict in the region."[202] The second base is located on the Aegean seashore town of Izmir, which allows the United States to strategically cover the Aegean, Black, and Mediterranean.

The South Caucasus has traditionally occupied a significant place in Russia's vital national interests and its identity. Caucasus had always some sort of a mysteriously romantic attraction for Russia: its greatest poets (Pushkin, Lermontov, to name a few) wrote their best pieces here; the Caucasians, as they are called in Russia, were instrumental for the Russian and Soviet empires as their statesmen and leaders, the most prominent of which being Stalin and Beria. During the initial Russian territorial expansion, Moscow turned its eyes to the region for its strategic location. Beginning in the sixteenth century, with varying degrees of success, Russia fought twelve wars against the Ottoman empire for access to the Black Sea. It was during the Crimean

War of 1853–56 that Crimea eventually fell within the borders of the Russian empire.

With the collapse of the Soviet Union, Russia lost the majority of Soviet ports connecting to Europe and beyond. The marine foreign trade of Russia became costly and somewhat limited. This was due to the nature of its seaports, located mainly in the cold north and far east of the country, and only operating a few months out of a year, with the exception of St. Petersburg by the Baltic Sea and Novorossiysk by the Black Sea. Georgian Abkhazia, now separate from it and under the Russian protectorate, alone offers the latter cost-effective year-round transit access to the Black Sea and the Mediterranean for commercial trade due to its mild subtropical climate. Abkhazia has five marine outposts that can be used as marine ports (Sokhumi, Gagra, Gudauta, Pitsunda, and Ochamchira). During the Soviet Union numerous sea resorts were major destination points for summer holidays. Even after more than a decade of no development, due to its exceptional location Abkhazia remains highly attractive to potential foreign investment.

Here, too, similar to the western direction, several scenarios are possible with only one constant assumption: Russia will not give up the idea of keeping the region within its geopolitical sphere of interest. This can be achieved in a number of ways. First, the least costly method that Russia has already used has proven successful: its short and small-scale interventions in the Georgian regions of Abkhazia and South Ossetia brought the desired result of destabilizing the domestic climate in this rapidly westernizing country with possible reversal of the previous democratic gains. The same can be said about Russian foreign policy toward Armenia and Azerbaijan: Russia could continue playing these two countries against each other by promising full political and military support to the former while selling millions worth of military equipment to the latter.

The second scenario entails more active participation of Russia in the domestic political processes of the three countries while keeping its political presence to a minimum. This option is also possible, especially taking into account the close integration of at least one of them

(Armenia) within the Russian sociopolitical and economic fields, as well as strategic connections with Baku over the transportation of Caspian oil. The Georgian case is the hardest nut to crack for Russia, since there are no societal groups, unlike the Abkhazians and Ossetians, which could, while living in Georgia proper, transmit Russian policies there.

The third way for Russian foreign policy to proceed is the costliest of all but, if successful, would bring the highest dividends: direct interventions, as in 2008 in Georgia, or hybrid war, as in Ukraine, in the three countries with their ultimate incorporation, like Crimea, as a part of the Russian state's administrative lands. This option could be possible, taking into account the presence of the Russian military base in Gyumri, Armenia, which could act as the hub for prospective military actions. However, it is also the least likely one because it lacks common borders with Russia. Also, Armenia does not have continuous, uninterrupted access to the aforementioned base. Last, but not the least, none of the three countries has significantly large ethnic Russian or Russian-speaking populations that would be used by Russia as the bases for claiming its right over the land they occupy.

"Strange" Wars in Georgia

Located "at a major commercial crossroads and among several power neighbors" (not all of them quite friendly) and right in the middle of the Great Silk Road, a halfway point between the East and the West, Georgia had its identity and culture historically exposed to the influences of diverse cultures, religions, languages, and the mostly authoritarian regimes of regional powers.[203] The Russian reign for Georgia started in 1783, when its eastern kingdom willingly joined the Russian empire followed by its western royal domain's forceful incorporation in 1810.[204] The end of the Russian empire gave a glimpse of hope of sovereignty to the Georgian polity, which soon established its modern independent state in 1918. In reality, however, this was a short intermission between the two empires—the Russian one and that of the Soviet Union in the making. In 1921, Georgia, along with its immediate Caucasian neighbors, Armenia and Azerbaijan, was conquered by the Russian military and incorporated into the Transcaucasian Socialist Federative Republic.[205] Fifteen years later, this entity dissolved with its members becoming separate but not sovereign republics within the Soviet Union.

Like other ethnic republics, Georgian society fell victim to the process of cultural homogenization of the Soviet nations. The pinnacle of this endeavor, as rendered by its mastermind, Joseph Stalin, was "the flourishing of the cultures, which are national in form and socialist in content, under the dictatorship of the proletariat in one country with the purpose of merging them into a single socialist (both in form and content) culture with a common language."[206] *Korenizatsiya* was prevalent in Georgia: according to J. W. R. Parsons, "Soviet policy has given active encouragement to the *rastsvet*, or flourishing, of Georgian culture (as of that of the other nationalities) in the belief that by providing for both the socioeconomic development of the republics and for political and cultural equality, attachment to national differences would, by itself, subside."[207] As a result, neither the Georgian language nor the Georgian orthodoxy was stifled by early Soviet authorities. Perhaps this is due to the fact that the Georgian language and culture were so alien to the Slavic language and culture that complete Russification efforts were not rationally justifiable. Besides, like what happened in other post-Russian imperial nations, the Georgian elite had already been quite tightly integrated within the Russian political environment since the country joined the Russian empire in eighteenth and nineteenth centuries, which made the process of socialization between these nations easy. Last but not least is the personality of Joseph Stalin, an ethnic Georgian, *quis fabricates* of Soviet policy on nationalities, who was strict with the Georgian establishment in political matters but was somewhat lenient toward the expression of their national self-consciousness.[208] In 1978, however, the Russian language was elevated to the level of official language along with Georgian, which was vehemently rejected by the Georgian establishment.

The first official Russian interventions in the conflicts in Georgia took place under the aegis of peacekeeping missions with conflict resolution mechanisms after the military clashes of the early 1990s between the Georgian nation and its Abkhazian and South Ossetian minorities. In some respects, the dynamics of the conflicts in Georgia followed that of the Transdniestrian confrontation. The tensions started from the so-called War of Laws, when in the late 1980s and early 1990s the national center in the capital of Tbilisi limited the rights and competencies of the autonomous entities of Abkhazia and South Ossetia. The legal confrontation culminated in a full-scale interethnic security dilemma when, according to A. G. Zdravomislov, the "imperial components of Georgian policies toward Abkhazians stimulated Abkhazian nationalism, which gave an impetus to Georgian nationalism."[209] The conflict in South Ossetia erupted in December 1990 and lasted for a year and a half, resulting in approximately three thousand battle deaths, complete economic devastation of the region, severance of mountainous transport routes connecting Georgia with Russia, and the de facto separation of the region.[210] In June 1992 Georgian president Shevardnadze signed a cease-fire agreement with Russia as a guarantor of peace and security, which established a peacekeeping organ in the form of the Joint Control Commission (JCC), composed of representatives from Georgia, South Ossetia, North Ossetia, and Russia.[211] From its very birth, the JCC brought forth the phenomenon of a "credible commitment problem" between Georgians facing their three opposing, potentially unfriendly, and untrustworthy counterparts.[212]

The warfare in Abkhazia started in 1992 soon after the end of military activities in South Ossetia. Under the pretext of protection from looting of the rail-cargo transit to Russia, Georgian troops entered Abkhazia in August 1992 and occupied its capital, Sokhumi. After receiving considerable assistance from mercenaries from the Northern Caucasus and the Baltic States, and Cossacks from the southern provinces of Russia, and military support from Russian military bases in Abkhazia, Abkhazians managed to retake Sokhumi in September 1993. The conflict in Abkhazia with the participation of unrecognized paramilitaries and the inability (or, rather, unwillingness) of Russia to seal firmly its southern borders was, in many respects, a dry run for the hybrid war in Ukraine in 2014. The conflict resulted in 20,000 deaths on both sides and more than 250,000 Georgian internally displaced persons.[213] To avoid a large-scale confrontation with Russia, Shevardnadze had to sign another cease-fire agreement with Russia in July 1993 and bring his country into the CIS to avoid further Russian aggression. Under the agreement, CIS peacekeeper troops, formed exclusively by the Russian military, arrived in Abkhazia and became guarantors of de facto peace.

The relative calm around neither-war-nor-peace situations in both de facto states, which seemed to satisfy Russia and Georgia as well as the authorities of the breakaway regions, was shaken by the 2003 coup against Shevardnadze. In November 2003, as a result of parliamentary elections orchestrated by Shevardnadze's corrupt political circles (and called by the OSCE a "spectacular fraud"), the progressive forces, led by young Georgian pro-American politician Mikheil Saakashvili, flooded the streets of Tbilisi and other major Georgian cities in what became known as the bloodless "Rose Revolution."[214] Saakashvili accused Shevardnadze of a massive manipulation of votes; his followers stormed Parliament, bringing democracy to Georgia with a single red rose. Since then the color adjective of the Georgia revolution has become a terrifying synonym in Russia of a forceful change of government in post-Soviet states orchestrated from outside.

In summer 2008 the frozen conflict reerupted in South Ossetia with Russia's official and full-scale military intervention in support of the South Ossetian minority.[215] Firing from the South Ossetian side of the border culminated at dusk on August 7 as a response to a unilateral cease-fire declared by Georgian president Saakashvili.[216] Georgian troops tasked with "restoring constitutional order" and bringing peace to the whole territory of Georgia started occupying village after village in South Ossetia, predominantly populated by ethnic Georgians. By the end of the next day Georgians were practically in control of the whole territory of South Ossetia, but not for long. Even before the renewed military clashes, South Ossetian authorities had been seeking Russian military help in protecting its citizens, which the majority of South Ossetians were. The assistance was soon provided in the form of Russian peacekeepers and "the unlawful presence of regular Russian military units [the Fifty-Eighth Army], that is to say, units not attached to the Russian peacekeeping contingent, in South Ossetia before the outbreak of the conflict" and volunteers from Northern Ossetia and other North Caucasian autonomies of Russia.[217] Russia entered the scene of the conflict with a peacekeeping agenda but also with its own wording—what Russian president Dmitri Medvedev called "enforcing peace upon Georgia" and Russia ambassador to NATO Dmitry Rogozin called "asking NATO not to meddle in this affair."[218]

Two days from the start of the operation, Georgian forces were pushed away from South Ossetia, suffering heavy losses. The Russian military continued its offensive toward Georgia proper, bombing its military facilities and destroying military airports adjacent to the conflicted territory and beyond it. De facto peace was reinstated on August 12 after a six-point peace agreement was signed between Medvedev and Saakashvili with mediation by French president Nicolas Sarkozy. This plan gave Moscow the opportunity to save face after the Georgian campaign and to conduct the "system restore" to the initial pre-intervention point in time.

> This plan opened up good diplomatic and political prospects for Russia. Had Moscow implemented this plan, Russia would have emerged as a responsible and reasonable player on the international arena. It would have helped to minimize the damage done to Moscow's relations with the West and to improve its international moral standing. At the same time, Moscow could demonstrate that it had the military capacity and political will to be a dominant force in the post-Soviet space and that it could defend its interests by all available means, including force.[219]

None of these milestones, however, except for perhaps the last one, was in Russia's agenda in its interventions in Georgia. As noted *ex post factum* from the Ukrainian interventions, the operations in Georgia were the precursors and first signs of a larger plan to regain influence and territories in the former Soviet Union.

As a result of continuous pressure from the EU, a group of 340 military observers was deployed in the fall of 2008 to monitor the situation in the conflict zone. The five-day war, according to South Ossetian sources, brought the deaths of 1,692 people and wounded 1,500 more.[220] Russian sources give similar figures—1,600 casualties among peaceful residents of South Ossetia; 74 Russian military dead, including 11 peacekeepers; and 171 wounded.[221] In four months Russian casualty estimates changed dramatically. According to the report of the Investigation Committee of the General Prosecutor's Office issued at the end of December 2008, 48 Russian military and 162 Ossetian civilians died during the war.[222] Georgian casualties reached 413, among which 169 were military personnel and 228 were civilians.[223]According to the UNHCR, 192,000 Georgian nationals fled from South Ossetia and nearby Georgian settlements.[224]

The conflict also "unfroze" in Abkhazia in August 2008, almost at the same time as the military actions in South Ossetia. Abkhazian forces were in full mobilization along the border during South Ossetian fighting and feared no attacks, since Georgia was clearly not prepared to wage wars on two fronts simultaneously. Inspired by the victorious advancement of Russian troops in South Ossetia, Abkhazian forces seized the momentum and launched a successful attack on the Georgian troops in the Upper Kodori region, the only part of Abkhazia previously controlled by Georgians. Not long after the cessation of hostilities in South Ossetia, Russia legally institutionalized the results of its intervention by officially recognizing South Ossetia and Abkhazia as new independent states and members of the international community. Currently South Ossetia and Abkhazia are strengthening their political gains by seeking further military assistance from and political alliance with Russia with the establishment of military bases on their territories and aspiring to join the Commonwealth of Russia and Belarus.

There are a number of reasons for Russia's actions in Georgia in the 1990s and in 2008. Changes in the Georgian government after the Rose Revolution, especially with increased interest in it on the part of the United States and European countries, drew several red flags for Moscow. Saakashvili's open pro-Western political orientation was seen as endangering the status quo for Russian influence in Georgia and in the South Caucasus region as a whole. Besides, small but uncorrupted

Georgia was a constant eyesore for Russia, which could not boast having the same levels of civil society. Therefore, it contained a dangerous example for the Russian population, who, seeing the successes of Saakashvili, could demand the same from Putin.

North Ossetia, which was a part of Russia, also felt alarmed seeing what Niklas Nilsson called the increased "zeal for territorial integrity"[225] coming from Tbilisi. The first harbinger that the new Georgian authorities would wish to bring back the refugees was the abolition of the black market of stolen cars right in between Georgia proper and South Ossetia, used by corrupt officials on both sides as a major source of income (for Georgia) and goods (for South Ossetia).[226] This was followed by large-scale social development programs and construction launched by pro-Georgian Ossetians in the Georgia-controlled territories adjoining the de facto state.[227] Most of that was accomplished by American and European grant and credit monies. This was also a negative sign for Moscow, which viewed Georgia as a thoroughfare, where the entry of the West meant its automatic departure.

Georgia's new leadership's foreign policy directions were equally alarming. Among the external reasons for the Russian interventions, in Jim Nichol's interpretation, are "coercing Georgia to accept Russian conditions on the status of the separatist regions, to relinquish its aspirations to join NATO, and to depose Saakashvili as president. In addition, Russia may have wanted to 'punish' the West for recognizing Kosovo's independence, for seeking to integrate Soviet successor states . . . into Western institutions such as the EU and NATO, and for developing oil and gas pipeline routes that bypass Russia."[228] Saakashvili and "the new generation of politicians swung defiantly to the West, striving for NATO and EU membership" with strong domestic support in Georgia: in 2008, 68.9 percent of the population wanted to join NATO.[229] As early as 2003 in his interviews with Russian newspaper *Komsomol'skaya Pravda*, Saakashvili declared, "As to our policy toward NATO, it is historically justified. Russia is absent; and the vacuum in the region was immediately filled by other countries. That is why the only guarantor of the security of my country today is the United States and the West."[230]

He further warned that any intervention into Georgian affairs would be broadcast by CNN. The Russian side did not hide their highly negative assessment of possible moves of Georgia toward closer integration with NATO: President Medvedev was quoted telling Saakashvili at the CIS summit in St. Petersburg that "Georgia's accession to NATO would increase bloodshed in South Ossetia and Abkhazia."[231] By this statement, Russia warned Georgia far ahead of the conflict of its potential reaction to Georgia's western drift.

Further along this line, the deployment of NATO radar installations in Eastern Europe was another irritant for Russia. One of the most outspoken critics of NATO, Rogozin, declared, "We will, of course, build a system that would overcome and suppress any antimissile defense. If anyone thinks that we can be surrounded by a missile fence, let them recall: under Peter [the Great] we 'cut through the window' to Europe, and now we will crush the whole wall if someone tries to isolate us or tries to bring us to our knees."[232] From this perspective, not only are the two currently proposed directions (Russia versus NATO) impossible to be pursued simultaneously, but they are also oxymoronic by definition.

There is a potentially valid circumstantial explanation for Russia's aggression against Georgia: personal dislike between the leaders. According to Tatiana Mikhailova, Putin "seems less tolerant of other kinds of jokes about his person, the most memorable example being his reaction to Mikheil Saakashvili's alleged 'Liliputin' (Lilliputian) joke, referring to Putin's diminutive stature, which some interpreted as one of the triggers of the Russian-Georgian war."[233] In the aftermath of the war, in his private conversation with French president Sarkozy, Putin said in rage, "I am going to hang Saakashvili by the balls."[234] Apparently this animosity started from the first meeting between the two presidents, when Putin allegedly warned Saakashvili not to make any hostile steps in South Ossetia and Abkhazia, which was disregarded by the Georgian leadership as their subsequent steps in the western direction show.[235]

Another major point in Russia's wish to keep Georgia in check was their disruption of energy supplies to Europe from the Caspian. The oil and gas deposits hidden there are significant: according to the January

2007 report of the U.S. Energy Information Administration, the volumes of proven and probable reserves are 48 billion barrels of oil and 292 trillion cubic feet of natural gas.[236] The Baku-Tbilisi-Supsa and Baku-Tbilisi-Ceyhan oil pipelines and the Baku-Tbilisi-Erzerum gas pipeline, operated by British Petroleum with strong support from Europe and the United States, connected the Caspian Sea with Europe via Turkey, bypassing Russia. This step was taken with the sole purpose of providing alternative supplies of energy to Europe and curtailing Russia's overall political influence in the region.

The war and high susceptibility to failure of the pipelines as a result of any successful attack on them caused serious concern for their Western owners and lobbyists. British Petroleum's leadership decreased the volume of oil passing through Georgia twice before the conflict and even shut down its pipelines during August 2008.[237] As a result of the war in South Ossetia and having been seriously concerned with the fate of its own oil revenues, Azerbaijan started negotiations with Russia to double the volume of oil transit from the Caspian via the northern route. According to some estimates, complete transfer of the current oil to the Baku-Novorossiysk would bring Russia $1.3 million per month.[238] Worth rather a small amount, this rerouting coupled with the transit of other energy carriers would leave the control over oil flows in the hands of Moscow and almost completely out of the reach of the West. According to some experts, the energy cause of the war was to show the West the volatile nature of the southern routes by swaggering and even applying hard power tools.[239] The hostilities in Georgia in 2008 revealed how vulnerable oil transit is when the Russian side bombed the territories adjacent to the route of the Caspian pipelines.

After the war, Russia's subsequent policy attention toward Georgia slowly subsided. As a result of the parliamentary election in Georgia, the pro-Russian government of Bidzina Ivanishvili, an ethnic Georgian tycoon from Russia, came to power. Saakashvili, who could not run for the third time, had to give his chair away to Giorgi Margvelashvili, Ivanishvili's candidate. This somewhat changed the mutually hostile attitudes between the two countries. The signs of "thawing" relations with Russia are mostly directed at gaining popular support at home by reviving the economic and cultural nostalgia of older generations of Georgians with Russia. The new government is taking some steps to reestablish political, economic, and cultural relations with Russia, which is not quite well received by a considerable part of the Georgian population.[240] Quite recently, Ivanishvili promised to follow another geopolitical course: toward integration with NATO, while blaming Georgian society for a "low level of political culture."[241] This move seems quite out of touch with the real geopolitical situation in the region.

Russia should not be expected to get into any more hot water with Georgia. The only new development that would strengthen Russia's upper hand in South Ossetia is the new legislative initiative prepared for ratification by both sides in 2015. According to the unofficial document, the sides agree "to coordinate their foreign efforts which involve mutual interests . . . in various fields of cooperation, informing each other of the actions committed in this regard, as well as closely cooperating in promoting peace, stability, and security in the Caucasus region." Russia and South Ossetia also agree to "form a common defense and security space" for which the "military forces and security agencies of the Republic of South Ossetia are included in military forces and security agencies of the Russian Federation."[242] This means another step toward incorporating this region into Russia, which is not surprising in light of Russia's similar, more aggressive steps in Ukraine.

Other than that, no major redrafting of the already shrunken Georgian map is on the Russian agenda for their short-term involvement in the South Caucasus. For starters, Georgia is not making any more or less viable efforts to retrieve its lost lands by force. Nor it is in an economic or military position to do so. No additional territorial encroachments should be expected on the part of Russia, either. To put it bluntly, Georgia has run out of territories that Russia can lay claim to—at least for the time being. There are no other parts of Georgia, except for Abkhazia and South Ossetia, which have been tightly integrated with Russia legally (through common Russian citizenship) and morally (through their external homelands), that can entice future Russian military involvement. On the other side of the equation are the United States and the European Union, neither of which is committed to taking up the daunting task of intervening on behalf of Georgia in the matters of Abkhazian and South Ossetian. As Danilov noted, "Relations [between the EU and Russia after the 2008 war] normalized quite quickly. The European Union has recognized that it is not willing to translate its discord with the Kremlin's policy on Georgia to the whole range of Russian-European relations and change its course and previously formulated approaches."[243] In simple terms, as long as Georgia, with its newly less pro-American government, does not take a blatantly anti-Russian stance, it should presume a less hostile stance from Russia. In longer perspective, however, the situation may change for the worse for Georgia: Russia is repeatedly proving to be an unpredictable international player.

"Estranged Partnership" with Armenia

On January 12 Valery Permyakov, a soldier from the Russian 102nd Military Base in Gyumri, Armenia, voluntarily left his guard duty, took up his service weapon, and left in the direction of the city. This was a typical move of a deserter. In his own words, Permyakov was heading toward the border with Turkey, located some 15 km (9 miles) from the city center and only 6 km (3.7 miles) from the closest Russian military installation. For some inexplicable reason, however, he ended up in the city's suburbs that lay in a different direction. On his own accounts, Permyakov got thirsty, entered one of the houses, and killed a whole family surnamed Avetisyan, who were awakened by a noise at their door. Seven lives were taken, including a two-year-old and her six-month-old brother, whom Permyakov slaughtered with his bayonet after his AK-47 jammed.[244] After the gruesome mass murder, he changed clothes, leaving his military uniform and boots with his name and rank in the house, and headed this time in the right direction. Permyakov was soon detained by Russian border guards who control the Armenian-Turkish border and brought back to the base.

The news rocked the Armenian public, usually very loyal to everything Russian. In the country heavily dependent on the Russian economic and security presence, Russians are welcome as allies and viable deterrents against possible Turkish aggression. The ensuing anti-Russian demonstrations were something truly out of the ordinary. People flooded the streets of Gyumri and organized mass actions of protests against the Russian embassy and the consulate, demanding the surrender of Permyakov and his prosecution in accordance with Armenian law. They called for the complete removal of the Russian base and its installations from Armenia.

This tragedy was not, however, the only one in otherwise cloudless relations between Russia and its Southern Caucasian ally. On April 14, 1999, two drunken Russian soldiers from the base in Gyumri randomly opened fire in the local market, killing two Armenians and wounding another two. They were detained and sentenced to fifteen and fourteen years in Armenian prison. One of the soldiers spent eleven years and the other only two before they were transferred without proper bureaucratic records to the Russian side. In 2003, four Armenian citizens illegally entered the base: two of them were killed and the other two wounded. Ten years later, two teenagers were blown up by Russian explosive ordinance on the territory of the shooting range belonging to the base.[245] In none of these incidents were the culprits duly prosecuted by the Armenian legislative system.

The reaction of Russia, officially from Moscow and by the public in general, was peculiar. For several days, Russian mass media had been ignoring this potentially explosive case between the two nations, fueling rumors in the Armenian mainstream that Russia was not going to turn Permyakov over to Armenian justice. This option went against the letter and the spirit of the agreement between Russia and Armenia related to the legal issues regarding the presence of the Russian military in the host country. According to its Article 4, "In cases of crimes and other offenses committed by members of the Russian military base and their family members on the territory of the Republic of Armenia, the legislation of the Republic of Armenia applies with its competent authorities."[246] The next article, however, states that Armenian law does not apply in the case of crimes committed within the base. These clauses came to a legal crux, since Permyakov is both a deserter (by Russian law) and a criminal suspect (by Armenian law). Eventually a shaky compromise was reached: Permyakov will be tried in Armenia but by a Russian court.[247] The deal, however, is not acceptable to many, and the forthcoming trial will possibly bring along additional disturbances in Armenia.

There were several allusions in the official Russian mass media to American influence in the tragedy. The Internet video project Pravda (Truth) brought up some expert opinion on the suspicious nature of the quickly organized protests: "The killing of the Avetisyan family became the reason for inciting anti-Russian sentiment in one of the countries most friendly to us. It is also suspicious that the American mass media reacted so quickly to the crime in Gyumri. In an hour after the crime, the *Washington Post* issued detailed information about the events in Armenia, where journalists kept pointing out the nationality of the killer."[248] The top Russian newsman, Dmitry Kiselev, could not resist dragging in the American factor: "He [Permyakov] is a native of the Chita region, an adherent of one of the many Protestant churches based in the United States."[249] This statement was meant to redirect the attention of the public of both countries away from the origins, citizenship, and mission of the perpetrator of the hideous crime to the "real" root: the United States. The nationalistic part of the general public is also unhappy: almost immediately several social media groups have sprung up supporting Permyakov, one of which under the title "Anti-Maidan Armenia" claims, "We, the Russian patriots, will not allow our enemies to win the information war and say our decisive 'NO!' to the attempts of the West and its cronies to blacken the name of the Russian Knight Valery Permyakov."[250] Everywhere, the United States is seen and presented by Russian political culture as the source of all evil, great or small, that comes to Russia from any direction.

The reaction of the Russian side toward this matter in Armenia shows the highly asymmetric nature of the relationship between the two countries, heavily skewed in favor of the former. There is a largely accepted view in the Russian political mainstream that Armenia "owes" its existence to Russia. Russia's acquisition of historically Armenian lands happened as a result of multiple bloody wars against the eastern and western Muslim empires. Persia and Turkey owned different parts of Armenia starting in the sixth century when the country lost its independence to outside invaders. The nineteenth century marked Russian rule over the Armenian provinces. As a result of the Russian-Persian War (1828), Russia took control over eastern Armenia. The Treaty of Adrianopole (1829) ended one of numerous Russian-Turkish wars on the Caucasus and the Black Sea, when the Ottoman empire ceded the parts of its land populated by the majority of Christian Armenians. Half a century and another war with Turkey later, the Treaty of San Stefano (1878) augmented Russia's possessions of Armenian land by incorporating Artvin, Kars, Beyazit, and other minor cities held by the Armenians, into the Russian empire. Article 16 of the Treaty focused on the situation with the Armenian minority still living in the rest of Turkey, forcing the former to conduct social and economic reforms and to protect the Armenian population from the attacks of Kurdish and Circassian nomads. The Congress of Berlin (1829) reaffirmed Russian control over these territories and stressed the Armenian question. This land remained in the Russian empire until World War I, from which conflict Russia withdrew as a result of the Bolshevik revolt.

After Russian troops had left, the newly created Democratic Republic of Armenia was immediately attacked by Turkey and lost the short war. Except for the Ararat Valley, Aragats, a major part of Echmiadzin, Kars, Olti, and Ardagan were taken back by Turkey. When Germany, Turkey's ally, lost World War I and surrendered to the terms of the Armistice of Mudros (1918), the Turkish army rolled back from the better part of these territories. The Treaty of Sèvres (1920), following World War I, transferred Erzerum, Bitlis, Van, and the port of Trabzon to the Armenian Republic, also known as Wilsonian Armenia. The beginning of the twentieth century marked a time of domestic turmoil in Ottoman Turkey. The new Turkish leadership under Mustafa Kemal Ataturk denounced the terms of Sèvres as illegitimately concluded by the extinct Ottoman empire. Another Turkish-Armenian war was waged, which was also won by Turkey. The Armenian Republic was forced to become part of the Soviet Union to retain even the smallest portion of land. In March 1921 Turkish representatives met with Bolsheviks in Moscow and agreed to keep the Armenian-populated land within its modern-day borders. It is noteworthy that the Moscow Agreement was signed without the presence of the Armenian side. Finally, the Treaty of Kars (1921), now with representatives from Armenia, reaffirmed the Moscow Agreement.

Russia had a significant input in the nation-building processes: it saved Christian Armenia from complete annihilation by hostile Muslim forces. Overall, but for Russia, according to Christopher Walker, "it is perfectly possible that the word Armenia would have henceforth denoted only an antique geographical term."[251] That said, Russia took that action not based on its altruistic nature but out of its own best interest: it was an ongoing battle to dominate the Caucasus with its ultimate access to the Black and Caspian Seas, and Russia left it victorious.

Like Georgia, Armenia had its couple of years of independent intermission between the two empires from 1918 until 1920, after which it became another member of the Transcaucasian SFSR, and since 1936 it became part of the Soviet Union. The Soviet years extended the severe Russification processes implemented in Armenia by the Russian/Soviet imperial government. aAs Hooman Peimani states, "In the 1880s, Armenian parish schools were closed and replaced by Russian-language schools, and the Armenian language was suppressed."[252] The ethnic suppression was overwhelming: Armenian last names acquired the typical-*ov/ova* ending to sound more Russian (as the last name of this book's author testifies). But that was not enough: the Armenian language was changed to create a new Soviet identity. The fact is that the Armenian nation became divided along ideological lines when the land became Soviet.

In order to separate Soviet Armenians from the "corrupting influence" of the West, Soviet language architects designed a whole new language: Eastern Armenian. Ulrich Ammon describes the process as "active language reform [that was attempted], in particular, in the fields of word formation and terminology building. A series of orthographic reforms resulted in a break with tradition and widened the distance between the

Eastern and Western variants. Ideological considerations led the Eastern variant of Armenian to being considered as 'Armenian' par excellence, and the very existence of a Western Armenian literary language was denied."[253] The later Soviet years, according to Mark Malkasian, saw an acceleration of the Russification process, "particularly after Stalin began to stress in the mid-1930s the importance of Russian as the lingua franca of the USSR."[254] The Russian language was omnipresent in Armenian culture; it was, in fact, considered a *mauvais ton* to enroll children in the Armenian national schools, since the Russian-language ones promised better chances for them to get into universities and institutes once they graduate.

Armenia's Soviet political life, too, was heavily infused with reverence for the Russian spirit. Like his Georgian colleague, long-term Armenian communist leader Karen Demirchyan (murdered at the Armenian Parliament in 1999) praised the historical Russian inputs into the Armenian future: "Blessed be the sacred hour when Russians set foot on our soil!"[255] It all changed after independence in 1991, when Armenia reversed the externally imposed Russification into "back to the roots" policies. Jasmine Dum-Tragut claims, "The first years of Armenian independence were characterized by 'De-Russification' and 'Re-Armenization' in a wide range of former Russian domains, such as public administration, education, and military."[256] Many Russian schools were closed down, and the use of the Russian language severely decreased, also due to the Language Law of Armenia of 1993.

This was not well received in Russia. When invited to an Armenian TV show on the cultural ties between that country and Russia, a highly controversial Russian journalist and the head of the government-sponsored foreign propaganda tool *Russia Today* warned Armenia of serious security consequences if it did not grant the Russian language an official status. Kiselev declared, "Russia is the guarantor of Armenia's security, but the Russian language is not widespread in Armenia. . . . You have banished Russian from Armenia. That means you have banished Russia from Armenia. . . . Let's talk honestly. It is in Armenia's interests to reinstate Russian."[257] What saved the country from the fate met by

Moldova and Georgia was its ethnic composition. During Soviet times, Armenia was called "the mono-ethnic republic," since the majority of its population were ethnic Armenians.

Independence from the Soviet Union for Armenia started with the conflict in Nagorno-Karabakh. This was one of the first signs of the USSR's slowly loosening its grip on domestic politics and of its inability to quench the primordial ethnic grievances that had been in place long before its existence. The roots of the conflict go back to ancient ages when the currently disputed "Black Garden" (this is its combined translation from Turkish-Armenian) was also the battleground between various nations, including modern-day Armenia and Azerbaijan.[258]

In 1924, on the wave of sovietization, the region was transferred to Azerbaijan to placate Turkey, which communists hoped to convert to their ideology. As the U.S. Library of Congress country study explains, "The Soviet Union created the Nagorno-Karabakh Autonomous Region within Azerbaijan in 1924, when over 94 percent of the region's population was Armenian. . . . As the Azerbaijani population grew, the Karabakh Armenians chafed under discriminatory rule, and by 1960 hostilities had begun between the two populations of the region."[259] Interethnic settings where a part of a nation is estranged from its core and encapsulated in another nation's territory were the "time bomb," as Ronald Suni described, in Stalin's politics of nationalities: "National self-determination to the point of separatism had been enshrined in a constitutional guarantee of a right of secession from the union, a time bomb that lay dormant through the years of Stalinism, only to explode with the Gorbachev reforms."[260] This way Soviet autonomies represented "a perceived and essential relationship to a real, i.e., historically recognized, territory or to a homeland to which they can only aspire."[261] The Soviet Union was already incapable of standing for the old social contract: new realities demanded change, which in most similar cases (in Georgia and in Moldova) ended in bloody conflicts.

Ethnic enclaves all over the Soviet Union, just as in Nagorno-Karabakh, created grave security problems for the ethnic groups, who by the late years of the Soviet Union found themselves sitting on a gunpowder keg with a lit wick.[262] Tensions started escalating in 1988 when Perestroika and Glasnost allowed for nationalist sentiments to be raised and to remind their respective kin who came to their lands first. This led to massive demonstrations on both sides, advocating for ethnic sovereignty and political independence from Moscow. After the collapse of the Soviet Union, the Armenian leadership of Nagorno-Karabakh Autonomous Oblast' (region) followed the Azerbaijani republican center and, likewise, declared independence from Baku, its capital. After severe fighting in 1994, Russia and Kyrgyzstan tried to broker a cease-fire agreement but failed to establish a peacekeeping force due to chronic disagreements between the parties.[263] According to Belfer Center's research, by 1994 the conflict had "left more than 30,000 dead and created more than a million refugees—more than 800,000 Azerbaijanis and 300,000 Armenians."[264] The CIS peacekeepers were never deployed in the region because Baku refused to ratify the Bishkek Agreement on establishing the peacekeeping force, fearing that the Russians stationed in Nagorno-Karabakh would support Christian Armenians over Muslim Azerbaijanis. As Schnabel stated, "Although Russian efforts to arrange for deployment of Russian peacekeepers failed, the amount of pressure exercised on Azerbaijan to accede to Russian troops in Nagorno-Karabakh suggests that Russia actively pursued a prominent role as stabilizer and hegemon in the context of this conflict."[265] In this case, which was not the worst outcome of all, Russia managed to maintain its presence in the region with minimal costs to itself.

Russia's involvement in Armenia began with its independence. Russia wanted to keep the historical linkages between the two Christian nations of the Caucasus, clearly seeing the advantages of this political cohabitation in the face of the NATO threat coming from Turkey. Moscow was also concerned with Georgia's slow drift toward the West and wanted to ensure its extended political, economic, and military presence in the region. At the same time, Russia had to approach the interethnic tensions between Armenia and Azerbaijan very carefully and not upset the latter with which it also had strong economic ties. With regard to the Nagorno-Karagakh conflict, as Ronald Donaldson et al.

believed, "Russia used [it] . . . to exert influence over both countries. Moscow played little role in sparking the initial dispute, but it has sought to monopolize the mediation and peacekeeping efforts to settle the conflict."[266] Thus its alleged neutrality jeopardized its standing with both belligerents, who could clearly see what was going on across the border with regard to Russian participation.

The Russian contribution to fueling the Nagorno-Karabakh was dubious from the very start. At the beginning of the 1990s there was complete chaos in Russia proper with regard to nearly all aspects or parts of its society, including the military. The strict control of its defense structures, for which the USSR was well known, vanished in the first years after the collapse. If the center still managed to show some signs of discipline, the further the Russian regiments were from Moscow the more lax the attitudes of the local commanders became. According to Rajan Menon, "The disarray in the Soviet armed forces led soldiers from units in the south Caucasus . . . to sell arms to the warring parties and to join the fighting on both sides—out of conviction or as mercenaries."[267] In a way, it was a strange form of participation where Russian troops stationed in the former Soviet republics developed friendly and sometimes even family links with local populations by marrying the locals. When conflict struck, they naturally supported their friends and family. This was also the case during the early stages of the conflicts in Georgia. Fariz Ismailzade and Kevin Rosner corroborate, "Russia actively supplied weapons, military and technical assistance to both Armenia and Azerbaijan in order to deepen each state's dependence on Russia. . . . The military assistance was provided at the state level and through corrupt local military officers. Although Moscow was interested in weakening both states, its primarily objective was to maintain its military presence in the region"—an adaptation of an old Roman "divide and conquer" policy to the multiethnic Caucasian realities.[268]

Current Russian foreign policy in Armenia is multifaceted and multidimensional. In the energy sector, Russia has undertaken the role of provider for energy security in Armenia. During the conflict with Azerbaijan, Armenia was blocked from all sides except for Iran, with which

Armenia has traditionally good neighborly relations. Russia was the only supplier of natural gas to the country. Domestic distribution capacities in Armenia also belong to Russia: 80 percent of shares of the national company ArmRosGazprom belong to the Gazprom, which since 2006 has owned an Armenian heat power plant. The Russian Inter RAO EES manages the Metsamor nuclear plant, the only one in the Caucasus, and also owns the electricity distribution networks in Armenia.[269] Possession of both production and distribution lines of energy was what got the South Stream project hacked by the European Union at the end of 2014, but which under the conditions of absence of any other sources puts the other countries in highly dependent positions toward Russia.

The economic components of Russian foreign policy include retaining prevalent leverage in most of the economic sectors in Armenia. The Russian giant RZhD—Russian Railroads' subsidiary—manages Armenian Railroads for a thirty-year term starting in 2008. There are significant shares of Russian capital in the Armenian banking sector, represented by VTB, ArExImBank (a part of the Gazprombank), and other smaller entities. Russian cellular companies also hold considerable shares of the mobile service providers' market. Russia has consistently hit the top list of trade partners of Armenia. According to the data collected by the Armenian National Statistical Service, in 2011 trade turnover between Russia and Armenia was $1.1 billion. Russia, with its 16.7 percent, is the most important destination for Armenian exports, and the same stands true for imports at 21.5 percent.[270]

From geopolitical and military perspectives, Russia's role in the Nagorno-Karabakh War was connected with "Russian attempts to cement its military presence in Armenia, and preventing interventions of Turkey and Iran" in its own Caucasian backyard.[271] A significant long-term objective is to keep Russia's interest in controlling Caspian Sea oil and energy reserves. Russia has business interests in the Azerbaijani companies that cannot go unnoticed in Armenia. For instance, the Russian company Lukoil holds 10 percent of Shah-Deniz gas deposits.[272] Currently there are three routes used to transport Caspian oil to European markets: the northern Baku-Novorossiysk through Russia and two southern ones, Baku-Supsa and Baku-Tbilisi-Ceyhan, both through Georgia. None of them crosses Armenia, the shortest and the most efficient route; however, having a Russian military presence in Armenia in the form of its 102nd Military Base has guaranteed the constant threat of fast military deployment for nearby nations in case Russia needs to protect or even damage the pipelines, if need be.

Russia has another form of leverage on Armenia: institutional. Armenia is an active member of the CIS and the CSTO, and in 2015 it joined the Customs Union with Russia, with which it has no common borders. From a geopolitical perspective, as Michael Croissant claims, the CSTO defense treaty played the role of a viable deterrent, since "a Turkish attack on Armenia would have been treated as an attack on Russia, and since Turkey is bound to the United States and Western Europe by similar terms under the North Atlantic Treaty, the stage would have been set theoretically for a conflict between NATO and Russia."[273] As a consequence of Armenia's joining the CSTO in 1992, much worse regional and possibly global confrontation was prevented with the accession of Azerbaijan a year later. The CSTO agreement bound the hands of the states in their aggressive intents, but it did not cover intrastate conflicts, of which Nagorno-Karabakh is a hybrid example. Thus having Russia bound to defend Armenia had positive and negative aspects, especially when it came to further economic integration with the former.

The hard power intimidation exercised by Russia proved the only way of persuading this, perhaps, most loyal friend, who initially refused to join the Customs Union in 2013. "We do not want to choose between friends—we want to have as many friends as possible," stated Armenian president Serzh Sargsyan at the EU Eastern Partnership summit in April 2014. This supposedly ecumenical message met the cold shoulder of Russian maximalism. It took Putin's one visit to Azerbaijan and his promises to expand military trade with them that forced Armenia to hastily join the Union. Even when superpower appeal is included as a noble aim of foreign policy, it is still achieved by coercion. Armenian refusal to sign the Association Agreement with Europe was essentially a big leap backward to its previous Soviet-style subordination to

Russia. For Armenia, joining the Customs Union with Russia, according to Portnikov, was "the first stage of the collapse of Armenian statehood because Russia does not need an independent Armenia. . . . Russia wants . . . Armenia to become a part of the Russian empire, as it was essentially until 1991."[274] Not only is Russia making a back-to-the-Soviet-future move in its foreign policy. It is also trying to drag its former Soviet entourage back together.

"Oil-Based Partnership" with Azerbaijan

Azerbaijan is the last country in the scope of the southern regional interests of Russia. Historically, it was a part of different empires and had experienced marvelous mixes of various cultures, ranging from Byzantine, Caucasian Albanian, Arab, Turkish, Mongol, and Persian. Linguistically and culturally, Azerbaijan has strong connections with Turkey, which communist rule attempted to break. Russia conquered the region in the early nineteenth century as a result of one of its numerous wars with Persia. Here, too, as with the Georgians and Armenians, Russian rule strived to eradicate signs of national self-awareness in the Azeri nation due to its cross-border links with Turkey and Persia, potentially dangerous neighbors for Russia. Audrey Alstadt comments, "Russian control, with its Christianization and Russification policies and discriminatory laws, was pervasive and obvious. The Russian state strove to intrude even into spheres it could not directly control, such as religion and culture. Yet this pressure rarely led to Russification. The Azerbaijan Turks' cultural inheritance . . . was of greater antiquity. . . . Adoption of Russian culture was regarded by many as a retrograde step."[275] This process also entailed a transformation of the written language: the traditionally used Arabic script was replaced by Latin in the second and third decades of the twentieth century, and then by Cyrillic until 1991, when Azerbaijan gained independence and reversed to Latin.[276]

The early years of independence for Azerbaijan after the collapse of the Soviet Union were marked by the bloody conflict in Nagorno-Karabakh, which it lost to the Armenian minority, together with other land comprising, by Thomas de Waal's estimates, 14 percent of its internationally recognized territory.[277] At this point, Azerbaijan is struggling hard to regain the lost land and to use international pressure as well as small-scale military skirmishes along the borders controlled by the Armenian side.

Since the first exploration for oil in the Caspian Sea, this part of the Caucasus fell within the regional and geopolitical interests of different nations. After the collapse of the Russian empire, Azerbaijan, like the other two Caucasian nations, had a brief period of independence from 1918 to 1920, which was toppled by the Soviets, who were seeking access to oil. The Caspian Sea oil reserves attracted the young Soviet Russia like a magnet, causing it to intervene militarily and forcefully nip Azerbaijani independence in the bud. Beryl Williams wrote, "Lenin had urged the taking of Azerbaijan, with its vital oil reserves. 'It is extremely essential that we should take Baku,' he wrote."[278] Nasib Nassibli quotes Lenin after the sovietization of Azerbaijan was completed: "We all know that our industries stood idle because of lack of fuel. . . . [N]ow we control the basis for an economy capable of supporting our industries."[279] It was, therefore, not surprising that among its Caucasian counterparts, Azerbaijan was the first state to become Soviet in 1920.

Not only Russia, however, was vitally interested in controlling the flows of energy resources from the Caspian Sea. Even prior to sovietization, Caucasian geopolitics was already in full swing: the British were deployed in Baku to secure Caspian oil. After their withdrawal in 1919, the Soviets acted quickly. During World War II, Baku was one of the strategic targets of Nazi Germany. According to Emmanuel Karagiannis, "Hitler was determined to conquer Azerbaijan from the beginning of the war because the interruption of Azerbaijani oil supplies on any large scale could possibly result in the collapse of the Soviet war effort. Moreover, Hitler was convinced that the Third Reich would be self-sufficient within its own borders, and thus invulnerable."[280] During the Cold War Azerbaijan was within the Soviet Union, which largely took the variable of oil off the international agenda.

The most important aspect in bilateral Russian-Azeri relations is the process of delimitation of the Caspian Sea shelf and the transit of Caspian oil to European markets. By the U.S. Energy Information Administration's estimation, Caspian energy reserves amount to "48 billion barrels of oil and 292 trillion cubic feet of natural gas in proved and probable reserves in the Caspian basins. Almost 75 percent of oil and 67 percent of natural gas reserves are located within 100 miles of the coast."[281] Russia is interested in common usage of the shelf while Azerbaijan demanded its split between the parties.[282] In 1993 Russia created three joint-stock companies—LUKOil, Surgutneftegaz, and Yukos—which split the Soviet oil monopoly, which was engaged in the Caspian Sea region. Foreign actors also started entering the market: ExxonMobil, BP, and Chevron have extraction contracts with Azerbaijan.

With multiple interests present in the Caspian, the region has become a geopolitical battleground. According to Farid Guliyev and Nozima Akhrarkhodjaeva, "The West has promoted transportation projects that would carry Caspian energy bypassing the Russian territory, such as the BTC, whereas Russia has used its power to keep almost all Central Asian energy exports under control and to prevent any major shift in Central Asian energy exports."[283] By the end of the 1990s, Russia had a monopoly over the transit of Azerbaijani oil to Europe through numerous oil and gas pipelines. The monopoly starting eroding in the 2000s with the development of several energy projects connecting the Caspian Sea with Europe beyond Russia's reach. Several pipelines were constructed in addition to the initial Baku-Novorossiysk in the 2000s, including the South Caucasus Gas Pipeline (also known as Baku-Tbilisi-Erzerum, with 10 percent of shares belonging to the Russian Lukoil), the Baku-Tbilisi-Ceyhan (BTC, with no Russian participation), and Baku-Supsa pipelines (BS, also without Russia), which started delivering Azerbaijani and Kazakh Caspian energy sources to European markets.[284] Russia does have its own resources in the Caspian: "There are sizable oil and gas deposits under development in the Russian offshore section of the Caspian Sea. For example, in the Lukoil-operated Yuri Korcharin oil and gas field, discovered in 2000, production started in 2010 and is expected to plateau at 50 kb/d and the large Vladimir Filanovskoye field, discovered in 2005, which may produce as much as 210 kb/d after 2015–16."[285] Having both the production capacities and the distribution facilities of oil and gas would turn Russia into the real monopolist in the region and significantly endanger the European Union's own energy security.

From political and military standpoints, Azerbaijan is a member of the CIS, although it left the CSTO in 1999. One of the main reasons why Azerbaijan decided not to continue its participation in the military treaty organization was its perception of Russia as an interested party in the Nagorno-Karabakh conflict on the side of Armenia. "Russia, as the founder and main sponsor of the CST, did not seek to find some incentive to keep Azerbaijan within the organization. Instead, it acted as if it were hurt, accusing Baku of refusing to cooperate in the military sphere. In despair, Azerbaijan . . . started more and more turning toward the West in matters of military cooperation," says Niyazi Niyazov.[286] At the end of 2009, CSTO leadership repeated its attempts to bring Azerbaijan in, but the latter refused until "Armenia is acknowledged as an aggressor state by the member states of this organization."[287] Apart from this bump in relations with the CSTO, there are no sizable benefits Azerbaijan can reap by joining this organization, since no resumption of fire by the Armenian side is foreseeable (after all, they got what they wanted and even more). Nor does Baku plan to resume large-scale hostilities in Nagorno-Karabakh, out of fears of Armenia's enacting Article 4 of the CST.

From geopolitical considerations, the Azerbaijani government also abstained from closer economic and political integration with Russia, declining to sign the Customs Union agreement. In a poll conducted by the Eurasian Development Bank in 2012, only 38 percent of Azerbaijani respondents considered the Customs Union a positive development.[288] Azerbaijani diplomatic games look especially perturbing to Russia taking into account the cultural closeness of the former with Turkey, Russia's long-term rival in the region. There is another variable in this game: Armenia, which is Russia's strategic and cultural partner in the region and which looks at any moves of Turkey and Azerbaijan in the region with suspicion. Russia is bound with Armenia by the CST

Treaty to provide military assistance in case of threats to its sovereignty and territorial integrity, which, however, did not stop it from attacking Georgia back in 2008.

During and in the first decade after the Nagorno-Karabakh conflict, Russia/Armenia and Azerbaijan/Turkey created a real interstate security dilemma in that part of the South Caucasus region. Kamaludin Gadjiev described the situation as a zero-sum game: "under the conditions when Russia carries out direct deliveries of arms to Armenia and deepens its cooperation with this country, Azerbaijan is forced to establish military cooperation with Turkey and the United States, as well as to strengthen the process of rapprochement with NATO and other Western military structures, including offering its territory for foreign military bases."[289] Azerbaijan's position is that "Russia's policy in the conflict between Azerbaijan and Armenia was influenced by the Armenian lobby, which had a strong standing in the Kremlin. In fact, Moscow counted on Yerevan as its main strategic ally in the Caucasus."[290] Turkey, too, fueled the tensions. "One nation, two states" logic in relations with Turkey increased its influence in the region and came into dangerous proximity with Russia's own aspirations.[291] Primordial memories of multiple confrontations between Russia and Turley are still vivid in the memory of both nations notwithstanding good partnership relations between them, especially ongoing negotiations to start a new pipeline from the Caspian Sea through Turkey to Europe as a substitute for the failed South Stream.

The basis for the improvement of bilateral relations was laid down in the Declaration of Friendship and Strategic Partnership signed in 2008 by Putin and Ilham Aliyev, president of Azerbaijan. The Declaration defined future areas of cooperation between the countries. This led to some eighty intergovernmental and bilateral treaties cementing good neighborly relations.[292] Currently economic cooperation between Russia and Azerbaijan is striving. This, however, was not always the case: apart from the deep economic crisis that struck Azerbaijan immediately after the collapse of the Soviet Union and in 1998, there were serious issues that cast a shadow on its economic interactions with Russia. Raphael

Ultanbayev mentioned several reasons for slowing down mutual trade and investment between the two countries: "discontent of the Baku leadership with Moscow's official position on the Karabakh problem and close Armenian-Russian relations; closure of the border with Azerbaijan during the Chechen war; and Baku's striving to expand connections with Western countries, setting up strategic partnership with the United States, the EU states, and Turkey."[293] Nevertheless, by early 2000, economic and fiscal cooperation between Moscow and Baku took an upturn, mostly due to the desire of the former to fill the financial vacuum in the latter without letting others do so.

Spheres of interaction include "opening new production capacities in Azerbaijan, active development of Russian enterprises in the Azerbaijani market, [and] close cooperation in financial matters, which also strengthens the integrative interaction" between the two countries.[294] According to an economic bulletin of the Russian embassy in Baku, "Trade turnover between Russia and Azerbaijan in 2013 . . . had reached $2.583 billion (an increase of 10.3%). Russian exports to Azerbaijan amounted to $1,505.2 billion. . . . Azerbaijani exports to Russia amounted to $1,077.8 billion."[295] Sectors of economic cooperation, besides oil and gas, include food commodities, transportation, mineral products, timber, and financial products. The same website mentions some five hundred Russian companies active in the Azerbaijani market, mostly in the energy sectors. These include such large ones as Gazprom, Rosneft', VTB Bank, Gazprombank, Alfa-Bank, Uralsib Bank, Nomos-Bank, Lukoil, Baltika Beer Factory, and car manufacturer Lada, which either have shares in the local companies or fully own them.[296]

Bilateral military cooperation between Russia and Azerbaijan have also intensified lately. In 2014 Russia sold heavy military equipment to Azerbaijan, including two divisions of SA-10 Grumble long-range surface-to-air missile systems, 100 T-90C tanks, two batteries of anti-aircraft missile systems Tor-2ME, 70 helicopters, 100 units of VMP-3, an artillery unit MSTA-C, and a complex of "Smerch" for the total sum of $5 billion.[297] As CSTO secretary general Nikolay Borduzha explained the deal, Russia wishes to keep arms parity in the region.[298] This was received highly negatively in Armenia, whose leadership felt played by Russia into joining the Customs Union. At the same time, Azerbaijan tries to play its own games, not being fully dependent on Russia. Azerbaijan tries to play politics where the interests of the most important regional players are balanced. Its closeness with the United States and the European Union in providing alternative energy carriers and thus contributing to the energy security of the latter raises Moscow's hackles.

Neighbors to the East

Multiple nomadic tribes of ancient Huns, Turkic people, and Mongols used to roam the endless steppes of Central Asia, interacting with each other—sometimes peacefully, sometimes not—along the Great Silk Road that bridged the cultural gap between the West and the East. The unique geopolitical location made the region a junction of political, cultural, and economic influences. In the eighth century, Islam started slowly getting hold in the region, adding the religious variable into the melting pot of various cultures and political influences.[299] Numerous nations ruled Central Asia, ranging from the Tibetan empires, the Arab Caliphate, China, the Mongol Horde, and eventually Russia. Russian exploration of the Central Asia started in the sixteenth century when the rapidly expanding Moscovia came into close proximity to the Kazakh tribes. In 1730 Abul-hair, khan of the Lesser Kirgiz Horde, asked for military support from Russia but was rejected with a counteroffer: a full "protectorate."[300] In the nineteenth century, Russia's gradual territorial expansion into Central Asia was accomplished with a mix of peaceful negotiations and military expeditions: the Kokand and Bukhara Khanates (1866), Khiva (1873), and the Turkmen land (1881), to mention a few. It was only a matter of time before the Russian quest for land would clash with the British Crown's interests in the region. During the short Battle for Kushka (1886), a Russian expeditionary battalion attacked Afghan cavalry under British command igniting the "Great Game," where the interests of Moscow clashed with those of London's colonial policies in the adjacent Afghanistan and India.[301]

The collapse of the Russian tsarist empire led to the creation of the independent but short-lived country of Alash Orda, with its center in Semipalatinsk, present-day Kazakhstan. Alash Orda happened to be between the two evils: the Bolsheviks to the west and the Russian royalists to the east; the struggle between the two forces largely presupposed its impending fall.[302] In 1920 its government was taken over by the Kazakh/Kyrgyz revolution committee. The same fate met lesser khanates in the territory of modern Uzbekistan: Khorezm, Bukhara, Tashkent. The takeover, however, was not peaceful as the Soviets had expected. In spreading their rule they faced the vicious guerrilla opposition of local militants, the *basmachi*, a loosely structured term used "by Bolshevik propagandists to label the Muslims who resisted Bolshevik rule in Central Asia," which lasted up until 1930.[303]

During the Soviet Union, the republics of Central Asia, from a geopolitical perspective, experienced the same policies of Russification as their other, non-Russian counterparts. According to Peimani, "To secure the Central Asians' loyalty to the Soviet State, the Soviet regime implemented a systematic policy to change Central Asia's ethnic and linguistic structure . . . employing mainly ethnic engineering and Russification. They aimed at replacing the Central Asians' culture and history with an artificial sense of belonging to distinct ethnic and religious groups."[304] At the same time, their entrance into the Soviet Union brought positive results for the people living there as far as their standard of living was concerned. The biggest improvements were in health care and education through the *likbez* program that eradicated illiteracy in the region. Geoffrey Jukes writes, "It could be said that through association with Russia the nationalities of Soviet Central Asia had achieved living standards, insofar as these may be expressed by wages, health, and education opportunity, somewhat lower than those of the European USSR, but a great deal higher than those of their independent neighbors."[305] So for them it was definitely a step up from the late feudalist public administrative settings, which numerous Central Asian khanates were known for.

The Central Asian region is important for the eastern direction of Russian foreign policy, where the notion of borders plays a geopolitical role as presented by the general views in Russian political culture. Russia does not feel immediately threatened by any of the eastern neighbors in the region or beyond. It is well protected, from the conventional standpoint, by the huge landmass of Kazakhstan, except for the drug trafficking and illegal movements of personnel and commodities. This issue, however, deserves a lesser focus for Russian national security concerned with dimensions of territorial expansionism. There are no natural enemies that, are encroaching upon its identity and place in the region. China is Russia's close strategic partner, as the countries share the same communist past (and present, for that matter). The same is true of India, with which Russia has mutually beneficial trade, embodied in the sales of arms and military machinery.

An additional factor contributing to the lower intensity of Russia's involvement in the region is its perceived lack of immediate threat in Russian political culture, which does not consider the countries of Central Asia as somehow part of the Russian identity construct. Closeness with the Muslim countries of Iran, Afghanistan, and Turkey is viewed as something normal, in the nature of things. There is no feeling of betrayal or grievance looking on the return of the countries in question to their historical roots, which in other instances (such as in Ukraine) is considered an affront to Russia's perceptions of self. To put it simply, in most of the Central Asian countries, Russia does not have any viable grounds to build the "Russian world," except for Kazakhstan, which may become a real security concern for this country in the foreseeable future.

Among the factors prioritizing this region for Moscow and affecting the nature of its responses to regional challenges and their frequencies are retained linguistic connections and availability of Russian-speaking local populations; presence of large Russian diasporas in the region and pro-Russian national elites that are connected to Russia mostly economically; existing cultural affinities and economic links; threats to its own national security emanating from transborder terrorism; drug smuggling and illegal movements of personnel across porous borders with Kazakhstan, the common Russia–Central Asian frontier; economic rationales for cooperation and control over energy resources; and geopolitical inputs from global tensions within U.S./Western interests in the region. Russia uses diverse instruments of negative pressure (sticks) and positive stimulation (carrots) to secure its areas of involvement: according to Bakhtier Rashidov, "in Tajikistan it is using its military-political trump card . . . ; in Kyrgyzstan where there are practically no serious industrial and raw bases—it uses economy; in Kazakhstan—it is ethnic (presence of a large Russian diaspora)."[306] Such tools are used to provide its vital national interests, which are framed by the overarching objectives of keeping its engaged presence in the region and protecting its own borders from local contingencies.

Transnational Terrorism

National security considerations for Russia focus on the destructive forces of Islamic extremism and international terrorism threatening to cross its southern borders. Russia is vitally interested in keeping regional stability under control to avoid spillovers of insecurity. The problem is exacerbated by dangerous proximity with the two most virulent failed states in the world, Afghanistan and Pakistan. These countries are characterized by high domestic political volatility, which can transfer to the Central Asian states bordering Russia, making it a secondhand sufferer of regional unrest. During the early 1990s the Taliban movement started gaining momentum in Afghanistan and by the early 2000s had established itself as a viable military and political force. Al Qaeda, another terrorist organization, has been partnering with local Islamic extremist organizations in Central Asia, the most notorious of which are the Islamic Movement of Uzbekistan (IMU) and Hizb Ut-Tahrir (Islamic Liberation Party), which pose significant regional threats to Uzbekistan, Kyrgyzstan, Tajikistan, and beyond.

The IMU was created in the 1990s by Salafis in the Ukzbek city of Fergana "calling for the adoption of Shariah and the creation of an Islamic state."[307] In 2001 it changed its name to the Islamic Movement of Turkestan, or the IMT. It is a highly ideological group made up of violent youth using the Salafist Wahabist doctrine to spread their anti-governmental influence in Uzbekistan and Kyrgyzstan by "ruthlessness and brutality. Police officers who were kidnapped were beheaded; . . . if forced to withdraw they would shoot their own wounded rather than let them fall into the hands of their enemies; even those among their own ranks who tried to take advantage of an Uzbek government amnesty were executed."[308] The second movement, Hizb Ut-Tahrir, is truly transnational, with adherents and cells in forty countries. According to Suha Taji-Farouki, it "posits the worldwide Islamic community of faith as every Muslim's exclusive focus of allegiance and source of identity. . . . Hizb Ut-Tahrir operates as a social movement that does not offer immediate concrete solutions but a single, utopian response to all problems, whether political, economic, or social," which is an order governed by Shariah law.[309] Initially largely an Uzbek phenomenon, it more recently has spread to nearby Central Asian states and even into Russia by claiming Russian converts to Islam.[310] The group positions itself as extremely antinationalist and "calls for jihad in order to establish the Islamic state. Hizb Ut-Tahrir opposes all existing Arab and Muslim states . . . as apostates and favors a limitless Islamic state without national boundaries."[311] Such an outlook makes Hizb Ut-Tahrir and similar organizations globalist or even postmodernist, from the Muslim fundamentalist perspective, of course.

This, and not their proximity to Russia's borders, is why these organizations are troubling to Russia's national security: by various estimates, the number of Russian citizens who consider themselves Muslims ranges between 12 and 13.5 million, which is more than 9 percent of the registered population in Russia.[312] In addition, there are about 9.5 million immigrants (one-third of whom are nonregistered illegals), most of whom are from CIS countries, including from Central Asia, and this presents fertile ground for radical Islamist movements.[313] Madawi Al-Rasheed et al. believe that "the appeal of [such] organizations . . . demonstrates that the desire to reestablish an Islamic political institution is still very strong among Central Asian Muslims, manifesting itself in active campaigning for the reinstatement of a form of governance inspired by both the historical caliphate and Islamic political theorizing."[314] This makes the country extremely susceptible to Islamic extremism, especially taking into account its long-lasting struggle with terrorists in Chechnya, who are connected with global terrorist networks. Russia's security interests in the region are, therefore, fueled by fears of cross-contamination of its own Muslims by Islamic extremist emissaries crossing less than perfectly controlled borders within Central Asia.

The proliferation of extremist and terrorist organizations in Central Asia and in its immediate vicinity poses indirect threats to Russian security in the areas closest to the region. Initially the so-called concept of "strategy of two borders" was adopted by the Russian Federal Border Service, which entails protection of the national interests of the former Soviet republics on their external borders and the protection of Russian national interests on its own border. Marlène Laruelle and Sébastien Peyrouse write, "Although Kazakhstan is the only Central Asian state that shares borders with Russia, Moscow sees the security of its southern borders as a question of domestic security born not out of 'imperialism' but of pragmatism. . . . Moscow therefore thinks of Central Asia as a buffer zone with a 'South' increasingly subject to strategic uncertainty and non-traditional threats."[315] After Russia removed its troops from Kazakhstan, Kyrgyzstan, Turkmenistan, and Uzbekistan, and reduced troops in Tajikistan, this strategy was seriously jeopardized.

Illegal Immigration

Porous borders between the Central Asian countries present another significant problem for Russian national security, mostly from the economic and criminal side: uncontrolled immigration. For a number of the transborder regions of Russia close to Kazakhstan, illegal immigration is also connected with the possibility of changing their ethnic composition and, as a consequence, increasing potential separatist and irredentist aspirations. Russia was traditionally the target of internal immigration during the Soviet Union, where people from the union republics went for education, work, and subsequent settlement. After independence, the immigration issue became especially acute because of the dramatic fall in the standard of living in the peripheral republics. The *Gastarbeiter*, labor immigrants, started coming to Russia in large numbers. State information agency TASS counts 11.5 million immigrants currently living in Russia mentioned by the Federal Border Agency, most of which come from Uzbekistan, Kyrgyzstan, and Tajikistan.[316]

Working and living under terrible conditions, these labor immigrants create enclaves of unintegrated and unassimilated populations in Russian metropolitan areas. Such ethnic pockets have high crime rates and ethnically based organized crime. Immigrants commit 40,000 crimes annually, which is only 2 percent of all crimes in the country. However, when separate cities are taken, especially metropolitan areas like Moscow and St. Petersburg, the share of immigrants in overall crime rate reaches a staggering 45 percent.[317] A related issue is the low numbers of registered immigrants in comparison to their real numbers: according to Constantine Romodanovsky, head of the Federal Migration Service, there were 3.5 million illegal immigrants in 2013.[318] Additionally, data produced by the Russian International Affairs Council stated that 21 percent of previously registered immigrants have not renewed their visas but have not exited the country either, which makes them illegal.[319]

From a Russian nationalist perspective, illegal and unregistered immigrants present several threats to Russian national security, namely, "the replacement of the native Slavic population by newcomers, mostly Turkic ethnic groups, usually belonging to the Muslim culture, in regions where mortality is higher than fertility"; "displacement of the indigenous population from SMEs by an immigrant criminal diaspora"; "turning Western Siberia . . . into a predominantly Muslim region"; and "increase of Islamists among the immigrants."[320] A concomitant issue is potential infiltration of terrorists among immigrants entering Russia legally or not and their joining the extremists' ranks in the North Caucasus and beyond.

Drug Trafficking

It was Russia's desire to defend its external Central Asian borders shared with its most volatile neighbor, Afghanistan, that presupposed its involvement there to avoid dangerous spillovers of insecurity across the northern side of regional borders. In 1992 Tajikistan was struck by an ethnopolitical civil war between various identity factions and supporters of the central government, which severely deteriorated the situation at the Tajik-Afghani border. This coincided with various armed groups of former mujahedeen fighting against Soviet troops, gaining momentum, and exploring opportunities for state failure in Afghanistan after the withdrawal of the USSR from its domestic scene. It was only a matter of time before these groups crossed loosely controlled borders with Tajikistan and started spreading Islamic influence there. In May 1993 the Agreement between the Russian Federation and the Republic of Tajikistan on Cooperation on Border Issues was signed, resulting in the transfer of the duty of protecting the Tajik-Afghani borders to Russian troops.

The agreement laid the basis for establishing peacekeeping forces in Tajikistan and, subsequently, the 201st Russian Military Base in 2004, which was tasked with protecting common CIS borders. The base included ten military units belonging to various military services: artillery, intelligence, army, and several air force squadrons.[321] During his trip to Tajikistan, Putin visited the base, where he said, "The Russian military base in Tajikistan is one of the most important factors of stability in the country, with which we have a special brotherly and very close strategic relationship, which is an outpost of the Commonwealth of Independent States in this very complicated and responsible Afghan direction."[322] The result of this visit was the extension of the base's operation until 2042, at practically no cost to the Russian side.

The official reason for Russian military involvement was the protection of common CIS borders by Russian troops blended with the need to reinforce antidrug activities. At the same time, some sources allege that Russian border guards have partnered with Afghani traffickers in illicit drug transfers across the border with Tajikistan. Frank Shanti gives several examples of interviews with Russian intelligence officers and court hearings against Russia military serving in the 201st Division.[323] Regardless of these cases, there are well-documented instances of cross-border fights against Afghani militants spanning a decade. According to information provided by the Regional Public Fund of the Veterans of the Military Conflict in Tajikistan, "Between 1992 and 2005, Russian border guards in Tajikistan detained more than 3,000 violators of the state border. There were about 3,500 border incidents . . . during which 161 Russian border guards were killed and 362 more were wounded. . . . Russian border guards . . . detained and destroyed more than 30,102,741 kilograms of drugs, out of which 11 tons and 463.77 kilograms was heroin. During the clashes, about 3,000 militants from various armed groups, armed violators of the state border, and drug smugglers were killed."[324] One of the largest attacks happened in April 2003 when some 120 Afghani militants tried to cross the border with Tajikistan resulting in a three-hour fight and the death of most of them.

The porousness of borders in the region of Central Asia poses significant concerns for Russian national security, including the illegal smuggling of narcotic substances passing through Central Asia from Afghanistan, the hotbed of international drug production and trafficking. The UNODC report gives a comprehensive picture of the drug-smuggling routes: "Afghan opiates enter Central Asia via the borders of Tajikistan, Uzbekistan, and Turkmenistan and proceed to their destinations in the Russian Federation. . . . Within Russia, opiates travel in almost every direction, since Russia is a main destination country for Afghan opiates."[325] According to the Council of Europe's report, "Afghanistan is by far the main source of heroin and other opiates consumed in the Council of Europe member states. Europe, including Russia, is the main target market for opiates from Afghanistan."[326] Drugs produced in Afghanistan enter Central Asia, which is the key transit route to Russia. Another UNODC estimate claims that in 2009 alone about 90 metric tons of opiates entered Central Asia, out of which 77 metric tons went on to Russia.[327] These figures are extremely alarming, especially taking into account the porous borders between Central Asian countries and Russia.

In 2010 the government of Russia adopted the State Anti-Drug Strategy Policy of the Russian Federation 2020, which includes "smuggling the Afghani opiates and cannabinoids from Central Asia" among the main strategic threats in this area. The problem of drug trafficking looms large: Kromova mentioned the figure of 12 tons of pure heroin smuggled from Afghanistan and used in Russia by the so-called Silk Road crossing the Kazakh-Russian border, which is the "first" of the "two borders."[328] The endless current of drugs makes the regions of Russia that are especially affected by narcotics the bastion of support for radical Islamist groups. This problem, due to its transborder nature, can only be solved through international cooperation at multiple levels: the regional multinational level, such as with the Shanghai Cooperation Organization, and also bilaterally, through close cooperation with the United States, which has been closely involved in the antidrug activities in the region.

Great Game 2.0

Central Asia is a unique region because of the triangulation of three potent factors affecting present and future situations there: economics, energy interests, and Realpolitik. Triangulating them produces the new version of the Great Game played by Russia and Britain in the nineteenth century. Only now the actors are multiple and the stakes are much higher. The geopolitics of relations between Russia and the Central Asian republics is far more complicated than it may seem to an inexperienced eye. Gleason applied the following consideration about Russian influence in Central Asia: "It is based on a subtle but important . . . distinction between leading and dominating. Russian leaders are attempting to exert a leading but not dominating role within the former Soviet space."[329] This is, however, only visible in specific areas where Russian political culture does not feel threatened by outside influence.

Much interaction between Russia and Central Asian countries is carried out within the institutional frameworks of the Shanghai Cooperation Organization (SCO). Set up in 2001 on the basis of the expanded "Shanghai Five" (Russia, China, Kazakhstan, Kyrgyzstan, Tajikistan, and Uzbekistan) the SCO set the triple priorities of its operation: terrorism, separatism, and extremism. All the countries included in the organization, to various degrees, experienced the devastating effects of those phenomena. From the onset, the SCO was viewed by Central Asian countries as "the basic structure to ensure the stability of the regional system of international relations and at the same time allowing them, if necessary, to maneuver between Russia and China."[330] Upon their consent, "Russia and China . . . have decided to take into their hands the matter of full control over security in the region, while having agreed on the 'division of labor' with the CSTO."[331] Counterterrorism and drug enforcement activities across borders would fit naturally into the future development of the SCO's spheres of interest.

Recently, however, Russia has been interested in further expansion of the organization through the inclusion of other potential regional members, such as India, Pakistan, Mongolia, and Iran. Enlargement of the organization with the accompanying diplomatic resolution of existing disputes between members, as mediated by Moscow, would champion its efforts as a peacemaker and a regional power in Central Asia.[332] At the same time, Russia views the SCO as a potential counterbalance to NATO in the region, especially in light of its past involvement in Iraq and Afghanistan as well as the ongoing confrontation with the West over Ukraine.

Russian economic interests in the region have rational bases. According to Trenin et al., "President Putin wants economic integration to pave the way to a more comprehensive consolidation of the Eurasian space, to include security and supranational institutions. . . . [He] has been personally working hard to expand the integration effort to include Kyrgyzstan and Tajikistan. This will be difficult."[333] The main challenges to bilateral Russian–Central Asian cooperation stem from the need to keep the economies of the Central Asian countries within the sphere of influence of the Russian economy, especially within the context of trading energy resources with European countries and China. Vladimir Paramonov and Alexey Strokov noted the pragmatism of Russia's participation in regional economies: "Russia's increased attention to the Central Asian republics is mostly explained by the fact that the extraction of carbohydrates in the region is technologically easier and economically more efficient than in northern Russia, where most of the oil and gas deposits of the country are located. The RF is trying to involve as much Central Asian carbohydrate resources as possible in its own fuel-energy balance for sustaining internal consumption while not decreasing the export of carbohydrates to external markets, primarily in Europe."[334]

Most of the productive capacities of the Central Asian nations are owned by Russian companies: Gazprom has been leading negotiations with the Kyrgyz side on purchase of shares of national companies Kyrgyzneftgaz and Kyrgyzgaz. Gazprom is also the monopolist in Tajikistan, which does not have its own energy resources and has to purchase them from its partner Russia, which owns some 30–35 percent of the local market. There are several gas deposits in Uzbekistan spread across the land and the Uzbek part of the Aral Sea. They are being developed with the presence of Russian energy companies Lukoil and Gazprom. By 2012 Russian investment in the country's energy sector amounted to $6.2 billion. Turkmenistan is the energy giant with 600 million barrels of proven oil reserves and 265 trillion cubic feet of proven gas reserves (by 2012), which puts it among the top six countries with the largest gas reserves.[335] Most of its gas is pumped through the Central Asia–Center pipeline to Russia, where it is transported to European markets. Finally, the biggest interest of Russian business is in Kazakhstan; there the Russian oil and gas complex represented by Lukoil, Gazprom, and Rosneft' invested up to $7.5 billion.[336] Similar to Uzbekistan, the Kazakh oil is pumped to Russia via the Atyrau-Samara and Tengiz-Novorossiysk pipelines. In 2014 Kazakhstan proposed jointly with Russia to build a pipeline to China, which is under consideration in Moscow.

Along with Russia, China is also active in Turkmenistan: its national energy actor, the China National Petroleum Company (CNPC), invested $4 billion in Turkmen gas development in 2014.[337] China is building a Turkmenistan–Uzbekistan–Tajikistan–Kyrgyzstan–China pipeline with the annual capacity of 65 billion cubic meters per year, which would diversify the Turkmen demand markets. In addition, China has been investing in other non-energy-related projects in the region: about half a billion dollars in more than fifty other projects in Turkmenistan; a $10 billion loan to Kazakhstan and 49 percent of the shares of the energy company Mangistaumunaigas, which Gazprom wanted to buy, making China the third party to control Kazakh energy; total Chinese investments in Uzbekistan amounted to $362 million by 2008; 107 joint Chinese-Uzbek enterprises were established by 2009. China is a major investor in the construction of the TUUKKA (Turkmenistan-Uzbekistan-Kazakhstan-China) pipeline, with an estimated cost of $20 billion and with a capacity of 30 billion cubic meters by 2012.[338]

The participation of China in the exploration and sale of energy in the Caspian basin fits well within the general line of diversification of sales markets for their most important commodities. The Central Asian states that are rich with oil and gas (primarily Kazakhstan and Turkmenistan) are vitally interested in diversifying transit routes to European Union buyers. Participation of extraregional companies in the exploration and transportation of Caspian energy would decrease the economic and, subsequently, political dependence of countries in the region on Russia's will to transport them. In this respect, the region's countries accelerated their participation in regional integration and globalization processes, which would bring into the region players other than Russia: China, the United States, India, Turkey, Iran, and Israel. One of the effects of the inclusion of the Central Asian countries in the globalization process was the 9/11 Global War on Terror, which led to the entry of the United States in the region and the start of including those countries in international cooperation frameworks.

On the multilateral level, according to Dimitri Trenin, "In terms of foreign policy per se, Putin's main project is Eurasian economic integration. The Customs Union of Belarus, Kazakhstan, and Russia, in operation since 2009, is being upgraded to a single economic area of the three, with the goal of an economic union by 2015."[339] This is the year when the Russian-borrowed Kazakh initiative to create the Eurasian Union got two new members: Armenia and Kyrgyzstan. The latter, however, hesitated for quite a while before committing to such a decisive step that would define its geopolitical orientation for generations to come. Hesitation was both political and economic. Shevtsova claims, "President Almazbek Atambayev of Kyrgyzstan has also proved willing to use blackmail, demanding a $200 million loan from Moscow in addition to trade and economic preferences. When he did not get what he wanted, Mr.

Atambayev postponed his country's entry into the Eurasian Union."[340] Kyrgyzstan has been maneuvering between Moscow and Brussels for the past two decades. To make it attractive for Kyrgyzstan to side with Europe, the EU has allocated about $100 million to the country in projects like Technical Assistance to CIS Countries (TACIS) and Transport Corridor Europe–Caucasus–Asia (TRASECA), social protection, governance, education, agriculture, and rural development.[341]

Russia's offer turned out to be five times higher: to facilitate the integration of Kyrgyzstan into the Customs Union, a joint development fund was set up with Russian capital of $500 million, which is essentially a soft loan. Prior to that, Russia allocated $1.7 billion for the reconstruction of the Kambaratinsk hydropower plant in 2009 in addition to an earlier $450 million, partly in credit, partly in loans.[342] Some claim that these financial incentives were used to placate Kyrgyzstan and make it more tractable, especially with regard to their decision to close down the U.S. base in Manas. The military transit center was eventually shut down in 2014, after thirteen years of operation.

The integration of Kazakhstan into Eurasian structures is a completely different matter. From the Russian perspective, Kazakhstan is important simply because it has the longest land border with Russia. There are also a significant number of ethnic Russians and Russian speakers historically living in Kazakhstan. Besides, Kazakhstan has one of the most important objects of space infrastructure for Russia—the Baikonur space launch facility, inherited by Kazakhstan from the Soviet Union. Russia continues to use it on loan due to the extremely high costs of constructing one of its own. Kazakhstan is one of the most active members of the integration in the Central Asian and Eurasian space and plays an important role as a source for Russian transit of oil and gas to Europe.

Longtime Kazakh president Nursultan Nazarbayev wants his country to play an equal role with Russia, at best, and not a subordinate one. The most important issue here is the impact that the Eurasian Union would have on the sovereignty of Kazakhstan, especially considering the large Russian minority in the country's northern areas bordering Russia. As the reality of the past years has shown, borders play an important role in the Russian perception of threat and projection of its identity outside of them. Although after the collapse of the Soviet Union large numbers of Russians and Russian speakers had left Kazakhstan (Dave mentions 2 million in the decade after 1989), Russians still form more than 21 percent of the total population of Kazakhstan, making them the second largest ethnic group in the country.[343]

The presence of such a large geopolitical actor as Russia in the region, especially when this presence is fraught with certain binding obligations, troubles Kazakhstan. Putin's recent statement at Seliger 2014 made Kazakhstan frown even more on its future next to Russia in the Eurasian structure. When commenting on a question about Russian partnerships in the region, Putin remarked, "Kazakhs never had their statehood. He [Nazarbayev] created it."[344] Nazarbayev did not make the public wait long for a reply: in his interview with the Habar TV channel, he threatened that his country would leave the Eurasian structure: "Astana [Kazakh capital] will never be a member of an organization that poses a threat to the independence of Kazakhstan."[345] Such statements coming from the president of a neighboring country, and the largest in the world, who prior to that denied the raison d'être to another former Soviet nation, Ukraine, should raise all possible warning flags of a questionable future for Kazakh-Russian relations.

Conclusion

There is never a dull moment in Russia's relationship with its former Soviet brothers and sisters. In a quarter of a century after the collapse of the Soviet Union, the Near Abroad does not stop evoking emotions in Russian political culture, which by inertia continues to view them as an extension of its political and territorial self. These emotions range from protecting those who are open to the idea of a Russian presence in domestic and international political choices (like the Central Asian countries) and patronizing those who shilly-shally between Russia and the West, its newly constructed nemesis (for example, Armenia and Belarus), to open aggression against those who dare deny the Russian restoration of historical justice and their own understanding of international law (Georgia and Ukraine immediately come to mind here, but Moldova and potentially Belarus can also be considered examples).

Russia has been closely involved in the former Soviet region since the very collapse of the empire. Yet there are some variations in the character of its involvement in each specific case that make Russian foreign policy diverse. Several factors affect the nature and scope of Russian involvement with its Near Abroad, which predisposes Russian foreign policy toward a benevolent or tightfisted approach. The first is the border factor: the closer the former Soviet republics are to Russia—even more so, if they share a common border—the more intense and involved Russia becomes in their domestic politics and their foreign policy orientations. The nearer the Near Abroad is to Russia, the less it is seen as "abroad" per se. Conversely, the farther the former Soviet nations are from Russia, the less likely they are to expect her close attention to their local and international political processes. This consideration does not apply to the three Baltic States, which are within the completely different supranational political, economic, cultural, and military frameworks of the EU and NATO, which shield them from incessant Russian involvement. The second outlier is Armenia, with no common border and farther away from Russian than the three aforementioned countries. There is, however, another variable that makes Armenia so dependent on Russia's political will: being surrounded by volatile and potentially hostile nations, this country simply has no other choice but to side with Russia in most of its moves.

The second factor affecting the intensity of Russian foreign policy is the presence of ethnic Russian populations and Russian speakers. These societal groups act as Trojan horses for the slow but deliberate takeover of their lands by Russia, claiming its historical birthright on the basis of the prevalent Russian cultural spectrum in the target countries. Clear cases of the presence of this variable are the Russian wars against Georgia in support of the South Ossetian and Abkhazian populations, the former being a divided nation with the North Ossetians in Russia proper and the latter having an almost complete Russian orientation in its domestic and foreign policies. Another example is Ukraine, which is also a split nation and which failed to establish a single civil identity during the past twenty-five years of its independent existence. This also attracted Russia's interests, coupled with the desire to reinforce its geopolitical status by getting a military foothold in the Black Sea and slowing down Ukraine's economic and energy revival. The third case is Transdniestria, with perhaps the closest ties with Russia. Having been on hiatus for a time, the conflict may resume with increased involvement of the Russian troops already stationed there. Keeping this in mind, the next one up is Belarus, with a foggy ethnic identity, allowing for loose distinctions between ethnic Russians and Belarusians. The Baltic States are again outliers here, which can also be explained by their affiliations within the European Union and NATO, remaining out of Russia's reach.

Speaking of Western politico-military institutions, other nations' proximity to them is another factor that affects the foreign policy choices that Putin's Russia has recently made. The closer the Near Abroad is to the EU and NATO, the less "near" it is to Russia. Guided by a Cold War mentality, Russia has painstakingly constructed an image of the West as hostile to everything Russian. It has entrenched itself in the Russian world, which extends mentally beyond its physical borders,and is encountering perceived enemies through its collision of values with the West. Any move of the former Soviet republics in the direction of closer affiliation with the West means by definition their betrayal of centuries of brotherly relations (as they are perceived in Moscow) while living within different Russian empires. The desires of Ukraine, Georgia, Moldova, and Armenia to be economically affiliated with the EU are one trigger irritant, as is the wish of some of them to become part of NATO structures, including membership. In parts of the Near Abroad where Russian does not feel threatened externally, such as in Central Asia, its foreign policy is more lax and amenable to various political frivolities, such as the U.S. base in Kyrgyzstan. Here, too, the Baltic States are the falsifiers of this variable by being directly parts of the EU and NATO.

5

European Dimensions of Russian Foreign Policy

European values is the result of agitated minds of intellectuals of the North Atlantic propaganda; these values do not exist.

—VLADIMIR MEDINSKY, minister of culture, 2013

We cannot lose Europe. Europe without Russia is not Europe. Russia has time and again saved Europe from Europe itself.

—SERGEY LAVROV, minister of foreign relations, December 2014

On November 12, 2014, millions of curious viewers all over the globe were glued to computer and TV screens with news that just a few decades ago would have seemed directly out of a science fiction movie. The Rosetta Mission spacecraft of the European Space Agency, covering more than 6 billion kilometers in ten years, delivered the robotic lander *Philae* to the surface of the Churyumov-Gerasimenko Comet orbiting between Earth and Jupiter at the unimaginable speed of 84,000 MPH. For the first time in human history, it became possible to have a "feel" for an elusive (and for some a fateful) celestial body, a comet. Even though *Philae*'s mission was not 100 percent successful (its battery life was shortened by several landing and drilling attempts), it managed in a matter of hours to collect very important data on the comet's surface, its composition, and sounds and take some close-ups of the comet's surface. In preparation for more than a decade, this experiment of a few hours proved to be groundbreaking for astronomy.

The reaction from some parts of the Russian political spectrum was interesting. A typical adept of the "Russian world" would say, "The comet is ours, because it was our people who found it in space." At first glance, this may sound quite funny, as though it were from a piece on the satirical website, the *Onion*. The reality, however, is less amusing. Sergey Malinkovich, chair of the Central Committee of the Communists of the Leningrad District, posted the following statement on that group's website:

> This is . . . a continuation of the Star Wars, or rather, starry raiding from the European Union. This comet was discovered by the Soviet scientists in 1969 and, therefore, is under the jurisdiction of our country. Any descent of a foreign spacecraft on the comet . . . is illegal. The European Union should pay a large sum to the budget of the Russian Federation for the spy shots of the dark side of the comet Churyumov-Gerasimenko, made by the *Philae*. . . . Russian Space Forces should start patrolling the comet Churyumov-Gerasimenko and detain all offenders![1]

The Russian nationalists (including communists) seem to completely forget that the comet was named for two ethnic Ukrainians and that Churyumov is a professor at Kiev National University.

Political Roller Coaster with Europe

In the aftermath of World War II, Europe was at a crossroads. The atrocities of the war were over, but their long-term effects on the people's lives were yet to be fully assessed. Yet there was some unexpected optimism about the future of Europe. This "noble continent, comprising on the whole the fairest and the most cultivated regions of the earth," "the fountain of Christian faith and Christian ethics," and the "origin of most of the culture, arts, philosophy and science," according to one of its most prominent sons, had to be consolidated into the "United States of Europe"[2] or vanish from the face of the earth. The "tragedy of Europe" was to be averted by unification of the European nations and not by their separation, which was the cause of the two world wars.

Less than fifty years later, Europe faced a similar dilemma when the

Soviet Union collapsed. This left Europe with an immense terra incognita to its east with some fifteen previously unheard of nations appearing as snippets of the Soviet ethnic patchwork quilt. Europe was thus faced with a dilemma: to embrace or to cast away the new Russia. Europe chose the first path, but with very slow and gradual integration.

At first, the West and Europe held illusions that Russia would readily embrace the principles of respect for human dignity and fundamental rights and freedoms upon which the European Union was built, but of which Soviet citizens were long deprived. Accepting the normative environment was, in fact, considered a sine qua non of future EU-Russia relations. Russia, in the words of Hanna Smith, has three objectives vis-à-vis the European Union: "a common economic area, a visa-free border, and some possibility to participate in EU decision-making."[3] These objectives were initially accepted by the European Union, which at the dusk of the past millennium was open to the idea of bringing Russia and other new eastern nations into the European family.

These illusions quickly vanished in the horror of the first and second Chechen wars and the subsequent limitations imposed by the Russian central governments on their own civil society. The previous European stance of inclusivity was replaced by one of exclusivity; this was clearly visible in the Kosovo crisis of 1999, when Russia was practically neglected in the matters of establishing peace in Europe. The events in Ukraine brought the interactions between the European Union and the Russian Federation below the freezing point where mutually imposed sanctions are only hurting their economies. Europe felt threatened by the growing and potentially insatiable territorial appetite of Putin's government.

To many in Russia, however, the explanation was reversed: according to Elena Frolova, Europe was "afraid of another Russia—a country which has become stronger and more confident in itself after several years of stability and continuity of economic growth. It has enhanced its reputation as a responsible participant of the international processes, conducting pragmatic policies aimed at satisfying the interests of internal development, dedicated to promoting dialogue with the rest of the world, including in the security issues."[4] These milestones, which are enhancing Russia's multidimensional inclusion in pan-European affairs and which, in principle, should make Europe happy, are viewed in Russia as major irritants for the Brussels supranational governance. So the grand question in EU-Russian relations is whether it is Europe that is deliberately shutting its doors to integration with Russia, or is it Russia's domestic and international actions that are making Europe turn a cold shoulder to Russia and treat it with increasing suspicion?

Partnering for Discontent

There are several communication channels for deliberation and decision making between the European Union and the Russian Federation. True to the spirit of Liberalism, these channels have been flowing in different directions and on multiple levels. The foundation of the EU-Russia relations was laid down by the Partnership and Cooperation Agreement (PCA) back in 1997.[5] The Agreement is a framework document defining the main direction of the bilateral interactions in the areas of promoting political dialogue between the Russia and the EC members (at that time, the European Communities); encouraging trade and investment; defending human rights and fundamental freedoms; promoting intercultural exchanges; and fostering cross-border movements of goods and services and other relevant forms of cooperation.[6] Nine similar PCAs were signed with the remaining former Soviet republics with the same purpose of promoting democracy, political dialogue, and economic development.

Northern Dimension

In addition to the PCA, there are two regional cooperation projects active between the EU and Russia. The first one is Northern Dimension (ND), which the EU initiated in 1999. The ND entails cooperation between the EU and non-allied European countries: Norway, Iceland, and Russia. The goal of the ND is to strengthen the links between these countries in democratic institutionalization, environmental security, transportation, public health, and cultural cooperation.[7] Participants were involved in the creation and implementation of its policies. Lannon Erwan and Peter Van Elsuwege noted, "The fact that these partner countries have become involved in the process from the very beginning and participated in the Foreign Ministers' conferences on the Northern Dimension is rather unusual in the EU context. In other words, the partner countries were expected to be not only policy-takers but also policymakers."[8] This is, however, quite understandable, taking into account Russia's attitude toward retaining its own sovereignty in decision making.

The ND was renewed in 2006 at the EU-Russia Helsinki summit, which defined its evolved goals as "a common framework for the promotion of dialogue and concrete cooperation, strengthening stability, well-being and intensified economic cooperation, promotion of economic integration and competitiveness and sustainable development in Northern Europe."[9] For the European countries, the program presented opportunities to foster their own regional agendas: Norway needed to include Russia to promote Norwegian roles in the region; Sweden wished to further complement its bilateral relations with Russia; and Finland wished to normalize bilateral relations with Russia.[10] The program was a good opportunity for Russia as well to promote its view in the region.

For Russia, the ND offered "an additional possibility to attract the attention of partners to the use of resources located in underdeveloped areas, as well as to find joint solutions to the problems of the Russian northwest border crossing areas."[11] Alexander Sergunin gives a rather precise outline of Russia's stake in the program:

> Given Moscow's growing isolation from Europe because of NATO enlargement and the Kosovo and Chechen wars, this is perhaps the only window of opportunity for Russian cooperation with European countries. Moreover, Russia is concerned about Kaliningrad—detached from the mainland and sandwiched between Poland and Lithuania. With Poland integrated into NATO and both Poland and Lithuania expected to join the EU, Kaliningrad could finally become an exclave rather than an enclave. At the same time, Russia sees the Northern Dimension as a "part of the whole": regional cooperation should facilitate the pan-European process, including pan-European security.[12]

Black Sea Synergy

The other program is the Black Sea Synergy (BSS), which was created in 2007. The program "aims to bring together different policy elements at EU's disposal including sectorial partnerships with Black Sea states."[13] In many ways this endeavor was caused by the EU enlargement itself. The accession of Bulgaria and Romania to the EU in the same year turned the land borders of the EU into the sea frontiers. This also brought the European Union closer to the insecurities that are either directly connected to the Black Sea (for instance, the conflicts in the Caucasus) or are occurring around it (such as the gas wars between Russia and Ukraine). At the inception of the BSS, there were discussions about supplying energy carriers to Europe through the Black Sea (for instance, the currently defunct "South Stream"), which would be enhanced by increased regional cooperation.

The Black Sea Synergy was the EU's extended hand of regional cooperation. Its program objectives were diverse: fostering democratic institutionalization, economic development, political stability, implementing projects of actual concern to the program participants, and contributing to the peaceful solution of regional conflicts. This was yet another way of including (and not ostracizing) Russia in the European family.

From the beginning, however, Russia's lack of interest and involvement, as well as its own views on the nature and forms of the regional partnership schemes, "generated concerns over the actual potential of the Synergy. Russia's lack of support to the Synergy and its insistence that the Synergy develop on an equal basis with BSEC [Organization of the Black Sea Economic Cooperation] and under BSEC- EU partnership has undermined the potential of BSS since its inception. To a large extent, difficulties with BSS implementation mirror those of the EU-Russia partnership."[14] The implementation of the program was further impeded by the involvement of the EU in regional affairs on the bilateral level: for instance, in color revolutions in Georgia and Ukraine with further slow but deliberate rapprochement of these countries with the EU. Moscow frowned upon this because it wanted to play the chief role in the policy engine of the region.

Euroregions

Finally, less institutional cooperation between the European Union and Russia is taking place on a subnational level between their bordering regions. The Euroregions' cooperation program entails closer economic and cultural ties between the countries of the EU bordering non-allied states. So far, cooperation with Russia on the regional levels occurs in the following regions: Euroregion Baltic (Russia, Denmark, Lithuania, Poland, and Sweden); Barents Euro-Atlantic Council (Russia, Finland, Norway, and Sweden); Euregion Karelia (Russia and Finland); and Neman Euroregion (Russia, Belarus, Lithuania, and Poland). Some regions do not include the European countries: Yaroslavna (Russia and Ukraine), Slobozhanshchina (Russia and Ukraine), and Dnepr (Russia, Belarus, and Ukraine).[15] After the worsening of the intergovernmental situation between Russia and Ukraine, future prospects for development of the Euroregions are quite vague.

Even before the Ukrainian crisis, development within the Euroregions left much to be desired, both Russian and EU standpoints. Aleksei Kuznetsov contends,

> If the main goal of the EU is to create a more or less safe socioeconomic development area at its borders and the main goal of Russia is to rise to certain local challenges with the help of the EU financing . . . then the prospects look quite bright. . . . But if we expect Russian society to get close to the societies of the neighboring EU countries in a few years, if we expect the common economic space to be formed on a different basis than that of large corporations, we will only face new problems.[16]

Aleksandr Sergunin further develops this pessimistic outlook on the subregional cooperation between the EU and Russia, "The Euroregions are basically reduced to what common Russians call 'bureaucratic tourism' (i.e., exchanged between municipalities). With rare exceptions, they do not promote economic cooperation and horizontal links at the people-to-people or NGO levels. There is no clear division of labor between Euroregions. . . . In some cases, there is an unhealthy competition for funds (EU and Russian) between different Euroregions. In other words, the Euroregion concept—being a potentially important tool for subregional cooperation—does not work properly."[17]

Evgeny Vinokurov and Alexander Libman agree that the problem was hidden in the design of the Euroregions such as inclusion of the regions with diverse cultural, social, and political contents:

> For Euroregions to function successfully, their participants must have sufficient financial capacity to participate actively in the projects and sufficient autonomy to make decisions without oversight by the nation-states. The FSU [Former Soviet Union] countries fail on at least one and usually both counts. Furthermore, the functioning of Euroregions often falls victim to conflict between individual countries. Finally . . . substantial trade restrictions exist in the regions [of Eastern Europe] and rules often change depending upon the current economic situation.[18]

Inequality within the Euroregions is of concern to the EU from another standpoint. As Oksana Antonenko and Kathryn Pinnick write, "The border regions are notorious for widening the economic and social gaps that exist along the EU-Russia frontier. . . . For the EU the asymmetry represents not merely an economic and social problem on its external borders, but also a potential security threat in terms of organized crime and illegal migration."[19] With the Euroregions, the European Union was entering an unknown terrain with diverse laws, practices, and norms.

European Union's Democracy Promotion

With all the pros and cons, the normative proximity was the main purpose of the aforementioned endeavors of the EU. Loyal to the Liberal Neofunctionalism view on the European integration, where "political integration is a more or less inevitable side-effect of economic integration,"[20] the process that brought the European countries to the EU was considered to be transferable also during the further stages of the European integration. This is especially true in the case of democratic institutionalization, where the norm of democratic governance is introduced to a new environment from outside. Later, via complex normative spillovers to other areas (health care, education, urban planning, social security, etc.) it starts to involve increased numbers of institutional actors. The final stage of the democratic normative life cycle is when a norm becomes a part of the political culture of a nation, an inherent component of its "moral fit" and the core of its identity. This fits well within the Constructivists' take on the European integration, which postulates that the norms, or "shared expectations about appropriate behavior held by a collectivity of actors," are socialized among the widest spectrums of institutional actors by looking at each other's performance and learning from the outcomes in each specific case.[21]

This is essentially what the EU was striving to achieve as a result of its cooperation programs and initiatives involving Russia as well as other former Soviet states. The problem was the different interpretation of those goals in Brussels and Moscow. While the EU was targeting the normative aspect of cooperation, Russia was feeling uneasy with the externally imposed values. Andrey Makarychev and Alexander Sergunin gave good accounts of the inherent incongruence in the EU-Russia dyad from the normative perspective.

> Normative unification is based on the presumption of Russia's acceptance of EU's values as guiding principles facilitating its inclusion into a wider Europe. In the EU reading, normative unification is a value-ridden model, grounded in a concept of the EU as a "soft power" that ought to "civilise," "democratise," "pacify," and "discipline" its "periphery." . . . Along these lines, the integration processes in Europe's new neighbourhood is viewed as an inevitable and natural result of "spill-over" and "ramification" effects. This model was more applicable to EU-Russia relations in the 1990s and is overtly challenged by the Putin regime.[22]

This is about thwarting the process of democratic reforms that started in the early 1990s and ended up with Putin's building the vertical of power. An example of the normative incongruence, which is especially related to interregional cooperation, was the end to regional self-governance put to sleep twice in its embryonic form by Putin when he revoked elections of regional governors first in 2004 after the terrorist act in Beslan and then again in 2013.

Institutional Grounds for Discord

On the regional level the important political and security issues between the EU and Russia are approached within the institutional framework of the Organization for Security and Cooperation in Europe (OSCE). Established in 1975 during the Conference on Security and Cooperation in Europe, OSCE remains the largest regional security organization involving all the European countries. The core functions of OSCE are divided into three "dimensions": politico-military, economic-environmental, and human security.[23] These wider umbrellas include such activities as arms control, border management, counterterrorism, conflict prevention, democratization, economic development, education, and human rights. Russia has been an active participant in the OSCE ever since its inception. Russian is one of the official languages of the organization.

In 1991 Russia initiated the so-called Moscow Mechanism, which is based on the "human dimension" of the OSCE: protection of human rights and promotion of democracy. This tool for international participation in political issues includes the creation of ad hoc groups of experts with the purpose of "resolution of a particular question or problem relating to the human dimension. . . . Such a mission may gather the information necessary for carrying out its tasks and, as appropriate, use its good offices and mediation services to promote dialogue and cooperation among interested parties."[24] The Moscow Mechanism was enacted several times in relation to the human rights violations committed in Croatia and Bosnia-Herzegovina (by the European Community and the United States in 1992) and NATO's Yugoslavia operations (enacted by Russia in 1999).

The Moscow Mechanism was, without a doubt, a significant step in developing the UN-type form and essence for the OSCE, where teams of experts would resemble those of the UN special rapporteurs, elevating the prestige of this regional organization on the international arena. The Moscow Mechanism also gave Russia an opportunity to raise its voice in matters related to European political affairs. It was the first real step toward the inclusion of Russia into the post–Cold War European security architecture as a full-fledged member who is relied upon. Finally, OSCE was the only European political organization in which Russia had veto power.

Because it is a nonbinding intergovernmental organization, OSCE offers its member states the opportunity to openly address many issues that other organizations, including the UN, cannot. This is also its major drawback, because to many, including Russia, the organization is viewed as merely paying lip service to the vital issues. Also, as Victor-Yves Ghebali noted "Russian grievances about insufficient military-security dialogue within OSCE, non-updating of the CSBMS regime, and the nonratification of the adapted treaty on Conventional Armed Forces in Europe (CFE)" as several stumbling blocks in its political interactions with Europe.[25]

If initially Russia aimed at transforming OSCE into a counterweight to NATO's involvement on the European continent and possibly beyond, it was greatly disillusioned with the OSCE and its various agencies openly chastising Moscow's violations of the very principles the organization was based on. OSCE's subunit, the Office of Democratic Institutions and Human Rights (ODIHR) took a highly critical stance on the issues of human rights violations by Russia, especially pertaining to the atrocities of the Russian troops in Chechnya and the elections in Russia.[26] The Russian government was outraged because Russia had made significant financial contributions to the organization, which was now criticizing Russia's domestic conduct. In the Russian view, this was tantamount to biting the hand that feeds you while questioning the very morals and true intentions of this hand and the whereabouts of the food.

Presidential elections of 2004 in Russia marked the beginning of an open conflict with the OSCE. At the CIS summit in Moscow in July 2004, Russia accused the OSCE of practicing "double standards" and showing "unwillingness to take into account the realities and peculiarities of individual states." Russia further urged the OSCE to reorganize in order to "bring it back to first principles," which were, in its view, the collective security without the unnecessary burden of human rights.[27] At the end, for three months Moscow had been blocking approval of the OSCE budget for 2005 under the pretext that it refused to fund activities contrary to its interests and principles. During his last presidential press conference in 2008, before giving the supreme seat to his substitute, Dmitri Medvedev, Putin blasted the ODIHR for imposing its terms and conditions on Russia. He even suggested that its election observers should stay at home and teach their wives how to cook *shchi* (a Russian vegetable soup) instead of coming to Russia and teaching it how to live.[28] As a result, the OSCE election monitors were unable to enter Russia because of unresolved visa issues, which Russia used as a pretext to prevent the OSCE from doing its mandated job.[29]

Continuing to resent OSCE's involvement in Russia's domestic political matters, in 2005 Foreign Minister Lavrov repeated the mantra of Russia's "double standards" toward the OSCE and its leadership and said he had enough "grounds to suspect that electoral monitoring under the OSCE roof is used as a trigger to destabilize the situation in a particular country," that country being, of course, Russia.[30] To reinforce its argument, according to Thomas Ambrosio, "Russia has even gone so far as to call into question the core mission of the CoF and the OSCE to spread and consolidate the liberal values in Europe."[31] Further extending the line of political alienation from the organization it had helped, established, and supported, during the December 2006 meeting of OSCE foreign ministers, for the first time Lavrov made threats about the possibility of Russia leaving the OSCE. He said that this could happen if the OSCE did not shift the focus of activity with human rights monitoring in the military-political and economic cooperation.[32] Perhaps the biggest boiling point in the Russia-OSCE relations was the so-called Vilnius Resolution of the OSCE Parliamentary Assembly in 2009, where the parliamentarians mentioned the Nazi and Soviet regimes as "two major totalitarian regimes . . . which brought about genocide, violations of human rights and freedoms, war crimes and crimes against humanity."[33] Needless to say, this was negatively received in Russia, which had already made the necessary changes in its criminal law that make the "rehabilitation of Nazism" punishable with three years in prison.

Because it resents the OSCE's criticism, the Russian political establishment is unable or unwilling to comprehend that in contemporary political times, collective institutionalized security is impossible without the joint compliance with the democratic principles, norms, and standards from which the very organization derives its existence. Historically, Russia had no problem in fulfilling the institutional requirements of collective political decision making. Even when collective security had been based on the principles of totalitarian intimidation, such as the Warsaw Pact, the Soviet Union had to satisfy its ideational cravings by strictly monitoring compliance of its members with the principles and postulates of communism. Yet now the principles were imposed by the USSR on its followers, whereas within the OSCE Russia had to take a parity standing with others. The cognitive dissonance in the Russian political culture was growing deep. Whereas in the Warsaw Pact the USSR was the producer and creator of institutional frameworks, in the OSCE Russia was a mere actor in the institution of the European collective security. The switch from being the leader of the whole institution to being one of the many followers seems to be very difficult for the Russian political culture.

In practice, Russia refused to comply with the OSCE's foundation principles (for which it was mandated and endorsed by Russia itself) because it saw them as encroachments on its sovereignty. Complaints that the OSCE had "departed from its original mission to act as a pan-European security agency and had become little more than the self-appointed monitor of elections and judge on the state of democracy in the post-Communist era" are devoid of any grounds.[34] Overreliance on the spirit of collective action and overemphasis of the domestic human dimensions of the regional security were what made the organization unique and internally impartial. Had the OSCE not engaged in Russia's criticism, this would mean the failure of fulfillment of the very mandate by which the organization was guided. The OSCE had not created the violations: it was merely reporting them. Thinking of NATO as America's pet project in Europe, Russia wanted to do the same with the OSCE. However, NATO's view of European security and its collective nature facilitated Russia's participation in the OSCE. As Adler held, "To make the enlargement process more palatable to Russia . . . NATO has engaged the latter in cooperative security dialogue, which includes military, political, economic and environmental OSCE-like community-building activities."[35] The problem was that Russia wanted "to enter a foreign monastery with its own statute," as the Russian proverb goes, namely, to change the rules of the same. It would not agree that "when in Rome, do as the Romans do," and it wanted to impose its own vision on the institutional actors.

The discord between Russia, the OSCE, and the European Union brought results that may not be what Russia expected, but to a certain degree they favored the Russian side. As Vladimir Shkolnikov states, "Russia, despite the crudeness of its methods, has achieved some of its objectives. As further bureaucratization forced staff turnover, the Russian veto on the extension of the OSCE Mission to Georgia and the successful change of mandate of the OSCE Office in Tashkent which could monitor and report on internal developments, meant that it changed to become merely a project office, focusing on assistance to government structures. Therefore, it is clear that the OSCE is in decline, not only in the human dimension, but overall."[36] Indeed, part of Russia's success in its war against Georgia in 2008 was the absence of strong international monitoring mechanisms. Russia refused to include any other side in the multilateral commission that it has co-chaired to add a more "impartial" arbiter status.

The biggest blow to the OSCE, however, happened in 2007, when Russia denounced the CFE treaty. Concluded in the final months of the Soviet Union, the CFE treaty set limits on the ceilings and "flanks" of the NATO and Warsaw treaty's military deployment in Europe. The flanks contain five groups of heavy conventional weapons: tanks, armored combat vehicles, artillery, aircrafts, and helicopters, which, as the Russian side admitted, it was in violation of by the time of its entry into force in 1995 for deployment of its troops in Chechnya.[37] As a successor state to the USSR, Russia undertook the same responsibilities, but was on numerous occasions, such as in 1998, found in violation of the "flank" limits.[38] As some form of concession to Russia, the United States and NATO decided "to update the CFE treaty in a significant and constructive way to ensure its continued viability and its stabilizing influence."[39] The adapted CFE, presented to its signatories in 1999, reviewed the structure and essence of the flank limitations per countries instead of per blocks (one of which was already extinct). Together with that, at the OSCE Istanbul summit of 1999, Russia pledged to remove its troops from Moldova and Georgia, which it never did. Consequently, the adapted CFE never entered into force, since "the NATO states committed themselves not to ratify the . . . Treaty until Russia had fulfilled these obligations."[40] The reason given was that the treaty required full legal ratification by its signatories.

This impasse from unwillingness of Russia to accept the proposed frameworks of the new CFE treaty resulted in Russia's withdrawal in 1999.[41] The Russian side justified this move by "extraordinary circumstances . . . which affect the security of the Russian Federation and require immediate measures": the advance of the antimissile defense in Eastern Europe and the failure of the NATO countries to ratify the adapted treaty (caused by non-fulfillment of Russia's obligations in the first place).[42] Some Russian scholars saw this move as a completely justified act of a nation that wanted to protect itself in the face of impending political disasters. For instance, C. V. Arapina and C. A. Pfetzer called the CFE a "political misunderstanding" and concluded, "The decision to suspend Russia's participation in . . . [the CFE] is a completely natural act entirely within the national interest of the Russian Federation. . . . Its formal existence meets the main military and political objectives of the West: removal of the Soviet troops from Europe, the maximum reduction in military capabilities, and instating western control over it."[43] As for the Adapted CFE, some call the U.S. and NATO concessions in it, such as more than 80 percent increase in the flank quotas for Russia, "political blackmailing from the Russian government on every minor issue, such as removal of the Russian forces from Georgia and Transnistria."[44] Azhdar Kurtov also saw the elements of security dilemma in the increase of quotas for Russia: according to him, this was not an important compromise, because under the adapted treaty, NATO would still have three times more military troops than Russia,[45] and this cannot be balanced by the increase in flanks.

Back in the early 2000s with the climate of the EU-Russia relations being rather optimistic, such a confrontational stance was difficult to foresee. There were even talks of possible Russian membership in the EU. Commenting on the future place of Russia within the European family, Swedish ambassador Sven Hirdman gave the following scenario: "I have a firm conviction that Russia's integration into the European structures should continue and deepen. . . . The globalization processes, unifications of the world economies, information revolution, freedom of movement, geography, and also history and culture push Russia in this direction."[46] In 2006 such elevated discussions were common: Putin's Munich speech would be made in a year; Russia would attack Georgia in two years, and the prospects of further integration of Russia into the European community would suffer an almost lethal blow with Russia's Crimean Anschluss and the following turmoil in eastern Ukraine.

Intergovernmental Forum for Cooperation

The programs between the European Union and Russia were designed and implemented within the general political intergovernmental cooperation between the EU and Russia. The umbrella medium of the EU-Russia relations are the biennial summits where the parties talk about the results achieved, lessons learned, the issues that can be improved, and future milestones. The most recent EU-Russia summit took place in January 2014, very close to the start of the Winter Olympic Games in Sochi. President of the European Council Herman Van Rompuy tried to assure the Russian leadership that the next level of integration of the former Soviet Union nations within the European family, the conclusion of the Eastern Partnership Association Agreements, was in no way threatening Russia's vital strategic and economic interests. Van Rompuy stated,

> A more stable economic and institutional environment, improved market access and intensified trade relations will strengthen demand and create new business opportunities for all. . . . The Eastern Partnership does not affect Russia's economic, trade, social, human and cultural links to many of our common neighbours. These links will not be put at risk, but on the contrary, stimulated by more dynamic and successful economic development in the partner countries.[47]

Essentially these agreements, as subsequent attempts to harmonize the vital areas of politics and economy of the post-Soviet countries, were directly based on the same APCs that Russia concluded, too, with the European Union. Russia, however, believed that these agreements, especially between the EU and Ukraine, were threatening its interests and decided to act appropriately, leading to its alleged participation in the Ukrainian crisis.

In 2008 the EU-Russia summit in Khanty-Mansiysk started the negotiations over a substantially new agreement. The proposed agreement would expand the previous PCA to reflect a more comprehensive nature of the relations between the European Union, as a supranational entity, and the Russian Federation, as the largest country on the European continent. The progress of the new legal document cementing the relationships between the parties, however, was slowed down by some issues of concern to the EU that were present from the beginning of negotiations and due to the past and present complications of the interactions with Russia. Apart from the purely legal quandary of the nonexistence of legal guidelines and references in the European Constitutional Treaty and the European Court on any compatible documents, there are substantial political concerns related to the feasibility of the new agreement.

EU's reservations about the potential agreement follow domestic and international political lines. Sami Andoura and Marius Vahl draw attention to the fact that "the EU has never concluded such an ambitious and comprehensive agreement with any third country, and the EU treaties do not provide any clear guidance as to how such an agreement might be concluded. Second, the bilateral relationship has become closer and more challenging in the last few years, and the numerous contentious issues encountered will have to be addressed by the new agreement."[48] Third, the newly concluded Customs Union between Russia, Belarus, Kazakhstan, and Armenia also impeded the economic part of the treaty with regard to the harmonization of the investment and trade procedures in the Customs Union and the EU.[49] These and other issues of concern resonate with the domestic situation in Russia with regard to the quality of fulfillment (or, rather, lack thereof) of the human rights and the conditions of the civil society, as well as the war against Georgia and its questionable involvement in the conflict in Ukraine. Instead of the new agreement, the PCAs have been annually renewed to keep the relations between the EU and Russia running.

The EU-Russia St. Petersburg summit 2003 launched sectorial cooperation between the EU and Russia and builds on the four "common spaces" where the EU and Russia overlap. These spaces include economy and the environment (trade and economic cooperation); freedom, security, and justice (enhancing the cross-border cooperation with regard to the movements of goods, services, and personnel; and also partnership in the counterterrorism activities); external security (multilateral cooperation in the field of regional security entailing nonproliferation, crisis management, and civil protection), and research and education (enhancing cooperation in joint research endeavors, cultural exchanges, language learning, and academic interactions).[50] In 2005, the parties at the Moscow summit agreed to further develop the instruments, or so-called road maps, which would allow the European Union and Russia to implement the "common spaces."

Development of cooperation in some of these "common spaces" was fruitful, such as in the economic space. An example of successful cooperation is Russia's accession to the World Trade Organization in August 2012 after years of painful negotiations with the WTO member countries "striving to achieve favorable access conditions to the internal Russian market, maximum lowering of tariff barriers . . . [and] Russia pressing on keeping the level of tariff and non-tariff protection of own producers."[51] Also, Ukraine and Georgia were blocking Russia's WTO membership due to their own problems with Russia, which was overcome upon successful negotiations with these states.

In other "spaces," however, cooperation was stalled by concerns the European Union had with numerous "reports of violence by law enforcement authorities in the North Caucasus, no progress in media pluralism, difficulties in holding public demonstrations, torture and ill treatment in detention centres and increased racism, xenophobia and homophobia . . . the situation of human rights defenders and independent journalists,"[52] noncompliance with the ECHR's judgments, and failure to ratify Protocol 6 of the ECHR on the abolition of the death penalty. Resolution 2789 of the European Parliament showed concern about the cases of "intimidation, harassment, and arrests of the representatives of opposition forces and non-governmental organisations, the recent adoption of a law on the financing of NGOs, on the right of assembly, the law on defamation, the law on the internet restrictions as well as the increasing pressure on free and independent media and minorities in sexual orientation and religious belief."[53] The domestic political situation in Russia, including imprisonment of the human rights activists (Mikhail Khodorkovsky's trial and punishment); breaches of the due process of law (in the Magnitsky case); unresolved assassinations of known journalists (Anna Politkovskaya), and the treatment of civil society organizations continue to bear negative inputs in EU-Russia relations.

Tensions over Extended Cooperation with Others

In the new millennium the European Union launched several regional partnership programs with other former Soviet nations. The most important of them were the European Neighborhood Policy (2004) and the Eastern Partnership (2009), both of which the Russian Federation viewed negatively. The European Neighborhood Policy (ENP) aimed at "avoiding the emergence of new dividing lines between the enlarged EU and our neighbours and instead strengthening the prosperity, stability and security of all. It is based on the values of democracy, rule of law and respect of human rights."[54] The ENP was offered to six former Soviet republics (Armenia, Azerbaijan, Belarus, Georgia, Moldova, and Ukraine), but not to Russia. Through the EPN the European Union offers its participants cooperation in specific sectors, such as closer economic ties and trade with the EU, transfer of expertise and sharing of experience in democratic institutionalization, as well as technical harmonization with the EU standards.

In 2009 the EPN was further enriched by the Eastern Partnership (EaP) initiative to the same countries, which was considered by many as the next step toward their further integration in the European Union's economic, political, and cultural structures with the ultimate purpose of their possible membership. To some, "The EaP was a direct product not just of the EU's internal inability to form a consensus on any 'single' way forward . . . but also of the increased perception of insecurity, threat, and risk resulting from events such as the Russia-Georgia war of August 2008, the violence in the Moldovan elections (2009), and the Ukraine-Russia gas crisis (2009)."[55] To tackle these possible challenges to Europe's security emanating from its eastern borders, the EU decided to act in the only way acceptable to its multilateralism: to further tighten the mutually beneficial web of liberal economic interdependence. The cooperation flew along multiple channels, most important of which were democratic and social development, energy security, and various sector-specific reforms.

In many respects, the ENP and the EaP were considered the necessary parts of the potential EU membership, although the EU accession process is free from exclusions. The closest the European Union ever came to integrating the former Soviet republics were the Association Agreements offered to their governments. The purpose of these agreements is to establish closer relations with the EU and the third states, including economic liberalization and political cooperation. In general, according to Vassilis Monastiriotis et al., "Signing of such agreements became in a way a kind of endorsement by the EU of the transition policies deployed in each of these countries and transmitted strong signals to the markets, at home and abroad, about the position of each country in its path to post-communist transition and accession to the EU."[56] The agreements essentially meant privileged relations with the EU while not offering any tangible or promising guarantees for becoming its member per se. Nothing precludes, however, the countries that have Association Agreements with the EU from gaining full membership. At some point, even the United Kingdom, before becoming an EU member, was offered an Association Agreement, but rejected it.[57] The countries that joined the European Union after the Cold War, including Hungary, Bulgaria, Cyprus, Croatia, Latvia, and Lithuania, all went through the stage of the agreement. There were others, too, including Turkey, which remained under the agreement for decades, never making it to full EU membership.

Russia rejected attempts by the European Union to extend the hand of friendship to former communist nations. The ENP/EaP did not offer more or less tangible answers to the Eastern European countries, especially those farther away from Brussels, related to their potential membership. In essence, it was a small carrot that carried no specific promise of potentially bigger carrots in the future. To worsen the matter, as Elena Korosteleva noted, "This positive experience [was] counter-balanced by the increasing anxiety in relation to the choice the partner countries feel they have to make: a closer integration with the EU or with Russia?"[58] The closer the countries were to Moscow, their former center of Soviet gravity, the more difficult it was for them to make a pro-Europe or pro-Russia choice, especially when the benefits and end results of at least the first direction, the uber-vague European conditionality applied to them were not fully and clearly visible. The benefits of the second direction, too, were not specific at that point, but the potential losses incurred by moving away from Russia and closer to Europe, especially from a political standpoint, loomed large. Some of the ENP/EaP countries, including Moldova, Georgia, Azerbaijan, and Armenia, had the "weak points"—the unresolved conflicts on their territories—which Russia can use as political leverage in case of their "dwindling" away.

Given this effete character of the ENP/EaP initiatives, they were nevertheless viewed similarly to other "encroachments" on Russia's own, as the NATO enlargement, happening almost the same time. As stated by Michael Johns, "Russia sees the Eastern partnership as the EU attempting to become involved in a part of the world that it sees as their sphere of influence."[59] The perceptional security dilemma present in Russia's approach to the politics of the United States in Europe also tainted Russia's ability to correctly understand the nature of the EU's extended cooperation. The main reason perhaps was the coincidental parallel in the developments of the two regional multinational organizations, one of which, for being a past military adversary of the USSR, was augmenting its influence in Europe at the expense of the territories that formerly were under Russian/USSR control.

The EU's wish to come closer to the non-allied members of the European family was assessed as highly negative and threating in Russia. Its political establishment thought of them as a challenge presented to it by the EU in the region that the Russian Federation considers a zone of its own interests. According to Irina Busigina and Mikhail Filippov, there was a widespread view in Russia that the EU, while openly advocating for the elimination of dividing lines in Europe, was actually drawing them again and forcing the post-Soviet countries, which have certain political and legal obligations with Moscow, to make a strategic choice: to follow the EU or Russia.[60] This view is essentially oxymoronic: why would Russia, who was striving for closer integration with the EU and promoting the contextually deeper association with the EU, deny essentially the same thing for other post-Soviet nations?

There is only one possible answer to this question: Russia still regards post-Soviet space as essentially neo-Russian. Otherwise, Putin would not have declared that the EU's "Eastern Partnership" was "an alternative to NATO's expansion to the East" and "a partnership against Russia."[61] Neither would Foreign Minister Lavrov have commented that the Eastern Partnership was an EU attempt to expand its "sphere of influence" in the quest for hydrocarbons.[62] The ultimate goal of Russian foreign policy in the European direction is the removal of the prefix "post" in the adjectives describing the political past of the newly independent states. This is the very reason for Russia's rejections of the EU mediations during the conflict in Georgia, its current stance vis-à-vis the unresolved fate of the Transdnistria part of Moldova, the start of tensions with Ukraine over the vectors of its economic development, and the attempts to create the Customs Union as a direct contender to the EU.

Europe in Russian Foreign Policy and National Security

The European direction has traditionally been one of the most important in Russian foreign policy. Its 2000 concept paper calls the relations with the European countries "traditional priority direction of Russia's foreign policy. The main goal of Russian foreign policy in Europe is to create a stable and democratic system pan-European security and cooperation." Further along its narrative, the document mentioned, "The relations with the European Union (EU) are of paramount importance. The processes taking place in the EU have an increasing impact on the dynamics of the situation in Europe. These include enlargement of the EU the transition to a single currency, institutional reforms, and establishment of the Common Foreign and Security Policy and Defense Policy (CFSP) and the European Security and Defense Identity (ESDI). Regarding these processes as an objective component of the European development, Russia will seek due respect for its interests."[63] The keyword here is the "objective development," which means that in 2000 Russia was opposed neither to the European integration processes nor its eastward enlargement. At the break of the new millennium, these processes were viewed as a normal outcome of the decade following the collapse of the bipolar system in the European continent. The foreign policy discourse at the end of Yeltsin's era and the beginning of Putin's era placed Russia as an interested, engaged, but not disruptive participant of the rapidly changing European security architecture.

Similarly pro-active was the Russian stance in its midterm strategy toward Europe, which defined the main priorities of the bilateral relations as "creation a reliable European collective security system, attraction of the economic potential and managerial experience of the European Union to promote socially oriented market economy in Russia." Among other aims of the strategy are "creation and strengthening of the partnership between Russia and the European Union in European and world affairs; prevention and resolution of local conflicts through joint efforts in Europe with a focus on international law and the use of force . . . [c]onstruction of a united Europe without dividing lines."[64] All these priorities that seemed quite legitimate and understandable, taking into account strong economic ties between Russia and many of the European Union members, were tossed away as a result of the Russian actions in Ukraine. The analysis of the latter shows either dual standards in approaching the matter of the European integration at least in economic terms or pure deception from the very start. For the Associated Agreement between Ukraine and the European Union, which the former was about to sign in November 2013 and which became the stumbling block in its relations with Russia, was nothing but what it was striving to achieve with the EU. If, of course, the aforementioned policy guidelines were taken seriously by the Russian leadership and not just the smokescreen western direction of Russia.

The National Security Concept Paper 2000 presents a different outlook on the relations with Europe. The European direction was mentioned there as the very ground zero of the hostile forces trying to hurt Russia and damage its international prestige. The Concept Paper lists "the attempts of other states to oppose the strengthening of Russia as one of the centers of influence in the multipolar world; to prevent exercise of its national interests and to weaken its positions in Europe."[65] This makes Europe not the place of natural habitat for Russian but the birthplace and the battleground of hostile forces for Russia. The dual character of the Russian foreign policy also extends in the rift between its visions on the international system per se and its place there, on the one hand, and the construction of perception of threats to its vital national interests, on the other. In Putin's first two presidential terms, Russia attempted to embrace Europe; it strived to become a full-fledged member of the European family, but viewed the actions of the European NATO members (and the United States, too) as threatening its national security.

The Foreign Policy Concept Paper of 2008 was drafted when Medvedev replaced Putin as president of Russia. Its language and spirit are far more liberal than its predecessors and any of other successors. The Concept Paper defined Russia's main aim in the European direction as "creation of a truly open, democratic system of collective regional security and cooperation ensuring the unity of the Euro-Atlantic region—from Vancouver to Vladivostok, without its fragmentation and reproduction of bloc approaches still persisting in the European architecture, developed as a result of the Cold War. The collective security thinking permeates the whole document, with references to the commitment of Russia to play an active role in strengthening the "positions of the Euro-Atlantic region in the global competition" and fortifying the roles of the intergovernmental organizations, such as the Council of Europe and the Organization for Security and Cooperation in Europe (where Russia has a membership), in the matter of provision of the regional security, economy, and humanitarian affairs.

European Security Treaty: From Success to Failure

The Russian translation of the spirit of liberalism was presented to the European countries during the June 2008 visit of President Medvedev to Germany, at which he proposed reorganization of the whole architecture of the European security. As the result of the preliminary proposal, the document further produced the name "European Security Treaty" advocated for the close integration of Russia within the political and economic institutional frameworks of the EU. Most of its key postulates, such as the "principles of indivisible and equal security; not endangering the security of each other, taking into account the security interests of all its Members," respect for territorial integrity, including nondeployment on its own territory of the military personnel or equipment that might endanger the sovereignty of the member states, arms control, and the variety of the consultation channels were, in principle, dear to the highly liberal environment of the EU.[66]

There were several reasons why the treaty was doomed from its very deliberation stages. First, there was no practical need for it because it was not going to threaten Russian security in the perceivable future. The European security architecture was set up as a result of the intergovernmental negotiations, discussions at the Brussels level, domestic deliberations, and voting, which was embodied in various common security documents, including the Common Foreign and Security Policy and the Common Security and Defense Policy. Besides, the first enlargement of NATO by bringing in the three Visegrad states (Hungary, Poland, and the Czech Republic) happened in 1999 as a result of the years of negotiations of these aspirant countries with NATO HQ. Their decisions to join NATO were not forcefully imposed upon them by the Alliance but by revelations of their sovereign national principle, the very societal pillar Russia proposed to withhold. Denying the notion of sovereignty to others while striving to uphold one's own was something that threw the European countries into the inexplicable cognitive dissonance.

Second, two months after Medvedev's visit, the war between Russia and Georgia broke out, for which many in the West placed the blame on Russia's shoulders. If Russia were sincere in proposing open and peaceful relations with the European countries based on the principles discussed in the proposed treaty, then its own actions in Georgia in support of the separatist movements in Abkhazia and South Ossetia (both of which were on numerous occasions proclaimed by the European Union to be indivisible parts of Georgia) did an incredibly poor job of assuring the EU of its peaceful intentions.[67] As President Medvedev explained during his visit to Evian, France, on October 8, 2008, it was the current system of the European security that failed in Georgia and not the Russian support to the separatists and irredentists starting from the first conflict in 1991–92 in South Ossetia and 1992–94 in Abkhazia. As a result, according to the Russian side, the "existing security system in Europe is unable to adequately respond to the contemporary challenges."[68] Thus the new basis for the joint security on the European continent should be developed. However, the only failure of the existing European security architecture was NATO's shilly-shallying about potential membership of Georgia (and Ukraine, for that matter), which might have given false hopes to these countries but very correct hopes to Russia in its lack of action.

If closely scrutinized, the proposed text of the treaty, according to its drafters, should bear "clear statement of the basic principles of security and intergovernmental relations in the Euro-Atlantic area. These should include the commitment to the good faith fulfillment of the international obligations; respect for the sovereignty, territorial integrity and political independence of the States . . . inadmissibility of the use of force or threat of its use in international relations."[69] To extend Medvedev's proposal for the treaty, in October 2012 the Russian Council of Federations issued a separate decree eulogizing Russia's role in upholding the European collective security. The decree read,

> The Russian Federation efforts to transform the relations on the European continent; overcome the legacy of the Cold War, cessation of ideological confrontation expanded the possibilities of cooperation in the European space and significantly reduced the risk of military conflicts in Europe. . . . The Council of Federations . . . declares inadmissibility of erosion of the key principles of international law . . . exclusion from the world practice of the actions aimed at suppressing the sovereignty and territorial integrity of States, interfering in the internal affairs of States, and attempts to solve internal conflicts and crises through military actions not authorized by the UN Security Council.[70]

The main and true recipient of the decree was the local public, however, which the Russian government tried to assure of its peaceful intentions of the proposed institutional rapprochement with the European Union by convoluting their true meaning. The international public and especially its European part were presented with a completely opposite picture of "sovereignty and territorial integrity" of Georgia in 2008 and later in Ukraine. These instances of application of the international law by Russia in practice went against the very spirit of the EST it was proposing. At the end, Russia presented the treaty to the EU countries as the solution to the problems on the European continent it had created in the first place.

Another probable reason for the EU's rejection of the EST was that in case of its approval the EU was *ex post factum* endorsing the Russian intervention in Georgia. Loyal to the spirit of "it was long time ago and never happened anyway" of the Russian political culture, the preliminary design of the treaty proposed to the EU to prohibit all the actions that Russia already had committed in 2008 against another member of the Council of Europe. Quite possibly, this specific part of the treaty was influenced by the thought that the EU had largely "forgiven" Russia for its Georgia war and showed, as the Russians thought, all signs it was ready to start from a clear slate with it. Alexei Smirnov verbalized these expectations, stating, "Even the August war between Russia and Georgia in 2008 should have become to be a new landmark of confrontation between Russia and the West. However, not only did the EU not reject Russia, but itself proposed to begin negotiations on a new Partnership and Cooperation Agreement (PCA) with Russia."[71] In the language of the Russian political culture it meant that the EU was content, at least nominally, with the status quo ensuing after the war and was understood as Europe's conniving attitude toward Russia's de facto territorial gains. Thus if something worked once (in Georgia), why not repeat it a second time (in Crimea) and even a third time (somewhere else)?

The war in Georgia cast seriously negative shadows on the future of the EU-Russia security treaty, where the institutional role of NATO, as a political-military, intergovernmental organization, was concerned. There was a part in the treaty directly related to the notion of collective security and Russian potential participation in the European security architecture: "Not to provide for own security at the expense of security of others. Not to allow the actions (within military alliances or coalitions), which would undermine the unity of common security space. . . . Not to allow the development of military alliances to happen to the detriment of the other parties to the treaty."[72] This very passage, according to some, contained the no-no's for the Euro-Atlantic views on security. Atayan and Cherepova gave the following explanation of the lack of success of the treaty: "Comprehensive security in the Western interpretation includes military-political, economic, and humanitarian blocks. Since the last two were ignored, the treaty was not comprehensive enough in the eyes of the Euro-Atlantic partners."[73] In other words, the proposed treaty focused only on the military aspect of the alliance/non-allied member interactions and would not allow for inclusion of other aspects of the aforementioned relations.

In reality, however, it was the potential stance toward the collective

European security, where the allied actions of the European Union members of the NATO would be scrutinized by a non-NATO member (and a priori hostile to it) that gave the grounds for yet another explanation for not accepting the treaty. As Marcel de Haas noted with regard to NATO's view of the EST, "The emphasis on legally binding decisions by the signatories' conference of the proposed treaty would make any independent Western actions in the realm of security virtually impossible."[74] Inclusion of the NATO countries in the European Security Treaty "would effectively give Moscow a veto over further NATO expansion and would de facto recognize Moscow's self-proclaimed sphere of privileged interests. . . . [It] would prevent NATO from acting independently of Moscow," as McNamara from the Heritage Foundation explained.[75]

Having a blocking say in the political matters on the European continent was exactly Russia's core aim at proposing the European Security Treaty, to start with. Danilov considers the Treaty a result of Russia's dissatisfaction with the existing state of affairs within the NATO-Russia Council. According to him, "Russia's claims are, first of all, directed to the fact that the NATO countries are still present in Council not in their national capacities . . . but from preliminarily agreed upon positions. Often Russia cannot make the [Council] partners to include the topics that it wants to discuss into the agenda. According to Moscow, the Council failed to reach the level of large-scale cooperation projects."[76] Russia continues to accuse the United States of meddling in European affairs, which was perhaps the main reason for the proposed treaty.

For Russia, Europe will always be the battleground for American imperialism. This is the main and concurrent message coming from the Russian political establishment to its domestic audience with the purpose of consolidating it around Putin's leadership and against the constructed Wester/European/NATO threat. Andrei Isayev, Vice Speaker of the Russian Duma, when addressing the National Front, a French nationalist political organization, further developed this viewpoint: "We regret to see how the sovereignty of our esteemed powerful nation-states of Europe . . . is lost in the name of so-called Atlantic integration; we see how the will of the peoples of the European countries is being replaced by the will of little-known EU officials who are essentially the American puppets."[77] Russia's ideal image of Europe is the continent without the United States and NATO without its main actor and contributor. This is what Naryshkin proposed: "I have a fantastic offer: I would suggest to our European partners to expel the United States from the [NATO] block. And I am sure that [after that] the level of stability and security in Europe will quickly return to its proper condition."[78] In return, Russia aspires to fit into the NATO shoes and play the leading role in European security. This wish is not fully verbalized or documented yet, but it is in the air surrounding the messages Russia sends to Europe concerning the future of its security architecture.

Europe under America

Europe is increasingly viewed as losing its identity and sovereignty to the onslaught of Americanism. The first loss is greatly lamented by Russia while the second is considered as irreparable. Europe is considered as devoid of any significantly strong voice on the international arena, and even if it does say something, it does so under the insurmountable pressure from the United States. A good example of the sanctions the EU imposed on Russia is the case of the Russian railroads, whose owner, Vladimir Yakunin, fell among the first victims of the Ukrainian situation. Commenting on Russian banks filing a lawsuit against the EU for the sanctions in October 2014, the Russian tycoon sees both Russia and the EU as "bearing the burden of a hawkish and unilateral U.S. policy that is being dictated to leading EU nations over the Ukrainian crisis."[79] Absence of the single potent voice in the European multilateralism proves the pressure from outside: this is the opinion of the Russian political elites that praises sovereignty higher than any other virtue.

Russia's paternalistic attitude toward Europe being a victim of American imperialism extends to seemingly bizarre grounds that are merely borderline normal. For instance, when Europe "dares to raise its voice" against American politics, it gets punished by the former: the terrorist attacks in France in early 2015 were increasingly presented in the Russian mainstream media and social networking as an act of the vindictive CIA. The source of this statement, Russian political scientist Alexey Martinov, building on the argument that Islamic terrorism is the creature of the Central Intelligence Agency, presents national sovereignty as the biggest loathed target for the United States: "We know last year many European countries limited their cooperation with Russia in the fight against international terrorism under U.S. pressure. If you give up your sovereignty in the area of security, be prepared to be treated as France was," referring to the terrorists attacks.[80]

On the institutional level, notwithstanding the fact that the NATO-Russian Council had resumed its routine after the reset, NATO leadership had a very clear view of Russia's "king's pawn" move with the treaty.[81] Soon it was presented with another proof of Russia's hostile intentions in Europe. The National Security Strategy 2020, drafted during the second year of Medvedev's reign, identified potential deployment of the missile defense systems in Eastern Europe as a direct threat to Russia's national security interests and the regional stability in Europe. With this, Russia wanted to contribute to "comprehensive strengthening of cooperation with the European Union, including the establishment of common spaces in economy, external and internal security, education, science, and culture." It was also striving "to develop relations with the North Atlantic Treaty Organization on the basis of equality and to strengthen global security in the Euro-Atlantic area, the depth and breadth of which would be determined by the willingness of the Alliance to take into account the legitimate interests of Russia in the implementation of the military and political planning."[82] Thus Russia pledged to become a responsible member of the European community of states and uphold the common issues of security concern on the Euro-Atlantic space on its own terms only—in stark contrast to the omnipresent spirit of supranationalism in the EU and multilateralism in the NATO.

Legitimacy and Justice

The part on the "legitimate interests" of Russia is quite tricky here. To start with, in the context of international relations, semantically the word "legitimate" is vague and subjective. From the point of view of the domestic politics, the relations between citizens and their government is a clear-cut controlled environment where the former give portions of their sovereignty to the latter to define what is legitimate and what is not. On the level of the international system, states enter the gray area of quasi-supranationalism in its form but not fully in the content. There, what is legitimate for one state can be illegitimate for others, unless, of course, the states are part of international/supranational governance, which extends the frameworks of legitimacy equally over its members. Russia, however, shuns any alliances, which would limit its sovereignty, thus allowing for the contradiction in understanding of the notion of legitimacy on the international level.

To many, Russia's "legitimate interests" remained obscure until March 18, 2014, when Putin lifted the veil of uncertainty convoluting this term. In his speech to the Federal Assembly, Putin based his decision to annex Crimea on his "convictions based on truth and justice."[83] He also made the reference to just and legitimate interests of his country in the Seliger patriotic camp in summer 2014: "We must restore historical justice, which was broken with the transfer—the illicit transfer, I should emphasize—of Crimea to Ukraine."[84] Apart from taking it upon himself to judge in retrospect on the legality of the internal normative acts of the currently derelict country (the Soviet Union), Putin heralded the start of a contextually new revisionist policy of Russia in Europe. This policy stance rejects multilateralism as a form of governance inherently deleterious to Russia's understanding of its own sovereignty.

For a country such as Russia, which cherishes its sovereignty (i.e., the ability of rulers to take any domestic and international actions without external judgments or interference) above all other values, the mere thought of giving it up to a supranational entity even with the purpose of higher individual benefits is quite egoistic. Makarychev and Sergunin noted this visionary incongruence in their following comment on the ideational clashes between the EU and Russia: "Brussels's approach, being intrinsically contradictory, is split between normative unification and multi-regionalist models and spheres of influence. Yet Moscow either denies or ignores the normative components in EU policies, and views them as an undue expansion into Russia's presumed sphere of interests. Meanwhile, the EU views Russia as a revisionist power trying to regain its former control over the post-Soviet space."[85] Russia wants to be a part of the multilateral European governance, including in the security, politics, economy, and culture, while rejecting its supranationalism by individual definitions of what is just and unjust.

Current Views on European Security

Currently active Russian Foreign Policy Concept 2013 is a much broader document in terms of the issue-area coverage as well as the depth of Russia's proposed involvement in regional and global politics. It was written during Putin's third presidential term and aimed at consolidating the responses to new challenges for Russian statehood. For the first time, European economic problems, including the debt crisis and possible dive of the Eurozone into recession, were listed among the threats to Russia's stable future of building a common market with the EU. Here, too, Russia strived to become an "integral and organic part of the European civilization" within the four common spaces on the basis of a newly proposed partnership agreement with the EU. With specific emphasis on the political component of partnership, Russia pledged to uphold European security by "maintaining an intensive and mutually beneficial political dialogue with the European Union on the major issues of foreign policy agenda . . . in order to foster collaborative decision making with their subsequent joint implementation."[86] The expressed wish to become a part of Europe's common governance by participation and collaboration in political deliberations is clearly visible in this part of the concept paper, yet again based on Russia's unilateral understanding of legitimacy and justice.

The latest document that raised waves of concerns in wider circles in the Russian political spectrum was the controversial military doctrine prepared as a political retort to the Western reaction to Russia's alleged involvement in the crisis in Ukraine. With the general anti-NATO rhetoric, Russia's new military outlook rejects the European direction and participatory and inclusive cohabitation within the European security architecture as framed by previous policy papers. Instead, it limits interactions with the EU and NATO to "maintaining equal dialogue in the field of European security . . . based on collective non-block principles."[87] The main emphasis is on the role of NATO expansion as a growing threat to Russian national security.

Russia's muscling in with the EU and NATO over the scope and form of participation in European politics is a symptom of much deeper issues. This rift has been artificially created by the contemporary Russian leadership with regard to the differences on the views on the political place of Russia in Europe. The conflict is the incompatibility of Russia's wish to play the solo violin in the Concert of Europe and the EU/NATO ensemble approach to the same performance. While Russia strives to closely participate in the political, cultural, and economic processes in Europe, it wants to so do on its own terms and based on its political culture, which is not always compatible with the cardinal values that "Europeanness" is based on.

Clashes of Values

There is no single view on the nature of the inputs of Europe in the Russian national identity and the role Russia plays among the European nations. For some, it is quite positive: Russia is an integral member of the European family, both contributing to its diversity and solidifying it beyond its geographic borders. Smitienko presents the following tribute to EU-Russia relations from the historical and cultural perspectives: "Ideas of united Europe are inconceivable without Russia, because the history of our country is closely intertwined with the history of Europe. Russia is the most important part of Europe. . . . Russia's significance to the rest of Europe . . . cannot be overestimated. . . . [The] European civilization would never have gotten to its present level without Russia's contribution to its culture, science and education, medicine, literature, music and art. . . . We have civilizational, cultural, and . . . religious kinship, mutual interdependence and common interests in ensuring national, European, and global security."[88] For the advocates of this viewpoint, Russia is indeed a part of Europe.

The other diametrically opposed view rests on the premise of Russia as an organism separate from Europe with its distinct history, culture, economics, and politics, which overlap those of Europe but never merge with them. Such a view is rooted in the belief that "the dialogue between Russia and the EU based on the common values has lost its momentum, if it ever had it."[89] Yevgeni Shestakov contends, "Russia no longer sees itself as part of modern Europe. The idea of creating a common European space from Vladivostok to Brest has failed. The ongoing rapid change of the European model prompts Moscow to take any long-term projects involving Europe with a big pinch of salt."[90] Living on the outskirts of European civilization gave Russia the distinctive air of sovereignty that extends well beyond the political realm. It is the identity sovereignty that drives Russia in a direction away from the European world and finds its embodiment in the irreconcilable political tensions between the EU, as a postmodernist supranational entity, on the one hand, and the Russian Federation, as a primordialist state, on the other.

Eurocentric Values

There was a time at the end of the sixteenth century when a young Russian tsar (quite an accidental one, to be more precise) decided to link the fate of his country with Europe. Pyotr Alexeyevich Romanov, later to become Peter the Great, first official emperor of Russia, built St. Petersburg, the city on the Neva River to fast forward the country into the modernity that it had been deprived of by over 250 years of Mongol rule. It took the titanic efforts of thousands of Russians serfs and hired labor to build the true pearl of Renaissance architecture, which stood out among larger Russian cities, including Moscow, due to its ultramodern design.

Even more exceptional was the true purpose of the city. In the words of the Italian encyclopedian Count Francesco Algarotti, St. Petersburg became a "great window . . . opened in the north through which Russia looks on Europe."[91] The great Russian poet Pushkin used the parlance "hacked through the window" when he referred to Peter's building of the city. The word choice here is not accidental: according to Joost van

Baak, this phrase "suggests the prior existence of some less open building, or at least a wall, rather than a construction of a completely new house, and thus implies a symbolic and paradigmatic 'opening up' of the closed, defensive wall of the old House of Russian Culture."[92] In other words, the building of St. Petersburg signified a providence-predestined future for the Russian nation, which is directed toward Europe.

The "window" allegory also means that Peter's decision to revolutionize Russian society was not accidental or forced upon him by some uncontrollable convergence of outside events. It was a conscious decision to pull the country out of the centuries of darkness imposed externally by the numerous conquerors and domestically cultivated by the *boyare* ultratraditionalist landlord elites shunning change. It was, in a way, a long-awaited continuation of the Europeanization of the country initiated by Vladimir Svyatoslavovich at the end of the tenth century with the conversion of the Kievan Rus' to Christianity, stipulated, as Thomson claims, by "the close commercial and political ties that Kiev had developed with Byzantium over the preceding hundred years."[93] Peter I conducted rigorous reforms aimed at boosting the centuries-dormant enormous economic, cultural, and political potential of the Russian nation. P. A. Krotov described Peter's vision as "turning a backward country into the great power with flourishing culture, advanced science, modern and highly developed economy and powerful professional military . . . to attach the due weight to the actions of the Russian state on the international arena."[94] The vision required gigantic institutional change, and Peter was not afraid to impose his will to implement such monumental transformations in Russian society.

The modernizing vision of Peter translated into a number of reforms in the spheres of public administration, directed toward building an essentially different type of the social contract, in which, as E. S. Kul'pin noted, "the government is recognized as the main value and is delegated the main decision-making rights."[95] This was perhaps the first example of regime mimicry in the Russian society. Externally proposed institutional frameworks were imposed in the recipient country's domestic political, cultural, and economic environment with the insurmountable force of the autocrat. The monetary and financial reforms, leading to completely new forms of taxation; the regional reform dividing Russia into the provinces with the governors appointed by the emperor; the legal reform creating the Supreme Court and lower-level provincial courts; the epochal military reforms, rebuilding the Russian army and creating the Russian navy from scratch; the educational reform, creating higher educational institutions in hard sciences; the cultural reform, one of the most notable of which was switching Russia off its traditional Byzantine chronology (since the creation of Adam) to the European (since the Birth of Christ, or Anno Domini) Julian calendar—all were mimicked, this way or another, from the parts of the governance regimes existing in the European countries, which Peter visited during his Grand Embassy trip to Europe in 1697 and 1698.

Peter's reforms in almost all sectors of society were fortified by hundreds of expats from Europe, whom he invited to come to Russia and to educate its population in their respective fields. These Europeans enjoyed considerable privileges, including highly paid jobs and even legally and spiritually: as Robert Massie notes, "Foreigners in Russia were permitted to have their own councils to rule on marriage and other ecclesiastical matters without being subject to Russian laws or the control of the Russian church."[96] The foreign experience combined with Peter's enormous energy and coercive force brought the unseen titanic industrialization to Russia; according to Evgenii Anisimov, "The industrial build-up of the Peterine epoch proceeded at a tempo never seen before that time: over the years 1695–1725 no fewer than two hundred enterprises of different sorts arose—that is, ten times more than there had been at the end of the seventeenth century."[97] In a century after Peter's reforms, Russia became one of the most powerful states in Europe, militarily and economically speaking.

But there was much more to erecting the Western-oriented city-outpost for the Russian state and modernizing its economy and society: it was the identity transformations that Peter forced upon its subjects. The societal changes were enormous, ranging from ordering the *boyare* to shave their "long beards and [get rid of] oriental costumes which symbolized the arch-conservatism of old Russia"[98] to re-creating the Russian military in accordance with European standards. The new Russia of the eighteenth century was no longer a backward country; it was on strong rails of rapid Europeanization in many spheres of life, including its identity.

It was Peter the Great who created the primary foundation of the Europeanization project in Russia, which with different degrees of success continued until the second and third terms of President Putin. Under different rulers, Russia participated in the European affairs not as an outcast but as its integral and closely integrated part. A cursory examination of Russia-Europe interactions reveals a steady pattern of the Western orientation of the former in most of the spheres, including political, economic, and military. Even the Russian ruling class had more European blood in them than Russian. For instance, Prussian-born Carl Peter Ulrich, Peter's grandson, became Peter III. Peter III's paternal great-uncle was the Swedish king Charles XII, and he was initially raised to be the heir to the Swedish throne. In 1762 he was replaced on the Russian throne by his wife, a Prussian, Sophie Auguste Friederike von Anhalt-Zerbst-Dornburg, aka Catherine II, as a result of a coup. Their son, Paul I, who was deposed as a result of a military coup in 1801, was technically more Prussian (3/4) than Russian.[99] The last Russian tsar, Nicolas II, was half-Danish on his mother's side: she was a daughter of King Christian IX of Denmark and sister of Britain's Queen Alexandra and King George I of Greece. Nicolas's paternal grandmother, Marie von Hessen und bei Rhein, was German, and so was his wife, Victoria Alix Helena Louise Beatrice von Hessen und bei Rhein, aka Alexandra Fedorovna, as her Russianized name goes.

In the military sector, Peter's reforms were continued by his successors with increased rigor. With some minor bumps along the road, such as the overthrow of Paul I as too much pro-Prussian, the European-style military continued to exist in tsarist Russia up until the October 1917 revolution. Close economic integration with Europe also continued. Although even before Peter Russia was trading with Europe, it still, as Fernand Braudel defined, remained inward-looking because of "her unmanageable size, her still sparse population, her limited interest in the West. . . . Russia was the victim neither of her deliberate action, nor of some categorical exclusion on the part of the outside world. It was simply that Russia tended to manage her affairs on the margins of the rest of Europe."[100] With Peter breaching the mental borders between Russia and Europe, "18th century Russian trade with the rest of Europe, expanded . . . 15-fold to 26-fold," as noted by Victor Lieberman.[101]

Politically, too, Russia remained tightly involved in the vital internal affairs of the European countries and even beyond. Empress Catherine II established the First League of Neutrality in 1780 to ensure the rights of neutral American colonies to trade with the rest of the world without British intervention.[102] This may be considered "mediation with muscles" to a certain extent. The Russian government sent its ships in the Mediterranean, Atlantic, and North Seas to protect the American colonies from the assaults from the British in high seas. Paul's successor, Alexander I, brought Russia into the Quadruple Alliance with the United Kingdom, Austria, and Prussia, which defeated Napoleon and laid down the basis for the Concert of Europe. It was the balance-of-power-based peace on the European continent, based on "self-restraint . . . if the good of 'Europe,' as an entity was to prevail over the conflicting national interests of the individual powers."[103] The alliance, of which Russia was one of the main actors, lasted for almost a hundred years until World War I broke out in 1914.

With the close ties with Europe, Russia brought its own palate to the European "melting pot," if you will, of multiculturalism: it was always a bit different, a bit off-the-grid—although integrated in Europe, still a bit separate. Iver Neumann gives a very good overview of the European integration of Russia after Peter the Great: "The Russian state spent the eighteenth century copying contemporary European models, the nineteenth century representing the Europe of the *anciens régimes*, which the rest of Europe had abandoned, and the twentieth century representing a European socialist model which most of the rest of Europe never chose to implement."[104] Russia always had its "own path," which lay in the Euclidian parallel world with Europe.

Differences in cultural identity lines were exacerbated during the Soviet Union, which claimed to be building a better future for its own people and for most of the Eastern European countries, but still viewed Europe as its natural "place of residence." As Dostoyevsky noted, "Yes, beyond all doubt, the destiny of a Russian is pan-European and universal. For a true Russian Europe . . . is as dear to his heart as Russia, as the fate of his motherland. . . . To become a true Russian means to reconcile the European differences."[105] Latynina echoes Dostoyevsky in the twenty-first century by stating, ". . . the Russian culture became great only after Russian became Europe . . . [H]ad not Peter I made Russia a part of the European world, there would have been no Tolstoy-Turgenev. There would have been no Russian Empire, so cherished by our [Russian] patriots. It would simply have not existed."[106] These passages show the intangible link between the Russian nation and its identity, on the one hand, and the European values, on the other, which proved to be fragile under the constructs of the new "Russian world."

Eurasianism

In the middle of the nineteenth century, however, Russia began slowly drifting away from its European orientation and towards Asia. It started from a new perspective in Russian philosophical thought, according to which the elite viewed their country as having a noble destiny of uniting in itself the qualities of the two words: European and Asian, but eventually producing a new identity product. The birth of the idea of *Eurasianism* largely happened as a result of the defeat in the Crimean War of 1855, when the tsarist Russian authorities decided to abandon their course of European alignment and to turn to Asia for spiritual and cultural comfort and enlightenment.[107]

In its essence, Eurasianism advocates for a "return to the East" and proposes to view the Russian identity as the unique amalgamation of the Eastern and Western cultures.[108] However, this notion had territorial connotation: it located Russia between the two geographic extremes and adds to its cultural context. According to Yelena Nikitenko, Eurasianists view Russia as "a special cultural-historical world, which synthesizes the features of Eastern and Western cultures; the link between these worlds. . . . Russia as a geopolitical, political, and cultural entity . . . belongs both to Europe and Asia."[109] For them, "there was an organic link between the geographical area, the specifics of each culture, and the people living in the area. . . . Russia is neither Europe nor Asia, and therefore there is no European and Asian Russia, but only parts that lie to the west and east of the Urals."[110]

After the October 1917 revolution, when the Soviets came to power, Eurasianism received a boost from numerous Russian émigrés and refugees to the European countries and the United States led by Nikolai Trubetskoi, Petr Savitsky, and George Florovsky. As Sergei Nizhnikov notes, "Eurasianists emphasized the role of the Turan-Asian element in the history of formation of the Russian culture and statehood. All of them occupied anti-Western, but not all—anti-Soviet stance. . . . The Russian Revolution, some of them thought, "hacked through a window to Asia." They rejected cultural and historical "eurocentrism," based on the pluralist perception of culture and rejection of existence of universal progress."[111] This brought along the depiction of Russia as cultural interaction of the continent, whether or not other parts of it consented to such geospiritual leadership in Russia.

With its Asian-centric move, the Eurasianists' vision also emphasizes the quality of the discourse equal to the concept of the "Third Rome" developed by the medieval Russia priest and philosopher Filaret. According to this Slavophil vision, the Russian nation has a larger geopolitical meaning and a messianic destiny. Matthew Johnson claims that in this identity vision, "Rome did not refer to a place. . . . Rome was a concept; it was historical, legal, theological and, certainly, in the poetic sense, mythical and mystical."[112] It was the receptacle of the most developed civilization among its contemporaries, and Russia was meant to inherit this engine of progress and spread it around to lesser cultures under its influence. From this standpoint, "the Eurasianists synthesized old Slavophil views on the 'people's truth' and the contemporary theories of public democracy of the twentieth century," which later became a very peculiar form of Russian nationalism.[113]

As inherited from Slavophils, a special place in Eurasianism was given to Russian Orthodoxy as the governing religion of the nation, but with a twist. George Florovsky defines the view of the Eurasianists of their Christian origins as their "cultural and everyday need; as historical heritage of Russia. Eurasians feel the Orthodox elements, experience and understand Orthodoxy as historical and everyday fact; as the subconscious 'center of gravity' of the Eurasian world; as (only) its potency. And yet . . . Russia is turning in their minds into the 'legacy of Genghis Khan.' Thus Russia is taken out of 'from the prospects of the history of Christian, baptized the world' and its 'Byzantine heritage' becomes obscured by a 'Mongol' one."[114] Spiritually Russia becomes an idiosyncratic amalgamation of Christianity, as a faith, with Asia, as a geohistorical point of reference.

With the collapse of the Soviet Union and rebirth of Russia, the Eurasianist school of thought acquired a strong scent of nationalist identity. This, however, was not a novel embodiment for the Eurasianists. Back in the 1920s, a prominent Russian thinker and minister of foreign affairs of the Russian Provisional Government after the Revolution of February 1917, Pavel Milyukov, named political concepts of Eurasianism as the "Russian racism."[115] The neo-Eurasianists reanimated century-old vistas of their predecessors on "the problems of choosing an original social and cultural strategy for Russia; return to the social-ontological cultural grounds; definition of the primary purpose of the value-based worldview potential of the Russian mentality; return to the cultural-aesthetic space; quest for new meanings in the fundamentals of art and many more."[116] The central part of the neo-Eurasianism became the Russian neo-nationalism. Europe was philosophically but not territorially left out from this quest.

The Eurasianist discourse was taken to an extreme in its "neo-" form by Alexander Dugin, one of the main ideological gurus of the contemporary, revived Russian nationalism. Dugin asserts, "The presence of the Western *logos* to universality refuses to recognize this universality as inevitable. . . . It considers Western culture as a local and temporary phenomenon and affirms a multiplicity of cultures and civilizations which coexist at different moments of a cycle."[117] I. A. Smaznov defined two main directions in the contemporary "neo-Eurasianism": *theoretical Eurasianism*, which develops the concept of "the Eurasian empire built on the territory of the former Soviet Union," and *economic Eurasianism* with the aim of "rebuilding of the economic interactions of the former Soviet Union republics."[118] Dugin belongs to the first category, which heralds the revival of Russia not only as *primus inter pares* on the post-Soviet space, as it was during the USSR, but as the main potent actor in the whole Eurasian space, stretching from Lisbon to the Ural Mountains.

In more practical terms, the recently reemerged concept of "Third Rome" is translated into the "Russian world," which has the goals, as defined by Dugin, of "restoration of a Greater Russia, crushing American hegemony, creation of the multipolar world; liberation of Russia from its fifth and sixth columns, the triumph of the Russian spirit, and the flourishing of Russian civilization," which is promoted as an antipode of the Western civilizations.[119] Dugin's Eurasianism is linked to the quest for defining the "Great Russian Idea": the Russian identity. Here is where the geographic dimensions of Europe come to light. In one of his interviews, Dugin gave the following definition of the Russian idea: "We need to take over Europe! Conquer her! And annex her! . . . And then, if we define the national idea as the annexation of the European Union into the Eurasian Union and our expansion into Europe—only then can we actually, by and large, get together around a great goal. Just imagine: to annex Europe! This would be so Russian of us! . . . We would just establish a protectorate over them—that's all!"[120] Opponents of such a view on the Russian civilization as destined to rule the world are those who consider the Russian way of life to be "compensatory" in which its routine failures in most aspects of life, including agriculture and industry, are compensated for by the "bully" logic of intimidation of those who succeeded.[121]

With the ascent of Putin to power, neo-Eurasianism undertook a slow but deliberate crossing of the very cultural Rubicon separating Russia and Europe. According to Jeffrey Mankoff, "Eurasianism in contemporary Russia is in many ways the recipe for the reconstruction of a state looking very much like the USSR, both in terms of frontiers and in terms of its authoritarian political system."[122] The regime, beyond the identity divide, artificially created and cultivated by the contemporary Russian political establishment, exacerbated the us-versus-them separation between Russia and Europe proper. Every subsequent clash between Russia and the European nations, be that in the cultural, economic, political, or military fields, became much worse than the previous one. Putin, in a sense, became an antipode of Peter the Great: he is on the path towards closing the circle of Europeanization of Russia by bolting the window, once hacked through by Peter, with the iron dowels of misunderstanding, prejudice, and envy.

Eurovision's "Gay" Fallout

Loyal to the Russian political culture's tradition of accusing others of their own deeds, the present-day Russian mainstream thinks it was betrayed by Europe, which, having been misguided by America, placed it on the edges of its identity, culture, and politics. A seminal example of the clashes of identities and values between Europe and Russia happened at the 2014 Eurovision Song Contest. This televised vocal competition is less known to the American public but is highly renowned in the music field in Europe, watched by millions of TV viewers all over the continent. Every year, European nations send their musicians to the Eurovision, where their musical talents are judged as well as the prestige and "weight" of the countries of Europe.

Through several stages of the selection process, the jury, together with the citizens of the contesting countries who, voting via phone calls and text messages, choose the country-winner, which will host the Eurovision in the following year. A peculiar character of the Eurovision voting is its ethnic polarization, where the representatives of a given nation, who cannot vote for their own representative, give their votes to their ethnic or otherwise cultural brethren. Gad Yair was the first academic to point out the political nature of the Eurovision contest, where the voting "bias represents the underlying political and cultural structure of Europe; European unity and solidarity, national rifts and ethnic conflict are reflected in the result of the contest."[123] Further along the same lines, Derek Gatherer's statistical analysis identified several "voting blocs" who traditionally vote for each other: the "Western Block" (Western Europe); the "Viking Empire" (Ireland, Scandinavian, and Baltic States); the "Warsaw Pact" (Russia, Romania, and the former Yugoslavia); the "Balkan Bloc" (Romania, Serbia, and Albania), and the "Pyrenean Axis" (Andorra and Spain).[124] Within these blocs, according to Victor Ginsburgh and Abdul Noury, "vote trading" is a "sincere voting based on the "quality," and linguistic and cultural proximities."[125] Regardless of the quality of the song and the *artistique* of the performers, the citizens of the European countries traditionally give their votes to the singer they consider as their identity kin.

The winners of Eurovision have been such world-class musicians as ABBA, Céline Dion, and Toto Cutugno. For them, winning the contest was a door opening to the larger musical stage. The Soviet Union never participated at the Eurovision; Russia entered the contest for the first time in 1994. In 2008 Russian singer Dima Bilan (originally from North Caucasus) assisted by Yevgeny Plyushchenko (four-time Olympic medalist in figure skating, three-time world champion, seven-time European champion, and ten-time Russian national champion) and world-class Hungarian violinist Edvin Marton won the Eurovision.

In 2014 Russia was represented by seventeen-year-old twins Maria and Anastasiya Tolmachevs, winners of the Junior Eurovision Song Contest in 2006. To many Russians the Tolmachev sisters embodied traditional virtues of purity and chastity that are ascribed to the Russian nation at large. The sisters ended up taking seventh place. The winner of Eurovision 2014 was Thomas Neuwirth, aka Conchita Wurst, an Austrian bearded drag queen and a LGBT activist. The outrage of representatives of the Russian establishment (actors, musicians, politicians, and general audience) gathered at the studio of the Russia 1 TV channel airing live had no limits. Zhirinovsky was yelling, "This is the end of Europe! It has rotted! They do not have 'a man' and 'a woman' anymore: they have 'it': Europe of the neutral gender!"

The cacophonic audience echoed him: "This is degeneration of Europe! This is the end of Europe! It has finally revealed its true face! It is a requiem for Europe, European Union, and traditional values in Europe!" Zhirinovsky crowned the overwhelming uproar of the audience by yelling, "This is the diagnosis for Europe: Europe has diarrhea with blood and foam!"[126]

A defeat in any prestigious international competition is an unfortunate occurrence but still is within the limits of normalcy, and the Eurovision contest is no exception. But the defeat to the openly gay and flamboyant European over the two true Russian "innocent beauties" sent a powerful message to the supporters of the Russian world: the emasculate and effeminate Europe (or what the Russian mainstream calls the *Gay-rope*) had finally come out of the closet. It is not the future habitat for the macho and spiritual Russian identity. A Russian nationalist organization, Sputnik and Pogrom (deriving its name from the two most commonly used Russian words in a Western world) even blamed Peter the Great for switching the Russian "spiritual time" to the "spiritless" European: "Prior to 1696, Russia was the Holy Russia, the land of sweetness and sanctity, awarded God's blessings for its holiness, and, therefore, having no need for time, since any change, any violation of the holy order is blasphemy and the reason for the deprivation of God's blessing."[127] The progress, economic development, state strengthening, and consolidation of the Russian society under Peter thus violated the perfect balance of the Russian people's communion with God, currently hinging on the feeble and ephemeral "staples."

The danger for the Russian identity, be that Slavophil or Eurasianist, is that these "staples" are now being pulled apart from the Russian identity by the Europeans, and this is happening not only in the musical sphere. In November 2013, the TV program *Special Correspondent* on Russia 1 discussed the danger of the European gay expansion into Russia: "The European sodomites are trying to infiltrate Russia and organize the political protest movement here, among our Russian perverts. This increasingly strong minority—by the way, very aggressive and impertinent—is holding by the throat the governments of France, Denmark, Britain . . . and now comes our turn. . . . Normalcy is in opposition; abnormalcy is in opposition to all humanity."[128] The anti-gay law with the lengthy title "On Amendments to Article 5 of the Federal Law, On protection of children from the information harmful to their health and development," and some other legislative acts of the Russian Federation in order to protect children from information that promotes the negation of traditional family values gave immediate results. Several days after its adoption in June 2013, gay activists from the Netherlands were arrested in Murmansk for assisting the Russian gays in organizing protest actions against violations of human rights. To make matters even worse, at the end of 2014 Medvedev's government issued a decree "On the List of Medical Contraindications, Medical Conditions and Medical Restrictions to Driving," which banned driving rights to people with adult personality and behavioral disorders.[129] This category, according to the Association of Lawyers of Russia for Human Rights, can include "all transgender, bi-gender and asexual people, transvestites, cross-dressers, and those seeking gender realignment," which would widen the population gap in Russia.[130]

The normative acts and the general anti-gay stance in Russia boiled down to inclusion of the following passage in the new Russian Military Doctrine, which defined "actions with intended information impact on the population, especially young citizens of the country, with the aim of undermining the historical, spiritual, and patriotic traditions in the matter of defense of the Fatherland" as one of the national security threats.[131] This paragraph, with extremely obscure wording, gives quite a liberal interpretation of the national security threats. It essentially allows Russian authorities to view a hypothetical visit of Conchita Wurst to their country as engendering the historically developed pillars of the edifice of the Russian nation and its national security by pulling apart the spiritual staples this edifice is based on. Wurst was, indeed, planning to visit Russia in 2014 to meet with Putin, but received very cold treatment from the Russian officialdom. As one of the hard-core apologists of the principal Russian values and a member of the St. Petersburg Legislative Assembly, Vitaly Milonov commented on her proposed visit: "I think we should send her as some kind of a comfort start sent to the CTO (Counter-Terrorist Operation of the Ukrainian officials in the South-Eastern Ukraine), where the soldiers from the National Guard and the volunteer will actually Euro-integrate themselves with her . . . and to better understand what the real modern European trends are."[132] Needless to say, after such a "warm" welcome, Ms. Wurst should think more than twice before being willing to commit herself to the charms of the Russian world.

Division between "us" versus "them" based on the value context is not a novelty in the Soviet/Russian political discourse. What is new, however, is the pace within the negative vision on Europe being the center for unholy defilement and infernal profanation of Christianity, and traditional Russian family values had been created, cultivated, and promoted within the ordinary Russian citizens by the state propaganda. Dmitri Trenin et al. note, "Moscow has not only accepted the values gap between itself and the EU but has begun to proudly advertise its own more conservative values, such as national sovereignty, religious faith, and traditional family. These priorities stand in contrast to Europe's unchecked freedoms which, in the Kremlin's view, erode society and will eventually doom it."[133] To withstand the negative vibes coming from the European capitals, various Russian nationalist movements, inspired by Dugin, are promoting the idea of "the full Russian Renaissance, the 'Russian Spring.' [They] are starting to feel pride for our country. The Russians are starting to realize that they are not only as passive objects in the world but also the subjects of history."[134] Even in this particular case of the Eurovision contest, giving the first place to a representative from Austria—on the basis of politicized voting (plus the performance "quality," of course)—was viewed as an organized conspiracy against Russia with the aim of eroding its traditional family and Christian values. The problem with this statement is that no one actually has ousted Russia from Europe or has infringed upon its identity or even denied them the basis for their pride. No one except the Russian political establishment itself, which—once again, as so often in Russian history—is attempting to turn its wheels backward and stall the natural societal and cultural evolution.

The idea of separation from Europe on the basis of the value conflict is currently being cultivated at the highest echelons of power in Russia. The apogee of this "unique Russia" perspective was given in two forms: one of the preparatory versions of the document "The Bases for the State Cultural Politics" prepared by the Russian Minister of Culture in 2014, which is supposed to define the state's vision on the place and role of the country in the world; and the other is being developed by the World Russian National Sobor. The initial text of the "Bases" contained the following passage: "Russia should be considered as a unique and a distinctive civilization, which cannot be reduced either to the West (Europe) or to the East. A brief statement of this position is the thesis: 'Russia is not Europe,' confirmed by the entire history of the country and its people."[135] After being leaked to the press, the "Bases" caused hurricanes of negative feedback in the mass media. Eventually, under pressure from the civil society, this paragraph was removed.

The image of Conchita Wurst will continue to haunt the traditionally wired minds in Russia. Immediately after the Eurovision finals, the Russia Church issued a statement in which it called the result of the Eurovision the "process of legalization of what the Bible calls none other than abomination."[136] Even on a higher political level, the disruptive role of European Union vis-à-vis Russia is seen, according to Glaz'ev, in "pursuit of its own expansionism by the EU, which applies the methodology of double standards, uses force, uses deception and political technologies. . . . They are ready to use violence, including organization of coups in order to absorb countries. . . . The European Union behaves as a bureaucratic empire utterly unscrupulous to use any means to expand its power and territory. It seems a vestige of the 21st century!"[137] On the popular level the anti-European stance is translated in the overwhelming rejection of the idea of the European Union and even (hypothetically) membership.

In a video program, *Polite Nastya* (the reference here is to the "polite people" of the Russian military in Crimea), the reporter presented the Swedish children's song about sex education. Happy characters "Snipp" and "Snopp"—the male and female genitals—of the song were ridiculed in the program as "absolutely normal for Europeans who are already accustomed to such kinds of sex-education and perversions of the tender children's souls. This is how monsters grow up, win the Eurovision contests, and teach us how to live. Thank God, we are smart enough not to accept mindlessly those Western 'values.'"[138] Such views on the incompatibility and even conflict between European values and Russian traditional lifestyles seem to be shared by the wider societal layers in Russia. The public opinion poll conducted by the Levada Center in September 2014 revealed massive (68 percent of the respondents) discontent with the EU, with approximately the same numbers of respondents (64 percent) believing that Russia should abstain from seeking membership in this organization in the future.[139]

Supranational Threats to Russia

The value rift between the European and Russian lies on a much deeper existential level and is based on the clashes between the two nations' sovereignty, two outlooks on political deliberation, two engines of development. The very spirit and letter of the contemporary political and economic processes in Europe are based on the notion of supranationalism. The heart and soul of this endeavor is the voluntary membership of the countries obtained as the result of the years of bringing their domestic political, cultural, and economic parameters into compliance with the commonly shared European standards. John Van Oudenaren defines this peculiar governance regime in Europe as "an approach to international integration under which national government cede sovereignty over certain matters to transnational institutions. These institutions then can make laws and policies that are binding upon those governments. Key features of supranationalist . . . integration include an executive authority independent of national government control."[140] Furthermore, the supranational institutions of the European nations "are based on a particular mandate, which grants them a certain degree of institutional independence from the member states. This involves the competence to make decisions and command over autonomous bureaucratic resources."[141] This stance on the decision-making process comes into direct conflict with the traditional and strictly hierarchical national bureaucracy that the Russian governance has been returned into by Putin.

The European supranationalism is offered to its potential member states through the lengthy process of harmonizing their legal, political, economic, and cultural environments with those already existing in and shared by the countries of the European Union. In the literature of the European Union, this process is called "the European conditionality," including the *acquis communautaire*, the enormous body of the European legislature, comprising "all the EU's treaties and laws . . . , declarations and resolutions, international agreements and the judgments of the Court of Justice. It also includes action that EU governments take together in the Area of Freedom, Security and Justice and under the Common Foreign and Security Policy."[142] Within the process of their accession to the European Union, the aspirant countries have to accept the European conditionality and the prevalence of the *acquis* in their domestic legislature.

The very idea of allowing someone from outside to control the domestic political environment in Russia is appalling to its current establishment, which takes pride in their country's nonalignment with any alliance or union. To a limited extent this is already done by the European Court of Human Rights, where the Russian citizens can submit claims against the violations of their rights by the Russian state. In case of closer integration of Russia with the European Union, supranational intrusions into Russia's domestic politics would happen on more systemic grounds. The following are some of Putin's statements on the democracy in Europe, supranationalism, and the *acquis* in the European Union, which he denies exists: "Protection of the so-called common European and Western values to the detriment of one's own national interests usually carries a few problems. First, what are those interests? There are no criteria. These are some general discussions on democracy; it's not the right for a coup or genocide."[143] The spirit of the Europeanness and its supranationalism, the purpose of which is to solve the problems common for diverse nations living on a limited territory of the Continental Europe, is clearly misunderstood in Russian political circles.

During the value clashes with Europe, the Russian norm entrepreneurs, those who "are turning individually held ideas into broader normative beliefs,"[144] present the European norms, values, and standards to their supporters as inherently detrimental to the notion of the Russian sovereignty and the infallible right of its government to act on its own discretion within its borders. In return, the majority of Russians view the European values as fundamentally alien to the traditionally Russian ones. In the country where the central authorities in Moscow keep strong domestic political control, including cancellation of the elections of the governors between 2005 and 2011, any intrusion and advice from outside into the internal public administration processes in Russia are rejected. In other words, in the area of Moscow supranationalism upon its regions and federative entities, there is no place for other forms of supranationalism, European or any other for that matter.

Russian Energy Politics: The Weapons of Choice

In the early twentieth century, Halford Mackinder developed the "Heartland" theory of regional politics, which he presented at a meeting of the British Royal Geographical Society. Further elaborated on in his later works, the Heartland theory explains the mechanics of the political processes in Europe by the following: "Who rules East Europe commands the Heartland: Who rules the Heartland commands the World-Island: Who rules the World-Island commands the World."[145] The reality of Russia's energy politics in Europe that started with the increase in the world's oil prices in the beginning of the new millennium, brought forth a customized definition of the Heartland theory. The new wording applies in relation to the ongoing gas battles with Ukraine and the rest of Europe: "Who controls the export routes controls the oil and gas; who controls the oil and gas controls the Heartland," the Heartland being Europe.[146] Putin turned out to be a good student of both Mackinder's and the revised theories. With regard to oil and gas exports to Europe, Putin strives to prove that his country is a reliable and indispensable trade partner for Europe and may use coercion, if needed, to keep Europe buying oil and gas from it. The Russian Federation has been in the process of spreading its economic influence in the region of wider Europe, which it considers within its historical area of interests and which falls within the general line of the post-Soviet Great Russia's revival. This resurrection includes imposition of its policies on the countries of the European Union, especially via energy carriers, which Russia uses as a weapon (not a tool) of its foreign policy.

Fluctuating Oil Dynamics

Currently Russia is one of the largest world energy producers, with its 87.2 billion barrels of proven oil reserves, which constitute 5.2 percent of the total share of the oil existing on Earth. In 2012 it produced 10,643 million barrels a day, which is 12.8 percent of global oil production. Out of this amount, it exported 240 million barrels of oil worth $181 billion; 88 percent went to European countries and the rest to CSI countries.[147] In terms of natural gas deposits and production, Russia, too, is the second largest owner in the world (next only to Iran): in 2012 its proven gas reserves amounted to 32.9 trillion cubic meters (tcm), or 17.6 percent of the global oil reserves. In 2012 it produced 592.3 billion cubic meters (bcm), which is a slight decline (-2.7 percent) from the previous year, but still about 17.6 percent of the share of the total production.[148] This is what the supply side looks like, which makes Russia a very powerful player on the European and global markets of energy carriers, enabling it to apply the energy-centric view in its foreign policy when dealing with the countries and regions that are dependent on Russian imports.

Abundance of the natural resources that are its main trade commodities puts Russia in a vulnerable position within the supply and demand equation. In late 1990, the market odds were not in new Russia's favor. Global oil prices fluctuated between $20 and $30 per gallon.[149] With that, as Peter Oppenheimer and Sergei Maslichenko noted, "At the world prices and ruble exchange rate . . . Russian oil exports were not strongly profitable. The high oil prices prevailing from 2000 were unforeseeable; in their absence the lower ruble exchange rate would have been decisive in underpinning production."[150] Between 1999 and 2003, the budgetary revenue shares from sales of oil and gas as a percentage of the GDP fluctuated between 3.2 to 5.9 percent. By 2003, Russia was one of the least dependent members of OPEC on the oil export in its GDPs: 12 percent.[151] Although the oil prices were comparatively high at that time, Russia also faced one of the most severe economic crises so far when it was forced "to default on both its public debts (valued at around $45 billion on the peg), and private external debt. . . . Russian debt, $36 billion at the start of the year, had leapt by $16 billion between 1 and 24 July alone."[152] Late twentieth-century economic prospects, coupled with skyrocketing corruption and organized crime, looked precarious for Russia.

Putin's entry into the political science coincided with the rise of oil prices and market stabilization. Russia's oil sales slowly took an upward turn reaching, on average, $100 to $115 per gallon by 2013.[153] However, during his first presidential term, oil revenues were not the main source of funding for the state budget. For instance, Olga Oliker et al. claim that "non-oil revenues amount for the bulk of government revenues (they accounted for 61.4 percent of total government revenues in 2006)."[154] The second term saw an increased realignment of the country's foreign trade pattern and the budgetary revenue structure toward energy carriers, which made Russia's economy overly dependent of their principal trading stock. Already in 2008, "oil and gas exports accounted for two-thirds of all Russian exports by value, while oil and gas revenue amounted to a third of general government revenue."[155] It was not accidental that the budgetary division into "non-oil" and "oil" revenues (with the latter aggregating mineral extraction tax and export duties and oil and gas products-related tax proceeds) in Russia happened in 2008, the year that Russian sales of energy carriers started to gain momentum.[156] In more recent data from the Russian Federal State Statistics Service, only in the first quarter of 2012, the share of oil exports in the total volume of Russian exports was 35.2 percent and the share of exports of energy products was 48.3 percent.[157] When the revenues from the extracting industry are prevalent in a country's GDP and, more important, when they do not go to the development of other industrial or service sectors (depending on the countries' specificities), the country is suffering from what is called the "Dutch Disease."

Coming Down with It?

This state of economy is associated with the Dutch economy in 1960. According to Mwanza Nkusu, the "Dutch Disease refers to the "adverse structural changes that economies undergo as a result of sectoral booms associated with factors such as positive external terms of trade shocks and large capital inflows, including aid."[158] Rudiger Ahrend describes the situations "where the discovery and subsequent export of large quantities of natural resources raises the equilibrium exchange rate and/or general wage level, thereby putting pressure on the competitiveness of the other tradable sectors in the economy."[159] In simple terms, the Dutch Disease occurs, according to Giancarlo Gandolfo, during "the contraction of the traditional manufacturing sector, due to the rapid expansion of the extractive sector," and the lack of reinvestment of the revenues from the sales of the extractive commodities into other sectors.[160]

In many respects, the Dutch Disease in Russia has been caused by skyrocketing oil prices. They were so high that they skewed the production balance to its favor overshadowing the other sectors of the Russian economy and not letting them fully and properly evolve. Marco Fantini confirms, "Largely because of the strong increase of oil prices, the ruble has appreciated strongly since 1999. Although non-extractive industrial output and productivity have risen, industry is under pressure from foreign imports."[161] In case of oil and gas exports, rates usually increase, which makes them less competitive on the international markets. Indeed, why develop the industries, which would generate lower and longer returns on investments from the sale of their relevant commodities when the ones with much higher and quicker yields can be given priority? Capital, on the other hand, is attracted by higher returns, which is in the aforementioned extractive industries. As long as oil and gas prices stay high, the economic situation is easier to control; things change rapidly and for the worse when the prices on international markets for those commodities go down. This is exactly what happened in 2014 when the oil prices on the global markets fell from $130 in June to $57 per barrel in December. Coupled with the refusal of the OPEC members to decrease their oil sales in the world market, this led to the spiraling downfall of the Russian ruble, which by December 2014 had "lost half of its weight" vis-à-vis the U.S. dollar and even more to the euro.

The possibility of the Russian economy's coming down with the Dutch Disease have been putting out red flags for the Russian governance for quite some time. In 2009 in his article "Russia, Forward!" then president Medvedev raised well-substantiated concerns about oil and gas dependence on Russia. He complained, "Twenty years of tumultuous change have not spared our country from its humiliating dependence on raw materials. . . . Domestic business with a few exceptions does not invent anything; it does not create the necessary commodities and technologies for people. It sells what it has not created: raw materials or imported goods."[162] Four years later, Medvedev, now prime minister, made the same comment on the dire need of Russia to get rid of its overreliance on revenue from the sale of energy carriers. In an interview to the Brazilian channel Globo, he foretold, "Indeed, we have a very high degree of dependence on the export of raw materials, including hydrocarbons, oil, and gas. This is not a critical situation, but it is very difficult for us. We now have a little less than 50 percent of budget revenues created by the oil and gas sales—it is too large a degree of dependence," and he expressed the need to decrease this by 25 percent.[163]

Demand and Supply Battle

The demand side of the energy equation in Europe looks equally impressive but not in favor of the latter. According to the European Commission's report "EU Energy in Figures" for 2011, Europe consumed 1,698 Mtoe (millions of tons of oil equivalent—a common denominator of energy usage), out of which the largest share (35 percent) was of oil and oil products followed by gas (24 percent) and solid fuels (17 percent). Most of it Europe had to import: 84.9 percent of oil and oil products, 67 percent of gas, and 41 percent of solid fuels. Most of it comes from Russia: 35 percent of oil, 30 percent of natural gas, and 26 percent of solid fuels.[164] These figures alone do not tell much, especially if the uneven import patterns across Europe are considered. Since the European Union is a unique supranational institution that deals with such important issues in its member states' lives, as the foreign and security policies, not individual but joint pan-EU oil and gas vulnerabilities should be considered.

Three issues should be paid particular attention in the matter of defying European dependence on the Russian energy carriers. First, the absolute (or unified) and not relative (or individual) energy dependence should be defined. Otherwise, the uneven distribution of the Russian energy carriers throughout Europe will skew the calculation of the overall energy dependence of Europe on Russian supplies as in the situation with a hospital report giving a median indicator of the patients' temperature, as the famous Russian saying goes. Thus, while several European countries are highly dependent on the energy commodities coming from Russia, others are getting their energy fix elsewhere. For instance, Lithuania gets 92 percent of its gas from Russia; Poland, 91 percent, Slovakia, 98 percent, Bulgaria, 90 percent, Hungary, 86 percept, Finland, 76 percent, Sweden, 46 percent, Greece, 40 percent, and Germany, 30 percent.[165] Other EU states are less dependent on Russia: Spain, 14 percent; Portugal, 10 percent; the United Kingdom, 13 percent, and France, 17 percent. Uneven distribution of the volumes of Russian gas also created political rifts within different EU members, where the attitudes toward Russia depend on the degree of its energy supplies: those who see Russia as a security threat are opposed by those who view it as a partner in potentially other spheres.[166]

Another consideration in determining the nature of EU-Russia energy relations is that the imports of energy carriers from Russia to Europe have been steadily declining since the collapse of the Soviet Union. According to Casier, "the Russian share in the EU's import of gas has declined drastically. In the late Soviet years, in 1990, the Russian share in EU imports was 55 percent . . . a lot higher than it is today."[167] To a certain degree, this decline is a general theme in the contemporary Europe, which is committed to limiting its consumption of fossil fuels by 2050 and to slowly substituting them for renewable energy, such as wind and solar, and the automobiles' hybrid engines revolution in the early

2000s.[168] Finally, a part of Russia's imported oil and gas to Europe is a transit from Kazakhstan and Turkmenistan via the Baku-Novorossiisk, Atyrau-Samara, and Tengiz-Novorossiisk pipelines, sometimes even to its short-term economic loss, but long-term political gain. For instance, in 2006, according to Tomberg, the Russian state gas giant Gazprom signed a sales agreement with Turkmenistan, where it "overpaid $6 billion for the Turkmen gas than it planned but would control all export of the Central Asian gas to Europe till 2010," which will make it as a de-factor monopolist on the European gas market.[169]

Complex Energy Interdependence

In the buyer-seller relations in which most of the importing side's imports and the exporting side's exports come from the same sources lead to the situations where, in principle, all the parties should mutually benefit. Both the buyer and the seller would have stable supply and demand markets, leading to long-term interconnectedness from an economic standpoint, which could possibly bring them to political stability, too. According to Debra Johnson, "Whilst the EU's main concern in its energy links with Russia is security of supply, Russia's main strategic priority is security of markets."[170] Nataliya Esakova noted, "The Russian side is highly dependent on the revenues from energy imports and in particular its dependence on the EU's energy market. A substantial part of Russia's energy goes to the EU, which constitutes a large part of state revenues. Therefore, supply disruptions to the EU would be costly to Russia."[171] The settings where both sides of the trade equation, the market and the supplier, can equally hurt each other belong to the realm of a midrange liberalist theory of Complex Economic Interdependence. According to the founding fathers of this specific outlook on the geopolitical economy, disruptions in supplies or demands can lead to the "situations characterized by reciprocal effects among countries or among actors in different countries."[172] Situations like these are almost always negative, where both sides lose to different degrees, depending on their comparative economic strengths and availability of the substitute sales or import markets.

Complex interdependence decreases the possibility of conflicts between the parties, since both the supplier and the market would prefer to cooperate in order to avoid the costly process of looking for mutual substitutes. Specifically in the Russia-EU energy relations, there are two views on the application of this theory in the actual context. According to a largely optimistic view for Europe, "The Russian exports . . . take the form of undramatic business relations and technical cooperation from which both Russia and the EU profit. . . . The main threat is not that Russia, for political reasons, would deliberately disrupt its gas supplies to Europe, but rather that its gas industry might fail."[173] Under such circumstances, it is in Europe's best interests to prevent such instances of market failures in Russia by further cooperating with its extracting sector in the matters of technical support and innovations. Ilya Matveev gave another argument in support of interdependence: he explained the fears of the Russian side in that "most of the oil and gas pipelines connect Russia with the countries of the European Union, which puts the buyer (EU) in a more advantageous position: Russia has no alternative markets for such large amounts of energy resources, while the EU can import gas and oil from other countries in significant volumes."[174] Under such circumstances, the European Union, as a major buyer, has considerable leverage over Russia, as a supplier, and can put the latter in a vulnerable situation by forcing upon it its own terms of sales of energy carriers.

The second viewpoint conceptualizes the rather negative impact of the Russian energy policy on Europe, which uses oil and gas as a "soft weapon." Notwithstanding the mutual benefits that the peculiar settings can bring all the participants of the energy game, Russia uses combination of several coercive strategies directed at making Europe, as a whole, and separate countries victims or hostage of its parochial strategies of energy carriers. First, according to Richard Weitz, "Moscow's EU energy policy is to approach the different EU states on an individual basis in order to price discriminate and get the maximum price possible from each. Additionally, Russia attempts to lock in supply by consolidating control over strategic energy infrastructure throughout Europe and Eurasia."[175] For instance, Russia charges the Eastern European countries the highest among the EU members, with Macedonia topping the list with $564 per thousand cubic meters (tcm) while the Western European countries, like Germany, Austria, and France, all pay less than $400.

Such price discrimination, as James Henderson at Oxford Institute for Energy Studies defined, is based on "what the [gas] alternatives in those countries are. . . . It [Russia] essentially acts as a discriminating monopolist. If it has a significant market share in a country, or if it can see that a country has limited alternatives, then it prices accordingly."[176] From this perspective, Russia treats Europe within the macroeconomic laws of supply and demand, which is quite understandable given the fact that the sale of energy carriers constitutes a significant part of its aggregate revenues. In 2013 the share of the oil and gas revenues in the Russian federal budget was 68 percent.[177] The problem is that on top of that, Russia uses energy carriers to put pressure on Europe for different purposes, be that political or economic, which is a very peculiar understanding of the complex economic interdependence.

The other side of the "soft weapon" usage of the energy carriers is the policy of blackmailing with the power to turn on and off the oil and gas pipelines' valves at will. Currently Russia supplies external energy sources to the European Union through the export pipelines of Druzhba, Baltic Pipeline System, North-West Pipeline System, Tengiz-Novorossiysk, and Baku-Novorossiysk. Natural gas is also being transported through the recently opened Nord Stream, an underwater pipeline in the Baltics, connecting Russian with Germany directly, bypassing Ukraine and carrying 40 to 50 percent of Europe's gas imports.

The issue of transit of gas through the territory of Ukraine has been the matter of tensions between Ukraine and Russia. There are several major pipelines connecting Russia with Europe through Ukraine: the Bratstvo (Brotherhood), Soyuz (Union), and Trans-Balkan. Since the early 1990s, Russia has repeatedly accused Ukraine of stealing its transit gas, which is, of course, refuted by the latter.[178] In fact, the former prime minister of Ukraine, Timoshenko, was accused of "smuggling Russian natural gas, tax evasion in especially large sizes, forgery" in 2001 and even was imprisoned for several years by the ousted president, Yanukovich, for signing the energy carriers' contract with Russia, which, according to the latter, was a betrayal of Ukraine's national interests.[179]

It was the winter of 2006 when Europe felt for the first time the result of its dependence on Russian energy supplies. To punish Ukraine for allegedly stealing transit gas, Russia completely cut off the transit of gas via its pipelines to Europe. Several days without gas nearly resulted in almost a complete energy collapse in Eastern Europe. The European Commission had to act as a mediator between Russia and Ukraine, urging the former to resume gas supplies. Nevertheless, the problems with uninterrupted gas supply through Ukraine continue. According to the European Commission's Directorate General for Economic and Financial Affairs, "The Russia-Ukraine gas disputes over natural gas supplies, prices, and debts have threatened natural gas supplies in numerous European countries dependent on imports from Russian suppliers, transported through Ukraine. In January 2009, eighteen European countries reported major drops in or complete cut-offs of their gas supplies."[180] The regime of international sanctions imposed on Russia by the United States, the European Union, and their partner states and also self-imposed by Russia on itself in 2014 would only aggravate the situation and may endanger the interdependence between Russia and the EU with regard to supplies of energy carriers.

Europe is under severe stress from the situation in Ukraine, and potential disruption of energy supplies looms large. The EU countries, especially those who have high dependence on Russian oil and gas, face the daunting task of enhancing their energy security via diversification of the sources of energy supplies and exploring domestic and foreign alternative types of energy. There are several ways to achieve this. One option is to buy gas from the United States, which is quickly becoming a world leader in oil and gas production. According to the BP Statistical Review 2014, oil production in the United States amounted to 10.8 percent of the total world's production in 2014 (only by 2.1 percent less that Russia's). With its proved natural gas deposits of "only" 9.3 trillion cubic meters (which is three times less than 1,103.6 trillion in Russia), in 2013 the United States produced more gas than Russia in comparative terms (20.6 percent of the global production in the United States versus 17.9 percent in Russia).[181] With regard to its gas production, the United States is in a good position to fine-tune its energy policy and programs in support of the European Union's energy security by not compromising its own. However, taking into account high cost calculations of transportation of the American gas to the European markets, buying American gas will be more expensive than continuing to procure it from Russia. The European Union needs to look for additional alternative energy sources.

Another possible solution is lifting the sanctions and trade embargo imposed on Iran by the United States and the European Union. As a part of the "Critical Dialogue" policy adopted in 1992, the EU had been trading with Iran while keeping watch over the issues vital to its normative fields, such as "the MEPP [the Middle East Peace Projects], human rights, terrorism, WMDs, and the *fatwa*, or death sentence, against Salman Rushdie."[182] The dialogue was halted with the assassinations of prominent Kurdish opposition leaders in Berlin in the same year, for which the Iranian side was blamed. A decade later, with more moderate forces in power in Iran, the EU renewed its collaboration with Iran under the "Comprehensive Dialogue" by offering it the Trade and Cooperation Agreement.[183] This rapprochement also was abandoned when in 2005 the IAEA decided that Iran was not complying with nuclear disarmament and the NPT. In January 2012 the EU banned Iranian oil imports to the EU and also froze the assets of the Iranian Central Bank.[184] Too many variables are at play in the EU-Iran relations, and the Russian factor is one of them. Others, according to Adebahr, include regional dimensions of security, which have the aim "to deter Israel from a unilateral military strike against Iranian nuclear facilities," which would inflict serious human and economic damage in the Middle East.[185]

Moving away from the Iranian sanctions to opening up cooperation would allow Iran to increase its sales of oil and gas to Europe. This would also help Europe switch from Russia to Iran as its main suppliers of energy carriers. In 2011, for example, 18 percent of the European oil imports came from Iran—about half a million barrels daily.[186] This would also mean closer integration of Iran into the European energy markets, which is fraught with possible repetition of the current dependency problems with Russia due to the political unpredictability of Iran.

Another avenue would be to continue negotiations with the OPEC countries to increase their oil outputs to the world markets with the purpose of dropping the overall price on this commodity. This could have been one of the negotiating points of President Obama's resent visit to Saudi Arabia, which was followed by one notable occurrence. Putin called Obama on his initiative and, among other things, "mentioned the actual blockade of Transdniestria." Bringing up an unrelated but disputed region of Europe with the similar issue—ethnic Russians in a third country—could mean strengthening the assumption of high vulnerability of Russia when faced with the potential of losing its oil and gas revenues and that it is willing to extend its militaristic rhetoric to blackmail the West with the purpose of retaining its influence in Europe.

The final option is perhaps the most viable: to contribute to strengthening political stability in Ukraine with the ultimate purpose of developing its fracking gas resources. Removal of some of the Russian troops from the vicinity of the Ukrainian eastern border is a positive development, but in light of Russia's recent erratic behavior, we should not raise hopes for trusting it. The United States should undertake similar steps as it did in Azerbaijan and Georgia; it should lobby exploration of the Ukrainian gas while, at the same time, pacifying Russia's possible aggression against Ukraine by strengthening defense and security along the NATO lines in its eastern member states.

True to the spirit of liberalism in its regional politics, as embodied by the economic interdependence with Russia, the European Union had been urging Russia to sign the treaties that would limit its further involvement in the European region, which Russia has been systematically rejecting. According to Vladimir Milov, "Considering the opportunistic instincts and severe lack of institutionalism in the approaches in the current Russian administration, it is very hard to imagine that Russia would suddenly wish to join any long-term, comprehensive, legally binding international agreements in the area of energy. Realistically, Russia would continue to prefer opportunistic behavior."[187] Such an attitude is very much in line with Russia's views on any possible infringements upon its own sovereignty by the European *acquis* and thus detrimental to its vital national interests. This was one of the most important reasons why the deal with the South Stream fell through.

Originally, the South Stream gas pipeline was meant to provide another gas tributary from Russia to Europe. According to its blueprint, the pipeline would have been built on the Black Sea bed from the Russian port of Anapa to Bulgaria and then through the Eastern European countries to Austria. Projected capacity of the offshore part of the pipeline was 63 billion cubic meters of natural gas per year.[188] However, in December 2014 the South Stream project was officially closed by the European Union, not even having started. This happened notwithstanding the objections of the government of Bulgaria, which would lose some 400 million euros annually for the transit of Russian gas through its territory to the rest of Europe. Arkadii Rotenberg's company Stroygazmontaj was supposed to be in charge of the construction of the pipeline, for which it had already received a sizable down payment of $5 billion from the Russian government, which can be already counted toward its losses.[189]

From the very beginning of the talks on the pipeline's construction, the EU raised serious concerns about the political motivation of Russia and its feasibility. On the one hand, as Krišjānis Karins, a Latvian MP of the European Parliament, stated, "South Stream is dead because it was a political project, not based on economics, but on the wish of the Putin government to circumvent Ukraine vis-à-vis gas supplies to Europe."[190] It was a political project designed to punish Ukraine by leaving her out of the energy transit revenues for its unwillingness to follow the general course of aligning its policies with those of the Russian leadership. Besides, the South Stream would rival another projected pipeline, the Nabucco West, planned to run from Turkey through Bulgaria to Austria with the starting capacity of 10 billion cubic meters of gas per year, reaching the ultimate projected 30 bcm.[191] Finally, the EU's own antimonopoly laws embodied in its "Third Energy Package" the rules that do not allow a gas supplier to be both an exclusive owner of the pipeline capacities as well as the controller of such an infrastructure.

Not willing to abandon plans for energy domination in Europe, the Russian government, immediately after the announcement of the closure of the South Stream, declared that it would build yet another pipeline to Turkey with the same throughput capacity as the failed South Stream. Economic profits for Russia from this endeavor (let alone much lesser political benefits) would be considerably lower than in the former, since Turkey has traditionally insisted on a special role of a transit country. It does not merely offer its territory, as Georgia did, for the transit of energy carriers; it buys them and later resells them as its own. The European Union, too, did not sit idle; after the fiasco with the South Stream, it decided to expand the currently working Baku-Tbilisi-Erzerum gas pipeline to TANAP-TAP (Trans-Anatolian Pipeline/Trans-Adriatic Pipeline), eventually rejuvenating the Nabucco West pipeline project. These pipelines would bring the gas from the Caspian Sea port of Shah-Deniz to Italy through Georgia, Turkey, Greece, and Albania by 2019.

Ukrainian Apple of Discord

Starting from the very onset of the destabilization of the situation in Ukraine, the EU and its selected countries were highly critical of any Russian involvement there. The matter, again, boils down to the identity clashes among the European countries, the family of which Ukraine has been striving to join since its Orange Revolution. Russia, on the other hand, was promoting the archaic imperial vision on the "Russian world." This hypothetical ethno-territorial could, in principle, be expanded to include other Slavs, Ukrainians the most, which flourish under the wing of an elder brother, Russia. Several factors were at play in the worsening of Europe-Russia relations in 2014. The primordial memory of the Russian political culture strives to keep the Russian ethnos placed as *primus inter pares* in the post-Soviet space, just as it was during the Soviet Union. Russia wants to retain leadership in the post-Soviet world and very emotionally approaches any dwindling of its former communist brethren toward the West, purely in terms of personal human betrayal. Several post-Soviet republics showed their desires for Westernization, including Georgia and, at some point, Armenia, but the situation is even worse with the Ukrainians, who are largely considered the same as Russians but with an accent. By offering the agreement of association with Ukraine, the EU is viewed in the mainstream Russian culture as an evil neighbor driving a wedge between two twin brothers, one of which is older.

The tendency of the former Soviet nations to integrate themselves with the EU is not a new phenomenon. First, Georgia and then Ukraine on various occasions expressed political aspirations for close integration with the political, economic, and military structures of the West, broadly defined, and the EU, in particular. The political course of Ukraine, under Yushenko and, since 2014, Poroshenko, was strongly pro-European, which is even reflected in the popular name for the 2013–14 revolution: EuroMaidan. In a highly suspicious Russian political culture seeing its enemies at every corner, the facts of closeness of the former Soviet nations with the EU and the United States were approached, quite literally, from territorial and geopolitical perspectives: every single step taken toward the West means a step away from the East.

For the post-Soviet countries, integration with Europe may also mean potential membership in the North Atlantic Treaty Organization and vice versa, just as for the Eastern European countries, NATO membership was the forerunner to their EU membership. Georgian ex-president Shevardnadze in his election campaign in 2000 made the promise to bring his country to NATO in 2005. Ukraine is trying to accomplish the same by abandoning its non-bloc status that was proclaimed in its Declaration on State Sovereignty of Ukraine adopted in 1990. In August 2014, Prime Minister Arsenii Yacenuk submitted a draft law to the Ukrainian parliament on revoking the non-bloc status and potential membership of the country in NATO. The two organizations—the European Union and NATO—although inherently different, are thus recognized as the two heads of the same evil hydra by the Russian political culture engulfed in the perceptional security dilemma deadlock.

The European Union views Russia's actions in Crimea and Ukraine as "illegal annexation of territory and deliberate destabilisation of a neighbouring sovereign country [that] cannot be accepted in 21st century Europe."[192] After Russia's alleged military and economic support for the illegal armed militia bringing turmoil in eastern Ukraine with subsequent shooting down in its skies of the Malaysian flight MH17, the EU launched its own line of sanctions. This is not the first time the EU had introduced restrictive measures against certain countries that were acting contrary to the EU normative environment. Traditionally, the purpose of the sanctions within the European Union's contest, as defined by its External Action Service, is "to bring about a change in activities or policies such as violations of international law or human rights, or policies that do not respect the rule of law or democratic principles" that the European supranationalism is based upon.[193] With regard to the regional and international peace, the Council of the EU's view on the sanctions is to "maintain and restore international peace and security . . . [to] reduce to the maximum extent possible any adverse humanitarian effects or unintended consequences for persons not targeted or neighbouring countries."[194] Such an outlook means application of the liberalist "soft power" with the purpose of altering the utility calculation of the state under the sanctions by making its current course of actions prohibitively costly.

As a part of the EU's "soft power" approach, it uses the political and economic sticks to promote the Common Foreign and Security Policy postulates of its supranational governance. Introduced as early as March 17, 2014, the European sanctions against Russia aimed at compelling Russia to change its course of actions in Ukraine.[195] Eight months later, British prime minister David Cameron verbalized the EU's stance toward the sanctions: "We should keep those sanctions in place until Russia changes its behaviour and stops the aggression in Ukraine." German Chancellor Merkel added, "The measure for lifting sanctions will be [the] territorial integrity [of Ukraine]."[196] Both statements of the high-level EU member states' officials referred to the unwillingness of Putin's government to completely fulfill the terms of the Minsk Protocols of September 2014.

From their start, the sanctions targeted economic interests of those who the EU thought were responsible for the Ukrainian debacle, and not the wider Russian population or economy, wholly or in part: Putin's pocket oligarchs (132 individuals and 28 companies); suspensions of the banking loans and credits to several major Russian state-controlled banks (Sberbank, VTB, Gazprombank, Vneshekonomobank, and Rossel'khozbank); embargos on arms trade with Russia as well as financing and transfer of specific energy installations and equipment that can be used for oil extraction by Rosneft, Transneft, and Gazpromneft.[197] The last step was taken to a considerable dislike of the major American and European oil producers. British Petroleum, for instance, which owns 19.75 percent of the Russian oil giant Rosneft, warned its stockholders in July 2014 that the sanctions "could adversely impact our business and strategic objectives in Russia."[198] The decisions of the EU in relation to enacting sanctions against Russia are based on the principles of the European supranationalism and its view toward nondemocratic states. Anatolii Pronin notes that the provisions of the March 17 decision of the EU are "semantically similar to the previously adopted acts of the European Union on the sanctions against other countries and do not contain any fundamentally . . . new regulations," in particular, to the European Union sanctions of October 2012 against Belarus.[199]

Perhaps the most sizable targets of sanctions were designated the extractive sectors of the Russian economy. According to Michael A. Levi from the Council of Foreign Relations, "The biggest edge that Western energy companies still have is their technological edge—that's why these sanctions have the potential to have significant impact."[200] Coupled with the decrease of the oil prices in 2014, the rapid devaluation of the Russian currency exchange rate from 50 rubles per euro in September 2014 to 84 in December 2014, the fall of the Russian Trading System Index by 40 percent since July 2014, and the effects of the European sanctions against Russia aggravated by its own self-embargo against the European companies trading with it, this could become quite serious. The trade interdependence between the EU and Russia places the latter in a more vulnerable position. The Russian Federal Customs Agency of the Russian Federation statistics reflects almost half (49.2 percent) of its total foreign trade turnover between January and August 2014 with the EU.[201] The same is confirmed by the other side: Russia is the EU's second largest food export market holding 10 percent of its food trade translating into €11.8 billion in 2013.[202] This means that the mutual sanctions imposed by the EU and the Russian government will hurt the Russian demand side more, which is the export-oriented extractive industry.

There was also an institutional component to the EU sanctions. In January 2015 the Parliamentary Assembly of the Council of Europe (PACE), which Russia joined in 1996, suspended Russian membership as part of the common vision of the Council on Russia's involvement in the prolonged hostilities in Ukraine. By this, the Council extended the suspension imposed on Russia earlier in April 2014.[203] In response, the head of the Russian delegation, Alexey Pushkov, declared that Russia is voluntarily leaving the CoE until the end of 2015.[204] The reaction from the Russian legislators was even more startling. As a response to the EU "punishing" Russia for Crimea (as the whole matter of sanctions is considered in Russia), Speaker of the Russian Duma Naryshkin initiated a parliamentary statement, introduced by a communist MP to one of the Duma committees, condemning "the annexation of the GDR (German Democratic Republic) by the Federative Republic of Germany" in 1989.[205] Another MP, Mikhail Degtyarev from the Liberal-Democratic Party of Russia (LDPR), initiated creation of a working group in the State Duma with the purpose of developing legal grounds for demanding reparations from Germany with the sum of €3 trillion for the damage the Soviet Union suffered from Hitler's Germany.[206] If accepted, this statement goes contrary to all previously existing international agreements and treaties between Russia and Germany, as well as, technically, between Russia and the EU, whose integral part the unified Germany was ever since the collapse of the Berlin Wall.

Others were even more ecstatic at the prospects of Russia leaving the PACE: Aleksei Didenko, an MP and deputy head of the LDPR, declared, "Exit of the Russian Federation from the Council of Europe would lead to denunciation of several international conventions; we would have, among others, legal grounds to revoke the death sentence moratorium. . . . All we need is 24 hours to leave the Council of Europe to execute millions and millions of perverts, rapists, and pedophiles in our prisons. This will give us enough groups to reopen the case. . . . Most Russians are in favor of the death sentence."[207] If nothing else, this is a clear sign of the irreconcilable value and identity differences between the European Union and Russia, which needed some political shocks to reveal their true colors.

Responding to the European sanctions, Russia imposed the ban on a number of high-end food commodities from the EU plus Norway, which includes such items as wines, meats, seafood, various processed food, cheeses, and fruits and vegetables (which are mostly luxury items, like the Spanish *jamon*, French *foie gras*, Norwegian salmon, and the Italian *Parmigiano-Reggiano*). On August 6, 2014, Putin issued Decree #560 banning and/or restricting "foreign economic operations on the imports into the territory of the Russian Federation of certain types of agricultural products, raw materials, and foodstuffs from the countries of origin, which had to impose economic sanctions against Russian legal or physical entities or joined such decisions."[208] The government followed up with its own Decree #791 that limited the governmental purchases of light industrial commodities from foreign suppliers with the aim of protecting the vital national interests of the Russian state.[209]

The effectiveness of these self-embargos measured by the overall damage to the economy of the EU is, in fact, insignificant. Although Deputy Foreign Minister Alexey Meshkov estimated the loss of €40 billion in 2014 and another €50 billion in 2015 for the EU, the share of food and life animals (as embargoed by Russia) in the combined export of twenty-eight European countries is only 4.3 percent.[210] With this, the EU-28 has a negative trade balance with Russia, which before the mutual sanctions in 2013 was $86 billion, most of which was achieved by importing energy carriers from Russia.[211] Besides, the share of the exports to Russia in the combined export of the EU is only 6.9 percent. The largest exporting commodity to Russia is machinery and transport equipment: 47.4 percent.[212] The statistics on trade between the EU and Russia sends several analytical messages, among which the most important is the fact that most of the non–oil and gas trade between the EU and Russia is quite limited.

By imposing restrictions on the access of the European food products to the tables of Russian citizens, their government does not target the economy of the EU per se. It does not want to punish the European countries it trades with for supporting the American sanctions or tacitly following them. Had it wished to do so, the Russian government would have either bumped up the prices for energy carriers for European consumers or would have severely cut the amounts of oil and gas sold to them. It would have "turned the valve off," thus putting to life Mackinder's worst nightmare of controlling the European Heartland from outside. Its aim here is to punish its own citizens and to present it as the deed of the evil West.

In addition to seriously damaging the economic situation in the European countries that are highly dependent on the Russian energy supplies, cutting them off from oil supplies would have put the EU in the textbook condition of vulnerable, complex economic interdependence, under which Brussels would have been forced to rapidly look for alternative sources of energy supplies. Instead, the Russian government pursues a single aim: by essentially punishing its own people by banning European foods, it tries to consolidate the Russian society around the perceptional security and identity threat that the EU poses to Russia and to amalgamate its support to the political course chosen by the current leadership under Putin.

Contrary to the expected effects of the Russian self-embargo on the economy of the European countries, their impact on Russian citizens, although not fully evaluated yet, shows the clear signs of heading toward the negative side of the economic spectrum. Stagnation of the Russian economy caused by the Western sanctions and its own was admitted by the Russian side as early as in July 2014 with the decrease of its GDP by 0.5 percent and the flight of $75 billion outside of Russia since January 2014.[213] As reported by CNN's Ivana Kottasova, quoting the Russian Ministry of Finances, "Economic sanctions imposed over the crisis in Ukraine have triggered huge capital outflows—estimated at $125 billion this year. As much as $80 billion could flow out of Russia in 2015, according to new official forecasts. Inflation in 2014 is expected to hit 9.7 percent, as opposed to an earlier forecast of 7.5 percent, and around 9 percent in 2015."[214] The Central Bank of Russia published an increased figure: net export of capital by banks and enterprises in 2014 reached the record figure of $151 billion, which is 2.5 times more than in a previous year.[215] Individually, entrepreneurs, as estimated by the Bloomberg's Billionaires Index, also suffered substantially from the sanctions; in just two days of the most severe downfall of the Russian ruble in December 2014, the top twenty Russian billionaires lost $10 billion.[216]

A part of the view on the sanctions explains their success from the point of impacting the political decisions on the highest level. The combined U.S. and European sanctions triggered by the Russian aggression against Ukraine deterred the former from expanding its presence in Ukraine beyond Crimea. The pro-Russian separatists in the south-eastern Ukraine are confined to a small portion of two mining areas of Lugansk and Donetsk. No further moves of the Novorossiya militia have been made beyond their initial stronghold, including thwarting plans to take the strategic port of Mariupol. No official Russian military forces have started de jure intervention into Ukraine within Novorossiya by establishing an active corridor of the military equipment, machinery, and manpower, nor further beyond, to the nominal areas of Novorossiya (as claimed by the separatists) that extend to surpass Odessa on the Black Sea.

Even more so, Putin's reference to Moldova's breakaway Transdniestria region as having the "pro-Russian population and a lot of Russian citizens with their own vision on how to build their future and their lives" immediately threw out red flags but had no further consequences.

There is yet a pessimistic outlook on the success of the sanctions on the Russian political actions in Ukraine, which is backed up by a substantial bulk of literature on the effectiveness of economic sanctions used as a tool for interstate compellence. Sanctions are applied by different countries against other countries with diverse economies, political cultures, domestic power settings, and governing regimes, which makes all talk about the effectiveness of sanctions moot. For instance, the success of the sanctions against the South African apartheid regime in the 1980s is applicable only in the case of South Africa and only in that timeframe; therefore, the failure of the sanctions against North Korea cannot be explained by their success in South Africa on the basis of general scientific falsifiability. In simple terms, if certain sanctions (with specific scope and content) have been successfully applied against country A, this does not mean that the sanctions (with the same or different scope and content) would necessarily work against country B.

Nevertheless, some generalization can still be drawn between these diverse cases. David Leyton-Brown put it well: "Compellant purposes of sanctions are the most difficult to achieve,." keeping in mind the differences between other purposes of sanctions, such as symbolic or signaling.[217] While acknowledging the positive role of sanctions as one of the tools of state foreign policies, Gary Hufbauer et al. are of a similar opinion about the utility of economic sanctions. In their seminal work, *Economic Sanctions Reconsidered,* they concluded, "Sanctions are of limited utility in achieving foreign policy goals that depend on compelling the target country to take actions it stoutly resists. In some cases, the security, political, or other costs of complying with the sender's demands may simply be higher than any pain that can be imposed with sanctions."[218] One can also add to this list the role of identity and national prestige in withstanding the external economic pressure.

Extending the discussion into the positivist field, some scholars present their vision on the design of successful sanctions. Among others, George Lopez gives the following criteria for the success of the sanctions: first, the multilateral nature of the sanctions will greatly contribute to their success; second, sanctions as "sticks" should be combined with the "carrots," including offering possible economic assistance in case of altering the course of actions in favor of the sanction-sender; third, economic sanctions alone will not work—they should be applied in conjunction with other measures, including political and military pressure; finally, "the structure of sanctions must be clear and credible. Both the imposers and the target must be in a reasonably tight agreement on what constitutes compliance."[219] Kenneth Rogoff is more pessimistic: "Economic sanctions usually have only modest effects, even if they can be an essential means of demonstrating moral resolve."[220] This reasoning is based on the fact that in the modern globalized environment only strong multilateral resolve can push the sanctions toward their success. Hufbauer et al. state that sanctions "sometimes fail because sender countries have cross-cutting interests and conflicting goals in their overall relations with the target country. Tensions among economic interests in the sender country that could either benefit or lose from a disruption in trade, finance, and investment often lead to tepid measures timidly imposed."[221] There are countries which, due to growing interdependence, are disproportionally affected by the negative influence of the sanctions on the recipient countries. In this case they would act as "strikebreakers" within the multilateral efforts slowing down or even backstabbing the very spirit of sanctions by threatening to leave or leaving the senders' coalition.

Current state of affairs with the European sanctions against Russia backs up the scholarly dualism on this subject. For starters, as German intelligence found out, the foreign currency reserves of Russia amount to $620 billion, which constitutes 162 percent of its budgetary expenditures for 2014. Such a gigantic sum means that even if hypothetically Russia remains without any possible revenues, it can survive off its accumulated savings for four years.[222] The veracity of this statement is subject to careful economic calculations, but the mere fact of the Russian reserves questions the effectiveness of the sanctions, at least in the short run. Besides, the longer the sanctions are imposed on Russia, the more damage will be inflicted on the European side of the interdependence dyad, putting it in a vulnerable position looking for replacements in the import markets of energy carriers (in case Russia retaliates and stops pumping oil and gas in the European direction) and the export markets of food and other commodities. These will not be easy to find, taking into account the nature of the trading links of the EU.

Last, but not least, the sanctions have hurt Russian and European tourist industries, which had become interdependent. The collateral effect of the Western sanctions on the Russian economy has been shrinking the consumer baskets of the ordinary Russian citizens who were used to traveling to Europe for holidays. Thomas Frellesen and Clelia Rontoyanni noted, "Millions of Russians visit the EU as tourists annually making Russia the most important new source of income for the European tourist industry."[223] The statistics from the EU corroborates on the gloomy future of Russian tourism in Europe. The European Travel Commission's statistics show the remarkable figure of 41.1 million Russians tourists in 2013. Before the sanctions, the ETC estimated the increase between 25 and 50 percent of the Russian tourists in different geographic parts of Europe.[224]

In 2001 the European Environmental Agency's forecast concerning tourism in Europe was quite optimistic. By the Agency's estimates, "Tourism will be soon the largest service industry in the EU, generating more than 13 percent of GDP (direct and indirect), 6 percent of employment and 30 percent of external trade. . . . Tourism demand will grow by almost 50 percent by 2010 in comparison with 1996 while capital investment in the sector will double to about 13 percent of national accounts (EU average)."[225] According to the data of the *Invest in EU*, a European development and investment magazine, "The European Union tourism sector is a major industry in EU that generates a lot of foreign revenue and contributes significantly to the EU GDP, the sector accounts for more than 5 percent of the total EU union. More than 1.8 million enterprises are engaged in the business and the sector accounts for providing employment to more than 5.2 percent of the total labor force in European Union. The sector is responsible for generating more than 9.7 million jobs in the European Union."[226] These indicators show how vulnerable the European tourism industry is to the potential decrease of the demand. The Russian side also confirms the worst worries of the European countries that become accustomed to hosting high-spender Russians: according to Alla Manilova, Russian deputy minister of culture, "The sanctions regime has resulted in a decline of the number of Russian citizens visiting Europe. . . . The scale will be defined by the end of the season. The decline can reach from 15 to 30 percent in some countries."[227] These were the estimates at the beginning of the Ukrainian crisis, and the real impact of the decline of the Russia tourism in Europe has yet to be evaluated.

With the low level of demand for major tourist routes, the well-off Russians who were used to spending their summers in Spain and Greece and winters in Austria and Switzerland have to look for alternative places to spend their money. This, in turn, would negatively affect the economies of tourism-oriented European countries. For instance, in Finland, according to the estimates of its government, "about 30 percent of tourists come from Russia and in 2013 they brought over €1.2 billion in revenue to Finland."[228] In Austria, too, "A major role in bilateral relations belongs to tourism. Austria has become a favourite tourism destination for well-to-do Russians. While in 2005 about 530,000 visited Austria, the number soared to 1.2 million in 2010; in 2011 alone, tourism increased by about 30 percent."[229] In the longer run, severely contracted revenues from tourism from Russia would be detrimental both to the European economies and to the average Russians. Yet, as presented in the previous chapter, 78 percent of Russians have never been abroad, which decreases significantly the impact of the declining tourist industry.[230] Just as with the self-embargo, only the thin upper-middle-class layer of Russian society will appear the most vulnerable from the sanctions.

Another part of the pessimistic view of the efficiency of the sanctions against Russia is rooted in the knowledge of the Russian political culture and domestic politics of the elites and their supporters. In the opinion of the European security experts Yana Dreyer and Nicu Popescu, economic sanctions would not "make Russian concessions on Ukraine any more likely: the worse the economic pressure, the more the Kremlin's propaganda will drum home the message that it is the Evil West, denying Russia its holy Crimean birthright, that is to blame."[231] History knows this phenomenal Russian trait: whenever the external pressure either in the form of economic or political influence would seem to be overwhelming and aim at undermining Russian statehood, the Russian nation would consolidate around its leadership, tighten its belt, and continue pushing through. The current autocratic governance would only contribute to tacit approval of the austerity measures imposed by Putin on Russia.

Finally, a real danger for the EU's economy is the possible complete stoppage of supplies of energy carriers to Europe from Russia. Europe is far from being immune to such an act of a desperate man. A study by the French energy giant Total finds that "by scrambling, Europe could cope with a cutoff of Russian gas exports through Ukraine this winter. But it would be severely affected by a halt in Russian deliveries. . . . If Russia interrupted these Ukraine flows, the study forecast[s] that it would be 'feasible' to compensate through adjustments. . . . Unless Gazprom agrees, it would be impossible to reroute flows through the Baltic and Belarus pipelines, for example."[232] The same fears were expressed by the British wholesaler Wingas, which warned the EU of "potentially some additional risk premium on the back of the recent sanctions being built into prices over fears of any impact this may have on Russian supplies into western Europe."[233] These forecasts look especially true taking into account Europe's dependence on Russian gas supplies. Pushed to the wall, Russia could completely stop supplies of energy carriers to the European countries, which would lead to expansion of the austerity measures the government had sentenced its population to since the Ukraine crisis.

Instead of fortifying the Western leverage over Russian aiming at igniting the people's push for their government to take corresponding actions to stop the sanctions, they would only reinforce Putin's rule. There is a Russian saying that became popular after the sanctions: "If everyone is against us, this means that we are doing everything right." Given this logic, the 84 percent of Putin's electorate would be very difficult to be persuaded otherwise. On the one hand, if Europe drops its sanctions, this move would only prove to those living by the saying above that they succeeded in their righteous stance toward Ukraine, including annexation of the Crimean peninsula and the involvement on the Russian troops there, and their past actions, including the wars in Georgia. The biggest danger, however, is that loosening or removing the sanctions would free their hands for similar actions in the future. The Russian world, as it is presented, has no boundaries. It is where Russians live, which means that Russia could possibly use the same tactics of "gathering" the Russian/Soviet land in other parts of Europe: in the Moldovan Transdniestria and possibly in the Baltic countries with a high percentage of Russians and Russian speakers (26 percent in Latvia and 25 percent in Estonia in 2014).[234]

Conclusion

If Europe continues its policy of toughening sanctions, it will also lose, at least in the short run. In order for the sanctions to be efficient and not to lose their momentum, they cannot be static. They may start from the lowest level possible, but in case of lack of compellence power, they would increase in the depth and breadth of their application. This is exactly where the West began by targeting Putin's closest entourage. Later, seeing Russia's adamant and uncompromising behavior in Ukraine, the sanctions increased their scope, targeting institutions as well as individuals. So far, this has not worked as intended, either. If the sanctions continue on their level, there will grow the aura of normalcy for an average Russian and become a part of their daily routine. The initial shock from sanctions will wither away, especially if they are stalled for longer periods or are withdrawn completely.

The future of Russia- EU relations remains under the transparent guise of political, economic, and cultural incongruences. Europe is important for Russia just as Russia is important for Europe. The root cause of the problems is hidden in the misconception regarding the modus of the relations, which is present in the both dyadic parties. Technically speaking, Russia is not against the settings of interdependence with Europe: it does not reject the notion of mutually beneficial economic relations with the latter and is highly surprised to see the EU endangering this balance by following the collective action. In the Russian political culture, placing sovereignty in *SAMOderjavie* (literally translated as SELF rule) in the hands of collective management is next to impossible. The EU, too, is stunned in disbelief at how Russia could place its own citizens in economic peril under the conditions of growing international resolve against Russia's actions in Ukraine.

The ongoing quagmire in EU and Russia relations is purely theoretical. According to Stephen Wegner, "The EU is simultaneously Russia's most important economic partner and a multilateral, sovereignty-questioning, value-based organization that fits uncomfortably with Moscow's state-centric view on international relations. . . . [T]he organizing principles of Russian politics and foreign policy are far removed from those at the heart of the EU."[235] For the EU, its interdependence with Russia (or any other non- EU partner, for that matter) is fully *complex*, embracing multiple aspects and areas of interstate interactions. It is hardly just economic: it does stem from the neofunctionalist logic of having "pragmatic goal(s) of practically organising good-neighbourly relations and selecting the institutions, programmes, instruments, and procedures that better serve the bilateral agenda," but extends into the normative context.[236] On top of the purely rational choice arguments for the tangible benefits for the EU, as a supranational institution, it seeks also normative compliance with its core principles that are enshrined in the foundation of various treaties, starting from Maastricht and ending with Lisbon, and the EU conditionality given in the bulk of *acquis*.

For Russia, the situation is much simpler. It employs the interdependence based on the cost-and-benefit analysis. Even if the larger synergy between the EU and Russia can be visualized in the future (for instance, the latter playing the key political role on the European continent and the former following it), this will happen in detachment from its normative meaning. Russia is not and will not sacrifice its individual sovereignty, its precious generational achievement, for some ephemeral collective security. The very notion of collective security embodied in the CFSP, as the second pillar of the European Union, is utterly alien to the Russian political culture and unacceptable by mere definition.[237]

Divergence of the views on cooperation leads to disagreements where the boiling point is when the parties' actions are deemed mutually unacceptable. Russia's resentment of the EU's overemphasis on its domestic situation, especially with regard to the human rights violations and the EU's nonacceptance of Russia's current revisionist foreign policy stance, would inevitably tear the dyad apart. Two scenarios of possible future of the Russian steps towards the EU can be envisaged: pessimistic and optimistic (with regard to the peace and security on the European continent). Both scenarios are equally credible and hypothetical at the same time.

The first direction in Russian foreign policy is continuation of reshaping the European map, at minimum, within the borders of the former Soviet Union. This rather retrograde action could include additional chunks of the former Soviet Union brethren, either in part or as a whole. After all, if a sovereign ownership of a portion of land can be considered illegal (such as, in case of the Crimea, the Novorossiya [which includes southeastern Ukraine], Abkhazia, and Ossetia), nothing prevents Russia from applying the same logic to the fact of decomposition of the Soviet Union as an illegal act in its entirety. The revisions politics in the Western direction could possibly include also the Transdniestria region of Moldova, whose marionette government has been dying to join Russia even since the conflict broke in 1989. In this case Russia would be filling the role of Dr. Frankenstein in the most bizarre attempt to put together the bits and pieces of the decaying body of the Cold War giant.

The second possible scenario is more malleable to European security. In this world Russia would stop at the point of annexation of Crimea and hope for another form of détente with Europe. The report of the Carnegie Center Moscow presents the following picture: "In the foreseeable future, Moscow is unlikely to emerge as a security risk to Europe, either because of its domestic developments or its foreign policy. The country will neither implode nor explode, and a Russian invasion of EU territory can be safely ruled out."[238] This will happen only if the logic of economic interdependence would prevail between the EU and Russia over the sanction rhetoric of the former and territorial encroachments of the latter. The reality, however, shows that this option is less probable, at least at this stage. The Russian Bear, as eulogized by Putin in his Valdai speech, has awakened. Retired Major-General Alexander Nikitin, currently the prominent member of the nationalist Party of Defense of the Russian Constitution, gave a vivid depiction of the Russian views on Europe: "The Bear is big and strong. It is much stronger than any other forest dwellers and can tear all apart, individually or as a group. It is difficult and scary for the Europeans to live with such a neighbor to the east."[239] The Bear itself, however, is deeply puzzled by seeing such an odd reaction from his neighbors to the west: it thinks it has done nothing wrong to scare the Europeans and was just protecting what it believed belonged to him.

6

Identity Meets Money in Asia and the Pacific

There are so many beautiful places in Russia! Kunashir.

—DMITRI MEDVEDEV's Twitter entry on his visit to the Kuril Islands, 2010

During the Valdai Discussion Club meeting in October 2014, Putin presented Russian relations with the countries of Asia-Pacific as a reboot of the interactions between the actors on multiple levels and diverse issues, which are deeply rooted in the history of the regional conflict and cooperation. He said, "Our active politics in the region of Asia-Pacific started not today and not in connection with [Western] sanctions but several years prior to that." Putin noted that the main rationale for Russia's new initiative in the region was the growing importance of the East in global politics and economics and, therefore "cannot be neglected." Bringing the geographic factor into the picture of bilateral interactions with the countries of the region, Putin noted, "We have a large part of our territory located in Asia—why should we not use our own advantages; that would be short-sighted."[1] The speech was meant to set Russia's foreign policy priorities in the region, and in the case of the Asia-Pacific region they fit with the historically path-dependent Russian political moves.

The importance of regional economic and political integration was also noted in the Russia foreign policy concept papers. The 2008 vision emphasized the belonging of Russia to the Asia-Pacific region, its interests in using regional capacities in funding the economic revival of Siberia and the Far East, and the need to strengthen regional cooperation in counterterrorism, security, and civilizational dialogue. Its 2013 version was more assertive about the importance of the region in global economic and political processes. The 2013 version paid significantly more attention to "this most dynamically developing geopolitical space, toward which the center of gravity of the world economy and politics is consistently being shifted." In Russian views, the region has "considerable conflict potential; augmenting military arsenals, increasing the risk of proliferation of weapons of mass destruction," and Russia strives to play a leading role in mitigating the security situation in Asia-Pacific.

Several directions in regional cooperation priorities can be extracted from Putin's words. First, Russia is vitally interested in being present in Asia-Pacific where it aspires to play not a secondary but a leading role in regional politics and cooperation. Second, cooperation with specific countries will be based on Russia's vital national interests and the projections of its concave identity vision to the region. Some of the most important areas of cooperation include mutual economic trade and the sales of energy resources. Third, although Russia borders China (in fact, this is the world's sixth longest international land border, over 3,500 kilometers in length), Russia does not feel threatened by having the giant neighbor across the Amur River, but plans to use the territorial proximity to its advantage. Finally, the region is important for spreading Russia's economic vision beyond the territorially confined geopolitical dimensions. Activation of Russia's efforts in this geopolitical direction will inevitably clash with the interests and involvement of other powers, including Japan and the United States, which are not welcoming Russian influence in the region, especially in light of the developments in 2014 in Europe.

Regional Integration

Economic dimensions of Russian foreign policy in the region have always been important for peaceful interactions with the regional players. Recently, however, they became of pivotal importance to Russia, which, when faced with the growing opposition and economic pressure from the West following its (alleged and not proven) aggressive actions in Ukraine, turned to the East for economic and moral support. Oil and gas remain the main trading commodities of Russia. According to Dmitri Trenin et al., "Moscow seeks to capitalize on its energy resources. Diversifying Russian energy trade toward the Asia-Pacific region, which is already under way on a modest scale, is based on a strategic geopolitical and geoeconomic rationale rather than a purely economic one. . . . Moscow is seeking to balance the established European market with a new and growing Asian one."[2] The Asia-Pacific region is perhaps most important for Russia in increasing the exports of not only energy carriers but also other industrial and consumer commodities that the Soviet Union used to supply to its ideological brethren.

Unfortunately for Russia, the collapse of the Soviet Union and the retreat of Russia from the regional economic scene coincided with the economic boost in the region (especially in China and Vietnam). Russia's return to the regional trading table is thus a relatively long-term priority because it must catch up with the regional standards of economic production and trade, especially in such fields as arms trade, hydrocarbons, fishery, and timber.[3] Since 2012, Russia has been determined to accelerate bilateral cooperation with the key regional actors to offset the negative consequences of international economic pressure following its actions in Ukraine, as well as within the multilateral cooperation frameworks. This initiative, according to Irina Troekurova, "was mostly coming from Russia and is being implemented in multilateral format, which signifies Russia's determination to be included in the integration processes in Asia."[4] Of the regional cooperation frameworks, the most important for Russia is the Asia-Pacific Economic Cooperation (APEC).

Multilateral Institutional Cooperation

In 1998 Russia became a member of APEC, a regional, multilateral organization tasked with developing and strengthening intra- and interregional cooperation frameworks, free trade, and its liberalization. At the time of Russia's accession, some were quite pessimistic about the joint benefits: "Membership [in APEC] alone will not strengthen the interdependence of Russia's economy with the Asia-Pacific or increase the influx of foreign capital into the country. . . . The slow process of political and economic reform in the Russian Far East and the region's nationalistic atmosphere created by its serious economic problems make Russia a less constructive partner in the Asia-Pacific."[5] Nevertheless, soon after joining the regional partnership network, Russia quickly engaged both within the organization and outside of its geographic borders. In just six years it doubled its trade with the APEC member states ($44.93 billion) and doubled its shares of the APEC's export ($28.66 billion) and import ($16.27 billion).[6]

In terms of trading commodities, as President Medvedev noted, "Russia will continue facilitating development of such a system of energy supplies in the region of Asia-Pacific, which will allow its energy users to diversify the geography of imports and ensure steady and uninterrupted supplies."[7] The 2012 APEC summit in Vladivostok, Russia, is notable for changing the geopolitical dimensions of Russian trade, as well as enlarging financial networks of potential partners from the region. According to Russian experts, the share of the APEC countries in the Russian foreign trade will increase from 20.7 percent in 2009 to 35 percent by 2025, while the volume of its trade with Europe will steadily decrease to 36 percent. This shift of geography of foreign trade will be achieved mostly by increasing energy resource supplies to China, North Korea, and Japan.[8] Thus Moscow expects the Asia-Pacific region to take an important place and role in its trade relations with the world, as is currently Europe, which will fully justify the Asian component of its "Eurasianist" geopolitical orientation.

Another regional organization that Russia is actively participating in is the Shanghai Cooperation Organization (SCO). The SCO was founded in 2001 by the Central Asian states of Kazakhstan, Kyrgyzstan, Uzbekistan, Tajikistan, Russia, and China. The organization grew out of the Shanghai Five, an organization set up in 1996 with considerably limited goals of territorial delineation and start-up economic cooperation. The new entity had very ambitious goals, among which some of the most important were strengthening mutual trust and friendship between its members, developing multi-profile cooperation in diverse fields, joint counterterrorism activities, and regional law enforcement against trans-border crime, facilitation of regional cooperation in economic, political, defense, and cultural fields. An additional area of development within the organization is economic cooperation and trade, which are slowly becoming priority areas within the organization.

There were also many opinions on the feasibility of Russian participation in the SCO, especially in the regional power games. Some analysts claimed that the members of the organization will be squashed by the domination of China, the main player in the region. According to Vilya Gelbras, "The creation of the Shanghai Cooperation Organization, praised by almost all its participants, in fact means that Russia and its partners in the CIS publicly and politically accepted the expansion of the sphere of China's vital interests over the whole of Central Asia. That way they objectively made all the contribution they could to 'the great revival of the nation of China.'"[9] Similarly, Vasily Mikheev believes that Russia should not strengthen the SCO because it will only contribute to increasing China's influence in the region.[10]

Economically, too, according to Andrei Kazantsev, "Moscow is afraid of Chinese economic hegemony inside the organization and is concerned that cheap Chinese goods will fully occupy not only Central Asian but also domestic Russian markets, and all SCO members could turn simply into raw material suppliers dependent on China."[11] Others refute these allegations by noting the absence of hard evidence of domination on the part of China and Russia's equal participation in the SCO, both budget-wise and the scope of membership.[12] This can be explained, however, by the very essence of the organization where the power balance is naturally skewed toward regional actors, such as China and Russia, who put lesser members (basically, all the others) into a disadvantaged position with regard to their relative bargaining powers. This is true especially for the international security frameworks, the creation of which, as Stephen Aris states, "is complicated by the caveat that the weaker states are willing to cede any form of national sovereignty decision-making power to a common regional body, due to concerns that this is tantamount to surrendering sovereignty to the stronger states."[13] If such vision prevails in the internal management of the organization, the SCO will remain alive as long as its mostly weaker members consider it beneficial to be under the wing of the regional powers.

The presence of Russia may help alleviate the influence China has over the smaller actors, such as former Soviet member states, all of which (except for Uzbekistan) are, in fact, the members of another regional organization with a stronger security and defense focus: the Collective Security Treaty Organization (CSTO). These countries can be expected to use their membership into the SCO to counterbalance Russia's towering influence in the CSTO. Russia can also be accused of selfish reasoning behind its joining the organization: "Russia may attempt to enforce the role of SCO as a counterweight to the EU and the use of SCO's framework in order to increase the level of vulnerability and sensitivity interdependence of the EU and, consequently, recharacterize its relationship with the EU."[14] The same can be said of Russia's stance on minimizing the role America plays in the region. With the intensification of political and economic tensions between Russia and the European Union, especially with the ostracism Russia is facing from the G7, G20, and the Council of Europe, it may further reinforce the security frameworks of the Shanghai Cooperation Organization and try to steer its members to increased anti-Western and anti-American agendas in the Asia-Pacific region.

China: Together Against All (?) Odds

Russia has very close relations with China based on three factors: historical path-dependency and continuous ideological rivalry with the West, geographic proximity, and economic cooperation.[15] During the Cold War the Soviets and Chinese were closest friends based on their mutual rejection of capitalist values. Throughout the early 1950s, the Soviet Union economically supported China, which allowed the latter to build its own industrial production.[16] In return, "Mao [Tse-tung] . . . openly proclaim[ed] that the Chinese Communists would lean to the Soviet side in the Cold War. The newborn People's Republic of China signed a treaty of alliance and other agreements with the Soviet Union. . . . Mao granted the Soviet Union mining and port rights in China."[17] With Stalin's death in 1953 and the rejection of the "personality cult" initiated by Nikita Khrushchev in 1956, Mao decided to distance his country from the Soviet developmental model. And then the relationship worsened: Khrushchev became an avid critic of the Chinese "Great Leap Forward," a Chinese economic reconstruction that was, in fact, a step aside from Soviet-style industrial management.[18] This moved the countries further apart, which culminated in a short border dispute that broke out in 1969 over the ownership of the island Damansky (Zhenbao in Chinese) in the Ussuri River. This incident and the subsequent deterioration of the quality of interactions tarnished Sino-Soviet relations for twenty long years and ended only when Gorbachev's Perestroika got hold of the Soviet Union.

During Putin's presidency, modern Russia's relations with China have significantly improved in two layers: politically and economically. From a political standpoint, the recent rapprochement of Russia with China is nothing but an attempt to jump-start the Cold War rivalry within the dimensions of the Asia-Pacific region where there are already substantial political and economic interests of the United States. Robert Legvold notes this move from previous views Russia had on regional security toward the substantially new level: "After favoring a path focused on 'multilateral security' that had little appeal to other states, such as the United States and Japan, which were already secure in their own bilateral alliance, Russian leaders joined China in calls for 'multipolarity' that again seemed to challenge the United States' role in Asia."[19] As a source in the Chinese Foreign Ministry noted, "The United States seeks to curb the development of both Russia and China, so Moscow and Beijing both share a common task of neutralizing these attempts of the United States."[20] Ekaterina Belousova also mentioned the "back-to-Cold-War" nature of modern Russian-Chinese relations: "Naturally, such a rapprochement between the two giants—vast Russia and rich China—cannot be overlooked in other countries, causing them resentment and fear. . . . Gaining strength China is looking for the equally strong partners to leverage together the existing hegemonic bloc of liberal capitalist states."[21] Like Russia, China strongly disapproves of any developments by NATO and its expansion eastward. The Chinese worry that NATO would forcefully incorporate the countries of Eastern Europe (Ukraine and Russia), which would strengthen its global position as a military alliance. Also, "NATO's eastward expansion . . . would disrupt the balance of power and lead to a deepening of the contradictions between the United States and Western Europe, the United States and Russia, which may distance these countries from the United States."[22] Needless to say, such opinions regarding NATO in general, and the United States in particular, are fully shared in Moscow.

Presently there is nothing that could prevent two Cold War buddies from being together again, especially if the political reunion is backed up by a solid economic base, which is subordinate to the Russian political culture's cornerstone of individual sovereignty. As Sergey Glaz'ev noted, "China is our largest trading partner, along with the European Union. Economically, the integration is already happening in terms of growth in turnover, increasing the cooperation ties, investments, etc. But, at the same time, there are no plans to create supranational bodies, because China, as well as Russia, prioritizes the sovereignty of their country."[23] Without a strong institutional base that both countries strongly shun, the integrating moves to China initiated by Russia are nothing but a short-term marriage of convenience, where even the terms of the prenuptial agreement are not clearly defined.

Mutual economic cooperation is still one of the most positive parts of bilateral relations. According to the statistics on trade turnover, Russia is China's ninth largest trading partner with 2.24 percent in Chinese total sales for the first nine months of 2014. China has for four consecutive years been Russia's primary trading partner.[24] The countries are planning to bring the bilateral trade level up to $100 billion by 2015 and to $200 billion by 2020 via diversification of the structure of trade turnover.[25] The major field of cooperation is the sale of Russian gas to China. In May 2014 the parties concluded an agreement worth $400 billion for up to 38 billion cubic meters of gas per year for thirty years.[26]

The countries made another significant step forward during the Ukrainian crisis. The Western sanctions forced Russia to look for alternative sources of financing, including the banking energy sector. The most notable from this is the Power of Siberia gas pipeline that has been shelved since 2012, but in 2014 this received the needed impetus after Russia signed the aforementioned contract with China. The gas transportation system would supply gas from the Irkutsk and Yakutsk gas deposits via Khabarovsk to Vladivostok and farther on to China. The projected throughput capacity of the Power is 61 billion cubic meters, out of which 38 billion cubic meters a year will go to China. The first phase of the project, with the total cost of $60 to $70 billion, is scheduled for the end of 2017.[27]

Those impressive figures under detailed scrutiny lose their "impressiveness" if confronted with the rough economic reality. After concluding the contract, Russia was going to sell 1,000 cubic meters of gas to China for $350, which is, according to Ariel Cohen, head of the International Market Analysis, $30 less than the average price of the same gas Russia sells to Europe. There are no pipelines, no pumping stations, and no gas storage facilities, which makes all the talk about the cost-efficiency of the pipeline for China and its profitability for Russia moot.[28] Political analyst Yulia Latynina is more skeptical about the whole feasibility of the project: she brings up the information that the final draft of the contract for the Power of Siberia has not been signed yet, and China already gets enough gas from Turkmenistan for 5 percent less per unit than Russia wants to sell it.[29] The Bloomberg analysis is even more skeptical. Apart from the vagueness with the price for gas (which really cannot be predicted by the end of the construction, which has not started yet), the project cannot withstand the feasibility inquest. "Even if the government is successful in expanding gas as planned in the years ahead, it will only comprise 10 percent or so of China's energy mix by the end of the decade. The two Russian gas deals together, if realized, would meet just 1.7 percent of China's overall energy demand; the second one on its own would amount to less than 1 percent of China's overall energy consumption."[30] This goes contrary to the numerous statements of the Russian officials (mainly directed toward calming down their own public at home and diminishing the looming economic problems) that the gas supplies to China will exceed those to Europe.

This clearly inefficient project serves two political goals: Russia wants to show the West and its own people that it is keeping its options open in the matter of economic security and that it has powerful friends able to assist in times of troubles. Russia also made several additional moves to "lure" China into supporting it politically and economically. First, on December 23 the State Duma adopted Law # N 473-ФЗ, the aim of which was to create zones with free economic development, which are meant to boost Russia's own economic state. Most notable are its Articles 18 and 27, which revoke the Russian laws on those specifically designated territories. Article 18 annuls the Russia immigration law: "Residents of the territories of advancing social and economic development, performing the functions of employers attracting and using foreign nationals as employees . . . are not required to obtain permits for foreign workers." Also, "invitations to enter the Russian Federation for work purposes as well as work permits for foreign citizens . . . are issued without quotas." Article 27 repels the property rights of Russian citizens in favor of the companies active in those zones: "For the purposes of creation and development of the infrastructure of the areas of advancing socioeconomic development, expropriation of land and (or) real estate or other assets located thereon is allowed."[31] The term of this law is seventy years, during which it is expected that hundreds of foreign companies and thousands of foreign workers will come to Russia and receive the land with all its building and its resources previously owned by Russian companies and citizens practically for free.

It is difficult to imagine any country other than China with its overpopulation problem being very keen to utilize the perks of this law. The first fruits of this curtsey towards China did not take long to ripen: in February 2015 the Chinese company SGCC and the Russian energy holding Inter RAO initiated negotiations for developing coal deposits in the Amur region of Russia. The $15 billion project will proceed in three stages: coal exploration with the output capacity of 35 million ton per year, construction of a power plant, and distribution of electricity to China.[32] China made other steps forward as it proposed "expanding a currency swap between the two nations" as "making increased use of yuan for bilateral trade would have the greatest impact in aiding Russia."[33] China will help Russia replace the U.S. dollar in mutual trade with yuan, the agreement for which was signed in October 2014 for the sum of 150 billion yuan, which makes $24 billion. Chinese help is thus meant to alleviate the economic problems for Russia in light of the downslide of its ruble and the fall in global oil prices.

Russia-China strategic partnership also extends to the sphere of arms trade, most notably in air warfare and defense. According to Henry Meyer and Evgeniya Pismennaya, "The S-400, which only Russia currently uses, would extend China's reach to encompass all of Taiwan's airspace, while the Su-35 would allow the Chinese to use the technology to expand their air force. . . . Russia has long been reluctant to further empower a neighbor that already has four times the economic output and almost ten times the population. Sanctions changed all that and Putin now risks playing a role he's not used to playing: junior partner."[34] If the talks find their reality, this will seriously alter the balance of power in the region, where there are other players, namely, Japan, South Korea, and Vietnam, who are very attentive to Chinese militarization.

Japan: Old Rivalry Never Dies

The biggest issue in Russian-Japan relations is the ongoing dispute over the ownership of what Russians call the Kuril Islands and the Japanese refer to as the Northern Territories. This squabble goes back centuries of exploration of the land, which has become the convergence point of geopolitical strategic control: a steady source of income and a receptacle of socially constructed identities. The vanished nation of Ainu used to occupy the Kuril Islands between the Sea of Okhotsk and the North Pacific Ocean before the arrival there of Russian and Japanese explorers. It was the Ainu who gave the name to the archipelago; in their extinct language, the word "kuru" meant "a man," hence the name Kuril.[35] The first references to the islands in both Russian and Japanese historic records go back to the mid-seventeenth century when these nations started exploring the island chains with the aim of territorial expansion for fishing purposes. It was not until two centuries later that Russia and Japan faced the need to clarify the issue of territorial possession of the Kurils.[36] In February 1855 they signed the first Russian-Japanese agreement, the Treaty of Shimoda on Trade and Borders. The document set the boundaries between the disputed islands of Iturup and Urup. Japan was to own Iturup, Kunashir, Shikotan, and Habomai Islands, whereas the rest were recognized as Russian possessions. That day, February 5, is sealed in the Japanese identity as the Day of the Northern Territories, which is currently celebrated in Japan as a national holiday.

In May 1875 the parties concluded the Petersburg Treaty, in accordance to which Russia surrendered to Japan the rights to all eighteen Kuril Islands in exchange for the Japanese portion of the Sakhalin Island, the biggest one in the Sea of Okhotsk.[37] This step concluded the final settlement over the islands until the Russian-Japanese War of 1904, initiated by Japan as a response to Russian expansion eastward and its annexation of the Liaodong Peninsula. In 1905 the war ended with loss of the Russian side leading to the Portsmouth Treaty, according to which Russia ceded to Japan the previously gained southern part of Sakhalin. In January 1925 the parties reestablished diplomatic relations by signing the Beijing Treaty. Already a new entity, the USSR was forced to recognize the condition developed as a result of the Portsmouth Treaty but refused to recognize the "political responsibility" for it. Through a series of negotiations and agreements during World War II, including the Cairo Declaration, the Teheran Conference, and the Yalta Agreement, the Soviet Union tried to legally justify occupying these islands when it joined the war against Japan in August 1945.[38]

The end of the war in Europe marked the start of military activities on the eastern front when in August the Soviet Union officially declared war against Japan and occupied South Kuril Islands. Japan capitulated a month later, and Soviet troops were deployed in the Lesser Kuril Ridge.

In September 1951 Japan concluded the Peace Treaty with the Allies, according to Article 2 of which it "renounce[d] all right, title and claim to the Kuril Islands, and to that portion of Sakhalin and the islands adjacent to it over which Japan acquired sovereignty as a consequence of the Treaty of Portsmouth of 5 September 1905."[39] This Article, in fact, recognized the legal possession of the islands as forthcoming from the aforementioned treaty. To ensure its full control over the islands, the Soviet authorities deported their Japanese population back to Japan proper or transferred them as POWs to the Soviet detention camps.[40]

Firmly believing that these islands were illegally seized by the Soviet Union in 1945, for the last sixty years the Japanese government has been engaged in various means of peaceful pressure on Soviet Union and later Russia: political, legal, and economic. In 1956 the parties almost reached an agreement to transfer of the isles of Shikotan and Hamobai to Japan in exchange for Kunashir and Iturup, but the United States stepped in by breaking the deal, fearing that this would give the Soviet Union increased leverage in the Asia-Pacific region.[41] The U.S. position on this matter somewhat abated after the end of the Cold War and Russia's cooperation during the Global War on Terror. Throughout the second half of the twentieth century, the question of ownership of the southern Kuril Islands remained the major stumbling block in Soviet-Japanese and later Russian-Japanese interactions. Russia, as a legal successor of the Soviet Union, continues rejecting the mere idea of having a territorial dispute with Japan. Even though the diplomatic interactions and economic linkages between Russia and Japan have improved considerably in recent years, the Kuril Islands issue has still soured their relations and could still trigger a crisis on a much deeper level.[42]

The situation with the Kuril Islands hit a clear stalemate where neither Japan nor Russia is willing to back off. Japan's stand is verbalized by its foreign minister: "The Northern Territories are inherent territories of Japan that continue to be illegally occupied by Russia."[43] The Russian position is equally adamant: according to Dmitri Gorenburg, the Russian officials "claim that the islands belong to Russia, and that Japan has to accept the idea that Russia's sovereignty extends to all four islands before proceeding to any further discussions of this matter."[44] With this, the pressure and resistance remain within nonmilitary confrontation lines. For example, when Prime Minister Dmitry Medvedev visited one of the islands in 2012, the bilateral relations deteriorated immediately to the point of recall of the Japanese ambassador to Russia. The Russian response has been systematically point-blank: as Foreign minister Lavrov stated, "There is no connection between the . . . visit of President of the Russian Federation to the Kuril Islands and the Russian-Japanese relations. . . . President Medvedev himself decides what parts of the Russian Federation he will visit."[45] On their part, the Japanese also keep the peaceful "political poking" from growing into open military confrontation with the Russians. For instance, earlier in 2002 then foreign minister of Japan, Ioriko Kavaguti, flew over the islands by helicopter, which caused a major uproar in the Russian political establishment.[46]

There are at least three explanations for why the standoff between Russia and Japan over the Kuril Islands remains one of the longest unresolved territorial disputes in East Asia. The strategic geography is so imperative that neither party wants to make any concessions. Geographically, the chain is a natural gateway for Russian trade and communications with Japan and the rest of the world. Strategically, the control of these islands would effectively cut off the Sea of Okhotsk from outside reach.[47] Mihoko Kato points out the importance of the region to the military goals of both nations: "An ice-free Northeast Passage could also provide the Russian navy with the shortest way to mobilize from the European theater to the East Asian theater, and vice versa. . . . The modernization of the Russian military forces around the Kuril Islands can be seen to reinforce Russia's control against Japan's claim for sovereignty."[48] Both Japan and Russia strive to control the "instability curve" along the Kuril Islands called so by ex-KGB general U. A. Drozdov.[49] The curve extends from the Horn of Africa to western China and is a focal point of their maritime security. Zbigniew Brzezinski refers to the Kuril Islands a bit differently but with the same outlook: as one of the "three strategic fronts" of confrontation of the Western civilization with the

Sino-Soviet bloc.[50] According to Andrew Mack and Martin O'Hare, the islands "are strategically located in that they guard the southern gateways to the Sea of Okhotsk from the Pacific and provide the most secure passage for Soviet surface combatants and submarines in and out of the Pacific Ocean" in case of possible hostilities in the region.[51]

Ownership of the islands also brings tangible economic benefits. The island of Iturup is the world's largest deposit of rhenium (opened in 1992 on the volcano Kudryavii), which is an indispensable component of air jet engines and high-octane lead-free gasoline. According to the Institute of Volcanology and Geodynamics of the Russian Academy of Natural Sciences, the volcano annually produces 36.7 tons of rhenium, which is almost 90 percent of its global output.[52] There are also possible oil and gas deposits across the islands with estimated reserves of over 300 million tons of oil capable of covering the needs of the region in energy carriers for thirty to forty years.[53] In addition, there is an alleged presence of gold all around the islands. Last, but not least, the islands give an additional 200-mile fishing zone to their owner, which is of major industrial importance in the region.

Possession of the islands is inextricably connected with the relevant identity constructs of the Russian and Japanese nations. Political elites and general public at both ends at various points in time have included the Kuril Islands as part of their national attributes and signs of honor. Tessa Morris-Suzuki claims that the disputed borderline in the Kuril Islands has had a significant role in creation of the corresponding identities of the Russian and Japanese people, galvanizing their separate raisons d'être.[54]

The question of the Kuril Islands is constructed by the Russian political establishment as the centerfold of the Russian identity. To return the Kurils would mean to lose the land (however small it is)—a historically important denominator of the Russian nation. Any territorial concessions made by Russia to Japan will be inevitably viewed by the domestic Russian constituencies as giving in on their identity.[55] When in the summer of 1992 Boris Yeltsin was considering returning the islands, his opponents successfully drew on nationalism to rally the people against him, capitalizing on the idea that "there were no Russian territories to be given away to others."[56] The public stance in Russia on transferring the Kuril Islands to Japan has remained increasingly negative for more than a decade. A poll by the Levada Center showed that the overwhelming majority of Russians do not favor this move: those against giving up the Kurils increased from 67 percent in 1991 to 90 percent in 2011.[57] In a recent survey quoted by Randall Newnham, the rising nationalism in Russia contributed to the rejection by the majority of the islands' residents of the idea of joining Japan, even though they are suffering from major economic hardship.[58] The same reasoning applies to the Japanese. Dropping the territorial claims by any Japanese administration would be considered a major weakness and betrayal to their history and future. Since many Japanese believe that the Kurils are such indivisible parts of their territory as to be elevated to the status of a national holiday, any leader willing to abandon the policy of peaceful compellence against Russia would likely run the risk of losing political support and be branded a traitor as well.

With all Russian and Japanese political "swaggering" used, in Robert Art's words, "to enhance the national pride of a people or to satisfy the personal ambitions of its ruler," the situation is highly unlikely to grow into an open military confrontation.[59] Except for several insignificant skirmishes along the maritime borders of the Kuril Islands, such as the Russian coast guards firing at the two Japanese fishing boats close to the disputed islands in 1994, the situation is largely under control and remains within the peaceful compellence frameworks.[60] Russia and Japan are well aware of the negative consequences by moving from peaceful compellence to military deterrence or even offense, and neither is willing to jeopardize the shaky political balance in this highly sensitive region.

During Putin's third presidential term, the discourse on the fate of the Kuril Islands was reactivated. At the G20 summit in Los Cabos, Mexico, Putin met with Japanese prime minister Yoshihiko Noda and talked about reopening negotiations concerning the ownership of the Kurils. According to Kato, "Noda . . . expected tangible progress such as the realization of the LNG project in Vladivostok and the participation of Japanese enterprises in the Sakhalin-3 project. Unlike the former president Medvedev . . . Putin seems to have had an incentive to promote territorial negotiations with Japan."[61] With the worsening of the international climate around Russia and keeping in mind Japan's joining the Western-imposed sanctions against Russia in 2014, Russia will become considerably intractable regarding any discussions around the potential transfer of the ownership of the Kuril Islands to Japan.

North Korea: Together against All Odds

The relationship between North Korea and Russia represents an interesting case from the point of view of the role of the past in their current joint opposition to everything Western. The Soviet Union contributed to creating the part of the formerly uniform country and became the first state formally recognizing the Democratic People's Republic of Korea. During the Korean War of 1950–53 the Soviet Union actively supported North Korea.[62] After the collapse of the Soviet Union, Russia–North Korea relations took a significant downturn, a sign of which was the absence of official condolences from the Russian side upon the death of the longtime leader, Kim Il-sung.[63] Putin was the first Russian leader who visited North Korea in 2000, activating bilateral relations. Russia also became an active member of the Six Party talks on a peaceful solution of the confrontation on the Korean Peninsula until they were suspended in 2009.

The modern dynamics of interactions between the two countries resembled a cautious courting between an amicable but yet not fully close couple. Vilen Kim made the following observation of Russian foreign policy toward North Korea: "Russia . . . has a realistic position in relation to the region, is interested in the unification of the peninsula, but under the condition of independence of Korean from any military alliances. . . . Russia needs a politically stable partner in the region, with which it can have good neighborly relations and develop mutually beneficial cooperation for the purpose of peace and security in northeast Asia."[64] Seeing South Korea partnering with the United States made

Russia highly sensitive to the prospects of the unification of the Korean Peninsula, since it is well aware of the tenacious U.S. military and political presence in South Korea. Having the unified Korea siding with the United States would be a nightmare for Russia.

After the first ten years of relative calm in bilateral relations, Russia started looking more closely at the developments in the Peninsula. According to Georgy Toloraya, "Russia has learned well the lesson of the 1990s; without intensive dialogue with the North, it is marginalized in Korean affairs. Therefore, Moscow started to implement the doctrine of 'standing on both legs' on the Korean Peninsula since the early 2000s and established basic agreements between President Putin and Kim Jong-il that continue to bear fruit today."[65] This tactic, however, did not immediately bring its desired results. Even in 2009, bilateral relations were far from perfect. As the Russian Foreign Ministry regretfully noted, "Pyongyang's desire to get more substantial political and economic support from Moscow . . . , as it was during the Soviet period, is supported neither by their sincere approach to dealing with us nor by their willingness to cooperate on the principles of trust and mutual benefits. We continue to act consistently with the position of not accepting the North Korean nuclear weapons program."[66] Later on, with Putin's third presidential turn, there appeared signs of significant improvement. Since then North Korea has sided with many Russian decisions in the international area, including recognizing its annexation of the Crimean Peninsula in 2014.

From the economic standpoint, Russia remains the major trade partner for North Korea, although the amount of bilateral trade turnover, by contemporary measures, is quite low: in 2011 it was equal to a bit more than $110 million and fell to $80 million in 2012.[67] With that, Russia supports North Korea by periodically sending humanitarian aid. For instance, on August 1, 2004, Russia sent 34,700 tons of wheat worth $10 million via the World Food Program as a part of its donor contributions to this humanitarian endeavor.[68] In September 2012, Russia agreed to pardon 90 percent of North Korea's debt amounting to $11 billion.[69] This was what North Korea owed to the Soviet Union and technically it should have been shared by the new independent states after its collapse. However, since Russia became the official heir of the USSR, it inherited both its debts and loans.[70]

Starting in 2014, bilateral economic interactions received additional impetus. Russia declared its interest in developing three projects in North Korea: connection of the railroads between the two Koreas with the Russian TransSiberian Railroad, construction of the gas pipeline, and power distribution lines from Primorye to South Korea via North Korea, in which Russia had already invested substantially.[71] The Russian Railroads opened the Hasan-Rajin section of the North Korean Railways in 2013 and the cargo terminal on pier 3 of Port Rajin a year later.[72] In 2014 during a visit to North Korea by Alexander Galushka, Russian minister of development of the Far East, the parties agreed to accelerate mutual trade to reach the point of $1 billion by 2020.[73]

A separate point of concern is the nuclear weaponization program of North Korea. Bilateral cooperation in the field of nuclear energy started back in 1965 when the Soviet Union built the Yongbyon Nuclear Research Center and the first light water reactor (LWR) IRT-2000 with the total capacity of 2 MWe.[74] North Korea was also asking for 440 MWe graphite reactors. But after the Chernobyl nuclear disaster of 1985, the Soviets agreed to build only three LWRs with the expanded capacities of 650 MWe, which, however, never materialized.[75] The Soviets also assisted North Korea in its nuclear weapons development program. With that, modern-day Russia is increasingly uncomfortable having a nuclear power close to its borders. On a number of occasions the Russian authorities were highly critical of North Korea's attempts to build its own nuclear weapons. For instance, in 2006 Russia supported United Nations Security Council Resolution #1695 condemning the 2006 North Korean missile test, which, according to Seung-Ho Joo, "clearly demonstrated its preference for stability in Korea."[76] In 2012 it condemned another test by North Korea; the Ministry of Foreign Affairs of Russia "urged the DPRK to avoid new actions that run counter to the UN Security Council resolutions. At the same time, we hope that other parties will refrain from steps that could further escalate the atmosphere."[77] It repeated its strong condemnation within the frameworks of G8 of Pyongyang's nuclear test in April 2013.

Worsening relations between the West and Russia added additional momentum to Russian–North Korean relations. The Russian political culture would dictate to Russia, when confronted with threat, to look for like-minded partners who can back it up economically, politically, and militarily. In January 2014, Valery Gerasimov, chief of staff of the Russian armed forces, announced that Russia was having "preliminary negotiations" with some of its contemporary allies, including North Korea and Cuba for holding joint naval, air, and ground exercises.[78] There are also rumors circulated at the highest levels on Kim Jong-un's possible visit to Moscow for the ceremonies commemorating the seventieth anniversary of Russia's victory over Nazi Germany. Foreign Minister Lavrov even talked about a positive "first signal" on the attendee coming from Pyongyang. If it turns to be true, Moscow's visit would mark the first official out-of-country trip for young Kim.[79] As surprising as this may sound, such a step can be explained by Russia's desperate quest for allies in the difficult times for her, politically and economically speaking.

India: Old-New Alliance

Official relations with India started soon after its independence in 1947 from Great Britain and partition of the former colony into India, Pakistan, and Bangladesh. Due to its nature, which was the union of proletariats against the reign of capitalists, the Soviet Union viewed the process of separation of India from its colonial estate within the context of the global ideological battle between capitalism and communism. India was on the side of those who fought against imperial domination and thus, by definition, should have been pro-Soviet. Political support focused on support to the Indian ownership over the Kashmir and the former Portuguese territories provided by the Soviet Union within the premises of the United Nations in 1957.[80] Economic aid went hand in hand with politics; according to Stanley Kochanek and Robert Hardgrave, "India benefited from Soviet aid and technical assistance for India's public-sector heavy industry, Indo-Soviet barter trade, and the favorable terms the USSR extended for arms purchases."[81] This led to serious deterioration of the Sino-Soviet relations and contributed to the tensions Soviets were having with China, who had its own sensitive policy toward India. China accused the USSR of supporting India economically and militarily, including provision of the fighter jets and building of the MiG factory in India on the background of the Sino-Indian war over the contested Himalayan border in 1962.[82]

There are several areas of cooperation between Russia and India, toward which both sides have pragmatic attitudes. Former Indian foreign secretary Ranjan Mathai mentioned five such possibilities: political (Russian support to India's permanent seat at the UN Security Council), counterterrorism cooperation, defense (for instance, joint military exercises INDRA and the arms trade), civil nuclear energy, and space exploration. Mathai called the cooperation with Russia "special and privileged," which made it possible to accelerate bilateral interactions after sanctions were imposed on Russia in 2014.[83] In post-Soviet times, Russia strived to continue good relations with India, seeing the evident rapprochement of the United States with this country.

Starting in 2000, Putin and Medvedev visited India seven times. The Strategic Partnership Agreement concluded between the countries in 2000 opened up new areas of bilateral and multilateral cooperation, including those within the frameworks of the BRICS. Prior to that, in 1998 former foreign minister Primakov advocated for the development of the strategic partnership triangle Russia-India-China (RIC), a "relationship with strategic significance to counterbalance the United States' dominance and unilateralism" without provoking the United States directly.[84] This is perhaps why the tripartite union had never reached the projected strengths of a full-blown strategic cooperation in the absence of a viable strategic threat (or unwillingness to have one). Such was the situation within the RIC throughout most of its existence and especially prior to the last troika summit in 2013. Now that Russia has turned the tables on the West and the United States in particular, the RIC may gain the required momentum. Its success again depends on how much China and India are pragmatically willing to upset the United States by siding with Russia.

From an economic standpoint, mutual trade between Russia and India is higher than with several other peripheral countries but still has much to be desired. In 2012/13, the trade turnover between Russia and India amounted to $6.52 billion. Currently Russia is #31 foreign trade partner of India with the share of only 0.8 percent in its foreign trade. Russian exports to India in 2012–13 dropped in comparison with the previous year and amounted to $4.23 billion. The major trading items were precious stones and metals (17.5%), ferrous metals (12.4%), nickel (10.4%), fertilizers (8.0%), oil and oil products (7.9%), copper (6.8%), and plastering materials, lime, and cement (5.1%).[85] Two areas of cooperation with India particularly stand out: the energy sector and arms trade.

Russia has been involved in supporting India's energy (in)dependence for quite a while: it is eager to get its foot in the door of the $30 billion energy market of India where it has to compete with French and American companies.[86] On the basis of the intergovernmental agreement in 1988, Russia built two energy units of the Indian nuclear power plant Kudankulam with the output capacity of 1,000 MW each in 2002.[87] The first reached its fully projected capacity by June 2014. In addition, India signed a $700 million deal with Russia to supply 2,000 tons of nuclear fuel for the reactors.[88] Overall, Russia plans to build two more blocks, which is in line with Putin's vision for Russian cooperation with India, which has "plans to build over 20 nuclear power units in India . . . , the joint extraction of natural uranium, production of nuclear fuel, and waste elimination," which would improve standings for both countries as an external provider (for Russia) and domestic supplier (for India) in the world's nuclear energy arena.[89] In the oil and gas sector, the countries made significant progress with regard to mutual financing and extraction of the energy carriers. In 2001 the Indian state energy company ONGC bought 20 percent of the oil project Sakhalin-1, which makes it the largest Indian investor in Russia. In 2007 the output of Sakhalin-1 reached 250,000 barrels per day.[90] In 2011 the Russian Gazprom concluded a multimillion dollar, twenty-five-year deal with the Indian companies GAIL, GSPC, and Petronet for supplies of liquefied natural gas, which is planned to start in 2016. Another contract concluded in 2012 envisions supplies of 2.5 million tons of gas to India for twenty-five years.[91] The latest development was the signature of the Memorandum of Understanding between the Russian Rosneft and the Indian company OVL (a branch of the ONGC) for cooperation in the Russian Arctic shelf in May 2014.[92]

During Putin's visit to New Delhi in December 2014, Indian prime minister Nrendra Modi "has given the Russians both official as well symbolic reassurance that it does not support Western sanctions. In return, India has got its own set of guarantees at the highest level from the Russians for spares for existing Russian-origin military hardware, with Moscow agreeing to move more quickly on transferring technology for the equipment to Indian firms."[93] CNN drew interesting conclusions after Putin's visit: "As you read about and see images of Vladimir Putin's grand reception in New Delhi this week, keep an eye not on the rhetoric, but the outcomes and deals struck. Russia is the world's second largest exporter of arms; India is the world's biggest importer. Russia is one of the world's biggest producers of oil and gas; India is one of the biggest consumers."[94] Indeed, during this visit, Russia and India concluded twenty high-level economic agreements with the total amount of $100 billion in commercial contracts, which include "$40 billion in nuclear energy, $50 billion in crude oil and gas, and $10 billion in a host of other sectors, including defense, fertilizers, space, and diamonds."[95] In a way, the Western sanctions played into Russian and Indian hands: they need each other for the new investment markets for Russian goods.

Arms trade is another major line of business between Russia and India. A significant distinction should be made between nuclear and conventional weaponization. General discourse in India on the issue of weapons of mass destruction (WMD) follows from the inherent dilemma of their usage. WMDs can be viewed as strengthening the potential of the states in the international arena, contributing to their prestige and value. The reverse effect of this proliferation of expensive nuclear programs is destabilization of the relations with other states possessing similar weapons.

According to Rajesh Basrur, the Indian state attaches limited practical utility to nuclear weapons as a source of national security and considers their added-value highly limited.[96] Muthiah Alagappa, too, sees the need to have the nuclear weapons but to keep further development under control: "India's nuclear weapon program had its roots in the confrontations with China and Pakistan. . . . [T]he need for and direction of the Indian nuclear weapon program was driven in large part by the security rationale while its pace may have been influenced by limited technological capabilities in the 1960s and by domestic political and bureaucratic factors."[97] It was the domestic political environment in India—in fact, its political culture, which determined the form and scope of its future weaponization program.

In the matter of developing nuclear weapons in India, much depended on its strategic culture's minimalist approach to security in the nuclear age. India is more interested in political and not technological benefits of WMDs. Once it acquired the nuclear weapons, India decided to slow down in their modernization. WMDs are morally unacceptable for their uncontrolled damage to the areas they cover, high level of civilian casualties, and destruction of intangible assets. Nuclear weapons also contain high environmental threat and other associated risks, such as accompanying diseases, even several decades after their actual use. In the modern age, however, their possession is a necessary prerequisite for security of an anarchic international system: a state having a nuclear arsenal feels itself invulnerable to outside threats because it can threaten outsiders itself.

Historically, Indian leaders have now and again rejected nuclear weapons and nuclear deterrence as morally unacceptable and overall harmful. However, living under constant outside threats from the very moment of their country's independence, they still acknowledged the importance of possession of WMDs in the system of their national defense. For example, Mahatma Gandhi "rejected nuclear weapons and deterrence outright as immoral," but "could not abandon using force for national defense."[98] The minimalist vision continued throughout successive Indian leadership, including Prime Minister Rajiv Gandhi, who advocated for military modernization, including its naval expansion through close and active engagement in the world and regional politics. Gandhi argued for universal and total nuclear disarmament, but failed to persuade other nuclear states to completely destroy their nuclear arsenals. Eventually Gandhi authorized the Indian Weaponization Program, again without any allusion to nuclear deterrence as such.[99] It was for this very reason that India relied mostly on its own scientific and technical resources and limited its military cooperation with the Soviet Union–Russia to the conventional weapons.

With regard to the conventional means of warfare, India relies on Russia for arms supplies. Rajan Kumar noted this imbalanced nature of the arms trade: "The Indian defense sector is highly dependent on Russian defense supplies. Twelve out of 16 Indian navy submarines are of Russian origin. Its five destroyers . . . and three . . . frigates are of Russian origin. . . . Indian Air Force (IAF) is equally dependent on Russia; 32 of 41 fighter squadrons are of Moscow origin. . . . In army Russian T-72 and T-90 models constitute 60 percent of the . . . main battle tanks."[100] An important area of military-technical cooperation between Russia and India was the construction of ships for the Indian navy. The first three types of 1135.6 frigates were built between 2000 and 2004.[101] From 2008 alone, Russia sold India an impressive list of items: 250 units of Igla-S/SA-24 missile system ($26 million), 80 Mi-8MT/Mi-17/Hip-H helicopters ($1.3 billion), 5 Ka-31/Helix AEW helicopters ($198 million); 29 MiG-29SMT/Fulcrum-F aircrafts ($1.2–1.5 billion), 100 KAB-500/1500 guided bombs, 50 Kh-35 Uran/SS-N-25 anti-ship missiles, 500 RVV-AE/AA-12 Adder BVRAAM missiles ($463), 10,000 9M113/AT-5 Konkurs antitank missiles ($225), 80 Zhuk-AE Combat AC radars, 2 A-50EhI AEW&C aircrafts, and 68 Mi-8MT/Mi-17/Hip-H helicopters ($1.3 billion).[102] One notable part of such defense cooperation is the joint venture to produce the BrahMos, the only short-range ramjet supersonic cruise missile, which can be launched from practically anywhere. Russia and India set up a joint venture in 1998 with shared investments of $250 million.[103] In 2012 Russia and India concluded another significant deal: 42 Sukhoi Su-30 fighter jets and 71 Mil Mi-17 helicopters for the impressive sum of $2.9 billion.[104] The arms trade between the two nations shows all the tendencies for upward trajectory in the near future with lowering the trade, including in arms, of Russia with the Western world.

Conclusion

The Asia-Pacific region represents a perfect case for the convergence of the two behavioral logics in Russian foreign policy: appropriateness and expected consequences. For the first, Russia sees its location on the geopolitical map of the world as lopsided more toward Asia than Europe. The uniqueness of this region is in the mutual coexistence of the two logics, both on the levels of separate countries and within the geographic region of Asia-Pacific. Russia's dual grand political objective is to closely integrate with the countries of Asia-Pacific while continuing to receive tangible benefits from political and economic cooperation.

The "Russia is not Europe" slogan finds its enactment in various moves Russia has been making toward the most important regional players, China, Japan, and North Korea. Siding with China would allow Russia to improve its standings in the international arena but, more important, for its own people. The social media networking sites are full of drawings of the two warriors dressed up in traditional Russian and Chinese armory and military attire, confronting a creature several times exceeding them in size. The picture may have multiple variations: the warriors can be dressed in medieval style, wear the clothes of World War II, or have modern outfits; likewise, the creature ranges from a dragon spitting fire to a slimy hydra with many heads. The content, however, is the same: the two warriors (while being bigger than an average man) bearing the positive visual attributes (colors, open face features, decisive postures) are facing a much larger negative force whom they always win over. The new growing alliance with China is a marriage of convenience: Russia needs China as a political prop against the United States and as a potential source of income and investments; China needs Russia for a slightly different purpose: to play Russia as one of the many trump cards it has hidden up its sleeve in the geopolitical poker game against the United States and use its vast lands and subterrestrial resources for its own benefit.

North Korea is a relatively new reference point in contemporary Russian foreign policy. Here is where the logic of consequentiality best coexists with its appropriate counterpart. Russia does not necessarily side with North Korea on the basis of the similarity of their respective identities. On the contrary, while it suits North Korea to be one of the world's rogue nations and to oppose the rest at all odds, even at the cost of total isolation, Russia wants to be in the center of regional and global processes. Russia sees its place as a bridge between the West and the East and wants to play significant roles in both directions. With North Korea, Russia can have a relatively loyal ally, which is, like itself, a huge eyesore for the neighbors and nevertheless powerful enough to prevent the neighbors from overtaking. North Korean behavioral patterns fit perfectly well within Russian political culture, which sees itself as at the edge of the civilization and can present a viable menace for immediate surroundings and way beyond. The only negative side in Russia–North Korean relations is the growing military power of the latter, which can eventually represent a threat even for Russia, which is by its very nature highly cautious of any other nation possessing nuclear weapons. North Korea may, indeed, at some point become uncontrollable for Russia, which must continue to embrace North Korea at arm's length.

Russia's relations with India gravitate more toward the logic of consequentiality. India is openly anti-American. It has its own problems, among which are the always present threat of terrorism, border dispute with Pakistan, and territorial rivalry with China over the Himalayas, which make it focus more on the regional politics than give it grounds for the aspirations for regional and world domination. Besides, India has very peculiar views on its nuclear arsenal, which makes it an uneasy partner in the ideological rivalry with the West. It realizes that the United States is having hard times with its nemesis, Pakistan, and tries to benefit from this situation. Russia should not expect strong and long-lasting strategic alliance with India as with China, but will be content with arms trade with India at the present level.

7

Peripheral Politics

> Syrian Army is fighting for us. Those who fight in Syria and who survive will return to us.
>
> —MIKHAIL LEONT'EV, journalist, 2013

> Chavez was an outstanding leader and manager, a close friend of Russia. . . . He was an extraordinary and powerful man who looked to the future and always set the highest bar for himself.
>
> —VLADIMIR PUTIN, 2013

Russia's involvement in Latin America, the Middle East, and Africa has been peripheral to its national security interests from the very start of its independent existence. Whereas the Soviet Union was actively involved in the political lives of its loyal ideological supporters from all around the world, new Russia was somewhat confined to its borders in the first decade after the collapse of the Soviet colonial empire. The implosion of Russian foreign policy prior to 2000 was completely understandable; the country was undergoing a combination of shrinking pains following post–Cold War territorial reduction as well as a crisis of identity. The question of whether Russia would continue to be a superpower was off the agenda for a number of reasons. First, the country was no longer in ideological rivalry with the United States. The existential conflict with the West was over by the late 1980s, replaced by overwhelming acceptance of new free-market economic relations and its culture. Another factor that pushed new Russia out of the political markets of former Soviet allies was economy: for a country undergoing an enormous transformation—from the communist command-and-control economy to the capitalist economic bases—it was awfully hard to continue economically supporting proxy regimes far outside its borders.

Starting in the 2000s, Russia began slowly changing its foreign policy to focus on the regions and countries/societal groups it once supported in its struggle against American imperialism. The deliberate rapprochement with outsiders of Russian foreign policy was happening in the background of significant internal transformations in Russia directed at building the vertical of power, consolidating and strengthening groups loyal to the Russian presidency. The interest of returning to the lands far, far away resumed after the end of Putin's second presidential term with the development of new foreign policy (2008) and national security concepts (2009), which were further renewed in his third term in 2013. Looking beyond Russia's immediate borders in foreign policy was heralded in Putin's famous Munich speech in 2007, where he declared the unwillingness of Russia to accept the unipolar vision of the world imposed on it by the United States. In the Foreign Policy Concept drafted a year later, the peripheral regions for the Russian foreign policy were referred to as areas that disturb global peace and security and were placed in a long-term Russian foreign policy agenda.[1]

The relatively slow pace of Russia's reengagement with its former Cold War allies and new partners can be explained by a number of reasons pertinent to both Russia's internal situation as well as world dynamics resulting from rapid globalization. First, it was the sluggish economic recovery in Russia after the financial crisis of 2008 that significantly confined its global political outreach. The end of the global financial crisis in 2009 saw a rapid increase in oil prices, which almost tripled in 2011 following the epic fall in 2008 from $143 per barrel to $43.[2] Russia now had enough resources to support autocratic regimes all over the world that opposed the American "hegemony." From the geopolitical perspective, these regions are indeed in periphery of Russia's political scope, as well as beyond the scope of its threat perception.

Countries of Latin America, the Middle East, and Africa were either too far away and too costly to support (such as always loyal Cuba and lumpen Venezuela spearheading anti-Americanism on a global scale), or had their own share of internal unrest and conflict (e.g., Afghanistan, Syria, and Libya).

Ghost of the Cold War Future

By 2009, political and economic conditions in Russia were ripe for expanding the depth and breadth of its foreign policy, which had been dormant in Latin America, the Middle East, and Africa. Russia's renewed interests in these diverse directions were born out of Putin's "multi-vector" policy design. In his 2009 address to the Federal Assembly, President Medvedev declared Russia's wish to reinforce multipolarity in the world as an alternative to the unipolar world domination of the United States in global affairs.[3] As theorized by Eurasianist Alexander Dugin, the very basis of the multipolar world is power asymmetry between the nations, which defies their absolute equality in existing in contemporary international law. Dugin gives the following definition of the new world order that Russia strives to achieve in its peripheral foreign policy, where the balance of power is more visibly skewed in Russia's favor:

> A multipolar world is different from the classical Westphalian system in its non-recognition of the status of a full-fledged center of polarity as belonging to a legally and formally acknowledged sovereign nation-state. . . . Multipolarity, as a system of international relations, does not consider the legal equality of the nation-state as given. . . . Multipolarity operates with the situation that exists not only de jure, but also de facto, and is based on the fact of fundamental inequality between nation-states in the modern and empirically observable model of the world.[4]

It is clear from this passage that Russia does not negate the global domination of the United States, as an objectively powerful country, but wants to oppose it with its own growing power. Thus the recipients of the Russian power test are meant to be the peripheral regions, since, based on its multipolar vision on the world, these countries are less powerful in comparative terms and thus are not equal.

The multipolar vision of international affairs is born out of the revived self-consciousness of Russia as an aspirant for regional and possibly global domination. The adverb "possibly" is not just a slip of a tongue or a futile excuse for shelving the global character of Russian foreign policy for years to come. The scope, volume, and engagement dynamics of Russia beyond its immediate borders and relatively wider geographic habitat, which is wider Eurasia, depend on such pragmatic issues as economic power to provide the incentives and military might to impose its will on potential followers.

Size does matter, after all: obsession with power transcends geographical borders. Andrey Nikitin explained Russia's renewed interest in distant regions by its multidimensional identity construct: "Russia as a Eurasian power has to play a stabilizing role in the world affairs, contributing to reduction of conflicts between East and West, North and South, religions and civilizations."[5] The bridgelike identity of new modern Russia is reinforced by the fact that "Russia, being the largest Eurasian country in the world in terms of its territory, should develop a multi-vector foreign policy."[6] Indeed, why shouldn't it, especially if the size is appropriate and the potential is sufficient? If not in the immediate future, the engagement in the regions of Latin America, the Middle East, and Africa is still within the general superpower agenda.

A part of Russia's return to the peripheral geographic areas is stipulated by the historical memory that primordialists hold dear to their hearts. During the Cold War, different parts of the world turned into the battlegrounds for the bipolar rivalry between the Soviet Union, as the stronghold of everything anti-Western and anti-American, and the United States, as the embodiment of capitalism. Ideological belief, and also purely pragmatic reasoning, drove the countries under the wings of either of the global centers of polarity. Political affiliations and preferences of their leaders coupled with the variables pertinent to their domestic political environs largely defined the sides they would take in the so-called proxy wars between the global superpowers. Karl Deutsch was one of the first to define this type of a political-military confrontation as "an international conflict between two foreign powers, fought out on the soil of a third country; disguised as a conflict over an internal issue of that country; and using some of that country's manpower, resources and territory as a means of achieving preponderantly foreign goals and foreign strategies."[7] Relative power considerations, such as conventional warfare means and, even more so, nuclear capabilities, prevented the superpowers from open, mano a mano military confrontation with each other. The superpowers, as Rajesh Basrur notes, being "aware of the risk of escalation . . . have kept to a relatively less risky level below that of conventional warfare. This has allowed them to engage in marginal combat . . . or in proxy wars through third parties, as the United States and Soviet Union did in Vietnam, Afghanistan, and numerous other theatres."[8] Unable to effectively hurt the other to further compel the other side to follow its course, each of the power poles turned to distant lands to test their might and that of the other side.

Thus the scope of warfare moved far beyond the statutory dividing lines in Europe, where neither the United States nor the USSR were capable of waging decisive military operations against the military alliances (NATO and the Warsaw Pact) at both sides. For instance, in Africa, "the Cold War conflict and competition and the virtual partitioning of [the continent] into ideological spheres of influence led to the support for client states and the propping up in power of brutal, anti-democratic and authoritarian regimes that owed allegiances and their very survival to the superpowers. . . . The Cold War security dictum was based on maintaining order and stability in client states."[9] Some of the leaders of client states supported by the Soviet Union are still thriving (e.g., Fidel Castro in Cuba), were in political scenes until quite recently (e.g., Kaddafi before the Libyan unrest), or are the descendants of previous loyal allies (e.g., Bashar Al-Assad in Syria).

Proxy wars entailed diverse forms and intensities of Soviet Union participation in the domestic politics of target regions. In some cases, the USSR provided economic support to opposition parties, mostly in more distant areas outside of its immediate reach, such as offering the financial assistance to Marxist guerrilla movements in Latin America (e.g., the FMLN in Latin America).[10] It also used to send its troops to locations geographically closer to its borders, as in its intervention in Afghanistan between 1979 and 1989.[11] There were also cases of so-called double proxies in the form of sending the militaries of the allies to communist camp, as it happened during the war in Angola, where the local MPLA, supported by the Cuban military, fought against the U.S.-backed UNITA from 1975 to 2002.[12] In some instances, which are not numerous but still should be mentioned, the Soviet Union supported both sides of the interstate or intrastate conflicts, just to prove that it could. A good example of such double-sided action was the Ogaadeen War between Somalia and Ethiopia in 1977–78, where both parties were backed up by Soviet money and military equipment and Cuban troops.[13] The Soviet Union also provided instructors and advisors to the allies engaged in military activities with their regional foes, as it did in Egypt prior to the Yom Kippur War in 1973.[14]

An interesting part of the post–Cold War legacy of proxy wars is that, in some cases, the confrontation even continued beyond the existence of the Soviet Union (e.g., Angola) or resumed with new actors filling the power vacuum after the withdrawal of Soviet troops, as with the mujahedeen in Afghanistan beyond 1989. Mostly, however, the end of the Cold War brought the cessation of proxy wars, since, without external help, it was difficult for the warring factions to further sustain confrontation. For instance, as Brands notes, at the height of the Cold War, "the Kremlin was providing hundreds of millions of dollars per year in aid to Nicaragua and $8–10 million *per day* to Cuba."[15] The same was with El Salvador, where the FLMN was forced to go on concessions with its rival, the ARENA party, after the USSR cut its assistance at the end of 1980s.[16]

However, not all peripheral regions witnessed the proxy wars between the United States and Soviet Union during the Cold War. There are foreign policy directions of modern Russia that involve regions that did not participate in the bipolar rivalry, but with which Russia's interactions go way beyond the twentieth-century Cold War confrontation. Such is the example of a historically grounded involvement of Russia is its supporting of the nuclear endeavors of Iran and acting as its lobby in the international arena, especially within the framework of the United Nations Security Council.

The Foreign Policy Concept of 2013 shows a remarkable consistency with the moves reinforcing the place and role of Russia in world politics. The Concept is infused by the revisionist vision on global affairs and the wish to overthrow the unilateral hegemony of the United States. The Concept tries to persuade the readers that "the capacity of the historical West to dominate the world economy and politics continues to shrink. Global potential of strength and development is being dispersed and shifted to the East. . . . The wish of the Western states to retain their positions is fraught with increase of global competitiveness, which leads to increase of instability in the international relations."[17] The task that Russia puts forth thus is to limit Western influences in the peripheral regions and to curtail the transfer of Western values to the world around Russia.

Ultimately, Russian foreign policy in the regions of Latin America, the Middle East, and Africa, as seen in this guidelines-setting document, becomes the fight against globalization. And here is why. The Concept promotes the incompatibility of "the desire to return to their civilizational roots in the Middle East and South Africa," as well as in other regions, with "the attempts to impose their own value scale leading to xenophobia, intolerance, and conflicts in international affairs."[18] Such are the conditions in global politics, as seen in Moscow. Russia aims at playing an increased role in the regions outside its geographic borders, as much as its economic power and military force would allow. Until recently, Russia was boosting its involvement within countries that shared its anti-Western and anti-American affinities. Burdened by the sanctions and self-embargo, Russia might slow down its global engagement in the perceivable future but not completely shelve it.

Latin America

The Russian foreign policy approach to the countries of Latin America is pretty straightforward and follows the general faults of Cold War superpower confrontation. According to Marvin Astrada and Félix Martin, starting from the end of the Cold War, Russia initiated "extensive and intensive ties with Latin America . . . based on trade, investment, development aid, diplomatic relations, and promoting the view of Russia as an alternative source of political and economic support" to the Latin American countries that were traditionally unhappy with the American "imperialistic" domination in the region.[19] Bringing international matters back to the bipolar rivalry, when the Soviet Union was feared and therefore respected, also fits with the general lines of the convex and concave identity of Russia. As an aspiring superpower, Russia has to intensify its involvement in regions where it can build, just as it did during the Cold War, coalitions of those who are not happy with the United States and who are willing to accept Russia's role in gaining momentum for global confrontation. This is the main reason for intensifying Russia's engagement in Latin America, especially considering that it is the only region where Russia can technically come the closest to the United States' borders. Russia's modern pattern of involvement is not much different from that of the Soviet Union, but perhaps is of quite limited scale.

Russian foreign policy in the region of Latin America, according to Stephen Blank, is "not driven by Latin America's views, but by classical desires for profit and influence, mainly at the expense of the United States, and a visceral anti-Americanism."[20] The recent Russian rapprochement with Latin America, especially with Brazil and Argentina and the traditional communist "stoics" (Venezuela, Cuba, Peru, and Bolivia), on the background of economic sanctions imposed on it externally and internally, shows a remarkable continuity with the Soviet Union's amiable relations in the region. Historically, Soviet Union has provided financial support and military aid to its traditional allies, but has also strived to establish partnership with newly gained friends, who, for one reason or another, criticize the politics of the United States in the region. Now, together with bilateral relations, Russia pays particular attention to the institutional settings where it can play, if not the main role, at least as a leading actor. Such an organization that spans across regions and high seas is the BRICS (Brazil, Russia, India, China, and South Africa), whose member Brazil is a significant player in Latin America. Russia strives to elevate the role and international prestige of BRICS as the counterweight to the forces of globalization and as an opposition to the United States' influence in the world.

Evolution of Russia's foreign policy documents closely follows the main line of its growing superpower identity and its projection to the outer world. In 2008, Russia was aiming at "building strategic partnership with Brazil, setting political and economic cooperation with Argentina, Mexico, Cuba, Venezuela, and other Latin American countries."[21] The most recent Foreign Policy Concept takes interactions with the aforementioned countries a step further in the matters of "deepening political cooperation, promoting trade, economic links, investments, innovations, cultural and humanitarian exchanges; search for joint responses to new challenges and threats; consolidating Russian companies in the fastest growing sectors of industry."[22] The signs of intensifying bilateral and multilateral cooperation between Russia and Latin American countries are evident in the multiple reciprocal visits of the heads of states (according to Foreign Minister Sergey Lavrov, the record between 2008 and 2011 includes twenty-two summits and more than sixty high-level meetings, as well as billions of dollars in economic contracts.[23] An indicator of the increased attention Russia started paying to the Latin American regions since the end of Putin's second presidential term is the number of bilateral cooperation agreements (over seventy) signed between 2009 and 2012 between Russia and Latin American states, which is, in fact, half of all the treaties concluded in the past two decades.[24]

Economic Cooperation

Two areas of cooperation are especially important in presenting the full picture of Russia's relations with Latin American countries: economics and weapons trades. Carl Meacham from the Center of Strategic and International Studies put it very well: "The past decade has seen a new and revived tenor to Russian involvement in Latin America, focusing primarily on establishing its place in the region through general commercial trade, but particularly the weapons trade."[25] According to the brief prepared by the Council for Hemispheric Affairs, "Russia's foreign policy towards Latin America under the Putin presidency focuses not on macro-deals and dominating large trading blocs, but on arms sales and economic agreements with ideologically driven nations like Venezuela, Nicaragua, and Cuba."[26] Such a stance means that Russia is on the starting phase of building partnerships with the Latin American countries but prefers to follow the trodden paths of the Soviet Union: to join sales with the pleasure of annoying America.

From an economic standpoint, Latin America provides the markets for a wide array of Russian goods that are cheaper than their local counterparts and those imported from the United States or China, but which still have to compete with them in quality. According to Yuri Paniyev, "Among new important developments here is the growth of private business activity, which is considering the region not only as a source for imported goods, primarily food products, but also a sizable market for Russian industrial goods, including high-tech, as well as promising area for investment. After all, Latin America is a huge and solvent market with a half billion consumers."[27] Comparative statistics also follow this upward running pattern of economic interactions: as the data of the Russian Federal Customs Service shows, in 2008 the trade turnover between Russia and Latin American states was more than $13 billion with the top trading partners being Brazil (about $6 billion), Argentina ($2 billion), and Mexico ($1.2 billion).[28] In 2014, however, there was a slight decrease of trade indicators: trade with Brazil went down to $5.5 billion and with Argentina to $1.2 billion, but a slightly increased with Mexico ($1.9 billion).[29]

With the relatively low level of bilateral trade, the comparative trade climate between Russia and select Latin American countries is positive. For instance, in first decade of the new millennium Russia, as Valery Chistov stated, became the main partner of Mexico in Central and Eastern Europe. The data on mutual trade is characterized by significantly positive growth indicators: in 2011, in comparison with the previous year, export of meat products from Mexico to Russia increased more than three times and comprised $100 million. In relative terms, the export of Mexican goods to Russia was notable for the 17.2 percent of annual growth in the first ten years of the new millennium.[30] This, of course, is in no way comparable to the gargantuan trade balance between Mexico and its closest economic partner, the United States ($226 billion in exports and $280.5 in imports), but, in itself, it is a promising indicator of potential future growth.[31] Russian companies are also present in construction and investment markets: the company Silovie Mashini (Power Machines) built three hydropower plants in the Mexican states of Nayarit and Halisco. Another line of cooperation is arms sales: the Russian aircraft manufacturer Sukhoi sold twenty Superjet-100s to Mexico in 2013.[32]

Cuba has traditionally been Russia's preferred trading partner in Latin America. Putin visited Cuba in 2001, and that year marked the restart of the Russia-Cuban relations slowed by a decade of calming down of the consequences of the imperial collapse in Russia. In a move to encourage foreign investments and further improve relations to open up military options, Moscow decided in late December 2013 to forgive 90 percent of the $32 billion debt that Cuba had held since the Soviet era.[33] Additionally, Russia and Cuba signed two more oil agreements in May with the intent of providing joint offshore drilling opportunities.[34] In 2014, within the climate of sanctions, Putin visited Latin America, and Cuba in particular, in an attempt to cement the relationships with the former on the background with the slow rapprochement of the island nation with the United States. A number of partnership agreements were signed, among which the most notable are cooperation in the fields of metallurgy, chemical and light industry, as well as transport and special machinery. Russian companies will participate in modernizing a number of Cuban light and heavy enterprises. So far Russian trade with Cuba is insignificant: in 2013 the total turnover equaled $185 million, which Russia plans to expand.[35]

Economic and financial interactions with Venezuela are focused on a number of sectors, where the energy sources play the dominant role. Russia's trade with Venezuela in 2012, according to the Federal Customs

Service of Russia, has increased compared with 2011 by 12.1 percent and reached $1.9 billion. Most of the Russian exports to Venezuela by the end of 2012 were heavy industry commodities—machinery, equipment, and vehicles: 50.3 percent.[36] Lately the Russian oil-extracting sector has accelerated cooperation with Venezuela. The parties will engage in offshore oil extraction near the port of Mejillones and Rio Caribe, with the capacity of 600 mcm of gas per day and 20,000 barrels of condensate. There are already twenty Russian wells drilling oil in Venezuela, and the Russian side promised to bring in fifty more. There are several Russian joint ventures with Pdvsa—the Venezuelan, state-owned natural oil and gas company—which extracts 230,000 barrels of oil per day. By 2019, this amount is expected to reach 930,000 barrels. For this, the joint ventures will invest $46.9 million, $17 million of which is the share of the Russian companies. As Rafael Ramirez, president of Pdvsa, said, "By 2021, we plan to produce 1.123 million barrels of oil per day. . . . The Russian Federation is the largest oil producer in the world, with great technological potential and resources for development, which is essential for the expansion of the oil industry in Venezuela."[37] Together, Russia and Venezuela could create a sizable counterbalance to American and Middle Eastern oil production, especially under the conditions of fluctuating oil prices in 2014–15.

On the multilateral level, too, there is a high level of cooperation between Russia and subregional and international organizations involving the countries of Latin America. With regard to the sanctions imposed on Russia, Brazil, and other members of the BRICS countries, in their summit declaration in July 2014, declared, "We condemn unilateral military interventions and economic sanctions in violation of international law and universally recognized norms of international relations. Bearing this in mind, we emphasize the unique importance of the indivisible nature of security, and that no state should strengthen its security at the expense of the security of others."[38] This statement was made on the background of Russia's own interventions in Ukraine and the overall worsening financial situation within the organization, with the exception of China.

Together against Sanctions

As a side effect of the Western economic sanctions and its own self-embargo following the Ukrainian crisis of 2014–15, the share of selected Latin American nations in Russian foreign trade is projected to increase exponentially. The effects of complex interdependence between Russia and the European Union placed Russia in a vulnerable position where the changes of the trade policies (in this case, the sources of import commodities) by Actor A toward Actor B led to the search for Actors N+, which would provide substitutes to balance the effects of the policy change.[39] The Russian government's own estimate largely supports the vulnerable nature of its (inter)dependence on European supplies: they import about 85 percent of all goods that fell under the sanctions and self-embargo can be channeled by other countries, mostly Latin America. The vulnerability is explained by the fact that not all of the goods can be fully substituted, and it would take a year and a half to two years to find other goods somewhere else, especially in such distant areas as Latin America, and to set up their uninterrupted constant supplies.[40] Besides, the transportation costs are a matter here since the European supply chains are located closer to Russian borders than those from any other region. In the case of Russia, some Latin American countries appeared as such actors, eager to pump up the production of their food commodities for Russian domestic consumption.

In October 2014, the Russian Ministry of Agriculture brought up the first statistics of the effects of Western sanctions and its own embargo on the Russian consumers markets. According to its head, Nikolai Fedorov, between 25 and 30 percent of food products produced in the countries that fell under the ban are expected to disappear.[41] Some Latin American countries eagerly answered Russia's quest for new food sources, which are mostly frozen food items, such as meat, fish, and dairy products. For instance, as Rapoza from *Forbes* magazine points out, "Brazil does not produce enough to immediately meet Russian appetites. Sharp price rises seem inevitable. . . . Brazil's massive food industry could use this time to firm relations with Russian importers in hopes to replace rival companies once the bans are removed. Russia's Agriculture Ministry increased the number of Brazilian meat packing facilities it can import from now—going from thirty to ninety."[42] As a representative of the Brazilian Ministry of Agriculture commented in relation to the potential widening agricultural trade with Russia, "Measures to ban food imports to Russia from the EU and the United States can have revolutionary consequences for the Brazilian agricultural sector."[43] This statement has a lot of credibility in it. Brazil is vitally interested in trade expansion into Russia. In a country with skyrocketing poverty and high unemployment, increased trade with Russia would be highly beneficial not only economically but also from domestic political perspectives. The riots prior to the World Soccer Cup of 2014 signaled brewing social tensions between the "haves" and the "have-nots." Many Brazilians were angered by exceedingly high inflation, sharp rises in prices on food commodities, and poor conditions with social services. Those tensions could be alleviated or even quenched at some point by increased economic activity connected with the opening up of additional export routes to Moscow.

There is yet another variable that presupposes Brazil's heightened interest in cooperating with Russia economically in spite of American and European sanctions. Edward Snowden, the disgruntled former employee of the U.S. National Security Agency, currently hiding away from the U.S. law in Russia, and his contact in Brazil, journalist Glenn Greenwald, published a report in which they presented leaked evidence of the NSA spying on Brazilian president Dilma Rousseff in the form of copied communications between her and her advisors. Brazilian Justice Minister Jose Eduardo Cardozo suggested that this fact "should be considered very serious and constitutes a clear violation of Brazilian sovereignty. . . . This [spying] hits not only Brazil, but the sovereignty of several countries that could have been violated in a way totally contrary to what international law establishes."[44] President Rousseff called "the illegal . . . interception of the communications and data of citizens, companies, and members of the Brazilian government constitutes events of the utmost gravity and are a threat to national sovereignty and individual rights."[45] As the result of this setback in the otherwise friendly relations between the two partnering countries, Rousseff indefinitely postponed her long-planned visit to the United States, marking an all-time low in the level of intergovernmental relations between Brazil and the United States. Russia and Brazil can jointly capitalize on the deterioration of their individual interactions with the United States and open up additional channels of bilateral economic, trade, political, and military cooperation.

Other countries are also eager to jump on the bandwagon of alternative food suppliers to Russia. Recently, the Russian Ministry of Agriculture lifted its 2013 ban on the products of eighteen Chilean fish factories. Nicaragua expressed a wish to substitute for the Canadian shrimp.[46] Peruvian and Ecuadorian dairy industries were willing to join the sanctions-breaking league of Latin American countries. Ecuador made it known to Russia and the European Union that thirty-six companies were ready to increase the supply of fish and seafood, and another twenty-three are interested in the Russian markets. For that, the Ecuadorian government has set up a special governmental commission under their vice president, Jorge Glass. According to its minister of foreign trade, Francisco Rivadeneira, "We are preparing a specific list of items to be proposed to our Russian partners. We plan to start delivery of agricultural products both on the short- and long-term basis."[47] Such products would include fish, seafood, vegetables, and fruits. The ambassador of Ecuador, Patricio Alberto Chávez Závala, said that his country plans to increase sales of agricultural items to Russia regardless of the potential negative international reaction. This especially concerns dairy and fish products, which, according to the ambassador, can compete with its Norwegian counterparts.[48] In 2009, the two countries signed the Agreement on Strategic Association, which set up future bilateral partnership frameworks.

Another country with significant agricultural export potential is Argentina, who also wants to export its meat and berries to substitute for the banned European products. There are, however, certain hurdles, which can represent difficulties in filling up the sales channels to Russia abandoned by the Europeans. For instance, in Argentina, an increase in exports to Russia directly depends on its state policy of restricting exports. Almost all of the beef produced in the country goes to the local markets to control the growth of domestic meat prices. The president of the Center for Dairy Producers, Miguel Paulón, has said that Russia's self-embargo of agricultural and food products from countries that have imposed sanctions against Moscow will allow Argentina to increase exports of dairy products to the Russian market: "By the end of the year [2014] we sell to Russia milk and dairy products at the sum of $250 million."[49] Jorge Capitanich, Argentinian head of the Cabinet of Ministers, expressed expectations of boosting trade with Moscow to $5 billion.[50] The ball is now in the local lobbyists' court to lift the ban completely and allow local Argentinian producers to trade with Russia.

The ongoing transformation of global trade between Latin America and Russia in food commodities resulting from European and Russian embargoes led to the severely negative reaction of the European Union to those countries that are acting as strikebreakers and jeopardizing the intended severity of the economic tools of political pressure. The nature of economic sanctions dictates that the severity of their effects on policy change can only be achieved in cases of consent among the majority of states. Those who disagree and provide substitutes for the goods under the embargoes and sanctions are watering down their effects. In response to Brazil and Chili's increase of agricultural productions, especially with regard to meat products, the European Union announced impending talks with the aforementioned countries. An EU representative quoted in the *Financial Times* said, "We will be talking to the countries that would be potentially replacing our exports to indicate that we would expect them not to profit unfairly from the current situation."[51] One possible way to import from those "secondary" countries of Latin America is to re-export: sales of their commodities to third-party countries, which would act as intermediaries between them and the final destination of their products. One such rapidly growing re-export hub is Belarus, which picked up the lion's share of the European imports to Russia, where sources are other countries, including Latin American ones.

Military Cooperation

Political and military interactions between Russia and Latin American countries bear the resemblance of the Cold War confrontation when the continent was split between the followers of either side of the bipolar dyad. Currently Russia strives to achieve a much lighter version of its involvement in the region (at least, in the short run) from the point of view of military cooperation with select countries. So far, there have been no official and widely known talks about deployment of the Russian military, as there was during the Cuban Missile Crisis of 1962. However, looking at the dynamics of Russia's slow entry into the Latin American military sector, this option should not be completely discarded. Such a move, if taken and if connected with deployment of the ICMBs, would violate the letter and spirit of the Non-Proliferation Treaty, especially Article 1, which states that "each nuclear-weapon state party to the treaty undertakes not to transfer to any recipient whatsoever nuclear weapons or other nuclear explosive devices or control over such weapons or explosive devices directly, or indirectly; and not in any way to assist, encourage, or induce any non-nuclear-weapon state to manufacture or otherwise acquire nuclear weapons or other nuclear explosive devices, or control over such weapons or explosive devices."[52] However, seeing how Russia treats other binding international agreements dealing with limitations on nuclear weapons, such as the Budapest Memorandum of 1994, this option should be discarded completely in the mid- to long-term future, depending on the escalation or de-escalation of the tensions between the West and Russia.

The idea of deployment of the Russia military in the closest vicinity possible to the borders of the United States might seem somewhat bizarre, but Russia has already started making certain moves that closely resemble those of the Cold War. Notable from this point of view is the interview with Colonel (ret.) Vladimir Yevseev, head of the Center of Public Policy Research, regarding the prospects of Russian military involvement in Latin America. Here are some excerpts from this interview, which followed Putin's visits to the region in 2014:

> The mere fact of a naval presence in the Caribbean Russia is important because from a military point of view, there is a good reach of the United States. . . . [This] would also be a very serious response to the United States, who believes that Russia has no national interests outside its own territory and the U.S. interests span around the world, and they still believe that Latin America is the backyard of the United States. . . . The United States wants us to begin war with Ukraine, but we can show them that there can also be threats in other areas that are much closer to them, where America is quite vulnerable. And it is not even a territory where they have forward-deployed bases—this is directly the United States. . . . Russia must enter the region for a long time, and the United States must understand that the period of their domination is over, and that Russia will be there as long as it needs to, regardless of what they think in Washington or Brussels.[53]

Russia is indeed on the quick rails of revamping its presence in the lost geographic areas of interest. For starters, the bilateral military cooperation would have the shape of building docking and communication infrastructures for the Russian military. Deputy Defense Minister Antonov, commenting on Putin's visit, also noted that Russia was going to increase its military-technical cooperation with Venezuela, Cuba, and Nicaragua by building logistic facilities for ships and by using local airports.[54] The visit of Defense Minister Sergei Shoigu to Venezuela, Nicaragua, and Cuba in February 2015 following Putin's own served the same purpose of laying the foundations for the Russian military bases in this "soft underbelly" of the United States. Antonov confirmed this motive of the visit by a high-level Russian military delegation, which had basically anti-American meaning,

> In this part of the world, the Americans have created 24 military bases, essentially surrounded the whole. The idea was that the Americans impose alien values upon those countries [Venezuela, Nicaragua, and Cuba]. They are trying to change the governments, who conducted politics not approved by Washington. The leaders of the countries visited by Sergei Shoigu clearly understand that the problem of the color revolutions, which today are facing many countries in North Africa, the attempts of their organization in

> the territory of the former Soviet Union, represent serious challenges to the security of the Latin American states. In this regard, we support the efforts of the leadership of Venezuela, Cuba, and Nicaragua to strengthen national security, and I would say the real sovereignty and independence.[55]

The statements above have "Cold War" written all over them, and overlooking them would mean having significant military problems in the future. Although the full details of both visits are secret, the experts can guess what was happening behind closed doors.

In addition to the agenda of building and reconstructing military transportation facilities, Russia has long been known for providing arms and other military equipment to Latin American countries. Being one of the world leaders in arms sales, between 2004 and 2007 alone, Russia made $39.3 billion, more than the United States for the same period.[56] Between 2001 and 2014, according to Ilan Berman, Russia sold arms to the tune of $14.5 billion, most of which were bought by Venezuela.[57] Vladimir Davidov, director of the Institute of Latin America, mentioned the sales of Russian military helicopters in Brazil, Argentina, Peru, and Mexico with the prospects for selling them the Sukhoi fighter jets.[58] Venezuela bought Mig-35 helicopters, T-72S tanks, Smerch missiles, and advanced aircraft defense systems.[59] Brazil is not a newcomer, either, to the Russian military export: for instance, in 1992 Brazil became an exclusive dealer of MiG-29 fighter jet sales in Latin America.[60] In 2008 Russia sold twelve helicopters for the total amount of $150 million. In 2013, Defense Minister Shoigu visited Brazil and Peru to promote a $1 billion deal of the missile systems in Brazil and $700 million worth sales of armored personnel carriers and tanks.[61]

Cuba holds a special place in the future Russian military plans in the region. Until 2001, there was the Russian radar station in Lourdes, which was capable of intercepting data from U.S. communication satellites and ground-based telecommunication cables, as well as messages from NASA in Florida. When it was closed, its annual rent to the Cuban government was $200 million.[62] Currently there are talks with Cuban authorities about reopening the base. If such a possibility were indeed given serious consideration by Russia and the green light by the Cuban government, this would allow Russia to conduct intelligence gathering not only in Florida but also in a much wider area. Existence of the presence of such a facility would give Russia a considerable advantage over the United States in obtaining intelligence directly from its own territory.

The Middle East

Russia's interest in Middle Eastern politics ranges from purely pragmatic cost calculation to its own identity formation and views on its place in the region. This is also a peripheral direction for the Russian foreign policy, since it doesn't seem immediately threatened by the turbulent regional politics there. Moreover, as simplistic as that may sound, the absence of common borders with Russia predestines the low level of its present-day political and military participation in the domestic politics of the countries of Middle East. There were times, however, when the Soviet Union was intimately involved in the politics of countries like Syria, Egypt, and Libya by selling them millions of dollars worth of military equipment and sending them their political and military advisors, as well as supporting their position during the negotiations and voting at the UN Security Council.[63] At that time, the Middle East, in the words of Russian diplomatic mastermind Yevgeny Primakov, was the USSR's "soft underbelly."[64] The Middle East—especially Mediterranean-Muslim nations, including Turkey—was in the vicinity of Russia's historically defined national interests of access to the sea and controlling trade routes, such as the Silk Road.

For the decade after the collapse of the Soviet Union, Russia took a time-out in the region to bring to order its domestic political and economic mess. With the ascent of Putin to power, Russia's interests involving in the Middle East grew exponentially. According to Dmitri Trenin, "Russia's presence in the region has been guided by a combination of commercial interests, concerns about the support that comes from the region for insurgents and terrorists in Russia's North Caucasus, and the newly discovered spiritual attractions of the Holy Land and the more mundane beaches of the Mediterranean, the Red Sea, and the Gulf."[65]

The trinity of Russian foreign policy in the Middle East—security, business, and spirituality—found their reflection in the combination of two behavioral logics: consequentiality and appropriateness. The calculated consequentiality plays a role in Russia's wish to limit U.S. involvement in the Middle East and to get back the niche of arms trade and general political influence in the region. From this perspective, the events of the Arab Spring in the Middle East are viewed in Moscow with increased suspicion and disdain.

The Cold War confrontation is still ongoing in the minds in Moscow, which has led to repeated voting against U.S.-sponsored international actions under the UN, as it was in 2011 with the blocked Syria resolution. Yet Moscow is not alone; it is followed by its Cold War ally China: "There is an informal agreement between China and Russia to vote in solidarity in the UN Security Council. When Russia voted for sanctions against Iran, China did the same. When Russia abstained in Libya, China did the same. When Russia was opposing on Syria, China did the same."[66] Here, support to Syria resurrects sweet memories of the Cold War when Russia was the Soviet Union and could influence the regional politics on a much wider scale. For Putin, who considered the dissolution of the Soviet Union "the biggest geopolitical tragedy of the 20th century," return to the Middle East would mark, in a way, revival of the tarnished Soviet glory. MacFarquhar makes an interesting point by commenting on this veto: "Both the Chinese and the Russians are determined to reassert their long opposition to anything that smacks of domestic meddling by outside powers."[67] The Russian part of the veto combines business with pleasure: the Soviet Union and its successor, Russia, have been consistent supporters of Syria in terms of political lobby on the international stage and most contemporary military sales.[68]

Solidarity of Russia and China in the face of the international actions against another is based on their specific views on governance born out of their visions on sovereignty. Trenin contends, "The wrangling over Syria represents a contest of different views of the global order, of the issues of sovereignty and human rights, of the use of force, and of the responsibility to use force rather than allow a conflict to 'burn itself out.'"[69] The United States and most of the European countries insist on the notion of "shared sovereignty" where what is happening within the territorial borders of a single country in terms of human rights and freedoms is no longer the matter of that country alone. Because of their universality, the democratic international community is insisting of universal oversight with regard to mass violations of individual freedom, dignity, and life conducted or sponsored by state or non-state actors.

Russia—and other states with strong authoritarian tendencies in their governance—is a follower of the individual version of sovereignty. The fact of an autocrat opposed by the civil opposition, as it was in most of the Arab Spring countries, brings in the Elizabethan syndrome discussed in chapter 4 on the Near Abroad. No matter how cruel and inhumane a regime is, because of the ideational power alliance with the latter, Russia is willing to support it to prevent the international community from "meddling" in local business. Another explanation of the support is the wish to prevent appearances of *vox populi* capable of overthrowing a dictator, no matter how "democratically" he or she is elected. The simple reasoning dictates that if the people who are unhappy with the autocratic regime can take it down in other countries, they can do so at home.

The factor of religion plays a paradoxical role in the special relationship Russia has with some countries of the Middle East. As a country with strong Christian tradition, Russia is gravely concerned with the fragile Christian-Muslim balance in the region. At the same time, Russia always has to look over its shoulder to its Muslim population in order not to aggravate it by supporting anti-Muslim initiatives in the region as well at the UN Security Council's meetings. Simultaneously being mostly conniving and generally regretting the Soviet past, the Russian political establishment started promoting Putin's very vague concept of the "spiritual staples," an ephemeral embodiment of the Russian spirituality based on their national values. Yet, in order to irritate the followers of Islam and with the purpose of reinforcing the nature of the Russian nation as different from the Western world, Putin claimed that Russian is unique with regard to its Christian denomination: "We have the Eastern Orthodoxy, and some Christian theoreticians say that it is closer to Islam than to Catholicism."[70] Without commenting on the nature of this statement, a reflection on the versatility of the Russian identity construct should be made. In 2013, the state-owned TV channel Russia 1 launched the online project "Russia10," where the viewers could vote on ten visual symbols of Russia. Seven out of ten frontrunners were religious tokens; the one with most of the votes at some point during the voting process was the mosque in Chechnya named after Akhmad Kadyrov, the assassinated former president and the father of the current president of Chechnya, Ramzan Kadyrov.

The mélange of business views, identity formation, and religious affiliations found its due reflection in the evolution of the Russian foreign policy. In its 2000 version, Russia had a goal of achieving stability in the Middle East. Viewing itself as a "co-sponsor of the peace process, Russia intends to pursue an active part in the normalization of the situation in the region after the crisis. In this context, Russia's priority will be to restore and strengthen its positions, particularly economic, in these rich and important interests around the world."[71] Medvedev's foreign policy vision saw a considerable departure from the "selfish" realist view on the global arena and introduced a more liberalist attitude with its emphasis on international cooperation as the cornerstone of world politics. The Foreign Policy Concept is infused with liberalism: in 2008, Russia aimed at "using its status as a permanent member of the UN Security Council . . . to mobilize collective efforts to achieve comprehensive and lasting settlement of the Arab-Israeli conflict on the internationally recognized frameworks. . . . Such a settlement should be achieved with the participation of and taking into account the legitimate interests of all the states and people, which the stability of the region depends on. The Russian Federation was in favor of increasing collective efforts, based on mutual respect."[72] The spirit and the letter of liberalism prevails in these proposals on respecting the role the United Nations plays in the world. But, truth be told, the concept paper was adopted a month before Russia attacked Georgia in 2008.

In the 2013 version of the Foreign Policy Concept, the liberalist voice was significantly toned down. Although Russia still pledged "to make a significant contribution to the stabilization of the situation in the Middle East and North Africa; to follow a consistent line of promotion of the civil peace and harmony in all the countries of the Middle East and North Africa and in the region, as a whole," it proposed to do so "on the basis of respect for sovereignty and territorial integrity and noninvolvement in their internal affairs."[73] As a departure from the collectivist vision on sovereignty as embodied by the international community of states regulated by the intergovernmental organizations, the Foreign Policy Concept of 2013 puts the individualist approach to sovereignty on the pedestal of international relations. Russia promotes the policy of not interfering in the affairs of Middle Eastern states, namely, Syria and Iran, as a poke in the eye to the United States for the Iraqi and Afghani campaigns. The subliminal message of this approach is the Russia's own obsession with sovereignty, which it indirectly reflects in the concept paper. The direct source here is the growing self-awareness of a constructed superpower-in-the-making vision of world affairs in Russian political culture, which it projects in various regional dimensions, including the Middle East.

Syria: There Is No Friend Like an Old One

The Soviet Union has been a loyal ally to Syria ever since Syrian independence from France in 1946. In 1980, the two countries concluded the Treaty of Friendship and Cooperation, which institutionalized their relations to a point where Syria was one of the few countries that supported Soviet intervention in Afghanistan. After the Ba'ath Party came to power in Syria in 1963 with the motto "Unity, Liberty, Socialism," it would be difficult to perceive the region without Soviet interests. Soon the Soviet military foothold became Tartus, the only Russian military base in the Middle East. The base was established in 1971 and had been used by the fifth operational naval squadron in the Mediterranean Sea. Collapse of the Soviet Union left the base largely unattended, and only in 2008 did Russia resume talks about its modernization and restored usage.[74] Russia jump-started relations with Syria in 1993 with a new intergovernmental agreement on trade, economic, and technical cooperation, which prioritized oil extraction, agricultural development, and industrial construction.

Russia inherited from the Soviet times this line of cooperation with Syria and since its rebirth in the 1990s has been the primary supplier of major military equipment, including conventional weapons and surface-to-air missiles. The true picture of the Russian-Syrian military deals is shrouded in the veil of secrecy with full details known to the duo alone. The military cooperation has been striving ever since. Every now and then rumors appear about the Moscow's military sales to Damascus, like the one regarding the $1.2 billion spent by Syria between 1992 and 1994 on modernization of its equipment from Russia, which reportedly included T-72A tanks for the amount of $270 million; between 1989 and 1999 they sold Syria antitank guided-missile systems Kornet-E ($65 million) and Metis-M ($73 million).[75] This is, however, just the tip of the military sales iceberg. By the time the Soviet Union collapsed, Syria had accrued more than $13 billion in debt for the Soviet equipment.[76] Three-quarters of this debt was pardoned by Russia in 2005 and the remaining was to be used for joint development projects, among which was the development of Syrian oil and gas fields by the Russian companies, construction of hydroelectric and irrigation systems, and modernization of Syrian ports.[77] The same year, Russia sold Syria SA-18 surface-to-air missiles in violation of its commitment under the Helsinki Agreement not to support terrorist regimes, and also air defense systems Strelec, Pantsir-C 1 (known in the West as SA-22 Greyhound) with Buk-M2 (SA-17 Grizzly).[78]

Worsening of the relations between the West and Syria provided Russia with the opportunity to reinstate its political influence in the region. In 2011, civil war broke out between the Syrian government and opposition forces to Bashar Al-Assad. Russia, together with China, repeatedly blocked several anti-Syrian resolutions, including those on imposition of sanctions on Assad's regime. In March 2013, chemical weapons were used in the vicinity of the city of Aleppo with twenty-five dead and several dozens wounded. The incident was followed by the series of mutual accusations, with the Russians taking the side of government forces accusing the rebels of firing what appeared to be sarin gas.[79] The incident caused severe negative international reaction and heated discussions in the UN Security Council. Russia, followed by China, again vetoed the SC resolution on starting multilateral military actions against Syria and proposed its inputs in resolving the conflict, mostly related to peaceful disposal of chemical weapons to avoid Libya-type military strikes on Syria. The United States agreed, and Russia mediated the agreement and assisted in the handover of Syrian chemical weapons.[80]

Averting the potential large-scale conflict in Syria was presented in Russia as the major point scored in the Middle East for the Russian diplomatic action, which was possible only with the green light from the United States. In his annual address to the Federal Assembly in 2013, Putin claimed that attempts by some countries to impose "progressive development models" on Syria and other Near Eastern and North African countries had resulted in great bloodshed. He also asserted that Russia's foreign policy, in contrast, was based on "international law, common sense, and the logic of peace." Such a "mature and responsible" policy resulted in placing Syria's chemical weapons under international control and heading off "military intervention."[81] Immediately after that, Russia started negotiations for selling to Syria its long-range, surface-to-air missile C-300 IIMY-1 (SA-10 Grumble) to assist it in defending itself from possible air strikes. Due to its radius of 200 miles, the missiles would be instrumental in intercepting aircrafts, cruise missiles, and ballistic missiles at low altitudes. In the face of opposition from the European Union, which imposed an embargo on sales of arms to Syria, Russia was forced to destroy the missiles.[82]

Iran: Traditions Rule

Similarly amiable are the Russian interactions with Iran, which is another power player in the region. The history of bilateral relations knows ups and downs, wars (in 1804–13 and 1826–28), and territorial tensions. The Russian-Iranian cooperation in trade and political support can be characterized as the historical path-dependence on the background of their common will to curtail the influence of the United States in the region of the Middle East. Russia and Iran have similar positions, primarily related to the geopolitical situation in the region, the issue of oil and gas extraction in the Caspian Sea, and NATO eastward expansion. The main foreign policy priorities of Russia toward Iran are summarized by Gelashvili.[83] Iran is Russia's traditional political partner in the region in restraining radical Sunni groups. It also helps to prevent isolation of Armenia in the Caucasus, which is Russia's close ally. It takes an active stance in anti-Taliban actions in Afghanistan. Iran is a good although not quite steady trading partner with Russia (in 2013 trade turnover between the two countries was almost $1.6 billion, which was one-third less than in 2012—$2.3 billion—which, in turn, was 38 percent less than in 2011). Finally, it is a regional competitor for Turkey, with which Russia has quite sensitive relations, also due to the NATO membership of the former.[84] Russia largely views its good relations with Iran as a precondition for its continuous influence in the Middle East.

One such field of cooperation is nuclear energy, which has been subject to additional restrictions from the international community unhappy with the militaristic attitudes of Iran and its connections with the rogue North Korea. Iran has been living under multinational and unilateral sanctions for most of the 2000s. The United Nations adopted numerous resolutions, which, according to Rizwan Ladha, were "all designed to single out Iran for its various IAEA (International Atomic Energy Agency) violations and somehow stop it from continuing its nuclear activities."[85] The most recent actions were introduced by the UN Security Council's Resolution #1929 (June 9, 2010), which "strengthens previous bans on dual-use technologies for nuclear and missile use as well as conventional military hardware, like tanks, aircraft, and warships; prevents Iranian involvement in nuclear mining outside Iran; calls on states to ban further banking interests by Iran in their territories if those interests could contribute to nuclear proliferation or missile technology."[86] The EU, on its part, also imposed several rounds of bans on Iran throughout the 2000s, only, in this case, they were about the oil embargo and freezing the assets of the Iranian central bank, which significantly reduced the budgetary revenues from the sales of oil.[87]

Under such tight conditions, Russia managed to build a close partnership with Iran in a number of directions. Cooperation was going on notwithstanding Moscow's support for Resolution #1929, which was received negatively in Teheran. In Moscow, this resolution was presented positively as a major breakthrough in the international negotiations process and the victory of Russian diplomacy, which managed to remove from the text of the Resolution otherwise "stifling" clauses for Iran.[88] In 2011, Moscow introduced a so-called step-by-step plan to ease the sanctions on Iran in exchange for the promises of peaceful utilization of the nuclear energy and lower the volumes of weaponization. The plan had a highly skeptical reception in the West, particularly in the United States, which did not trust in peaceful Iranian intentions and considered it merely a respite from full-blown nuclear weaponization programs.[89] With the purpose of showing to the international community that it has the Iranian nuclear development program under control, Russia pushed through the project that it has been dragging since Soviet times: the Bushehr nuclear power plant. The USSR initiated the construction of this power plant back in 1975 at the height of its power; its collapse conserved the project until 1995. The initial construction works were completed by the Iranian companies under close supervision by Russian experts.

Bending to international pressure yet being reluctant to abandon its power ally in the region, Russia, according to Jeffrey Mankoff, "dragged out the work at the Bushehr for years before finally agreeing to provide fuel to allow the plant to begin operations in mid-2010 (a step the United States grudgingly accepted, since Russia would retain custody of the Iranian fuel throughout the entire power cycle)."[90] In September 2011, the station was turned on notwithstanding the significant pressure from the international environment, the most active representative of which was the United States, suspicious of the dual-use technologies and fulfillment of the agreement providing for the return of the used nuclear fuel to Russia.[91] The problem, as noted by Alexander Pikaev, was that "theoretically these facilities will allow Iran to develop nuclear explosive devises based on weapon-grade uranium instead of plutonium, which could have been potentially extracted from the spent nuclear fuel from the Bushehr power plant."[92] The international quarrel over Iran's nuclear plans took the "he-said-I-said-he-said" form with the international community claiming that the power plant gives Iran "a justification to enrich uranium [whereas] the Russians counter that the reactor itself is harmless if viewed separately from the effect to enrich uranium."[93] On its part, the United States showed the signs of tacit approval of the power plant provided Russia controls the return of processed uranium.[94] As a result of the improving international climate and regardless of international pressure, the plant has been fully operational with insignificant technical problems.

Another area of the modern-day cooperation between Russia and Iran is the arms trade. The first arms deal was made back in 1989, and after the collapse of the Soviet Union, Russia emerged as the major arms supplier for Iran. Lionel Beehner gave an in-depth description of this engagement:

> Since 1992, Russia has sold Iran hundreds of major weapons systems, including twenty T-72 tanks, ninety-four air-to-air missiles, and a handful of combat aircraft like the MiG-29. Late last year, Russia agreed to sell Iran a $700 million surface-to-air missile defense system (SA-15 Gauntlet) along with thirty TOR M-1 air-defense missile systems, ostensibly to defend its soon- to-be-complete, Russian-built nuclear reactor at Bushehr. Moscow also plans to upgrade Tehran's Su-24, MiG-29 aircraft, and T-72 battle tanks. Iran has shown interest in S-300 antiaircraft missiles from Russia and Belarus, which can intercept enemy aircraft 90 to 180 miles away.[95]

In 2000, Moscow left the agreement with the United States, which restricted military sales to Iran and soon after became the major arms seller to Iran.[96] For instance, in 2005 it sold several S-200 (SA-5 Gammon) and 29 TOR-M1 (SA-15 Gauntlet) surface-to-air defense systems to Iran.[97] In 2010, following the requirements of Resolution #1929, "Moscow cancelled the S-300 contract as part of its contribution to the improvement in U.S.-Russian relations sparked by the Obama reset, recognizing that it had more to gain from cooperation with the United States than by trying to remain in Iran's good graces at the expanse of mounting hostility from Washington"[98] With that, the Russian weapons sold to Iran are mostly of a defensive nature. Besides, as Anthony Cordesman and Khalid Al-Rodhan note, "The Tor is too range-limited to have a major impact on U.S. stealth attack capacity," and it does not represent a significant threat to regional security.[99]

Saudi Arabia: Neither Foes nor Friends

Relations between Saudi Arabia and Russia are based on the mix of business interests with politics, where the latter plays the role of the guiding light for the former. There are several points of interactions, where cooperation in the sphere of oil and gas extraction does play a role but not the most important one. Saudi Arabia and Russia are traditionally the world's two most productive oil countries with the daily outputs of 10.5 and 11.6 million barrels, respectively.[100] With this, according to the economic service of the Vesti New network, twenty-five Russian companies are planning to start actively investing in the economy of Saudi Arabia in the medical, agricultural, educational, and industrial areas.[101] Prospective investment interests are developing as Russia's relations with the United States have worsened since the Syrian crisis.

Saudi Arabia and Russia have a number of joint initiatives with the presence of the Saudi capital and the Russia technology in oil and extraction, oil refining and mining. The foot in the door initiation project for Russia in Saudi Arabia was the contract in 2003 for launching the ARABSAT communication satellites by the International Launch Service (ILS), a joint U.S.-Russian enterprise using the Russian PROTON launch vehicles.[102] Larger-scale endeavors started in 2004 with the Russian oil giant Lukoil concluding the deal for exploration and development of Saudi gas and condensate. This was the first case of a Russian company entering the Saudi market, which has been traditionally dominated by the British and American energy holdings. Russia became part of a multinational (together with Chinese and European investors) and multimillion ($800 million) gas exploration initiative. As the Saudi minister of petroleum and mineral resources, Ali Al-Naimi, declared at the signing ceremony, "We already have strong relations with Russia and excellent cooperation in managing market stability. . . . And there is no question in my mind that strengthening economic relations will strengthen other areas of cooperation."[103] Investing in a country that is the direct and major rival in the market of your most important trading commodity sounds outlandish only if it is not within the agenda of getting increased personal benefits from the ruling elites in Russia involved in the oil business.

This was as good as done: in 2008, the Russian railroad company got a share of constructing the Saudi "Landbridge" Railroad. The rout, spanning 4,000 km across the whole Arabian Peninsula linking the Persian Gulf with the Red Sea, had the total cost exceeding $6 billion. The construction of the project was split into four stages, one of which, for the sum of $800 million, was won by Russia.[104] This project was yet another sign of Russia diversifying its spheres of economic influence and wanting to play a positive role in the region. A more recent side deal with the Saudi sponsorship was concluded in 2014 when Egypt paid over $2 billion credited by Saudi Arabia for Russian military equipment, including MiG fighter jets, air defense systems, Mi-35 helicopters, and other armaments.[105]

With the worsening of the situation in Ukraine connected with the annexation of the Crimean Peninsula by Russia in 2014, and the hybrid war in the southeastern parts of the country, Russia came under the economic fire of Western sanctions. The economic pressure went hand in hand with the fall of global oil prices, which some viewed as politically motivated. The price on Brent crude oil (the brand the Russian oil is hooked up to pricewise) took a staggering fall from $113 per barrel in June 2014 to $60 per gallon in February 2015.[106] More than half of the price decrease had a tremendous impact on the Russian economy, which is almost completely dependent on revenues from the sale of energy carriers to Europe and beyond. The main reason for such a situation in the global oil market was the increase in oil output by Saudi Arabia.

Two theories were up in the air: that the Saudis wanted to punish the American oil extraction companies by making it economically unprofitable for them to continue to operate and that it was connected with the situation in Syria. In December 2014 Saudi officials dismissed the political bearing of the price change, declaring, "We do not seek to politicize oil. . . . For us it's a question of supply and demand. It's purely business" and "There is no conspiracy, there is no targeting of anyone. This is a market and it goes up and down."[107] In a couple of months, the Saudi stance changed: according to a *New York Times* article, Saudi Arabia has been trying to persuade Putin to stop supporting Assad, using its oil resources as the bargaining tool. The article quoted a Saudi diplomat confessing, "If oil can serve to bring peace in Syria, I don't see how Saudi Arabia would back away from trying to reach a deal."[108] Under such pressure, Russian-Saudi Arabian relations are expected to deteriorate in the near future.

Turkey: Old Rivalry, New Realities

Turkey is another country with which Russia has historically experienced high turbulence and continues to do so today. On many international policy issues, Moscow and Ankara play in tune. As Murat Akkaya noted, "Russian and Turkish foreign policies are similar with reciprocal behavioral patterns in some foreign policy issues. Both Russia and Turkey hold the same position on the peaceful solution to the problems of Iran and Syria, and oppose the U.S. attempts to place its navy in the Black Sea. Common perceptions of foreign policy, historical and cultural ties between the two countries encourage them to take on the role of a bridge between East and West."[109] Economic cooperation is a good sign of the convergence of foreign policy interests. According to the Russian Federal Customs Service, in 2013 the Russian-Turkish trade turnover amounted to $32.7 billion. This makes Turkey the seventh largest foreign trade partner of Russia with the share of 3.9 percent in Russia's foreign trade.[110]

During the American operations in Iraq in 2003, Turkey did not let U.S. troops use its territory as a transit point for the attacks on Iraqi land, which gave it some credit in Moscow appreciating such a rumble within NATO.[111] Another Turkish anti-American action that found warm appreciation in Russia was the ban it imposed on the entry of the American military vessels to the Black Sea during Russia's war against Georgia. By the Monteaux Convention, "Vessels of war belonging to non–Black Sea Powers shall not remain in the Black Sea more than twenty-one days, whatever be the object of their presence there." This was strictly enforced by Ankara "to prevent the deployment of NATO's Operation Active Endeavour in the Black Sea. Turkey abided strictly by the terms of Montreux and even reportedly denied access to two large U.S. hospital ships."[112] These moves showed Russia that Turkey was planning to play a role in the region independent of the United States, which also falls under the general Russian plan to fence itself against NATO.

A seriously destabilizing factor in the bilateral Russian-Turkish relations is the Nagorno-Karabakh conflict between the Armenians and Azerbaijanis, ethnic kin of Turks. Although Russia had not explicitly participated in the conflict on behalf of either side, Russian soldiers were rumored to be selling arms to the belligerents. The interaction within the dyad is aggravated by the presence of the Russian military base in Gyumri, Armenia, the soldiers of which are tasked with border patrolling. Russia is bound with Armenia by the Collective Security Treaty, which presupposes joint defense between all the members of the Collective Security Treaty Organization in case of an attack on one of their member. Regardless this fact, Russia is cooperating with Turkey on the bilateral basis as well as within regional organizations.

Another area of divergence of Russian and Turkish interests is the Syrian conflict. While both sides agree on the need for peaceful resolution of the civil war, Russia has in mind keeping Assad in power, which is not what Turkey wants. In their joint statement concerning the resolution of the conflict in Syria, Putin and Turkish prime minister Recep Erdoğan declared, "We share the same goal, but differ on how to get there," which means only that the parties decided to peacefully approach this matter.[113] Russia approaches the Syrian conflict from the point of view of its vision on individual sovereignty, which prioritizes territorial integrity and not interfering. Possible regime changes with the deposition of Assad would mean the failure of the legal postulates that Russian society is based on. It would also mean defeat of Russia's political interests and influence in the Middle East as well as economic influence. Finally, from a military perspective, Russia could lose its foothold in the port of Tartus if Assad is defeated.

Most of these priority areas are reversed for Turkey. First off, according to Habibe Özdal et al., "Syria outranks all other Arab countries when it comes to its significance to Turkey. How Syria's future takes shape as well as its inter-ethnic, inter-religious dynamics are beyond mere Syrian internal matters: they carry regional implications. The border separating Syria and Turkey is not contiguous with economic and cultural zones; rather, they intersect historically united regions. Syria is a natural extension of the Anatolian human terrain. The cross-border affinities have tremendous political import in how the countries behave toward one another. Therefore, Turkey choosing to watch events in Syria from the sidelines may be tantamount to allowing the instability to spill over into its own house."[114] According to the Turkish government estimates, about 400,000 ethnic Syrians currently live in Turkey.[115] Turkey is thus vitally interested in containing the violence across the common border with Syria and would also consider intervening, which would bear interesting implications for the NATO as an alliance based on collective decision making.

Arab-Israeli Conflict

Finally, Russian involvement in the resolution of the Arab-Israeli conflict is notable in its path-dependency during Putin's reign. Russian policy in this matter is framed by its wish "to do its best to strengthen its position in the Middle East by striving to actively participate in the resolution of various conflicts, to protect its own interests and its citizens."[116] Russia is a member of the "Quartet of the Middle East," where it is involved with the UN, the United States, and the European Union in elaboration and implementation of the so-called road map for peaceful resolution of the conflict. With this, Moscow does not hide that creation of the state of Palestine is a consistent aim for Russia as shown by the two Foreign Policy Concept papers of 2008 and 2013.

Russia was the first country that Hamas, viewed by many as a terrorist organization, visited in 2007 after its win in the elections for the Palestinian legislative council, which Putin called "legitimate democratic elections."[117] Similar statements and the general course of Russia in support of the Palestinian statehood are made despite strong economic ties with Israel, which in 2011 amounted to $2.8 billion and existence of strong cultural ties in the form of over a million Russian-speaking Jewish émigrés to Israel.[118] Russia also recognized Palestine as an independent state in 2011 and continues to lobby for its interests in the international arena.[119]

Africa

The African continent represents the geographic region with the least priority point for the contemporary Russian foreign policy. In this geographic direction, Russia follows the policies of political benefits but mostly pragmatic economic gains. The biggest interests for Russia are channeled into the explorations of the natural resources of the continent. As Jonathan Thompson rightly noted, "Russia's reemerging foreign policy in Africa as a whole is based on status considerations and economic pragmatism including Moscow's interest in hydrocarbon exploitation projects and access to uranium and other raw materials to sustain its domestic industry."[120] Yes, in order to deconstruct these focal points in the Russian views on its current and future involvement in Africa, multiple factors pertinent to the history of the Soviet Union's presence in the region as well as geopolitical and economic considerations should be taken into account.

In Africa, as in other regions, the Russian foreign policy assesses the situation from the point of threats and opportunities. Present low interest in Africa can also be explained by the absence of the current systemic confrontation between the West and Russia, which was the normal environment during the Cold War. The African continent was used by the Soviet Union as a playground for its communist experiments and the ideal source for proxy wars with the West. During the Cold War pro-communist countries of the region were the recipients of lavish support from the Soviet Union in the form of financial and military donations. The stepping-stone for the Soviet Union in Africa was Egypt, with which it concluded its first trade agreement soon after the end of World War II. Agreements with other African nations followed: Soviet Union was one of the first non-African countries to extend the partnership hands to the newly de-colonized nations of the continent.

The main variable stipulating the Soviet aid for the selected African nations was the quality and spirit of their struggle against the colonial powers. Since Moscow viewed the de-colonization in Africa as a regional extension of the ideological conflict between communism and capitalism on the systemic level, it was ready to assist the fight against the imperial forces. As Oleg Bogomolov concurs, "'The socialist' cooperation with the developing world . . . is mainly extended to those countries that are most active in the national liberation struggle and have embarked on a progressive political development."[121] James Mulira lists the following conditions for sending economic aid by the Soviet Union to Africa: "the actual or potential strategic importance of the recipient to Soviet security interests; the potential of the USSR to reduce American and Chinese influence in the recipient country or region; the ideological stand of the recipient, and, finally, the importance of the recipient to Soviet markets."[122] In short, the more the countries were doing (or just expressing their affiliations with the Soviets, as Siyaad Barre's Somalia did in the 1970s) in the matter of their fight against the imperialist suppressors, the more gravitas was added to the Soviet economic and military assistance to the countries for their ideological strive.

Most of the agreements were focused on economic assistance, trade, and construction projects in the main sectors of the new and developing African nations. Soviet assistance hit its peak during the 1950s, when the Cold War was in full swing. According to Robert Grey, "In the decade 1967–76, the average annual value of such transfers was $2,200 million whereas during the half-decade 1976–80 the comparable figure was $7,700 million, a multiple of 3.5."[123] Colin Lawson brings the amount of $273 million disbursed to the African countries by the COMECON (Council of Mutual Economic Assistance), a Soviet economic organization between 1982 and 1985, which was split between Ethiopia (57.9 percent), Mozambique (13.8 percent), Egypt (6.6 percent), Madagascar (4.2 percent), Congo (2.6 percent), Angola (2.8 percent), and Tunisia (2.1 percent).[124] In 1985, the total amount of the Soviet aid to the African counties quadrupled and reached the amount of $1.7 billion.[125] On top of that, there were thousands of Soviet technicians, aid workers, and military advisors who worked in Africa in Soviet-sponsored projects.[126] It was, however, the growing arms transfers to Africa that made this region of special importance to Moscow: according to George Hudson, Soviet arms transfers to Africa had ballooned from $400,000 in 1959 to a stunning $55.2 million in 1970.[127] The soaring stockpiling of Soviet arms in Africa signified this involvement as long-term investment projects.

Such was the picture of Soviet-African relations at the height of the Cold War when the Soviet Union was spending billions of dollars to sustain its unwinnable confrontation with the United States. After the collapse of the Soviet empire, Africa almost fell off the radar in Russian foreign policy priorities. Recently, however, this region has been increasing its value to Russian foreign policy decision makers who feel a strong urge to seek supporters for their international actions. Together with China, Russia has increased its involvement in Africa (Mali, Angola, Nigeria, South Africa) in the fields of "mineral resources, energy, infrastructure, telecommunications, fishing, education, health, tourism, and defence."[128] Also, Russia has been traditionally active in the international peacekeeping efforts on the African continent, a good example of which is its anti-piracy activities in the Gulf of Aden. While Russia, unlike France, cannot claim to have historically developed cultural links with the African countries, it can still appeal to past cooperation during Soviet times, which, depending on specific instances, can indeed be successful.

For the present-day Russia the African countries are still sufficiently too far from Moscow to represent any significant threat to its sovereignty. Besides, there are no common borders with Russia, which lowers Moscow's interest in political and economic developments on the African continent. There is only one American military base in Djibouti, Camp Lemonnier hosting Combined Joint Task Force-Horn of Africa (CJTF-HOA), that cannot realistically create perceptions of threat for the Russian identity or its national security.

There is yet another factor contributing to putting the region in the background of Russian political mechanisms: African nations are too detached from the pan-Slavic Russian identity to even be considered a distant part of the "Russian world." Finally, from a purely rational perspective, peculiarities of the African geopolitical environment, including hot climate and lack of the infrastructure, make the main Russian sales commodity, energy carriers, useless in the region: transportation of Russian oil and gas to the African continent would be costly enough to dissuade any attempts to do so, which would also decrease the temptation to use the energy resources as a foreign policy weapon, as Russia is doing in Europe.

The Foreign Policy Concept papers of 2008 and 2013 both paid due attention to the growing importance of the African continent for the Russian political and economic expansions. The 2008 version plans "to expand multi-vector interaction with the African countries on a bilateral and multilateral basis . . . [and] to promote the prompt resolution of regional conflicts and crisis situations in Africa. Political dialogue with the African Union and other subregional organizations will further develop, including the opportunities for Russia's involvement in economic projects in the continent." The same main points were reiterated in the latest concept paper, which shows that not much has changed since then in the Russian foreign policy outlook toward Africa. The recent developments in Europe, on the other hand, might lead to an increase in bilateral and multilateral contacts between African countries and Russia, seeking political support and a destination for its foreign direct investments.

Strategic Economic Cooperation

The current rhythm of economic interactions between Russia and African states is on its upward trajectory. The relations are developing under the conditions of both cooperation and competition. Russia is interested in the African continent as a good investment opportunity for its own companies, which are left off-board the European markets. With this, Russia is one of the leaders for writing off the foreign debt for the African countries: several years prior to 2010, Russia "forgave" some $20 billion to the African states, which is a token of its goodwill and the long-term political investment in the region.[129] Russia is also one of the largest extraregional donors in Africa; according to the information given by the Russian Foreign Ministry, Russia's aid to Africa quadrupled from $50 million in 2003 to $210 million in 2007, making Russia a leader in the G8 humanitarian assistance (that is, until it was out of the G8 in 2014).[130]

The level of mutual trade between Russia and Africa, as the statistics show, is the lowest among Russia's economic interactions with the rest of the world. The data of the United Nations Conference on Trade and Development for 2012 contain the following indicator for Russian trade with Africa: over $7.2 billion for the combined foreign trade turnover, which was a fivefold increase from 2000. Out of this sum, $2.1 billion were imports. The main Russian export commodities are fossil fuel, grain, fertilizers, metals, and their products. From the heavy industry trading in 2012, the highest revenue came from the sale of telecommunications equipment ($42 million).[131] According to L. L. Fituni, "The average annual trade turnover of Russia with the African countries for the last five years [between 2008 and 2013] remained on average about $4.5 billion.... Some of the leading Russian companies ... have large shares in the African companies in the spheres of extraction of oil, bauxite, uranium, and other raw materials. A realistic assessment of Africa's place in Russian foreign policy tells us that neither now nor in the near future.... can [Russia] be considered one of the main actors on the African scene."[132] Fituni is absolutely right here: these figures of mutual trade are significant indicators of the low level of Russian participation in the African economies.

The picture is different with the Russian direct investments in Africa. Between 2004 and 2008, several leading Russian heavy industry companies, including Nornikel, RUSAL, Renova, and ALROSA, invested more than $5 billion in the industrial markets in Africa. Russian energy giants Lukoil, Rosneft, and Stroygaz signed contracts for another $3 billion for development of the oil deposits of Algeria, Angola, Nigeria, Egypt, and Côte d'Ivoire.[133] Another oil company, Tatneft, bought the shares in the Libyan oil deposits of Gadamis and Sirt in 2005 and was planning to start oil extraction together with the Libyan National Oil Company. Operations were suspended during the Libyan revolution in 2011, but the company is planning a comeback.[134] Lukoil Overseas, a branch of Lukoil, entered Africa with over $200 million for the sea oil extraction in Ghana and Côte d'Ivoire and has plans for twelve more mines in Ghana and Sierra Leone. The total amount of Lukoil's investments in the region in 2011 amounted to $700 to $900 million.[135]

The road for the Russian energy businesses to Africa has not always been smooth, though. In its approach to the possibility of building a pipeline to the African continent, Gazprom bumped into the European Union building its own Trans-Saharan gas pipeline. Announced in 2007, the pipeline would have the throughput capacity of 30 billion cubic meters by its start-up phase. It will start in Nigeria and connect with the existing Trans-Mediterranean pipeline, which would further transport the African gas to Algeria, Spain, Italy, and the rest of Europe. It is expected to be completed by 2015 and will cost some $10 billion.[136] Gazprom, fearing that this Trans-Saharan pipeline could endanger its own operations in Africa, created a joint venture with the Nigerian National Oil Corporation in 2009 with the investment capital of $2.5 billion. The Russian-Nigerian pipeline will have comparable costs with the Trans-Saharan one. Even if this pipeline is not built, "developing the relationship with Nigeria helps in its efforts to control gas distribution options for many Central and Eastern European countries"—a unique opportunity, which the joint venture would still offer in case the construction falls through.[137]

Arms Trade: Old Habits Die Hard

Together with the economic cooperation and investments in the extractive industry of Africa, Russia has been very keen to sustain another lucrative line of business: arms trade. Apart from the over-the-counter "clean" intergovernmental deals, there are loners, like an alleged Russian shadow arms dealer, Victor Bout, currently in the FBI custody, who smuggled guns and ammunitions all over the world, but mostly to the continents on fire, including Africa.[138] Bout is the figure behind the Hollywood movie *Lord of War* main character personified by Nicholas Cage, but the Russian government is involved in much harder games. Soviet Union/Russia has been trading/transferring arms to African countries with the short intermission pretty much from their independence from the colonial powers. Newly created countries or those that were in existence prior to colonization had multiple identity groups who were not happy with the postcolonial settings and wanted to remake the African map. Within three decades from the start of the de-colonization process, the African continent was struck with eighty violent conflicts in forty-eight countries, mostly in Sub-Saharan Africa.[139] The warring factions needed weapons, and it did not take Russia long to recover the old Soviet routes for arms trade with its African clients.

Russian weapons proved to be among the highly successful means of warfare, both in terms of their battlefield performance and cost-effectiveness. Second only to the United States with respect of the volumes of foreign sales of arms, Russia sold the weapons for $13.2 billion in 2011.[140] Its main state-owned enterprise, Rosoboronexport, sells 90 out of 100 units of Russian warfare a year with a stunning $34 billion in total sales in 2010. Most of its arms and military equipment goes to the countries of Africa and Asia.[141] Analytical review of the think tank African Executive points to 2012, when Russia concluded export contracts for $15 billion. Most of that arms trade went through the Rosoboronexport to its supply points in Algeria, Angola, Burkina Faso, Botswana, Ethiopia, Ghana, Libya, Morocco, Mozambique, Namibia, Sudan, South Africa, and Uganda.[142]

It is next to impossible to credibly calculate the full amount of Russian arms supplied to the African nations due to the existence of multibillion dollar shadow markers of weapon sales. Even rough approximation cannot give a complete picture of the condition of the arms market in

Africa. Nevertheless, the open-source data give some glimpse into the trade deals. The following data were pulled out of the Stockholm International Peace Research Institute Arms Transfer database between 2000 and 2013. For example, for this period, Algeria, the largest client of Russia (11 percent of Russian global arms) received the following weapons from Russia: 42 Mi-28N/Havoc combat helicopters and 6 Mi-26/Halo helicopters (both parts of the $2.7 billion deal); 305 T-90S tanks ($1.470 billion); 30 Kh-35 Uran/SS-N-25 anti-ship missiles; 28 Su-30MK/Flanker FGA aircrafts ($1.2–1.8 billion); 2 Project-636E/Kilo submarines ($400 million); 42 Mi-8MT/Mi-17/Hip-H helicopters ($180 million), 25 Su-24/Fencer Bomber aircrafts, among the most significant buys.[143] Egypt bought 24 Mi-8MT/Mi-17/Hip-H helicopters ($300 million) and hundreds of portable missile systems.

These are the old Soviet "clients" who have the memory and experience of the trouble-free performance of the Russian weaponry. Yet there is a significant difference between how the weapons were sold by the Soviet Union during the Cold War and their contemporary sales patterns by Russia. According to David Shinn, former U.S. ambassador to Ethiopia and Burkina Faso, "The current Russian arms transfers to Africa should not be interpreted the same way as they occurred under the Soviet Union. The Soviet Union provided huge quantities of arms to client states such as Ethiopia and Angola during the Cold War. It also provided a significant amount of military training to select African countries. The focus was to counter Western interests in Africa. [By contrast today] military transfers and training by Russia are commercial deals as a way to make money. Ideology is not a significant factor."[144] What were at some point ideology-driven arms transfers based on the logic of appropriateness changed into the nothing-personal, pure-business approach in the modern Russian arms trade with Africa.

Conclusion

Interactions with the countries of Latin America, the Middle East, and Africa fall into the category of peripheral cooperation. Russia is not threatened by the processes under way in the countries of these regions, nor does it feel particularly at home with multiple issue-areas oversaturating their domestic politics. One thing is clear: Russia will try to accelerate its foreign policy, mainly in the form of economic cooperation with the key players for the sake of improving its political and economic standings in the key areas of its foreign policy: Europe, New Neighborhood, Asia/Pacific, and its interactions with the United States. Other parts of the world will continue to be within marginal interests of Russia, which would try to continue its presence, either because of the profits it seeks to gain from the investments in the domestic economies or the arms sales, or because this is what, in general, superpowers do. A country cannot have the prefix "super" if it does not have global geopolitical coverage.

Heterogeneity of the local political, economic, and cultural terrain in the Latin American, Middle Eastern, and African states presupposes diverse approaches and treatments in Russia. While some enjoy preferential treatments, others, even old friends, can come under fire if Russia decides to do so. This was the case with the Libyan arms embargo, imposed by Russia on Libya in March 2011 under the UN-imposed sanctions and lifted a year later.[145] Regardless of the nature of its involvement, Russia—like many other countries in their own rights—is not an altruist. Even if it acts out of humanitarian reasoning, it wants to achieve specific tangible benefits in return.

8

Quo Vadis?

> In fact, we are at a juncture. Russia may continue very slow development . . . or make a big step forward. Following the first scenario with the hypothetical possibility of retaining the gains is even more dangerous. This is a direct road to their loss. The road to the abyss.
>
> —DMITRI MEDVEDEV, interview to news agency Vedomosti, 2013

In 2014, the Golden Globe Award for Best Foreign Language Film went to the Russian *Leviathan*. Its plot was loosely based on the tragic life story of Marvin John Heemeyer, a blue-collar American worker who clashed with local officials over zoning rights and city ordinance fines, and the Mountain Park Cement Factory, which took over (he believed, illegally) his land. In July 2004, Heemeyer took off on a rampage in his modified and bullet-proofed bulldozer, destroying over a dozen administrative buildings and eventually committing suicide. The crux of Heemeyer's story hinges on the failure of an individual to fight for his rights and the failure of a government to ensure effective protection of those rights: essentially, the failure of the social contract.

Leviathan took the viewer to a distant town on the shores of the Barents Sea, neighboring on the Arctic Ocean, where it adapted Heemeyer's storyline to Russian realities of corrupt government, mischievous clergy, and overwhelming feelings of powerlessness to change the enveloping apathetic reality. The movie was critically acclaimed and a chief contender for a 2014 Oscar. Completely different was its reception at home. Against a backdrop of cool to almost freezing coverage of the film's international success by Russian central mass media, prominent pro-governmental politicians and artists issued harshly negative reviews. The backlash ranged from commenting on the low level of cinematographic art to accusing its director, Andrei Zvyagintsev, of intentional denigration of Russia, a fitting accusation amid the general anti-Russian hysteria in the West. The most interesting element was that the shooting of the film was partially sponsored by the Russian Ministry of Culture. Perhaps the apex of the avalanche of wrath that rained down on *Leviathan* came from a prominent anti-gay activist and St. Petersburg MP, Vitaly Milonov:

> The movie is full of Russophobic stereotypes aiming at creating a negative image of the Russian society and the state. . . . Zvyagintsev de facto committed an ideological sabotage against his homeland. . . . With the people's money, he drew a false picture of his people, which is clearly in discord with traditional Russian culture . . . and incites hatred in the society. The state must fine this director, who seems to have forgotten that his customer and the viewer is Russia and not the United States. . . . Movies distorting the history, traditions, and culture of the country must be banned.[1]

It is hard to imagine what the reaction of the mainstream pro-Kremlin Russian society would have been if *Leviathan* had won the Oscar in 2015.

Russian Political Culture in Distress

Reaction of the general Russian public and its officials to *Leviathan* reflects what is currently occurring in Russian political culture and its echoes in Russian foreign policy. Rejection of the movie, which ironically is based on the corruption, bribery, and governmental despotism of the United States, of all countries, stems from the Russian social contract. The mere notion of individualism is deeply abhorred in Russian political culture, which praises political conformity and social homogeneity above all other political virtues. Though the movie is fiction, it dramatizes the worst nightmare of the contemporary Russian political establishment and 84 percent of Putin's supporters: that an individual can rise against the system. Using this reasoning, Zvyagintsev's film details not a rebellion of an individual but, rather, a rebellion against the collective being, which is the state. Such a rebellion is ultimately translated as a rebellion against the Russian Leviathan itself, a sovereign who takes away the rights and responsibilities of its citizens as individuals and gives them in return a sense of stability on the collective level.

The story of *Leviathan* is also spiced up by its American origins, an element even more deeply resented in Russia. The fact that foreign problems in purely endemic American reality were implanted into contemporary Russia casts a veil over actual domestic issues and is presented as an outside attack by the vicious West. The ensuing chain reaction builds upon a perception of the West as an entity aimed at shaking the very foundation of the collectivist Russian society. Such a perspective leads Russian society to further consolidation around its own Leviathan, the government. With a general picture depicting Russia as the target of external fire, the only response from its political culture is further resentment and rebuff. When feeling threatened, Russia, as dictated by its political culture, congregates around its leader and envelops him in a cuirass of righteousness and highest trust. The Russian vice prime minister, Igor Shuvalov, gave a vivid description of this process:

> If a Russian feels any pressure from the outside, he will never give up his leader. Never. And we will endure any hardships that will be in the country—we will eat less, use less electricity, I do not know, some other things that we are used to. But if we feel that someone from the outside wants to change our leader and it is not our will that this influence our will, we will unite as never before.[2]

Political discourse has changed significantly since Putin came to power in 2000. In stark contrast to Boris Yeltsin, who would periodically entertain the public with impromptu bursts of personal charm, Colonel Putin embodies everything that "getting off its knees" Russia holds dear. The metaphor of Yeltsin's Russia as a dynamically developing part of the world striving to become a respected and responsible member of even more advanced democratic nations morphed into the metaphor of Putin's Russia as a bear pulled from its taiga layer in the midst of winter hibernation by reckless intruders. This bear-Russia consciously put itself on the outskirts of Western civilization and is proud to oppose everything of value to the West. Protection of sovereignty became as much Putin's mantra as protection of its taiga for the bear.

The notion of an external threat plays a significant role in cementing the domestic social contract in Russia. Here, again, Putin's bear metaphor comes in handy. The bear did not wake up on his own: he was awakened by hostile outside forces aimed at destroying his immediate den and its surroundings. This vision of international affairs is filtered by way of Russian political culture and socially constructed for its general domestic public in order to whitewash its own deeds and present others as culprits. Commenting on the second round of Minsk negotiations to halt the hostilities in southeastern Ukraine, Sergei Karaganov, dean of the faculty of the Higher School of Economics, said:

> The war began in Ukraine . . . not so much because there was a coup but because the West, for more than twenty years, by expanding their area of influence and control, refused to recognize the legitimate security interests of the Russian Federation. Eventually, Russia got tired of it and realized that persuasion cannot do anything. This is the root cause of the current conflict. . . . The main cause [of the conflict] is that the Cold War was de facto not over and remained an open wound. The West refused to agree on new rules of the game, believing that it could continue expanding its zone of influence and military, economic, and political control.[3]

Karaganov's statement is the quintessential example of the element of Russian political culture that always presents Russia as a victim, defender, protector, and responder to threats from the outside, never their initiator. It was not Russia who annexed Crimea from Ukraine. The West made it do so. This was not a Russian-orchestrated military coup in Crimea and southeastern Ukraine; rather, the Russian military was forced to respond to Western influences. During his visit to Egypt in 2015, Putin granted an interview to a local newspaper in which he directly blamed the United States for the Russian annexation of Crimea and the war in Ukraine:

> The Ukrainian crisis is not Russians' fault. It is the result of the attempts of the United States and its Western allies, who considered themselves "winners" in the Cold War—to impose their will everywhere. NATO promised the Soviet leadership not to expand eastward, which were merely empty words. Notice how NATO infrastructure is moving closer to Russia's borders; how it is ignoring Russia's interests? . . . We have repeatedly warned the United States and its Western partners about the harmful effects of interference in the internal affairs of Ukraine.[4]

It does not matter to Russian political culture whether or not such promises were ever made, either individually or collectively, by the Alliance to any Soviet or Russian officials. All that matters is that Russia felt insulted and hurt by the West. Such a stance, regarding the West as the source of all evil, was not always the case. In fact, in an interview in 1999, Putin blamed Russia for its problems, not the West, asserting, "Constantly pushing the blame abroad as the source of all our troubles is inherently wrong. All our troubles are in ourselves. Everything comes from our own carelessness and weakness."[5] At that time, Prime Minister Putin, who was on the rise, was eager to look good to the West, to whom Russia had turned for economic, political, and institutional guidance since its independence.

The change began with Putin's Munich 2007 and culminated in his Munich 2014. Anti-Western sentiment in Russia reached an all-time high in 2015, as shown by a survey of the Levada Center, in which 81 percent of the respondents had negative attitudes toward the United States (a statistic that has doubled since 2014).[6] Such findings roughly correlate with the percentages of those who have supported Putin throughout the Ukrainian crisis. Also interesting is another figure: the number of those who consider the relationship between Russia and the United States "hostile" increased more than ten times in one year: leaping from 4 to 42 percent. Similarly, 71 percent have negative feelings about the European Union and another 24 percent feel hostile toward it (increasing from merely 1 percent in 2014). At the same time, 40 percent still believe that relations with the West should be strengthened, while only 26 percent support further distancing from the West. The number of those who believed that Russia stood on par with the most influential world powers decreased from 45 percent in 2008 to 27 percent in 2015. With regard to the causes of the increased tension between Russia and the United States and Europe, Putin's press secretary, Dmitry Peskov, blamed the West:

> The West is trying to make Putin a side in the conflict; to isolate him in international politics; to strangle Russia economically in favor of their own interests, to achieve Putin's overthrow, while requiring him to resolve the crisis in the neighboring country.... The West will never leave us alone. And it is not the matter of Crimea or Ukraine. If it weren't Crimea, they would have come up with something else.[7]

In order to promulgate the idea of the West putting such a personalized hit at Putin, that is, Russian statehood, Russian political culture relies heavily on the very core of the "Just War" theoretical tradition, in which it presents itself as a protector of the noble cause.[8] Even international law is used to justify its hostile actions against Ukraine, a state that Russia officially vowed to protect: at the Munich Security Conference in 2014, Sergey Lavrov mentioned, "We have much in common with Europe.... First,... the principles of sovereign equality, noninterference in internal affairs, settlement of all disputes by peaceful means, the inadmissibility of the use of force or threat of force."[9] Russia violated each and every one of these postulates of international law, while presenting its actions as self-defense. However, brandishing weapons and blaming others for doing so is not a new tactic in Russian political culture. During his 2011 preparation for reelection, at a banquet packed with invited foreign guests, Putin claimed that the only reason the United States had any interest in relations with Moscow was that Russia was the only country that could "destroy America in half an hour or less."[10] This comment came prior to his post-Ukraine promises to turn America into nuclear ashes; together they reveal the Cold War–oriented character of current Russian political culture.

Back to the USSR

A quarter century after the band Scorpions sang their iconic song about the Wind of Change, it began blowing in the reverse direction. Russia is back on the rails toward a new Cold War and is committed to moving fast. In her book *Hard Choices*, Hillary Clinton gave the following reason for this turnaround: "Russia under Putin remains frozen between the past they can't let go of and the future they can't bring themselves to embrace."[11] Putin's task is not to revive Great Russia or to build the future for a postmodern nation. It is to reanimate the stale Soviet Union with the new flavor of elitist capitalism. When Putin mentioned that the collapse of the Soviet Union was for him the greatest geopolitical catastrophe of the twentieth century, he was not lying. Neither was it a clumsy joke made by a socialite novice eager to mingle with senior members of an exclusive club. Rather, it was a sincere, nostalgic outcry of excruciating pain, due to Russia's failures both in preserving the USSR and keeping its promise to mend its faults.

The Soviet Union is the only reference point that Putin-colonel has for Putin-president. Gerasimov gives interesting statistics on this matter. He conducted content analysis of over 85,000 documents in the language base National Corps of the Russian Language for presence and frequency of the usage of the words "Soviet Union" and "USSR." These are some of his findings:

> The "memory" of the USSR intensifies in language in the public space of the post-Soviet period not since 1991 but with the beginning of Putin's second term, in 2005. A relative peak comes in 1990 with the heated discussions about the fate of the Soviet Union, followed by a sharp dip in the number of references and rapid growth since 1996. After 1998 (the Kosovo crisis? Default?) a slow drop until 2004, where the absolute champions are the years of 2005 through 2007 exceeding even the level of 1950.[12]

The Soviet Union is Putin's final destination as leader, and all his actions on this post fit as jigsaw puzzle pieces into the grand picture of the USSR ruled by Russia. This is the main reason for Russian involvement in Ukraine: by denying its people the right to civil participation and deliberative democracy, Putin wants to re-create the Soviet society, where the people deprived of these rights were turned into the faceless lethargic crowd. The forms may differ, of course—the CIS, the Customs Union, or the Eurasian Union—but the content is always the same. It is ultimately the *Pax Russiana* that Putin is driving his nation to and forcing others to follow. However, a return to the political system of the Soviet Union is as doomed to failure as trying to get back together with an ex-lover. If it didn't work the first time, odds are it will not work in the future, regardless of how hard you may try. Nevertheless, the USSR continues to be romanticized, especially by those with no actual adult cognitive memory before the 1990s. Why are people, like journalist Ulyana Skoybeda, nostalgic about a phenomenon for which they have, at best, only vague empirical accounts? An explanation for this puzzle can be found in the depths of Russian political culture, steeped in an obsession for power embodied by territorial expansionism. Putin gave the Russian people what previous leaders could not: a feeling of power; of collective menace from the regional and global neighbors, as manifested by the fear of others, which in the Russian consciousness denotes respect. Insatiable cravings for respect permeates the multiple cognitive layers of concave and convex Russian identities and sentiments, bleeding into a quest for individuals who can satisfy such cravings. Herein lies the greatest paradox of Russian political culture: although inherently collectivist, individualism matters only at the highest echelons of power.

Powerful individual rulers enjoy immense and unquestionable respect in Russian domestic politics; likewise, those without power are collectively loathed. Prime examples of such powerful individualism can be seen in Russian foreign policy. Ivan the Terrible was a ruthless leader of Moscowia who governed it with an iron fist. Yet when he decided to resign, crowds of people—many of whom he later prosecuted—begged him to change his mind. Peter I turned the country inside out forcing it to accept Western standards of public administration, economy, and culture. Another strong leader was Lenin, who spearheaded the transformation of tsarist Russia into communist rule, which, seventy years later, was singlehandedly destroyed by Gorbachev. Yeltsin's rule was the least successful in bringing Russian political culture back to the motifs of fear and power. Putin significantly improved on the works of his predecessors and is currently leading Russia along the sure path back to the Soviet Union. As the USSR was both feared and hated, in Russian political language that meant it boasted immense international respect as a superpower. For that reason, the positive attitude of the general public toward Stalin hit an all-time high in 2015: a combined share of 82 percent believe that Stalin played an "unconditionally positive" (52 percent) and "positive" (30 percent) role in the history of Russia. In contrast, the considerably less powerful figure of Yeltsin received appreciation from only 11 percent.[13] It was Stalin who gave the Russian people what they needed: an illusion of the West as fearful of the Soviet Union at the expense of the individual well-being of its citizens. Yeltsin, on the other hand, squandered the resources to ensure fear and intimidation to the West in the 1990s. Now Putin is giving it all back, so how not to support him?

This is perhaps the best explanation for why liberalism and liberals (or, to use the contemporary Russian parlance, *liberasts*) are hated in Russian society: its collective nature considers itself violated by any unwelcome intrusion of individualism with its threats of a supremacy of human rights and free market economy. The collectivist nature of Russian political culture is also reflected in the peculiar balance between its domestic "inputs" and "outputs," all of which are channeled toward foreign policy decision making. In societies like Russia, the people are not the policy producers (in the form of inputs) but rather the policy witnesses and recipients (of the outputs). Therefore, in order to remain in power, governments must limit the outputs for citizens as individuals, while increasing them for citizens as a collective entity. This stands true for all autocratic societies around the globe: North Korea, Zimbabwe, Cuba, and Iran, to name a few. Under such conditions, notwithstanding the low level of individual prosperity, people will still remain happy because, as a collective organism, their mediocre needs are largely satisfied by feelings of moral superiority over others.

Time and again autocracies have offered their citizens outputs of various forms that ultimately quenched their individual dissatisfaction with the quality of their lives. Such tactics ensured that citizens remained largely content with the domestic and international choices of their governments. In ancient Rome, for example, it was *panem et circenses* (bread and circuses), a bulletproof formula for universal happiness of the masses. The Roman citizens were kept more or less fed and entertained, thus freeing the government's hands to make decisions without civic contributions. Fast forward to Nazi Germany, where Hitler offered mass outputs of a totally different variety: those fueled by a collective hatred for the Jews and other *Untermenschen* (lesser humans). The resulting constructed feelings of moral superiority as *Übermenschen* (super humans) blindfolded German society to their everyday problems and filled their hearts with a common sense of moral superiority over their own non-German fellow citizens. Putin employed this very process, but in a different direction. On the collective level, his outputs resulted in feelings of moral superiority over anyone outside Russian borders. According to this conviction, the West is envious of Russia, of its achievements, of its spirituality. The fact that Russia is "getting off its knees" makes it a constant irritant to the West. Putin said this himself when commenting on the Western sanctions against Russia: "As soon as Russia starts talking about protection of its own people and interests, it immediately becomes bad. . . . Do you think it's about our position on Ukraine or Crimea? Absolutely not! If not that, they [the West] would have found something else. That was always the case."[14] Here Putin verbalized the motto of the Russian world: "They hate us because they ain't us," which became the common mantra among key supporters of current Russian governance.

What the Future Holds for Russia

Russia is on the fast track to becoming a regional (short-term) and global (long-term) superpower. Mostly this will be ensured by developing the nuclear potential—the mega-club it inherited from the Soviet Union. Russian foreign policy is based on a four-prong approach: building a rivalry of power with the United States; spreading economic and military influence in priority regions of Europe and Asia; maintaining its presence in the peripheral areas of Latin America, the Middle East, and Africa; and expanding territorial possessions close to its borders by incorporating chunks of the Near Neighborhood—all in all, a foreign policy trip back to the USSR.

With regard to the first three objectives, Russia would continue to apply tit-for-tat policy tools, mimicking the U.S. moves 180-out. The primary battleground would, of course, be Europe, but also other primary and, to a lesser extent, peripheral regions, as bridgeheads to restore the superpower rivalry. On a multilateral level, Russia would also use veto leverage (with potential help from the Chinese) to block any U.S.-sponsored resolutions. In order to implement the last objective, Russia would further develop behavioral "anchors" to bind its identity to specific land plots close to its borders. These anchors, or "spiritual staples," as Putin christened them, were found in Crimea in 2014, yet they exist anywhere in the world with Russian-speaking populations. Next in line is Latvia, Moldova, Northern Kazakhstan, or even Belarus: anywhere with a pro-Russian population bordering Russia proper. These Russian diaspora are, in essence, the Trojan horses of the former USSR, now time bombs waiting to explode—and Putin stands ready to annex their lands and name them sacred places for the Russian nation, just as it happened with the Crimean Peninsula.

Predictability of the future moves of the Russian political culture also extends to its equally predictable intractability to external political and economic forces. It is widely forecasted that the Russian economy will suffer considerably from economic pressure, sanctions, outflow of capital, and decrease of global oil prices. Such a recession could reach 9 percent by 2015.[15] Morgan Stanley claims that Russia "is doomed": in 2014, it predicted the consumer price inflation at 13.7 percent and annual real GDP growth at −1.7 percent.[16] The Russian government has an even gloomier outlook: according to the minister of economic development, Alexey Ulyukayev, the Russian economy could shrink by 3 percent in 2015.[17] Yet despite such sizable economic hardships, the toughening of Western sanctions against Russia would bring only marginal results. Russia will not give up Crimea or any other land it considers part of its identity of *velikoderzhavnost'*. People will feel individual deprivation, materialized in increased prices for commodities and lower consumer baskets. However, their political culture will tell them not to bend to such external pressure, due to the unique outputs they receive from their government, outputs they have been craving since the dissolution of the Soviet Union: feelings of being feared, that is, respected, by their neighbors.

Such a gloomy outlook on Russian foreign policy can be explained by the peculiarities of the social contract between its government and its people. Russian citizens' absence of responsibility for their own lives was discussed in chapter 2 on the Russian political culture. There it was explained why common citizens prefer to accept the lies their government has been telling them: because they want to avoid long-term responsibility for their lives. It is always easier to blame someone else if, at the end of the day, something does not work the way you had hoped. However, the same forces that work in the case of Russia's domestic social contract have disastrous effects on its foreign policy. Until the Russian population accepts full responsibility for the foreign policy of its government—just as it should on the domestic level—until they hold their leaders fully accountable for the choices and actions their government and the military are taking—until that time comes, no change can be expected in Russian foreign policy.

So what can the West do? Nothing really different from what it has been doing so far and was doing during the Cold War. The Soviet Union did not succumb to external political force: it did not withdraw its troops from Afghanistan and Eastern Europe because of political pressure from the West. It did so on its own because it could not sustain the costs of further confrontation superpower-style. It even changed its foreign policy outlook from strictly hostile to tractable and even friendly at the very end of its rule. In that particular time, the West was united against Soviet aggressive actions across the globe, and so should it be now. The matter is not whether Russia and its foreign policy are capable of change. They, of course, are. The real problem lies in the fact that, when a new Gorbachev comes, as he inevitably will, it will be hard to trust him.

NOTES

1. Continuity without Change

1. Huntington, *The Clash of Civilizations and the Remaking of World Order.*

2. Simes, "America and the Post-Soviet Republics," 73.

3. Bobrov, "God Russkogo Yazika."

4. McElroy, *Morality and American Foreign Policy*, 23.

5. Kutchins and Zevelev, "Russian Foreign Policy: Continuity in Change," 149.

6. Andrey Kozyrev, "USSR Left a Bad Inheritance for the Foreign Policy," *Nezavissimaïa Gazeta*, April 1, 1992.

7. Gray, *The Geopolitics of Super Power*, 38.

8. Frolova-Walker, "National in Form, Socialist in Content," 331–71.

9. Mearsheimer, *The Tragedy of Great Power Politics*, 30–31.

10. Wendt, "Anarchy Is What States Make of It," 391–425.

11. Keohane and Nye, *Power and Interdependence*; Russett, *Grasping at the Democratic Peace.*

12. Waltz, *Theory of International Politics.*

13. Waever et al., *Identity, Migration, and the New Security Agenda in Europe.*

14. Popescu, "Hybrid Tactics: Neither New nor Only Russian," 1–2.

15. Nietzsche, Tille, and Haussmann, *A Genealogy of Morals.*

16. Greenfield, "Types of European Nationalism," 170.

17. Renan, *Qu'est-ce qu'une nation? Conférence faite en Sorbonne, le 11 mars 1882.*

18. Anderson, *Imagined Communities.*

19. Caldwell, "Russian Concepts of National Security," 316.

20. "Vistuplenie I Diskussiya na Munkhenskoi Konferencii Po Voprosam Politiki Bezopastnosti" [Speech and discussion at the Munich Security Politics Conference], February 10, 2007, http://archive.kremlin.ru/appears/2007/02/10/1737_type63374type63376type63377type63381type82634_118097.shtml.

21. Dmitri Trenin, "The Putin Doctrine," *Security Times*, February 1, 2013, http://carnegieeurope.eu/publications/?fa=51085.

22. Kozyrev, "Russia: A Chance for Survival."

23. "Putin: Rossiiskiy Medved' Nikomu Ne Otdast" [Putin: Russian Bear will not give his Taiga to anyone], Russian State TV New Channel Vesti, October 24, 2014, http://www.vesti.ru/doc.html?id=2071417.

24. Putin's interview with French journalists, June 10, 2010, http://rutube.ru/video/065e023456d7f580b28d4a2302b99ff4/.

25. Kozyrev, "Russia: A Chance for Survival," 9.

26. "Yeltsin's Secret Letter on NATO Expansion," Mlada Fronta Dnes, Prague, December 2, 1993, 6, in Foreign Broadcast Information Service (FBIS) Daily Report Eastern Europe.

27. Waltz, *Man, the State, and War*, 209.

28. Johnston, "Thinking about Strategic Culture," 41.

29. Winston Churchill, BBC broadcast, London, October 1, 1939.

30. Morgenthau, Thompson, and Clinton, *Politics among Nations* (2005), 5.

31. Viacheslav Morozov, "Nationalization of the Elites and Its Impact on Russian Foreign Policy," *Russia's Global Engagement* (PONARS Eurasia Policy Perspective: 2013), 8.

32. Gvosdev and Marsh, *Russian Foreign Policy*; Petro and Rubinstein, *Russian Foreign Policy from Empire to Nation-State*; Tsygankov, *Russia's Foreign Policy: Change and Continuity in National Identity*; Donaldson, Nogee, and Nadkarni, *Foreign Policy of Russia*; Oliker et al., *Russian Foreign Policy.*

33. Oliker et al., *Russian Foreign Policy*, iii; Mankoff, *Russian Foreign Policy.*

34. "Avgustovskie Reitingi Odobreniya" [August ratings of support], Levada Center, August 6, 2014, http://www.levada.ru/06–08–2014/avgustovskie-reitingi-odobreniya.

35. Lakatos, "Falsification and the Methodology of Scientific Research Programs."

36. "Chuck Schumer: 'Russia Has Stabbed Us in the Back,'" *U.S. News*, August 1, 2013 http://www.usnews.com/news/blogs/washington-whispers/2013/08/01/chuck-schumer-russia-has-stabbed-us-in-the-back.

37. O'Hara, "Great Game or Grubby Game?" 48.

38. Hahn, "Continuity and Change in Russian Political Culture"; Gibson, "Becoming Tolerant? Short-Term Changes in Russian Political Culture"; Kuchins and Zevelev, *Russian Foreign Policy: Continuity in Change.*

39. Yin, *Case Study Research: Design and Methods.*

2. Fear and Loathing in Russian Political Culture

1. Statements by Presidents Bush and Yeltsin at their Camp David meeting of February 2, 1992.

2. Dmitri Kiselev, "Vesti Nedeli" [Weekly Digest], State Channel Russia 1, March 15, 2014.

3. Kazantsev, Ignato, and Chichkanov, *Vertikal' Vlasti* [Vertical of power].

4. Hanley, "Beyond the Tip of the Iceberg," 9–12.

5. Weaver, "Understanding and Coping with Cross-Cultural Adjustment Stress."

6. North, *Institutions, Institutional Change, and Economic Performance*, 37.

7. Ditmer, "Political Culture and Political Symbolism," 566.

8. Ake, "A Definition of Political Stability," 271.

9. Laitin and Wildavsky, "Political Culture and Political Preferences," 589.

10. Wilson, DiIulio, and Bose, *American Government*, 80.

11. Almond and Verba, *The Civic Culture*, 13.

12. Chilton, "Defining Political Culture," 431.

13. Renan, "What Is a Nation?" 42–55.

14. Gellner, *Nations and Nationalism*, 6.

15. Anderson, *Imagined Communities*.

16. Tsygankov, *Russia's Foreign Policy: Change and Continuity in National Identity*, 1–33.

17. Comprehensive accounts of the discourse on two logics are given in March and Olsen: *Ambiguity and Choice in Organizations*; *Rediscovering Institutions*; *Democratic Governance*; and "The Institutional Dynamics of International Political Orders."

18. Hicks, "Is Political Sociology Informed by Political Science?" 1221.

19. Hechter and Kanazawa, "Sociological Rational Choice Theory," 193–94.

20. Goldmann, "Appropriateness and Consequences," 44.

21. Regan, *Civil Wars and Foreign Powers*, 39.

22. Hicks, "Is Political Sociology Informed by Political Science?" 1223.

23. Goldmann, "Appropriateness and Consequences," 44.

24. March and Olsen, "The Logic of Appropriateness," 690.

25. Weber, Kopelman, and Messick, "A Conceptual Review of Decision Making in Social Dilemmas," 281.

26. March and Olsen, "Understanding Institutions and Logics of Appropriateness," 3.

27. March and Olsen, "Understanding Institutions and Logics of Appropriateness," 5.

28. Weinstein, "The Concept of a Commitment in International Relations," 46.

29. Finnemore and Sikkink, "International Norm Dynamics and Political Change," 888.

30. Pelevin, *Generation P*, 175.

31. Roccas and Brewer, "Social Identity Complexity," 89.

32. Reid and Deaux, "Relationship between Social and Personal Identities," 1084–91.

33. Deaux, "Social Identity," 2.

34. Ting-Toomey and Chung, *Understanding Intercultural Communication*.

35. Ellemers, Spears, and Doosje, "Self and Social Identity," *Annual Review of Psychology* 53 (2002): 161–86.

36. Goffman, *The Presentation of Self in Everyday Life*.

37. Clarke, "Culture and Identity," 511.

38. Clowes, *Russia on the Edge*.

39. "Russkie Kak Mirostroitel'naya Naciya" [Russians as a peacebuilding nation], All-Russian People's Sobor, August 4, 2014, http://www.vrns.ru/experts/3142/#.VGJxEocf_6g.

40. Bill Keller, "Major Soviet Paper Says 20 Million Died as Victims of Stalin," *New York Times,* February 4, 1989. This expression "hacking through" is borrowed from a passage from Alexandr Pushkin's poem *Bronze Horseman*, which talks about the founding of the city of St. Petersburg.

41. "Vyacheslav Nikonov: Otnosheniye K Strane Vo Mnogom Zavisit Ot Togo, Chto Budet Napisano V Uchebnike Istorii" [Vyacheslav Nikonov: Your relationship with the country largely depends on what is written in its history books], State Duma website, April 7, 2014, http://www.duma.gov.ru/news/273/646438/?sphrase_id=1250977.

42. Vujacic, "Stalinism and Russian Nationalism: A Reconceptualization," 51.

43. Renan, "What Is a Nation?" (1882).

44. "Deputaty Gosdumy Predlozhili Prazdnovat' Den' Vzyatiya Parizha" [State Duma deputies suggest celebrating "Day of Occupation of Paris"], *Argumenti I Fakti*, January 14, 2015.

45. Christiano, Swatos, and Kivisto, *Sociology of Religion*, 6; circular letter #10 of the Central Committee of the Communist Party, "On Strengthening of Anti-Religious Work," Commission on the Issues of the Cults under the Presidium of the Central Executive Committee 2, no. 7 (1929): 1–2.

46. Hutten, *Iron Curtain Christians*, 11.

47. Pospelovsky, *Russkaya Pravoslavnaya Cerkov' v XX Veke* [Russian Orthodox Church in the twentieth century], 168.

48. Anna Dickinson claims that 97.6 percent of all churches open in 1916 had been closed by 1940. See Dickinson, "Quantifying Religious Oppression," 330. According to Ol'ga Vasil'yeva, the numbers of Orthodox priests decreased by more than 90 percent between 1916 and 1940. See Vasil'yeva, *Russkaya Pravoslavnaya Tserkov' i Kommunisticheskoye Gosudarstvo 1917–1941* [Russian Orthodox Church and communist state], 298.

49. Trenin, Lipman, and Malashenko, "The End of Era in EU-Russian Relations."

50. Speech of Minister of Foreign Affairs of Russia S. V. Lavrov on the Jubilee International Conference, "Russia in the World of Force of the XXI Century," dedicated to the twentieth anniversary of the Council on Foreign and Defense Policy and the tenth anniversary of the journal *Russia in Global Affairs*, Moscow, December 1, 2012, www.mid.ru/bdomp/brp_4.nsf/e78a48070f128a7b43256999005bcbb3/1eeac193a9c09f3d44257ad1003777.

51. Trenin, "The Mythical Alliance: Russia's Syria Policy," 13.

52. "Deklaraciya Russkoi Identichnosti" [Declaration of Russian Identity], Russian Orthodox Church, November 12, 2014, http://www.patriarchia.ru/db/text/508347.html.

53. "Putin Pozdravil Rossiyan s Paskhoi" [Putin's Easter address to the Russian citizens], *RIA Novosti*, May 5, 2013, http://ria.ru/society/20130505/935875322.html.

54. "Rossiyane O Staline" [Russian citizens on Stalin], Levada Center, March 5, 2010, http://www.levada.ru/05-03-2010/rossiyane-o-staline.

55. Mendelson and Gerber, "Failing the Stalin Test," 2.

56. Project "Name of Russia," TV Rossiya in partnership with Fund "Public Opinion," 2008, http://www.nameofrussia.ru/rating.html.

57. "Kolichestvo Negativnykh Otsenok Lichnosti Stalina Sredi Rossiyan za 15 let Sokratilos' Pochti v Tri Raza" [The number of negative assessments of Stalin among Russians within fifteen years decreased by almost three times], Levada Center, October 18, 2012, http://www.levada.ru/18-10-2012/kolichestvo-negativnykh-otsenok-lichnosti-stalina-sredi-rossiyan-za-15-let-sokratilos-poc.

58. Dmitry Rogozin, Twitter entry, June 11, 2014, https://twitter.com/Rogozin/status/476962746777751552.

59. Brandenberger, "Debate: Stalin's Populism and the Accidental Creation of Russian National Identity," 729.

60. Satter, *It Was a Long Time Ago, and It Never Happened Anyway*, 6.

61. Jaspers, *The Question of German Guilt*, 26.

62. Article 354.1 of the Federal Law № 128-ФЗ of the Russian Federation "Rehabilitation of Nazism."

63. "West Is Moving Away from Russia Because of Its Return to Orthodoxy, Believes Lavrov," June 5, 2014, http://www.interfax-religion.ru/?act=news&div=55525; speech of Sergei Lavrov, minister of foreign affairs of the Russian Federation, on the 69th session of the United Nations General Assembly, September 27, 2014.

64. Article 28, Vienna Convention on the Law of Treaties, May 23, 1969, UN Doc. A/CONF. 39/27 (1969).

65. Gramsci, *Selections from the Prison Notebooks*.

66. Nye, *Soft Power: The Means to Success in World Politics*, x. Bismarck made the following statement in the Prussian House of Deputies on January 28, 1886: "This policy cannot succeed through speeches . . . and songs; it can be carried out only through blood and iron."

67. Nye, "Soft Power," *Foreign Policy* 80 (1990): 160.

68. Lasswell, *Psychopathology and Politics*, 203.

69. Thucydides, *History of the Peloponnesian War* (1954), 402.

70. Andreas Antoniades, "From 'Theories of Hegemon' to 'Hegemon Analysis' in International Relations," paper presented at 49th annual ISA convention (2002), 2.

71. Ikenberry and Kupchan, "Socialization and Hegemonic Power," 287–88.

72. Clausewitz, *On War*, 75.

73. Gramsci, *Selections from the Prison Notebooks*, 201.

74. Gilpin, *War and Change in World Politics*.

75. Thompson, *Russia and the Soviet Union*, 2.

76. "Population density (people per sq. km of land area)," World Bank data.

77. Astolphe-Louis-Léonor, marquis de Custine, *La Rusiie en 1839*, 341.

78. The full account of the "gathering" is given in Ruslan G. Skrynnikov, *Ivan III*.

79. Perrier and Pavlov, *Ivan the Terrible*.

80. Shubinsky, *Istoricheskie Ocherki I Rasskazi* [Historical essays and stories], 44–51.

81. Smith, *Soviet Politics*, 2.

82. Lehovich, "The Testament of Peter the Great," 111–24.

83. Semen Novoprudsky, "Rossia Vmesto Novorossii" [Russia instead of Novorossiya], *GazetaRU*, June 27, 2014, http://www.gazeta.ru/comments/column/novoprudsky/6087957.shtml.

84. Wilson, "Hard Power, Soft Power, Smart Power."

85. Mittelman, *Hyperconflict: Globalization and Insecurity*, 7.

86. Semen Novoprudsky, "Pepel V Golove" [Ashes in the head], *GazetaRu*, June 6, 2014, http://www.gazeta.ru/comments/column/novoprudsky/6061157.shtml.

87. Gyorkei, Kirov, and Horvath, *Soviet Military Intervention in Hungary, 1956*.

88. Persak, "The Polish-Soviet Confrontation in 1956 and the Attempted Soviet Military Intervention in Poland," 1285.

89. Morgenthau, "Inquisition in Czechoslovakia," 20–21; Bennett, *Condemned to Repetition?* 127–66, 215–46.

90. Gachechiladze, *The New Georgia*, xix.

91. Bolukbasi, *Azerbaijan*, 19–44.

92. Hovannisian, *The Republic of Armenia*, 4:373–408; Marshall, *The Caucasus under Soviet Rule*, 175–94.

93. For full accounts of the process of sovetization of the Baltic States, see Lane et al., *The Baltic States: Estonia, Latvia, and Lithuania*; Senn, *Lithuania 1940: Revolution from Above*; Cox, *The Soviet Takeover of Latvia*.

94. Sander, *The Hundred Day Winter War*.

95. Hale, "The Parade of Sovereignties."

96. Scott Wilson, "Obama Dismisses Russia as 'Regional Power' Acting out of Weakness," *Washington Post*, March 25, 2014.

97. Thucydides, *History of the Peloponnesian War* (1972), 402.

98. Fund for Fighting against Corruption, "Skol'ko Stoila Olimpiada" [How Much Did the Olympics Cost?], http://sochi.fbk.info/ru/price/.

99. Max Weber, quoted in Weber, Owen, Strong, and Livingstone, *The Vocation Lectures: Science as a Vocation, Politics as a Vocation*.

100. Plato, *Crito*.

101. Locke, *Second Treatise of Government* (2013), 3.

102. Hobbes, *Leviathan* (1968), 188.

103. John Locke, *Second Treatise of Government* (1980), 9.

104. Lipset, "Some Social Requisites of Democracy," 86–87; Wildavsky, "Choosing Preferences by Constructing Institutions," 6.

105. Call, "Beyond the 'Failed State': Toward Conceptual Alternatives," 308.

106. Lipset, "Some Social Requisites of Democracy," 86.

107. Goldstone, "Pathways to State Failure," 285.

108. Shepherd, "Political Stability: Crucial for Growth?" 9.

109. Feng, "Democracy, Political Stability, and Economic Growth," 398.

110. Kant, *Perpetual Peace and Other Essays on Politics, History, and Morals*, 112.

111. Gutmann and Thompson, *Why Deliberative Democracy?* 3.

112. Habermas, "Popular Sovereignty as Procedure."

113. Silitski, "From Social Contract to Social Dialogue," 156.

114. Haiduk, "Social Contract: A Conceptual Framework," 22.

115. Nathan, "China's Changing of the Guard."

116. Przeworski and Limongi, "Political Regimes and Economic Growth," 58.

117. "Chem Mi Dorojom? O Samom Vazhnom V Zhizni Rossiyan" [What are our values? On the most important in the lives of Russians], *FOM*, July 18, 2013.

118. Rothstein and Teorell, "What Is Quality of Government?" 169.

119. Maslow, "A Theory of Human Motivation."

120. McAuley, *Soviet Politics, 1917–1991*, 5.

121. Moon, *The Russian Peasantry, 1600–1930*, 242.

122. Kesey, *One Flew over the Cuckoo's Nest*, 64.

123. Payne, *Ivan the Terrible*, 222–27.

124. Zimin, *Oprichnina Ivana Groznogo* [Oprichnina of Ivan the Terrible]; Riasanovsky and Steinberg, "The Time of Troubles, 1598–1613."

125. Saynakov, *Oprichnina Ivana Groznogo glazami tekh, kto vyzhil* [Oprichnina of Ivan the Terrible as seen by those who survived].

126. Courtois et al., *The Black Book of Communism*, 71–80.

127. Figes, *A People's Tragedy*, 525.

128. Pipes, *The Unknown Lenin*, 10.

129. Conquest, *The Harvest of Sorrow*, 4; Kulchytsky, *Terror-Holodomor Kak Instrument Kollektivizacii* [Terror-famine as an instrument of collectivization], 34; Dolot, *Execution by Hunger*.

130. For extensive accounts of Stalinist violence and fear, see Hollander, *From the Gulag to the Killing Fields*.

131. Hagenloh, *Stalin's Police*.

132. Snyder, *Stalin and Europe*, 19.

133. McLoughlin, "Mass Operations of the NKVD, 1937–8," 119.

134. Gregory, *Terror by Quota*, 166; Getty, Naumov, and Sher, *The Road to Terror*, 243; data of the State Archive of the Russian Federation, mentioned in Getty et al., 276.

135. Lynn Berry, "Putin's Promises Sound Like a 2012 Campaign Spiel," Associated Press, *Moscow World*, April 21, 2011.

136. Sakwa, *Putin and the Oligarch*, xviii.

137. Federal Law on Making Changes to Article 148 of the Criminal Code of the Russian Federation and Separate Legislative Acts of the Russian Federation with the Purpose of Countering the Insults to the Religious Beliefs and Feelings of the Citizens, June 26, 2013.

138. Article 354.1 of the Criminal Code of the Russian Federation; Decree of the Government of the Russian Federation #733 "On Approval of the Rules of the Federal Migration Service and Its Territorial Units of Registering the Written Statements of the Citizens of the Russian Federation the Citizenship of Another State," July 30, 2014; Fed-

eral Law No. 65-Ф3 "On Making Amendments to the Code of Administrative Offenses and the Federal Law No. 54-Ф3 (19.06.2004) "On Demonstrations, Rallies, Marches and Picketing," August 6, 2012; Federal Law "On Amendments to Certain Legislative Acts of the Russian Federation in the Regulation of Nonprofit Organizations Acting as Foreign Agents," July 20, 2012.

139. ODV-INFO, "Chelovek is Avtozaka: Politicheskie Zaderjaniya v Moskve" [Man from a prison car: Political detentions in Moscow], annual report of ODV-INFO for 2012, http://reports.odvinfo.org/2012/report/.

140. "Putin: U Rossii Net Sopernikov" [Putin: Russia has no rivals], *RosBusiness-Consulting*, February 2, 2014, http://top.rbc.ru/politics/02/02/2014/902911.shtml.

141. Lenin, "Maevka Revolucionnogo Proletariata," 23:300; Lenin, "Krakh II Internatsionala" [Collapse of II International], 26:219.

142. Livy, *The Rise of Rome*, 83–84.

143. "Vneshnepoliticheskie Vragi I Partneri Rossii" [Foreign policy enemies and partners of Russia], Levada Center, October 21, 2014, http://www.levada.ru/21–10–2014/vneshne politicheskie-vragi-i-partnery-rossii.

144. Jervis, "Cooperation under the Security Dilemma."

145. Thucydides, *History of the Peloponnesian War* (1972), 402.

146. Thompson, *Russia and the Soviet Union*, 60.

147. For instance, starting from the mid-sixteenth century, Russia has waged twelve wars against the Ottoman empire and five against Persia with the purpose of getting access to the Caucasus and the Black and Caspian Seas.

148. Thompson, *Russia and the Soviet Union*, 60.

149. De Juvenelle, *Tito—Boss of Traitors*; Order #1 of Marchall Konev, Supreme Allied Commander of Soviet troops in Europe, November 4, 1956; Sergei Shelin, "Tekhnologiya Rasstavaniya" [Technology of farewell], *GazetaRU*, April 2, 2014, http://www.gazeta.ru/comments/column/shelin/5976781.shtml.

150. Pipes, *The Russian Revolution*, 603.

151. Benjamin Welles, "Khrushchev Bangs His Shoe on Desk: Khrushchev Adds Shoe-Waving To His Heckling Antics at UN," *New York Times*, 13 Oct 1960: 1.

152. "Syria—Russia Puts Qatar to Order," *Algeria ISP*, February 6, 2012, http://www.algeria-isp.com/actualites/politique-syrie/201202-A8523/syrie-russie-remet-qatar-ordre-fevrier-2012.html.

153. "Zhirinovsky's Threats Angered Poland and Latvia," BBC Russian Service, August 13, 2014.

154. Vladimir Zhirinovsky, speech at the State Duma meeting, 2015, https://www.youtube.com/watch?v=bxM9Zx9ZOOg.

155. "Il ricatto dello zar sul vertice europeo 'Se voglio prendo Kiev in due settimane'" [The blackmail of the tsar on the European summit, "If I want, I will take Kiev in two weeks"], *Le Republica*, September 1, 2014, http://ricerca.repubblica.it/repubblica/archivio/repubblica/2014/09/01/il-ricatto-dello-zar-sul-vertice-europeo-se-voglio-prendo-kiev-in-due-settimane10.html?ref=search.

156. Daniel Brössler, "Putin Soll Europa Massiv Gedroht haben" [Putin massively threatened Europe], *Süddeutschen Zeitung*, September 18, 2014, http://www.sueddeutsche.de/politik/berichte-des-ukrainischen-praesidenten-putin-soll-europa-massiv-gedroht-haben-1.2134168.

157. In 2013 Russia's share in Armenia's foreign trade was 22.6 percent and 24.8 percent of export/import. Ministry of Economic Development of the Russian Federation, "Armenia: Foreign Trade Activity."

158. Araks Martirosyan, "S. Markedonov: Vozmojno, Svoim Vizitom V Baku Putin Okazivaet Psixologicheskoe Davlenie Na Erevan" [S. Markedonov: Maybe his visit to Baku Putin is exerting psychological pressure on Yerevan], *Armenian News and Analysis*, August 15, 2013, http://ru.1in.am/34056.html.

159. "Putin Posetil 102-u Voennuyu Bazu v Gyumri" [Putin visited 102nd Military Base in Gyumri], *RIA Novosti*, December 12, 2013, http://ria.ru/defense_safety/20131202/981289923.html.

160. Masha Gessen, "Russia Is Remaking Itself as the Leader of the Anti-Western World," *Washington Post*, March 30, 2014.

161. Address of the President of the Russian Federation to the Federal Assembly, March 18, 2014, http://kremlin.ru/news/20603.

162. "Putin: Rossiya Budet Narashivat Yadernii I Voennii Potentsial" [Putin: Russia will build up its nuclear and conventional military potential], *GazetaRU*, August 29, 2014, http://www.gazeta.ru/politics/news/2014/08/29/n_6436465.shtml.

163. Machiavelli, *The Prince*, 66.

164. Maria Zheleznova, "Levada Centr: Dolya Schitaushikh Rossiu Velikoi Derzhavoi Dostigla Maksimuma za 15 Let" [Levada Center: Numbers of those who think that Russia is a great power reached all-time high for 15 years], *Vedomosti*, March 17, 2013, http://www.vedomosti.ru/politics/news/24033871/velikoderzhavnost-vmesto-dostatka.

165. Ulyana Skoybeda, "Ya Bol'she Ne Zhivu v Zavoevannoi Strane" [I no longer live in a conquered country], *Komsomolskaya Pravda*, March 25, 2014.

166. Mayakovky, *Vladimir Ilyich Lenin: A Poem*.

167. Dostoyevsky, *A Writer's Diary. Volume 1: 1873–1876*, 161–62.

168. National Research University, Higher School of Economics, "The Level and Lifestyle of the Russian Population in 1989–2009" (Moscow: Higher School of Economics, 2011), 11.

169. Hofstede, *Cultures and Organizations*.

170. Thompson, *Russia and the Soviet Union*, 6.

171. Vasilii Kluchevsky, quoted in Lawrence and Vlachoutsicos, *Behind the Factory Walls*, 16.

172. Richmond, *From Nyet to Da*, 25.

173. *Vestnik Obshestvennogo Mneniya* [Public Opinion Gazette] 16, nos. 3–4 (July–December 2014): 165.

174. Article 131, para. 2 of the Constitution of the Union of the Soviet Socialist Republics, adopted by the VIII Extraordinary Congress of the Soviets of the USSR on December 5, 1936.

175. Svetlana Alexievich, "Those Who Are Not Happy Are Public Enemies," http://www.faz.net/aktuell/feuilleton/debatten/svetlana-alexijewitsch-ueber-putins-russland-12895308.html#.

176. North, Wallis, and Weingast, *Violence and Social Orders*, 18

177. Cross and Sherbowitz-Wetzor, *The Russian Primary Chronicle*, 59.

178. Kluchevsky, "Readings in Russian History," lecture 42.

179. Teper, "Elections in Soviet Russia."

180. Sakwa, *The Crisis of Russian Democracy*, 53.

181. D'Agostino, *Soviet Succession Struggles*.

182. Artem Kochetnikov, "Khronika Putcha. Chast II" [Chronicles of Putch. Part II], *BBC Russian Service*, August 18, 2006, http://news.bbc.co.uk/hi/russian/russia/newsid_5261000/5261982.stm.

183. Ellison, *Boris Yeltsin and Russia's Democratic Transformation*, 43.

184. Gessen, *The Man without a Face*, 12–13.

185. Yuri Tsiganov, "Farewell to Oligarchs?" 82; Kotz and Weir, *Russia's Path from Gorbachev to Putin*, 268–69.

186. Treisman, *The Return: Russia's Journey from Gorbachev to Medvedev*, 138.

187. Black, *The Russian Presidency of Dmitry Medvedev, 2008–2012*, 16.

188. Medvedev's speech at the State Duma nominating Putin for prime ministerial position, May 8, 2008.

189. Treisman, *The Return*, 138.

190. Andrei A. Amal'rik, "Prosushestvuet li Sovetskii Soyuz Do 1984 goda?" [Will the Soviet Union last beyond 1984?], Alexander Herzen Foundation, 1969, http://royallib.ru/book/amalrik_andrey/prosushchestvuet_li_sovetskiy_soyuz_do_1984_goda.html.

191. Valery Zor'kin, "Sud Skoriy, Praviy I Ravniy Dlya Vsex: Sudebnaya Reforma Alexandra II: Uroki Dlya Pravovogo Razvitiya Rossii" [Swift, fair, and equal court: Court reform of Alexander II: Lessons for the legal development of Russia], *Rossiiskaya Gazeta*, September 26, 2014, http://www.rg.ru/2014/09/26/zorkin.html.

192. Mironov, *Social'naya Istoriya Rossii Perioda Imperii* [Social history of Russia in the times of empire], 1:413.

193. Wortman, *The Development of a Russian Legal Consciousness*, 9.

194. Kordonsky, *Rossiya: Pomestnaya Federaciya*, 23.

195. Yevgenii Minchenko, "Doklad: 'Politburo 2.0.' Nakanune Perezagruzki Elitnix Grupp" [Report: "Politburo 2.0." On the eve of reset of the elite groups], Minchenko Consulting Group, January–February 2013, 1.

196. Hofstede, *Cultures and Organizations*; Murav, *Russia's Legal Fictions*, 24.

197. Mulder, *The Daily Power Game*, 4.

198. Bruins and Wilke, "Upward Power Tendencies in a Hierarchy," 253.

199. Medvedev and Medvedev, *Unknown Stalin*, 96; Yossi Melman, "Yesh Eyzeshehu Neum Shel Khruzhev Mehaveida" [Here is a speech of Khrushchev from the Congress], *Ha-aretz*, March 7, 2006, http://www.haaretz.co.il/misc/1. 1089815.

200. Barth, *Ethnic Groups and Boundaries*, 27.

201. Robert Collins, "Marked for Life: Songbun. North Korea's Social Classification System," Committee for Human Rights in Korea, 2012, 1.

202. "Lives of Soviet Leaders Are Very Private Indeed," *Hour*, February 16, 1984, 22.

203. Roland Oliphant, "'Putin and Kabayeva Are Crowned': Guard's Remark Suggests Russian President Has Married His Mistress," *Telegraph*, September 26, 2013, http://news.nationalpost.com/2013/09/26/putin-and-kabayeva-are-crowned-guards-remark-suggests-russian-president-has-married-his-mistress/?__federated=1.

204. Alla Yaroshinskaya, "The Big Lie: The Secret Chernobyl Documents," *Eurozine*, Index on Censorship 2/2006, 1.

205. Shlyakhter and Wilson, "Chernobyl: The Inevitable Results of Secrecy," *Public Understanding of Science* 1, no. 3 (1992): 253–54.

206. *Larry King Live,* "Russian President Vladimir Putin Discusses Domestic and Foreign Affairs," CNN transcripts, aired September 8, 2000.

207. Burleson, *Kursk Down*, 189.

208. "Putin: Rossiya Ne Vvodila Voiska v Krim: Oni Tam Uje Bili" [Putin: Russia did not bring its troops into Crimea: They were there already], *Vedomosti*, March 18, 2014, http://www.vedomosti.ru/politics/news/24117601/putin-rossiya-ne-vvodila-vojska-v-krym-oni-tam-uzhe-byli.

209. "Shoygu Sdelal To Zhe, Chto Grachev v 1994 v Chechne—Otreksya Ot Svoikh Soldat" [Shoigu did the same as Grachev in 1994 in Chechnya—He renounced his soldiers], *Online812*, March 5, 2014, http://www.online812.ru/2014/03/05/014/.

210. "Shoygu: Lyudi V Forme Bez Opoznavatel'nykh Znakov V Krymu Ne Imeyut Otnosheniya K Armii RF" [Shoigu: Uniformed people without badges in Crimea do not belong to the Russian Federation military], *ITAR TASS*, March 5, 2014, http://itar-tass.com/politika/1022832.

211. Tomasz M. Korczynski, "Żołnierze Rosyjscy Gubią Się Tysiącami" [Russian soldiers are lost by thousands], *Nasz Dziennik*, August 29, 2014, http://naszdziennik.pl/swiat/94295,zolnierze-rosyjscy-gubia-sie-tysiacami.html.

212. "Osada I Bombezhki Grozyat Millionnomu Donetsku" [The siege and bombardment facing millions of Donetsk], Russia 1 TV channel, aired on July 13, 2014, http://www.1tv.ru/news/world/263022.

213. "Ukrainskiye Siloviki Nakachali Narkotikami I Prevratili V Shpiona 13-letnego Mal'chika" [Ukrainian military drugged a 13-year-old boy and made him a spy], NTV, aired on November 11, 2014, http://www.ntv.ru/novosti/1258211/.

214. Ministry of Interior of Ukraine, Missing Children Billboard, http://mvs.gov.ua/mvs/control/investigation/card/missedPerson?ID=533269.

215. Sergei Podosenov and Vladimir Dergachev, "Za Desantnikov Sprosyat" [Someone should ask about the paratroopers], *GazetaRU*, August 27, 2014, http://www.gazeta.ru/politics/2014/08/27_a_6192281.shtml

216. Fund of Public Opinion, "About Mass Media" [O Sredstvax Massovoi Informacii], March 27, 2014.

217. Bergson, "Reliability and Usability of Soviet Statistics," 13–16.

218. George Bovt, "Rossiiskiy Informacionnii Zapovednik" [Russian informational zoo], *GazetaRU*, September 29, 2014, http://www.gazeta.ru/comments/column/bovt/6239489.shtml.

219. Ponsard, *Russia, NATO, and Cooperative Security*, 58.

220. Putin's speech at the extraordinary session of the government, *Izvestia*, September 17, 1999.

221. "Talking to Vladimir Putin. Continuation," Russia 1 TV channel, December 18, 2010.

222. Clinton, *Hard Choices*, 227.

223. Natalia Gevorkian, "Acid Test," Radio Liberty, April 9, 2014, http://www.svoboda.org/content/article/25327376.html.

224. "Surkov Nazval Putina Belim Ricarem Boga" [Surkov called Putin white knight of God], Forbes Russian Service, July 27, 2013, http://www.forbes.ru/news/242710-surkov-nazval-putina-belym-rytsarem-boga.

225. Gleb Pavlovsky, "Vlasti, Emocii I Protesti V Rossii" [Authorities, emotions, and protests in Russia], Gefter 2/952, http://gefter.ru/archive/12661; full interview of Putin to the French mass media, Pravda-TV, June 5, 2014, http://www.pravda-tv.ru/2014/06/05/63243.

226. Dmitry Nikolayev, "Posle Patriotizma" [After patriotism], *GazetaRU*, June 4, 2014, http://www.gazeta.ru/comments/column/nikolaev/s62993/6057849.shtml.

227. Solov'ev, *Velikii Spor I Khristianskaya Politica* [Great dispute and Christian politics], 4.

228. "Self-Austerity in Exchange for Superpower Status," interview with Alexander Auzan, dean of the Department of Economics, Moscow State University, October 29, 2014, http://www.gazeta.ru/comments/2014/10/29_a_6281141.shtml.

229. "Zhirinovsky Predlojil Zapretit Partii I Vibrat' Imperatora" [Zhirinovsky proposed banning the parties and electing an emperor], *GazetaRU*, August 23, 2014, http://www.gazeta.ru/politics/news/2014/08/23/n_6419397.shtml.

230. Interview with Evgeni Yasin, "Ne Sil'naya Ruka A Sil'nie Mozgi" [Not a strong hand, but a strong mind], *Argumenti I Fakti*, February 11, 2009.

231. "Opros: Peiting Putina Dostig Pika V Avguste I poshel Vniz" [Poll: Putin's rating reached its peak in August and then went down], BBC Russian Service, August 27, 2014, http://www.bbc.co.uk/russian/russia/2014/08/140827_levada_center_survey_putin.

232. "Moralnie Avtoriteti" [Moral authorities], *FOM*, September 24, 2014, http://fom.ru/TSennosti/11719.

233. Vladimir Medinsky, "Zadacha Kulturnoi Politiki—Virastit Pokolenie Pobeditelei" [The task of the cultural policy is to raise a generation of victors], *Komersant,* September 18, 2014, http://www.kommersant.ru/doc/2569559.

234. Stanislav Kucher, "Putin—Eto Lubov' Grajdan Rossii K Samim Sebe" [Putin means love of the Russian citizens to themselves], *Moskovsky Comsomolec,* September 22, 2014, http://www.mk.ru/politics/2014/09/22/putin-eto-lyubov.html.

235. Russia-Reborn, http://russia-reborn.ru/vk/index.html.

236. "O Natsional'nom Velichii Velikorosov" [On national greatness of the great Russians], February 2, 2007, *VCIOM,* February 2, 2007, http://wciom.ru/index.php?id=269&uid=3957.

237. "Velichie Rossii, Po Mneniu Bol'shinstva, Obespechivaetsya Agressivnim Otnosheniem k Sosedyam" [Russia's greatness is defined by its aggressive stance toward its neighbors], *Komersant,* June 16, 2014, http://www.kommersant.ru/doc/2492248.

238. VCIOM, press release #2672, "Rossiya: Strana Vozmojnostei" [Russia: A country of opportunities], September 2014.

239. VCIOM, press release #2573, "Schast'e—Est'!" [There is happiness!], March 30, 2014.

240. Levada Center, Public Opinion Poll, "How Often Do You Go Outside of the Country?" April 2014.

241. An example of mimicry is a frog, *Lithodytes lineatus* (commonly known as *Sapito Listado*), living in Pan-Amazonia. *Lithodytes* is a harmless creature that is often confused with a highly poisonous *Allobates femoralis.* During the process of physical evolution, *Lithodytes* adopted the form of its poisonous look-alike without its poisonous characteristics to avoid being eaten by other creatures.

242. Philipp Krause, "Of Institutions and Butterflies: Is Isomorphism in Developing Countries Necessarily a Bad Thing?" Overseas Development Institute, *Background Note,* April 2013, 1.

243. Sherratt, "The Evolution of Imperfect Mimicry," 821.

244. Krause, "Of Institutions and Butterflies," 2.

245. Evans, "Development as Institutional Change," 33.

246. The "Greenbook," U.S. Overseas Loans and Grants, Obligations and Loan Authorizations, 2012.

247. Financial Cooperation with Russia, European Union website, http://eeas.europa.eu/russia/financial_cooperation_en.htm.

248. "EU-Russia Common Spaces," Progress Report 2009, European Union, March 2010.

249. Hedlund, "Russia and the IMF: A Sordid Tale of Moral Hazard," 109.

250. Glaz'ev, "Kak Dobit'sya Ekonomicheskogo Rosta?" [How to achieve economic growth?]; Velichenkov, "Kuda Idem Mi S IMF" [Where are we going with IMF?].

251. Vitalii Tret'yakov, "Pravitel'stvo Kholopov" [Government of kholops], *Novaya Gazeta,* December 19, 1997.

252. Vyacheslav Dashichev, "Obval Rossii v 90-ye Gody: Prichiny I Posledstviya V Otsenkakh Sovremennikov" [Collapse of Russia in the 90s: Causes and consequences in the estimates of the contemporaries], *KM.RU*, February 5, 2013, http://www.km.ru/spetsproekty/2013/02/05/istoriya-rossiiskoi-federatsii/703236-obval-rossii-v-90-e-gody-prichiny-i-po.

253. Heritage Foundation, "The IMF's $22.6 Billion Failure in Russia," *Executive Memorandum #548*, April 24, 1998.

254. Luke Harding, "Russia Orders British Council Offices to Be Shut Down," *Guardian*, December 12, 2007, http://www.theguardian.com/world/2007/dec/13/russia.lukeharding.

255. "Zakritie Programi FLEX: Rol' Gomosexualizma v Rossisko-Amerikanskix Otnosheniyax" [Closure of FLEX program: Role of homosexuality in Russian-American relations], *Moskovsky Komsomolets*, October 5, 2014, http://www.mk.ru/politics/2014/10/05/zakrytie-programmy-flex-rol-gomoseksualizma-v-rossiyskoamerikanskikh-otnosheniyakh.html.

256. Yevgeni Yasin, "Rinochnie Reformi I Democratiya V Rossii. 1991" [Market reforms and democracy in Russia], Radio Station Ekho Moskvi, September 9, 2011, http://www.echo.msk.ru/blog/yasin/810298-echo/.

257. Jim Nichol, "Russian Political, Economic, and Security Issues and U.S. Interests," *Congressional Research Service*, January 9, 2014, 2.

258. McFaul, Petrov, and Ryabov, *Between Dictatorship and Democracy*, 1.

259. Huntington, *The Clash of Civilizations and the Remaking of World Order.*

260. Fukuyama, *The End of History and the Last Man*.

261. Shalom H. Schwartz, "An Overview of the Schwartz Theory of Basic Values," *Online Readings in Psychology and Culture* 2, no. 1 (2012): 8, http://dx.doi.org/10.9707/2307–0919. 1116.

262. Galtung, "Institutionalized Conflict Resolution: A Theoretical Paradigm," 348.

263. Theiler, "Societal Security and Social Psychology," 261.

264. Sanders, "Ethnic Boundaries and Identity in Plural Societies," 328.

265. Ross, "Psychocultural Interpretations and Dramas: Identity Dynamics in Ethnic Conflict," 159.

266. De Vattel, *The Law of Nations*, 2.

267. Dugin, *The Fourth Political Theory*, 79.

268. Will Gunham, "Kerry Condemns Russia's 'Incredible Act of Aggression' in Ukraine," Reuters, March 2, 2014, http://www.reuters.com/article/2014/03/02/us-ukraine-crisis-usa-kerry-idUSBREA210DG20140302.

269. Krasner, "Sharing Sovereignty: New Institutions for Collapsed and Failing States," 90.

270. Bull and Hurrell, *The Anarchical Society*, 13.

271. Carment and Harvey, *Using Force to Prevent Ethnic Violence*, 129

272. Fenwick, "Intervention: Individual and Collective," 663.

273. "Volodin Otozhdestvil Rossiu I Putina" [Volodin equalized Russia with Putin], October 22, 2014, *LentaRU*, http://lenta.ru/news/2014/10/22/waldai/.

274. Meeting of the Security Council, July 22, 2014, http://www.kremlin.ru/transcripts/46305.

275. Fedorov, "Dve Morali" [Two morals], 46.

276. Nalbandov, *Democratization and Instability in Ukraine, Georgia, and Belarus.*

277. Ward-Perkins, *The Fall of Rome and the End of Civilization*, 167.

3. Russia and the United States

1. "Shoigu: Glavnie Ugrozi Dlya Rossii: Terrorism I NATO" [Shoigu: Main threats to Russia are terrorism and NATO], *GazetaRU*, November 9, 2013, http://www.gazeta.ru/politics/news/2013/11/09/n_3312969.shtml.

2. Ceasar, "The Origins and Character of American Exceptionalism," 6.

3. Murray, *American Exceptionalism*, 7–38.

4. Pease, *The New American Exceptionalism*, 10.

5. Vladimir V. Putin, "A Plea for Caution from Russia: What Putin Has to Say to Americans about Syria," *New York Times*, September 11, 2013.

6. Herpen, *Putin's Wars*, 32–46.

7. Mendras, *Russian Politics: The Paradox of a Weak State*, 258.

8. Tocqueville, *Democracy in America*, 413.

9. Oneal and Russett, "The Kantian Peace."

10. Ivan Kurilla, "Mneniye: Pochemu Rossiya Rugayet Ameriku, no Khochet Eyu Stat'" [Op-Ed: Why Russia scolds America but wants to be it], *RosBusinessConsulting*, August 19, 2004.

11. March, "Is Nationalism Rising in Russian Foreign Policy?" 26.

12. Legvold, "The Role of Multilateralism in Russian Foreign Policy," 40.

13. Putin interview on the situation in Ukraine, March 4, 2014, http://kremlin.ru/news/20366.

14. "Putin Sravnil Yujnuyu Osetiu S Kosovom" [Putin compared South Ossetia with Kosovo], BBC Russian Service, September 21, 2008, http://news.bbc.co.uk/hi/russian/international/newsid_7627000/7627723.stm.

15. Yulia Latynina, "Rossiya ne Uvelichivaet Russkii Mir—Ona Ego Umen'shaet" [Russia does not expand the Russian world—It is shrinking it], *Novaya Gazeta* #61, June 6, 2014, 3.

16. Dostoyevsky, *Crime and Punishment*, 403.

17. Satter, *It Was a Long Time Ago, and It Never Happened Anyway*, 304–5.

18. "Direct Line with Vladimir Putin," aired on *Russia Today*, April 17, 2014.

19. Herz, "Idealist Internationalism and the Security Dilemma," 171–201.

20. Jervis, "Cooperation under the Security Dilemma," 167–241.

21. Walter, "The Critical Barriers to Civil War Settlement," 338.

22. Gvozdev and Marsh, *Russian Foreign Policy: Interests, Vectors, and Sectors*, 71.

23. "Poslanie Prezidenta Federal'nomu Sobraniu" [Presidential address to the Federal Assembly], December 4, 2014, http://www.kremlin.ru/transcripts/47173.

24. Clinton, *Hard Choices*, 212.

25. Wales Summit Declaration, issued by the heads of state and government participating in the meeting of the North Atlantic Council in Wales, September 5, 2014.

26. "Kommentarii MID Rossii V Svyazi s Sammitom NATO V Uel'se" [Comments of the Ministry of Foreign Affairs of Russia in relation to the NATO summit in Wales], Ministry of Foreign Affairs of the Russian Federation, September 5, 2014. http://www.mid.ru/brp_4.nsf/newsline/0AC3CA478290549A44257D4A004D4A54.

27. Global Firepower Index 2014, http://www.globalfirepower.com/countries-listing.asp ; Amanda Macias, Jeremy Bender, and Skye Gould, "The 35 Most Powerful Militaries in the World," *Business Insider*, July 10, 2014, http://www.businessinsider.com/35-most-powerful-militaries-in-the-world-2014–7.

28. Sam Perlo-Freeman et al., "Trends in World Military Expenditure, 2012," Stockholm International Peace Research Institute (SIPRI), April 2013.

29. "Russia, China Driving Return to Growth in Global Defense Market," *IHS Quarterly*, Q2–2014.

30. Fedorov, "Gosudarstvennaya Programma Voorujenii-2020: Vlast' I Promishlennost" [State Armament Program 2020: Government and industry], 41.

31. "Rossiya Obognala SSHA Po Dole Raskhodov Na Oboronu" [Russia has higher defense spending than the United States], *FinMarket*, March 28, 2014, http://www.finmarket.ru/main/article/3666352.

32. Van Evera, *Causes of War*, 6.

33. Glaser, "The Security Dilemma Revised," 183.

34. Finnemore and Sikkink, "International Norm Dynamics and Political Change," 897.

35. White, *Nobody Wanted War*.

36. "Striking the Balance: U.S. Policy and Stability in Georgia," report to the Committee on Foreign Relations, U.S. Senate, December 22, 2009, S. Rep. No. 111–37, p. 17.

37. "Russian Jet Makes 'Provocative and Unprofessional' Pass at USS Donald Cook," *CBS News*, April 14, 2014, http://www.cbsnews.com/news/russian-jet-makes-provocative-and-unprofessional-pass-at-uss-donald-cook/.

38. "Komanda Esmintsa VMS SSHA "Donal'd Kuk" Chut' Ne Razbezhalas' Posle Poleta Rossiyskogo Su 24" [USS *Donald Cook* crew almost ran away after the flight of the Russian Su 24], *PiterTV*, April 23, 2014, http://piter.tv/event/esminec_donal_d_kuk_i_su_24/.

39. Interview of Sergey Glaz'ev, advisor to President Putin, in TV program *Politika*, April 23, 2014.

40. "Chuck Schumer Sees Damaged Relations with Russia over Edward Snowden," *Huffington Post*, June 23, 2013, http://www.huffingtonpost.com/2013/06/23/chuck-schumer-russia_n_3486621.html.

41. Levada Center, "Vneshnepolitiheskie Vragi I Partneri Rossii" [Foreign policy foes and partners of Russia], press release, October 21, 2014, http://www.levada.ru/21-10-2014/vneshnepoliticheskie-vragi-i-partnery-rossii.

42. Dmitry Kiselev, *Vesti Nedeli*, aired on October 19, 2014, http://russia.tv/video/show/brand_id/5206/episode_id/1137717.

43. Alexey Pushkov, Twitter entry, September 28, 2014, https://twitter.com/Alexey_Pushkov/status/516244954688270336.

44. Sergey Glaz'ev, *Genocide: Russia and the New World Order*, 125–26.

45. Victoria Nuland, quoted in Simes, "Losing Russia: The Cost of Renewed Confrontation."

46. Website of the National Liberation Movement, http://rusnod.ru.

47. "Russia Expels USAID Development Agency," *BBC News Europe*, September 19, 2012.

48. U.S. embassy in Moscow, "U.S. Regrets Russian Government Decision to Cancel Participation in FLEX Program," press release, September 30, 2014, http://moscow.usembassy.gov/st-flex-09302014.html.

49. Putin, speech, Forum of Independent Local and Regional Media, St. Petersburg, April 24, 2014, http://eng.kremlin.ru/transcripts/7075.

50. Medvedev and Borisenko, "Non-Systemic Opposition in the Political Space of Modern Russia," 154.

51. Tashterov, "Fenomen 'Tsvetnix Revolucii': Ot Klassicheskoi Teorii K Nepredskazuemoi Praktike," 40.

52. Alexander Khokhlov, "Veronika Krasheninnikova: «Pyatuyu kolonnu» amerikantsy vykarmlivali 20 let" [Veronica Krasheninnikova: Americans were nurturing the "Fifth Column" for 20 years], *Vechernyaya Moskva*, February 14, 2014.

53. Horvath, *Putin's Preventative Counter-Revolution*, 31–46.

54. "Meeting of the Valdai International Discussion Club," http://eng.news.kremlin.ru/news/23137.

55. "Gosdepartament SSHA Podderhivaet Terroristov, A Sovet Evropi Zashishaet Ix Prava" [U.S. State Department supports terrorists and the Council of Europe protects their rights], *Komersant* newsline, 3, January 15, 2000.

56. Gvozdev and Marsh, *Russian Foreign Policy*, 85.

57. Bespalov, "Transnational'nii Islamskii Terrorism—Global'naya Problema" [Transnational Islamic terrorism—Global problem], 76.

58. Doyle, *Ways of War and Peace*, 308.

59. Sobek, Abouharb, and Ingram, "The Human Rights Peace: How the Respect for Human Rights at Home Leads to Peace Abroad," 519.

60. Moravcsik, "The Origins of Human Rights Regimes," 229.

61. *Congressional Record*, proceeding and the debate, 108th Cong., 2d sess., vol. 150, part 14, 2004, 19062.

62. Aslund, Guriev, and Kuchins, *Russia after the Global Economic Crisis*, 215.

63. Overall, eighteen officials have been included in the Magnitsky Act. See "Magnitsky Sanctions Listings," U.S. Department of the Treasury, April 12, 2013, http://www.treasury.gov/resource-center/sanctions/OFAC-Enforcement/Pages/20130412.aspx; Philip Aldrick, "Russia Refuses Autopsy for Anti-Corruption Lawyer," *Daily Telegraph* (London), November 19, 2009, http://www.telegraph.co.uk/finance/newsbysector/banksandfinance/6608505/Russia-refuses-autopsy-for-anti-corruption-lawyer.html.

64. Russia and Moldova Jackson-Vanik Repeal and Sergei Magnitsky Rule of Law Accountability Act of 2012, Pub. L. No.112–208, 126 Stat. 1496 (2012); Roxburgh, *The Strongman*, 341.

65. Stent, *The Limits of Partnership*, 252.

66. Gardner, *NATO Expansion and the U.S. Strategy in Asia*, 61.

67. Sakwa, *Putin Redux*, 201; "A Law on Sanctions for Individuals Violating Fundamental Human Rights and Freedoms of Russian Citizens Has Been Signed," December 28, 2012, http://eng.kremlin.ru/acts/4810.

68. Jim Nichol, *Russian Political, Economic, and Security Issues and U.S. Interests*, Report RL 33407 (Washington DC: Congressional Research Service, 2014), 19.

69. The Founding Act on Mutual Relations, Cooperation, and Security between NATO and the Russian Federation signed in Paris, May 27, 1997; Andrey Makarychev, "Remember the Mutual Commitments of the Russia-NATO Partnership?" PONARS Eurasia, September 4, 2014, http://www.ponarseurasia.org/article/remember-mutual-commitments-russia-nato-partnership.

70. "Meeting of the Valdai International Discussion Club," October 24, 2014, http://eng.kremlin.ru/news/23137#sel=21:4,21:10.

71. "National Security Strategy of the Russian Federation 2020," National Security Council of the Russian Federation, http://www.scrf.gov.ru/documents/99.html.

72. "Military Doctrine of the Russian Federation 2010," http://news.kremlin.ru/ref_notes/461.

73. Kipp, "Russian Military Doctrine: Past, Present, and Future," 65.

74. "Pressa Rossii: Kakoi Budet Novaya Voennaya Doktrina Kremlya" [Russian press: What will be the new military doctrine of the Kremlin?], BBC Russian Service, September 3, 2014, http://www.bbc.co.uk/russian/russia/2014/09/140903_rus_press.

75. De Haas, "Russia's Military Doctrine Development (2000–10)," 16.

76. "Military Doctrine of the Russian Federation," December 26, 2014, 5.

77. "Putin Predlozhil BRIKS Protivostoyat' Travle Gosudarstv, Nesoglasnykh S SSHA I Ikh Soyuznikami" [Putin: The BRICS countries should resist the persecution of those who disagree with the United States and its allies], ITAR TASS State News Agency, July 15, 2014.

78. "Developmental Trends of the Largest World Economies," *Center of Macroeconomic Analysis and Short-Term Forecast* 7, no. 28 (2014): 36.

79. Lucy O'Carroll, "The BRICS Bank and Bretton Woods," *Financial Times*, July 23, 2014.

80. "Patrioti Edinnoi Rossii Protiv Demokratii" [Patriots of Edinnaya Rossiya against democracy], *GazetaRU*, October 31, 2014, http://www.gazeta.ru/politics/2014/10/31_a_6284789.shtml.

81. Figes, *Natasha's Dance*, 377.

82. Hartley, *Siberia: A History of the People*, 1.

83. Lincoln, *The Conquest of a Continent*, 46.

84. Wood, *Russia's Frozen Frontier*, 116; Okladnikov, *Istoriya Sibiri S Drevneyshikh Vremon Do Nashikh Dney* [History of Siberia from ancient times to the present day], 2:25.

85. Verkhoturov, *Pokorenie Sibiri: Mifi I Realnost* [Conquest of Siberia: Myths and reality], 138.

86. "Rossiyskiye Protivniki Odnopolykh Brakov Potrebovali U SSHA Vernut' Alyasku" [Russian opponents of gay marriages demand return of Alaska from the United States], Forbes Russian Service, March 15, 2013, http://m.forbes.ru/article.php?id=235729.

87. "Deputat Prosit MID Proverit', Komu Prinadlezhit Fort-Ross" [MP asks the Foreign Ministry to check who owns Fort Ross], *Izvestiya*, September 26, 2014, http://izvestia.ru/news/577183.

88. "Ne Privykli Kollegi iz SSHA, Kogda Ne Oni V Pobeditelyakh" [The colleagues from the USA are not used to not being among the winners], TV program *Glavnaya Tema*, online streaming on April 29, 2014, http://www.gazeta.ru/video/main/ne_privykli_amerikanskie_kollegi_k_situatsiyam_kogda_ne_oni_v_pobeditelyah.shtml.

89. Fawn and Nalbandov, "The Difficulties of Knowing the Start of War in the Information Age"; Baev, *The Russian Army in a Time of Troubles*, 103–9.

90. "Mamsurov: Vsya istoriya SSHA-eto nepreryvnaya tsep' prestupleniy" [Mamsurov: The entire history of the United States—Continuous chain of crimes], interview with Teimuraz Mamsurov, head of the North Ossetian Autonomous Republic, March 21, 2014, *Severo-Kavkazskie Novosti*, http://www.sk-s.ru/rsoa/news/authority/40200/.

91. John W. Garver talks about close ties of the Soviet Union with Nazi Germany: "Soviet-Nazi cooperation was manifested in numerous ways. . . . Soviet exports of strategic ores, petroleum, and cotton to Germany expanded rapidly. . . . Soviet railways carried goods from the entire Pacific littoral through Siberia to Germany. . . . [M]ilitary cooperation occurred during Germany's invasion of Poland and . . . during the Soviet attack on Finland." See Garver, *Chinese-Soviet Relations, 1937–1945*, 90. For more detailed insights into the Soviet-Nazi military and economic cooperation, see Ericson, *Feeding the German Eagle*, esp. 1–10, and Kantor, *Zaklyataya druzhba* [Curse of friendship].

92. Evgeniy P. Maslin, "Cooperation between the Russian Military of Defense and the U.S. Defense Department on Nuclear Weapons Safety," paper, conference on "The Nunn-Lugar Cooperative Threat Reduction Program: Donor and Recipient Country Perspectives," Monterey, California, August 20–22, 1995, 77.

93. "Cooperative Threat Reduction Annual Report to Congress, Fiscal Year 2009," 4.

94. Mankoff, "The Politics of U.S. Missile Defence Cooperation with Europe and Russia," 334.

95. "Russia Could Aim Rockets at European Missile Shield—Putin," *RIA Novosti*, February 14, 2008, http://en.ria.ru/russia/20080214/99201375.html.

96. Lilly, *Russian Foreign Policy towards Missile Defense*, 72–73.

97. Donaldson and Nogee, *Foreign Policy of Russia*, 370.

98. Leichtova, *Misunderstanding Russia*, 93.

99. "Edinstvennaya Garantiya—Polnii Otkaz Ot PRO" [Complete halt to the antimissile defense: The only guarantee], *GazetaRU*, May 2, 2012, http://www.gazeta.ru/politics/2012/05/02a4569905.shtml.

100. National Security Strategy of the United States of America, White House, Washington DC, May 2010, 4.

101. National Security Strategy of the Russian Federation 2020, Kremlin, Moscow, May 13, 2009.

102. *Cold Politics*, Russia 1 TV, aired on February 2, 2012.

103. "Gabala Radar for Both Russia and U.S.?" *RT News*, aired on March 12, 2009.

104. "Putin Compares U.S. Shield to Cuba," *BBC News*, October 26, 2007, http://news.bbc.co.uk/2/hi/7064428.stm.

105. "Russia in Defense Warning to U.S.," *BBC News*, April 26, 2007, http://news.bbc.co.uk/2/hi/europe/6594379.stm.

106. Natalya Kovalenko, "U.S. Using Missile Defense System in Europe to Make Russia Change Its Ukraine Policies," Voice of Russia Radio, March 20, 2014.

107. Lilly, *Russian Foreign Policy towards Missile Defense*, 78.

108. Dmitry Rogozin, Twitter entry, February 10, 2010, https://twitter.com/Rogozin/status/8900971605.

109. "Strakha Pered NATO U Nas Net, No Nas Vynuzhdayut K Otvetnym Deystviyam: Putin" [Putin: We don't fear NATO, but we are forced to retaliatory actions], Regnum News Agency, March 17, 2014, http://www.regnum.ru/news/polit/1792376.html#ixzz3IY9evj9Q.

110. Christian Neef, "A Sober Look: It's Time to Stop Romanticizing Russia," *Spiegel International*, April 10, 2014, http://www.spiegel.de/international/europe/why-it-is-time-for-germany-to-stop-romanticizing-russia-a-963284.html.

111. Sarotte, "A Broken Promise? What the West Really Told Moscow about NATO Expansion."

112. Kramer, "The Myth of a No-NATO-Enlargement Pledge to Russia," 41.

113. Anne Applebaum, "The Myth of Russian Humiliation," *Washington Post*, October 17, 2014.

114. "Der traurige Held der Perestroika" [The sad hero of Perestroyka], interview of Mikhail Gorbachev with the German TV channel ZDF, November 8, 2014, http://www.zdf.de/ZDFmediathek/beitrag/video/2273826/Der-traurige-Held-der-Perestroika#/beitrag/video/2273826/Der-traurige-Held-der-Perestroika.

115. "Shoygu Obespokoyen Namereniyem Pentagona Gotovit'sya K Bor'be s Armiyei Rossii [Shoigu is concerned with Pentagon's plan to prepare for the fight with the Russian army], *GazetaRU*, http://www.gazeta.ru/politics/news/2014/10/16/n_6568649

.shtml; "Russia–U.S. Relations Reset 'Impossible': PM Medvedev," interview, CNBC, aired October 15, 2014, http://www.cnbc.com/id/102086463.

116. March and Olsen, "The New Institutionalism," 736

117. March and Olsen, *Rediscovering Institutions*, 160.

118. Kolodziej and Kanet, *From Superpower to Besieged Global Power*, 313

119. Mitchell, *Uncertain Democracy*, 2–3.

120. Sushko and Prystayko, "Western Influence," 125–44.

121. Ortmann, "Diffusion as Discourse of Danger," 143.

122. Luzyanin, "'Tsvetnie Revolucii' V Central'no-Aziatskoi Proekcii: Kyrgyzstan-Uzbekistan-Kazakhstan" ["Color revolutions" in Central Asian projection: Kyrgyzstan-Uzbekistan-Kazakhstan], 8–9.

123. Shamin, "'Tsvetnaya' ('Barkhatnaya') Revoluciya Kak Instrument Obespecheniya Interesov SSHA Na Mejdunarodnoi Arene v Konce 1990x-Nachale 2000x Godov" ["Colored" ("velvet") revolution as the instrument of provision of the U.S. interests in the international arena in 1990–2000] , 93.

124. U.S. Overseas Loans and Grants, United States Agency for International Development. Country files are available from http://gbk.eads.usaidallnet.gov; Steven Woehrel, "Ukraine: Current Issues and U.S. Policy, May 24, 2013," Congressional Research Service, 7–5700, RL33460.

125. Jim Nichol, "Georgia [Republic]: Recent Developments and U.S. Interests," Congressional Research Service, 7–5700, 97–727.

126. Tian, "Ot Central'noi Azii k Bol'shoi Central'noi Azii: Celi I Korrektirovki Strategii SSHA V TsA" [From Central Asia to the Greater Central Asia: Goals and corrections of the USA strategy in the Central Asia], 84.

127. Jim Nichol, "Kyrgyzstan: Recent Developments and U.S. Interests," Congressional Research Service, 7–5700, 97–690, 21.

128. Ipek, "Challenges for Democracy in Central Asia: What Can the United States Do?" 102.

129. "Poteri Rossiyskikh Bankov na Ukraine Otsenili v $25 mlrd" [Loss of the Russian banks in Ukraine estimated at $25 billion], Forbes Russian Service, http://www.forbes.ru/news/272023poteri-rossiiskikh-bankov-na-ukraine-otsenili-v-25-mlrd.

130. "Nikolay Patrushev: Otrezvlenie Ukrainicev Budet Jestkim I Boleznennim" [Nikolay Patrushev: Sobering up of Ukrainians would be rough and painful], *Rossiyskaya Gazeta*, October 15, 2014, http://www.rg.ru/2014/10/15/patrushev.html.

131. Goldman, *How Civilizations Die (and Why Islam Is Dying Too)*, 267.

132. Wallensteen, "Characteristics of Economic Sanctions," 248–49.

133. "Ukraine and Russia Sanctions," U.S. Department of State, http://www.state.gov/e/eb/tfs/spi/ukrainerussia/.

134. For the consolidated list of the individuals sanctioned by the United States and its allies, see Risk Advisory Group data at http://www.riskadvisory.net/pdfrepository/Sanctions_individuals_Russia_Ukraine_ys.pdf.

135. U.S. Department of Treasury, "Announcement of Expanded Treasury Sanctions within the Russian Financial Services, Energy and Defense or Related Materiel Sectors," press release, September 12, 2014, http://www.treasury.gov/press-center/press-releases/Pages/jl2629.aspx .

136. Spisok ofitsial'nykh lits i chlenov Kongressa SSHA, kotorym zakryvayetsya v"yezd v Rossiyskuyu Federatsiyu na osnove vzaimnosti v svyazi s amerikanskimi sanktsiyami po Ukraine i Krymu [List of officials and members of the U.S. Congress banned from entry into the Russian Federation on the basis of reciprocity in relation to the U.S. sanctions on Ukraine and Crimea], Ministry of Foreign Affairs of the Russian Federation, http://www.mid.ru/brp_4. nsf/newsline/177739554DA10C8B44257CA100551FFE.

137. "MID RF Sergei Lavrov Na 69oi Sessii General'noi Assamblei OON v N'u Iorke, SSHA" [Minister of Foreign Affairs Sergei Lavrov at the 69th session of the UN General Assembly, New York, USA], *RT News,* September 9, 2014, http://russian.rt.com/article/51918#ixzz3IKRWMO2g.

138. Ukaz O Primenenii Otdel'nykh Spetsial'nykh Ekonomicheskikh Mer V Tselyakh Obespecheniya Bezopasnosti Rossiyskoy Federatsii [The decree on the application of certain special economic measures to ensure the security of the Russian Federation], August 6, 2014.

139. "Russia Hits West with Food Import Ban in Sanctions Row," *BBC News*, August 7, 2014, http://www.bbc.com/news/world-europe-28687172 .

140. For the full list of the industrial and consumer products, see http://government.ru/media/files/41d4f8cdfeeb731522d2.pdf.

141. "Peskov: Ataki Zapada Na Rossiyu Fokusiruyutsya Na Lichnosti Putina" [Peskov: Western attacks focus on Putin's personality], *GazetaRU,* November 6, 2014, http://www.gazeta.ru/politics/news/2014/11/06/n_6627661.shtml.

142. Drezner, *The Sanctions Paradox*.

143. Hart, "Democracy and the Successful Use of Economic Sanctions," 267–68.

144. Allen, "The Domestic Political Costs of Economic Sanctions," 917.

145. Allen, "The Domestic Political Costs of Economic Sanctions," 923, 925.

146. Krain, *Repression and Accommodation in Post-Revolutionary States.*

147. Pape, "Why Economic Sanctions Do Not Work," 97.

148. Baldwin and Pape, "Evaluating Economic Sanctions," 192.

149. Drury, "Sanctions as Coercive Diplomacy," 489.

150. Putnam, "Diplomacy and Domestic Politics: The Logic of Two-Level Games."

151. "Vneshnyaya Torgovlya Rossiyskoy Federatsii Po Osnovnym Stranam Za Yanvar'-Avgust 2014 g." [Foreign trade of the Russian Federation with key countries, January–August 2014], Federal Customs Agency of the Russian Federation, August 10, 2014, http://www.customs.ru/index2. php?option=com_content&view=article&id=19997&Itemid=1976.

152. Russian-American Business Cooperation," website of the U.S. embassy in Moscow, http://www.russianembassy.org/page/russian-american-business-cooperation.

153. Zimovec, "O Problemakh I Perspektivakh Pereorientacii Ekonomiki Rossii S Zapada Na Vostok" [On the problems and perspectives of reorientation of the Russian economy from west to east], 34.

154. Porter, *Economic Sanctions against Oil Producers*.

155. Robert Mitkowski, "Turmoil in Iraq and Ukraine Is Roiling the Energy Markets," ValueLine Research, June 19, 2014, http://www.valueline.com/Stocks/Commentaries/Turmoil_in_Iraq_and_Ukraine_is_Roiling_the_Energy_Markets.aspx#.VF5wa4cf-3V.

156. Caroline Bain quoted in Claudia Assis, "Oil Futures Rise as Russia Sanctions Loom," MarketWatch.Com, July 21, 2014, http://www.marketwatch.com/story/oil-futures-choppy-as-russia-sanctions-loom-2014–07–21–31034729.

157. Crude Oil Prices: West Texas Intermediate (WTI), Cushing, Oklahoma (DCOILWTICO), Federal Reserve Economic Data (FRED), U.S. Department of Energy: Energy Information Administration, http://research.stlouisfed.org/fred2/series/DCOILWTICO/downloaddata.

158. "Crude Oil and Commodity Prices," Oil-Price-Net, February 19, 2015, http://www.oil-price.net.

159. Jacob Mirkin, "Political Chernogo Zolota" [Black gold politics], interview, *GazeraRU*, September 17, 2014, http://www.gazeta.ru/comments/2014/09/16_x_6216621.shtml.

160. Azarova, "Izmenenie Sprosa I Tseni Na Energonositeli" [Changes in demand and price for energy carriers], 66.

161. Saygadachnaya, "Budgetnie Pravila I Principi Budgetnoi Sistemi: Sootnoshenie I Transformaciya" [Budgetary rules and principles of budgetary system: Correlation and transformation], 57.

162. Azarova, "Izmenenie Sprosa I Tseni Na Energonositeli" [Changes of demand and price for energy carriers], 67.

163. "Zaklyucheniye Instituta Ekonomicheskoy Politiki Im. Ye.T. Gaydara Na Proyekt Federal'nogo Budzheta Na 2013 God I Na Planovyi Period 2014 I 2015 Godov" [Conclusion of the Gaidar Institute for Economic Policy on the draft federal budget for 2013 and the planning period of 2014 and 2015], Gaidar Institute, 5, http://www.iep.ru/files/text/other/IEP_zakluchenie_na_proekt_FB_2013–2015. pdf.

164. Goldman, "The Russian Ruble and Why It Collapsed," 12.

165. Julia Joffe, "Russia's Currency Is Plummeting and Putin's Billionaires Are Cannibalizing Each Other," *New Republic*, November 7, 2014, http://www.newrepublic.com/article/120201/russias-ruble-value-collapsing-due-sanctions-stagnation.

166. Yelena Tregubova, "Devalvacia V Voprosax I Otvetax. Chto Nujno Znat' On Obescenivanii Rublya" [Devaluation FAQ: What you should know about the ruble devaluation], *Argumenti I Fakti*, November 7, 2014.

167. Dmitry Bulin, "Skol'ko Eshe Budet Padat' Rubl'?" [How long will the ruble fall?], BBC Russian Service, October 30, 2014, http://www.bbc.co.uk/russian/business/2014/10/141030_russia_currency_future.

168. "Vneshnii Dolg Rossiiskoi Federacii" [Foreign debt of the Russian Federation], Central Bank of the Russian Federation, http://www.cbr.ru/statistics/print.aspx?file=credit_statistics/debt.htm&pid=svs&sid=itm_16709 ; "Ocenka Vneshnego Dolga Rossiiskoi Federacii Po Sostoyaniu na 1 Yanvarya 2015" [Assessment of the foreign debt of the Russian Federation, January 1, 2015], Central Bank of the Russian Federation, http://cbr.ru/statistics/print.aspx?file=credit_statistics/debt_est_new.htm&pid=svs&sid=itm_56777

169. "Moody's Assigns Negative Outlook to Russia's Baa1 Government Bond Rating; Confirms Rating," Moody's Investors Service, June 27, 2014, https://www.moodys.com/research/Moodys-assigns-negative-outlook-to-Russias-Baa1-government-bond-rating—PR_301804; "Moody's Downgrades Russia's Sovereign Rating to Ba1 from Baa3; Outlook Negative," Moody's Investors Service, February 20, 2015, https://www.moodys.com/research/Moodys-downgrades-Russias-sovereign-rating-to-Ba1-from-Baa3-outlook—PR_318857.

170. "Mezhdunarodnie Rezervi Rossiiskoi Federacii" [Foreign reserves of the Russian Federation], Central Bank of the Russian Federation, http://cbr.ru/hd_base/default.aspx?Prtid=mrrf_m.

171. Tatyana Grigor'eva and Elizaveta Antonova, "Sberbank CIB Predrek Rossiyskim Kompaniyam Problemy S Vyplatami Dolgov" [Sberbank CIB predicted problems for Russian companies paying debts], *RosBusinessConsulting*, October 24, 2014.

172. Cracraft and Rowland, *Architectures of Russian Identity*.

173. Donnelly, *Realism and International Relations*, 9.

174. Morgenthau, *Politics among Nations* (1948), 440.

175. Waltz, *Man, the State, and War*, 16.

176. Goldmann, "Appropriateness and Consequences: The Logic of Neo-Institutionalism," 44.

177. Soltan, Uslaner, and Haufler, *Institutions and Social Order*, 7.

178. Stigler and Becker, "De Gustibus Non Est Disputandum," 67, 76–90.

179. Hobbes, *Leviathan* (2009), 57.

180. Weber, *International Relations Theory*, 16.

181. Thucydides, *History of the Peloponnesian War* (2004), 271.

182. Rousseau, *The Social Contract*, 15.

183. Kant, *Perpetual Peace: A Philosophical Essay*, 11.

184. Hobbes, *Leviathan*, 56–57.

185. D'Anieri, *International Politics*, 78.

186. Daddow, *International Relations Theory. The Essentials*, 87.

187. Oneal and Russett, *Triangulating Peace*.

188. Keohane and Nye, *Power and Interdependence*.

189. Wendt, "Anarchy Is What States Make of It," 394.

190. Klotz and Lynch, *Strategies for Research in Constructivist International Relations*, 3.

191. Barkin, *Realist Constructivism*, 80.

192. Wendt, "Levels of Analysis vs. Agents and Structures: Part III," 183.

193. Zehfuss, *Constructivism in International Relations*, 16.

194. Burchill et al., *Theories of International Relations*, 212–36.

195. Goldmann, "Appropriateness and Consequences," 44.

196. Wendt, "Collective Identity Formation and International State."

197. Heikka, "Beyond Neorealism and Constructivism," 59.

198. Secretary Clinton's interview with Ekho Moskvy Radio, U.S. Department of State, October 14, 2009, http://www.state.gov/secretary/20092013clinton/rm/2009a/10/130546. htm.

199. Levy, "Misperception and the Causes of War," 79.

200. Stoessinger, *Why Nations Go to War*, esp. chaps. 1 and 7.

201. George Bovt, "Nenujnaya America" [Unnecessary America], *GazetaRU*, August 12, 2013, http://www.gazeta.ru/comments/column/bovt/5549633.shtml.

202. George Bovt, "Bush Kak Putin" [Bush is like Putin], *GazetaRU*, November 9, 2004, http://www.gazeta.ru/column/bovt/254531.shtml.

203. Barack Obama, "United States National Security Strategy 2010," May 2010, http://www.whitehouse.gov/sites/default/files/rss_viewer/national_security_strategy.pdf.

204. Scott Willson, "Obama Dismisses Russia as 'Regional Power' Acting Out of Weakness," *Washington Post*, March 25, 2014, http://www.washingtonpost.com/world/national-security/obama-dismisses-russia-as-regional-power-acting-out-of-weakness/2014/03/25/1e5a678e-b439–11e3-b899–20667de76985_story.html.

4. Russia and Its Near Abroad

1. Spencer and Wollman, *Nationalism*, 27.

2. Wegner, *Return to Putin's Russia: Past Imperfect, Future Uncertain.*

3. Mearsheimer, "Back to the Future."

4. Richard Lugar quoted in Rhodes, "U.S. Perspectives on NATO," 40.

5. Burganova, "Scenarii Mezhgosudarstvennoi Integracii Na Post-Sovetskom Prostranstve v Ramkax SNG" [Scenarios of interstate integration in the former Soviet space within the CIS], 27.

6. Joireman, *Nationalism and Political Identity*, 28.

7. Castells, *The Power of Identity* 2:41.

8. Gaidar, *Collapse of an Empire*, 17.

9. Strayer, *Why Did the Soviet Union Collapse?* 72.

10. Anderson, *Imagined Communities.*

11. Kudryavcev, "Postcovetskoe Prostranstvo Kak Otdel'nii Region: Integracionnie Perspectivi" [Post-Soviet space as a separate region: Prospects for integration], 261.

12. Mandelbaum, *The Rise of Nations in the Soviet Union*, 4.

13. Rezvani, *Conflict and Peace in Central Eurasia*, 74.

14. "Podpisan Zakon, Napravlennyy Na Protivodeystviye Popytkam Posyagatel'stv Na Istoricheskuyu Pamyat' V Otnoshenii Sobytiy Vtoroy Mirovoy Voyny [The law aimed at counteracting attempts to undermine the historical memory regarding the events of World War II is signed], May 5, 2014, http://www.kremlin.ru/acts/20912.

15. Eduard Shevardandze's speech at the 25th Congress of the Georgian Communist Party, 1983, quoted in Nahaylo and Swoboda, *Soviet Disunion* (2010), 189.

16. "Georgia-NATO: Friends Forever," News Agency Utro, September 26, 2000, http://www.utro.ru/articles/politics/2000/09/26/200009260332183024.shtml?2000/09/26.

17. Wastl-Walter, *The Ashgate Research Companion to Border Studies*, 554.

18. Horowitz, *Ethnic Groups in Conflict*.

19. Salih and Wohlgemurth, "Somalia: State and Society in Turmoil," 79–82.; Nalbandov, *Foreign Interventions in Ethnic Conflicts*.

20. Schmidt, *Foreign Intervention in Africa*, 165–92.

21. Chaigneau, *La Politique Militaire de la France en Afrique*, 28.

22. Korolev and Mukhamedjanov, *Sodruzhestvo Nezavisimykh Gosudarstv: Istoriya Sozdaniya, Problemy, Perspektivy Razvitiya* [Commonwealth of Independent States: History, problems, and prospects of development], 106.

23. Prunier, *The Rwanda Crisis*, 103.

24. "Putin: Rossiiskiy Medved' Nikomu Ne Otdast" [Putin: The Russian Bear will not give his Taiga to anyone], Russian State TV New Channel Vesti, October 24, 2014, http://www.vesti.ru/doc.html?id=2071417.

25. Moravcsik, "De Gaulle between Grain and Grandeur," 5; Cerny, *The Politics of Grandeur*.

26. "Indexes of Social Development," International Institute of Social Studies, http://www.indsocdev.org/home.html; "GDP per Capita" World Bank Data Indicators for 2013 placed Russia with its $14,612 in 63rd place in the world, between Argentina and Venezuela.

27. Dolenko, Konichenko, and Petukhov, "SNG Kak Prioritet Rossii" [CIS as Russia's Priority], 135.

28. Bliakher, "Vozmozhen li Post-imperskii Proekt: Ot Vzaimnykh Pretenziy k Obschemu Buduschemu" [Is the post-imperial project possible: From mutual claims to common future], 15.

29. Joshua Kuchera, "Russia: Transit Facility at Ulyanovsk Ready for NATO," EURASIANET, September 24, 2012, http://www.eurasianet.org/node/65951.

30. "NATO and Central Asia: The two elephants that never meet," *EUCAM Watch EU-Central Asia Monitoring* 11 (February 2012): 1.

31. Genadiy Zyuganov quoted in Isingarin, *Problemi Integracii V CNG* [Problems of integration in the CIS], 216.

32. Brubaker, *Nationalism Reframed*, 29.

33. The Alma Ata Declaration, December 21, 1991.

34. Nalbandov, "Living with Security Dilemmas."

35. Vorob'ev, "Etapi Formirovaniya Sodruzhestva Nezavisimix Gosudarstv v 1990-e Godi" [Stages of creation of the Commonwealth of Independent States in 1990s], 90–94.

36. Biryukova, "Sodrujestvo Nezavisimix Gosudarstv: Poisk Optimal'noi Modeli Integracii" [Commonwealth of Independent States: Search of optimal integration models], 89.

37. Landman and Robinson, *The SAGE Handbook of Comparative Politics*, 138.

38. Katrin Elborgh-Woytek, "Of Openness and Distance: Trade Developments in the Commonwealth of Independent States, 1993–2002," Working Paper 03/207, International Monetary Fund, 2003, 17.

39. Chernyavsky, "SNG: Ot Istorii K Budushemu" [CIS: From history to the future], 31.

40. *Commonwealth of Independent States Industry*, 9.

41. Torjesen, "Russia, the CIS, and the EEC," 155.

42. "SNG Bilo Zaprogramirovanno Pod Raspad, Zayavil Vladimir Putin" [Vladimir Putin: CIS was programmed for collapse], *NewsRU*, March 25, 2005, http://www.newsru.com/russia/25mar2005/doomed.html

43. Kubicek, "The Commonwealth of Independent States: An Example of Failed Regionalism?" 237.

44. "Ostanovistes': Turkmenbashi Sxodit" [Stop: Turkmenbashi is getting off"], *GazetaRU*, August 27, 2005, http://www.gazeta.ru/2005/08/27/oa168736.shtml.

45. Fawn and Nalbandov, "The Difficulties of Knowing the Start of War in the Information Age."

46. Shoemaker, *Russia and the Commonwealth of Independent States 2014*, 138.

47. "Vykhod iz SNG Dlya Ukrainy eto Katastrofa—Suslov" [Suslov: Withdrawal from the CIS for Ukraine Is a Disaster], *RIA Novosti*, December 9, 2014, http://rian.com.ua/interview/20141209/360557205.html.

48. Turisbekov, "20 Let Nezavisimosti" [Twenty years of independence], 62.

49. Trenin, Lipman, and Malashenko, "The End of an Era in EU—Russia Relations," 11.

50. Vladimir Putin, "Novyy Integratsionnyy Proyekt Dlya Evrazii—Budushcheye, Kotoroye Rozhdayetsya Segodnya" [The new integration project for Eurasia—The future born is today], *Izvestiya,* October 3, 2011.

51. Makarychev and Mommen, *Russia's Changing Economic and Political Regimes*, 158.

52. Dutkiewicz and Sakwa, *Eurasian Integration*, 98.

53. Torjesen, "Russia, the CIS, and the EEC," 156.

54. Shoemaker, *Russia and the Commonwealth of Independent States 2014*, 138.

55. Liliya Shevtsova, "Putin's Attempt to Recreate the Soviet Empire is Futile," *Financial Times*, January 7, 2014.

56. Dmitri Trenin, "Realpolitik Moskvi" [Moscow's realpolitik], *Nezavisimaya*, February 9, 2004.

57. Kembayev, *Legal Aspects of the Regional Integration Processes in the Post-Soviet Area*, 134.

58. Alexander Prokhanov, "Svyachennie Kamni Imperii" [Sacred stones of empire], *Zavtra*, 41 (2011): 1.

59. Sergey Lukianenko, "Aprel'skie Tezisi" (April theses), April 10, 2014, http://dr-piliulkin.livejournal.com/518667.html.

60. Collective Security Treaty, May 15, 1992.

61. Chernov, "Formirovanie Sistemi Collektivnoi Bezopasnosti Post-Soveskikh Gosudarstv" [Creation of the collective security system of post-Sovietstates], 98–99.

62. Izotov and Khachaturyan, "Sostoyanie I Perspektivi Razvitiya Voenno-Tekhnicheskogo Sotrudnichestva Gosugarstv-Chlenov Organizacii Dogoovra O Kollektivnoi Bezopastnosti" [Current state and prospects of development of military-technical cooperation between member states of the Collective Security Treaty Organization], 74.

63. "OON i ODKB koordiniruyut usiliya v bor'be s terrorizmom v Tsentral'noy Azii" [UN and the CSTO coordinate efforts in the fight against terrorism in Central Asia], Information Agency "Russian Weapon," September 30, 2014, https://arms-expo.ru/news/politics_and_society/oon_i_odkb_koordiniruyut_usiliya_v_borbe_s_terrorizmom_v_tsentralnoy_azii/?sphrase_id=3831242.

64. "SMI: Bakiyev Poprosil Strany ODBK Vvesti Voyska V Kyrgyzstan" [Bakiyev asks CSTO countries to send troops to Kyrgyzstan], Korrespondent.NET, May 12 2010, http://korrespondent.net/world/1075168-smi-bakiev-poprosil-strany-odkb-vvesti-vojska-v-kyrgyzstan.

65. "ODKB Osudila Gruziu Za Voennii Konflikt v Yuzhnoi Ossetii" [CSTO blamed Georgia for the military conflict in South Ossetia], *NewsRU,* August 13, 2008, http://www.newsru.com/arch/world/13aug2008/odkb.html.

66. "Uzbekistan Vyshel iz ODKB iz-za 'Nepriyatnykh' Sosedey i v Ugodu Amerikantsam, Schitayut Eksperty" [Experts: Uzbekistan withdrew from the CSTO because of "unpleasant" neighbors and to please the Americans], *NewsRU,* June 2012, http://www.newsru.com/world/29jun2012/uzb.html.

67. Mukhametov, "Voennoe Sotrudnichestvo Rossii So Stranami Blizhnego Zarubezh'ya" [Military Cooperation of Russia with Near Abroad Countries], 14–15.

68. "Raspredeleniye Naseleniya Po Natsional'nosti I Rodnomu Yazyku" [Distribution of the Population by Nationality and Native Language], State Statistics Committee of Ukraine, http://2001. ukrcensus.gov.ua/rus/results/nationality_population/nationality_popul1/select_51/?botton=cens_db&box=5. 1W&k_t=00&p=0&rz=1_1&rz_b=2_1%20%20%20%20&n_page=1

69. Brubaker, "Nationhood and National Question in the Soviet Union and Post-Soviet Eurasia"; Jenne, "A Bargaining Theory of Minority Demands: Explaining the Dog That Didn't Bite in 1990 Yugoslavia."

70. Sergei Shtukarin, "Ukrainian Identity Matrix," *CPS Non-Paper,* June 25, 2013.

71. Serhy Yekelchyk, *Ukraine: Birth of a Modern Nation*, 5.

72. Subtelny, *Ukraine*, 19–41.

73. Reid, *Borderland*, 1.

74. Tomashivsky, *Istoriya Ukrainy: Starynni viku i seredni viku* [History of Ukraine: Old ages and middle ages].

75. Magocsi, *A History of Ukraine: The Land and Its Peoples*, 133–43.

76. Aslund, *How Ukraine Became a Market Economy and Democracy*, 11.

77. Pritsak, "The First Constitution of Ukraine (5 April 1750)."

78. Cresson, *The Cossacks.*

79. Reid, *Borderland*, 64.

80. Kaufmann, "Possible and Impossible Solutions to Ethnic Civil War," 274.

81. Brzezinski, "The Premature Partnership?" 80.

82. Brzezinski, "The Premature Partnership?" 43–56.

83. Kuchma was accused by some in Ukraine of ordering the kidnapping and assassination of local journalist Georgiy Gongadze (coincidentally an ethnic Georgian), who was famous for his anticorruption articles. See Wilson, *Ukraine's Orange Revolution*, 53–54.

84. Asluns and McFaul, *Revolution in Orange*, 39.

85. D'Anieri, *Orange Revolution and Aftermath*.

86. Schneider, "The Partnership and Cooperation Agreement (PCA) between Ukraine and the EU—Idea and Reality70.

87. Hale, *Patronal Politics*, 235.

88. Rustem Falyakhov, Jana Milyukova, and Constantine Shiyan, "Ukraine Ne Daut Dobro" [No green light for Ukraine], *GazetaRU,* August 14, 2013, http://www.gazeta.ru/business/2013/08/14/5566285.shtml.

89. Trenin, Lipman, and Malashenko, *The End of an Era in EU-Russian Relations*, 12.

90. "Associirovannoe Chlenstvo Ukraini v ES Zakroet Dlya Need Put' V Tamojennii Soyuz" [Ukraine associated membership in the EU would close the doors for her in the Customs Union], REX Information Agency, October 15, 2013, http://www.iarex.ru/news/42200.html.

91. Miszlivetz, "The Post-Euromaidan Future for Europe," 250.

92. Shevel et al., *Great Decisions 2015*.

93. Kaufmann, Kraay, and Mastruzzi, "The Worldwide Governance Indicators: Methodology and Analytical Issues"; Transparency International," *Transparency International,* http://gcb.transparency.org/gcb201011/results/

94. Wilson, *Ukraine Crisis: What It Means for the West*, 66–68.

95. Max Fisher, "Ukraine's Parliament Just Threw President Yanukovych under the Bus. That's Great News," *Washington Post*, February 20, 2014.

96. "Ukraine President, Protest Leaders Agree on Truce," The Associated Press, February 19, 2014, http://www.gainesville.com/article/20140219/WIRE/140219514.

97. "Tri lidera Oppozitsii I Prezident Ukrainy Podpisali Dokument Ob Uregulirovanii Politicheskoy Situatsii" [Three opposition leaders and president of Ukraine signed the document on the settlement of the political situation], TvI TV station, February 21, 2014, http://ru.tvi.ua/new/2014/02/21/polnyj_tekst_soglasheniya_oppozicii_i_yanukovicha.

98. "Maidan Polnost'u Kontroliruet Kiev—Parubiy" [Parubiy: Maidan Fully Controls Kiev], *Segodnya*, February 22, 2014, http://www.segodnya.ua/politics/pnews/maydan-polnostyu-kontroliruet-kiev-parubiy-497737.html.

99. "Putin: Russia Helped Yanukovych to Flee Ukraine," *BBC News Europe*, October 24, 2014, http://www.bbc.com/news/world-europe-29761799.

100. Byshok, Kochetkov, and Semenov, *Neonazis & Euromaidan: From Democracy to Dictatorship*, 11.

101. Naples and Mendez, *Border Politics*, 318.

102. Vibory-2014. "Rezul'tati Golosovaniya" [Elections 2014. Results], UNIAN News Agency, http://www.unian.net/elections/ ; "'Perviy Kanal' Rossii Soobshaet, Chto Na

Viborax Presidenta Ukraini Pobejdaet Yarosh" ["Channel 1" of Russia: Yarosh is winning in the presidential elections in Ukraine], iPress news agency, http://ipress.ua/ru/news/perviy_kanal_rossyy_soobshchaet_chto_na_viborah_prezydenta_ukrayni_pobezhdaet_yarosh_66384.html.

103. Streissguth, *Vladimir Putin*, 103.

104. Nygren, *The Rebuilding of Greater Russia*, 62–63.

105. Miller, *To Balance or Not to Balance*, 136.

106. Liliya Shevtsova, "Putin's Attempt to Re-create the Soviet Empire Is Futile," *Financial Times*, January 7, 2014, http://carnegie.ru/2014/01/07/putin-s-attempt-to-recreate-soviet-empire-is-futile/gxrl

107. Zweig, *Mary Stuart*, 323.

108. "'Antimaydan' Ne Dopustit Povtoreniya Ukrainskikh Sobytiy" ["Antimaidan" will not allow repetition of the Ukrainian events], State TV Channel Vesti, January 15, 2015, http://www.vesti.ru/videos/show/vid/632759/.

109. "Shestvie Dvizheniya "Antimaidan" V Moskve" [Demonstrations of the movement "Anti-Maidan" in Moscow], *GazetaRU*, February 21, 2015, http://www.gazeta.ru/politics/photo/shestvie_dvizhenie_antimaidan_v_moskve.shtml.

110. Tsygankov, *Russia's Foreign Policy*, 162.

111. Laruelle, *Russian Nationalism and the National Reassertion of Russia*, 198.

112. "Rossiya Ne Rassmatrivayet Variant Prisoyedineniya Kryma k Rossii" [Russia is not considering the option of joining the Crimea to Russia], *Interfax News Agency*, http://www.interfax.ru/362633.

113. "Shoygu: V Krymu Rossiyskikh Voysk Net" [Shoigu: There are no Russian troops in the Crimea], Interfax News Agency, March 5, 2014, http://www.interfax.ru/russia/362895.

114. "Rasshirennoye Zasedaniye Kollegii Ministerstva Oborony" [Expanded meeting of the Collegium of the Ministry of Defense], December 19, 2014, http://news.kremlin.ru/news/47257/print.

115. "Zayavleniye MID Rossii po Sobytiyam na Ukraine" [Russian Foreign Ministry Statement on the Events in Ukraine], Ministry of Foreign Affairs of Russia, August 29, 2014, http://www.mid.ru/brp_4. nsf/0/5A4CB5306FC0ABD344257D4300415026.

116. Robert Evans, "Ukraine Death Toll Rises to More than 4,300 Despite Cease-fire: UN," Reuters, November 20, 2014, http://www.reuters.com/article/2014/11/20/us-ukraine-crisis-un-idUSKCN0J40XC20141120.

117. "Igor Girking vs. Nicolay Starikov," *Polit-Ring*, January 22, 2015, http://neuromir.tv/tsentrsily-silatsentra/.

118. "Address by the President of the Russian Federation," March 18, 2014, http://eng.kremlin.ru/news/6889.

119. "Public Opinion Poll: What Is Happening in Ukraine, Crimea, and Russia's Reaction," Levada Center, March 26, 2014, http://www.levada.ru/26-03-2014/proiskhodyashchee-v-ukraine-krymu-i-reaktsiya-rossii.

120. Grigorii Vanin and Alexander Zhilin, "Pochemu Tak Stremitel'no Reshalsya Vopros O Prisoedinenii Krima K Rossii" [Why the question of accession of the Crimea to Russia was solved so fast], REX Information Agency, May 5, 2014, http://www.iarex.ru/articles/47561.html.

121. Paul N. Schwartz, "Crimea's Strategic Value to Russia," Center for Strategic and International Studies, March 18, 2014, http://csis.org/blog/crimeas-strategic-value-russia.

122. Frank Umbach, "The Energy Dimensions of Russia's Annexation of Crimea," *NATO Review*, http://www.nato.int/docu/review/2014/NATO-Energy-security-running-on-empty/Ukraine-energy-independence-gas-dependence-on-Russia/EN/index.htm.

123. "Presidential Address to the Federal Assembly," December 4, 2014, http://eng.kremlin.ru/news/23341.

124. Sofia Kornienko, "Pidzhak Rvetsya Po Shvu" [Jacket is torn at the seam], Radio Liberty, January 23, 2015, http://www.svoboda.org/content/article/25362031.html.

125. "Putin Uveren, Chto Desantniki RF, Zaderzhannyye na Ukraine, Zabludilis'" [Putin: The Russian paratroopers who were detained in Ukraine lost their way], RIA News Agency, August 29, 2014, http://ria.ru/incidents/20140829/1021929011.html.

126. "Putin Nazval Ukrainskuyu Armiu Natovskim Legionom" [Putin: The Ukrainian army is NATO's legion], Russia 24 TV, January 26, 2015, http://www.vesti.ru/doc.html?id=2305612

127. Pavel Kanygin, "Kto Tam Shagaet Pravoi? Levii" [Who is in the right? The left], *Novaya Gazeta*, January 29, 2015, http://www.novayagazeta.ru/society/67041.html.

128. Sergey Ryabkov's interview with Russian State News Agency TASS, December 13, 2014, http://itar-tass.com/politika/1644983.

129. "Sergey Lavrov: Ukraina Stala Zhertvoy Politiki Zapada" [Sergei Lavrov: Ukraine has become a victim of western politics], September 27, 2014, http://www.kp.ru/daily/26288. 7/3165545/.

130. Alexander Dugin, "Geopolitika Novorossii: Spasti Putina" [Geopolitics of Novorossiya: Save Putin].

131. "Nas Deystvitel'no Khotyat Unichtozhit', Ili Tak Dumat'—Opasnaya Paranoyya?" [Do they really want to destroy us, or it is dangerously paranoid to think so?], *RIA Novosti News Agency*, January 8, 2015, http://m.ria.ru/zinoviev_club/20150108/1041766413.html.

132. Brooks, *Just War Theory*.

133. "Konflikti Rossii I Zapadnix Strffjan Vokrug Ukraini" [Conflicts of Russia and the Western Countries around Ukraine], Levada Center, November 21, 2014, http://www.levada.ru/21–11–2014/konflikt-rossii-i-zapadnykh-stran-vokrug-ukrainy.

134. U.S. Council on Foreign Relations, "Budapest Memorandum on Security Assurances," December 5, 1994, www.CFR.org/nonproliferation-arms-control-and-disarmament/budapest-memorandums-security-assurance-1994/p32484.

135. "Ministr Inostrannykh Del Rossii Sergey Lavrov Dal Razvernutuyu Press-konferentsiyu V Shveytsarskom Bazele" [Russian Foreign Minister Sergey Lavrov gave

a detailed press conference in Basel, Switzerland], Russian State TV Channel 1, December 5, 2014, http://www.1tv.ru/news/social/273255.

136. Zaprudnik, *Belarus: At a Crossroads of History*, 2, 10–20.

137. Wilson, *Belarus: The Last European Dictatorship*, 59.

138. Plokhy, *The Origins of the Slavic Nations*, 360–61.

139. Krajhanovski, "Zhivaya Krynitsa Ty, Rodnaya Mova" [Living source you are, my native tongue], 65–66.

140. Wilson, *Belarus: The Last European Dictatorship*, 124.

141. Marples, *Belarus: From Soviet Rule to Nuclear Catastrophe*, 4.

142. Bennett, *Last Dictatorship in Europe*.

143. Čavusau, "Belarus' Civic Sector," 9.

144. Medvedev, *Aleksandr Lukashenko: Konturi Belarusskoi Modeli* [Alexander Lukashenka: Contours of the Belarusian model].

145. Danilovich, *Russian-Belarusian Integration*, 73.

146. Black, *Russia Faces NATO Expansion: Bearing Gifts or Bearing Arms?* 119.

147. Alexeenko and Gurova, "Osnovkie Tendencii i Prioriteti V Dinamike Pryamix Inostrannix Investicii v Ekonomiku Respubliki Belarus'" [Main tendencies and priorities in the dynamics of direct foreign investments in Republic of Belarus], 2.

148. Ministry of Foreign Affairs of Belarus, "Facilitation of Investments" [Sodeistvie Investiciyam], http://www.mfa.gov.by/investments/.

149. "V 2012 godu inostrannyye investitsii v Belarusi sokratilis' na 25%" [In 2012 foreign investments in Belarus decreased by 25%], *TelegrafBY*, February 1, 2013, http://telegraf.by/2013/02/v-2012-godu-inostrannie-investicii-v-belarusi-sokratilis-na-chetvert; "Potok Inostrannykh Investitsiy v Belarus' Zametno Umen'shilsya" [Foreign investments in Belarus drastically decreased], *TUT.BY*, February 2, 2013, http://news.tut.by/economics/333001.html.

150. "Rossiyskiye Investitsii v Belarus' v 2009 Godu Uvelichilis' v 2,8 Raza" [Russian investments in Belarus in 2009 increased 2.8 times], *TUT.BY*, March 18, 2010. http://news.tut.by/economics/164391.html.

151. Ejednevnik, "Rossiyskiye Investitsii v Belarus' v 2009 Godu Uvelichilis' v 2,8 Raza" [By the volumes of the Russian investments, Belarus is far ahead of Austria and Germany], November 23, 2011, http://www.ej.by/news/economy/2011/11/23/po_ob_emam_nakoplennyh_rossiyskih_investitsiy_belarus__operezhaet_avstriyu_i_germaniyu____.html.

152. Alexander V. Kharlov and Dnitry Y. Nozhenko, "Obshie Itogi Funktsionirovaniya Tamojennogo Soyuza" [Common results of functioning of the Customs Union], *Regional Economics* 4, no. 32 (2012): 210.

153. "Ob'yem Investitsiy iz Belarusi v Rossiyu v 2010 Godu Uvelichilsya V 2,2 Raza, Iz Rossii V Belarus'-Na 7,9%" [The investment volume from Belarus to Russia in 2010 increased by 2.2 times, from Russia to Belarus—by 7.9%], *Belta*, May 18, 2011, http://www.belta.by/ru/all_news/economics/Objem-investitsij-iz-Belarusi-v-Rossiju-v-2010-godu-uvelichilsja-v-22-raza-iz-Rossii-v-Belarus-na-79_i_555312.html.

154. Antonina Doleva, "Pryamie Inostrannie Investicii V Belarus" [Foreign direct investments in Belarus], *NovaBelarus*, September 7, 2012, http://ru.novabelarus.com/ekonomika-belarusi/pryamyje-inostrannyje-investicii-v-belarus/.

155. Balmaceda, *Belarus*, 26.

156. Balmaceda, "Russian Energy Companies in the New Eastern Europe," 79.

157. Jeffries, *Economic Developments in Contemporary Russia*, 230.

158. "Lukashenko: 'Rossiiskie Negodyai' Obvalili Kaliinii Riniok" [Lukashenka: "Russian Scoundrels" Crushed the Potassium Market], Regnum News Agency, September 10, 2013, http://www.regnum.ru/news/1705815.html.

159. "Minsk Menyaet Moskvu Na Pekin" [Minsk dumps Moscow for Beijing], *GazetaRU*, July 17, 2013, http://www.gazeta.ru/politics/2013/07/17_a_5433737.shtml.

160. Lilia Shevtsova, "Putin's Attempt to Re-create the Soviet Empire Is Futile," *Financial Times*, January 7, 2014.

161. "Lukashenko o Kryme: Nedopustimo Narushat' Garantirovannuyu Territorial'nuyu Tselostnost', no Ukraina Sama Dala Povod" [Lukashenka about Crimea: Violation of guaranteed territorial integrity should not be allowed, but Ukraine has itself to blame], TUT News Agency, October 17, 2014, http://news.tut.by/politics/419983.html.

162. Denis Lavnikevich and Danila Rozanov, "Lukashenko Flirtuet S NATO" [Lukashenka is flirting with NATO], *GazetaRU*, February 2, 2015, http://www.gazeta.ru/politics/2015/02/19_a_6419169.shtml.

163. Interview with Tamara Vikkikova, former head of the Belarusian National Bank, exiled in Great Britain, *Komersant*, March 9, 2001, http://www.kommersant.ru/doc/281285?fp=.

164. "Sensacionnii Fil'm o Lukashenko na NTV: Polnaya Versiya" [Sensational movie on Lukashenka on NTV: Uncut version], Charter 97, July 4, 2010, http://charter97.org/ru/news/2010/7/4/30348/.

165. "Belarusskii Kanal Obozval Putina 'Durakom'" [Belarusian TV channel called Putin "a fool"], Newsland, September 3, 2010. http://newsland.com/news/detail/id/553972/

166. Alla Bron', "Alla Bron'. Belarusskie Vishinvantsi, Dobro Pojalovat v Srednevekov'e" [Belarus "Vishivanka," welcome to the Middle Ages!], Information Agency REGNUM, January 23, 2015, http://www.regnum.ru/news/polit/1887390.html.

167. Viktor Granin, "Bonusy Belarusi v Tamozhennom Soyuze Okazalis' Mimoletnymi" [Bonuses in the Customs Union of Belarus are fleeting], BBC Russian Service, January 21, 2013,

http://www.bbc.co.uk/ukrainian/ukraine_in_russian/2013/01/130121_ru_s_bilorus_cu.

168. Ol'ga Samofalova, "Ravnopraviye V Ego Pol'zu" [Equality in his favor], *Vzglyad*, October 17, 2014.

169. Constantine Eggert, "Lukashenko V Odinochku Pokhoronil Tamozhennyy I Budushchiy Yevraziyskiy Soyuzy" [Lukashenka singlehandedly buried the Customs

and future Eurasian Unions], *Komersant*, December 12, 2014, http://kommersant.ru/doc/2629909.

170. Koval'chuk, "Mezhdunarodnyye otnosheniya v SNG: pol'skaya perspektiva" [International relations in the CIS: The Polish perspective], 290.

171. Balmaceda, *Belarus: Oil, Gas, Transit Pipelines, and Russian Foreign Energy Policy*, 30.

172. Karina Romanova, "Belorussiya Zarabatyvayet Na Sanktsiyakh" [Belarus makes money off sanctions], *GazetaRU*, September 20, 2014, http://www.gazeta.ru/business/2014/09/19/6222133.shtml.

173. Veronika Lisovskaya and Vladimir Todorov, "Belarusiya Ne Sdaetsya" [Belarus is not giving up], *GazetaRU*, January 12, 2015, http://static.gazeta.ru/business/2015/01/12/6372861.shtml.

174. Protocol of the Meeting of the National Security Council of Belarus, December 16, 2014, http://president.gov.by/ru/news_ru/view/zasedanie-soveta-bezopasnosti-belarusi-10444/.

175. Q&A session with President Lukashenko after the annual address to the Belarus people, REGNUM News Agency, April 22, 2014, http://www.regnum.ru/news/polit/1794155.html.

176. Bell, *Eastern Europe, Russia, and Central Asia 2003*, 263.

177. Vasiliy Stati, "Mejdu Russkimi I Ruminami" [Between the Russians and Romanians], *Rusin* 1, no. 27 (2012): 132.

178. Batalden and Batalden, *The Newly Independent States of Eurasia*, 65.

179. Roper, "Regionalism in Moldova," 103.

180. Casey-Maslen, *The War Report: Armed Conflict in 2013*, 68.

181. Bibilunga, "Raspad SSSR I Krizis Moldavskoi Gosudarstvennosti" [Dissolution of the Soviet Union and the crisis of Moldovan statehood], 116.

182. Kharitonova. "Pridnestrov'e: Voina I Peremirie" [Transdnistria: War and armistice], 191.

183. Nechayeva-Yuriychuk, "Osobennosti Formirovaniya Moldavskoi Gosudarstvennosti Posle Obreteniya Nezavisimosti" [Peculiarities of the creation of Moldovan statehood after gaining independence], 136.

184. Lieven, *Chechnya: Tombstone of Russian Power*, 247; Pavkovic and Radan, *The Ashgate Research Companion to Secession*, 532.

185. Dailey, *Human Rights in Moldova*, 7.

186. Eriksson, *Targeting Peace*, 72.

187. "Transdnistrian Conflict: Origins and Main Issues," OSCE Background Paper, Vienna, June 10, 1994, CSCE Conflict Prevention Center 4.

188. The term was designed by the Russian government to define people who after the dissolution of the Soviet Union ended up outside of Russia but who identified themselves ethnically, linguistically, or culturally with the Russian nation.

189. Tsukanova, "Etapi Moldovo-Pridnestrovskogo Konflikta" [Stages of the Moldovo-Dnestr conflict], 247.

190. Walter, von Ungern-Sternberg, and Abushov, *Self-Determination and Secession in International Law*, 163–64.

191. Katchanovski, *Cleft Countries*, 101.

192. Danks, *Politics Russia*.

193. "Glamurnyy Ministr Pridnestrov'ya Nina Shtanski: Sravneniye s Krymskim Prokurorom—Kompliment Dlya Menya" [Glamorous minister of Transnistria Nina Shtanski: Comparison with the Crimean prosecutor is a compliment for me], *Komsomol'skaya Pravda*, April 14, 2014.

194. "Lavrov: Pridnestrov'ye Mozhet Stat' Nezavisimym, Esli Moldaviya Izmenit Svoy Vneblokoviy Status" [Lavrov: Transnistria can become independent if Moldova changes its neutral status], Russian State TV Channel Vesti, October 20, 2014, http://www.vesti.ru/doc.html?id=2060323.

195. Ol'ga V. Tsukanova, "Rol' Rossii V Processe Uregulirovaniya Moldovo-Prindnestrovskogo Konflikta" [Role of Russia in the process of resolution of the Moldova-Transdnistria conflict], *Problems in the Russian Legislature*, 4 (2010): 295.

196. Heenan and Lamontagne, *CIS Handbook*, 113.

197. Bugajski, *Cold Peace*, 104.

198. Sobják, "The Romania-Moldova Gas Pipeline: Does a Connection to the EU Mean a Disconnect from Russia?" 1.

199. Ogneva and Brysyakina, "Rossiya I Moldova v Poiske Optimal'nogo Formata Sotrudnichestva" [Russia and Moldova in search of optimal cooperation format], 2.

200. "Moldova Inaugurates New Gas Pipeline, Will Get Gas from Romania to Lessen Dependence on Russia," *Fox Business News*, August 27, 2014, http://www.foxbusiness.com/markets/2014/08/27/moldova-inaugurates-new-gas-pipeline-will-get-gas-from-romania-to-lessen/.

201. Svetlana Gamova, "Rossiya Snyala Pridnestrov'ye S Dovol'stviya" [Russia stopped its allowances in Transnistria], *Nezavisimaya*, January 26, 2015.

202. Uslu, *The Turkish-American Relationship between 1947 and 2003*, 103.

203. Curtis, *Armenia, Azerbaijan, and Georgia: Country Studies*, 157; Berdzenishvili et al., *Istoriya Gruzii. S Drevneishix Vremen Do 60-x Godov XIX Veka* [History of Georgia: From ancient times to the 1860s].

204. Rayfield, *Edge of Empires*, 250.

205. Allen, "The New Political Boundaries in the Caucasus," 431.

206. Stalin, *Sochineniya*, 12:369.

207. Parsons, "National Integration in Soviet Georgia," 548.

208. According to Pavel Stephanovski, Stalin "hated the Georgian intelligentsia as a class enemy" and ordered Beria to lead the execution squads to eliminate the Georgian elite in 1924. See Pavel Stephanovski, *Razvoroti Sud'bi: Avtobiografiya* [Crossroads of fate: An autobiography], *RUDN*, 200201502003, http://www.sakharov-center.ru/asfcd/auth/?t=page&num=9748.

209. Zdravomislov, *Mezhnatsionalnye konflikty v postsovetskom prostranstve* [International conflicts in post-Soviet space], 21. One example of many, an interview with Gam-

sakhurdia, gives a glimpse into the situation of ethnic minorities in early independent Georgia: "We wanted to persuade the Ossetians to give in. They took flight, which is quite logical since they are criminals. The Ossetians are an uncultured, wild people—clever people can handle them easily." See interview with Zviad Gamsakhurdia, "We Have Chatted Too Long with the Separatists: A Conversation with the Chairman of the Georgian Supreme Soviet," *Moscow News*, December 2, 1990, 11.

210. As reported by the Uppsala Conflict Dataset, http://www.pcr.uu.se/research/UCDP/our_data1.htm.

211. Mulaj, "International Actions and the Making and Unmaking of Unrecognized States," 53.

212. Fearon, "Commitment Problems and the Spread of Ethnic Conflict."

213. As reported by the Uppsala Conflict Dataset, http://www.pcr.uu.se/research/UCDP/our_data1.htm.

214. Rob Parsons, "Unrest Rises in Georgia," *Sunday Herald*, November 14, 2003, www.sundayherald.com/38065; Coppieters and Legvold, *Statehood and Security*.

215. Fawn and Nalbandov, "The Difficulties of Knowing the Start of War in the Information Age."

216. Asmus, *A Little War That Shook the World*, 19.

217. Dunlop, "The August 2008 Russo-Georgian War?" 94.

218. Dmitry Rogozin, *Yastrebi Mira: Dnevnik Russkogo Posla* [Hawks of peace: A diary of the Russian ambassador], 424.

219. Fedorov, "The Return of History: Hard Security Issues in the Russia-Europe Relationship," 123

220. Teimuraz Khugaev, Prosecutor General of South Ossetia, online interview, http://www.gazeta.ru/news/lastnews/2008/08/28/n_1263719.shtml.

221. "Tsifri Voini" [Numbers of war], *Rossiyskaya Gazeta*, week 4729, August 14, 2008, http://www.rg.ru/2008/08/14/voyna.html.

222. Public statement of the Investigation Committee of the General Prosecutor's Office, December 23, 2008, http://www.gazeta.ru/politics/2008/12/23_a_2916550.shtml.

223. "Georgia Update," Government of Georgia, December 5, 2008, http://georgiaupdate.gov.ge/doc/10006968/Microsoft%20Word%20-%205.11.pdf.

224. United Nations High Commissioner for Refugees, "UNHCR Chief Visits South Ossetia," August 22, 2008, http://www.unhcr.org/news/NEWS/48aef0dc4.html.

225. Nilsson, "Georgia's Rose Revolution: The Break with the Past," 91.

226. Nalbandov, "Living with Security Dilemmas," 52.

227. Wheatley, "The Case of Asymmetric Federalism in Georgia: A Missed Opportunity," 226.

228. Jim Nichol, "Russia-Georgia Conflict in August 2008: Context and Implications for U.S. Interests," *Congressional Research Service* (2009), 12.

229. Sumbadze, "Saakashvili in the Public Eye," 100.

230. Vladimir Vosrobin, "Kandidat v Prezidenty Gruzii Mikhail Saakashvili: Lyuboye Vmeshatel'stvo v Nashi Dela Budet Translirovat'sya SNN" [Presidential candidate Mikhail

Saakashvili: Any interference in our affairs will be televised on CNN], *Komsomol'skaya Pravda*, December 22, 2003, http://www.kp.ru/daily/23181/25517.

231. Zhungzhi and Huirong, "Chinese Views of the Russia-Georgia Conflict and Its Impact," 201.

232. "Rogozin Pro Sistemi PRO: Vilomaem Vsu Steny, Esli Nas Kto-to Popitaetsya Izolirovat" [Rogozin's take on antimissile defense: We will crush the whole wall if isolated], *GazetaRU*, June 29, 2012, http://www.gazeta.ru/politics/news/2012/06/29/n_2414157.shtml.

233. Mikhailova, "Putin as the Father of the Nation: His Family and Other Animals," 67.

234. "Vladimir Putin Threatened to Hang Georgia Leader 'By the Balls,' *Telegraph*, November 13, 2008, http://www.telegraph.co.uk/news/worldnews/europe/russia/3454154/Vladimir-Putin-threatened-to-hang-Georgia-leader-by-the-balls.html.

235. Asmus, *A Little War That Shook the World*, 75.

236. "Overview of Oil and Natural Gas in the Caspian Sea Region," U.S. Energy Information Administration, August 26, 2013, http://www.eia.gov/countries/regions-topics.cfm?fips=csr.

237. Kakachia, "Energeticheskaya Bezopasnost V Svete Rossiisko-Gruzinskoi Voini" [Energy security in the light of the Russian-Georgian war], 76.

238. Philip Hanson, "The August 2008 Conflict: Economic Consequences for Russia," *Chatham House Policy Brief*, REP BN 08/06, 2008, http://www.chathamhouse.org.uk/files/12219_0908rep_hanson.pdf.

239. Haitun, *Energetichskaya Politika Rossii Na Evropeiskom Kontinente* [Energy politics of Russia on the European Continent], 175.

240. "The Hopes of Ivanishvili Regarding Russia," *Messenger Online*, October 11, 2012 http://www.messenger.com.ge/issues/2712_october_11_2012/2712_edit.html.

241. "Ivanishvili Yeshche Raz Podtverdil Namereniye Uyti iz Politiki do Novogo Goda" [Ivanishvili once more confirmed his desire to leave politics before the New Year], *Georgia Online News Agency*, August 23, 2013, http://www.apsny.ge/2013/pol/1377319338.php.

242. Draft "Treaty on Cooperation and Integration between the Russian Federation and Republic of South Ossetia," *Caucasian Knot*, January 24, 2013, http://www.kavkaz-uzel.ru/articles/256095/.

243. Dmitry Danilov, "Dogovor O Evropeiskoi Bezopasnosti v Kontekste Treugol'nika ES-SShA-NATO" [Treaty on the European security in the context of the EU-USA-NATO triangle], *Security Index* 3, no. 94 (2010): 69.

244. "V Armenii soobshchili podrobnosti rassledovaniya ubiystv v Gyumri" [Armenia tells the details of the investigation of the Gyumri murders], *Regnum New Agency*, January 17, 2015, http://www.regnum.ru/news/society/1885439.html.

245. "Gyumri: Kak Rossiyskaya Baza Gubila Mestnykh Zhiteley" [Gyumri: How the Russian base killed the locals], *Caucasian Knot*, January 21, 2015, https://www.kavkaz-uzel.ru/articles/255581/.

246. Agreement #19970191, "Soglashenie Mejdu Rossiikoi Federaciei I Respublikoi Armenia Po Voprosam Yurisdikcii I Vzaimnoi Pravovoi Pomoshi Po Delam, Svyazannim S Naxojdeniem Rossiiskoi Voennoi Bazi Na Territorii Respubliki Armenia" [Agreement between the Russian Federation and the Republic of Armenia on jurisdiction and mutual legal assistance in cases related to the presence of the Russian military base in the Republic of Armenia], August 29, 1997.

247. "Peskov: Voyennosluzhashchiy, Obvinyayemyy V Ubiystve Sem'i V Gyumri, Predstanet Pered Sudom Rossii" [Peskov: Soldier accused of murdering family in Gyumri will appear before the Russian court], Russian State News Agency TASS, January 21, 2015, http://itar-tass.com/politika/1711693.

248. "Tragediya v Gyumri ranila Armeniyu" [Gyumri tragedy wounded Armenia], *Pravda.RU*, January 16, 2015, http://www.pravda.ru/video/news/15889.html.

249. Dmitry Kiselev, "Tragediya v Gyumri: Rossiyskiy Soldat Rasstrelyal Armyanskuyu Sem'yu" [Tragedy in Gyumri: Russian soldier shot an Armenian family], *Vesti Nedeli*, Russia 1 TV, January 18, 2015, http://vesti7.ru/news?id=45204.

250. "Anti-Maidan Armenia: Valeriy Permaykov," https://vk.com/antimaidan__zaria.

251. Walker, *Armenia: The Survival of a Nation*, 254–55.

252. Peimani, *Conflict and Security in Central Asia and the Caucasus*, 237.

253. Ammon et al., *Sociolinguistics*, 1901.

254. Malkasian, *Gha-ra-bagh!* 111.

255. Nahaylo and Swoboda, *Soviet Disunion* (1990), 189.

256. Dum-Tragut, *Armenian*, 6.

257. "Kremlin-Linked Media Chief Warns Armenia," Radio Liberty in Armenia, September 21, 2014.

258. De Waal, *Black Garden*.

259. *Azerbaijan: A Country Study*, U.S. Library of Congress Federal Research Division, March 1994, http://lcweb2. loc.gov/cgi-bin/query/r?frd/cstdy:@field(DOCID+az0024).

260. Suni, *The Revenge of the Past*, 143–44.

261. Donnan and Wilson, *Borders*, 6.

262. Posen, "The Security Dilemma and Ethnic Conflict."

263. Nygren, *The Rebuilding of Greater Russia*, 105.

264. Belfer Center for Science and International Affairs, "A Conflict That Can Be Resolved in Time: Nagorno-Karabakh," op-ed from *International Herald Tribune*, November 29, 2003.

265. Schnabel, *Southeast European Security*, 54.

266. Donaldson, Nogee, and Nadkarni, *Foreign Policy of Russia*, 200.

267. Menon, "After Empire: Russia and Southern 'Near Abroad,'" 129.

268. Ismailzade and Rosner, *Russia's Energy Interests in Azerbaijan*, 7.

269. Merabyan, "Sovremennaya Politika Rossii Ya Yuzhnom Kavkaze" [Modern Russian politics in South Caucasus], 94.

270. National Statistical Service of the Republic of Armenia.

271. Yaz'kova, "Rossiya I Nezavisimie Gosudarstva Kavkaza" [Russia and the independent state of the Caucasus], 27.

272. Kavkaz, *Tendencii I Problem Razvitiya (1992–2008)* [Tendencies and problems of development (1992–2008)], 65.

273. Croissant, *The Armenia-Azerbaijan Conflict: Causes and Implications*, 82.

274. "I Krim, I Karabakh—Rossiiskie Lovushki: Vitali Portnikov" [Vitaly Portnikov: Both Crimea and Karabakh are the Russian traps], First Armenian Informational Channel, October 7, 2014, http://ru.1in.am/1064489.html.

275. Alstadt, *The Azerbaijani Turks*, 39.

276. Hatcher, "Script Change in Azerbaijan: Acts of Identity," 106.

277. De Waal, *Black Garden*, 3.

278. Williams, *Lenin*, 183.

279. Nassibli, "Azerbaijan: Oil and Politics in the Country's Future," 103.

280. Karagiannis, *Energy and Security in the Caucasus*, 17.

281. "Caspian Sea Region," U.S. Energy Information Administration, August 26, 2013, 8.

282. Vylegjanin, "Basic Legal Issues of Management of Natural Resources of the Caspian Sea," 167.

283. Farid Guliyev and Nozima Akhrarkhodjaeva "Transportation of Kazakhstani Oil via the Caspian Sea (TKOC): Arrangements, Actors and Interests," *RussCasp Working Paper*, November 18, 2008, 6.

284. Peimani, *Conflict and Security in Central Asia and the Caucasus*, 262.

285. Christof Van Agt, "Caspian Oil and Gas: New Perspectives beyond Projects and Pipelines," Clingendale International Energy Program Paper, January 2014, 32–33.

286. Niyazov, "Vzaimootnosheniya Azerbaijana I ODKB V 1994–2011 gg" [Relations between Azerbaijan and CSTO in 1994–2011], 99.

287. "Borduzha Xochet Videt' Azerbaijan V Voennom Bloke S Armeniei" [Azerbaijan wants to see Azerbaijan in a military block with Armenia], News Agency AZE, March 25, 2009, http://news.bakililar.az/news_%20bordyuja_xochet_%20videt_22586.html.

288. "Integratsionnii Barometer EABR 2012" [Integration barometer of EBD 2012], Eurasian Development Bank, #4, 2012, 10.

289. Gadjiev, *Geopolitika Kavkaza* [Caucasian geopolitics], 383.

290. Ezhiev, "Geopoliticheskie Aspekti Etnopoliticheskix Confliktov V Kavkazsko-Kaspiiskom Regione" [Geopolitical aspects of ethnopolitical conflicts in the region of Caucasus], 40.

291. "MID Turtsii: Logika 'Odin Narod Dva Gosudarstva' S Azerbaydzhanom—Neizmenna" [Turkish FM: The Logic 'One Nation, Two States' with Azerbaijan is Unchanged], News Agency REGNUM, December 31, 2009, http://www.regnum.ru/news/polit/1240319.html.

292. Chernyavsky, "Rossiya I Azerbaijan: Osobennosti I Osnovnie Napravleniya Mejgosudarstvennogo Sotrudnichestva V Post-Sovetskii Perion" [Russia and Azer-

baijan: Particulars and main direction of intergovernmental cooperation in the post-Soviet period], 37.

293. Ultanbayev, "Rossiya I Strani Zakavkaz'ya: Real'nost' I Strategii Ekonomicheskogo Sotrudnichestva" [Russia and the Transcaucasian countries: Reality and strategies of economic cooperation], 156.

294. Voronina, "Razvitie Integracionnogo Sotrudnichestva Mezhdu Rossiei I Azerbaijanom v Ramkax SNG" [Developing integrated cooperation between Russia and Azerbaijan within CIS], 241.

295. "Torgovo-Ekonomicheskiye Svyazi Mezhdu Rossiyskoy Federatsiyey i Azerbaydzhanskoy Respublikoi v 2013 godu" [Trade and economic relations between the Russian Federation and the Republic of Azerbaijan in 2013], embassy of the Russian Federation in the Republic of Azerbaijan, http://embrus-az.com/economic_partnership.html.

296. Zeynalov and Mamedov, "Problemi I Perspektivi Razvitiya Azerbaidjansko-Rossiyskogo Sotrudnichestva v Finansovo-Bankovskoi Sfere" [Problems and perspectives of development of the Azerbaiani-Russian cooperation in the financial-banking sphere], 332–33.

297. Merabyan, "Sovremennaya Politika Rossii Ya Yuzhnom Kavkaze" [Modern Russian politics in South Caucasus], 93; "Rossiiskoe Orujie Azerbaijanu Na 5 Milliardov Dollarov" [Russian arms to Azerbaijan for $5 billion], Inosmi, October 30, 2014, http://inosmi.ru/sngbaltia/20141030/223990422.html.

298. "Rossiya Prodayet Oruzhiye Azerbaijanu Dlya Sokhraneniya Pariteta Sil V Zakavkaz'ye—Borduzha" [Borduzha: Russia sells weapons to Azerbaijan to preserve the balance of power in the Caucasus], News Agency REGNUM, June 26, 2013, http://www.regnum.ru/news/polit/1676314.html.

299. Levi and Sela, *Islamic Central Asia*.

300. Ewans, *The Great Game: A Narrative of the Russian Military Expedition to Khiva in 1839*, 3:11.

301. A. A. Danilov and A. V. Philippov, *Pribaltika I Srednyana Aziya V Sostave Rossiiskoi Imperii I SSSR* [Baltics and Central Asia under the Russian empire and USSR], Fund for Preparation of the Personnel Reserve "State Club," 2010, 114; Ewans, *The Great Game: Britain and Russia in Central Asia*.

302. Tomhiko, "The Alash Orda's Relations with Siberia, the Urals, and Turkestan," 271–87.

303. Dowling, *Russia at War*, 102.

304. Peimani, *Conflict and Security in Central Asia and the Caucasus*, 198.

305. Jukes, *The Soviet Union in Asia*, 48.

306. Rashidov, "Rossiya V Central'noi Azii: Perekhod k Pozitivnoi Vneshnei Politike" [Russia in Central Asia: Move to a positive foreign policy], 132.

307. Naumkin, *Radical Islam in Central Asia: Between Pen and Rifle*, 38.

308. Johnson, *Oil, Islam, and Conflict*, 114.

309. Taji-Farouki, "Hizb ut-Tahrir," 49.

310. Karagiannis, *Political Islam in Central Asia*, 58.

311. Farmer, *Radical Islam in the West*, 40.

312. Malashenko, "Russkiy Nacionalizm I Islam" [Russian nationalism and Islam], 94.

313. "Vlasti RF Podschitali Migrantov: Ikh Deystvitel'no Milliony" [The Russian authorities count the migrants: There really are millions], *KM.RU*, March 22, 2012, http://www.km.ru/v-rossii/2012/03/22/mezhnatsionalnye-otnosheniya-v-rossii/vlasti-rf-podschitali-migrantov-ikh-deistv.

314. Al-Rasheed, Kersten, and Shterin, *Demystifying the Caliphate*, 27.

315. Laruelle and Peyrouse, *Globalizing Central Asia*, 14.

316. "Nelegal'naya Migraciya v RF" [Illegal migration in RF], Russian State News Agency TASS, August 21, 2014, http://itar-tass.com/info/691935.

317. Buryak, "Protivodeistvie Nelegal'noi I Kriminal'noi Miracii v Deyatel'nosti FMS Rossii" [Countering illegal and criminal migration in the practice of FMS of Russia], 7.

318. "Glava FMS: Na Territorii Rossii Nakhodyatsya Pochti 3,5 mln Nelegalov" [The head of the Federal Migration Service: There are almost 3.5 million illegal immigrants in Russia], *BaltInfo News Agency*, December 9, 2013, http://www.baltinfo.ru/2013/12/09/Glava-FMS-Na-territorii-Rossii-nakhodyatsya-pochti-35-mln-nelegalov-395752.

319. Ekaterina Egorova, "Nelegal'naya Migraciya V Rossii" [Illegal migration in Russia], Russian International Affairs Council, June 21, 2013, http://russiancouncil.ru/inner/?id_4=2003#1.

320. Benediktov et al., "Immigraciya Kak Vizov Natsional'noi Bezopastnosti Rossii" [Immigration as a challenge to the Russian national security], 4–5.

321. Alimjonova, "O Voenno-Tekhnicheskom Sotrudnichestve Rossii I Respubliki Tajikistan" [On military-technical cooperation between Russia and Republic of Tajikistan], 107.

322. "Vstrecha S Lichnym Sostavom 201-y Rossiyskoy Voyennoy Bazy" [Meeting with staff of the 201st Russian Military Base], October 5, 2012, http://news.kremlin.ru/news/16605/print.

323. Shanty, *The Nexus* 39.

324. "Gruppa Pogranichnykh Voysk v Respublike Tadzhikistan" [Group of border troops in Tajikistan], Regional Public Fund of the Veterans of Military Conflict in the Republic of Tajikistan, http://fondedinstvo.ru/colleagues/history/210/.

325. "Addiction, Crime and Insurgency. The Transnational Threat of Afghan Opium," United Nations Office on Drugs and Crime, 2009, 65, http://www.unodc.org/documents/data-and-analysis/Afghanistan/Afghan_Opium_Trade_2009_web.pdf.

326. "Drug Traffic from Afghanistan as a Threat to European Security," Committee on Political Affairs and Democracy, Parliamentary Assembly of the Council of Europe, September 2013, 3.

327. "The Global Afghan Opium Trade: A Threat Assessment," United Nations Office on Drugs and Crime, July 2011, 8, http://www.unodc.org/documents/data-and-analysis/Studies/Global_Afghan_Opium_Trade_2011-web.pdf.

328. Ya, "Kontrabanda Narkotikov kak Naibolee Social'no Opastnaya Raznovidnost' Nelegal'noi Transgranichnoi Aktivnosti Mejdu Stranami Central'noi Azii I Rossiei"

[Drug smuggling as the most socially dangerous form of illegal cross-border activity between Central Asia and Russia], 43.

329. Gleason, "Relationship with Central Asia," 258.

330. Troitsky, "Stanovlenie I Razvitie Shanxaiskoi Organizacii Sotrudnichestva (2000–2007)" [Creation and development of the Shanghai Cooperation Organization (2000–2007)], 180

331. Arunova, "Shankhaiskaya Organizaciya Sotrudnichestva (2001–2011)" [Shanghai Cooperation Organization (2001–2011)], 30.

332. Starchak, "Shankhaiskaya Organizaciya Sotrudnichestva" [Shanghai Cooperation Organization], 153.

333. Trenin, Lipman, and Malashenko, "The End of an Era in EU-Russia Relations," *America-Russia: Towards Political, Security, and Economic Alliance*, November 5, 2013, http://us-russia.org/1894-the-end-of-an-era-in-eu-russia-relations.html.

334. Paramonov and Strokov, "Proekti I Investicii Rossiiv Gosudarstvax Central'noi Azii" [Projects and investments of Russia in the Central Asian states], 101.

335. "Turkmenistan Brief," *Country Analysis Briefs*, U.S. Information Agency, January 2012, 4.

336. Paramonov and Strokov, "Proekti I Investicii Rossii v Gosudarstvax Cental'noi Azii].

337. "Novosti. Gaz" [News. Gas], *NeftegazRU*, May 12, 2015, http://neftegaz.ru/news/view/123767.

338. Igor Tomberg, "Neochevidnyye Posledstviya Gazovogo Vtorzheniya Kitaya v Tsentral'nuyu Aziyu" [Non-obvious consequences of the gas invasion of China in Central Asia], *Open Economy*, Higher School of Economics, January 20, 2010.

339. Dmitri Trenin, "The Putin Doctrine," *Security Times*, February 2013, 9.

340. Liliya Shevtsova, "Putin's Attempt to Re-create the Soviet Empire Is Futile," *Financial Times*, January 7, 2014, http://carnegie.ru/2014/01/07/putin-s-attempt-to-recreate-soviet-empire-is-futile/gxrl.

341. "Kyrgyzstan Country Profile," European Commission, https://ec.europa.eu/europeaid/countries/kyrgyzstan_en.

342. Yana Milyukova, Petr Netreba, and Yuliya Zabavina, "Druz'ya Na Milliard: Kak Rossiya Zarabatyvayet Loyal'nost' Soyuznikov" [Billion-dollar friends: How Russia earns the loyalty of its allies], RosBusinessConsulting, August 12, 2014, http://top.rbc.ru/economics/12/08/2014/942271.shtml.

343. Dave, *Kazakhstan: Ethnicity, Language, and Power*, 128; Ethno-demographic Collection 2014, Statistics Agency of the Republic of Kazakhstan, http://www.stat.gov.kz/getImg?id=ESTAT081783.

344. "Putin O Kazakhstane: 'U Kazakhov Ne Bilo Gosudarstvennosti'" [Putin on Kazakhstan, "Kazakhs never had statehood"], *Voice of America Russian Service*, September 2, 2014, http://www.golos-ameriki.ru/content/putin-about-kazahstan-osharov/2434090.html.

345. "Nazarbayev Prigrozil Vykhodom Kazakhstana iz Tamozhennogo Soyuza: Tsena Vyskazyvaniy Putina" [Nazarbayev threatened to withdraw Kazakhstan from the Customs Union: The cost of Putin's remarks], *Sobesednik*, August 31, 2014, http://sobesednik.ru/politika/20140831-nazarbaev-napomnil-putinu-o-neobhodimosti-sledit-za-yazykom.

5. European Dimensions of Russian Foreign Policy

1. "Malinkovich: Modul' Fila Ne Imeet Prava Spuskat'sya Na Kometu, Otkrituyu Sovetskimi Uchennimi" [Malinkovich: "The *Philae* robotic has no right to land on the comet discovered by the Soviet scientists"], http://kplo.ru/content/view/3459/5/.

2. Winston Churchill, "Speech to the Academic Youth," University of Zurich, September 19, 1946.

3. Smith, "Russian Foreign Policy, Regional Cooperation, and Northern Relations," 25.

4. Frolova, "Rossiya V Sisteme Evropeiskoi Bezopasnosti" [Russia in the system of European security], 55.

5. 97/800/EC, ECSC, Euratom: "Council and Commission Decision of 30 October 1997 on the Conclusion of the Partnership and Cooperation Agreement between the European Communities and Their Member States, of the One Part, and the Russian Federation, of the Other Part," *Official Journal of the European Communities*, November 28, 1997, L327, 1.

6. "Agreement on Partnership and Cooperation Establishing a Partnership between the European Communities and Their Member States, of the One Part, and the Russian Federation, of the Other Part," EU-Russia, December 1, 1997, L327, 3.

7. "9th May 2014. Europe Day. Europe in the World," Fact Sheet on Northern Dimensions, European Union External Action Service.

8. Erwan and Van Elsuwege, "The EU's Northern Dimension and the EMP-ENP," 25.

9. "Northern Dimensions Policy Framework Document," adopted at the EU-Russia Helsinki Summit, November 24, 2006, 3.

10. Catellani, *The EU's Northern Dimension*, 6, 8, and 11.

11. Busigina and Filippov, "Severnoe Izmerenie": Strategii Uchastnikov" [Northern dimension: Participant strategies], 1.

12. Alexander Sergounin, "Russia and the European Union: The Northern Dimension," PONARS Policy Memo 138, 2.

13. Programming of the European Neighbourhood Instrument (ENI)–2014–2020, Regional East Strategy Paper (2014–2020) and Multiannual Indicative Programme (2014–2017), European Commission, Directorate General for Development and Cooperation, European External Action Service, 2014, 10.

14. "The EU's Black Sea Synergy: Results and Possible Ways Forward," European Union, Directorate-General for External Policies of the Union, EXPO/B/AFET/FWC/2009–01/Lot1/24, Brussels, 2010, 6.

15. "Regions List. Large-Scale Cross-Border Cooperation," Association of European Border Regions, http://www.aebr.eu/en/members/list_of_regions.php.

16. Kuznetsov, "Perspektivi Evroregionov S Rossiiskim Uchastiem S Uchetom Inovacii Regional'noi Politiki ES" [Perspectives of Euroregions with Russian participation in terms of changes in the EU regional policy], 6.

17. Sergunin, "Russian Foreign Policy Decision Making on Europe," 82–83.

18. Vinokurov and Libman, *Eurasian Integration*, 193.

19. Antonenko and Pinnick, *Russia and the European Union*, 8.

20. Rosamond, *Theories of European Integration*, 52.

21. Checkel, "Norms, Institutions, and National Identity in Contemporary Europe," 83.

22. Makarychev and Sergunin, "The EU, Russia, and Models of International Society in a Wider Europe," 318.

23. Van Ham, "EU, NATO, OSCE: Interaction, Cooperation, and Confrontation," 29.

24. "The Moscow Mechanism," OSCE MOSCOW 1991 (Par. 1 to 16) as amended by ROME 1993 (Chapter IV, par. 5).

25. Ghebali, "Where Is the OSCE Going?" 57.

26. "Russia, Referendum in Chechnya, March 23, 2003: Preliminary Statement," ODIHR/Council of Europe Joint Assessment Statement; Saari, *Promoting Democracy and Human Rights in Russia*, 102.

27. "Kak Ssorilis' Rossiya and OBSE" [How Russia quarreled with OSCE], *Kommersant*, №240 (3816), December 27, 2007.

28. "Putin Dal Poslednuyu Press-Conferenciu: "Pist' Jenu Svou Uchat Shchi Varit'" [Putin's last press conference, "Let them teach their wives to cook shchi"], *GazetaRU*, February 14, 2008, http://www.gazeta.ru/politics/2008/02/14_a_2636567.shtml.

29. Organization for Security and Co-operation in Europe, "OSCE/ODIHR Regrets that Restrictions Force Cancellation of Election Observation Mission to Russian Federation," press release, February 7, 2008, http://www.osce.org/odihr/elections/49438.

30. Vneshnepoliticheskie Itogi 2005 Goda: Razmishleniya I Vivodi [Foreign policy results of 2005: Thoughts and conclusions], Ministry of Foreign Affairs of the Russian Federation, December 2005, http://www.mid.ru/bdomp/brp_4. nsf/106e7bfcd73035f043256999005bcbbb/d094ec3478cf6571c32570e6004d14da!OpenDocument.

31. Ambrosio, *Authoritarian Backlash*, 54.

32. "Kak Ssorilis' Rossiya and OBSE" [How Russia quarreled with OSCE], *Kommersant*, №240 (3816), December 27, 2007.

33. Resolution "Divided Europe Reunited: Promoting Human Rights and Civil Liberties in the OSCE Region in the 21st Century," Meeting of the Parliamentary Assembly of the Organization of Security and Cooperation in Europe, Vilnius, June 29–July 3, 2009 AS (09) D 1 E, 48.

34. Sakwa, *The Crisis of Russian Democracy*, 215.

35. Adler, "Seeds of Peaceful Change," 143.

36. Vladimir D. Shkolnikov, "Russia and the OSCE Human Dimension: A Critical Assessment," in Russia, the OSCE and European Security, no. 12, EU-Russia Centre, 2009, 28.

37. Columbus, *Russia in Transition,* 109.

38. Boese, "CFE Compliance Report Issued; Treaty Adaptation Talks Continue."

39. Lugar and Nuland, *Russia, Its Neighbors, and an Enlarging NATO: Report of an Independent Task Force*, 27.

40. "Global Security: Russia," Second Report of Session 2007–08, House of Commons of the United Kingdom, Foreign Affairs Committee, Cm 7305, February 2008, 102.

41. Decree of the President of the Russian Federation #872 "On the Suspension by the Russian Federation of the Treaty on Conventional Armed Forces in Europe and Related International Treaties," July 13, 2007, and Federal Law # 276-ФЗ "On the Suspension by the Russian Federation of the Treaty on Conventional Armed Forces in Europe," November 29, 2007.

42. Zarakhovich, "Why Putin Pulled Out of a Key Treaty."

43. Arapina and Pfetzer, "Maratorii Na DOVSE Kak Prodoljenie 'Munkhenskoi Rechi' V.V. Putina" [Moratorium on the CFE as a continuation of V.V. Putin's "Munich speech"], 12.

44. Zagorsky, "Krizis Kontrolya Obichnix Voorujennix Sil V Evrope I Sud'ba Dogovora Ob Obichnix Voorujennix Silax" [Crisis of control over conventional forces and the fate of the CFE treaty], 49; Arapina and Pfetzer, "Maratorii Na DOVSE," 12.

45. Azhdar Kurtov, "ODKB I GUAM Kak Elementi Transormacii Prostranstva Bivshego SSSR" [CSTO and GUAM as elements of transformation of the former USSR space], *Central Asia and Caucasus* 3–4 (2008): 306.

46. Sven Hirdman, "Role of Russia in Europe," Moscow Carnegie Center (Moscow: Carnegie Endowment for Peace, 2006), 15, http://www.eurocollege.ru/fileserver/files/RF-role-in-Europe.pdf.

47. Remarks by President of the European Council Herman Van Rompuy following the 32nd EU-Russia summit, European Council, EUCO 27/14, PRESSE 38 PR PCE 21, Brussels, January 28, 2014, 1.

48. Andoura and Vahl, "A New Agreement between Russia and the European Union," 5.

49. EU-Russia Common Spaces Progress Report 2012, European Union, March 2013, 1.

50. "The European Union and Russia," House of Lords, European Union Committee, 14th Report of Session 2007–08, May 2008, 96.

51. Yakhnyuk, "Perspektivi Ekonomicheskoi Bezopasnosti Rossii V Usloviyax Prisoedineniya K Vsemirnoi Torgovoi Organizatsii" [Economic security prospects of Russia under its accession to the World Trade Organization], 143.

52. Raül Hernández i Sagrera and Olga Potemkina, "Russia and the Common Space on Freedom, Security, and Justice," *CEPS Paper in Liberty and Security in Europe* 54 (February 2013): 17.

53. "European Parliament Resolution on the Political Use of Justice in Russia," European Parliament, 2012/2789 (RSP).

54. "What Is the European Neighbourhood Policy?" European Union External Action Service, http://eeas.europa.eu/enp/about-us/index_en.htm.

55. Christou, "European Union Security Logic to the East," 79.

56. Vassilis Monastiriotis, Dimitris Kallioras, and George Petrakos, "The Regional Impact of EU Association Agreements: Lessons for the ENP from the CEE Experience," LEQS Paper No. 80, 2014, 5.

57. Bindi, "European Union Foreign Policy," 16.

58. Korosteleva, *Eastern Partnership*, 3.

59. Johns, "Russia-European Union Relations after 2012: Good, Bad, Indifferent?" 158.

60. Busigina and Filippov, "Evrosoyuz: Ot Chastnogo K Obshemu" [European Union: From specifics to generalizations].

61. "Putin's Customs Union and Eurasian Economic Union," *Rafiga's Blog*, March 1, 2014, https://grafiga.wordpress.com/2014/03/01/putins-customs-union-and-eurasian-economic-union/#_ftn33.

62. Valentina Pop, "Putin's Customs Union and Eurasian Economic Union," *EU Observer*, March 21, 2009,

http://euobserver.com/foreign/27827.

63. Foreign Policy Concept Paper 2000.

64. Mid-term Strategy of the Development of the Relations of the Russian Federation with the European Union (2000–2010),

http://www.mgimo.ru/files2/y11_2013/243404/4. 4. strategy_russia_relations_eu.htm.

65. "National Security Concept Paper," January 10, 2000, http://www.scrf.gov.ru/documents/1.html.

66. Draft document, "The European Security Treaty," November 29, 2009, http://kremlin.ru/news/6152.

67. "Conflict Resolution in the South Caucasus: The EU's Role," *International Crisis Report*, no. 173, International Crisis Group, Brussels, March 20, 2006, 11.

68. Komarov, "Iniciativa D.A. Medvedeva po Zaklucheniu DEB" [D. A. Medvedev's idea on concluding the EST], 19.

69. Keynote Speech of President Medvedev at the Conference on World Politics, Evian, France, October 8, 2008, http://archive.kremlin.ru/text/appears/2008/10/207422.shtml.

70. "O Roli Rossiyskoy Federatsii v Ukreplenii Sistemy Yevropeyskoy Bezopasnosti" № 308-СФ [Decree of the Council of the Federations of the Federal Assembly of the Russian Federation "On the role of the Russian Federation in strengthening the European Security System"], Moscow, October 31, 2012.

71. Smirnov, "Sovremennie Rossiiskie Podxodi K Obespecheniu Evropeiskoi Bezopasnosti" [Modern approaches to European security], 1.

72. Keynote speech of President Medvedev at the Conference on World Politics, Evian, France, October 8, 2008, http://archive.kremlin.ru/text/appears/2008/10/207422.shtml.

73. Atayan and Cherepova, "Dogovor O Evropeiskoi Bezopasnosti—Impul's K Razvitiu Sotrudnichestva" [European Security Treaty—Impetus for development of cooperation], 171–72.

74. De Haas, "Medvedev's Alternative European Security Architecture," 47.

75. Sally McNamara, "Russia's Proposed New European Security Treaty: A Non-Starter for the U.S. and Europe," backgrounder on Europe #2463, Heritage Foundation, September 6, 2010.

76. Danilov, "Dogovor O Evropeiskoi Bezopasnosti V Kontexte Treugol'nika EC-SSHA-NATO" [European security treaty in the context of the EU-USA-NATO triangle], 73.

77. "Vice-Spiker Gosdumi Andrei Isayev Nazval Chinovnikov Evrosoyuza 'Marionetkami SSHA" [Vice Speaker of the State Duma: The EU officials are American puppets], *GazetaRU*, November 29, 2014, http://www.gazeta.ru/business/news/2014/11/29/n_6697005.shtml.

78. "Naryshkin Predlozhil Evropeytsam Izgnat' SSHA iz NATO" [Naryshkin suggested to Europeans to expel the United States from NATO], TASS Information Agency, November 25, 2014, http://itar-tass.com/politika/1600972.

79. Vladimir Yakunin, "EU Is Bending to U.S. Pressure over Ukraine," *Financial Times*, October 20, 2014.

80. "Politolog: Terakt v Parizhe Ustroili Amerikanskiye Spetssluzhby" [Expert: Terrorist attack in Paris was staged by the U.S. intelligence], Lifenews Agency, January 8, 2014, http://lifenews.ru/news/148122.

81. Tonkikh, "Otnosheniya Rossii s NATO i OBSE v Kontekste Novoy Arkhitektury Evroatlanticheskoy Bezopasnosti" [Russia's relations with NATO and the OSCE in the context of the new Euro-Atlantic security architecture], 157.

82. National Security Strategy 2020.

83. "Address of the President of the Russian Federation," March 18, 2014, http://kremlin.ru/transcripts/20603.

84. All-Russian Youth Forum "Seliger-2014," August 28, 2014, http://kremlin.ru/news/46507.

85. Makarychev and Sergunin, "The EU, Russia, and Models of International Society in a Wider Europe," 320.

86. Foreign Policy Concept Paper 2013.

87. "Military Doctrine of the Russian Federation," December 26, 2014, 11.

88. Boris M. Smitienko, "Rossiya I Idei Ob'edinennoi Evropi" [Russia and the ideas of United Europe], *Age of Globalization* 1 (2010):149–50, 151.

89. Ryngaert, "Rossiya I Evropeiskii Soyuz: Efemernii Poisk Obshix Cennostei?" [Russia and European Union: Ephemeral quest for common values?], 126.

90. Yevgeni Shestakov, "Why We Have Finally Fallen Out of Love with Europe," *Valdai Discussion Club*, December 22, 2011, http://valdaiclub.com/europe/36480.html.

91. Francesco Algarotti, quoted in Cracraft, *The Revolution of Peter the Great*, 155.

92. Van Baak, *The House in Russian Literature*, 84.

93. Thompson, *Russia and the Soviet Union*, 18.

94. Krotov, "Opyt Gosudarstvennoi Reformi Petra Velikogo I Sovremennaya Rossiya" [Experience from the state reform of Peter the Great and modern Russia], 59.

95. Kul'pin, "Urki Petrovskoi Modernizacii: Socioestestvennii Vzglyad" [Lessons from Peter's modernization: Socionatural view], 101.

96. Massie, *Peter the Great*, 784.

97. Anisimov, *The Reforms of Peter the Great*, 70.

98. Bain, *The First Romanovs (1613–1725)*, 233.

99. Balitski, *Vremya Pavla I Ego Smert', Zapiski Sovremennikov I Uchastnikov Sobitii 11 Marta 2018 Goda* [Paul's time and death: Memories of the contemporaries and participants of the events of March 11, 2018], 315.

100. Braudel, *Civilization and Capitalism*, 442.

101. Victor Lieberman, *Strange Parallels*, 298.

102. Kulsrud, *Maritime Neutrality to 1780*, 296.

103. Lowe, *The Great Powers, Imperialism, and the German Problem*, 2.

104. Neumann, *Russia and the Idea of Europe*, 1.

105. Dostoyevsky, quoted in Timofeeva et al., *Vospominaniya I Issledovaniya O Tvorchestve F. M. Dostoyevskogo* [Memoirs and study of F. M. Dostoyevsky's works], 13:760.

106. Latynina, "If Not the West, Then Who Are We?" 19.

107. Laruelle, *Russian Eurasianism*, 3.

108. Shlapentokh, *Russia between East and West*, 145.

109. Nikitenko, "'Geopolitika' Evraziistva I Vizovi Sovremennosti" ["Geopolitics" of Eurasianism and contemporary challenges], 1.

110. Golenkova and Eremeev, "Evraziistvo Kak Geographicheskaya Ideologiya" [Eurasianism as geographic ideology], 40.

111. Nizhnikov, "Evraziistvo v Istorii Russkoi Misli I Georgii Florovsky" [Eurasianism in the history of the Russian thought and George Florovsky], 1.

112. Johnson, *The Third Rome*, 51.

113. Samokhin, "Kontseptsii Politicheskogo Ustroystva Rossii v Klassicheskom Yevraziystve" [The concept of Russia's political system in classical Eurasianism], 98.

114. Florovsky, *Iz Proshlogo Russkoi Misli* [From the past of the Russian thought], 336–37.

115. Milyukov, "Russkii Rassizm" [Russian racism].

116. Karabayeva, "Fenomen Evraziistva Kak Poisk Garmonii" [Phenomenon of Eurasianism as the quest for harmony], 4.

117. Dugin, *The Fourth Political Theory* (2009), 99.

118. I. A. Smaznov, "Evraziistvo v Post-Sovetskoi Rossii" [Eurasianism in post-Soviet Russia], *Izvestiya Rossiyskogo Gosudarstvennogo Pedagogicheskogo Universiteta Im. A. I. Gertsena*, 65, 2008, 298–99.

119. Dugin, "Strashnaya Pauza" [A frightening pause].

120. Dugin: We Have to Capture Europe, Conquer Her, and Annex Her."

121. Maria Shubina, interview with Boris Dubin, "We All Have to Carry the Payback Burden," *COLTA*, August 21, 2014, http://www.colta.ru/articles/society/4319.

122. Mankoff, *Russian Foreign Policy*, 65.

123. Yair, "'Unite Unite Europe': The Political and Cultural Structures of Europe as Reflected in the Eurovision Song Context," 150.

124. Gatherer, "Comparison of Eurovision Song Contest Simulation with Actual Results Reveals Shifting Patterns of Collusive Voting Alliances," 1, http://jasss.soc.surrey.ac.uk/9/2/1.html.

125. Victor Ginsburgh and Abdul Noury, "The Eurovision Song Contest: Is Voting Political or Cultural?" European Center for Advanced Research in Economics and Statistics (ECARES) publication, November 2006, 2.

126. "Zhirinovsky o Konchite Wurst, Evrovidenii I Evropi" [Zhirinovsly on Conchita Wurst, Eurovision and Europe], Russia 1 TV, May 10, 2014, https://www.youtube.com/watch?v=CFatRZtgCak.

127. "Mi Russkie. S Nami Vremya" [We are Russians: Time is ours], Sputnik I Pogrom, http://sputnikipogrom.com/mustread/25375/in-time-we-trust#.VH3rI4sf_6g.

128. "Special Correspondent. Hypocrites," Russia 1 TV, November 12, 2013, http://russia.tv/video/show/brand_id/3957/episode_id/699361.

129. Decree of the Government of the Russian Federation #1604 "O Perechnyakh Meditsinskikh Protivopokazaniy, Meditsinskikh Pokazaņiy i Meditsinskikh Ogranicheniy k Upravleniyu Transportnym Sredstvom" [On the list of medical contraindications, medical conditions, and medical restrictions to driving], December 29, 2014, 1.

130. "Pravitel'stvo RF Ogranichilo v Prave na Upravleniye Transportnym Sredstvom LGBT, Invalidov-amputantov I Dal'tonikov" [The Russian government restricted the right to drive for LGBT, amputees, and color-blind], *Association of Lawyers of Russia for Human Rights*, January 7, 2015, http://www.rusadvocat.com/node/996.

131. "Military Doctrine of the Russian Federation," December 26, 2014, 7.

132. "Deputat Milonov Poslal Borodatuyu Konchitu 'Uteshat' Boycov Natsgvardii" [Deputy Milonov sent bearded Conchita to "comfort" the National Guard soldiers], NTV, December 28, 2014, http://www.ntv.ru/novosti/1280220/.

133. Trenin, Lipman, and Malashenko, "The End of an Era in EU-Russian Relations."

134. Interview with Alexander Dugin on TV program *Pozner*, Russia 1, April 21, 2014, http://www.1tv.ru/sprojects_edition/si5756/fi30894.

135. "Ministry of Culture: The Cornerstone of the Foundations of the State Cultural Policy Should Be the Thesis of "Russia Is Not Europe," *Nezavisimaya Gazeta*, April 2, 2014, http://www.ng.ru/politics/2014-04-04/2_cultura.html.

136. "Russkaya Pravoslavnaya Tserkov' Obespokoilas' Rezul'tatami 'Yevrovideniya'" [Russian Orthodox Church concerned about the results of the "Eurovision"], Lenta.RU, May 11, 2014, http://lenta.ru/news/2014/05/11/neuwirth/?fb_action_ids=10202476792933979&fb_action_types=og.recommends.

137. "Sergey Glaz'yev: Ukraina Segodnya Okkupirovana Amerikantsami, Kotoryye Diktuyut Kadrovyye Naznacheniya I Rukovodyat Vsemi Deystviyami Natsistskoy Khunty" [Sergey Glaz'yev: Ukraine today is occupied by Americans who dictate appointments and manage all the activities of the Nazi junta], Rusinform News Agency, July 21, 2014, http://rusinform.net/sergej-glazev-ukraina-segodnya-okkupirovana-amerikancami-kotorye-diktuyut-kadrovye-naznacheniya-i-rukovodyat-vsemi-dejstviyami-nacistskoj-xunty/.

138. "Swedish Genitals as the Absolute European Values," *POLITRUSSIA Public-Political Internet Magazine*, January 14, 2015, http://politrussia.com/society/shvedskie-genitalii-kak-207/#comment-3814974.

139. "Rossiyane Protiv Vsex" [Russians against everyone], Levada Center, October 3, 2014, http://www.levada.ru/03–10–2014/rossiyane-protiv-vsekh.

140. Van Oudenaren, *Uniting Europe*, 8.

141. Puetter, *The European Council and the Council*, 43.

142. Vaughne Miller, "The EU's Acquis Communautaire," International Affairs and Defence Section, Library of the House of Commons, Parliament of the United Kingdom, 2011, 1; Sedelmeier and Epstein, "Beyond Conditionality: International Institutions in Postcommunist Europe after Enlargement," 795–805.

143. "Vladimir Putin: Demokratiya Ne Yavlyayetsya Pravom Na Genotsid I Gosperevorot" [Vladimir Putin: Democracy is not right for genocide and coup], Russia Today News Channel, November 18, 2014, http://russian.rt.com/article/60204#ixzz3JRHWHyph.

144. Checkel, "Social Construction and Integration," 552

145. Mackinder, *Democratic Ideals and Reality*, 106.

146. O'Hara, "Great Game or Grubby Game?" 48.

147. "Eksport Rossikoi Federaciei Siroi Nefti za 2000–2014 godi" [Export of crude oil by the Russian Federation for 2000–2014], http://www.cbr.ru/statistics/credit_statistics/print.aspx?file=crude_oil.htm.

148. "BP Statistical Review of World Energy," *British Petroleum*, June 2013, 6–7, 20–22.

149. "BP Statistical Review of World Energy," *British Petroleum*, June 2014, 15.

150. Oppenheimer and Maslichenko, "Energy and Economy," 22.

151. Gurvich, "Makroekonomicheskaya Otsenka Roli Rossiyskogo Neftegazovogo Sektora" [Macroeconomic assessment of the role of the Russian oil and gas sector], 10, 14.

152. "Oil Prices Fall from Record Highs," BBC Business Service, October 19, 2007, http://newsvote.bbc.co.uk/2/hi/business/7052071.stm; Keating, "Asia Catches Cold, Russia Sneezes," 108.

153. Pablo Gorondi, "Oil price gains to above $94 on weaker dollar," *News & Observer*, Associated Press, February 25, 2013, http://finance.yahoo.com/news/oil-price-gains-above-94-weaker-dollar-130714883-finance.html.

154. Oliker et al., *Russian Foreign Policy*, 61.

155. Brenton Goldworthy et al., "Evaluation of Oil Fiscal Regime in Russia and Proposals for Reform," working paper, International Monetary Fund, 2010, 3.

156. Vinhas de Souza, *A Different Country*, 55.

157. Rossstat-V Pervom Kvartale Eksport Nefti Iz Rossii Viros na 0.4% [Rosstat: Export of oil from Russia increased by 0.4% in the first quarter), *FinMarket*, http://www.finmarket.ru/news/2926127.

158. Mwanza Nkusu, "Aid and the Dutch Disease in Low-Income Countries: Informed Diagnoses for Prudent Prognoses," *IMF Working Paper* WP/04/49, 2004, 7.

159. Rudiger Ahrend, "Sustaining Growth in a Resource-Based Economy: The Main Issues and the Specific Case of Russia," Occasional Paper #6, *Economic Commission for Europe, the United Nations*, 2005, 5.

160. Gandolfo, *International Economics I*, 236.

161. Fantini, "The Economic Relationship between Russia and the EU," 249.

162. Dmitry Medvedev, "Rossiya, Vpered!" [Russia, forward!], *GazetaRU*, September 10, 2009, http://www.gazeta.ru/comments/2009/09/10_a_3258568.shtml.

163. "D. Medvedev: Neobkhodimo Vdvoye Snizit' Dolyu Neftyanykh Dokhodov V Byudzhete" [Medvedev: It is necessary to cut by a half the share of oil revenues in the budget], *RosBusinessConsulting*, February 2, 2013, http://top.rbc.ru/economics/26/02/2013/846979.shtml.

164. "EU Energy in Figures," European Commission, Statistical Pocket Book 2011, Brussels, 2013, 20–22.

165. "How Much Europe Depends on Russian Energy," *New York Times*, September 2014, http://www.nytimes.com/interactive/2014/03/21/world/europe/how-much-europe-depends-on-russian-energy.html?_r=0.

166. Leonard and Popescu, *A Power of EU-Russia Relations*.

167. Casier, "Russia's Energy Leverage over the EU," 139.

168. "Green Paper: A European Strategy for Sustainable, Competitive, and Secure Energy," European Commission, March 8, 2006.

169. I. Tomberg, "Energeticheskaya Politica I Energeticheskie Proekti V Central'noi Evraazii" [Energy security and energy projects in Central Eurasia], 53.

170. Johnson, "EU-Russia Energy Links," 181.

171. Esakova, *European Energy Security*, 176.

172. Keohane and Nye, *Power and Interdependence: World Politics in Transition*, 8

173. Högselius, *Red Gas*, 1–2.

174. Matveev, "Sotrudnichestvo Rossiiskoi Federacii I Evrosoyuza V Sfere Energetiki V Konce XX-Nachale XXI VV" [Cooperation between the Russian Federation and the EU in the energy sector at the end of the twentieth century and the beginning of the twenty-first century], 123.

175. Richard Weitz, "Can We Manage a Declining Russia," *Security & Foreign Affairs Monograph* (Washington DC: Hudson Institute, November 2011), 9.

176. Glenn Kates and Li Luo, "Russian Gas: How Much Is That?" Radio Free Europe/Radio Liberty, July 1, 2014, http://www.rferl.org/content/russian-gas-how-much-gazprom/25442003.html.

177. "Oil and Natural Gas Sales Accounted for 68% of Russia's Total Export Revenues in 2013," *Today in Energy*, U.S. Energy Information Administration, Russia Federal Customs Service, IHS Energy, Eastern Bloc Research, July 23, 2014, http://www.eia.gov/todayinenergy/detail.cfm?id=17231#.

178. "Prodan Oproverg Obvineniya RF v Krazhe Gaza" [Prodan denied Russian allegations of stealing gas], CenzonNET, October 23, 2014, http://censor.net.ua/news/308522/prodan

_oproverg_obvineniya_rf_v_kraje_gaza_ukraina_chetko_vypolnyaet_svoi_obyazatelstva_po_transportirovke.

179. "Reshetka Dlya 'Tigryuli'" [Cage for a "tigress")], *Obozrevatel,'* December 27, 2010, http://obozrevatel.com/news/2010/12/27/412566. htm

180. "European Economy Member States' Energy Dependence: An Indicator-Based Assessment," Occasional Papers 145, European Commission, Directorate-General for Economic and Financial Affairs Publications B-1049 Brussels, April 2013, 14.

181. "BP Statistical Review of World Energy," British Petroleum, June 2014, 8, 20, and 22.

182. Ginsberg, *The European Union in International Politics*, 200.

183. Engelbrekt and Hallenberg, *European Union and Strategy: An Emerging Actor*, 98.

184. Ladane Nasseri, "Iran Won't Yield to Pressure, Foreign Minister Says; Nuclear News Awaited," Bloomberg, February 12, 2012, http://www.bloomberg.com/news/2012–02–12/iran-won-t-yield-to-pressure-foreign-minister-says-nuclear-news-awaited.html.

185. Adebahr, "A Plan B, C, and D for an EU policy towards Iran."

186. Sadri and Vera-Muniz, "Iranian Relations with the South Caucasus," 141.

187. Milov, *Russia and the West*, 15.

188. "Gazprom Agrees to Boost Pipeline Capacity," *Downstream Today*, Deutsche Presse-Agentur, May 15, 2009, http://downstreamtoday.com/news/article.aspx?a_id=16386&AspxAutoDetectCookieSupport=1.

189. Arkadiy Krutikhin, "Yuzhnii Potok": Poluchitsya Li Voiti V Druguyu Dver'?" ["South Stream": Would it be possible to enter another door?], Forbes Russian Service, December 2, 2012, http://www.forbes.ru/mneniya-column/gosplan/274709-yuzhnyi-potok-poluchitsya-li-voiti-v-druguyu-dver.

190. "EU Consequences of South Stream Closure," Euranet Plus News Agency, December 8, 2014, http://euranetplus-inside.eu/south-streams-closure-towards-new-eu-energy-sources-or-eu-division/.

191. Vladimir Sokor, "'Nabucco-West': Abridged Pipeline Project Officially Submitted to Shah Deniz Consortium," *Eurasia Daily Monitor*, May 23, 2012.

192. "Statement by the President of the European Council Herman Van Rompuy and the President of the European Commission in the Name of the European Union on the Agreed Additional Restrictive Measures against Russia," European Council, EUCO 158/14, PRESSE 436 PR PCE, 140 Brussels, July 29, 2014.

193. European External Action Service, "Sanctions or Restrictive Measures," http://eeas.europa.eu/cfsp/sanctions/index_en.htm.

194. Council of the European Union, "Basic Principles on the Use of Restrictive Measures (Sanctions)," 10198/1/04 Rev 1, Brussels, June 7, 2004, paras 1 and 6.

195. Council of the European Union, Decision # 2014/145/CFSP of March 17, 2014, "Concerning Restrictive Measures in Respect of Actions Undermining or Threatening the Territorial Integrity, Sovereignty, and Independence of Ukraine," *Official Journal of the European Union*, March 17, 2014, 16–21.

196. Valentina Pop, "Merkel: EU Strategy Is to Maintain Russia Sanctions," *EUObserver*, December 19, 2014, https://euobserver.com/foreign/127002.

197. Council of the European Union, "List of Persons and Entities under EU Restrictive Measures over the Territorial Integrity of Ukraine," press release, December 1, 2014.

198. "BP Reports Jump in Profits, Warns of Russia Sanctions Impact," *Deutsche Welle*, July 29, 2014, http://www.dw.de/bp-reports-jump-in-profits-warns-of-russia-sanctions-impact/a-17816945.

199. Pronin, "O Pravovoi Prirode Sankcii EC V Otnoshenii RF" [On legal nature of the EU sanctions against the RF], 35; Council of the European Union, Decision # 2012/642/CFSP of October 15, 2012, "Concerning Restrictive Measures against Belarus," *Official Journal of the European Union*, October 17, 2012, 1–52.

200. Peter Baker, Alan Cowell, and James Kanter, "Coordinated Sanctions Aim at Russia's Ability to Tap Its Oil Reserves," *New York Times*, July 29, 2014, http://www.nytimes.com/2014/07/30/world/europe/european-sanctions-russia.html?_r=0.

201. "Vneshnyaya Torgovlya Rossiyskoy Federatsii Po Osnovnym Stranam Za Yanvar'–Avgust 2014 g." [Foreign trade of the Russian Federation with key countries in January–August 2014], *Federal Customs Agency of the Russian Federation*, August 10, 2014, http://www.customs.ru/index2. php?option=com_content&view=article&id=19997&Itemid=1976.

202. "Agricultural Trade in 2013: EU Gains in Commodity Exports," *European Commission, Monitoring Agri-Trade Policy*, MAP 2014–1

203. "Russia Delegation Suspended from Council of Europe over Crimea," *Guardian*, April 10, 2014, http://www.theguardian.com/world/2014/apr/10/russia-suspended-council-europe-crimea-ukraine

204. "PACE Strips Russia of Voting Rights until April over Ukraine; Russia Quits for One Year," TV channel RT, January 28, 2015, http://rt.com/news/227107-pace-resolution-against-russia/.

205. "Naryshkin Poruchil Prorabotat' Initsiativu o Prinyatii Zayavleniya Gosdumy ob Anneksii GDR" [Naryshkin ordered to prepare the initiative on the statement of the State Duma of the annexation of the GDR], Russian State News Agency TASS, January 28, 2015, http://itar-tass.com/politika/1727173.

206. "The State Duma Is Working to Collect from the Federal Republic of Germany €3 Trillion in Compensation for World War II," *RT News*, February 3, 2015, http://russian.rt.com/article/72075.

207. "State Duma MP Proposed Withdrawal from the PACE to Execute a Million Perverts," BigmirNet, February 1, 2014, http://news.bigmir.net/world/874332-Deputat-Gosdumy-predlozhil-vyjti-iz-PASE—chtoby-kaznit—million-izvracshencev.

208. "Ukaz O Primenenii Otdel'nykh Spetsial'nykh Ekonomicheskikh Mer V Tselyakh Obespecheniya Bezopasnosti Rossiyskoy Federatsii" [On application of certain special economic measures in order to ensure the security of the Russian Federation], decree #560 of the president of the Russian Federation, August 6, 2014.

209. "Ob Ustanovlenii Zapreta Na Dopusk Tovarov Legkoy Promyshlennosti, Proiskhodyashchikh Iz Inostrannykh Gosudarstv, V Tselyakh Osushchestvleniya Zakupok Dlya Obespecheniya Federal'nykh Nuzhd" [On prohibiting access of light industrial products originating from foreign countries with the purpose of procurement for the federal needs], order #791 of the Government of the Russian Federation, August 11, 2014.

210. "V MID RF Zayavili Ob Ushcherbe ES Of Sanktsiy Proton Rossii V Etom Godu v 40 mMlrd Evro" [The Russian Foreign Ministry: This Year Damage to the EU from Sanctions against Russia Is €40 Billion], *Interfax News Agency*, November 29, 2014, http://www.interfax.ru/world/410086.

211. "European Union in the World: Index," Directorate-General for Trade, the European Commission, November 8, 2014, 12 and 24.

212. "European Union, Trade in Goods with Russia," Directorate-General for Trade, the European Commission, August 27, 2014, 4–5.

213. Lidia Kelly, "UPDATE 2-Russian Economy Stagnates As Capital Flight Hits $75 billion," Reuters, July 9, 2014, http://www.reuters.com/article/2014/07/09/ukraine-crisis-russia-money-idUSL6N0PK43020140709.

214. Ivana Kottasova, "Russia Recession: It's Official Now," *CNN Money*, December 3, 2014, http://money.cnn.com/2014/12/02/news/economy/russia-economy-recession/.

215. "Otsenka Platezhnogo Balansa Rossiyskoy Federatsii Za 2014 God" [Assessment of the balance of payments of the Russian Federation for 2014], Central Bank of the Russian Federation, http://cbr.ru/statistics/print.aspx?file=credit_statistics/bal_of_payments_est_new.htm&pid=svs&sid=itm_45297.

216. Alex Sazonov, "Russian Rich Lose $10 Billion in Two Days as Ruble Drops," *Bloomberg News*, December 17, 2014, http://www.bloomberg.com/news/2014–12–17/russian-rich-lose-10-billion-in-two-days-as-ruble-drops.html.

217. Leyton-Brown, *The Utility of International Economic Sanctions*, 304.

218. Hufbauer et al., *Economic Sanctions Reconsidered*, 159.

219. Lopez, "Effective Sanctions: Incentives and UN-U.S. Dynamics," 50–51.

220. Kenneth Rogoff, "Do Sanctions Work?" *MarketWatch*, January 6, 2015, http://www.marketwatch.com/story/do-economic-sanctions-work-2015–01–06?page=1.

221. Hufbauer et al., *Economic Sanctions Reconsidered*, 160.

222. Von Peter Tiede, "Machtkampf Im Kreml: BILD Erklärt, Warum Putin die Nato Reizt" [Power struggle in Kremlin: BILD explains why Putin appeals to NATO], *BILD*, November 30, 2014, http://www.bild.de/politik/ausland/machtkampf/krebs-geruechte-ukraine-kampf-wie-angeschlagen-ist-putin-38348762. bild.html.

223. Frellesen and Rontoyanni, "EU-Russia Political Relations: Negotiating the Common Spaces," 232.

224. "European Tourism 2013—Trends and Prospects," European Travel Commission, Quarterly Report Q3/2013, 25.

225. "Indicator Fact Sheet Signals 2001—Chapter Tourism," European Environmental Agency, 2001, http://www.eea.europa.eu/data-and-maps/indicators/tourism-intensity/tourism-contribution-to-gdp.

226. "Tourism Sector in European Union," *Invest in Europe*, http://www.investineu.com/content/tourism-sector-european-union.

227. "Russian Tourists' Flow to Europe Falls by 30% after Sanctions," ITAR TASS News Agency, July 21, 2014, http://itar-tass.com/en/non-political/741603.

228. Ministry of Finance of Finland, "The Economic Effects of the EU's Russia Sanctions and Russia's Counter Sanctions," press release, September 2014, 11.

229. Lobjakas and Mölder, *EU-Russia Watch 2012*, 19.

230. Levada Center, Public Opinion Poll, "70% of the Russian Citizens Have Never Been Abroad," April 5, 2014, http://www.levada.ru/05–04–2012/70-rossiyan-nikogda-ne-byvali-za-granitsei.

231. Yana Dreyer and Nicu Popescu, "Do Sanctions against Russia Work?" *Issue Brief, European Union Institute for Security Studies* no. 35 (December 2014): 3.

232. David Ignatius, "The Risk of Tougher Sanctions on Russia," op-ed, *Washington Post*, July 17, 2014.

233. Isis Almeida and Anna Shiryaevskaya, "U.K. Gas Rises to 2-Week High on New Russia Sanctions," *Bloomberg BusinessWeek*, July 17, 2014, http://www.businessweek.com/news/2014–07–17/u-dot-k-dot-gas-rises-to-2-week-high-on-new-russia-sanctions.

234. Latvia: Resident Population by Ethnicity at the Beginning of the Year, http://data.csb.gov.lv/pxweb/en/Sociala/Sociala__ikgad__iedz__iedzskaits/IS0070. px/table/tableViewLayout1/?rxid=cdcb978c-22b0–416a-aacc-aa650d3e2ce0; Estonia: Population by Year, Sex, County, and Ethnic Nationality, January 2014, http://pub.stat.ee/px-web.2001/Dialog/varval.asp?ma=PO0222&lang=1.

235. Wegner, *Return to Putin's Russia: Past Imperfect, Future Uncertain*, 277.

236. Makarychev and Sergunin, "The EU, Russia, and Models of International Society in a Wider Europe," 313.

237. Nedergaard, *European Union Administration*, 51.

238. Trenin, Lipman, and Malashenko, *The End of an Era in EU-Russia Relations*, 14.

239. Alexandr Vladimirov, "Russkii Medved' I Evropeiskii Sosed" [Russian Bear and the European neighbor], *Zavtra* [Tomorrow], January 2, 2015, http://zavtra.ru/content/view/len-russkogo-medvedya/.

6. Identity Meets Money in Asia and the Pacific

1. Vladimir Putin, "The World Order: New Rules or a Game without Rules?" speech, Valdai International Discussion Club XI session, October 24, 2014, http://www.kremlin.ru/news/46860.

2. Trenin, Lipman, and Malashenko, "The End of Era in EU-Russian Relations."

3. Nazarchuk and Promski, "Osobennosti Rossiiskogo Eksporta I Ego Problemi v Aziatskom Regione" [Peculiarities of Russian export and its problems in the Asian region], 95.

4. Troekurova, "Rossiya I ATES: Of Formal'nogo Chlenstva K Real'nomu Uchastiu" [Russia and Asia-Pacific economic cooperation: From token membership to real participation], 133.

5. Chikahito Harada, "Russia and North-East Asia," International Institute for Strategic Studies, Adelphi Paper 310 (2005): 75.

6. Troekurova, "Poiski Putei I Opredelenie Mesta Rossii V Torgovle So Stranami ATEC" [Search for channels and definition of the place of Russia in trade with the APEC countries], 240.

7. Sevastyanov, "Rasshirenie Povestki Sotrudnichestva Kak Vozmojnii Put' k Povisheniu Roli ATES V Regione" [Enlargement of the cooperation agenda as a possible way toward enlargement of the APEC role in the region], 60.

8. Sitaryan, *Strategicheskie Orientiri Vneshneekonomicheskix Svyazei Rossii V Usloviyax Globalizacii: Scenarii Do 2025 Goda* [Strategic targets of foreign trade relations of Russia under the conditions of globalization: Scenario up to 2005], 113.

9. Gelbras, *Rossiya V Usloyakh Global'noi Migratsii* [Russia in the situation of global migration], 24–25.

10. Mikheev, *Kitai-Yaponiya: Strategicheskoe Sopernichestvo v Globaliziruyushemsya Mire* [China-Japan: Strategic rivalry and partnership in the globalizing world], 182.

11. Kazantsev, "Russian Policy in Central Asia and the Caspian Sea Region," 201–2.

12. Luki, "Russia's Identity Dilemmas," 94–95.

13. Aris, "The Shanghai Cooperation Organization: A Eurasian Security Actor?" 143.

14. Esakova, *European Energy Security*, 250.

15. Vladimir Y. Portyakov, "Rossiisko-Kitaiskie Otnosheniya: Sovremenoe Sostoyanie I Perspektivi Razvitiya" [Russia-China relations: Current state and perspectives for development], *China in Global and Regional Politics* 18, no. 18 (2013): 11.

16. Luthi, "Sino-Soviet Relations during the Mao Years, 1949–1969," 44.

17. Su, "The Strategic Triangle and China's Soviet Policy," 45.

18. King, *Heroes of China's Great Leap Forward: Two Stories*, 4.

19. Legvold, *Russian Foreign Policy in the Twenty-First Century and the Shadow of the Past*, 346.

20. Lukin and Ivanov, "Rossiisko-Kitaiskie Otnosheniya: Problemi I Perspektivi" [Russian-Chinese relations: Problems and perspectives], 314.

21. Belousova, "Vneshnyaya Politika KNR: Novii Lider–Novii Kurs" [Chinese foreign policy: New leader—new course], 120.

22. Kim, "Kitai I Vopros Rasshireniya NATO Na Vostok" [China and the NATO eastward expansion], 86.

23. "Sergey Glaz'ev: Ukraina Segodnya Okkupirovana Amerikantsami, Kotoryye Diktuyut Kadrovyye Naznacheniya i Rukovodyat Vsemi Deystviyami Natsistskoy Khunty" [Sergey Glaz'ev: Ukraine is occupied today by Americans who dictate appointments and manage all the activities of the Nazi junta], Rusinform.net, July 21, 2014, http://rusinform.net/sergej-glazev-ukraina-segodnya-okkupirovana-amerikancami-kotorye-diktuyut-kadrovye-naznacheniya-i-rukovodyat-vsemi-dejstviyami-nacistskoj-xunty/.

24. Russian-Chinese Trade and Economic Cooperation in 2014, Ministry of Economic Development of the Russian Federation, December 2014, http://www.ved.gov.ru/exportcountries/cn/cn_ru_relations/cn_ru_trade/.

25. Chernyavsky, "Istochniki Razvitiya Ekonomiki Kitaya I Rossiisko-Kitaiskie Ekonomicheskie Otnosheniya" [Sources for development of the Chinese economy and Russia-China economic relations], 417–18.

26. "Podpisan Gazovii Kontrakt s Kitaem" [The gas contract with China was signed], *GazetaRU*, May 21, 2014, http://www.gazeta.ru/business/news/2014/05/21/n_6168921.shtml.

27. Alexei Topalov, "Dorogaya Sila Sibiri" [Expensive power of Siberia], *GazertaRU*, June 9, 2014, http://www.gazeta.ru/business/2014/07/09/6107453.shtml.

28. Ariel Cohen, "Sekreti Rossiisko-Kitaiskogo Torgovogo Dogovora" [Secrets of Russian-Chinese trade agreement], Voice of America Russian Service, May 25, 2014, http://blogs.voanews.com/russian/us-russia/2014/05/25/секреты-российско-китайского-газово/.

29. Yulia Latynina, "Potok Soznaniya prirastaet "Siloi Sibiri" [Flow of consciousness gets "the power of Siberia"], *Novaya Gazeta*, December 17, 2014, http://www.novayagazeta.ru/columns/66562.html%20http://www.novayagazeta.ru/columns/66562.html.

30. "New China-Russia Gas Pact Is No Big Deal," *BloombergView*, November 14, 2014, http://www.bloombergview.com/articles/2014–11–14/new-chinarussia-gas-pact-is-no-big-deal.

31. Federal Law N 473-ФЗ of the Russian Federation "On the Territories with Advancing Socioeconomic Development in the Russian Federation," December 29, 2014.

32. "Kitai Ocenil Sovmestnii s 'Inter RAO' Proekt v $15 mlrd" [China: Joint project with "Inter RAO" costs $15 billion], *GazetaRU*, February 6, 2015, http://www.gazeta.ru/business/news/2015/02/06/n_6899073.shtml.

33. "China Offers Russia Help with Currency Swap Suggestion," *BloombergBusiness*, December 21, 2014, http://www.bloomberg.com/news/articles/2014–12–22/china-offers-russia-help-with-suggestion-of-wider-currency-swap.

34. Henry Meyer and Evgeniya Pismennaya, "Putin Deals China Winning Hand as Sanctions Power Rival," *BloombergBusiness*, October 12, 2014, http://www.bloomberg.com/news/articles/2014–10–12/putin-deals-china-winning-hand-as-sanctions-power-rival.

35. Marina I. Ishenko, "Korennoe Naselenie: Ainy" [Indigenous population: Aini], in *Istoriya Kuril'skikh Ostrovov* [History of the Kuryl Islands], ed. A. A. Vasilevski et al. (Yujno-Sakhalinsk: Sakhalin, 2008), accessed August 2, 2014, http://kurils-history.ru/book/.

36. Elleman, Nichols, and Ouimet, "A Historical Reevaluation of America's Role in the Kuril Islands Dispute," 489–504.

37. Trenin and Weber, *Russia's Pacific Future*.

38. Trenin and Weber, *Russia's Pacific Future,* 489–504.

39. Nimmons, *Treasure of War—Concealed by the Evil Ones*, 465.

40. Jason Lambacher, "Floating Habitats: Envisioning an International Peace Park in the Kurile Islands," paper, International Studies Association, Honolulu, 2005.

41. Goodby, Ivanov, and Shimotomai, *Northern Territories and Beyond*.

42. According to the Ministry of Economic Development of the Russian Federation, the trade turnover with Japan reached $31.2 million in 2012; services turnover was almost $1 billion, and with over $10 billion Japanese FDIs in the Russian economy. See "Torgovo-Ekonomicheskoe Sotrudnichestvo Mejdu Rossiiskoi Federaciei I Yaponiei" [Trade and economic cooperation between the Russian Federation and Japan], Ministry of Economic Development of the Russian Federation, http://www.ved.gov.ru/exportcountries/jp/jp_ru_relations/jp_ru_trade/.

43. "Northern Territories Issue," Ministry of Foreign Affairs of Japan, http://www.mofa.go.jp/region/europe/russia/territory/overview.html.

44. Dmitri Gorenburg, "Spor Za Yujnie Kurili" [Dispute over South Kuryls], *PONARS Eurasia*, Analytic Note, no. 226 (2008): 3.

45. "Yaponiya Zakrila Dlya Medvedeva Kurili" [Japan closed off Kurils for Medvedev], *Pravda*, November 1, 2010, http://www.pravda.ru/world/asia/fareast/01-11-2010/1055673-kurils-0/.

46. "Rossiiskaya Oficial'naya Poziciya Po Povodu Kuriskix Ostrovov Ostaetsya Neizmenna" [Russian official position regarding the Kuril Islands is unchanged], SakhalinInfo, August 26, 2002, http://www.sakhalin.info/kuriles.ru/list92/12672/.

47. Elleman et al., "A Historical Reevaluation," 489–504.

48. Kato, "Japan and Russia at the Beginning of the Twenty-First Century," 210–11.

49. Drozdov and Markin, *Operaciya "Prezident"* [Operation "President"], 172–73.

50. Brzezinski, *The Grand Chessboard*, xiv.

51. Mack and O'Hare, "Moscow-Tokyo and the Northern Territories Dispute," 387.

52. "Oboidemsya Bez Kudryavogo? Vulkan na Ostrove Iturup, Postavshik Redchaishego Metala, v Kotorom Nujdaetsya Strana, Poxoje, Malo Kogo Interesuet" [Can we do without the Kudryavi? Interest in the volcano on the Iturup Island supplying the rarest metal needed in the country is down], *Poisk*, October 7, 2011, accessed August 2, 2014, http://www.poisknews.ru/theme/science/2181/?print.

53. Il'ev et al., *Geologo-geofizichyeskaya Kharakteristika I Peerspektivi Neftegazonosnosti Sredinno-Kuril'skogo Progiba* [Geological and geophysical characteristics and petroleum potential of the mid-Kuril Bend].

54. Morris-Suzuki, "Lines in the Snow."

55. Gorenburg, "Spor Za Yujnie Kurili," 3.

56. Newnham, "How to Win Friends and Influence People," 253.

57. "Public Opinion 2011," Levada Center Annual Report (Moscow: Levada Center, 2012), 216.

58. Newnham, "How to Win Friends and Influence People," 254.

59. Art, "To What Ends Military Power," 10.

60. "Russo-Japanese Conflict in the Kuril Islands," *Washington Post*, August 16, 1994.

61. Kato, "Japan and Russia at the Beginning of the Twenty-First Century," 209.

62. Edwards, *The Korean War*, 4.

63. Bazhanov and Bazhanov, "The Evolution of Russian-Korea Relations," 794.

64. Kim, "Politicheskie Aspekti Vozmozhnix Putei Uregulirovaniya Problemi Koreiskogo Poluostrova" [Political aspects of possible resolution of the problem of the Korean Peninsula], 122.

65. Georgy Toloraya, "Russia-North Korea Economic Ties Gain Traction," U.S.-Korea Institute at SAIC, November 2014, http://38north.org/2014/11/toloraya110614/.

66. "Otnosheniya Rossii I Korei," Ministry of Foreign Affairs of the Russian Federation, February 19, 2009, http://www.mid.ru/bdomp/ns-rasia.nsf/1083b7937ae580ae432569e7004199c2/432569d80021985f43256bc0002a364d!OpenDocument.

67. Ludmila Zakharova, "Ekonomicheskie Otnosheniya Rossii I KNDR: Kurs Na Proriv" [Russian-DPRK economic relations: Toward a breakthrough], *New East Review*, June 4, 2014, http://ru.journal-neo.org/2014/06/04/rus-e-konomicheskie-otnosheniya-rossii-i-kndr-kurs-na-prory-v/.

68. Richard Lloyd Parry, "North Korean Floods Threaten Starvation," *Times*, August 3, 2004, 12.

69. Maya Dyakina and Lidia Kelly, "Russia Writes Off 90 Percent of North Korea's Debt," Reuters, September 18, 2012, http://www.reuters.com/article/2012/09/18/us-korea-north-debt-idUSBRE88H0NH20120918.

70. "Rossiya I KNDR Vozvrashautsya k Partnerstvu" [Russia and DPRK return to partnership], *Pravda*, September 19, 2012, http://www.pravda.ru/world/asia/fareast/19-09-2012/1128572-kndr-0/.

71. Alexander Vorontsov, "Novaya Faza Politiki Rossii na Koreyskom Poluostrove i v Otnosheniyakh s KNDR" [The new phase of Russian policy on the Korean Peninsula and in relations with the DPRK], *New Eastern Review*, http://ru.journal-neo.org/2014/04/24/rus-novaya-faza-politiki-rossii-na-korejskom-poluostrove-i-v-otnosheniyah-s-kndr/.

72. "Trade and Economic Cooperation," embassy of the Russian Federation in DPRK, http://www.rusembdprk.ru/ru/rossiya-i-kndr/torgovo-ekonomicheskoe-sotrudnichestvo.

73. "A. Galushka: Rossiysko–Severokoreyskiye Otnosheniya Natseleny na Kachestvenno Novyy Uroven' I Proryv v Torgovo-Ekonomicheskoy Sfere" [A. Galushka: North Korea–Russia Relations are aimed at a new level and a breakthrough in the trade-economic sphere], Ministry of Development of the Far East of the Russian Federation, March 28, 2014, http://minvostokrazvitia.ru/press-center/news_minvostok/?ELEMENT_ID=1905.

74. Tellis, Denmark, and Tanner, *Strategic Asia 2013–14: Asia in the Second Nuclear Age*, 165–66.

75. Park, "Nuclear Ambition and Tension on the Korean Peninsula," 18.

76. Joo, "Russia and North Korea: Nuclear Proliferation and Power Transition," 200.

77. "Moskva Boitsya Voini na Koreiskom Poluostrove" [Moscow is afraid of the war on the Korean Peninsula], BBC Russian Service, December 12, 2012, http://www.bbc.co.uk/russian/russia/2012/12/121212_korea_missile_russia_reaction.shtml.

78. Geoffrey Cain, "It looks like Kim Jong Un and Vladimir Putin Are Becoming BFFs," *Global Post*, February 10, 2015, http://www.globalpost.com/dispatch/news/regions/asia-pacific/north-korea/150209/kim-jong-un-vladimir-putin-military-exercises.

79. "North Korea's Kim Jong Un Picks Russia for First Foreign Trip as Leader," NBC News, January 28, 2015, http://www.nbcnews.com/news/world/north-koreas-kim-jong-un-picks-russia-first-foreign-trip-n295086

80. Sharma, *India-USSR Relations, 1947–1971*, 32.

81. Kochanek and Hardgrave, *India: Government and Politics in a Developing Nation*, 507.

82. Ray, *Sino-Soviet Conflict over India*, 104–5.

83. Rajeev Sharma, "Top Indian Diplomat Explains Russia's Importance to India," *Russia and India Report*, November 28, 2012, http://in.rbth.com/articles/2012/11/28/top_indian_diplomat_explains_russias_importance_to_india_19391.html

84. Fang, "The Past, Prospects, and the Problems of Forming the 'Chindia' Alliance," 84.

85. "Obzor Torgovo-Ekonomicheskix Otnoshenii Indii I Rossii za Yanvar-Oktyabr 2013 goda" [Review of trade-economic relations of India and Russia for January–October 2013], Ministry of Economic Development of Russia, http://www.ved.gov.ru/exportcountries/in/in_ru_relations/in_ru_trade/

86. Kaushik, "Changing Perspective of India-Russia Relations," 94.

87. Donaldson, Nogee, and Nadkarni, *Foreign Policy of Russia*, 339.

88. Oxenstierna and Tynkkynen, *Russian Energy and Security up to 2030*, 154.

89. "Putin: Russia Ready to Build 'More than' 20 Reactors in India," December 11, 2014, World Nuclear News, http://www.world-nuclear-news.org/NP-Putin-Russia-ready-to-build-more-than-20-reactors-in-India-11121401.html.

90. Tselichtchev and Debroux, *Asia's Turning Point*, 304.

91. "India Energy Report 2012," *Enerdata* (2012): 38.

92. "India Eyes Russia's Arctic Shelf Exploration," *RT News*, August 20, 2012, http://rt.com/business/india-russia-arctic-shelf-101/.

93. Saurav Jha, "Vladimir Putin's Productive India Visit," December 12, 2014, http://thediplomat.com/2014/12/vladimir-putins-productive-india-visit/.

94. Ravi Agraval, "Putin's Visit to India: Don't Focus on the Rhetoric," CNN, December 10, 2014, http://www.cnn.com/2014/12/10/world/asia/india-putin/.

95. Rajeev Sharma, "20 Deals in 24 Hours: Russia-India Relations Given $100 Billion-Worth Boost," *RT News*, December 12, 2014, http://rt.com/op-edge/213835-russia-india-contracts-nuclear/.

96. Basrur, "Nuclear Weapons and Indian Strategic Culture," 184.

97. Alagappa, *The Long Shadow*, 40.

98. Basrur, "Nuclear Weapons and Indian Strategic Culture," 186.

99. Basrur, *Minimum Deterrence and India's Nuclear Security*, 63.

100. Kumar, "Indo-Russian Defense Cooperation," 144.

101. http://www.newsru.com/russia/19apr2004/fregate.html.

102. Stockholm International Peace Research Institute Arms Trade Registry 2013.

103. Mishra, "'BraMox' Reaffirms Faith," 158.

104. "India, Russia Sign New Defence Deals," *BBC News India*, December 24, 2012, http://www.bbc.com/news/world-asia-india-20834910.

7. Peripheral Politics

1. "The National Security Strategy of the Russian Federation until 2020," May 13, 2009, http://news.kremlin.ru/ref_notes/424.

2. Energy Information Administration, "Crude Oil Price History Chart," *Macrotrends*, http://www.macrotrends.net/1369/crude-oil-price-history-chart.

3. Dmitry Medvedev, "Address to the Federal Assembly of the Russian Federation," November 12, 2009, http://www.kremlin.ru/transcripts/5979.

4. Dugin, *Theory of Multipolar World*, 18.

5. Nikitin, "Usilenie Mnogovektornoi Rossiiskoi Vneshnei Politiki" [Strengthening of multivector Russian foreign policy], 15.

6. Smitiyenko, "Rossiya I Idei Ob'edinennoi Evropoi" [Russia and the ideas of unified Europe], 155.

7. Deutsch, "External Involvement in Internal Wars," 102.

8. Basrur, *South Asia's Cold War*, 58.

9. Francis, *Uniting Africa*, 74.

10. Miller, *Soviet Relations with Latin America, 1959–1987*, 188–216.

11. Galeotti, *Afghanistan, the Soviet Union's Last War*.

12. Porter, *The USSR in Third World Conflicts*, 31.

13. Nalbandov, *Foreign Interventions in Ethnic Conflicts*, 105–28.

14. Asher, *The Egyptian Strategy for the Yom Kippur War*, 67–68.

15. Brands, *Latin America's Cold War*, 216. Italics added.

16. Bracamonte and Spencer, *Strategy and Tactics of the Salvadoran FMLN Guerrillas*, 36.

17. Foreign Policy Concept, 2013, approved by the president of the Russian Federation, February 12, 2013.

18. Foreign Policy Concept, 2013.

19. Astrada and Martín, *Russia and Latin America: From Nation-State to Society of States*, 68.

20. Blank, "Russia's Second Wind in Latin America," 1.

21. Foreign Policy Concept, 2008.

22. Foreign Policy Concept, 2013.

23. Sergey Lavrov, "The New Stage of Development of Russian-Latin American Relations," Rossiyskaya Gazeta Supplements in the Latin American Publications Clarin (Argentina), Folha de Sao Paulo (Brazil), and Observador (Uruguay), August 24, 2011, http://www.mid.ru/brp_4. nsf/0/A27D6F235094016DC32578F70042C31C.

24. Nunez-Sarantseva, "Torgovo-Ekonomicheskie Otnosheniya Merkosura S Vnezonal'nimi Partnerami" [Trade-economic relations of MERCOSUR with out-of-zone partners], 144.

25. Carl Meacham, "Is Russia Moving In on Latin America?" *Center for Strategic and International Studies,* March 25, 2014, http://csis.org/publication/russia-moving-latin-america.

26. "Russia and Latin America: Geopolitical Posturing or International Partnership?" *Council on Hemispheric Affairs,* June 20, 2014, http://www.coha.org/russia-and-latin-america-geopolitical-posturing-or-international-partnership/.

27. Paniev, "Russia Turning on Latin America," 39.

28. "Tamozhnya Vistraivaet Letinoamerikanski Korridor" [Customs are setting up the Latin American corridor], *Federal Customs Service of the Russian Federation,* July 3, 2009, http://customs.ru:8111/index.php?option=com_content&view=article&id=7420:Таможня%20выстраивает%20латиноамериканский%20коридор&catid=62:2011-01-24-16-54-55&Itemid=2055.

29. Foreign Trade of the Russian Federation with Main Countries and Groups of Countries, January–November 2014.

30. Chistov, "Ekonomiki Razvivaushikhsya Rinkov V Usloviyax Mezhkrizisnoi Globalizacii" [Economics of development markets in the conditions of inter-crisis globalization], 137.

31. "Top U.S. Trade Partners Ranked by 2013 U.S. Total Export Value for Goods," U.S. Department of Trade.

32. Russian embassy in Mexico, "Economic Relations," http://www.embrumex.org/ru/ekonomicheskie-otnosheniya.

33. "Russia Forgives $29 Billion of Cuban Debt from Soviet Era," *Aljazeera America,* December 10, 2013, accessed June 6, 2014, http://america.aljazeera.com/articles/2013/12/10/russia-forgives-29billionincubadebt.html.

34. "Russia Signs Oil Agreements," *Cuba Standard,* May 24, 2014, accessed June 6, 2014, http://www.cubastandard.com/2014/05/24/russia-signs-oil-agreements/.

35. Ministry of Industry and Trade of Russia, "Rossiya I Kuba Opredelili Preoritetnie Napravleniya Sotrudnichestva v Sfere Promishlennosti" [Russia and Cuba set priority directions in industrial cooperation], press release, July 12, 2014.

36. "Trade-Economic Cooperation between Russia and Venezuela," *Information Bulletin of the Ministry of Industry and Trade of Russia,* 2013.

37. "Rossiya I Venezuela Razvivaut Sotrudnichestvo V Neftyanom Sektore" [Russia and Venezuela cooperate in the oil sector], embassy of Venezuela in Russia, http://www.embavenez.ru/index.php?option=com_content&view=article&id=876%3Arusia-y-venezuela-estrechan-relaciones-con-acuerdos-de-cooperacion-en-el-sector-petrolero&catid=35%3Aeconomia&Itemid=103&lang=ru.

38. BRICS Sixth Summit, "Fortaleza Declaration and Action Plan," July 2014.

39. Keohane and Nye, *Power and Interdependence: World Politics in Transition,* 15.

40. Tamochkin, "Embargo v Konteste Rossiiskoi Gosudarstvennoi Politike Importozamesheniya" [Embargo in the context of Russian state policy of import replacement], 350–51.

41. "Evropeiskim Fermeram Nashli Zamenu" [Substitutes are found for the European farmers], *GazetaRU*, October 13, 2014, http://www.gazeta.ru/business/2014/10/10/6257157.shtml.

42. Kenneth Rapoza, "Putin's European Food Ban Bad for Russia, Good for Brazil," *Forbes*, August 10, 2014, http://www.forbes.com/sites/kenrapoza/2014/08/10/putins-european-food-ban-bad-for-russia-good-for-brazil/.

43. "La UE Impulsa un Boicotanti-Rusia en América Latina" [The EU promotes boycott of Russia in Latin America], August 12, 2014, http://www.cronista.com/financialtimes/La-ue-impulsa-un-boicotanti-Rusia-en-America-latina-20140812–0014.html.

44. "U.S. Spied on Brazil, Mexico Presidents: Report," Reuters, September 2, 2014.

45. Joe Leahy and Geoff Dyer, "Dilma Rousseff Postpones State Visit to U.S.," *Financial Times*, September 17, 2013.

46. "V Rossiyu Postavyat Myaso Krokodilov s Filippin i Krevetki iz Nikaragua" [Philippines crocodile meat and shrimp from Nicaragua will come to Russia], *GazetaRU*, October 9, 2014, http://www.gazeta.ru/business/news/2014/10/09/n_6548117.shtml.

47. "Gobierno Ecuatoriano Estudia Oferta Exportable a Rusia" [Government of Ecuador studies exportable offerings to Russia], *El Universo*, August 12, 2014, http://www.eluniverso.com/noticias/2014/08/12/nota/3393906/gobierno-ecuatoriano-estudia-oferta-exportable-rusia.

48. "Ekvador Narastit Eksport v Rossiu Vopreki Davleniu EC" [Ecuador will increase export to Russia notwithstanding the pressure from the EU], *LentaRU*, August 12, 2014, http://lenta.ru/news/2014/08/12/ecuador/.

49. "Exportadores de Carne y Lácteos se Entusiasman con el Mercado Ruso" [Exporters of meat and dairy products are enthusiastic with the Russian market], *La Nacion*, August 11, 2014, http://www.lanacion.com.ar/1717500-exportadores-de-carne-y-lacteos-se-entusiasman-con-el-mercado-ruso.

50. "Ecuador y Argentina Podrían Aumentar Sus Exportaciones a Rusia" [Ecuador and Argentina could increase their exports to Russia], *Juventud Rebelde*, August 12, 2014, http://www.juventudrebelde.cu/internacionales/2014–08–12/ecuador-y-argentina-podrian-aumentar-sus-exportaciones-a-rusia/.

51. Christian Oliver, "EU plans Russia sanctions talks with Latin America countries," *Financial Times*, August 11, 2014.

52. Treaty on the Non-Proliferation of Nuclear Weapons, July 1, 1968.

53. "Vladimir Yevseev: Rossiya Bol'she ne Stanet Sderzhivat' Svoye Sotrudnichestvo s Latinskoy Amerikoy" [Vladimir Evseev: Russia will no longer restrain their cooperation with Latin America], *Pravda*, July 14, 2014, http://www.pravda.ru/news/expert/14–07–2014/1216122-kuba-0/.

54. "Antonov: Rossiya Narastit Voyennoye Sotrudnichestvo s Latinskoy Amerikoy [Antonov: Russia will increase its military cooperation with Latin America," *RIA News Agency*, December 24, 2014, http://ria.ru/defense_safety/20141224/1039929684.html#ixzz3QfLfS1ck.

55. Interview of Anatoly Antonov, deputy minister of defense of the Russian Federation in the newspaper *Moskovsky Komsomolets*, February 15, 2015, http://www.mk.ru/politics/2015/02/15/chto-privez-shoygu-iz-latinskoy-ameriki.html.

56. Richard F. Grimmett, "Conventional Arms Transfers to Developing Nations, 2000–2007," Congressional Research Service, Library of Congress, October 23, 2008, 6.

57. Ilan Berman, "Russia pivots toward Cuba, Venezuela, Nicaragua," *Washington Times*, March 26, 2014, accessed June 5, 2014, http://www.washingtontimes.com/news/2014/mar/26/berman-russia-pivots-toward-latin-america/.

58. "Latinskaya Amerika Yavlyayetsya 'Rastushchim Partnerom' RF, Schitayet Analitik" [Latin America is a "growing partner" of the Russian Federation, says analyst], *RIA News Agency*, July 8, 2014, http://ria.ru/world/20140708/1015194710.html#ixzz3QfICmOaG.

59. O'Toole, *Politics Latin America*, 354.

60. Cooper, "Russia," 188.

61. Carl Meacham, "Is Russia Moving in on Latin America?" Center for Strategic and International Studies, March 25, 2014, http://csis.org/publication/russia-moving-latin-america.

62. "Rossiya Vse Zhe Khochet Razmestit' Svoi Bazy Na Kube" [Russia still wants to deploy its bases in Cuba], *NewsRU*, August 4, 2008, http://palm.newsru.com/russia/04aug2008/kuba.html.

63. Kreutz, *Russia in the Middle East: Friend or Foe?* 15; Cordesman, *A Tragedy of Arms*, 32.

64. Primakov, *Russia and the Arabs*.

65. Trenin, "The Mythical Alliance: Russia's Syria Policy," 8.

66. "The Positions of Russia and China at the UN Security Council in the Light of Recent Events," Policy Department, Directorate-General for External Policies, European Parliament (2013), 17.

67. Neil MacFarquhar, "With Rare Double UN Veto on Syria, Russia and China Try to Shield Friend," *Herald Tribune*, October 6, 2011, http://www.heraldtribune.com/article/20111005/ZNYT03/110053039?p=1&tc=pg.

68. Laird, "Soviet Arms Trade with Noncommunist Third World," 725.

69. Trenin, "The Mythical Alliance: Russia's Syria Policy," 4.

70. "Talking to Vladimir Putin. Continuation," Russia 1 TV channel, December 18, 2010.

71. Foreign Policy Concept, 2000.

72. Foreign Policy Concept, 2008.

73. Foreign Policy Concept, 2013.

74. Habibe Özdal, Hasan Selim Özertem, Kerim Has, M. Turgut Demirtepe, "Turkish-Russian Relations in the Post–Cold War Period: Current Dynamics—Future Prospects," International Strategic Research Organization, USAK Report no.13–06, 29.

75. Cordesman, *The Military Balance in the Middle East*, 210 ; Cordesman, Nerguizian, and Popescu, *Israel and Syria*, 163.

76. Weitz, *Global Security Watch—Russia: A Reference Handbook*, 30.

77. Sapronova, "Rossisko-Arabskoe Sotrudnichestvo Do I Posle 'Arabskoi Vesni'" [Russian-Arab cooperation prior and after the "Arab Spring"], 33.

78. Brookes, *A Devil's Triangle*, 223.

79. Oliver Holmes and Erika Solomon, "Alleged Chemical Attack Kills 25 in Northern Syria," Reuters, March 19, 2013, http://www.reuters.com/article/2013/03/19/us-syria-crisis-chemical-idUSBRE92I0A220130319.

80. "Rol' Rossii V Uregulirovanii Vooruzhennogo konflikta v Sirii, Dos'ye" [Russia's role in the settlement of the conflict in Syria, dossier], TASS News Agency, January 16, 2014, http://itar-tass.com/info/889036.

81. "Poslaniye Prezidenta Federal'nomu Sobraniyu" [Presidential address to the federal assembly], December 12, 2013, http://kremlin.ru/transcripts/19825.

82. "SA-10 to Syria," Global Security Analysis, http://www.globalsecurity.org/military/world/syria/sa-10.htm.

83. Gelashvili, "Iranskaya Problema na Fone Ukhudsheniya Rossiisko-Amerikanskix Otnoshenii" [Iranian problem on the background of deteriorating Russian-American relations], 39.

84. "Torgovie Otnosheniya Rossii I Irana, 2012–2013" [Trade relations between Russia and Iran, 2012–2013], Ministry of Economic Development of the Russian Federation, http://www.ved.gov.ru/exportcountries/ir/ir_ru_relations/ir_ru_trade/.

85. Ladha, "Squaring the Circle? 118.

86. Williams and Viotti, *Arms Control*, 166.

87. Cordesman, Gold, and Coughlin-Schulte, *Iran: Sanctions, Energy, Arms Control, and Regime Change*, 21–22.

88. Anna S. Tyumenkova and Alexey O. Kolobov, "Transformatsia Vneshnepolitichskoi Linii Rossii V Otnoshenii Irana v 2010 godu" [Transformation of the foreign policy of Russia toward Iran in 2010], *Bulletin of the N. I. Lobachevsky Nizhni Novgorod University*, 309.

89. Kemp and Gay, *War with Iran*, 169.

90. Mankoff, *Russian Foreign Policy,* 125.

91. Carol R. Saivetz, "Russia, Iraq, and Iran: Business, Politics, or Both?" 127.

92. Pikaev, "Iranian Nuclear Problem: Prospects for a Solution," 101.

93. Jeffries, *Political Developments in Contemporary Russia*, 545.

94. Nugzar Teg-Oganov, "Dinamika Razvitiya Rossiisko-Iranskogo Sotrudnichestva V Oblasti Yadernoi Energii: 1992–2006" [Dynamics of development of Russian-Iranian cooperation in the sphere of nuclear energy: 1992–2006], *Central Asia and Caucasus*, 2:56, 87.

95. Lionel Beehner, Russia-Iran Arms Trade, Council on Foreign Relations, Backgrounder, November 1, 2006, http://www.cfr.org/arms-industries-and-trade/russia-iran-arms-trade/p11869.

96. Aslund, Guriev, and Kuchins, *Russia after the Global Economic Crisis*, 118.

97. Ward, *Immortal, Updated Edition*, 318.

98. Mankoff, *Russian Foreign Policy*, 126.

99. Cordesman and Al-Rodhan, *Iranian Nuclear Weapons?* 34.

100. U.S. Energy Information Administration, "Petroleum Consumption, 2013," *International Energy Statistics*.

101. "7 Faktov Ob Otnosheniyakh Saudovskoy Aravii i Rossii" [Seven facts about the Saudi Arabia–Russia relations], *Vesti Economics*, June 4, 2006, http://www.vestifinance.ru/articles/43557.

102. Sapronova, "Rossisko-Arabskoe Sotrudnichestvo," 32.

103. Cordesman, *Energy Developments in the Middle East*, 170.

104. Oxford Business Group, "The Report: Saudi Arabia 2009," 125.

105. Bel Trew, "Egypt Spends $2bn of Saudi Money on Russian Arms," *Times* Middle East edition, February 13, 2014, http://www.thetimes.co.uk/tto/news/world/middleeast/article4004050.ece.

106. "Crude Oil and Commodity Prices," Oil-Price-Net, February 19, 2015, http://www.oil-price.net.

107. Mike Whitney, "Did the U.S. and the Saudis Conspire to Push Down Oil Prices? Irreversible Decline?" *CounterPunch*, December 29, 2014, http://www.counterpunch.org/2014/12/29/irreversible-decline/.

108. Mark Mazzetti, Eric Schmitt, and David D. Kirkpatrick, "Saudi Oil Is Seen as Lever to Pry Russian Support from Syria's Assad," *New York Times*, February 3, 2015.

109. Murat Akkaya, "Rossisko-Turetskie Otnosheniya v 2000–2006 gg" [Russian-Turkish relations in 2000–2006], *Power* 11 (2008): 70.

110. Ministry of Economic Development of the Russian Federation, "O Torgovo-Ekonomicheskom Sotrudnichestve Mezhdu Rossiyskoy Federatsiyey i Turetskoy Respublikoy" [On trade and economic cooperation between the Russian Federation and the Republic of Turkey], November 28, 2014, http://economy.gov.ru/minec/press/news/201411281300.

111. Fiona Hill and Omer Taspinar, "Rassiya i Turtsiya na Kavkaze" [Russia and Turkey in the Caucasus], *Politika*, November 20, 2011, http://www.politika-magazine.ru/78/245-rossija-i-turtsija-na-kavkaze.html.

112. Habibe Özdal et al., *Turkish-Russian Relations*, 22.

113. Serpil Çevikcan, "Ankara: Suriye'nin Ordusu Dağılmamalı" [Syria should disperse its army], *Milliyet*, December 5, 2012, http://www.milliyet.com.tr/ankara-suriye-nin-ordusu-dagilmamali/siyaset/siyasetyazardetay/05.12.2012/1637316/default.htm.

114. Habibe Özdal et al., *Turkish-Russian Relations,* 29.

115. Mehmet Güçer, Sema Karaca, and O. Bahadır Dinçer, "The Struggle for Life between Borders: Syrian Refugees," International Strategic Research Organization, USAK Report no.13–06, 13.

116. Kolobov et al., "Arabo-Izraelskii Conflict I Novaya Blizhnevostochnaya Politika Rossiiskoi Federacii" [Arab-Israeli conflict and the new Middle Eastern politics of the Russian Federation], 259.

117. Kreutz, *Russia in the Middle East: Friend or Foe?* 77.

118. Ministry of Economic Development of the Russian Federation, "Trade-Economic Cooperation between the Russian Federation and the State of Israel, 2011."

119. "Russia Recognizes Palestine," UPI, January 19, 2011, http://www.upi.com/Top_News/World-News/2011/01/19/Russia-recognizes-Palestine/UPI-86851295444898/.

120. Thompson, "The Global Players in the EU's Broader Neighborhood," 248.

121. Bogomolov, "CMEA and the Developing World," 32.

122. Mulira, "The Soviet Union, Angola, and the Horn of Africa," 109–10.

123. Grey, "The Soviet Presence in Africa," 511.

124. Lawson, "Soviet Economic Aid to Africa," 509.

125. Sorokine, "The Challenge of Africa's Economic Recovery and the Concept of International Economic Security," 280.

126. Cooper and Fogarty, "Soviet Economic and Military Aid to the Less Developed Countries, 1954–78," 65.

127. Hudson, "Soviet Arms Policy towards Black Africa: Opportunities and Constraints," 52.

128. Arkhangelskaya and Shubin, "Is Russia Back? Realities of Russian Engagement in Africa," 25.

129. "Rossiya I Afrika Razvivaut Sotrudnichestvo" [Russia and Africa are expanding cooperation], *Bridges* 2 (April 2010).

130. "Otnosheniya Rossii So Stranami Afriki k Yugu Sakhari v 2008 Godu" [Relations of Russia with sub-Saharan countries in 2008], Ministry of Foreign Affairs of Russian Federation, http://www.mid.ru/brp_4. nsf/itogi/010F5AF500657389C325752E003210B3.

131. United Nations Conference on Trade and Development, statistics, 2012, http://unctad.org/en/Pages/Statistics.aspx.

132. Fituni, "Afrika v Sovremennoi Mirovoi Sisteme Torgovli" [Africa in the modern global system of trade], 153.

133. A. M. Vasil'eva and L. L. Fituni, "Strategicheskoe Sopernichestvo Vedushix Eknomik Mira Za Afrikanskie Resursi" [Strategic competition of leading economies of the world for African resources], Africa Institute, Academy of Sciences of the Russian Federation, 2008, http://www.inafran.ru/node/48.

134. Daniel J. Graber, "Russia's Tatneft Plans Libyan Return," UPI News, April 2, 2014, http://www.upi.com/Business_News/Energy-Resources/2014/04/02/Russias-Tatneft-plans-Libyan-return/8321396443933/.

135. Tomberg, "Rossiiskii Neftegazovii Biznes v Afrike" [Russian oil and gas business in Africa], 102–7.

136. *Algeria Mineral and Mining Sector Investment and Business Guide* (Washington DC: International Business Publications, 2009), 45.

137. Oxford Business Group, *The Report: Nigeria, 2010*, 93.

138. Feinstein, *The Shadow World*, 115.

139. Adedeji, *Comprehending and Mastering African Conflicts*, 3.

140. Arun Mohanty, "Putin Articulates Arms Export Strategy towards BRICS," South African Foreign Policy Initiative, December 29, 2012, http://www.safpi.org/print/2976.

141. Panibratov and Lakukha, "Foreign Expansion of Russian Arms Based on Natural Resources and Technology," 145.

142. Klomegah, "Russia and Arms Sales to Africa," *African Executive* 27 (April 2013).

143. Nicolay Novichkov, "Ob'em Torgovli Orujiem Rastet" [Arms trade is growing], *Military-Industrial Courier*, March 26, 2014.

144. Keser Kenn Klomegah, "Arms Deals with Africa: From Russia with Love," *ThinkAfricaPress*, April 4, 2013, http://thinkafricapress.com/legal/russia-raising-arms-sales-africa.

145. Isabel Gorst, "Russia Imposes Arms Ban on Libya," *Financial Times*, March 10, 2011.

8. Quo Vadis?

1. "Milonov Potreboval Vzyskat' Den'gi, Potrachennyye na *Leviafan*" [Milonov demanded to recover money spent on *Leviathan*], LifeNews, January 17, 2015, http://lifenews.ru/news/148528.

2. "Shuvalov: Rossiyane ne Dopustyat Sverzheniya Svoyego Lidera [Shuvalov: Russians will not allow others to overthrow their leader], Russian State News Agency *TASS*, January 23, 2015, http://tass.ru/politika/1717116.

3. Ekaterina Zabrodina and Ariadna Rokossovskaya, "Itogi Peregovorov 'Normandskoy Chetverki': Pervyye Otsenki" [Outcomes of the negotiations of the "Normandy Four": First assessments], *Rossiiskaya Gazeta*, February 12, 2015, http://www.rg.ru/2015/02/13/itogi.html.

4. Vladimir Putin: Interview to the daily Egyptian newspaper *Al-Ahram*, February 9, 2015, http://www.kremlin.ru/news/47643.

5. Yuri Nureev, "Putin v 99-m" [Putin in 1999], video interview with Putin, Siapress, http://www.siapress.ru/blogs/36388.

6. "Mezhdunarodnie Otnosheniya" [International relations], Levada Center, February 9, 2015, http://www.levada.ru/09–02–2015/mezhdunarodnye-otnosheniya.

7. "Dmitry Peskov: "Uveren, Zapad ot nas ne otvyazhetsya nikogda" [Dmitri Peskov: I am sure the West will never leave us alone], *Argumenti I Fakti*, January 20, 2015.

8. Bethke Elshtain, *Just War Theory*.

9. Speech of Sergey Lavrov, minister of foreign affairs of Russia, and Q&A from the participants of the 50th Munich Conference on Security Policy, Munich, February 1, 2014, Ministry of Foreign Affairs of the Russian Federation, http://www.mid.ru/brp_4. nsf/0/BD142C4CC167050044257C72004E6957.

10. Schoen and Kaylan, *The Russia-China Axis*, 34.

11. Clinton, *Hard Choices*, 245.

12. Ilya Gerasimov, "Sovok Podkralsya Nezametno" [Sovok (Soviet Union) crept unnoticed], *Ab Imperio*, February 21, 2015, http://net.abimperio.net/node/3371.

13. "Za Stalina, Tsarya I Otechestvo" [For Stalin, tsar, and fatherland], Levada Center, January 21, 2015, http://www.levada.ru/21-01-2015/za-stalina-tsarya-i-otechestvo.

14. Semen Novoprodsky, "Unizhennyye I Oskorblennyye [Insulted and hurt], *GazetaRU*, November 28, 2014, http://www.gazeta.ru/comments/column/novoprudsky/6317549.shtml.

15. Anastasiya Bashkatova, "Rossiya–2015: Scenarii Khuzhe Nekuda" [Russia 2015: The worst scenario ever], *Nezavisimaya Gazeta*, October 16, 2014, http://www.ng.ru/economics/2014-10-16/1_russia2015.html.

16. "The Global Macro Analyst," Morgan Stanley Research, January 14, 2015, 9.

17. "Ulyukayev: VVP Rossii v 2015 Godu Mozhet Sokratit'sya Na 3%" [Ulyukayev: Russia's GDP in 2015 could fall by 3%], *GazetaRU*, December 25, 2014, http://www.gazeta.ru/business/news/2014/12/25/n_6780985.shtml.

BIBLIOGRAPHY

Adebahr, Cornelius. "A Plan B, C, and D for an EU policy towards Iran." Policy brief. European Policy Center, June 10, 2013.

Adedeji, Adebayo, ed. *Comprehending and Mastering African Conflicts: The Search for Sustainable Peace and Good Governance*. London: Zed, 1999.

Adler, Emanuel. "Seeds of Peaceful Change: The OSCE's Security Community-Building Model." In *Security Communities*, ed. Emanuel Adler and Michael Barnett, 119–60. Cambridge: Cambridge University Press, 1998.

Ake, Claude. "A Definition of Political Stability." *Comparative Politics* 7, no. 2 (1975): 271.

Alagappa, Muthiah, ed. *The Long Shadow: Nuclear Weapons and Security in 21st Century Asia*. Singapore: NUS Press, 2009.

Alexeenko, N. A., and I. N. Gurova. "Osnovkie Tendencii i Prioriteti V Dinamike Pryamix Inostrannix Investicii v Ekonomiku Respubliki Belarus'" [Main tendencies and priorities in the dynamics of direct foreign investments in the Republic of Belarus]. *Bulletin of the Sukhoi Gomel State Technical University* 1, no. 24 (2006): 2.

Algeria Mineral and Mining Sector Investment and Business Guide. Washington DC: International Business Publications, 2009.

Alimjonova, A. H. "O Voenno-Tekhnicheskom Sotrudnichestve Rossii I Respubliki Tajikistan" [On military-technical cooperation between Russia and the Republic of Tajikistan]. *Bulletin of the Tajik State University of Law, Business, and Politics* 4 (2009): 107.

Allen, Susan Hannah. "The Domestic Political Costs of Economic Sanctions." *Journal of Conflict Resolution* 52, no. 6 (2008): 917.

Allen, W. E. D. "The New Political Boundaries in the Caucasus." *Geographic Journal* 69, no. 5 (1927): 431.

Almond, Gabriel A., and Sidney Verba, eds. *The Civic Culture: Political Attitudes and Democracy in Five Nations*. Newbury Park CA: SAGE, 1989.

Al-Rasheed, Madawi, Carool Kersten, and Marat Shterin, eds. *Demystifying the Caliphate: Historical Memory and Contemporary Contexts*. New York: Oxford University Press, 2015.

Alstadt, Audrey L. *The Azerbaijani Turks: Power and Identity under Russian Rule.* Stanford CA: Hoover Institution, 1992.

Ambrosio, Thomas. *Authoritarian Backlash: Russian Resistance to Democratization in the Former Soviet Union.* Burlington VT: Ashgate, 2009.

Ammon, Ulrich, Norbert Dittmar, Klaus J. Mattheier, and Peter Trudgill, eds. *Sociolinguistics: An International Handbook of the Science of Language and Society.* Vol. 3 of *Handbooks of Linguistics and Communication Science.* Berlin: Walter de Gruyter, 2006.

Anderson, Benedict. *Imagined Communities: Reflections on the Origin and Spread of Nationalism.* New York: Verso, 2006.

Andoura, Sami, and Marius Vahl. "A New Agreement between Russia and the European Union." *EU-Russia Review,* no. 2 (November 2006): 5.

Anisimov, Evgenii V. *The Reforms of Peter the Great: Progress through Coercion in Russia.* Translated by John T. Alexander. New York: M. E. Sharpe, 1993.

Antonenko, Oksana, and Kathryn Pinnick. *Russia and the European Union: Prospects for a New Relationship.* Milton Park, UK: Routledge, 2005.

Arapina, C. V., and C. A. Pfetzer. "Maratorii Na DOVSE Kak Prodoljenie 'Munkhenskoi Rechi' V. V. Putina" [Moratorium on the CFE as a continuation of V. V. Putin's "Munich speech"]. *Bulletin of the Kemerovo State University* 2 (2008): 12.

Aris, Stephen. "The Shanghai Cooperation Organization: A Eurasian Security Actor?" In *Regional Organisations and Security: Conceptions and Practices,* ed. Stephen Aris and Andreas Wenger, 141–60. Milton Park, UK: Routledge, 2014.

Arkhangelskaya, Alexandra, and Vladimir Shubin. "Is Russia Back? Realities of Russian Engagement in Africa." *IDEAS Report SR016* (London: London School of Economics, 2013).

Art, Robert J. "To What Ends Military Power." *International Security* 4 (1990): 10.

Arunova, Marianna. "Shankhaiskaya Organizaciya Sotrudnichestva (2001–2011): Zadachi, Itogi, Perspektivi" [Shanghai Cooperation Organization [2001–2011)]: Tasks, outcomes, perspectives]. *Central Asia and Caucasus* 4, no. 14 (2011): 30.

Asher, Dani. *The Egyptian Strategy for the Yom Kippur War: An Analysis.* Translated by Moshe Tlamim. Jefferson NC: McFarland, 2009.

Aslund, Anders. *How Ukraine Became a Market Economy and Democracy.* Washington DC: Peterson Institute for International Economics, 2009.

Aslund, Anders, Sergei Guriev, and Andrew Kuchins, eds. *Russia after the Global Economic Crisis.* Washington DC: Peterson Institute for International Economics, 2010.

Aslund, Anders, and Michael McFaul. *Revolution in Orange: The Origins of Ukraine's Democratic Breakthrough.* Washington: Carnegie Endowment of International Peace, 2006.

Asmus, Ronald D. *A Little War That Shook the World: Georgia, Russia, and the Future of the West.* New York: Palgrave Macmillan, 2010.

Astrada, Marvin L., and Félix E. Martín. *Russia and Latin America: From Nation-State to Society of States.* New York: Palgrave Macmillan, 2013.

Atayan, A. V., and P. A. Cherepova. "Dogovor O Evropeiskoi Bezopasnosti—Impul's K Razvitiu Sotrudnichestva" [European Security Treaty—Impetus for development of cooperation]. In *Dogovor o Yevropeyskoy Bezopasnosti: Impul's k Razvitiyu Otnosheniy Rossii i Evropy* [European Security Treaty: Impetus to the development of relations between Russia and Europe], ed. M. B. Bratersky et al., 169–74. Moscow: High School of Economics, 2011.

Azarova, Antanina. "Izmenenie Sprosa I Tseni Na Energonositeli" [Changes in demand and price for energy carriers]. *Problems of Accounting and Finances* 2, no. 6 (2012): 66.

Baev, Pavel K. *The Russian Army in a Time of Troubles.* Oslo, Norway: International Peace Research Institute, 1996.

Bain, R. Nisbet. *The First Romanovs (1613–1725): A History of Moscovite Civilization and the Rise of Modern Russia under Peter the Great and His Forerunners.* London: Archibald Constable, 1905.

Baldwin, David A., and Robert A. Pape. "Evaluating Economic Sanctions." *International Security* 23, no. 2 (1998): 192.

Balitski, G., ed. *Vremya Pavla I Ego Smert', Zapiski Sovremennikov I Uchastnikov Sobitii 11 Marta 2018 Goda* [Paul's time and death: Memories of the contemporaries and participants of the events of March 11, 2018], part 1. Moscow: Russiaya Bil', Obrazovanie 1908.

Balmaceda, Margarita M. *Belarus: Oil, Gas, Transit Pipelines, and Russian Foreign Energy Policy.* London: GMB, 2006.

———. "Russian Energy Companies in the New Eastern Europe: The Case of Ukraine and Belarus." In *Russian Business Power: The Role of Russian Business in Foreign and Security Relations*, ed. Andreas Wenger, Robert Orttung, and Jeronim Perovic, 67–87. Milton Park, UK: Routledge, 2006.

Barkin, J. Samuel. *Realist Constructivism: Rethinking International Relations Theory.* Cambridge: Cambridge University Press, 2010.

Barth, Fredrik. *Ethnic Groups and Boundaries: The Social Organization of Culture Difference.* Long Grove IL: Waveland, 1998.

Basrur, Rajesh M. *Minimum Deterrence and India's Nuclear Security.* Singapore: NUS Press, 2009.

———. "Nuclear Weapons and Indian Strategic Culture." *Journal of Peace Research* 38, no. 2 (2001): 184.

———. *South Asia's Cold War: Nuclear Weapons and Conflict in Comparative Perspective.* Milton Park, UK: Routledge, 2008.

Batalden, Stephen K., and Sandra L. Batalden. *The Newly Independent States of Eurasia: Handbook of Former Soviet Republics.* Phoenix: Oryx, 1997.

Bazhanov, Eugene, and Natasha Bazhanov. "The Evolution of Russian-Korea Relations." *Asian Survey* 34, no. 9 (1994): 794.

Bell, Imogen, ed. *Eastern Europe, Russia, and Central Asia 2003*. London: Europa, 2002.

Belousova, Ekaterina S. "Vneshnyaya Politika KNR: Novii Lider–Novii Kurs" [Chinese foreign policy: New leader–new course]. *Bulletin of the Chelyabinsk State University* 4, no. 343 (2014): 120.

Benediktov, Cyril, Alexander Kostin, Mikhail Remizov, Il'yas Sarsembayev, Rais Suleymanov, and Marat Shibutov. *"Immigraciya Kak Vizov Natsional'noi Bezopastnosti Rossii"* [Immigration as a challenge to Russian national security]. Institute of National Strategy, 2014. www.instrategy.ru/pdf/276/pdf.

Bennett, Andrew. *Condemned to Repetition? The Rise, Fall, and Reprise of Soviet-Russian Military Interventionism, 1973–1996*. Cambridge: MIT Press, 1999.

Bennett, Brian. *Last Dictatorship in Europe: Belarus under Lukashenko*. Oxford: Oxford University Press, 2011.

Berdzenishvili, N. A., V. D. Dondua, M. K. Dumbadze, G. A. Melikishvili, and S. A. Meskhia. *Istoriya Gruzii. S Drevneishix Vremen Do 60-x Godov XIX Veka* [History of Georgia: From the ancient times to 1860s]. Tbilisi, Georgia: State Publishing House of Educational-Pedagogical Literature, 1962.

Bergson, Abram. "Reliability and Usability of Soviet Statistics: A Summary Appraisal." *American Statistician* 7, no. 3 (1953): 13–16.

Bespalov, S. V. "Transnational'nii Islamskii Terrorism—Global'naya Problema" [Transnational Islamic terrorism—globalp]. *PolitBook* 3 (2012): 76.

Bethke Elshtain, Jean, ed. *Just War Theory*. New York: New York University Press, 1991.

Bibilunga, Nikolay V. "Raspad SSSR I Krizis Moldavskoi Gosudarstvennosti" [Dissolution of the Soviet Union and the crisis of Moldovan statehood]. *Rusin* 4 (2010): 116.

Bindi, Federiga. "European Union Foreign Policy: A Historical Overview." In *The Foreign Policy of the European Union: Assessing Europe's Role in the World*, ed. Federiga Bindi, 13–41. Washington DC: Brookings Institution Press, 2012.

Biryukova, Ol'ga A. "Sodrujestvo Nezavisimix Gosudarstv: Poisk Optimal'noi Modeli Integracii" [Commonwealth of Independent States: Search of optimal integration models]. *Vlast'* 8 (2008): 89.

Black, Joseph Laurence. *Russia Faces NATO Expansion: Bearing Gifts or Bearing Arms?* Lanham MD: Rowman and Littlefield, 2000.

———. *The Russian Presidency of Dmitry Medvedev, 2008–2012: The Next Step Forward or Merely a Time Out?* Milton Park UK: Routledge, 2014.

Bliakher, L. "Vozmozhen li Post-imperskii Proekt: Ot Vzaimnykh Pretenziy k Obschemu Buduschemu" [Is the post-imperial project possible: From mutual claims to common future]. *Politia* 48, no 1 (2008): 15.

Bobrov, Aleksandr A. "God Russkogo Yazika." *Russkii Dom* 2 (2007).

Boese, Wade. "CFE Compliance Report Issued; Treaty Adaptation Talks Continue." *Arms Control Today*, June/July 1998.

Bogomolov, Oleg. "CMEA and the Developing World." *International Affairs* 7 (1979): 32.

Bolukbasi, Suha. *Azerbaijan: A Political History*. London: I. B. Tauris, 2011.

"BP Statistical Review of World Energy." *British Petroleum*, June 2013, 6–7 and 20–22.

Bracamonte, José Angel Moroni, and David E. Spencer. *Strategy and Tactics of the Salvadoran FMLN Guerrillas: Last Battle of the Cold War, Blueprint for Future Conflicts.* Westport CT: Praeger, 1995.

Brandenberger, David. "Debate: Stalin's Populism and the Accidental Creation of Russian National Identity." *Nationalist Papers* 38, no. 5 (2010): 729.

Brands, Hal. *Latin America's Cold War.* Cambridge: Harvard University Press, 2012.

Braudel, Fernand. *Civilization and Capitalism, 15th–18th Century: The Perspective of the World.* Berkeley: University of California Press, 1992.

Brookes, Peter. *A Devil's Triangle: Terrorism, Weapons of Mass Destruction, and Rogue States.* Lanham: Rowman and Littlefield, 2005.

Brooks, Thom, ed. *Just War Theory.* Leiden, Netherlands: Koninklijke Brill NV, 2013.

Brubaker, Rogers. *Nationalism Reframed: Nationhood and the National Question in the New Europe.* Cambridge: Cambridge University Press, 1996.

———. "Nationhood and National Question in the Soviet Union and Post-Soviet Eurasia: An Institutional Account." *Theory and Society* 23, no. 1 (1994): 55–76.

Bruins, Jan J., and Henk A. M. Wilke. "Upward Power Tendencies in a Hierarchy: Power Distance Theory versus Bureaucratic Rule." *European Journal of Social Psychology* 23 (1993): 253.

Brzezinski, Zbigniew. *The Grand Chessboard: American Primacy and Its Geostrategic Imperatives.* New York: Basic, 1997.

———. "The Premature Partnership?" *Foreign Affairs* 73, no. 2 (1994): 67–82.

Bugajski, Janusz. *Cold Peace: Russia's New Imperialism.* Washington DC: Center for Strategic and International Studies, 2004.

Bull, Hedley, and Andrew Hurrell. *The Anarchical Society: A Study of Order in World Politics.* New York: Columbia University Press, 2012.

Burchill, Scott, Andrew Linklater, Richard Devetak, Jack Donnelly, Terry Nardin, Matthew Paterson, Christian Reus-Smit, and Jacqui True. *Theories of International Relations.* 4th ed. London: Palgrave Macmillan, 2009.

Burganova, I. N. "Scenarii Mezhgosudarstvennoi Integracii Na Post-Sovetskom Prostranstve v Ramkax SNG" [Scenarios of interstate integration in the former Soviet space within the CIS]. *Proceedings of the Herzen Russian State Pedagogical University* 22, no. 4 (2006): 27.

Burleson, Clyde. *Kursk Down: The Shocking True Story of the Sinking of a Russian Nuclear Submarine.* New York: Grand Central, 2002.

Buryak, Yurii N. "Protivodeistvie Nelegal'noi I Kriminal'noi Miracii v Deyatel'nosti FMS Rossii" [Countering illegal and criminal migration in the practice of FMS of Russia]. *Psycho-Pedagogy in Law Enforcement* 2 (2009): 7.

Busigina, Irina M., and Mikhail G. Filippov. "Evrosoyuz: Ot Chastnogo K Obshemu" [European Union: From specifics to generalizations]. *Russia in Global Politics* 8, no. 1 (2010): 121–33.

———. "Severnoe Izmerenie: Strategii Uchastnikov" [Northern dimension: Participant strategies]. *Baltic Region* 1 (2009): 1.

Byshok, Stanislav, Alexei Kochetkov, and Alexei Semenov. *Neonazis and Euromaidan: From Democracy to Dictatorship*. Translated by Anna E. Nikiforova. Charleston SC: CreateSpace, 2014.

Caldwell, Lawrence T. "Russian Concepts of National Security." In *Russian Foreign Policy in the Twenty-First Century and the Shadow of the Past*, ed. Robert Legvold, 279–342. New York: Columbia University Press, 2007.

Carment, David, and Frank Harvey. *Using Force to Prevent Ethnic Violence: An Evaluation of Theory and Evidence*. Westport CT: Praeger, 2001.

Casey-Maslen, Stuart. *The War Report: Armed Conflict in 2013*. Oxford: Oxford University Press, 2014.

Casier, Tom. "Russia's Energy Leverage over the EU: Myth or Reality." In *European Security Governance and the European Neighborhood after the Lisbon Treaty*, ed. Christian Kaunert and Sarah Leonard, 139–48. Milton Park, UK: Routledge, 2013.

Castells, Manuel. *The Power of Identity: The Information Age: Economy, Society, and Culture*. Vol. 2. Chichester, UK: Blackwell, 2010.

Catellani, Nicola. *The EU's Northern Dimension: Testing a New Approach to Neighbourhood Relations?* Swedish Institute of International Affairs. Stockholm, Sweden: Utrikespolitiska Institutet, 2003.

Čavusau, Jury. "Belarus' Civic Sector." In *Hopes, Illusions, Perspectives: Belarusian Society 2007*, ed. Marta Pejda. Warsaw, Poland, and Minsk, Belarus: East European Democratic Center, 2007.

Ceasar, James W. "The Origins and Character of American Exceptionalism." *American Political Thought: A Journal of Ideas, Institutions, and Culture* 1 (2012): 6.

Cerny, Philip G. *The Politics of Grandeur: Ideological Aspects of de Gaulle's Foreign Policy*. New York: Cambridge University Press, 1980.

Chaigneau, Pascal. *La Politique Militaire de la France en Afrique*. Paris: Éditions du Centre des Hautes Études sur l'Afrique et l'Asie Modernes, 1984.

Checkel, Jeffrey T. "Norms, Institutions, and National Identity in Contemporary Europe." *International Studies Quarterly* 43, no. 1 (1999): 83.

Chernov, Vladimir. "Formirovanie Sistemi Collektivnoi Bezopasnosti Post-Soveskikh Gosudarstv" [Creation of the collective security system of post-Soviet states]. *Power* 8 (2009): 98–99.

Chernyavsky, A. A. "Istochniki Razvitiya Ekonomiki Kitaya I Rossiisko-Kitaiskie Ekonomicheskie Otnosheniya" [Sources for development of the Chinese economy and Russia-China economic relations]. *World of Science, Culture, and Education* 3, no. 40 (2013): 417–18.

Chernyavsky, Stanislav. "Rossiya I Azerbaijan: Osobennosti I Osnovnie Napravleniya Mejgosudarstvennogo Sotrudnichestva V Post-Sovetskii Perion" [Russia and Azerbaijan: Particulars and main direction of intergovernmental cooperation in the post-Soviet period]. *Caucasus and Globalization* 1–2, no. 4 (2010): 37.

———. "SNG: Ot Istorii K Budushemu" [CIS: From history to the future]. *MGIMO University Bulletin* 6 (2011): 31.

Chilton, Stephen. "Defining Political Culture." *Western Political Quarterly* 41, no. 3 (1988): 431.

Chistov, Valery A. "Ekonomiki Razvivaushikhsya Rinkov V Usloviyax Mezhkrizisnoi Globalizacii" [Economics of development markets in the conditions of intercrisis globalization]. *Journal of St. Petersburg University of Economics and Finances* 1, no. 79 (2013): 137.

Christiano, Kevin J., William H. Swatos, and Peter Kivisto. *Sociology of Religion: Contemporary Developments.* Lanham MD: Rowman and Littlefield, 2008.

Christou, George. "European Union Security Logic to the East: The European Neighborhood Policy and Eastern Partnership." In *European 'Security' Governance*, ed. George Christou and Stuart Croft, 77–95. Milton Park, UK: Routledge, 2012.

Clarke, Simon. "Culture and Identity." In *The SAGE Handbook of Cultural Analysis*, ed. Tony Bennett and John Frow. London: SAGE, 2008.

Clausewitz, Carl von. *On War.* Edited and translated by Michael Howard and Pater Paret. Princeton: Princeton University Press, 1989.

Clinton, Hillary R. *Hard Choices.* New York: Simon & Schuster, 2014.

Clowes, Edith W. *Russia on the Edge: Imagined Geographies and Post-Soviet Identity.* Ithaca NY: Cornell University Press, 2011.

Columbus, Frank, ed. *Russia in Transition.* Vol. 1. New York: Nova Science, 2008.

Commonwealth of Independent States Industry (International Business Publications USA, 2013).

Conquest, Robert. *The Harvest of Sorrow: Soviet Collectivization and the Terror-Famine.* Oxford: Oxford University Press, 1986.

Cooper, Orah, and Carol Fogarty. "Soviet Economic and Military Aid to the Less Developed Countries, 1954–78." *Soviet and Eastern European Foreign Trade* 21, nos. 1–3 (Spring–Fall 1985): 65.

Cooper, Julian. "Russia." In *Cascade of Arms: Managing Conventional Weapons Proliferation*, ed. Andrew J. Pierre, 173–201. Cambridge: World Press Foundation, 1997.

Coppieters, Bruno, and Robert Legvold, eds. *Statehood and Security: Georgia after the Rose Revolution.* Cambridge: MIT Press, 2005.

Cordesman, Anthony H. *Energy Developments in the Middle East.* Washington DC: Center for Strategic and International Studies, 2004.

———. *Israel and Syria: The Military Balance and Prospects of War.* Washington DC: Center for Strategic and International Studies, 2008.

———. *A Tragedy of Arms: Military and Security Developments in the Maghreb.* Westport CT: Praeger, 2002.

Cordesman, Anthony H., and Khalid R. Al-Rodhan. *Iranian Nuclear Weapons? The Options If Diplomacy Fails.* Washington DC: Center for Strategic and International Studies, 2006.

Cordesman, Anthony H., Bryan Gold, and Chloe Coughlin-Schulte. *Iran: Sanctions, Energy, Arms Control, and Regime Change.* Washington DC: Center for Strategic and Security Studies, 2014.

Cordesman, Anthony H., Aram Nerguizian, and Inout C. Popescu. *Israel and Syria: The Military Balance and Prospects of War.* Washington DC: Center for Strategic and International Studies, 2008.

Courtois, Stéphane, Nicholas Werth, Jean-Louis Panné, Andrzej Paczkowski, Karel Bartosek, and Jean-Louis Margolin. *The Black Book of Communism: Crimes, Terror, Repression.* Translated by Jonathan Murphy and Mark Kramer. Cambridge: Harvard University Press, 1999.

Cox, Craig. *The Soviet Takeover of Latvia: How Riga's Russian-Language Newspapers Chronicled Latvia's Occupation and Sovetization in 1940.* Amazon Digital Services, 2014. Kindle ed.

Cracraft, James. *The Revolution of Peter the Great.* Cambridge: Harvard University Press, 2003.

Cracraft, James, and Daniel Rowland, eds. *Architectures of Russian Identity, 1500 to the Present.* Ithaca NY: Cornell University Press, 2003.

Crane, Keith, et al. *Russian Foreign Policy: Sources and Implications.* Santa Monica: RAND, 2009.

Cresson, William Penn. *The Cossacks: Their History and Country.* Norwood MA: Plimpton, 1919.

Croissant, Michael P. *The Armenia-Azerbaijan Conflict: Causes and Implications.* Santa Barbara: Praeger, 1998.

Cross, Samuel Hazzard, and Olgerd P. Sherbowitz-Wetzor. *The Russian Primary Chronicle: Laurentian Text.* Cambridge: Medieval Academy of America, 2012.

Curtis, Glenn E. *Armenia, Azerbaijan, and Georgia: Country Studies.* Charleston SC: CreateSpace, 2013.

Custine, Astolphe, Marquis de. *La Rusiie en 1839* [Russia in 1839]. Translated by Vera A. Mil'china. Moscow: Sabashnikov's, 1996.

Daddow, Oliver. *International Relations Theory: The Essentials.* London: SAGE, 2013.

D'Agostino, Anthony. *Soviet Succession Struggles: Kremlinology and the Russian Question from Lenin to Gorbachev.* New York: HarperCollins, 1988.

Dailey, Erika. *Human Rights in Moldova: The Turbulent Dniester.* Washington DC: Human Rights Watch, 1993.

D'Anieri, Paul J. *International Politics: Power and Purpose in Global Affairs.* Boston: Wadsworth, Cengage Learning, 2014.

———, ed. *Orange Revolution and Aftermath: Mobilization, Apathy, and the State in Ukraine.* Baltimore: Johns Hopkins University Press, 2010.

Danilov, Dmitry. "Dogovor O Evropeiskoi Bezopasnosti V Kontexte Treugol'nika EC-SSHA-NATO" [European Security Treaty in the context of the EU-USA-NATO triangle]. *Security Index* 3, no. 94 (2010): 73.

Danilovich, Alex. *Russian-Belarusian Integration: Playing Games behind the Kremlin Walls.* Burlington VT: Ashgate, 2006.

Danks, Catherine. *Politics Russia.* Milton Park, UK: Routledge, 2013. Kindle ed.

Dave, Bhavna. *Kazakhstan: Ethnicity, Language, and Power.* Milton Park, UK: Routledge, 2007.

Deaux, Kay. "Social Identity." In *Encyclopedia of Women and Gender: Sex Similarities and Differences and the Impact of Society on Gender.* San Diego: Academic Press, 2001.

de Haas, Marcel. "Medvedev's Alternative European Security Architecture." *Security and Human Rights* 21, no. 1 (March 2010): 47.

———. "Russia's Military Doctrine Development (2000–10)." In *Russian Military Politics and Russia's 2010 Defense Doctrine*, ed. Steven J. Blank, 1–62. Carlisle PA: Strategic Studies Institute, U.S. Army War College Press, 2011.

de Jouvenel, Renaud. *Tito—Boss of Traitors.* Moscow: Inostrannaya Literatura, 1951.

Deutsch, Karl W. "External Involvement in Internal Wars." In *Internal War: Problems and Approaches*, ed. Harry Eckstein, 100–110. New York: Free Press of Glencoe, 1964.

de Vattel, Emmerich. *The Law of Nations; or, Principles of the Law of Nature Applied to the Conduct and Affairs of Nations and Sovereigns.* London: G. G. and J. Robinson, 1797.

de Waal, Thomas. *Black Garden: Armenia and Azerbaijan through Peace and War.* New York: New York University Press, 2003.

Dickinson, Anna. "Quantifying Religious Oppression: Russian Orthodox Church Closures and Repression of Priests, 1917–41." *Religion, State & Society* 28, no. 4 (2000): 330.

Ditmer, Lowell. "Political Culture and Political Symbolism: Toward a Theoretical Synthesis." *World Politics* 29 (1977): 566.

Dolenko, Dmitry V., Zhana D. Konichenko, and Alexey V. Petukhov. "SNG Kak Prioritet Rossii" (CIS as Russia's priority). *Social-Political Science* 1 (2012): 135.

Dolot, Miron. *Execution by Hunger: The Hidden Holocaust.* New York: W. W. Norton, 1987.

Donaldson, Robert H., and Joseph L. Nogee. *Foreign Policy of Russia: Changing Systems, Enduring Interests.* 4th ed. New York: M. E. Sharpe, 2009.

Donaldson, Robert H., Joseph L. Nogee, and Vidya Nadkarni. *Foreign Policy of Russia: Changing Systems, Enduring Interests.* Armonk NY: M. E. Sharpe, 2014.

Donnan, Hastings, and Thomas M. Wilson. *Borders: Frontiers of Identity, Nation, and State.* New York: Berg, 1999.

Donnelly, Jack. *Realism and International Relations.* Cambridge: Cambridge University Press, 2000.

Dostoyevsky, Fyodor. *Crime and Punishment.* Translated by Constance Garnett. New York: Cosimo, 2008.

———. *A Writer's Diary (Volume 1: 1873–1876).* Translated by Kenneth Lantz. Evanston IL: Northwestern University Press, 1994.

Dowling, Timothy C., ed. *Russia at War: From the Mongol Conquest to Afghanistan, Chechnya, and Beyond.* Santa Barbara CA: ABC-CLIO, 2015.

Doyle, Michael W. *Ways of War and Peace: Realism, Liberalism, and Socialism.* New York: W. W. Norton, 1997.

Drezner, Daniel W. *The Sanctions Paradox: Economic Statecraft and International Relations*. Cambridge: Cambridge University Press, 1999.

Drozdov, U. A., and A. G. Markin. *Operaciya "Prezident": Ot Xolodnoi Voini Do Peregruzki* [Operation "President": From the Cold War to the reset]. Moscow: Artstil-Poligrafiya, 2010.

Drury, A. Cooper. "Sanctions as Coercive Diplomacy: The U.S. President's Decision to Initiate Economic Sanctions." *Political Research Quarterly* 54, no. 3 (2001): 489.

Dugin, Alexander. *The Fourth Political Theory*. London: Arktos Media, 2009, 2012.

———. "Geopolitika Novorossii: Spasti Putina" [Geopolitics of Novorossiya: Save Putin]. *Okhranka*, September 30, 2014, http://ohranka.com/2014/09/геополитика-новороссии-спасти-путин/.

———. "Strashnaya Pauza" [A frightening pause], *Pravdinform*, June 16, 2014, http://trueinform.ru/modules.php?name=News&file=print&sid=27941.

———. "We Have to Capture Europe, Conquer Her, and Annex Her." *Snob*, March 13, 2014, http://snob.ru/profile/6090/blog/73552#comment_703769.

———. *Theory of Multipolar World*. Moscow: Eurasian Movement, 2013.

Dum-Tragut, Jasmine. *Armenian: Modern Eastern Armenian*. Amsterdam, Netherlands: John Benjamins, 2009.

Dunlop, John B. "The August 2008 Russo-Georgian War: Which Side Went First?" In *Russia and Its Near Neighbours*, ed. Maria Raquel Freire and Roger E. Kanet, 89–108. Basingstoke UK: Palgrave Macmillan, 2012.

Dutkiewicz, Piotr, and Richard Sakwa, eds. *Eurasian Integration: The View from Within*. Milton Park UK: Routledge, 2014.

Edwards, Paul M. *The Korean War*. Westport CT: Greenwood Press, 2006.

Elleman, Bruce A., Michael R. Nichols, and Matthew J. Ouimet. "A Historical Reevaluation of America's Role in the Kuril Islands Dispute." *Pacific Affairs* 71 (1998): 489–504.

Ellemers, Naomi, Russell Spears, and Bertjan Doosje. "Self and Social Identity." *Annual Review of Psychology* 53 (2002): 161–86.

Ellison, Herbert J. *Boris Yeltsin and Russia's Democratic Transformation*. Seattle: University of Washington Press, 2006.

Engelbrekt, Kjell, and Jan Hallenberg, eds. *European Union and Strategy: An Emerging Actor*. Milton Park UK: Routledge, 2008.

Ericson, Edward E., III. *Feeding the German Eagle: Soviet Economic Aid to Nazi Germany, 1933–1941*. Westport CT: Praeger, 1999.

Eriksson, Mikael. *Targeting Peace: Understanding UN and EU Targeted Sanctions*. Burlington VT: Ashgate, 2011.

Erwan, Lannon, and Peter Van Elsuwege. "The EU's Northern Dimension and the EMP-ENP: Institutional Frameworks and Decision-Making Processes Compared." In *The European Union and the Mediterranean: The Mediterranean's European Challenge*, ed. P. G. Xuereb et al., 5:3–70. Msida: EDRC, University of Malta, 2004.

Esakova, Nataliya. *European Energy Security: Analysing the EU-Russia Energy Security Regime in Terms of Interdependence Theory*. Frankfurt: Springer, 2012.

Evans, Peter. "Development as Institutional Change: The Pitfalls of Monocropping and the Potentials of Deliberation." *Studies in Comparative International Development* 38, no. 4 (Winter 2004): 33.

Ewans, Martin. *The Great Game: A Narrative of the Russian Military Expedition to Khiva in 1839*. Vol. 3. Calcutta: Office of Superintendent Government, 1867.

———. *The Great Game: Britain and Russia in Central Asia*. London: RoutledgeCurzon, 2003.

Ezhiev, Isa. "Geopoliticheskie Aspekti Etnopoliticheskix Confliktov V Kavkazsko-Kaspiiskom Regione" [Geopolitical aspects of ethnopolitical conflicts in the region of Caucasus]. *Power* 8 (2007): 40.

Fang, Tien-sze. "The Past, Prospects and the Problems of Forming the 'Chindia' Alliance." In *India and China in the Emerging Dynamics of East Asia*, ed. G. V. C. Naidu, Mumin Chen, and Raviprasad Narayanan, 75–88. New Delhi: Springer India, 2015.

Fantini, Marco. "The Economic Relationship between Russia and the EU: History and Prospects." In *Russia and Europe in the Twenty-First Century: An Uneasy Partnership*, ed. Jackie Gower and Graham Timmins, 247–66. London: Anthem, 2009.

Farmer, Brian R. *Radical Islam in the West: Ideology and Challenge*. Jefferson NC: McFarland, 2010.

Fawn, Rick, and Robert Nalbandov. "The Difficulties of Knowing the Start of War in the Information Age: Russia, Georgia, and the War over South Ossetia, August 2008." In *Georgia: Revolution and War*, ed. Rick Fawn. Milton Park: Routledge, 2013.

Fearon, James D. "Commitment Problems and the Spread of Ethnic Conflict." In *The International Spread of Ethnic Conflict*, ed. David A. Lake and Donald Rothchild, 107–26. Princeton: Princeton University Press, 1998.

Fedorov, Alexei V. "Dve Morali" (Two morals). *Russian Academic Journal* 1, no. 23 (2013): 46.

Fedorov, Yuri F. "Gosudarstvennaya Programma Voorujenii-2020: Vlast' I Promishlennost" [State armament program 2020: Government and industry]. *Security index* #4 (107), vol. 19 (2013): 41.

———. "The Return of History: Hard Security Issues in the Russia-Europe Relationship." In *Russia and Europe: Building Bridges, Digging Trenches*, ed. Kjell Engelbrekt and Bertil Nygre, 103–31. Milton Park UK: Routledge, 2010.

Feinstein, Andrew. *The Shadow World: Inside the Global Arms Trade*. New York: Picador, 2012.

Feng, Yi. "Democracy, Political Stability, and Economic Growth." *British Journal of Political Science* 27, no. 3 (1997): 398.

Fenwick, Charles G. "Intervention: Individual and Collective." *American Journal of International Law* 39, no. 4 (1945): 663.

Figes, Orlando. *Natasha's Dance: A Cultural History of Russia*. New York: Picador, 2003.

———. *A People's Tragedy: The Russian Revolution, 1891–1924*. New York: Penguin Books, 1998.

Finnemore, Martha, and Kathryn Sikkink. "International Norm Dynamics and Political Change." *International Organization* 52, no. 4 (1998): 897.

Fituni, Leonid L. "Afrika v Sovremennoi Mirovoi Sisteme Torgovli" [Africa in the modern global system of trade]. *Problems of Contemporary Economics* 3, no. 47 (2013): 153.

Florovsky, George. *Iz Proshlogo Russkoi Misli* [From the Past of the Russian Thought]. Moscow: UAgrafF, 1998).

Francis, David J. *Uniting Africa: Building Regional Peace and Security Systems*. Milton Park UK: Routledge, 2006.

Frellesen, Thomas, and Rontoyanni, Clelia. "EU-Russia Political Relations: Negotiating the Common Spaces." In *Russia and Europe in the Twenty-First Century: An Uneasy Partnership*, ed. Jackie Gower and Graham Timmins, 229–47. London: Anthem Press, 2009.

Frolova, Elena I. "Rossiya V Sisteme Evropeiskoi Bezopasnosti" [Russia in the system of European security]. *Power* 1 (2008): 55.

Frolova-Walker, Marina. "National in Form, Socialist in Content: Musical Nation-Building in the Soviet Republics." *Journal of the American Musicological Society* 51, no. 2 (1998): 331–71.

Fukuyama, Francis. *The End of History and the Last Man*. New York: Free Press, 2006.

Gachechiladze, Revaz. *The New Georgia: Space, Society, Politics*. College Station: Texas A&M University Press, 1996.

Gadjiev, Kamaludin S. *Geopolitika Kavkaza* [Caucasian geopolitics]. Moscow: International Relations, 2003.

Gaidar, Yegor. *Collapse of an Empire: Lessons for Modern Russia*. Translated by Antonina W. Bouis. Washington DC: Brookings Institution Press, 2007.

Galeotti, Mark. *Afghanistan, the Soviet Union's Last War*. Milton Park UK: Routledge, 2001.

Galtung, Johan. "Institutionalized Conflict Resolution: A Theoretical Paradigm." *Journal of Peace Research* 2, no. 4 (1965): 348.

Gandolfo, Giancarlo. *International Economics I: The Pure Theory of International Trade*. Wiesbaden, Germany: Springer, 1994.

Gardner, Hall. *NATO Expansion and the U.S. Strategy in Asia: Surmounting the Global Crisis*. New York: Palgrave Macmillan, 2013.

Garver, John W. *Chinese-Soviet Relations, 1937–1945: The Diplomacy of Chinese Nationalism*. New York: Oxford University Press, 1988.

Gatherer, Derek. "Comparison of Eurovision Song Contest Simulation with Actual Results Reveals Shifting Patterns of Collusive Voting Alliances." *Journal of Artificial Societies and Social Simulation* 9, no. 2 (2006): 1.

Gelashvili, Nana. "Iranskaya Problema na Fone Ukhudsheniya Rossiisko-Amerikanskix Otnoshenii" [Iranian problem on the background of deteriorating Russian-American relations]. *Caucasus and Globalization* 2, no. 2 (2008): 39.

Gelbras, Vilya G. *Rossiya V Usloyakh Global'noi Migratsii* [Russia in the situation of global migration]. Moscow: Muravei, 2004.

Gellner, Ernest. *Nations and Nationalism*. Ithaca NY: Cornell University Press, 1983.

Gessen, Masha. *The Man without a Face: The Unlikely Rise of Vladimir Putin*. New York: Riverhead Books, 2013.

Getty, J. Arch, Oleg V. Naumov, and Benjamin Sher. *The Road to Terror: Stalin and the Self-Destruction of the Bolsheviks, 1932–1939*. New Haven: Yale University Press, 2010.

Ghebali, Victor-Yves. "Where Is the OSCE Going? Present Role and Challenges of a Stealth Security Organization." In *European Security in a Global Context: Internal and External Dynamics*, ed. Thierry Tardy, 55–73. Milton Park UK: Routledge, 2008.

Gibson, James L. "Becoming Tolerant? Short-Term Changes in Russian Political Culture." *British Journal of Political Science* 32, no. 2 (2002): 309–34.

Gilpin, Robert. *War and Change in World Politics*. Cambridge: Cambridge University Press 1981.

Ginsberg, Roy H. *The European Union in International Politics: Baptism by Fire*. Lanham MD: Rowman and Littlefield, 2001.

Glaser, Charles L. "The Security Dilemma Revised." *World Politics* 50, no. 1 (October 1997): 183.

Glaz'yev, Sergei. *Genocide: Russia and the New World Order*. A Strategy for Economic Growth on the Threshold of the 21st Century. Translated by Rachel B. Douglas. Washington DC: Executive Intelligence Review, 1999.

Glaz'yev, Sergey. "Kak Dobit'sya Ekonomicheskogo Rosta?" [How to achieve economic growth?] *Russian Economic Journal*, nos. 5–7 (1996).

Gleason, Gregory. "Relationship with Central Asia." In *Return to Putin's Russia: Past Imperfect, Future Uncertain*, ed. Stephen K. Wegren, 257–76. Plymouth UK: Rowman and Littlefield, 2013.

Goffman, Erving. *The Presentation of Self in Everyday Life*. London: Penguin, 1969.

Goldman, David. *How Civilizations Die (And Why Islam Is Dying Too)*. Washington DC: Regnery, 2011.

Goldman, Marshall. "The Russian Ruble and Why It Collapsed." *Challenge* 41, no. 6 (1998): 12.

Goldmann, Kjell. "Appropriateness and Consequences: The Logic of Neo-Institutionalism." *Governance: An International Journal of Policy, Administration, and Institutions* 18 (2005): 44.

Goldstone, Jack A. "Pathways to State Failure." *Conflict Management and Peace Science* 25 (2008): 285.

Golenkova, Zinaida T., and Alexandr E. Eremeev. "Evraziistvo Kak Geographicheskaya Ideologiya" [Eurasianism as geographic ideology]. *Bulletin of the Tyumen State University* 4 (2009): 40.

Goodby, James E., Vladimir I. Ivanov, and Nobuo Shimotomai. *Northern Territories and Beyond: Russian, Japanese, and American Perspectives*. Westport: Praeger, 1995.

Gramsci, Antonio. *Selections from the Prison Notebooks*. Cambridge: Cambridge University Press, 1971.

Gray, Colin S. *The Geopolitics of Super Power*. Lexington: University Press of Kentucky, 1988.

Greenfield, Liah. "Types of European Nationalism." In *Nationalism*, ed. John Hutchinson and Anthony D. Smith, 165–70. Oxford: Oxford University Press, 1994.

Gregory, Paul R. *Terror by Quota: State Security from Lenin to Stalin*. New Haven: Yale University Press, 2009.

Grey, Robert D. "The Soviet Presence in Africa: An Analysis of Goals." *Journal of Modern African Studies* 22, no. 3 (1984): 511.

Guriev, Sergei, Anders Aslund, and Andrew Kuchins. *Russia after the Global Economic Crisis*. Washington DC: Peter G. Peterson Institute for International Economics, 2010.

Gurvich, E. T. "Makroekonomicheskaya Otsenka Roli Rossiyskogo Neftegazovogo Sektora" [Macroeconomic assessment of the role of the Russian oil and gas sector]. *Issues of Economics* 10 (2004): 10 and 14.

Gutmann, Amy, and Dennis Thompson. *Why Deliberative Democracy?* Princeton: Princeton University Press, 2004.

Gvosdev, Nikolas K., and Christopher Marsh. *Russian Foreign Policy: Interests, Vectors, and Sectors*. Thousand Oaks CA: CQ Press, 2013.

Gyorkei, Jeno, Alexandr Kirov, and Miklos Horvath, eds. *Soviet Military Intervention in Hungary, 1956*. Budapest: Central European University Press, 1999.

Habermas, Jürgen. "Popular Sovereignty as Procedure." In *Deliberative Democracy: Essays on Reason and Politics*, ed. James Bohman and William Rehg, 35–66. Boston: MIT Press, 1997.

Hagenloh, Paul. *Stalin's Police: Public Order and Mass Repression in the USSR, 1926–1941*. Baltimore: Johns Hopkins University Press, 2009.

Hahn, Jeffrey W. "Continuity and Change in Russian Political Culture." *British Journal of Political Science* 21, no. 4 (1991): 393–421.

Haiduk, Kiryl. "Social Contract: A Conceptual Framework." In *Social Contracts in Contemporary Belarus*, ed. Kiryl Haiduk, Elena Rakova, and Vital Silitski, 8–25. Minsk, Belarus: Belarusian Institute for Strategic Studies, 2009.

Haitun, A. D. *Energetichskaya Politika Rossii Na Evropeiskom Kontinente* [Energy politics of Russia on the European continent]. Moscow: Russian Academy of Sciences, 2008.

Hale, Henry E. "The Parade of Sovereignties: Testing Theories of Secession in the Soviet Setting." *British Journal of Political Science* 30, no. 1 (2000): 31–56.

———. *Patronal Politics: Eurasian Regime Dynamics in Comparative Perspective*. New York: Cambridge University Press, 2015.

Hanley, Jerome. "Beyond the Tip of the Iceberg: Five Stages toward Cultural Competence." *Reaching Today's Youth* 3, no. 2 (1999): 9–12.

Hart, Robert A., Jr. "Democracy and the Successful Use of Economic Sanctions." *Political Research Quarterly* 53, no. 2 (2000): 267–68.

Hartley, Janet M. *Siberia: A History of the People*. New Haven: Yale University Press, 2014.

Hatcher, Lynley. "Script Change in Azerbaijan: Acts of Identity." In *International Journal of the Sociology of Language* 192 (2008): 106.

Hechter, Michael, and Satoshi Kanazawa, "Sociological Rational Choice Theory." *Annual Review of Sociology* 23 (1997): 193–94.

Hedlund, Stefan. "Russia and the IMF: A Sordid Tale of Moral Hazard." *Demokratizatsiya* 9, no. 1 (2001): 109.

Heenan, Patrick, and Monique Lamontagne. *The CIS Handbook: Prospects onto the 21st Century*. Chicago: Fitzroy Dearborn, 1999.

Heikka, Henrikki. "Beyond Neorealism and Constructivism: Desire, Identity, and Russian Foreign Policy." In *Understanding of Russian Foreign Policy*, ed. Ted Hopf, 57–107. University Park: Penn State University Press, 1999.

Hernández i Sagrera, Raül, and Olga Potemkina. "Russia and the Common Space on Freedom, Security, and Justice." *CEPS Paper in Liberty and Security in Europe* 54 (February 2013).

Herpen, Van. *Putin's Wars: The Rise of Russia's New Imperialism*. Lanham MD: Rowman and Littlefield, 2014.

Herz, John H. "Idealist Internationalism and the Security Dilemma." *World Politics* 2 (1950): 171–201.

Hicks, Alexander. "Is Political Sociology Informed by Political Science?" *Social Force* 73, no. 4 (1995): 1221.

Hobbes, Thomas. *Leviathan*. Harmondsworth UK: Penguin Classic, 1968.

———. *Leviathan*. New York: Digireads, 2009.

Hofstede, Geert. *Cultures and Organizations: Software of the Mind*. 3rd ed. New York: McGraw-Hill, 2010.

Högselius, Per. *Red Gas: Russia and the Origins of European Energy Dependence*. New York: Palgrave Macmillan, 2013.

Hollander, Paul, ed. *From the Gulag to the Killing Fields: Personal Accounts of Political Violence and Repression in Communist States*. Wilmington DE: Intercollegiate Studies Institute, 2007.

Horowitz, Donald L. *Ethnic Groups in Conflict*. Berkeley: University of California Press, 1985.

Horvath, Robert. *Putin's Preventative Counter-Revolution: Post-Soviet Authoritarianism and the Spectre of Velvet Revolution*. Milton Park UK: Routledge, 2013.

Hovannisian, Richard G. *The Republic of Armenia*. Vol. 4: *Between Crescent and Sickle-Partition and Sovietization*. Berkeley: University of California Press, 1996.

Hudson, George E. "Soviet Arms Policy towards Black Africa: Opportunities and Constraints." In *The Gun Merchants: Politics and Policies of the Major Arms Suppliers*, ed. Cindy Cannizzo, 49–67. New York: Pergamon, 1980.

Hufbauer, Gary Clyde, Jeffrey J. Schott, Kimberly Ann Elliott, and Barbara Oegg. *Economic Sanctions Reconsidered*. 3rd ed. Washington DC: Peter G. Peterson Institute for International Economics, 2008.

Huntington, Samuel P. *The Clash of Civilizations and the Remaking of World Order.* New York: Simon and Schuster, 2011.

Hutten, Kurt. *Iron Curtain Christians: The Church in Communist Countries Today.* Minneapolis: Augsburg, 1967.

Ikenberry, John, and Charles Kupchan. "Socialization and Hegemonic Power." *International Organization* 44, no. 3 (1990): 287–88.

Il'ev, A.Ya., et al. *Geologo-geofizichyeskaya Kharakteristika I Peerspektivi Neftegazonosnosti Sredinno-Kuril'skogo Progiba* [Geological and geophysical characteristics and petroleum potential of the mid-Kuril bend]. Vladivostok, Russia: Dal'nauka, 2009.

Ipek, Pinar. "Challenges for Democracy in Central Asia: What Can the United States Do?" *Middle East Policy* 14, no. 1 (2007): 102.

Isingarin, Nigmatzhan K. *Problemi Integracii V CNG* [Problems of integration in the CIS]. Almati, Kazakhstan: Amatura, 1998.

Ismailzade, Fariz, and Kevin Rosner. *Russia's Energy Interests in Azerbaijan.* London: GMB, 2006.

Izotov, Mikhail A., and Arutyun A. Khachaturyan. "Sostoyanie I Perspektivi Razvitiya Voenno-Tekhnicheskogo Sotrudnichestva Gosugarstv-Chlenov Organizacii Dogoovra O Kollektivnoi Bezopastnosti" [Current state and prospects of development of military-technical cooperation between member states of the Collective Security Treaty Organization]. *Armiya I Obshestvo* [Army and society] 4 (2007): 74.

Jaspers, Karl. *The Question of German Guilt.* 2nd ed. Translated by E. B. Ashton. New York: Fordham University Press, 2001.

Jeffries, Ian. *Economic Developments in Contemporary Russia.* Milton Park UK: Routledge, 2011.

———. *Political Developments in Contemporary Russia.* Milton Park UK: Routledge, 2011.

Jenne, Erin K. "A Bargaining Theory of Minority Demands: Explaining the Dog That Didn't Bite in 1990 Yugoslavia." *International Studies Quarterly* 48, no. 4 (2004): 729–54.

Jervis, Robert. "Cooperation under the Security Dilemma." *World Politics* 30 (1978): 167–241.

Johns, Michael. "Russia-European Union Relations after 2012: Good, Bad, Indifferent?" In *Russia after 2012: From Putin to Medvedev to Putin—Continuity, Change, or Revolution?* ed. J. L. Black and Michael Johns, 153–66. Milton Park UK: Routledge, 2013.

Johnson, Debra. "EU-Russia Energy Links." In *Perspectives on EU-Russia Relations*, ed. Debra Johnson and Paul Robinson, 164–82. Milton Park UK: Routledge, 2005.

Johnson, Matthew Raphael. *The Third Rome: Holy Russia, Tsarism, and Orthodoxy.* Atlanta: Foundation for Economic Liberty, 2004.

Johnson, Rob. *Oil, Islam, and Conflict: Central Asia since 1945.* London: Reaktion Books, 2007.

Johnston, Alastair Iain. "Thinking about Strategic Culture." *International Security* 19, no. 4 (1995): 41.

Joireman, Sandra. *Nationalism and Political Identity.* London: Continuum, 2003.

Joo, Seung-Ho. "Russia and North Korea: Nuclear Proliferation and Power Transition." In *North Korea and Security Cooperation in Northeast Asia*, ed. Tae-Hwan Kwak and Seung-Ho Joo, 199–218. Burlington VT: Ashgate, 2014.

Jukes, Geoffrey. *The Soviet Union in Asia*. Berkeley: University of California Press, 1973.

Kakachia, Korneli. "Energeticheskaya Bezopasnost V Svete Rossiisko-Gruzinskoi Voini: Posledstviya Dlya Centralnogo Kavkaza" [Energy security in the light of the Russian-Georgian qar: Consequences for the Central Caucasus]. *Caucasus and Globalization* 3, no. 4 (2009): 76.

Kant, Immanuel. *Perpetual Peace: A Philosophical Essay*. Translated by Benjamin F. Trueblood. New York: American Peace Society: 1897.

———. *Perpetual Peace and Other Essays on Politics, History, and Morals*. Translated by Ted Humphrey. Indianapolis: Hackett, 1983.

Kantor, Yulia. *Zaklyataya druzhba: Sekretnoye sotrudnichestvo SSSR i Germanii v 1920–1930-ye gody* [Curse of friendship: Secret cooperation between the USSR and Germany in 1920–1930]. St. Petersburg: Piter, 2009.

Karabayeva, K. D. "Fenomen Evraziistva Kak Poisk Garmonii" [Phenomenon of Eurasianism as the quest for harmony]. *Bulletin of the Orenburg State University* 4 (2009): 4.

Karagiannis, Emmanuel. *Energy and Security in the Caucasus*. London: Routledge-Curzon, 2002.

———. *Political Islam in Central Asia: The Challenge of Hizb Ut-Tahrir*. Milton Park UK: Routledge, 2010.

Katchanovski, Ivan. *Cleft Countries: Regional Political Divisions and Cultures in Post-Soviet Ukraine and Moldova*. Stuttgart: Ibidem Press, 2014.

Kato, Mihoko. "Japan and Russia at the Beginning of the Twenty-First Century: New Dimensions to Maritime Security Surrounding the 'Kuril Islands.'" *UNISCI Discussion Papers* 32 (2013): 210–11.

Kaufmann, Chaim. "Possible and Impossible Solutions to Ethnic Civil Wars." In *Nationalism and Ethnic Conflict*, ed. Michael Brown, Owen R. Coté Jr., Sean M. Lynn-Jones, and Steven E. Miller, 265–304. Cambridge: MIT Press, 1997.

Kaufmann, D., A. Kraay, and M. Mastruzzi. "The Worldwide Governance Indicators: Methodology and Analytical Issues." World Bank Policy Research Working Paper no. 5430 (2010).

Kaushik, Devendra. "Changing Perspective of India-Russia Relations." In *New Trends in Indo-Russian Relations*, ed. V. D. Chopra, 91–100. New Delhi: Kalpaz, 2003.

Kavkaz, Yuzhnii. *Tendencii I Problem Razvitiya 1992–2008* [Tendencies and problems of development, 1992–2008]. Moscow: Krasnaya Zvezda, 2008.

Kazantsev, Andrei. "Russian Policy in Central Asia and the Caspian Sea Region." In *Power and Policy in Putin's Russia*, ed. Richard Sakwa. Milton Park UK: Routledge, 2011.

Kazantsev, V. G., V. G. Ignato, and V. P. Chichkanov et al. *Vertikal' Vlasti: Problemy Ukrepleniya Rossiyskoy Gosudarstvennosti v Sovremennykh Usloviyakh* [Vertical of Power: The Challenges to Strengthening Russian Statehood under Modern Conditions]. Rostov-na-Donu, Russia: North Caucasus Academy of State Service, 2001.

Keating, Michael F. "Asia Catches Cold, Russia Sneezes: The Political Economy of Emerging Market Crises in 1997–98." In *The Politics of International Political Economy: A Survey*, ed. Vassilis K. Fouskas, 95–118. Milton Park UK: Routledge, 2015.

Kembayev, Zhanis. *Legal Aspects of the Regional Integration Processes in the Post-Soviet Area*. Berlin: Springer, 2009.

Kemp, Geoffrey, and John Allen Gay. *War with Iran: Political, Military, and Economic Consequences*. Lanham MD: Rowman and Littlefield, 2013.

Keohane, Robert O., and Joseph S. Nye. *Power and Interdependence: World Politics in Transition*. New York: Little, Brown, 1977.

———. *Power and Interdependence*. 4th ed. Longman Classics in Political Science. New York: Pearson, 2011.

Kesey, Ken. *One Flew Over the Cuckoo's Nest*. New York: Signet, 1962.

Kharitonova, N. I. "Pridnestrov'e: Voina I Peremirie" [Transdnistria: War and armistice]. *New Historical Journal* 17 (2008): 191.

Kim, Valery S. "Kitai I Vopros Rasshireniya NATO Na Vostok" [China and the NATO eastward expansion]. *Bulletin of the Chelyabinsk State University* 40 (2009): 86.

Kim, Vilen V. "Politicheskie Aspekti Vozmozhnix Putei Uregulirovaniya Problemi Koreiskogo Poluostrova" [Political aspects of possible resolution of the problem of the Korean Peninsula]. *Bulletin of the Chelyabinsk State University* 13 (2008): 122.

King, Richard, ed. *Heroes of China's Great Leap Forward: Two Stories*. Honolulu: University of Hawaii Press, 2010.

Kipp, Jacob. "Russian Military Doctrine: Past, Present, and Future." In *Russian Military Politics and Russia's 2010 Defense Doctrine*, ed. Steven J. Blank, 63–152. Carlisle PA: Strategic Studies Institute, U.S. Army War College Press, 2011.

Klomegah, Keser Kenn. "Russia and Arms Sales to Africa." *African Executive* 27 (April 2013): 3.

Klotz, Audie, and Cecelia Lynch. *Strategies for Research in Constructivist International Relations*. New York: M. E. Sharpe, 2007.

Kluchevsky, Valisii O. "Readings in Russian History," lecture 42. St. Petersburg, 1904.

———. *Works in 9 Volumes*. Vol. 1: *Russian History*. Moscow: Misl', 1987.

Kochanek, Stanley, and Robert Hardgrave. *India: Government and Politics in a Developing Nation*. Boston: Thomson Wadsworth, 2008.

Kolobov, A. O., O. A. Kolobiv, R. U. Zhukarin, and O. O. Khokhlisheva. "Arabo-Izraelskii Conflict I Novaya Blizhnevostochnaya Politika Rossiiskoi Federacii" [Arab-Israeli conflict and the new Middle Eastern politics of the Russian Federation]. *Bulletin of the N. I. Lobachevsky Nizhni Novgorod University* 2 (2007): 259.

Kolodziej, Edward A., and Roger E. Kanet. *From Superpower to Besieged Global Power: Restoring World Order after the Failure of the Bush Doctrine*. Athens: University of Georgia Press, 2008.

Komarov, P. "Iniciativa D.A. Medvedeva po Zakluchenіu DEB" [D.A. Medvedev's idea on concluding the EST]. In *Dogovor o Yevropeyskoy Bezopasnosti: Impul's k Raz-*

vitiyu Otnosheniy Rossii i Evropy [European security treaty: Impetus to the development of relations between Russia and Europe], ed. M. B. Bratersky and S. V. Kortunov, 13–56. Moscow: High School of Economics, 2011.

Kordonsky, Simon. *Rossiya: Pomestnaya Federaciya* [Russia: An Estate Federation]. Moscow: Europa, 2010.

Korolev, Anatoly A., and Mansur M. Mukhamedjanov. *Sodruzhestvo Nezavisimykh Gosudarstv: Istoriya Sozdaniya, Problemy, Perspektivy Razvitiya* [Commonwealth of Independent States: History, problems, and prospects of development]. *Knowledge, Understanding, Skills* 4 (2012): 106.

Korosteleva, Elena, ed. *Eastern Partnership: A New Opportunity for the Neighbours?* Milton Park UK: Routledge, 2012.

Kotz, David, and Fred Weir. *Russia's Path from Gorbachev to Putin: The Demise of the Soviet System and the New Russia*. Milton Park UK: Routledge, 2007.

Koval'chuk, Alexandra. "Mezhdunarodnyye otnosheniya v SNG: pol'skaya perspektiva" [International relations in the CIS: The Polish perspective]. *MGIMO University Bulletin* 6, no. 27 (2012): 290.

Kozyrev, Andrey. "Russia: A Chance for Survival." *Foreign Policy* 71, no. 2 (1992): 9.

Krain, Matthew. *Repression and Accommodation in Post-Revolutionary States*. New York: St. Martin's Press, 2000.

Krajhanovski, M. "Zhivaya Krynitsa Ty, Rodnaya Mova" [Living source you are, my native tongue]. *Narodnaya Volya* (2008): 65–66.

Kramer, Mark. "The Myth of a No-NATO-Enlargement Pledge to Russia." *Washington Quarterly* 32, no. 2 (2009): 41.

Krasner, Stephen D. "Sharing Sovereignty: New Institutions for Collapsed and Failing States." *International Security* 29, no. 2 (2004): 90.

Kreutz, Andrej. *Russia in the Middle East: Friend or Foe?* Westport CT: Praeger, 2007.

Krotov, P. A. "Opyt Gosudarstvennoi Reformi Petra Velikogo I Sovremennaya Rossiya" [Experience from the State Reform of Peter the Great and Modern Russia]. *Works of the Department of History of the Saint Petersburg University* 15 (2013): 59.

Kubicek, Paul. "The Commonwealth of Independent States: An Example of Failed Regionalism?" In *Globalising the Regional, Regionalising the Global*, ed. Rick Fawn, 237–56. Cambridge: Cambridge University Press, 2009.

Kuchins, Andrew C., and Igor A. Zevelev. *Russian Foreign Policy: Continuity in Change*. Washington DC: Center for International and Strategic Studies, 2012.

Kudryavcev, Egor S. "Postcovetskoe Prostranstvo Kak Otdel'nii Region: Integracionnie Perspectivi" [Post-Soviet space as a separate region: Prospects for integration]. *Proceedings of the Herzen Russian State Pedagogical University*130 (2011): 261.

Kulchytsky, Stanislav. "Terror-Holodomor Kak Instrument Kollektivizacii" [Terror-famine as an instrument of collectivization]. In *Holodomor 1932–1933 rr. V Ukraini: prychyny i naslydki* [Terror-famine 1932–1933 in Ukraine: Causes and consequence]. Kyiv: Institut Istorii Ukrainiy NANU, 1995.

Kul'pin, E. S. "Urki Petrovskoi Modernizacii: Socioestestvennii Vzglyad" [Lessons from Peter's modernization: Socionatural view]. *Historical Psychology and Sociology of History* 1, no. 5 (2012): 101.

Kulsrud, Carl J. *Maritime Neutrality to 1780: A History of the Main Principles Governing Neutrality and Belligerency to 1780.* Clark NJ: Lawbook Exchange, 2000.

Kumar, Rajan. "Indo-Russian Defense Cooperation." In *Significance of Indo-Russian Relations in the 21st Century*, ed. V. D. Chopra, 141–56. New Delhi: Kaplaz, 2008.

Kurtov, Azhdar. "ODKB I GUAM Kak Elementi Transormacii Prostranstva Bivshego SSSR" [CSTO and GUAM as elements of transformation of the former USSR space]. *Central Asia and Caucasus* 3–4 (2008): 306

Kutchins, Andrew C., and Igor A. Zevelev. "Russian Foreign Policy: Continuity in Change." *Washington Quarterly* 35, no. 1 (2012): 149.

Kuznetsov, Aleksei V. "Perspektivi Evroregionov S Rossiiskim Uchastiem S Uchetom Inovacii Regional'noi Politiki ES" [Perspectives of Euroregions with Russian participation in terms of changes in the EU regional policy]. *Baltic Region* 2 (2009): 6.

Ladha, Rizwan. "Squaring the Circle? The Nuclear Non-Proliferation Treaty, Iran, and the Challenge of Compliance." In *Nuclear Scholars Initiative*, ed. Sarah Weiner, 108–22. Lanham MD: Rowman and Littlefield, 2014.

Laird, Robin F. "Soviet Arms Trade with Noncommunist Third World." In *Soviet Foreign Policy in a Changing World*, ed. Robin F. Laird and Erik P. Hoffmann, 713–30. New York: Aldine, 1975.

Laitin, David D., and Aaron Wildavsky. "Political Culture and Political Preferences." *American Political Science Review* 82, no. 2 (June 1988): 589.

Lakatos, Imre. "Falsification and the Methodology of Scientific Research Programs." In *Criticism and the Growth of Knowledge*, ed. Imre Lakatos and Alan Musgrave, 91–138. New York: Cambridge University Press, 1970.

Landman, Todd, and Neil Robinson, eds. *The SAGE Handbook of Comparative Politics.* London: SAGE, 2009.

Lane, Thomas, Artis Pabriks, Aldis Purs, and David J. Smith. *The Baltic States: Estonia, Latvia, and Lithuania.* Milton Park UK: Routledge, 2002.

Laruelle, Marlène. *Russian Eurasianism: An Ideology of Empire.* Washington DC: Johns Hopkins University Press, 2012.

———. *Russian Nationalism and the National Reassertion of Russia.* Milton Park UK: Routledge, 2009.

Laruelle, Marlène, and Sébastien Peyrouse. *Globalizing Central Asia: Geopolitics and the Challenges of Economic Development.* New York: M. E. Sharpe, 2013.

Lasswell, Harold D. *Psychopathology and Politics.* Chicago: University of Chicago Press, 1986.

Latynina, Yulia. "If Not the West, Then Who Are We?" *Novaya Gazeta* 101 (September 10, 2014): 19.

Lawrence, Paul, and Charalambos Vlachoutsicos, eds. *Behind the Factory Walls: Decision Making in Soviet and U.S. Enterprises.* Boston: Harvard Business School Press, 1990.

Lawson, Colin W. "Soviet Economic Aid to Africa." *African Affairs* 87, no. 349 (1988): 509.

Legvold, Robert. "The Role of Multilateralism in Russian Foreign Policy." In *The Multilateral Dimension in Russian Foreign Policy*, ed. Elana Wilson Rowe and Stina Torjesen, 21–45. New York: Routledge, 2012.

———. *Russian Foreign Policy in the Twenty-First Century and the Shadow of the Past*. New York: Columbia University Press, 2007.

Lehovich, Dimitry V. "The Testament of Peter the Great." *American Slavic and East European Review* 7, no. 2 (1948): 111–24.

Leichtova, Magda. *Misunderstanding Russia: Russian Foreign Policy and the West*. Farnham: Ashgate, 2014.

Lenin, Vladimir. "Krakh II Internatsionala" [Collapse of II International]. In *The Complete Works*, vol. 26. Moscow: Institute of Marxism-Leninism CC of the CPSS, 1967.

———. "Maevka Revolucionnogo Proletariata." In *The Complete Works*, vol. 23. Moscow: Institute of Marxism-Leninism CC of the CPSS, 1967.

Leonard, Mark, and Nicu Popescu. *A Power of EU-Russia Relations*. London: European Council on Foreign Relations, November 2007.

Levi, Scott Cameron, and Ron Sela, eds. *Islamic Central Asia: An Anthology of Historical Sources*. Bloomington: Indiana University Press, 2010.

Levy, Jack S. "Misperception and the Causes of War: Theoretical Linkages and Analytical Problems." *World Politics* 36, no. 1 (1983): 79.

Leyton-Brown, David, ed. *The Utility of International Economic Sanctions*. London: Croom Helm, 1987.

Lieberman, Victor. *Strange Parallels: Southeast Asia in Global Context, c. 800–1830*. Vol. 2 of *Mainland Mirrors: Europe, Japan, China, South Asia, and the Islands*. New York: Cambridge University Press, 2009.

Lieven, Anatol. *Chechnya: Tombstone of Russian Power*. New Haven: Yale University Press, 1998.

Lilly, Bilyana. *Russian Foreign Policy toward Missile Defense: Actors, Motivations, and Influence*. Lanham MD: Lexington Books, 2014.

Lincoln, Bruce. *The Conquest of a Continent: Siberia and the Russians*. Ithaca NY: Cornell University Press, 2007.

Lipset, Seymour Martin. "Some Social Requisites of Democracy: Economic Development and Political Legitimacy." *American Political Science Review* 53, no. 1 (1959): 86–87.

Livy, Titus. *The Rise of Rome: Books 1–5*. Translated by T. J. Luke. Oxford: Oxford University Press, 1998.

Lobjakas, Ahto, and Martin Mölder, eds. *EU-Russia Watch 2012*. Tartu, Estonia: Center for EU-Russia Studies, University of Tartu, 2012.

Locke, John. *Second Treatise of Government*. Edited by C. B. Macpherson. Indianapolis: Hackett, 1980.

———. *Second Treatise of Government*. Charleston SC: CreateSpace, 2013.

Lopez, George A. "Effective Sanctions: Incentives and UN-U.S. Dynamics." *Harvard International Review* 29 (Fall 2007): 50–51.

Lowe, John. *The Great Powers, Imperialism, and the German Problem, 1865–1925*. London: Routledge, 1994.

Lugar, Richard G., and Victoria Nuland. *Russia, Its Neighbors, and an Enlarging NATO: Report of an Independent Task Force*. New York: Council on Foreign Relations, 1997.

Luki, Alexander. "Russia's Identity Dilemmas: BRICS, the G8, and the Shanghai Cooperation Organization." In *Laying the BRICS of a New Global Order: From Yekaterinburg 2009 to Ethekwini 2013*, ed. Francis A. Kornegay Jr. and Narnia Bohler-Muller, 85–100. Pretoria, South Africa: Dalro, 2013.

Lukin, Alexander V., and Andrei V. Ivanov. "Rossiisko-Kitaiskie Otnosheniya: Problemi I Perspektivi" [Russian-Chinese relations: Problems and perspectives]. *Bulletin of the MGIMO* 2 (2011): 314.

Luthi, Lorenz M. "Sino-Soviet Relations during the Mao Years, 1949–1969." In *China Learns from the Soviet Union, 1949–Present*, ed. Thomas P. Bernstein and Hua-Yu Li. Plymouth: Lexington Books, 2010.

Luzyanin, Sergey. "'Tsvetnie Revolucii' V Central'no-Aziatskoi Proekcii: Kyrgyzstan-Uzbekistan-Kazakhstan." ["Color revolutions" in Central Asian projection: Kyrgyzstan-Uzbekistan-Kazakhstan]. *Central Asia and Caucasus* 5, no. 41 (2005): 8–9.

Machiavelli, Niccolo. *The Prince*. Translated by Luigi Ricci. London: Grant Richards, 1903.

Mack, Andrew, and Martin O'Hare. "Moscow-Tokyo and the Northern Territories Dispute." *Asian Survey* 30 (1990): 387.

Mackinder, Halford J. *Democratic Ideals and Reality*. Washington DC: National Defense University Press, 1981.

Magocsi, Paul Robert. *A History of Ukraine: The Land and Its Peoples*. 2nd ed. Toronto: University of Toronto Press, 2010.

Makarychev, Andrey, and Andre Mommen. *Russia's Changing Economic and Political Regimes: The Putin Years and Afterwards*. Milton Park UK: Routledge, 2013.

Makarychev, Andrey, and Alexander Sergunin. "The EU, Russia, and Models of International Society in a Wider Europe." *Journal of Contemporary European Research* 9, no. 2 (2013): 318.

Malashenko, Alexey V. "Russkiy Nacionalizm I Islam" [Russian nationalism and Islam]. *Eurasian Bulletin* 2 (1996): 94.

Malkasian, Mark. *Gha-ra-bagh! The Emergence of the National Democratic Movement in Armenia*. Detroit: Wayne State University Press, 1996.

Mandelbaum, Michael, ed. *The Rise of Nations in the Soviet Union: American Foreign Policy and the Disintegration of the USSR*. New York: Council of Foreign Relations Press, 1991.

Mankoff, Jeffrey. "The Politics of U.S. Missile Defence Cooperation with Europe and Russia." *International Affairs* 88 (2012): 334.

———. *Russian Foreign Policy: The Return of Great Power Politics*. 2nd ed. Lanham MD: Rowman and Littlefield, 2011.

March, James G., and Johan P. Olsen. *Ambiguity and Choice in Organizations*. Bergen, Norway: Universitetsforlaget, 1976.

———. *Democratic Governance*. New York: Free Press, 1995.

———. "The Institutional Dynamics of International Political Orders." *International Organization* 52 (1998): 943–69.

———. "The Logic of Appropriateness." In *The Oxford Handbook of Public Policy*, ed. Michael Moran, Martin Rein, and Robert E. Goodin, 689–708. New York: Oxford University Press, 2006.

———. "The New Institutionalism: Organizational Factors in Political Life." *American Political Science Review* 78, no. 3 (1984): 736

———. *Rediscovering Institutions: The Organizational Basis of Politics*. New York: Free Press, 1989.

———. "Understanding Institutions and Logics of Appropriateness: Introductory Essay," *ARENA Working Papers* 13 (2007): 3.

March, Luke. "Is Nationalism Rising in Russian Foreign Policy? The Case of Georgia." In *Russian Nationalism, Foreign Policy, and Identity Debates in Putin's Russia: New Ideological Patterns after the Orange Revolution*, ed. Marlène Laruelle, 11–40. Stuttgart: Ibidem Press, 2012.

Marples, David R. *Belarus: From Soviet Rule to Nuclear Catastrophe*. New York: St. Martin's Press, 1996.

Marshall, Alex. *The Caucasus under Soviet Rule*. Milton Park UK: Routledge, 2012.

Maslow, Abraham H. "A Theory of Human Motivation." *Psychological Review* 50 (1943): 370–96.

Massie, Robert K. *Peter the Great: His Life and World*. New York: Random House, 2011.

Matveev, Ilya N. "Sotrudnichestvo Rossiiskoi Federacii I Evrosoyuza V Sfere Energetiki V Konce xx–Nachale xxi vv" [Cooperation between the Russian Federation and the EU in the energy sector at the end of the 20th century–the beginning of the 21th century]. *Power* 4 (2014): 123.

Mayakovky, Vladimir. *Vladimir Ilyich Lenin: A Poem*. Honolulu: University Press of Hawaii, 2003.

McAuley, Mary. *Soviet Politics, 1917–1991*. Oxford: Oxford University Press, 1992.

McElroy, Robert W. *Morality and American Foreign Policy: The Role of Ethics in International Affairs*. Princeton NJ: Princeton University Press, 1992.

McFaul, Michael, Nikolay Petrov, and Andrei Ryabov. *Between Dictatorship and Democracy: Russian Post-Communist Political Reform*. Washington DC: Carnegie Endowment for International Peace, 2004.

McLoughlin, Barry. "Mass Operations of the NKVD, 1937–8: A Survey." In *Stalin's Terror: High Politics and Mass Repression in the Soviet Union*, ed. Barry McLoughlin and Kevin McDermott Houndmills, 118–52. Basingstoke UK: Palgrave Macmillan, 2002.

Mearsheimer, John J. "Back to the Future: Instability in Europe after the Cold War." *International Security* 15, no. 1 (1990): 5–56.

———. *The Tragedy of Great Power Politics*. New York: W. W. Norton, 2014.

Medvedev, N. P., and A. B. Borisenko. "Non-Systemic Opposition in the Political Space of Modern Russia." *Belgorod State University Scientific Journal* 8 (39), no. 4 (2007): 154.

Medvedev, Roy. *Aleksandr Lukashenko: Konturi Belarusskoi Modeli* [Alexander Lukashenko: Contours of the Belarusian model]. Minsk, Belarus: BBPG, 2010.

Medvedev, Zhores, and Roy Medvedev. *The Unknown Stalin*. London: I. B. Tauris, 2003.

Mendelson, Sarah E., and Theodore P. Gerber. "Failing the Stalin Test: Russians and Their Dictator." *Foreign Affairs* 85 (2006): 2.

Mendras, Marie. *Russian Politics: The Paradox of a Weak State*. New York: Columbia University Press, 2012.

Menon, Rajan. "After Empire: Russia and Southern 'Near Abroad.'" In *The New Russian Foreign Policy*, ed. Michael Mandelbaum, 100–166. New York: Council on Foreign Relations, 1998.

Merabyan, Karen. "Sovremennaya Politika Rossii Ya Yuzhnom Kavkaze" [Modern Russian politics in South Caucasus]. *MGIM University Bulletin* 4, no. 37 (2014): 94.

Mikhailova, Tatiana. "Putin as the Father of the Nation: His Family and Other Animals." In *Putin as Celebrity and Cultural Icon*, ed. Helena Goscilo, 65–81. Milton Park UK: Routledge, 2013.

Mikheev, Vasily V. *Kitai-Yaponiya: Strategicheskoe Sopernichestvo v Globaliziruyushemsya Mire* [China-Japan: Strategic Rivalry and Partnership in the Globalizing World]. Moscow: IMEMO, 2009.

Miller, Eric A. *To Balance or Not to Balance: Alignment Theory and the Commonwealth of Independent States*. Burlington VT: Ashgate, 2006.

Miller, Nicola. *Soviet Relations with Latin America, 1959–1987*. Cambridge: Cambridge University Press, 1989.

Milov, Vladimir. *Russia and the West: The Energy Factor*. Washington DC: Center for Strategic and International Studies, 2008.

Milyukov, Pavel N. "Russkii Rassizm" [Russian racism]. In *Istoricheskaya Nauka Rossiiskoi Emigracii: "Evraziiskii Soblazn"* [Historical science of Russian emigration: "Eurasianist temptations"], ed. Margarita G. Vandalovskaya, 331–35. Moscow: Institute of the Russian History of the Russian Academy of Sciences, 1997.

Mironov, Boris. *Social'naya Istoriya Rossii Perioda Imperii XVIII–XX vv* [Social history of Russia in the times of empire, eighteenth through the beginning of the twentieth century], vol. 1. St. Petersburg: Dmitri Bulanin, 2003.

Mishra, Ranjana. "'BraMox' Reaffirms Faith." In *Significance of Indo-Russian Relations in the 21st Century*, ed. V. D. Chopra, 157–72. New Delhi: Kaplaz, 2008.

Miszlivetz, Ferenc. "The Post-Euromaidan Future for Europe." In *Reframing Europe's Future: Challenges and Failures of the European Construction*, ed. Jody Jensen and Ferenc Miszlivetz, 249–59. Milton Park UK: Routledge, 2015.

Mitchell, Lincoln A. *Uncertain Democracy: U.S. Foreign Policy and Georgia's Rose Revolution*. Philadelphia: University of Pennsylvania Press, 2008.

Mittelman, James. *Hyperconflict: Globalization and Insecurity*. Redwood City CA: Stanford University Press, 2010.

Moon, David. *The Russian Peasantry, 1600–1930: The World the Peasants Made*. Milton Park UK: Routledge, 1999.

Moravcsik, Andrew. "De Gaulle between Grain and Grandeur: The Political Economy of French EC Policy, 1958–1970 (Part 1)." *Journal of Cold War Studies* 2, no. 2 (2000): 5.

———. "The Origins of Human Rights Regimes: Democratic Delegation in Postwar Europe." *International Organization* 54, no. 2 (2000): 229.

Morgenthau, Hans. "Inquisition in Czechoslovakia." *New York Review of Books*, December 4, 1969, 20–21.

———. *Politics among Nations: The Struggle for Power and Peace*. New York: Alfred A. Knopf, 1948.

Morgenthau, Hans, Kenneth W. Thompson, and W. David Clinton. *Politics among Nations: The Struggle for Power and Peace*. 7th ed. New York: McGraw-Hill, 2005.

Morris-Suzuki, Tessa. "Lines in the Snow: Imagining the Russo-Japanese Frontier." *Pacific Affairs* 72 (1999): 57–77.

Mukhametov, Ruslan S. "Voennoe Sotrudnichestvo Rossii So Stranami Blizhnego Zarubezh'ya" [Military cooperation of Russia with Near Abroad countries]. *Bulletin of the Chelyabinsk State University* 23, no. 314 (2013): 14–15.

Mulaj, Klejda. "International Actions and the Making and Unmaking of Unrecognized States." In *Unrecognized States in the International System*, ed. Nina Caspersen and Gareth Stansfield, 41–57. Milton Park UK: Routledge, 2011.

Mulder, Mauk. *The Daily Power Game*. Leiden, Netherlands: Martinus Nijhoff, 1977.

Mulira, James. "The Soviet Union, Angola, and the Horn of Africa: New Patterns in Afro-European Relations." In *Africa and Europe: From Partition to Independence or Dependence?* ed. Amadu Sesay, 104–28. Milton Park UK: Routledge, 2012.

Murav, Harriet. *Russia's Legal Fictions*. Ann Arbor: University of Michigan Press, 1998.

Murray, Charles. *American Exceptionalism: An Experiment in History*. Washington DC: AEI Press, 2013.

Nahaylo, Bohdan, and Victor Swoboda. *Soviet Disunion: A History of the Nationalities Problem in the USSR*. New York: The Free Press, 1990.

———. *Soviet Disunion: A History of the Nationalities Problem in the USSR*. London: Hamish Hamilton, 2010.

Nalbandov, Robert. *Democratization and Instability in Ukraine, Georgia, and Belarus*. Carlisle PA: Strategic Studies Institute, U.S. Army War College, 2014.

———. *Foreign Interventions in Ethnic Conflicts*. Burlington VT: Ashgate, 2009.

———. "Living with Security Dilemmas: Triggers of Ethnic Conflicts." *Transcience* 1, no. 1 (2010): 52.

Naples, Nancy A., and Jennifer Bickham Mendez, eds. *Border Politics: Social Movements, Collective Identities, and Globalization*. New York: New York University Press, 2014.

Nassibli, Nasib. "Azerbaijan: Oil and Politics in the Country's Future." In *Oil and Geopolitics in the Caspian Sea Region*, ed. Michael P. Croissant and Bülent Aras, 101–30. Westport CT: Praeger, 1999.

Nathan, A. J. "China's Changing of the Guard: Authoritarian Resilience." *Journal of Democracy* 14 (2003): 6–17.

Naumkin, Vitaliy V. *Radical Islam in Central Asia: Between Pen and Rifle*. Lanham MD: Rowman and Littlefield, 2005.

Nazarchuk, Dmitry N., and Nicolay I. Promski. "Osobennosti Rossiiskogo Eksporta I Ego Problemi v Aziatskom Regione" [Peculiarities of Russian export and its problems in the Asian region]. *Economic Journal* 26 (2012): 95.

Nechayeva-Yuriychuk, Nataliya V. "Osobennosti Formirovaniya Moldavskoi Gosudarstvennosti Posle Obreteniya Nezavisimosti" [Peculiarities of the creation of Moldovan statehood after gaining independence]. *Rusin* 4 (2010): 136.

Nedergaard, Peter. *European Union Administration: Legitimacy and Efficiency*. Leiden, Netherlands: Martinus Nijhoff, 2007.

Neumann, Iver B. *Russia and the Idea of Europe: A Study in Identity and International Relations*. London: Routledge, 1995.

Newnham, Randall E. "How to Win Friends and Influence People: Japanese Economic Aid Linkage and the Kuril Islands." *Asian Affairs: An American Review* 27 (2001): 253.

Nietzsche, Friedrich Wilhelm, Alexander Tille, and William August Haussmann. *A Genealogy of Morals*. Translated by William A. Hausemann. New York: Macmillan, 1897.

Nikitenko, Yelena. "'Geopolitika' Evraziistva I Vizovi Sovremennosti" ["Geopolitics" of Eurasianism and contemporary challenges]. *Interexpo Geo-Siberia* no. 1 (2012): 1.

Nikitin, Andrey. "Usilenie Mnogovektornoi Rossiiskoi Vneshnei Politiki" [Strengthening of multivector Russian foreign policy]. *Power* 12 (2009): 15.

Nilsson, Niklas. "Georgia's Rose Revolution: The Break with the Past." In *The Guns of August 2008*, ed. Svante E. Cornell and S. Frederick Starr, 85–103. New York: M. E. Sharpe, 2009.

Nimmons, Don Stewart. *Treasure of War—Concealed by the Evil Ones*. Fairfax VA: Xulon Press, 2003.

Niyazov, Niyazi. "Vzaimootnosheniya Azerbaijana I ODKB V 1994–2011 gg" [Relations between Azerbaijan and CSTO in 1994–2011]. *Bulletin of Tomsk State University* 2 (2011): 99.

Nizhnikov, Sergei. "Evraziistvo v Istorii Russkoi Misli I Georgii Florovsky" [Eurasianism in the history of Russian thought and George Florovsky]. *Bulletin of the Kant Baltic Federal University* 6 (2010): 1.

North, Douglass C. *Institutions, Institutional Change, and Economic Performance*. Cambridge: Cambridge University Press, 1990.

North, Douglass C., John Joseph Wallis, and Barry R. Weingast. *Violence and Social Orders: A Conceptual Framework for Interpreting Recorded Human History*. New York: Cambridge University Press, 2009.

Nunez-Sarantseva, Natalya N. "Torgovo-Ekonomicheskie Otnosheniya Merkosura S Vnezonal'nimi Partnerami" [Trade-economic relations of MERCOSUR with out-of-zone partners]. *Economics and Economic Science* 8 (2012): 144.

Nye, Joseph S., Jr. "Soft Power." *Foreign Policy* 80 (1990): 160.

———. *Soft Power: The Means to Success in World Politics*. New York: PublicAffairs, 2004.

Nygren, Bertyl. *The Rebuilding of Greater Russia: Putin's Foreign Policy towards the CIS*. Milton Park UK: Routledge, 2008.

Ogneva, V. V., and L. A. Brysyakina. "Rossiya I Moldova v Poiske Optimal'nogo Formata Sotrudnichestva" [Russia and Moldova in search of an optimal cooperation format]. *Scientific Newsletter of the Belgorod State University* 7, no. 102 (2011): 2.

O'Hara, S. L. "Great Game or Grubby Game? The Struggle for Control over the Caspian." In *The Geopolitics of Resource Wars: Resource Dependence, Governance, and Violence*, ed. Philippe Le Billon, 138–60. Milton Park UK: Routledge, 2007.

Okladnikov, A. P., ed. *Istoriya Sibiri S Drevneyshikh Vremon Do Nashikh Dney. Tom 2. Sibir' V Sostave Feodal'noy Rossii* [History of Siberia from ancient times to the present day. Vol. 2. Siberia as a part of feudal Russia]. Leningrad: NAUKA, 1968.

Oliker, Olga, Keith Crane, Lowell H. Schwartz, and Catherine Yusupov. *Russian Foreign Policy: Sources and Implications*. Santa Monica CA: RAND, 2009.

Oneal, John R., and Bruce Russett. "The Kantian Peace: The Pacific Benefits of Democracy, Interdependence, and International Organizations." *World Politics* 52, no. 1 (1999): 1–37.

———. *Triangulating Peace: Democracy, Interdependence, and International Organizations*. New York: W. W. Norton, 2000.

Oppenheimer, Peter, and Sergei Maslichenko. "Energy and Economy: An Introduction." In *Russia's Oil and Natural Gas: Bonanza or Curse?* ed. Michael Elman, 15–32. London: Anthem Press, 2006.

Ortmann, Stephanie. "Diffusion as Discourse of Danger: Russian Self-Interpretations and the Framing of the Tulip Revolution." In *Domestic and International Perspective on Kyrgyzstan's "Tulip Revolution": Motives, Mobilizations, and Meaning*, ed. Sally N. Cummings, 137–52. Milton Park UK: Routledge, 2009.

O'Toole, Gavin. *Politics Latin America*. Milton Park UK: Routledge, 2007.

Oxenstierna, Susanne, and Veli-Pekka Tynkkynen, eds. *Russian Energy and Security up to 2030*. Milton Park UK: Routledge, 2014.

Oxford Business Group. *The Report: Nigeria, 2010*. London: Oxford Business Group, 2010.

Panibratov, Andrei, and Marina Lakukha. "Foreign Expansion of Russian Arms Based on Natural Resources and Technology." In *Successes and Challenges of Emerging Economy Multinationals*, ed. Marin Marinov and Svetla Marinova, 128–57. Basingstoke UK: Palgrave Macmillan, 2014.

Paniev, Yuri. "Russia Turning on Latin America." *Austral: Brazilian Journal of Strategy and International Relations* 1, no. 1 (2012).

Pape, Robert A. "Why Economic Sanctions Do Not Work." *International Security* 22, no. 2 (Fall 1997): 97.

Paramonov, Vladimir, and Alexey Strokov. "Proekti I Investicii Rossiiv Gosudarstvax Central'noi Azii: Nefte-Gazovaya Sfera" [Projects and investments of Russia in the Central Asian states: Oil and gas sphere]. *Central Asia and Caucasus* 6, no. 60 (2008): 101–10.

Park, John S. "Nuclear Ambition and Tension on the Korean Peninsula." In *The North Korean Nuclear Weapons Crisis: The Nuclear Taboo Revisited?* ed. Jina Kim. London: Palgrave Macmillan, 2014.

Parsons, J. W. R. "National Integration in Soviet Georgia." *Soviet Studies* 34, no. 4 (1982): 548.

Pavkovic, Aleksandar, and Peter Radan, eds. *The Ashgate Research Companion to Secession*. Burlington VT: Ashgate, 2011.

Payne, Robert. *Ivan the Terrible*. New York: Cooper Square, 2002.

Pease, Donald E. *The New American Exceptionalism*. Minneapolis: University of Minnesota Press, 2009.

Peimani, Hooman. *Conflict and Security in Central Asia and the Caucasus*. Santa Barbara CA: ABC-CLIO, 2009.

Pelevin, Victor. *Generation P*. Moscow: Vagrius, 2000.

Perrie, Maureen, and Andrei Pavlov. *Ivan the Terrible*. Milton Park UK: Routledge, 2003.

Persak, Krzysztof. "The Polish-Soviet Confrontation in 1956 and the Attempted Soviet Military Intervention in Poland." *Europe-Asia Studies* 58, no. 8 (2006): 1285.

Petro, Nicolai N., and Alvin Z. Rubinstein. *Russian Foreign Policy from Empire to Nation-State*. New York: Longman, 1997.

Pikaev, Alexander. "Iranian Nuclear Problem: Prospects for a Solution." In *Nuclear Doctrines and Strategies: National Policies and International Security*, ed. Mark Fitzpatrick, A. I. Nikitin, and Sergeĭ Oznobishchev, 99–112. Amsterdam: IOS Press, 2008.

Pipes, Richard. *The Russian Revolution*. New York: Knopf Doubleday, 2011.

———, ed. *The Unknown Lenin: From the Secret Archive*. New Haven: Yale University Press, 1996.

Plato. *The Trial and Death of Socrates: Four Dialogues*. Mineola: Dover, 1992.

Plokhy, Serhii. *The Origins of the Slavic Nations: Modern Identities in Russia, Ukraine, and Belarus*. Cambridge: Cambridge University Press, 2010.

Ponsard, Lionel. *Russia, NATO, and Cooperative Security: Bridging the Gap*. Milton Park UK: Routledge, 2007.

Popescu, Nicu. "Hybrid Tactics: Neither New nor Only Russian." European Union Institute for Security Studies, *Issue-Alert* 4 (2015): 1–2.

Porter, Bruce D. *The USSR in Third World Conflicts: Soviet Arms and Diplomacy in Local Wars, 1945–1980*. Cambridge: Cambridge University Press, 1984.

Porter, Edward D. *Economic Sanctions against Oil Producers: Who's Isolating Whom? Issue Analysis #105*. Washington DC: American Petroleum Institute, August 1998.

Posen, Barry R. "The Security Dilemma and Ethnic Conflict." In *Ethnic Conflict and International Security*, ed. Michael E. Brown. Princeton: Princeton University Press, 1993.

Pospelovsky, Dmitry. *Russkaya Pravoslavnaya Cerkov' v XX Veke* [Russian Orthodox Church in the twentieth century]. Moscow: Respublika, 1995.

Primakov, Yevgeny. *Russia and the Arabs: Behind the Scenes in the Middle East from the Cold War to the Present*. Translated by Paul Gould. New York: Basic Books, 2009.

Pritsak, Omeljan. "The First Constitution of Ukraine (5 April 1750)." *Harvard Ukrainian Studies* 22, Cultures and Nations of Central and Eastern Europe (1998): 471–96.

Pronin, Anatolii V. "O Pravovoi Prirode Sankcii EC V Otnoshenii RF" [On the legal nature of the EU sanctions against the RF]. *Historical and Social-Educational Thought* 2, no. 24 (2014): 35.

Prunier, Gérard. *The Rwanda Crisis: History of a Genocide, 1959–1994*. London: Hurst, 1995.

Przeworski, Adam, and Fernando Limongi. "Political Regimes and Economic Growth." *Journal of Economic Perspectives* 7, no. 3 (1993): 58.

Puetter, Uwe. *The European Council and the Council: New Intergovernmentalism and Institutional Change*. Oxford: Oxford University Press, 2014.

Putnam, Robert. "Diplomacy and Domestic Politics: The Logic of Two-Level Games." *International Organization* 42, no. 3 (1988): 427–60.

Rashidov, Bakhtier."Rossiya V Central'noi Azii: Perekhod k Pozitivnoi Vneshnei Politike" [Russia in Central Asia: Move to a positive foreign policy]. *Central Asia and Caucasus* 2, no. 38 (2005): 132.

Ray, Hemen. *Sino-Soviet Conflict over India: An Analysis of the Causes of Conflict between Moscow and Beijing over India since 1949*. New Delhi: Abhinnav, 1988.

Rayfield, Donald. *Edge of Empires: A History of Georgia*. London: Reaktion, 2012.

Regan, Patrick M. *Civil Wars and Foreign Powers—Outside Intervention in Intrastate Conflict*. Ann Arbor: University of Michigan Press, 2002.

Reid, Anna. *Borderland: A Journey through the History of Ukraine*. Boulder CO: Basic Books, 2000.

Reid, Anne, and Kay Deaux. "Relationship between Social and Personal Identities." *Journal of Personality and Social Psychology* 71, no. 6 (1996): 1084–91.

Renan, Ernst. *Qu'est-ce qu'une nation? Conférence faite en Sorbonne, le 11 mars 1882*. Paris: Ancien Maison Michele Levy Freres, 1882.

———. "What Is a Nation?" In *Becoming National: A Reader*, ed. Geoff Eley and Ronald Grigor Suny, 42–56. Oxford: Oxford University Press, 1996.

Rezvani, Babak. *Conflict and Peace in Central Eurasia: Towards Explanations and Understandings*. Leiden, Netherlands: Brill Academic, 2014.

Rhodes, Matthew. "U.S. Perspectives on NATO." In *Understanding NATO in the 21st Century: Alliance Strategies, Security, and Global Governance*, ed. Graeme P. Herd and John Kriendle, 33–49. Milton Park UK: Routledge, 2013.

Riasanovsky, Nicholas, and Mark Steinberg, "The Time of Troubles, 1598–1613." In *A History of Russia,* 157–74. New York: Oxford University Press, 2010.

Richmond, Yale. *From Nyet to Da: Understanding the New Russia*. Boston: Intercultural Press, 1992.

Roccas, Sonia, and Marilynn B. Brewer. "Social Identity Complexity." *Personality and Social Psychology Review* 6, no. 2 (2001): 89.

Rogozin, Dmitry. *Yastrebi Mira: Dnevnik Russkogo Posla* [Hawks of Peace: A Diary of the Russian Ambassador]. Moscow: Alpina Non-Fiction, 2010.

Roper, Steven D. "Regionalism in Moldova: The Case of Transdnistria and Gagauzia." In *Ethnicity and Territory in the Former Soviet Union: Regions in Conflict*, ed. James Hughes and Gwendolyn Sasse, 101–22. Milton Park UK: Frank Cass, 2002.

Rosamond, Ben. *Theories of European Integration*. London: Macmillan, 2000.

Ross, Marc Howard. "Psychocultural Interpretations and Dramas: Identity Dynamics in Ethnic Conflict." *Political Psychology* 22, no. 1 (2001): 159.

Rothstein, Bo, and Jan Teorell. "What Is Quality of Government? A Theory of Impartial Government Institutions." *Governance: An International Journal of Policy, Administration, and Institutions* 21, no. 2 (April 2008): 169.

Rousseau, Jean-Jacques. *The Social Contract*. Hertfordshire UK: Wordsworth, 1998.

Roxburgh, Angus. *The Strongman: Vladimir Putin and the Struggle for Russia*. London: I. B. Tauris, 2013.

Russett, Bruce. *Grasping at the Democratic Peace: Principles for a Post-Cold War World*. Princeton: Princeton University Press, 1993.

Ryngaert, Cedric. "Rossiya I Evropeiskii Soyuz: Efemernii Poisk Obshix Cennostei?" [Russia and European Union: Ephemeral quest for common values?]. *Baltic Region* 4, no. 14 (2012): 126.

Saari, Sinikukka. *Promoting Democracy and Human Rights in Russia*. Milton Park UK: Routledge, 2010.

Sadri, Houman A., and Omar Vera-Muniz. "Iranian Relations with the South Caucasus." In *Iranian Foreign Policy since 2001: Alone in the World*, ed. Thomas Juneau and Sam Razavi, 140–56. Milton Park UK: Routledge, 2013.

Saivetz, Carol R. "Russia, Iraq, and Iran: Business, Politics, or Both?" In *Russian Business Power: The Role of Russian Business in Foreign and Security Relations*, ed. Andreas Wenger, Robert W. Orttung, and Jeronim Perovic, 114–32. Milton Park UK: Routledge, 2006.

Sakwa, Richard. *The Crisis of Russian Democracy: The Dual State, Factionalism, and the Medvedev Succession*. New York: Cambridge University Press, 2011.

———. *Putin and the Oligarkh: The Khodorkovsky-Yukos Affair*. London: I. B. Tauris, 2014.

———. *Putin Redux: Power and Contradiction in Contemporary Russia*. Milton Park UK: Routledge, 2014.

Salih, M. A. Mohamed, and Lennart Wohlgemurth. "Somalia: State and Society in Turmoil." *Review of African Political Economy* 21, no. 59 (1994): 79–82.

Samokhin, Alexandr V. "Kontseptsii Politicheskogo Ustroystva Rossii v Klassicheskom Yevraziystve" [The concept of Russia's political system in classical Eurasianism]. *Bulletin of the Sholokhov Moscow State Humanitarian University of History and Political Science* 2 (2010): 98.

Sander, Gordon F. *The Hundred Day Winter War: Finland's Gallant Stand against the Soviet Army.* Lawrence: University Press of Kansas, 2013.

Sanders, Jimy M. "Ethnic Boundaries and Identity in Plural Societies." *Annual Review of Sociology* 28 (2002): 328.

Sapronova, Marina A. "Rossisko-Arabskoe Sotrudnichestvo Do I Posle 'Arabskoi Vesni'" [Russian-Arab cooperation before and after the "Arab Spring"]. *Bulletin of the MGIMO* 3 (2014): 33.

Sarotte, Mary Elise. "A Broken Promise? What the West Really Told Moscow about NATO Expansion." *Foreign Affairs*, September/October 2014.

Satter, David. *It Was a Long Time Ago, and It Never Happened Anyway: Russia and the Communist Past.* New Haven: Yale University Press, 2012.

Saygadachnaya, Nadejda. "Budgetnie Pravila I Principi Budgetnoi Sistemi: Sootnoshenie I Transformaciya" [Budgetary rules and principles of budgetary system: Correlation and transformation]. *Problems of Accounting and Finances* 1, no. 9 (2013): 57.

Saynakov, Nikolay. *Oprichnina Ivana Groznogo glazami tekh, kto vyzhil: Lichnost' tsarya v kontekste oprichnogo vremeni: istoriograficheskie i metodologicheskie aspekty issledovaniya* [Oprichnina of Ivan the Terrible as seen by those who survived: Personality of a tsar in the context of the times of Oprichnina: Historical and Methodological Aspects of Research]. Hamburg: Lambert Academic, 2011.

Schmidt, Elizabeth. *Foreign Intervention in Africa: From the Cold War to the War on Terror.* New York: Cambridge University Press, 2013.

Schnabel, Albrecht. *Southeast European Security: Threats, Responses, Challenges.* New York: Nova Science, 2001.

Schneider, Klaus. "The Partnership and Cooperation Agreement (PCA) between Ukraine and the EU—Idea and Reality." In *Ukraine on the Road to Europe*, ed. Lutz Hoffmann and Felicitas Möllers, 66–78. Berlin: Physica Verlag Heilberg, 2001.

Schoen, Douglas E., and Melik Kaylan. *The Russia-China Axis: The New Cold War and America's Crisis of Leadership.* New York: Encounter Books, 2014.

Sedelmeier, Ulrich, and Rachel Epstein. "Beyond Conditionality: International Institutions in Postcommunist Europe after Enlargement." *Journal of European Public Policy* 15, no. 6 (2008): 795–805.

Senn, Alfred Erich. *Lithuania 1940: Revolution from Above.* Amsterdam: Rodopi, 2007.

Sergunin, Aleksandr. "Russian Foreign Policy Decision Making on Europe." In *Russian European Choice*, ed. Ted Hopf, 59–96. New York: Palgrave Macmillan.

Sevastyanov, Sergey V. "Rasshirenie Povestki Sotrudnichestva Kak Vozmojnii Put' k Povisheniu Roli ATES V Regione" [Enlargement of the cooperation agenda as a possible way toward enlargement of the APEC role in the region]. *Studies in the Humanities in Eastern Siberia and the Far East* 4 (2009): 60.

Shamin, I. V. "'Tsvetnaya' (Barkhatnaya) Revoluciya Kak Instrument Obespecheniya Interesov SSHA Na Mejdunarodnoi Arene v Konce 1990x-Nachale 2000x Godov" ["Colored" (velvet) revolution as the instrument of provision of the U.S. interests on the international arena in 1990–2000]. *Journal of the Volgograd State University* 4, no. 2 (2008): 93.

Shanty, Frank. *The Nexus: International Terrorism and Drug Trafficking from Afghanistan.* Santa Barbara: ABC-CLIO, LLC, 2011.

Sharma, Shri Ram. *India-USSR Relations, 1947–1971: From Ambivalence to Steadfastness.* Part 1. New Delhi: Discovery, 1999.

Shepherd, Ben. "Political Stability: Crucial for Growth?" *IDEAS Report, SU004-Resurgent Continent? Africa and the World* , March 2010, 9.

Sherratt, Thomas N. "The Evolution of Imperfect Mimicry." *Behavioral Ecology* 13, no. 6 (2002): 821.

Shevel, Oxana, Nuala O'Connor, Alethea Lange, Lawrence G. Potter, Barbara Crossette, Adekeye Adebajo, Rochelle Davis, Joseph Chamie, Juan de Onis, and Karen M. Rohan. *Great Decisions 2015.* Washington: Foreign Policy Association, 2015. Kindle ed.

Shlapentokh, Dmitry. *Russia between East and West: Scholarly Debates on Eurasianism.* Leiden, Netherlands: Brill Academic, 2006.

Shlyakhter, Alexander, and Richard Wilson. "Chernobyl: The Inevitable Results of Secrecy." *Public Understanding of Science* 1, no. 3 (1992): 253–54.

Shoemaker, M. Wesley. *Russia and the Commonwealth of Independent States 2014.* 45th ed. World Today series 2014–2015. Lanham MD: Rowman and Littlefield, 2014.

Shubinsky, Sergey N. *Istoricheskie Ocherki I Rasskazi* [Historical essays and stories]. 6th ed. Saint Petersburg: TIP, 1911.

Silitski, Vital. "From Social Contract to Social Dialogue: Some Observations on the Nature and Dynamics of Social Contracting in Modern Belarus." In *Social Contracts in Contemporary Belarus*, ed. Kiryl Haiduk, Elena Rakova, and Vital Silitski, 156–74. Minsk: Belarusian Institute for Strategic Studies, 2009.

Simes, Dimitri K. "America and the Post-Soviet Republics." *Foreign Affairs* 71, no. 3 (1992): 73.

———. "Losing Russia: The Cost of Renewed Confrontation." *Foreign Affairs*, November/December 2007.

Sitaryan, S. A., ed. *Strategicheskie Orientiri Vneshneekonomicheskix Svyazei Rossii V Usloviyax Globalizacii: Scenarii Do 2005 Goda* [Strategic targets of foreign trade relations of Russia under the conditions of globalization: Scenario up to 2005]. Moscow: Nauka, 2005.

Skrynnikov, Ruslan G. *Ivan III.* Moscow: ACT Tranzitkniga, 2006.

Smirnov, Alexei M. "Sovremennie Rossiiskie Podxodi K Obespecheniu Evropeiskoi Bezopasnosti" [Modern Approaches to European Security]. *Military and the Society* 5, no. 37 (2013): 1.

Smith, Gordon B. *Soviet Politics: Continuity and Contradiction.* New York: St. Martin's Press, 1988.

Smith, Hanna. "Russian Foreign Policy, Regional Cooperation, and Northern Relations." In *The New Northern Dimension of the European Neighbourhood*, ed. Pami Aalto, Helge Blakkinsrud, and Hanna Smith, 19–34. Brussels, Belgium: Center for European Policy Studies, 2008.

Smitiyenko, Boris M. "Rossiya I Idei Ob'edinennoi Evropoi" [Russia and the ideas of unified Europe]. *Globalization Age* 1 (2010): 155.

Snyder, Timothy. *Stalin and Europe: Imitation and Domination; 1928–1953*. New York: Oxford University Press, 2014.

Sobek, David M., Rodwan Abouharb, and Christopher G. Ingram. "The Human Rights Peace: How the Respect for Human Rights at Home Leads to Peace Abroad." *Journal of Politics* 68, no. 3 (2006): 519.

Sobják, Anita. "The Romania-Moldova Gas Pipeline: Does a Connection to the EU Mean a Disconnect from Russia?" *Bulletin of the Polish Institute of International Affairs* 93, no. 546 (2013): 1.

Solov'ev, Vladimir. *Velikii Spor I Khristianskaya Politica* [Great dispute and Christian politics]. Moscow: Kniga Po Trebovaniu, 2011.

Soltan, Karol, Erin M. Uslaner, and Virginia Haufler, eds. *Institutions and Social Order*. Ann Arbor: University of Michigan Press, 1998.

Sorokine, A. A. "The Challenge of Africa's Economic Recovery and the Concept of International Economic Security." In *The Challenge of African Economic Recovery and Development*, ed. Adebayo Adedeji, Patrick Bugembe, and Owodunni Teriba, 270–84. Milton Park UK: Routledge, 1991.

Spencer, Philip, and Howard Wollman. *Nationalism: A Critical Introduction*. London: SAGE, 2003.

Stalin, Joseph. *Sochineniya*. Vol. 12. Moscow: State Publishing House of Political Literature, 1949.

Starchak, Maxim. "Shankhaiskaya Organizaciya Sotrudnichestva: Vozmojnosti Dlya Rossii" [Shanghai Cooperation Organization: Opportunities for Russia]. *Central Asia and Caucasus* 2, no. 14 (2011): 153.

Stent, Angela E. *The Limits of Partnership: U.S.-Russia Relations in the Twenty-First Century*. Princeton: Princeton University Press, 2014.

Stigler, George, and Gary Becker. "De Gustibus Non Est Disputandum." *American Economic Review* 67, no. 2 (1977): 76–90.

Stoessinger, John G. *Why Nations Go to War*. 2nd ed. New York: St. Martin's Press, 1974.

Strayer, Robert. *Why Did the Soviet Union Collapse? Understanding Historical Change*. Armonk NY: M. E. Sharpe, 1998.

Streissguth, Thomas. *Vladimir Putin*. Minneapolis: Lerner Publications & A&E Biography, 2005.

Su, Chi. "The Strategic Triangle and China's Soviet Policy." In *China, the United States, and the Soviet Union: Tripolarity and Policy Making in the Cold War*, ed. Robert S. Ross, 39–64. Armonk NY: M. E. Sharpe, 1993.

Subtelny, Orest. *Ukraine: A History*. 4th ed. Toronto: University of Toronto Press, 2009.

Sumbadze, Nana. "Saakashvili in the Public Eye: What Public Opinion Polls Tell Us." In *War and Revolution in the Caucasus: Georgia Ablaze*, ed. Stephen F. Jones, 92–104. Milton Park UK: Routledge, 2010.

Suni, Ronald G. *The Revenge of the Past: Nationalism Revolution and the Collapse of the Soviet Union*. Redwood City CA: Stanford University Press, 1993.

Sushko, Oleksandr, and Olena Prystayko. "Western Influence." In *Revolution in Orange: The Origins of Ukraine's Democratic Breakthrough*, ed. Anders Aslund and Michael McFaul, 125–144. Washington DC: Carnegie Endowment for International Peace, 2006.

Taji-Farouki, Suha. "Hizb ut-Tahrir." In *Islamic Movements of Europe*, ed. Frank Peter and Rafael Ortega, 44–49. New York: I. B. Taurus, 2014.

Tamochkin, Pavel. "Embargo v Konteste Rossiiskoi Gosudarstvennoi Politike Importozamesheniya" [Embargo in the context of Russian state policy of import replacement]. *Science Time* 10, no. 10 (2014): 350–51.

Tashterov, Alisher. "Fenomen 'Tsvetnix Revolucii': Ot Klassicheskoi Teorii K Nepredskazuemoi Praktike." *Central'naya Aziya I Kavkaz [Central Asia and the Caucasus]* 1, no. 49 (2007): 40.

Tellis, Ashley J., Abraham M. Denmark, and Travis Tanner, eds. *Strategic Asia 2013–14: Asia in the Second Nuclear Age*. Washington DC: National Bureau of Asian Research, 2013.

Teper, Lazare. "Elections in Soviet Russia." *American Political Science Review* 26, no. 5 (1932): 926–31

Theiler, Tobias. "Societal Security and Social Psychology." *Review of International Studies* 29 (2003): 261.

Thompson, John M. *Russia and the Soviet Union: A Historical Introduction from the Kievan State to the Present*. 7th ed. Boulder CO: Westview Press, 2012.

Thompson, Jonathan. "The Global Players in the EU's Broader Neighborhood." In *The Neighbours of the European Union's Neighbours: Diplomatic and Geopolitical Dimensions beyond the European Neighborhood Policy*, ed. Sieglinde Gstöhl and Erwan Lannon, 243–68. Burlington VT: Ashgate, 2014.

Thomson, John M. *Russia and the Soviet Union: A Historical Introduction from the Kievan State to the Present*. 7th ed. Boulder: Westview Press, 2012.

Thucydides. *History of the Peloponnesian War*. Translated by Rex Warner. London: Penguin Classics, 1954.

———. *History of the Peloponnesian War*. London: Penguin Books, 1972.

———. *History of the Peloponnesian War*. Translated by Richard Crawley. Mineola NY: Dover, 2004.

Tian, Robert Guang. "Ot Central'noi Azii k Bol'shoi Central'noi Azii: Celi I Korrektirovki Strategii SSHA V TsA" [From Central Asia to the Greater Central Asia: Goals and corrections of the U.S. xtrategy in Central Asia]. *Central Asian and Caucasus* 3, no. 63 (2009): 84.

Timofeeva, V. V., et al. *Vospominaniya I Issledovaniya O Tvorchestve F.M. Dostoyevskogo* [Memoires and study on F. M. Dostoyevsky's works]. Moscow: DirectMEDIA, 2010.

Ting-Toomey, Stella, and Leeva C. Chung. *Understanding Intercultural Communication*. Oxford: Oxford University Press, 2011.

Tocqueville, Alexis de. *Democracy in America*. Vol. 1. Translated by George Lawrence. New York: Perennial Library, 1988.

Tomashivsky, Stefan. *Istoriya Ukrainy: Starynni viku i seredni viku* [History of Ukraine: Old ages and middle ages]. Munich: UVU, 1948.

Tomberg, Igor. "Energeticheskaya Politica I Energeticheskie Proekti V Central'noi Evraazii" [Energy security and energy projects in Central Eurasia]. *Central'naya Aziya I Kavkaz* [Central Asia and Caucasus)] 6, no. 54 (2007): 53.

Tomberg, Roman I. "Rossiiskii Neftegazovii Biznes v Afrike" [Russian oil and gas business in Africa]. *Bulletin of the MGIMO* 3, no. 3 (2011): 102–7.

Tomhiko, Uama. "The Alash Orda's Relations with Siberia, the Urals, and Turkestan: The Kazakh National Movement and the Russian Imperial Legacy." In *Asiatic Russia: Imperial Power in Regional and International Contexts*, ed. Uama Tomhiko, 271–87. Milton Park UK: Routledge, 2012.

Tonkikh, P. S. "Otnosheniya Rossii s NATO i OBSE v Kontekste Novoy Arkhitektury Evroatlanticheskoy Bezopasnosti" [Russia's relations with NATO and the OSCE in the context of the new Euro-Atlantic security srchitecture]. In *Dogovor o Yevropeyskoy Bezopasnosti: Impul's k Razvitiyu Otnosheniy Rossii i Evropy* [European Security Treaty: Impetus to the development of relations between Russia and Europe], ed. M. B. Bratersky et al., 152–68. Moscow: High School of Economics, 2011.

Torjesen, Stina. "Russia, the CIS, and the EEC." In *The Multilateral Dimension in Russian Foreign Policy*, ed. Elana Wilson Rowe and Stina Torjesen, 153–62. Milton Park UK: Routledge, 2009.

Treisman, Daniel. *The Return: Russia's Journey from Gorbachev to Medvedev*. New York: Free Press, 2012.

Trenin, Dmitri. "The Mythical Alliance: Russia's Syria Policy." Moscow: Carnegie Moscow Center, 2013.

Trenin, Dmitri, Maria Lipman, and Alexey Malashenko, eds. *The End of an Era in EU-Russia Relations*. Moscow: Carnegie Moscow Center, May 2013.

Trenin, Dmitri, and Yuval Weber. *Russia's Pacific Future: Solving the South Kuril Islands Dispute*. Moscow: Carnegie Moscow Center, 2012.

Troekurova, Irina S. "Poiski Putei I Opredelenie Mesta Rossii V Torgovle So Stranami ATEC" [Search for channels and definition of the place of Russia in trade with the APEC countries]. *Economic Journal* 13 (2006): 240.

———. "Rossiya I ATES: Of Formal'nogo Chlenstva K Real'nomu Uchastiu" [Russia and Asia-Pacific Economic Cooperation: From token membership to real participation]. *Herald of the Saratov State Socio-Economic University* 2 (2011): 133.

Troitsky, Evgeniy F. "Stanovlenie I Razvitie Shanxaiskoi Organizacii Sotrudnichestva (2000–2007)" [Creation and development of the Shanghai Cooperation Organization [2000–2007]. *Bulletin of the Tomsk State University* 323 (2009): 180.

Tselichtchev, Ivan, and Philippe Debroux. *Asia's Turning Point: An Introduction to Asia's Dynamic Economies at the Dawn of the New Century*. Singapore: Wiley, 2009.

Tsiganov, Yuri. "Farewell to Oligarchs? Presidency and Business Tycoons in Contemporary Russia." In *Russia after Yeltsin*, ed. Vladimir Tikhomirov, 79–102. Burlington VT: Ashgate, 2001.

Tsukanova, Ol'ga V. "Etapi Moldovo-Pridnestrovskogo Konflikta" [Stages of the Moldovo-Dnestr conflict]. *Problems in the Russian Legislature* 2 (2011): 247.

Tsygankov, Andrei P. *Russia's Foreign Policy: Change and Continuity in National Identity*. Plymouth UK: Rowman and Littlefield, 2013.

Turisbekov, Z. "20 Let Nezavisimosti" [Twenty years of independence]. *Rodina* 1 (2012): 62.

Ultanbayev, Raphael. "Rossiya I Strani Zakavkaz'ya: Real'nost' I Strategii Ekonomicheskogo Sotrudnichestva" [Russia and the transcaucasian countries: Reality and strategies of economic cooperation]. *Central Asia and Caucasus* 1, no. 37 (2005): 156.

Uslu, Nasuh. *The Turkish-American Relationship between 1947 and 2003: The History of a Distinctive Alliance*. New York: Nova Science, 2003.

van Baak, Joost. *The House in Russian Literature: A Mythopoetic Exploration*. Amsterdam: Rodopi, 2009.

Van Evera, Stephen. *Causes of War*. Ithaca: Cornell University Press, 2001.

Van Ham, Peter. "EU, NATO, OSCE: Interaction, Cooperation, and Confrontation." In *European Security in Transition*, ed. Gunther Hauser and Franz Kernic, 23–38. Burlington VT: Ashgate, 2006.

Van Oudenaren, John. *Uniting Europe: An Introduction to the European Union*. Lanham MD: Rowman and Littlefield, 2005.

Vasil'yeva, Ol'ga. *Russkaya Pravoslavnaya Tserkov' i Kommunisticheskoye Gosudarstvo 1917–1941* [Russian Orthodox Church and communist state]. Moscow: Bibleisko-bogoslovsky Institut sv. Apostola Andreya, 1996.

Velichenkov, A. "Kuda Idem Mi S IMF?" [Where are we going with IMF?]. *Russian Economic Journal*, no. 8 (1996).

Verkhoturov, D. N. *Pokorenie Sibiri: Mifi I Realnost* [Conquest of Siberia: Myths and reality]. Moscow: OLMA-PRESS, 2005.

Vinhas de Souza, Lúcio. *A Different Country: Russia's Economic Resurgence*. Brussels, Belgium: Center for European Policy Studies, 2008.

Vinokurov, Evgeny, and Alexander Libman. *Eurasian Integration: Challenges of Transcontinental Regionalism*. New York: Palgrave Macmillan, 2012.

Vorob'ev, Vladimir V. "Etapi Formirovaniya Sodruzhestva Nezavisimix Gosudarstv v 1990-e Godi" [Stages of creation of the Commonwealth of Independent States in the 1990s]. *Bulletin of the Chelyabinsk State University* 34 (2011): 90–94.

Voronina, T. V. "Razvitie Integracionnogo Sotrudnichestva Mezhdu Rossiei I Azerbaijanom v Ramkax SNG" [Developing integrated cooperation between Russia and Azerbaijan within the CIS]. *Bulletin of Volgograd State University* 2 (2011): 241.

Vujacic, Veljko. "Stalinism and Russian Nationalism: A Reconceptualization." In *Russian Nationalism and the National Reassertion of Russia*, ed. Marlène Laruelle, 49–75. New York: Routledge, 2009.

Vylegjanin, Alexandre N. "Basic Legal Issues of Management of Natural Resources of the Caspian Sea." In *The Caspian Sea: A Quest for Environmental Security*, ed. William Ascher and Natalia Mirovitskaya, 163–72. Dordrecht, Netherlands: Kluwer Academic, 1999.

Waever, Ole, Barry Buzan, Morten Kelstrup, and Piere Lemaitre. *Identity, Migration, and the New Security Agenda in Europe*. New York: St. Martin's Press, 1993.

Walker, Christopher J. *Armenia: The Survival of a Nation*. 2nd ed. New York: St. Martin's Press, 1990.

Wallensteen, Peter. "Characteristics of Economic Sanctions." *Journal of Peace Research* 5, no. 3 (1968): 248–49.

Walter, Barbara. "The Critical Barriers to Civil War Settlement." *International Organization* 51 (1997): 338.

Walter, Christian, Antje von Ungern-Sternberg, and Kavus Abushov, eds. *Self-Determination and Secession in International Law*. Oxford: Oxford University Press, 2014.

Waltz, Kenneth N. *Man, the State, and War: A Theoretical Analysis*. New York: Columbia University Press, 2001.

———. *Theory of International Politics*. New York: McGraw-Hill, 1979.

Ward, Steven R. *Immortal, Updated Edition: A Military History of Iran and Its Armed Forces*. Washington DC: Georgetown University Press, 2009.

Ward-Perkins, Brian. *The Fall of Rome and the End of Civilization*. New York: Oxford University Press, 2006.

Wastl-Walter, Doris. *The Ashgate Research Companion to Border Studies*. Burlington VT: Ashgate, 2011.

Weaver, Gary R. "Understanding and Coping with Cross-Cultural Adjustment Stress." In *Cross-Cultural Orientation: New Conceptualizations and Applications*, ed. R. Michael Paige, 134–46. Lanham MD: University Press of America, 1986.

Weber, Cynthia. *International Relations Theory: A Critical Introduction*. Milton Park UK: Routledge, 2005.

Weber, Mark J., Shirli Kopelman, and David M. Messick. "A Conceptual Review of Decision Making in Social Dilemmas: Applying a Logic of Appropriateness." *Personality and Social Psychology Review* 8, no. 3 (2004): 281.

Weber, Max, David S. Owen, Tracy B. Strong, and Rodney Livingstone. *The Vocation Lectures: Science as a Vocation, Politics as a Vocation*. Indianapolis: Hackett, 2004. Kindle ed.

Wegner, Stephen K. *Return to Putin's Russia: Past Imperfect, Future Uncertain*. Lanham MD: Rowman and Littlefield, 2013.

Weinstein, Franklin B. "The Concept of a Commitment in International Relations." *Journal of Conflict Resolution* 13, no. 2 (1969): 46.

Weitz, Richard. *Global Security Watch—Russia: A Reference Handbook*. Santa Barbara CA: ABC-CLIO, 2010.

Wendt, Alexander. "Anarchy Is What States Make of It: The Social Construction of Power Politics." *International Organization* 46, no. 2 (1992): 391–425.

———. "Collective Identity Formation and International State." *American Political Science Review* 88 (1994): 384–96.

———. "Levels of Analysis vs. Agents and Structures: Part III." *Review of International Studies* 18 (1992): 183.

Wheatley, Jonathan. "The Case of Asymmetric Federalism in Georgia: A Missed Opportunity." In *Asymmetric Autonomy and the Settlement of Ethnic Conflicts*, ed. Marc Weller and Katherine Nobbs, 213–30. Philadelphia: University of Pennsylvania Press, 2010.

White, Robert H. *Nobody Wanted War*. Garden City NY: Doubleday/Anchor, 1968.

Wildavsky, Aaron. "Choosing Preferences by Constructing Institutions: A Cultural Theory of Preference Formation." *American Political Science Review* 81 (1987): 6.

Williams, Beryl. *Lenin*. Milton Park, UK: Routledge, 2000.

Williams, Robert E., Jr., and Paul R. Viotti. *Arms Control: History, Theory, and Policy*. Santa Barbara CA: ABC-CLIO, 2012.

Wilson, Andrew. *Belarus: The Last European Dictatorship*. New Haven CT: Yale University Press, 2011.

———. *Ukraine Crisis: What It Means for the West*. New Haven: Yale University Press, 2014.

———. *Ukraine's Orange Revolution*. New Haven: Yale University Press, 2005.

Wilson, Ernest J. "Hard Power, Soft Power, Smart Power." *Annals of the American Academy of Political and Social Sciences* 616 (2008): 110–24.

Wilson, James Q., Jr., John J. DiIulio, and Meena Bose. *American Government: Institutions and Policies*. Boston: Cengage Learning, 2012.

Wood, Alan. *Russia's Frozen Frontier: A History of Siberia and the Russian Far East, 1581–1991*. London: Bloomsbury, 2011.

Wortman, Richard S. *The Development of a Russian Legal Consciousness*. Chicago: University of Chicago Press, 2010.

Ya, Kromova Al'bina. "Kontrabanda Narkotikov kak Naibolee Social'no Opastnaya Raznovidnost' Nelegal'noi Transgranichnoi Aktivnosti Mejdu Stranami Central'noi Azii I Rossiei" [Drug smuggling as the most socially dangerous form of illegal cross-border activity between Central Asia and Russia]. *Bulletin of the South Ural State University* 6, no. 223 (2011): 43.

Yair, Gad. "'Unite Unite Europe': The Political and Cultural Structures of Europe as Reflected in the Eurovision Song Context." *Social Networks* 17 (1995): 150.

Yakhnyuk, Alexander. "Perspektivi Ekonomicheskoi Bezopasnosti Rossii V Usloviyax Prisoedineniya K Vsemirnoi Torgovoi Organizatsii" [Economic security prospects of Russia under its accession to the World Trade Organization]. *Journal of the Saint-Petersburg University of Economics and Finances* 5 (2012): 143.

Yaz'kova, Alla. "Rossiya I Nezavisimie Gosudarstva Kavkaza" [Russia and Independent State of the Caucasus]. *Caucasus and Globalization* 1, no. 3 (2009): 27.

Yekelchyk, Serhy. *Ukraine: Birth of a Modern Nation*. New York: Oxford University Press, 2007.

Yin, Robert K. *Case Study Research: Design and Methods*. Thousand Oaks CA: SAGE, 2014.

Zagorsky, Alexei V. "Krizis Kontrolya Obichnix Voorujennix Sil V Evrope I Sud'ba Dogovora Ob Obichnix Voorujennix Silax" [Crisis of control over conventional forces and the fate of the CFE treaty]. *MGIMO University Bulletin* 4 (2010): 49.

Zaprudnik, Jan. *Belarus: At a Crossroads of History*. Boulder CO: Westview Press, 1993.

Zarakhovich, Yuri. "Why Putin Pulled Out of a Key Treaty." *Time*, July 14, 2007.

Zdravomislov, A. G. *Mezhnatsionalnye konflikty v postsovetskom prostranstve* [International conflicts in post-Soviet space]. Moscow: Aspekt Press, 1997.

Zehfuss, Maja. *Constructivism in International Relations: The Politics of Reality*. Cambridge: Cambridge University Press, 2002.

Zeynalov, Vidadi Z., and Z. H. Mamedov. "Problemi I Perspektivi Razvitiya Azerbaidjansko-Rossiyskogo Sotrudnichestva v Finansovo-Bankovskoi Sfere" [Problems and perspectives of development of the Azerbaiani-Russian cooperation in the financial-banking sphere]. *Problems of Modern Economy* 4 (2012): 332–33.

Zhungzhi, Sun, and Zhao Huirong. "Chinese Views of the Russia-Georgia Conflict and Its Impact." In *Eurasia's Ascent in Energy and Geopolitics: Rivalry or Partnership for China, Russia, and Central Asia?* ed. Robert E. Bedeski and Niklas Swanström, 199–213. Milton Park UK: Routledge, 2012.

Zimin, Aleksandr A. *Oprichnina Ivana Groznogo* [Oprichnina of Ivan the Terrible]. Moskva: Mysl', 1964.

Zimovec, A. V. "O Problemakh I Perspektivakh Pereorientacii Ekonomiki Rossii S Zapada Na Vostok" [On the problems and perspectives of reorientation of the Russian economy from west to east]. *Journal of Taganrog Institute of Management and Economics* 1 (2014): 34.

Zweig, Stefan. *Mary Stuart*. Translated by Eden Paul and Cedar Paul. New York: Viking, 1935.

INDEX

Other works by Robert Nalbandov

Foreign Interventions in Ethnic Conflicts (Burlington VT: Ashgate, 2009)